# Cross-Cultural Psychology

W9-AOB-089

This second edition of the bestselling textbook *Cross-Cultural Psychology* has been substantially revised to provide the student with the most comprehensive overview of cross-cultural psychology available in one volume. The team of internationally acclaimed authors have included the most up-to-date research in the field, and written two new chapters on language and on emotion. Within a universalist framework the book emphasizes not only research on basic processes and theory, but also methodology and applications of cross-cultural psychology with respect to acculturation, organizational processes, communication, health, and national development. The new format of the book is designed to make it even more accessible and reader-friendly, and includes chapter outlines, chapter summaries, further reading, and a glossary of key terms.

# Cross-Cultural Psychology

## Research and Applications

**SECOND EDITION**

JOHN W. BERRY

Queen's University
Kingston, Ontario, Canada

YPE H. POORTINGA

Tilburg University
Tilburg, The Netherlands

MARSHALL H. SEGALL

Syracuse University
Syracuse, New York, USA

PIERRE R. DASEN

University of Geneva
Geneva, Switzerland

CAMBRIDGE
UNIVERSITY PRESS

CAMBRIDGE UNIVERSITY PRESS
Cambridge, NewYork, Melbourne, Madrid, Cape Town, Singapore, São Paulo, Delhi

Cambridge University Press
The Edinburgh Building, Cambridge CB2 8RU, UK

Published in the United States of America by Cambridge University Press, New York

www.cambridge.org
Information on this title: www.cambridge.org/9780521646178

First published 1992
Reprinted Seven times 1992-1998
Second edition 2002
Seventh printing 2008

Printed in the United Kingdom at the University Press, Cambridge

*A catalogue record for this publication is available from the British Library*

*Library of Congress Cataloguing in Publication data*

Cross-cultural psychology : research and applications / John W. Berry ...[et al.]–2nd ed.
    p.    cm.
Includes bibliographical references and index.
ISBN 0 521 64152 7–ISBN 0 521 64617 0 (pb.)
1. Ethnopsychology. I. Berry, John W.
GN502 .C76 2002
155.8–dc21    2001052479

ISBN 978-0-521-64152-4 hardback
ISBN 978-0-521-64617-8 paperback

**Dedicated to our partners in life**

# Contents

# Figures

# Tables

# Foreword

When commenting on the original text, I congratulated the authors and predicted that it would remain unrivaled for some time to come. This prediction has proved correct for the past decade, but over the period the book has inevitably become somewhat dated. In the old days, and by that I mean the 1960s and 1970s (which rather dates me!), I was easily able to read virtually everything published in the general area of psychology related to culture. Since then the expansion of the literature has become exponential, so that no single person could fully keep up with it.

Hence it is indeed fortunate that the authors have undertaken the heroic task of updating their work in a second edition. I say "heroic," since it was necessary to scan the voluminous literature not only in cross-cultural and cultural psychology, but also in such neighboring fields as anthropology and evolutionary biology. Moreover, they faced the difficulties of selection, of separating the wheat from the chaff. Since they are among the most able and experienced scholars in the field, it was not unexpected that they did a brilliant job, reshaping the book in such a way that it broadly reflects the current state of knowledge. It is also gratifying to find that, as indicated above, they brought "cultural psychology" in from the cold where it had languished in the first edition.

After part I, which is relatively plain sailing, the difficulty level rises steeply in part II, and one can relax again in part III. However, it is important to stress that grappling with part II is well worth the effort, since it is concerned with fundamental issues of method and theory – exciting and sometimes contentious. This means that it is hard to resist the temptation of entering into the fray, and I shall do so briefly. On the topic of methods, let me say first of all that the inclusion of qualitative aspects, relating mainly but by no means exclusively to cultural psychology, is to be welcomed. Turning to quantitative approaches, the treatment here is extremely thorough and even more high-powered than in the first edition. Although admirable in its technical sophistication, it could be argued that its recommendations constitute more of a statement of ideal aims than a realistic target, because relatively few empirical studies come close to achieving them. Hence novice cross-cultural psychologists should not be unduly alarmed or discouraged!

As regards the aims of cross-cultural psychology, I may perhaps be allowed to ride my hobbyhorse once again. The ultimate goal is still declared to be that of arriving at universals and "approaching universal laws," seeking to justify this by reference to biology and other disciplines. There is, however, an important difference between "universals" and "universal laws." Throughout universals are repeatedly mentioned, e.g. greetings or attribution, which have cultural variations superimposed on common elements. Now "greetings" is hardly a psychological category, and to say that attribution is "a basic psychological process" is little more than using an imposing label to refer to the universal human tendency to look for explanations of events (incidentally, such attributions often tend to be to supernaturals, a fact rarely noted by psychologists). The comparison with biology *in this context* is also misguided: biologists would find it rather odd to hear eating, drinking, and sleeping described as "biological laws," though they are clearly biological universals. In sum, it would seem that the authors' concepts in this sphere are perhaps somewhat lacking in clarity.

One does, however, find a more promising pointer. It is likely that non-trivial and non-obvious universals will be revealed by studies based on an evolutionary framework. Hence this would be a worthwhile and realistic goal, as indeed stated towards the end of ch. 10 on "Biology and culture": "We expect that culture-comparative research will increasingly become the testing ground of [evolutionary] models and theories."

Let me stress that the above is one of the very few topics on which I find myself in substantial disagreement with the authors. Generally they present complex issues with lucidity, alternative views being given a fair hearing. The volume is also enriched by the addition of two chapters as well as the inclusion of fresh material and fresh perspectives throughout. It was pleasing–to this reader at any rate–that the authors took some sideswipes at postmodern approaches, though they fail to convey the extent to which these have influenced (I am inclined to write "subverted") American anthropology.

Altogether I have profited a great deal from reading this book, since no amount of time spent in the library could have been as informative about changes during the past decade. Hence I can do no better than cite the concluding paragraph of my foreword to the first edition:

> In sum, the dedicated labor of the authors has resulted in a most impressive volume that is stimulating as well as useful, packed with information and ideas. It is likely to remain unrivaled for some time to come, and as such will certainly prove indispensable to all serious students, teachers, and practitioners of cross-cultural psychology.

Gustav Jahoda

# Preface to the first edition

This book provides an examination of the rapidly growing field of cross-cultural psychology for students who have had at least some prior academic training in psychology and related disciplines, and who seek to extend their knowledge of the relationship between culture and behavior. In assuming prior courses in psychology the present book differs from another volume by the same authors (M. H. Segall, P. R. Dasen, J. W. Berry, and Y. H. Poortinga (1990), *Human Behavior in Global Perspective: An Introduction to Cross-cultural Psychology.* New York: Pergamon Press). The two texts were prepared in a way that minimizes overlap in content, which allows for the present volume to follow the earlier one in a student's program.

The book consists of three parts, preceded by an introductory chapter and followed by an epilogue. The introduction orients the reader toward the field by providing a general framework that has guided the organization of the book. Part I critically surveys empirical studies in important areas of human behavior that have long been treated in psychology: these include developmental, social, personality, cognition, and perception. Part II provides essential information from the cognate disciplines of anthropology and biology. It also contains two chapters on the methodological and theoretical foundations of cross-cultural psychology that are needed for a critical appraisal of the literature. Part III builds upon the knowledge and principles established earlier on to consider how cross-cultural psychology can contribute to areas such as acculturation, ethnic and minority groups, organizations and work, communication and training, health behaviour, and the role of psychology in the developing world. The brief epilogue makes some concluding observations.

Inevitably, only a portion of the relevant research has been included. The selection of materials was based upon explicit interests of the authors, but also upon some implicit personal and cultural biases. Readers with other cultural concerns are invited to reflect on this book from their own perspectives, informed by knowledge of other traditions.

The chapters are intended to be read in the order in which they appear in the book. However, most chapters can be read on their own by those with specific interests. The boxes provide background information, extensions of certain arguments, and items of particular interest. They are meant to be read along with the main text, but can be omitted without loss of continuity. For most topics, sufficient references have been provided to enable the reader to pursue them in more detail; such supplementary reading is encouraged. Readers should look, in particular, for supplementary sources rooted in their own culture.

# Preface to the second edition

Some years ago Cambridge University Press asked us to prepare a second edition of this textbook. Needless to say we were pleased with this request, which in our view reflects not only a positive reaction to the first edition, but also testifies to the growth and viability of cross-cultural psychology.

We have retained the overall structure of the first edition with three parts, the first giving an empirical survey of the field, the second part oriented towards theory and method, and the third part dealing with applications. In part I there are now two more chapters. One of these is on emotions, an area of cross-cultural research that has grown in size and importance during the past decade. The other new chapter is on language, an area where the balance between universal and culture-specific aspects has become a major focus of analysis. As a consequence of these additions, the chapter on personality has been changed and is now more focussed on topics that traditionally belong to personality research.

The most important changes in part II are in the chapters on methodology and theory. Throughout the book, but especially in these chapters, we have paid more attention than in the first edition to the concerns reflected in the approach of cultural psychology. For reasons that we explain in the text, the alleged controversy between relativist (culturalist) and universalist (culture-comparative) approaches that has dominated so much of the theoretical discussion of the 1990s in many respects overstates differences and understates common issues and objectives. Perhaps even more than in the previous edition we have indicated our own position in various debates. We believe that it is preferable to state one's position explicitly, rather than to present it only implicitly through selection of materials and arguments.

In part III there is one less chapter than in the previous edition. There is now a single chapter on acculturation and intercultural relations, instead of two chapters. Theoretical conceptions on acculturation have been integrated in part I, especially in ch. 3 on social behavior.

Even more than in the previous edition we had to leave out many interesting topics of research and many findings that we would have liked to include. The field of cross-cultural psychology continues to expand and this means that within the scope of a single textbook only a selection of the available information can be discussed. As in the previous edition we have limited the overlap in content with our other textbook: M. H. Segall, P. R. Dasen, J. W. Berry, and Y. H. Poortinga (1999, 2nd ed.), *Human behavior in global perspective: An introduction to cross-cultural psychology* (Boston, MA: Allyn and Bacon).

Finally we would like to draw attention to some new features, namely the addition to each chapter of a few suggested readings and a glossary of key terms. We hope that this, together with the improved page layout will make the book more attractive for students.

## Acknowledgments

We benefited greatly from the reading of some draft chapters by Fons van de Vijver, Seger Breugelmans, and several students of the 2000 class in cross-cultural psychology at the University of Leuven. Valuable assistance was provided by Bilge Ataca, who carried out bibliographic searches, and by Joan Berry, who helped prepare the manuscript.

Secretarial help was given by Kim Leveck at Queen's University and Rinus Verkooijen at Tilburg University. For the final preparation of the text, including the organization of the references, we relied also on Rinus.

For what the book looks like the responsibility, and the credit, goes to Sarah Caro at Cambridge University Press. She has been encouraging and patient throughout a process that lasted much longer than she, and we, had anticipated.

We are really grateful to all those mentioned.

John W. Berry
Ype H. Poortinga
Marshall H. Segall
Pierre R. Dasen

# Acknowledgments

Figure 3.1 reproduced from Schwartz S. and Sagiv L. (1995) Identifying culture specific in the content and structure of values, Journal of Cross Cultural Psychology, 26, 92–116 by permission of Sage Publications Inc, 2455 Teller Road, Thousand Oaks, CA 91320.

Figure 3.2 from Hofstede G. (1980) Culture's Consequences: International differences in work related values, copyright © Geert Hofstede, reproduced with permission from the author and copyright holder.

Figure 5.1 from Berry J. W. and Bennett J. A. (1992) Cree conceptions of cognitive competence International Journal of Psychology, 24, 429–50 by permission of Taylor and Francis Group, New York, Philadelphia, London, Singapore. 325 Chestnut Street Philadelphia, PA 1906.

Figure 5.2 Reaction time tasks for Iranian and Dutch respondents on four tasks during three days from Sonke, Poortinga and de Kuijer (1999) by permission of Swets and Zeitlinger Publications.

Figure 6.1 from Vorster J. and Schuring G. (1989) Language and thought: Developmental perspectives on counterfactual conditionals South African Journal of Psychology, 19, 34–38 by permission of the publishers.

Figure 6.2 and Figure 6.3 reproduced from Brent Berlin B. and Kay P. Basic Color Terms: Their Universality and Evolution, fig 3, p8 and sequence 2, page 4 by permission of the authors.

Figure 8.1 reproduced from Deregowski et al (1972) Pictorial recognition in a remote Ethiopian population, Perception, 1, 417–25 by permission of the author and Pion Ltd, 207 Brondesbury Park, London, NW2 5JN.

Figure 8.3 Two figures from the Symmetry Completion Test from Poortinga, Y. H. and Foden B. I. M. (1975) A comparative study of curiosity in black and white South African students, Psychologia Africana, Monograph, Suppl. 8 by permission of National Institute for Personnel Research, South Africa.

Figure 8.4 Hudson (1960) Pictorial depth perception in sub-cultural groups in Africa from Journal of Social Psychology, 52, 183–208. Reprinted with permission of the Helen Dwight Reid Educational Foundation. Published by Heldref Publications, 1319 Eighteenth St, NW, Washington DC 20036-1802 Copyright © 2002.

Figure 8.5 from Deregowski J. B. (1968) Difficulties in pictorial depth perception in Africa. *British Journal of Psychology, 59*, 195–204.

Figure 8.6 from Deregowski J. B. and Berkley A. M. (1987) Seeing the impossible and building the likely. *British Journal of Psychology, 78*, 91–97.

Figure 8.7, 8.8 from Poorkinga Y. H. and Foden B. I. M. (1975) A comparative study of curiosuky in black and white South African students. *Psychologia Africana*, Monograph, Supplement 8.

Figure 9.1 from Whiting, B. B. and Whiting, J. W. M. (1975) Children of Six Cultures Cambridge, MA: Harvard University Press Copyright © 1975 by the President of Fellows of Harvard College. Reprinted by permission of the Publishers.

Figure 11.1, Table 11.1 from Malpass R. S. and Poortinga Y. H. (1986) Strategies for design and analysis, in honner W. and Berry J. W. eds., *Field Methods for Cross-cultural Research*, p. 50. Reprinted by permission of Sage Publications, Inc.

Table 11.2 from Van de Vijver, F. J. R. and Leung K. (1997) Methods of data analysis of comparative research in J. W. Berry, Y. H. Poortinga and J. Pandey (eds.) Theory and Method (pp. 275–300) Vol. 1 of Handbook of Cross-Cultural Psychology (2ed) by permission of Allyn and Bacon, 75 Arlington Street, Suite 300, Boston MA 02116.

Table 11.4 An overview of three types of bias and their possible sources reproduced with permission from European Journal of Psychological Assessment, vol. 13, No.1: 1997, pp. 29–37 © 1997 by Hogrefe and Huber Publishers, Seattle, Toronto, Bern, Göttingen.

# 1 Introduction to cross-cultural psychology

## What is cross-cultural psychology?

The field of cross-cultural psychology is the scientific study of variations in human behavior, taking into account the ways in which behavior is influenced by cultural context. This initial definition directs our attention to two central endeavors: describing the diversity of human behavior in the world, and attempting to link individual behavior to the cultural environment in which it occurs. This definition is relatively simple and straightforward. A number of other definitions reveal some new facets and point to some complexities:

1 "Cross-cultural research in psychology is the explicit, systematic comparison of psychological variables under different cultural conditions in order to specify the antecedents and processes that mediate the emergence of behaviour differences" (Eckensberger, 1972, p. 100).
2 "Cross-cultural psychology is the empirical study of members of various culture groups who have had different experiences that lead to predictable and significant differences in behavior. In the majority of such studies, the groups under study speak different languages and are governed by different political units" (Brislin, Lonner, & Thorndike, 1973, p. 5).
3 "Cultural psychology is, first of all, a designation for the comparative study of the way culture and psyche make each other up" (Shweder & Sullivan, 1993, p. 498).
4 "Cultural psychology (is) the study of the culture's role in the mental life of human beings" (Cole, 1996, p. 1).

In all these definitions, the term "culture" appears. For the time being, we can define culture as "the shared way of life of a group of people." Later, in ch. 9, we will consider more elaborate meanings of the term. Despite this common focus each definition attends more specifically to a particular feature, highlighting it for our consideration. In the first, the key idea is that of identifying cause and effect relationships between culture and behavior ("specify the antecedents and processes that mediate"); the second is more concerned with identifying the kinds of cultural experiences ("speak different languages") that may be factors in promoting human behavioral diversity. In the third and fourth definitions, the adjective "cross-cultural" is replaced by "cultural"; this single change signifies a broader set of ideas that will also be elaborated in chs. 9 and 12. However, in essence, the core issues are whether "culture" and "behavior" are distinguishable entities, and whether the former is antecedent to, or even causes, the latter. In the "cultural" approach to the field, there is an emphasis on the mutual, interactive relationship between cultural and behavioral phenomena. In our view, the field of cross-cultural psychology incorporates both the "culture-comparative" and "cultural" perspectives represented in these definitions (Berry, 1997b, 2000a; Poortinga, 1997). This position will be elaborated and supported in ch. 12.

Limited attention is given in this set of definitions to some other interests. For example, cross-cultural psychology is concerned not only with diversity, but also with uniformity: what is there that might be psychologically common or universal in the human species (Lonner, 1980)? Moreover, there are other kinds of contextual variables (not usually included in the conception of culture) that have been considered to be part of the cross-cultural enterprise. These include biological variables (Dawson, 1971) such as nutrition, genetic inheritance, and hormonal processes which may vary across groups along with their cultures (see ch. 10) and ecological variables (Berry, 1976a) that are based on a view of human populations as being in a process of adaptation to their natural environment, emphasizing factors such as economic activity (hunting, gathering, farming, etc.) and population density. This view permeates much of this text.

Also not included in these definitions is any mention of the term "cross-national." As pointed out by Frijda and Jahoda (1966), while cross-national comparisons may be the same as in cross-cultural psychology, this term refers to studies carried out in two populations which are culturally closely related (such as Scots–Irish, or French–Spanish comparisons). Another kind of study has become increasingly important: this is the study of various ethnocultural groups within a single nation state which interact and change as they adapt to living together. The justification for such an ethnic psychology (Berry, 1985) being included in cross-cultural psychology is that most groups show continuity over time; some longstanding groups continue to express their original cultures (for example Aboriginal, African, and Spanish peoples in the Americas), while other more recent immigrant groups maintain distinctive cultures for generations after migration. This special focus on intercultural behavior in cross-cultural psychology is signaled in the following definition by the term "change" (which often results from contact between cultures), and is considered in detail in ch. 13.

We are now in a position to propose the general **definition of cross-cultural psychology** that will be used in this book:

> Cross-cultural psychology is the study: of similarities and differences in individual psychological functioning in various cultural and ethnocultural groups; of the relationships between psychological variables and socio-cultural, ecological and biological variables; and of ongoing changes in these variables.

## Goals of cross-cultural psychology

Implied in the various definitions given in the previous section are a set of goals for cross-cultural psychology; these may now be made explicit. Perhaps the first and most obvious goal is the testing of the generality of existing psychological knowledge and theories. This goal was proposed by Whiting (1968), who argued that we do cross-cultural psychology, using data from "various peoples throughout the world to test hypotheses concerning human behavior." Dawson (1971), too, emphasized this goal when he proposed that cross-cultural psychology was conducted, in part, "so that the universal validity of psychological theories can be more effectively examined." This point of view was further reiterated by Segall, Dasen, Berry, and Poortinga (1999), who have argued that it is essential to test the cross-cultural generality of these existing principles before considering them to be established.

This first goal has been called the transport and test goal by Berry and Dasen (1974); in essence psychologists seek to transport their present hypotheses and findings to other cultural settings in order to test their validity and applicability in other (and, eventually, in all) groups of human beings. As examples, we may ask whether it is everywhere the case that "practice makes perfect" (performance improves over trials in a study of learning), or that "antisocial behavior is a normal part of adolescence" (the storm and stress hypothesis). For this first goal, obviously, we start with what we know to be the case in our own culture and examine the question in another culture; the formulation of the question is not particularly sensitive to discovering psychological phenomena that may be important in the other culture.

To remedy this problem, a second goal was proposed by Berry and Dasen (1974): to explore other cultures in order to discover cultural and psychological variations which are not present in our own limited cultural experience. While we may be alerted to the presence of these other phenomena by our failure to find the same results when pursuing the first goal, we could simply come back from our study in the other culture with the conclusion that there were no performance effects in learning or social problems in adolescence. However, this second goal makes it clear that we should go beyond such a failure to replicate or generalize, and seek out the reasons for failure, or find alternative (perhaps culture-specific) ways in which learning progresses, or adolescents achieve adulthood. Moreover, this second goal requires us to keep our eyes open for novel aspects of behavior, even when we do find support for the generality of the phenomenon we are studying. For example, individuals may evidence different culturally based learning strategies. The recent rise of the "cultural" perspective has emphasized the importance of this need to understand human behavior as enmeshed in its particular cultural context.

The third goal is to attempt to assemble and integrate, into a broadly based psychology, the results obtained when pursuing the first two goals, and to generate a more nearly universal psychology that will be valid for a broader range of cultures. This third goal is necessary because of the distinct possibility that, in pursuing our first goal, we will find limits to the generality of our existing psychological knowledge, and that in pursuing our second goal, we will discover some novel psychological phenomena that need to be taken into account in a more general psychological theory.

It is a working assumption of this textbook that such "universal laws" of human behavior can be approached. That is, we believe that we can approach the underlying psychological processes that are characteristic of our species, *homo sapiens*, as a whole. Our belief is based upon the existence of such universals in related disciplines. For example, in biology, there are well-established pan-species primary needs (such as eating, drinking, sleeping) even though their fulfillment is achieved in very different ways in different cultures. In sociology, there are universal sets of relationships (such as dominance); in linguistics there are universal features of language (such as grammatical rules); and in anthropology, there are universal customs and institutions (such as tool making and the family). In psychology, it is therefore plausible to proceed on the assumption that we will also uncover universals of human behavior even though (as in these cognate disciplines) there will likely be wide variation across cultures in the ways in which these universal processes are developed, displayed, and deployed.

While not everyone agrees with our view that, eventually a pan-human or global psychology will be achieved (e.g., Boesch, 1996), others, who represent alternative perspectives, have also accepted it as a plausible outcome of our endeavors. For example, Greenfield (1994, p. 1) has noted that, "Developmental psychology, like other branches of psychology, desires to establish a universal science of the person"; and Yang (2000, p. 257) writing from the "indigenous psychology" perspective has argued that these psychologies "collectively ... serve the higher purpose of developing a balanced, genuine global psychology."

To help us distinguish these various points of view, three general orientations have been proposed (Berry, Poortinga, Segall, & Dasen, 1992). These three theoretical orientations are absolutism, relativism, and universalism (see ch. 12). The position of **absolutism** is one that assumes that psychological phenomena are basically the same (qualitatively) in all cultures: "honesty" is "honesty," and "depression" is "depression," no matter where one observes them. From the absolutist perspective, culture is thought to play little or no role in either the meaning or display of human characteristics. Assessments of such characteristics are made using standard instruments (perhaps with linguistic translation) and interpretations are made easily, without taking culturally based views into account.

In sharp contrast, **relativism** assumes that all human behavior is culturally patterned. It seeks to avoid ethnocentrism by trying to understand people "in their own terms." Explanations of human diversity are sought in the cultural context in which people have developed. Assessments are typically carried out employing the values and meanings that a cultural group gives to a phenomenon. Comparisons are judged to be conceptually and methodologically problematic and ethnocentric, and are thus virtually never made.

A third perspective, **universalism**, lies somewhere between the first two positions. It makes the assumption that basic psychological processes are common to all members of the species (that is, they constitute a set of psychological givens in all human beings) and that culture influences the development and display of psychological characteristics (that is, culture plays different variations on these underlying themes). Assessments are based on the presumed underlying process, but measures are developed in culturally meaningful versions. Comparisons are made cautiously, employing a wide variety of methodological principles and safeguards, and interpretations of similarities and differences are attempted that take alternative culturally based meanings into account. Universalism has sometimes been confused with absolutism. However, we see it as very distinct for two reasons. First, universalism seeks to understand the role of culture in stimulating behavioral diversity and, rather than dismissing culture, accepts it as the source of human variety. Second, while assuming that basic processes are likely to be common features of the human species, this approach permits the discovery not only of behavioral similarities (universals), but also of differences (cultural specifics) across human groups. Universalism is also clearly distinguishable from relativism, since comparisons are considered essential to the achievement of a global understanding of human behavior.

## Relationships with other disciplines

Clearly, cross-cultural psychology has all the hallmarks of an international and interdisciplinary enterprise (see box 1.1 for an overview of current activity in the field of cross-cultural psychology). This is also evident from our definition, in which we seek to discover systematic relationships between population-level data (from ecology, biology, and anthropology) and individual psychological data. Wherever scientists approach a topic from an interdisciplinary perspective, it is useful to deal with the issue of **levels of analysis**, which is concerned with the legitimacy of studying a phenomenon from various perspectives without the threat of reductionism (the tendency in interdisciplinary debate to reduce the phenomena of one discipline to the level of explanation commonly employed in the next "more basic" discipline). Thus, in our frame of reference, we need to avoid reducing culture to the level of psychological explanations, psychological phenomena to biological explanations, biological to chemical, and so on. That is, we must recognize

## Box 1.1 Current activity in cross-cultural psychology

Cross-cultural psychology is now an established, thriving intellectual enterprise peopled by hundreds of scholars from many parts of the world. As early as 1973, 1,125 cross-cultural psychologists were listed in a published *Directory of cross-cultural research and researchers* (Berry, Lonner, & Leroux, 1973) and presumably more were not listed. Although most such scholars are in departments of psychology in North American and European universities, many are to be found in the universities in Africa, Asia, Latin America, and Oceania. Wherever they may be, they are linked by a variety of institutions. In large numbers they belong to established professional organizations, including the International Association for Cross-Cultural Psychology (IACCP, founded in 1972), the Society for Cross-Cultural Research (SCCR, 1972), and the French-language Association pour la Recherche Interculturelle (ARIC, 1984). The increasing cadres of cross-cultural psychologists now enjoy a diversity of journals in which they publish their research findings. These include the *Journal of Cross-Cultural Psychology* (founded in 1970), the *International Journal of Psychology* (1966), *Ethos* (1972), the *International Journal of Intercultural Relations* (1978), *Mind, Culture and Activity* (1994), *Culture and Psychology* (1995), and the *Asian Journal of Social Psychology* (1998).

A brief introduction to cross-cultural psychology for beginning students of psychology was written by Serpell (1976), while a textbook by Segall (1979) was widely used during the 1980s (later revised by Segall, Dasen, Berry, & Poortinga, 1990, 1999). Other texts include Brislin (1997), Cole (1996) and Matsumoto (2000) in English, Camilleri and Vinsonneau (1996), Guerraoui and Troadec (2000) and Vinsonneau (1997) written in French, and Thomas (1993) in German.

A series on cross-cultural psychology (edited by W. J. Lonner and J. W. Berry) has been published since 1974. Since then, over twenty volumes have appeared, ranging from research methods to mental health, and from learning to social psychology. The bibliographies in all of these attest to the virtual explosion of interest and activity in cross-cultural psychology.

Conferences devoted largely or even exclusively to cross-cultural psychology are now frequent. The International Association for Cross-Cultural Psychology has met, starting in 1972 in Hong Kong, every two years until the present. Many regional meetings have also taken place in Africa, Asia, Europe, and the Americas. The proceedings of most such conferences are also published, thus adding to the regional materials available for study by cross-cultural psychologists.

A first comprehensive source of information for the field was the six-volume *Handbook of cross-cultural psychology* (1980) under the general editorship of H. C. Triandis. A second edition of the *Handbook of cross-*

**Box 1.1 (continued)**

*cultural psychology* appeared in 1997 in three volumes: vol. I: *Theory and method* (edited by J. W. Berry, Y. H. Poortinga, & J. Pandey); vol. II: *Basic processes and human development* (edited by J. W. Berry, P. R. Dasen, & T. S. Saraswathi); vol. III: *Social behavior and applications* (edited by J. W. Berry, M. H. Segall, C. Kagitcibasi). Students and other readers who seek a detailed exposition will be much rewarded by studying these handbooks.

that there are, for example, cultural phenomena which exist and can be studied at their own level. These phenomena cannot be rendered into psychological terms; the same is true for all the other disciplines with which we are concerned.

Cross-cultural psychology is related to a number of population-level disciplines (anthropology, biology, ecology, linguistics, sociology) that are largely concerned with describing, analyzing, and understanding features of whole populations, groups, or collectivities; in these disciplines there is not a primary concern with specific individuals. And, of course, the field incorporates the characteristic domains of psychology (such as development, social behaviors, personality, cognition, language, emotion, and perception) that are concerned with individual-level (including inter- and intra-individual) phenomena. From these disciplines cross-cultural psychology can draw a substantial amount of information. This can be employed to establish the general context for the psychological development and functioning of individuals, and for understanding variations in individual behavior displayed in different cultural populations. The field of cross-cultural psychology attempts to link these population and individual levels in order to provide insight into individual behavior as it relates to population-level phenomena. Note that the particular fields of individual behavior mentioned above are those that we consider in part I of this book, in our survey of the field.

Another way of thinking about these two levels is to note the argument that to a large extent the population-level disciplines are naturalistic, basically concerned with understanding things the way they are, and where they are, in nature. For example, for anthropology, Edgerton (1974, pp. 63–4) has argued that "at heart, anthropologists are naturalists whose commitment is to the phenomena themselves. Anthropologists have always believed that human phenomena can best be understood by procedures that are primarily sensitive to context, be it situational, social, or cultural." In contrast, psychologists often use more intrusive methods, such as experiments, tests, interviews, and other methods in which the researcher constructs an artificial situation within which to control or constrain behavior. Of course, many psychologists have used more naturalistic methods (such as observation) for a long time, and Edgerton points out that there is no inherent superiority of naturalism over experimentalism; they both are legitimate scientific approaches, at their own levels. He concludes that if there is to be a valid interdisciplinary domain, so that "a convergence between anthropology and psychology can come about, then it must somehow combine naturalism and experimentation" (p. 64). The same argument can be made when we wish to bridge psychology and other population-level disciplines (ecology, biology, population genetics, linguistics, and sociology). An attempt will be made in part II of this book to show in what way and to what extent this bridging can be done, when we consider cultural (including ecological), biological, and psychological approaches in more detail.

In detailed analyses, Jahoda (1990a; Jahoda & Krewer, 1997) has examined the relationship between anthropology and psychology, which is, in many respects, the most substantial of these interdisciplinary relationships. He has traced the long, but sporadic, interactions between the two disciplines from the time when they were largely undifferentiated (in the nineteenth century), through a period when many scholars were experts in both fields (around the beginning of the twentieth century). Then followed a period of mutual neglect, even hostility, with the exception of the field of "culture and personality" (now known as "psychological anthropology" – see ch. 9) up to the past few decades in which there has been a serious meeting of minds between a number of anthropologists and psychologists. Klineberg (1980) has also traced this on–off relationship, much of it from the point of view of an active participant.

## Ethnocentrism in psychology

The cross-cultural study of differences may lead to their being viewed as deficiencies; the differential evaluation of differences between groups (as in "us better–them worse") is known as **ethnocentrism**. The term was coined by Sumner (1906), who noted that there exists a strong tendency to use one's own group's standards as *the* standard when viewing other groups, to place one's group at the top of a hierarchy and to rank all others as lower. This tendency may even be a universal feature of cultural group relations (LeVine & Campbell, 1972). However, it need not be (and we argue, *should* not be) a feature of cross-cultural psychology. In its stead, a value-neutral position has been advocated for anthropology (Herskovits, 1948) and for psychology by many researchers who consider that we, too, must avoid absolute judgments that are rooted in our own culture. Essentially, this position is one that assumes no evaluative stance with respect to differences; each varying phenomenon is viewed in its own context, and described and interpreted relative to the cultural or ecological situation in which it occurs.[1] An obvious example, from the domain of social behavior, is that of greeting procedures; in many

---

[1] For some, relativism accords respect for, but not necessarily acceptance of, various cultural practices and individual behaviors. It is also useful to note here that Herskovits, who used the concept of cultural relativism, limited his concerns to the making of ethnocentric value judgments. He did not consider it necessary to prohibit the making of comparisons, nor did he argue that no cultural or psychological phenomena were common across cultural groups. In ch. 12 we will employ the term relativism to refer to the general position taken by some researchers that seeks to avoid both value judgments and comparisons.

Western cultures a firm handshake and direct eye contact are considered appropriate, while in other parts of the world, a bow, without eye contact, is proper. It is difficult to avoid imposing one's own cultural norms (feeling that looking down is inappropriate), or making attributions about the other person (as shy or lacking in manners) even when one has had frequent contact with other cultures. However, it is necessary to avoid these value judgments in cross-cultural psychology.

Apart from leading to incorrect interpretations of other people's behavior, the effects of ethnocentrism can enter into cross-cultural research at three more levels. An obvious danger is the introduction of culture-specific meaning with instruments that originally were designed in one particular culture. If there is one message that emerges from knowledge accumulated so far, it is that we should never assume an item or task in a psychological instrument to have the same meaning cross-culturally. A more subtle effect of ethnocentrism lies in the choice of research topics. Psychologists from developing countries have lamented the lack of societal relevance of cross-cultural research. There is another side to this complaint, namely that a hasty application of presumed scientific knowledge in the past has led to gross and serious errors. A final level at which ethnocentrism is likely to affect cross-cultural research is in the formulation of theories. Our notions and ideas about behavior have cultural antecedents. Consequently, even theory-driven research is likely to be affected by cultural biases.

Cross-cultural psychology attempts to reduce the ethnocentrism of psychology in one important sense: by recognizing the limitations of our current knowledge (cf. the first goal), and by seeking to extend our data and theory through the inclusion of other cultures (cf. the second and third goals), we can reduce the culture-bound nature of the discipline. The pursuit of this goal of reducing ethnocentrism exposes us to the risk of even more ethnocentrism since it involves collecting and interpreting data from other cultures. As a general rule, the greater the cultural or behavioral difference, the greater the potential for negative evaluations of the difference. Indeed, one critic (Nisbet, 1971) has argued that the (culture-)comparative method is "profoundly ethnocentric" (p. 95), and is just another way (now claiming scientific respectability) of placing other peoples in a hierarchy with European cultures at the top, and others ranked below. Similarly, in a thorough analysis of the discipline of history, Preiswerk and Perrot (1978) have shown the dangers that social scientists face when looking at their own past in relation to that of others: who can resist the temptation to accept even in subtle ways, his or her own superiority? However, resist we must, and an explicit recognition of the potential for ethnocentrism is a first step towards its control.

A second protection lies in a proposal made by Campbell (1970) to carry out every cross-cultural research project four times. If a researcher from one culture (A) studies a phenomenon in that culture (study 1), and no comparisons are made outside the culture, it remains culture bound. The usual cross-cultural research study is when a researcher from culture A does the study in another culture (B; study 2) and compares the results with those obtained in study 1. Campbell argues (1970, p. 70) that for both of these studies there is an inherent ambiguity: "for any given feature of the report, it is equivocal whether or not it is a trait of the observer or a trait of the object observed" that might account for the similarity or difference between the two studies.

To overcome this problem, Campbell recommends carrying out two more studies, 3 and 4. Here a second researcher, this time from culture B, studies his or her own culture (study 3) and then the other culture (A; study 4). In this way, comparison across the four studies will enable us to distinguish differences which arise from ethnocentric bias in the researcher from differences which are actually present between the two cultures. The first possibility (bias) would be signaled by a sharp disagreement between the outcome of studies 1 and 4, and between studies 2 and 3, usually in reciprocal ways. For example, in the first comparison (1 against 4) individuals from culture A might be judged to be superior on some trait, while in the second comparison (2 against 3) the reverse might be claimed for the same trait. The second possibility (valid differences) would be signaled by common findings in the two comparisons (1 and 4, and 2 and 3). To our knowledge, this type of multiple study has not yet been carried out in cross-cultural psychology. However, the scientific advantages of doing so are clear; so, too, are the disadvantages, in terms of cost, time, and effort. Still, the very existence of the proposal neatly identifies the nature of the problem, and shows us how we can tackle it, if resources are available.

Without meaning to minimize the dangers of ethnocentrism, the working assumption of this book is nevertheless that principles of behavior which have universal validity can be formulated. Psychology as it is known today in all probability contains strong ethnocentric elements reflecting specific manifestations of behavior from the industrial urban societies where psychological science has largely been developed. We acknowledge that until alternative approaches, focussing on other research topics and theories, rooted in other cultures, have been formulated and extensively tested, psychology will unfortunately remain a Western, ethnocentric, and incomplete, science.

The search for non-Western approaches has been gaining momentum; these have come to be known as **indigenous psychologies** (Kim & Berry, 1993; Sinha, 1997). However, such studies are still few in number and so far they have had little impact on psychology as a science, even in non-industrialized countries. In other words, the extent of scientific colonialism in psychology is rather great, but difficult to evaluate, and even more difficult to remedy (see ch. 17). We can only hope that we reflect in this book an awareness about the limitations inherent in contemporary psychological knowledge.

## A general framework for cross-cultural psychology

It is useful at the outset to have some conceptual framework within which the various bits and pieces the reader comes across can be meaningfully placed. Of course, no single framework can do justice to the variation or complexity of cross-cultural psychology, and as we acquire more information and insight, we

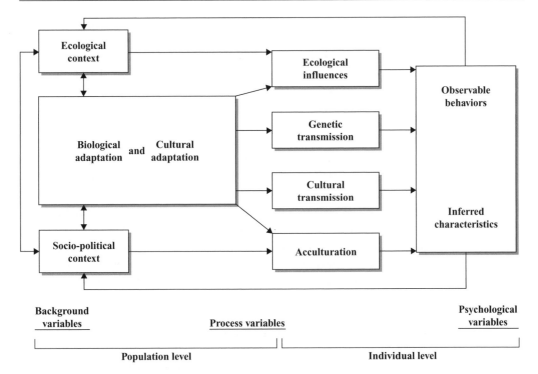

**1.1** An ecocultural framework of relationships among classes of variables
employed in cross-cultural psychology

become less comfortable with a simple model. Nevertheless, the advantages probably outweigh the disadvantages, and so we present a general framework that we
call the **ecocultural framework**, in fig. 1.1. This framework is a conceptual
scheme rather than a theoretical model from which specific testable hypotheses
can be derived. It is a general guide to classes of variables and their relevance
for the explanation of similarities and differences in human behavior and experience to be found across cultures.

This framework derives from thinking about how behavioral, cultural, and
ecological phenomena might be related, particularly the work of Malinowski
(1924) and Rivers (1924). For Malinowski (whose views are known as func-
tionalism) features of a culture are to be understood "by the manner in which
they are related to each other within the system, and by the manner in which
the system is related to the physical surroundings" (1924, p. xxx). Here the
linkages between ecology and culture are proposed. For Rivers, "the ultimate
aim of all studies of mankind . . . is to reach explanation in terms of psychology . . . by which the conduct of man, both individual and collective, is determined . . . by the social structure of which every person . . . finds himself a
member" (p. 1). Here the linkages between human behavior and the sociocultural context are proposed. Together, the sequence of ecology–culture–behavior
came to be part of thinking about how to account for psychological similarities

and differences around the world. This theme was carried forward by those who worked in the field of "culture and personality" (such as Kardiner & Linton, 1945; Whiting, 1974; see ch. 9), and by those who proposed an "ecocultural" approach in cross-cultural psychology (e.g., Berry, 1966, 1976a; Troadec, 2000). The framework used in this text is part of this long tradition of thinking about human diversity, continuing its use in the first edition of this text[2] and in Segall et al. (1999).

Earlier we distinguished between the population level and the individual level of analysis. This distinction is used in fig. 1.1, with the former on the left of the framework, and the latter on the right. The general flow of the framework is from left to right, with population-level variables (left part) conceived of as influencing the individual outcomes (right part). This general flow is intended to correspond to the interests of cross-cultural psychology; we wish to account for individual and group similarities and differences in psychological characteristics as a function of population-level factors. However, it is obvious that a full model (one that attempted to specify completely relationships in the real world) would have numerous feedback arrows representing influences by individuals back to the other variables in the framework.

The notion of feedback is necessary in order to avoid viewing the developing and behaving individual as a mere pawn in such a framework. According to many philosophical and psychological theories, human beings are active participants in their relationships with the physical and cultural contexts in which they operate. There is an interactive or dialectical relationship (Boesch, 1991; Eckensberger, 1996; see ch. 12) that can both filter and alter the very nature of these contexts, so that we must represent this possibility in any overall conception. However, for ease presenting the framework, only two feedback relationships are illustrated in fig. 1.1 (individuals influencing their ecological and sociopolitical contexts), and this should be taken to signal the presence of feedback in the framework more generally, even though not all such relationships are indicated in the figure.

At the extreme left are three major classes of influence: the two background variables of ecological and sociopolitical contexts; and the biological and cultural adaptations made by a population to these two contexts. At the extreme right are the psychological characteristics that are usually the focus of psychological research (including both observable behaviors and inferred characteristics, such as motives, abilities, traits, and attitudes). The middle sets of variables (process variables) represent the various kinds of transmission or influence to individuals from population variables (including the contextual, biological, and cultural adaptation factors).

In more detail, the ecological context is the setting in which human organisms and the physical environment interact; it is best understood as a set of relationships

---

[2] The position of the biological and cultural adaptation variables is now between the two contextual variables, rather than to the right (as in the first edition of this text). This change better communicates our view that biological and cultural adaptation occur together with (or even occasionally precede) ecological and cultural variables, rather than following from them.

that provide a range of life possibilities for a population. These possibilities include both opportunities, or affordances, and limitations, or constraints, on cultural and psychological development (see ch. 12). Such an interactive point of view is the essence of an ecological approach to understanding culture (see ch. 9), and allows us to avoid the pitfalls of earlier approaches, such as that of "environmental determinism" (Feldman, 1975; Moran, 1990); this interaction is signaled by the bidirectional arrow between the ecological and adaptation boxes.[3]

One central feature of this ecological context is economic activity, in which non-industrial cultural groups are examined with respect to their degree of reliance on five kinds of economic activity: hunting, gathering, fishing, pastoralism, and agriculture. Urban industrial societies have a way of life in which other dimensions of economic activity have emerged; in particular, socioeconomic status has come to be related to cultural or ethnic group characteristics in many societies. However, each form of economic activity implies a different kind of relationship between the local human population and the animal and physical resources of its habitat. These relationships in turn imply varying cultural, biological, and psychological outcomes, as we shall see in the chapters to come.

With respect to adaptation at the population level, we take the position that individual behavior can be understood across cultures only when both the cultural and biological features of our species are taken into account. This joint interest in cultural and biological influences on behavior appears to us to be not only balanced, but, indeed, the only possible point of view to adopt; the exclusion of either culture or biology as factors in the explanation of human variation makes little sense (Freeman, 1983; Boyd & Richerson, 1985; Massimini & Delle Fave, 2000). We shall later argue (in chs. 9 and 10) that these two major sources of influence are together adaptive to the contexts in which individuals live.

The framework also illustrates various ways in which features of the population (on the left) become incorporated into an individual's behavioral repertoire (on the right). These process variables include both genetic and cultural transmission; the first will be discussed in ch. 10, while the second will be elaborated in ch. 2, using the central concepts of **enculturation** and **socialization**.

Not all outcomes can be seen as being the result of ecological relationships. We also take the view that culture and individual behavior are affected by influences stemming from culture contact in the sociopolitical context of an individual's own group. These come about with contacts between populations arising from such historical and contemporary experiences as colonial expansion, international trade,

---

[3] In both anthropological and psychological theory, these interactions can proceed in two ways. One is for the population and its individual members to alter the context in some way in order to increase the fit between them and the environment; this "man over nature" strategy has been termed primary control (Weisz, Rothbaum, & Blackburn, 1984) or efficacy (Bandura, 1998), in psychology and is one of the cultural value orientations studied in anthropology (see ch. 3). The other is for the population and its members to seek to "live with nature" by altering their customs and daily behavior to fit into an ecosystem that they do not wish to (or cannot) change. The bidirectional arrows seek to represent this double strategy.

invasion, and migration. This contact leads to another process variable, that of acculturation, which involves mutual influence between the groups in contact; this process will be elaborated in ch. 13.

It is important to note that not all relationships between the two major background variables and psychological outcomes are mediated by cultural and biological adaptation or transmission. Some influences are direct and rather immediate, such as environmental learning in a particular ecology (leading to a new performance), nutritional deficiency during a famine (leading to reduced performance), or a new experience with another culture (leading to new attitudes or values). These direct influences are indicated by the upper and lower arrows that bypass the two forms of population adaptation, as well as the genetic and cultural transmission processes. Many of these direct influences have been the focus of work in the field of ecological psychology. We also adopt the position that individuals can recognize, screen, appraise, and alter all of these influences (whether direct or mediated); as a result, there are likely to be wide individual differences in the psychological outcomes, and return (reciprocal) influences on the background contexts and the various process variables.

To summarize, we consider that the distribution of psychological characteristics within and across groups can best be understood with the help of a framework such as this one. When ecological, biological, cultural, and acculturational factors are identified and taken into consideration, we should be able to account for how and why people differ from one another, and why they are also the same.

## Conclusions

We have argued that, in its content and approach, cross-cultural psychology draws upon various established scientific traditions: biology, which provides information on the structure and functioning of the human organism; general psychology, which is an individual-level discipline that studies human behavior in laboratory and field settings; and social sciences which reside, in particular cultural anthropology, at the population level, and emphasize more naturalistic, observational methods. As such, cross-cultural psychology is an "inter-discipline," operating in a space largely left vacant and unattended by these other disciplines, but one very much in need of attention. This need to understand population-level influences on individual-level psychological functioning is best met by attempting to adopt a non-ethnocentric standpoint, while remaining oriented toward the long-term possibility of generating universal psychological laws.

Our theoretical approach consists of two positions. The first is that we need to take cultural context seriously in understanding human psychological phenomena, and we need to do this work comparatively across cultures. Both aspects are necessary, neither being sufficient by itself: together, the "cultural" and the "comparative" approaches give us cross-cultural psychology. The second is that culture–behavior relationships are reciprocal: individual human beings produce culture, and individual behavior is influenced by culture. However, we believe that these are distinct levels of activity, and analysis, and need distinct levels of conceptualization and measurement; one cannot be reduced to, or subsumed within, the other.

Finally, we believe that two methodological positions will assist us in fulfilling this need. One is that on the continuum from pure phenomenology to unrestricted positivism we occupy an intermediate position (with some of us more, and some of us less, positivist). We believe that the basis of science is empirical studies, which are designed so that the data can show the beliefs and expectations of researchers to be incorrect. In other words, theoretical notions have to be open to empirical scrutiny. The second methodological theme of this book is the inherent ambiguity that attends the interpretation of any observed behavioral differences between cultural groups; are they a valid indication of differences in psychological functioning, or are they merely an artifact of the methods used? We adopt a critical perspective to the making of intergroup comparisons of psychological data. A cross-cultural psychology that looks critically at other areas of the behavioral sciences, but not at its own shortcomings, in our opinion would undermine one of its more important functions.

## Key terms

absolutism

(definition of) cross-cultural psychology

ecocultural framework

enculturation

ethnocentrism

indigenous psychologies

levels of analysis

relativism

socialization

universalism

## Further reading

Berry, J. W., Poortinga, Y. H., Pandey, J., Dasen, P. R., Saraswathi, T. S., Segall, M. H., & Kagitcibasi, C. (eds.) (1997). *Handbook of cross-cultural psychology* (2nd ed., vols. 1–3). Boston, MA: Allyn and Bacon. The three-volume handbook consists of thirty-one chapters which together represent the state of the art in much of cross-cultural psychology. This source is recommended as a first entry to a broader literature for a reader who wishes to learn more about a topic.

Brislin, R. (1997). *Understanding culture's influence on behavior* (2nd ed.). Fort Worth, TX: Harcourt. Brislin's text deals more than the present one with aspects of social behavior, paying ample attention to major dimensions on which cultural populations tend to be distinguished, like individualism–collectivism. It is particularly directed to an audience interested in the practical applications of cross-cultural psychology.

Cole, M. (1996). *Cultural psychology: A once and future discipline*. Cambridge, MA: Harvard University Press. This is a sophisticated text written from a culturalist (relativist) perspective. Cole attempts to integrate biological, sociohistorical, and psychological perspectives on behavior.

Jahoda, G., & Krewer, B. (1997). History of cross-cultural and cultural psychology. In J. W. Berry, Y. H. Poortinga, & J. Pandey (Eds.), *Theory and method,* pp. 1–42. Vol. I of *Handbook of cross-cultural psychology.* Boston, MA: Allyn and Bacon. Starting with classical Greece this chapter provides a historical overview of endeavors that today would be considered part of cross-cultural psychology. A leading theme is the distinction between the relativist and universalist approaches.

Matsumoto, D. (2000). *Culture and psychology* (2nd ed.). Pacific Grove, CA: Brooks/ Cole. This textbook provides a fairly wide coverage of the field of cross-cultural psychology, considering its size. It comes fairly close in orientation to the present book and the following one by Segall et al.

Segall, M. H., Dasen, P. R., Berry, J. W., & Poortinga, Y. H. (1999). *Human behavior in global perspective: An introduction to cross-cultural psychology* (2nd ed.). Boston, MA: Allyn and Bacon. This textbook, written by the same authors as the present one, is more oriented to students who have had little formal training in psychology. Like the present text, it provides a broad overview of the field, but differs from it in some aspects of content: for example, Segall et al. deals more extensively with education and socialization.

**1**

# Similarities and differences in behavior across cultures

# 2 Cultural transmission and individual development

At the end of ch. 1, we proposed a general framework (fig. 1.1) that related ecological and sociopoliticial contexts at the population level to psychological outcomes at the individual level. Two key elements of the model that serve as a way for the human species and for cultural groups to reproduce themselves and transmit their culture to new members are those of biological and cultural transmission. Obviously, human beings acquire patterns of behavior through experiences that are characteristic of the context in which they live. We begin with the concept of transmission because it is central to much of this chapter, indeed to much of this book. In subsequent sections we follow the development of the individual, often called **ontogenetic development**, through the lifespan. Hence, there is a section on early development and caretaking. Human infants cannot develop on their own; they need to be taken care of for a longer period of time than the young in any other species. In the section on enculturation and socialization we examine cultural practices in the transmission by adults, and the learning by children, of culturally appropriate behaviors. Here we draw upon both ethnographic reports and psychological studies. There is a brief section on adolescence, a period of life that has been much discussed in the cross-cultural literature. One section deals with a more specific topic, namely moral development. We have chosen this topic, among many others, because it deals with an aspect of behavior that has received explicit attention in research. Finally, we devote a section to conceptualizations of development, in which we outline some theories of ontogenetic development that are concerned explicitly with the role of culture.

## Cultural and biological transmission

The concept of **cultural transmission** was used by Cavalli-Sforza and Feldman (1981) to parallel the notion of **biological or genetic transmission** by which, through genetic mechanisms (see fig. 1.1), certain features of a population are perpetuated over time across generations. Biological transmission will be discussed in ch. 10 of this book (see also other sources like Keller, 1997, for theories of how these biological factors enter into cross-cultural psychology). Here we merely want to note the central biological feature of transmission, namely the passing on of the species-specific genetic material from two parents to the individual at the moment of conception. By analogy, using various forms of cultural transmission a cultural group can perpetuate its behavioral features among subsequent generations employing teaching and learning mechanisms. Cultural transmission from parents to their offspring is termed vertical transmission by Cavalli-Sforza and Feldman, since it involves the descent of cultural characteristics from one generation to the next. However, while vertical descent is the only possible form of biological transmission, there are two other forms of cultural transmission, horizontal and oblique (see fig. 2.1).

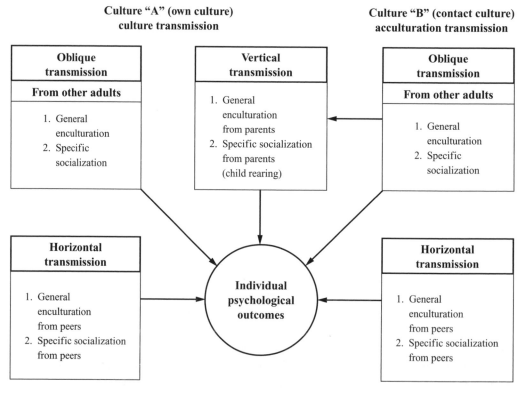

**2.1** Vertical, horizontal, and oblique forms of cultural transmission and acculturation
Modified from Berry & Cavalli-Sforza, 1986

These three forms of cultural transmission involve two processes: **enculturation** and **socialization** (see later section). Enculturation takes place by the "enfolding" of individuals by their culture, leading them to incorporate appropriate behavior into their repertoires. Socialization takes place by more specific instruction and training, again leading to the acquisition of culture-appropriate behavior.

In vertical transmission parents transmit cultural values, skills, beliefs, and motives to their offspring. In this case it is difficult to distinguish between cultural and biological transmission, since we typically learn from the very people who are responsible for our conception; biological parents and cultural parents are very often the same. In horizontal cultural transmission, we learn from our peers in day-to-day interactions during the course of development from birth to adulthood; in this case, there is no confounding of biological and cultural transmission. And in oblique cultural transmission, we learn from other adults and institutions (for example in formal schooling), either in our own culture or from other cultures. If the process takes place entirely within our own or primary culture, then cultural transmission is the appropriate term (see left side of fig. 2.1). However, if the process derives from contact with another or secondary culture, the term **acculturation** is employed (see right side of fig. 2.1). This latter term refers to the form of transmission experienced by individuals that results from contact with, and influence from, persons and institutions belonging to cultures other than their own. Acculturation is discussed in ch. 13.

While these forms of transmission have been shown in fig. 2.1 with arrows flowing toward the developing individual, reciprocal influences are known to be important, particularly among peers but also in parent–child relationships (Lamb, 1986). Thus, perhaps double-headed arrows, representing interaction and mutual influence, would more accurately represent what takes place during cultural transmission and acculturation.

## Early development and caretaking

The notion of development comes into this book at three levels. First, there is phylogenetic development, as exemplified in evolution theory. This deals with variation across species, and the emergence of new species over long periods of time. This form of development will be discussed in ch. 10. Second, the term "development" can refer to cultural changes in societies. Development in this sense will be touched upon in ch. 9 (where we discuss the anthropological tradition of cultural evolution), and in ch. 17 (where we focus on national development). In the present chapter we are mainly concerned with the development of individuals during their lifetimes, or ontogenetic development.

Individual development can be considered as the outcome of interactions between a biological organism and environmental influences. This means that we accept as a starting point for the discussion the distinction between nature and nurture. The relative importance of the biological and the environmental–experiential components of behavior has formed the major dimension that has accounted for the differences between the various schools of thinking on individual development in the psychological literature. Thus, there are maturational theories (e.g., Gesell, 1940) that place great emphasis on biological factors. In contrast, traditional learning theory (e.g., Skinner, 1957) emphasizes the role of the environment. In other theories more attention is paid to the interaction between the organism and the environment; an example is the theory of Piaget (1970), in which stages in cognitive development are distinguished. Piaget recognized that ontogenetic development is critically dependent on experience. However, he also thought that the sequence, and even the timing, of the various stages would show cross-cultural similarity, as each cultural environment would provide the stimulation and experiences that were needed for individual development. In differentiation theory (Werner, 1957, p. 126) development implies "increasing differentiation, articulation and hierarchic integration" in the child's psychological life. Greater differentiation implies specialization of psychological functions, as well as a more structured organization of these functions. These changes are largely the result of environmental experiences. Finally, there are theories in which ontogenetic development is seen as following essentially different pathways as a consequence of differences in the cultural environment in which the individual is growing up. The leading theorist in this tradition has been Vygotsky (1978), who postulated that the typically human forms of psychological functioning are societal rather than individual in nature. In the last section of this chapter we shall elaborate on some conceptualizations of development.

## Infant development

Biologists consider human beings to be adapted, anatomically and physiologically, to gathering and probably hunting, a way of life that they pursued for millions of years. The invention of agriculture leading to sedentarization, and later the change to industrialization, are only recent events to which humankind has been able to make only cultural rather than major biological adaptations (e.g., Konner, 1981). For humans more than any other species, neurological development continues after birth; this permits a large environmental influence on development. Although generally the plasticity of behavior increases as one goes up the phylogenetic scale, there is nevertheless great variability between closely related species. The level of development at birth depends on the specific adaptation to a particular ecological niche. Higher primates and human beings are precocious in their sensory systems, but less developed in their motor systems. Konner (1981) has hypothesized that the relatively slow motor development among human infants would be a recent adaptation (taking place perhaps over a million years) arising from the invention of the means for humans to carry babies while keeping their hands free.

Weaning takes place among primates at different times (at one year for most monkeys, at two years for baboons, and at four years for chimpanzees), but the nursing period represents a constant proportion (one-quarter to one-third) of the age until female sexual maturity. Among human nomadic hunters weaning takes place around three or four years of age (later if there is no new baby), and this corresponds to the same proportion. Most sedentary agricultural societies have a birth spacing (corresponding to the age of weaning) of two to three years. In recent decades, early weaning and bottle feeding have spread to much of the world's population, above all to the large cities of the **majority world**,[1] with the well-known risks of unclean water and poor preparation.

Just after birth, or at least in the first forty-eight hours, the pediatrician can carry out an examination to establish if the development of the neonate is normal. This examination looks at neuromotor characteristics, particularly at the "archaic" reflexes, which disappear after six to ten weeks in Euroamerican babies. These examinations are not easy to conduct, because of the rapid changes in the infant's state of wakefulness, but gradually stricter protocols have been established, for example, by Brazelton (1973).

The first cross-cultural study of infant performance, one that has had important repercussions, was carried out by Geber and Dean (1957). They examined full-term neonates who weighed more than 2,500 grams in the maternity hospital in Kampala, Uganda. They found a marked precocity in development in relation to Western pediatric norms: an advance of two to six weeks in holding the head, and a nearly complete absence of the archaic reflexes (indicating an advanced state of development). This has come to be known as African infant precocity.[2]

In retrospect, Geber and Dean's observations, and the way in which they presented the results, were flawed. The authors did not use statistical tests to establish African differences from the Euroamerican norms; and it would have been better to have both African and Euroamerican samples tested by the same experimenter. Other, more subtle, factors may also have affected the validity of their results. For example, birthing in Africa (even in a maternity hospital) does not take place under the same conditions as in Western hospitals; anesthetics, routinely used in the West up to the 1970s, are rarely employed in Africa, and can have marked effects on the performance of neonates. Furthermore, the mean weight at birth of African neonates (as well as Afro-Americans) is on average lower than that of Euroamerican babies, even under optimal nutritional conditions. Thus, the limit of 2,500 grams was not appropriate, and led to the elimination of one-third of the potential subjects, who were falsely considered to be premature. Finally, the examination rests in part on the absence of a phenomenon (the archaic reflexes), and should be subject to greater caution than if it had rested on behaviors actually observed. Later, studies (e.g., Warren & Parkin, 1974; Keefer, Dixon, Tronik, & Brazelton, 1978) using stricter methods (e.g., the Brazelton examination) soon showed that the neonatal precocity found by Geber and Dean was partly exaggerated: there is a certain precocity, but it is not as general as they described.

---

[1] For lack of a better distinction we follow Kagitcibasi (1996) in her manner of designating the non-Western part of the world, although we are reluctant to use such broad dichotomies.

[2] The term African precocity can be seen as an example of ethnocentrism. The equally appropriate term of Euroamerican retardation is used nowhere in the literature.

Differences at birth may be due to genetic factors, but certainly do not preclude pre-birth environmental influences, known as the intra-uterine experiences of the baby. Differences in birth weight can arise from differences in nutrition of expectant mothers, or from differences in their activity level. While in many Western societies expectant mothers are granted maternity leave enabling them to take more rest for several weeks before the date of birth, this is not the case in most other societies. Moreover, from the moment of birth explicit cultural practices provide for differences in context. For example, in many parts of Africa and the West Indies babies tend to be massaged extensively (e.g., Hopkins, 1977), while in quite a few Western countries babies born in hospitals are taken away from their mothers for most of the day and placed in cribs. These practices are likely to result in later motor development in Western neonates (Hopkins & Westra, 1990), as we shall see.

Part of the research on infant development across cultures has sought to observe, describe, and measure individual behavior (particularly in the psychomotor domain) in a variety of field settings. Following the work of the pediatricians Gesell and Amatruda (1947), who first systematized observations in this domain, various psychologists have constructed developmental scales called baby tests that allow for quantitative measurement (e.g., Bayley, 1969; Brunet & Lézine, 1951; Griffiths, 1970). Based on the IQ model these scales are composed of a number of items (observable behaviors that are characteristic of a given age), that can be used to determine the infant's developmental age. When developmental age is divided by the chronological age (and multiplied by 100), a "developmental quotient" (DQ) is obtained. These scales, in addition to giving a general DQ, also allow the distinguishing of partial DQs in particular areas, such as motor and eye–hand coordination, language, and sociability. They can be applied to infants aged between birth and three years.

Although neonatal precocity has been controversial, psychomotor precocity in the first year of life in different populations (above all in Africa, but elsewhere as well) has been well documented in many studies (e.g., Geber, 1958; Vouilloux, 1959; Werner, 1972). It is indicated by a general DQ on baby tests between 140 and 180 during the first months of development. It appears certain that this advance is due to particular child rearing practices: bodily and affective contact with the mother, care that promotes motor development (such as massage), and tactile, proprioceptive, visual, and auditory stimulation. Linked to this is the baby's participation in daily life, and its being in a vertical position (on the back of the mother), as compared to Western babies who spend most of the day lying in a separate quiet place. For several decades the gradual convergence of scores has been attributed to harsh weaning. However, Dasen, Inhelder, Lavallée, and Retschitzki (1978) and others have argued that the ill effects of harsh and sudden weaning have been exaggerated. The advantages of a physically stimulating environment probably begin to disappear when the infant becomes a toddler and starts moving around.

The use of baby tests has been criticized because the overall DQ masks interesting differences between specific items. Super (1976), by analyzing each item in the Bayley scale separately, found that sitting upright unassisted, and walking, were acquired very early by the Kipsigi in Kenya (about one month before the Bayley US norms). These motor developments are recognized as important by Kipsigi mothers; they are named and are specifically trained for. In contrast, other motor behaviors, for which infants receive little training (such as crawling), show a delay rather than an advance on the Western norm. Super (1976) studied six groups in East Africa to find out if crawling was valued and trained or not. The correlation between these data and the mean age of acquisition was 0.77, and reached 0.97 if the opportunity an infant had to practice this motor skill was taken into account. Kilbride (1980) has made the same argument concerning sitting and smiling comparing the Baganda (of Uganda) and the Samia (of Kenya). Thus, informed researchers no longer speak of general precocity, but look for a direct link between "parental ethnotheories" (see below) and psychomotor development.

Bril and colleagues (Bril & Sabatier 1986; Bril & Zack, 1989), and Nkounkou-Hombessa (1988) have made detailed observations on the different postures that accompany child rearing practices and the care of babies among French infant–mother dyads, and among the Bambara (of Mali) and the Kongo-Lari (of the Congo). Rabain (1989) observing African mothers and their babies in Paris, found that migration had little effect on these practices. There is thus evidence of a strong connection between parental ethnotheories and motor development: the Bambara believe that infants should sit at three to four months, and train them to this end; the Kongo-Lari believe that if an infant does not walk by eight months it is late in development, and go to seek a healer who practices a therapy which consists of motor manipulation and the application to the joints of a mixture made from the bones of ferocious animals and hot spices (Nkounkou-Hombessa, 1988).

For their rural Baoulé subjects, Dasen et al. (1978) found advances over the French norms on certain tasks, but not on all. There was a certain precocity in both motor development and sensorimotor intelligence, but as in the work of Super (1976) this was selective rather than general. Especially advanced over the French norms was the resolution of problems involving the use of instruments to increase the reach of the arm, and the combination of two objects. This result was a little surprising, since the literature suggested that the environment of the African infant was limited in variety of objects. For example, Knapen (1962) stated that for the Mukongo infant (of Zaire), "The daily environment of the Congolese child is striking in its poverty of intellectual stimulation" (p. 157). Moreover, African adults seldom use objects as intermediaries in their communication with young children. While a European mother offers a rattle or other toy to calm a crying baby, an African mother intervenes with body contact, especially by offering her breast (Zempléni-Rabain, 1970; Rabain, 1979). Despite the absence of this adult use of objects, and the absence of manufactured toys, behavior observations in natural settings show that, in fact, young Africans have available a host of different objects, which they are not prevented from using. Virtually nothing is forbidden, not even access to objects that would be considered dangerous by European mothers (Dasen et al., 1978).

These objects, unlike toys, do not have a single function. They are thus particularly relevant to symbolic play (Piaget, 1970), which marks the passage from the stage of sensorimotor intelligence to the pre-operational stage, and which begins by the acquisition of the symbolic function, of which language is a part. Behavioral observations made by Dasen et al. (1978) in natural settings, as well as those videoed under controlled situations, permitted the study of the stages of construction of this symbolic function. Again, there is no reason to doubt that this aspect of psychological development is universal, even if the content of symbolic play differs between cultures. At this stage, a Baoulé child pretends to carry a small bowl on its head, or a baby on its back, while a French child of the same age pretends to put the doll on the potty, or gives it something to eat with a spoon. The structure of these actions, carried out in the absence of the actual model being imitated, and with objects used symbolically, is nevertheless the same.

The emphasis on sensorimotor development in earlier studies can be explained in part by the central position of Piaget (1970) in developmental psychology during much of the second half of the twentieth century. Although he stressed development as an interactive process between the individual organism and the environment, Piaget focussed on the child rather than on the social context. A shift in emphasis is reflected in the growing attention to the social context in which children grow up, perhaps best exemplified in research on parenting (cf. Bornstein, 1991, 1995). Thus, we now turn to another aspect of development, namely the interaction patterns of parents with their infants. Not only are neonates equipped to start interacting with both the physical and the social environment, parents are also equipped to deal with babies, an idea reflected in the notion of intuitive parenting (e.g., Papoušek & Papoušek, 1995).

Although we are dealing here with the behavior of adults, parenting of infants is an area where remarkable cross-cultural invariance has been found. One example is the special intonation patterns of speech that mothers (and also fathers) use when they address the young baby. Among the characteristics of this way of speaking, called "motherese," are a generally higher pitch and larger variations in pitch (Fernald, 1992). Detailed analysis shows that tonal patterns can be distinguished according to communicative intent, for example, asking for attention, or comforting the baby (Fernald et al., 1989). Although there are some cross-cultural variations, these appear to be negligible compared to the similarities (e.g., Papoušek & Papoušek, 1992).

Such communication patterns tend to be interactive, as demonstrated, for example, in a study by Keller, Schölmerich, and Eibl-Eibesfeldt (1988). They analyzed communication patterns between infants two to six months old and parents in West German, Greek, Trobriand, and Yanomami societies. Quite similar interaction structures were found. For example, infants produce few vocalizations when adults are talking, and vice versa; adults respond differently to vocalizations with a positive and negative emotional tone. According to the authors these findings are compatible with the notion of intuitive parenting practices which rest on inborn characteristics which regulate behavior exchange between parents and children.

This is not to say that there are no cross-cultural differences in early parenting behavior. For example, findings by Bornstein et al. (1992) suggest that Japanese mothers more than mothers in Argentina, France, and the USA use "affect-salient" speech to five- and thirteen-month-old babies. This means that they used more incomplete utterances, song, and nonsense expressions. The mothers of the other cultures used relatively more "information-salient" speech. This is in line with previous findings to the effect that Japanese mothers empathize with the needs of their infants and try to communicate at the babies' level, while Western mothers encourage individual expression in their children. An important, but in our opinion so far rather unanswerable, question is to what extent these early differences are small and incidental, and to what extent they form the start of consistent ways in which societies socialize their youngsters.

## Attachment patterns

An important theme in developmental psychology is the **attachment** between the baby and its mother (Ainsworth, 1967; Bowlby, 1969; Kermoian & Leiderman, 1986). From ethology (see ch. 10) Bowlby derived the idea that behaviors of human infants such as crying and smiling will elicit care-giving reactions from adults. As a result of such interactions, especially with the mother, attachment develops. This provides the child with a secure base from which it can explore the world. The importance of security was demonstrated dramatically in experiments in which rhesus monkeys were reared in isolation (Harlow & Harlow, 1962). In their cages were two devices: one was constructed of wire and had a nipple from which the young monkey could drink; the other was padded with soft cloth. It was found that the monkey would cling to the "cloth mother" rather than to the "wire mother" when some strange and probably threatening object was put in the cage. Apparently it was not food but warmth and safety that determined the attachment behavior. Theorists in this area tend to assume that a secure attachment forms the basis for healthy emotional and social development.

Although attachment theory was originally largely rooted in field observations, the most frequent method of assessment is by means of a standard procedure called the 'strange situation' (Ainsworth, Blehar, Waters, & Wall, 1978). This consists of a sequence of situations in a laboratory room where at first the child is with the mother. After a while a stranger comes in. Subsequently the mother leaves, then the stranger leaves, and then the mother returns. The reactions of the child are observed during each of these episodes. One-year-old children who go to the mother when she returns and who will accept comfort if they felt distressed are considered securely attached. Children who avoid the mother or show signs of anger are considered insecurely attached (with a further division in to two or even three subcategories [cf. Main & Solomon, 1990]).

The cross-cultural **equivalence** (see ch. 11) of the strange situation as an assessment procedure is questionable. For example, in many societies young children are continually in the company of others. As a rule, the mother is the primary care giver for the young infant everywhere, but even here practices differ. For example, among the Aka Pygmies the father spends considerable time with the baby of a few months old (Hewlett, 1992). We mentioned earlier the long periods of bodily contact, with the baby held in a vertical position during the day, that are characteristic of many nomadic hunting societies but also frequent among agriculturalists. As the infant grows older, there is an increase in cross-cultural differences in the social interactions to which a child is exposed. In some settings children become part of an extended family or village community in which many adults and other children assume caretaking roles. In other settings the role of the mother as primary caretaker remains more central and exclusive. In urban Western settings, a new pattern has been developing recently: bringing children from a few months of age onward to a day care center. Is it to be expected that reactions to the strange situation can be interpreted in the same way for these one-year-olds who have such different experiences?

What are the consequences of these differences in cultural practices? Attachment theory as developed by Bowlby and Ainsworth emphasizes the importance of one primary caretaker, which in all societies is usually the mother. For the development of secure attachment patterns she has to be available when the infant needs her. If the child is confronted with various other adults as caretakers, especially relative strangers, this may be detrimental to the formation of secure attachment. Needless to say, this could have serious implications for developmentally optimal modes of child care, notably in day care centers. However, the question is not easy to answer, because not only the social settings per se, but also socialization goals, may differ across cultures. Thus, it has been argued that two orientations can be distinguished: in Western societies, socialization may be more oriented toward self-regulation and autonomy, while in many non-Western countries the orientation is more toward social interdependencies (e.g., Bornstein, 1994).

Keller and Eckensberger (1998) are among those who postulate continuity between these early child rearing themes and later differences in the nature of the self-concept (to be discussed in ch. 4). Convincing demonstration of the validity of this view requires longitudinal research from infancy to adulthood in societies with quite varying practices. More tenuous evidence is obtained by studying the continuity of attachment styles over shorter periods, or by asking adults to recall their early attachment experiences. In a small study conducted in western Kenya, frequency of mother-holding in infancy correlated positively with measures of affective disposition at age twelve, but not with measures of cognitive performance (Munroe, Munroe, Westling, & Rosenberg, 1997). These results suggest domain-specific consequences (affectiveness) rather than general developmental consequences (including cognition) of early experiences. Kornadt and Tibachana (1999) reported a high correlation between expressions of aggressiveness in young children and child rearing variables indicative of secure attachment in eight cultural groups from east Asia and western Europe. In a nine-year follow-up study (children were then fourteen years old) a relationship was found between early child rearing and later expressions of aggression in a projective test. A procedure that asks adults about their own past is the adult attachment interview (Main, Kaplan, & Cassidy, 1985). A relationship between interview results and adults' caretaking style has been reported in a meta-analysis based on a number of studies (Van Ijzendoorn, 1995), but the interpretation of this finding is debatable (Fox, 1995). Further extension of attachment patterns into adult life is thought to be reflected in the care provided for elderly parents in need of help (e.g., Ho, 1996; Marcoen, 1995).

The presumed long-lasting effects of early experiences have been debated extensively at least since Freud's (e.g., 1980) claims about the importance of the first six years of life. Culture-comparative research cannot resolve this debate, because ecocultural and sociopolitical contexts continue to have an influence at least for the lifetime of an individual. This makes it difficult to distinguish between effects that carry over from early in life and direct effects of present conditions. One danger of the sometimes speculative inferences about the long-term effects of quite subtle sociocultural variables is that we may overlook differences in actual ecological conditions. An example to illustrate this comes from a multi-country study by Whiting (1981) on infant carrying practices in relation to mean annual temperature. Whiting grouped infant carrying practices into three categories, the use of cradle, arms, and sling. Drawing a 10°C isotherm (coldest month) on a world map, and placing the three styles of carrying on the same map, revealed a striking correlation with temperature. In a sample of 250 societies, cradle carrying was predominant in those where the mean temperatures were lower than 10°C, while arm and sling carrying were predominant in warmer societies. The main exceptions were the Inuit, who carry their babies in the parka hood. One can speculate on the functional origins of such a relationship between climate and a child rearing practice. In this case, a very down to earth consideration may be at work: urine on the clothes is disagreeable in cold climates, while it can evaporate quickly in the heat. One can equally speculate on the long-term effects of such practices on young babies. Some of these possibilities will be further discussed in ch. 9 in the section on psychological anthropology.

## Enculturation and socialization

Two processes of cultural transmission were distinguished in fig. 2.1: **enculturation** and **socialization**. The concept of enculturation has been developed within the discipline of cultural anthropology, and was first defined and used by Herskovits (1948). As the term suggests, an individual is encompassed or surrounded by a culture; the individual acquires, by learning, what the culture deems to be necessary. There is not necessarily anything deliberate or didactic about this process; often there is learning without specific teaching. The process of enculturation involves parents, and other adults and peers, in a network of influences (vertical, oblique, and horizontal), all of which can limit, shape, and direct the developing individual. The end result (if enculturation is successful) is a person who is competent in the culture, including its language, its rituals, its values, and so on.

The concept of socialization was developed in the disciplines of sociology and social psychology to refer to the process of deliberate shaping, by way of tutelage, of the individual. It is generally employed in cross-cultural psychology in the same way. When cultural transmission involves deliberate teaching from within a group, we are dealing with the process of socialization; resocialization occurs when the deliberate influences come from outside an individual's own culture. The eventual result of both enculturation and socialization is the development of behavioral similarities within cultures, and behavioral differences between cultures. They are thus the crucial cultural mechanisms that produce the distribution of similarities and differences.

The processes of enculturation and socialization take place in a larger ecological and cultural context: the forms (or style) and the content (what) of transmission are generally viewed as adaptive to the ecocultural setting, and functional in that they ensure that the developing individual acquires the behavioral repertoire that is necessary to live successfully in that setting. It is for this reason that cultural transmission is placed in such a central position in the ecocultural framework (fig. 1.1). Even when developing children are biologically self-sustaining, they typically continue to live in the family group, and continue to acquire important features of their culture. There is a shift from physical dependency to social and psychological dependency: after puberty, individuals can meet their own physical needs, but their acquired social needs (such as for intimacy, love, social interaction, and social support) continue to be met largely by the family group. Thus, attachment remains but its basis gradually shifts from physical to social and psychological dependency, permitting continuing and substantial cultural transmission.

On the other hand, the process of cultural transmission does not necessarily lead to exact replication of successive generations; it falls somewhere between an exact transmission (with hardly any differences between parents and offspring) and a complete failure of transmission (with offspring who are unlike their parents). It usually falls closer to the full transmission end of this spectrum than to the non-transmission end. Functionally, either extreme would be problematic for a society: exact transmission would not allow for novelty and change, and hence the ability to respond to new situations, while failure of transmission would not permit coordinated action between generations (Boyd & Richerson, 1985).

Studies of how a society characteristically raises its children have been reported in the literature for over a century. As we shall see in ch. 9, many of these reports have been accumulated in an archive mainly composed of ethnographic reports known as the **Human Relations Area Files** (HRAF). One approach to the study of cultural transmissions is to employ these files to discover the major dimensions of variation in practices as they are used around the world. This approach provides us with a broad overview, and allows us to examine cultural transmission in the context of other ecological and cultural variables that have also been included in the archives. We are thus able to examine how enculturation and socialization fit into, or are adaptive to, other features of the group's circumstances.

Studies of cultural transmission employing ethnographic archives have been termed "holocultural," since they permit the examination of materials from cultures the whole world over. One such study, carried out by Whiting and Child (1953), attempted to link adult personality to **child training** by examining the ways in which societies typically explain illness. Ethnographic data from seventy-five societies were derived from the HRAF and five "systems of behavior" (defined as "habits or customs motivated by a common drive and leading to common satisfactions," p. 45) were examined: oral, anal, sexual, dependence, and aggression. The first three of these five behavior systems were derived from Freud's (1938) theory of psychosexual development, in which sexual gratification is thought to be associated, over the course of development, with different erogenous zones, beginning with the mouth (during the oral stage). Adult personality, in Freudian theory, is described in terms of these developmental stages. Whiting and Child employed them not only because of their status in psychoanalytic theory, but also because of their relationship to three primary needs or drives (hunger, elimination, and sex) that, along with the two other behaviors (dependence and aggression), are likely to be universally subjected to socialization. Judges made ratings of practices in each of these five domains on three dimensions: initial satisfaction or indulgence of the child, the age of socialization, and the severity of socialization.

Two very general conclusions resulted from this study. First "child training the world over is in certain respects identical . . . in that it is found always to be concerned with certain universal problems of behavior" (Whiting & Child, 1953, p. 63). Second, "child training also differs from one society to another" (p. 64). In this pair of conclusions are the two prototypical and most frequent empirical results found in cross-cultural psychology, and which are consistent with the "universalist" approach: there are some common dimensions that serve to link humankind together, while individuals and groups differ in their typical place on these dimensions. We shall see later (in chs. 11 and 12) that the first conclusion is essential if we are to have some valid basis on which to make cross-cultural comparisons, and that the second is essential if we are to have sufficient variance in our data to discover evidence that cultural and psychological observations are related in theoretically interpretable ways.

In another classic study, Barry and his colleagues (Barry, Bacon, & Child, 1957; Barry, Child, & Bacon, 1959) were able (1) to identify common dimensions of child training; (2) to place societies at various positions on these dimensions; (3) to show some characteristic differences between training for boys and girls; and (4) to relate all of these to features of ecological and cultural variation (such as economy and social structure), thus placing socialization in a broader context. Let us examine this pair of reports in some detail.

By the mid-1950s attention had become focussed, among users of the HRAF, on six central dimensions of child rearing thought to be common to all societies. As defined in the work of Barry et al. (1957, 1959) these were:

1  obedience training: the degree to which children are trained to obey adults;
2  responsibility training: the degree to which children are trained to take on responsibility for subsistence or household tasks;
3  nurturance training: the degree to which children are trained to care for and help younger siblings and other dependent people;
4  achievement training: the degree to which children are trained to strive towards standards of excellence in performance;
5  self-reliance: the degree to which children are trained to take care of themselves and to be independent of assistance from others in supplying their own needs or wants;
6  general independence training: the degree to which children are trained (beyond self-reliance as defined above) toward freedom from control, domination, and supervision.

Ratings of child rearing practices used in a particular society were generally made by two or more judges, on the basis of the descriptions of societies available in the HRAF. The samples of societies that were drawn from the Files represented quite a wide variety of cultures.

Armed with the ratings, Barry and his colleagues considered whether these six dimensions were independent of each other, or related in some systematic way across cultures. Their analyses showed that five of the six dimensions tended to form two clusters. One cluster (termed "pressure toward compliance") combined training for responsibility and obedience; training for nurturance was only marginally part of this cluster. The other cluster (termed "pressure toward assertion") combined training for achievement, self-reliance, and independence. These two clusters appeared to be negatively related. Thus, a single dimension was created, along which societies were placed, ranging from compliance training at one end and assertion training at the other. In this way the six initial dimensions were reduced to a single one.

Variations in cultural transmission along this dimension have also been described (Arnett, 1995) as "narrow" through to "broad" socialization. Narrow socialization (compliance) is characterized by obedience and conformity, and is thought to lead to a restricted range of individual differences, while broad socialization (assertion) is characterized by the promotion of independence and self-expression, and is thought to lead to a broad range of individual differences. While this new dimension appears to be consistent with the earlier research, the expectation that there will be concomitant differences in the range of individual variation has not yet been tested empirically.

The two remaining issues were the presence of sex differences in socialization, and how a society's place on the dimension might relate to a number of other ecological and cultural variables. To examine the first of these issues Barry et al. (1957) made ratings on five of the six basic dimensions (excluding general

**Table 2.1** Gender differences in child rearing

| Dimension of child rearing | Number of cultures | Percentage of cultures with evidence of gender difference in direction of | | |
|---|---|---|---|---|
| | | Girls | Boys | Neither |
| 1. Obedience | 69 | 35 | 3 | 62 |
| 2. Responsibility | 84 | 61 | 11 | 28 |
| 3. Nurturance | 33 | 82 | 0 | 18 |
| 4. Achievement | 31 | 3 | 87 | 10 |
| 5. Self-reliance | 82 | 0 | 85 | 15 |

Extracted from table 1, Barry et al., 1957

independence training) separately for boys and girls. Results showed a fairly clear-cut difference in four of the five dimensions (see table 2.1). With the exception of the dimension of obedience training, girls were socialized more often for "compliance" (evidenced in table 2.1 by ratings on responsibility and nurturance training); conversely, boys were socialized more for "assertion" (evidenced by ratings on achievement and self-reliance).

In a further analysis, Barry and his colleagues (Barry et al., 1957) found that the magnitude of these gender differences in socialization correlated with other features of the society. First, large gender differences in socialization are associated with "an economy that places a high premium in the superior strength, and superior development of motor skills requiring strength, which characterize the male"; and second, they are "correlated with customs that make for a large family group with high cooperative interaction" (p. 330). To interpret these differences it is useful to turn to the later analysis (Barry et al., 1959) in which the broader ecological and cultural context of socialization is explored more fully.

## Ecocultural factors

The following questions guided the analysis of Barry and his colleagues:

> Why does a particular society select child training practices which will tend to produce a particular kind of typical personality? Is it because this kind of typical personality[3] is functional for the adult life of the society, and training methods which will produce it are thus also functional? (Barry et al., 1959, p. 51).

---

[3]  Barry et al. use the term "typical personality" to refer to basic dispositions in the individual. In ch. 4 we question the validity of the notion that there are personality types characteristic of a particular society. We accept that there are culture-typical patterns of behavior that have been learned during the process of enculturation. However, we doubt whether this makes it necessary to postulate cross-cultural differences in internal dispositions. The issue is not of great concern here, as the results of Barry et al. appear to be quite meaningful if "typical personality" is read as meaning no more than "typical patterns of adult behavior."

They began their search for an answer to these questions by examining one of the most basic functions in a society: the economic relationship between a population and its ecosystem. For each society, the economic mode of subsistence was rated on dimensions of gathering, hunting, fishing, pastoralism, or agriculture. In the view of Barry et al. (1959, p. 52) with a dependence on pastoralism (raising animals for milk and meat) "future food supply seems to be best assured by faithful adherence to routines designed to maintain the good health of the herd." At the opposite extreme is hunting and gathering. Where "each day's food comes from that day's catch, variations in the energy and skill exerted in food-getting lead to immediate reward or punishment ... If the change is a good one, it may lead to immediate reward" (p. 52). Agriculture- and fishing-based societies are thought to lie between these two extremes.

On the basis of these observations, Barry and his colleagues argued that in pastoral and agricultural societies (which are high in "food accumulation"), people should tend to be relatively "conscientious, compliant and conservative," while in hunting and gathering societies (low in "food accumulation") people should be relatively "individualistic, assertive and venturesome" (p. 53). Assuming that societies will train their children for these appropriate adult behaviors, Barry et al. (1959) predicted a relationship between type of subsistence economy and child rearing practices. In a sample of forty-six societies the correlation between food accumulation and socialization practices was positive for responsibility and obedience training, and negative for achievement, self-reliance, and independence training. When the more global measure of socialization ("pressure toward compliance versus assertion") was employed, these relationships became even clearer. Using this overall compliance-assertion score, Barry et al. (1959) found a correlation of +.94 with degree of food accumulation. Of the twenty-three societies above the median on the compliance–assertion rating, twenty were high food accumulating, while of the twenty-three societies below the median, nineteen were low food accumulating. There was thus a strong similarity between socialization emphases, and the broader ecological and cultural context.

Since these original studies by Barry et al., more extensive codes have been produced by Barry (e.g. Barry, Josephson, Lawer, & Marshall, 1976; Barry & Paxson, 1971) which both increase the range of societies included, and the range of socialization variables covered. There has also been a critical reanalysis of the HRAF data by Hendrix (1985), who explored two questions: is the basic dimension actually present and are the reported variations in child rearing (and in gender differences in child rearing) related to subsistence economic activities? The first question was examined by a factor analysis of twenty-four socialization variables in 102 societies. One result was that the "assertion" variables (of self-reliance, achievement, and independence) formed one dimension, and that this was independent of the "compliance" dimension (formed by responsibility, obedience, and nurturance), rather than the two sets being opposite ends of a single dimension. Moreover, gender differences (see below) did not appear in either dimension. In Hendrix's view, his "re-examination of the links of socialization to the economy shows that the original conclusions were much overly simplified, somewhat misleading, but not completely off the mark" (p. 260).

## Gender differences

The issue of **gender** differences in socialization has received extensive treatment in the cross-cultural literature about gender differences in behavior, leading Munroe and Munroe (1975, p. 116) to conclude that there are modal gender differences in behavior in every society, and that every society has some division of labor by gender. These two phenomena, besides being universal, are also probably interrelated in a functional way.

The correspondence between gender differences in socialization emphases and gender differences in behavior is very strong. That the two genders behave in different ways is not surprising, but it still leads to interesting questions. For example, have all societies observed different inborn behavioral tendencies in males and females and then shaped their socialization practices to reinforce such biologically based tendencies? Or are societies' socialization practices merely influenced by certain physical differences between males and females, with those practices responsible for behavioral differences? (See the discussion of these possibilities in ch. 3.)

Risking oversimplification, we can summarize the picture of gender differences in behavior that is presented by these HRAF-based studies as showing males to be more self-assertive, achievement oriented, and dominant and females to be more socially responsive, passive, and submissive. One key to the explanation is the fact that the behavioral differences just summarized, although nearly universal and almost never reversed, range in magnitude from quite large down to virtually nil. A satisfactory explanation, then, will account for both the universality of direction of difference and the variation in magnitude of the difference.

Such an explanation takes into account economic facts, including division of labor and socialization practices. The argument begins with an early anthropological finding (Murdock, 1937) that a division of labor by sex is universal (or nearly so) and quite consistent in content. For example, food preparation is done predominantly by females in nearly all societies. Child care is usually the responsibility of females. Sometimes it is shared, but in no society is it the modal practice for males to have the major responsibility. These differences are widely viewed as arising from biologically based physical differences (and not behavioral ones), especially the female's lesser overall physical strength and, most of all, her child bearing and child caring functions. Different economic roles for males and females, with the latter consigned mostly to close-to-home activities, would have been a functional response. A second argument was to suggest that differential socialization evolved as a means for preparing children to assume their sex-linked adult roles. Then, the behavioral differences could best be viewed as a product of different socialization emphases, with those in turn reflective of, and appropriate training for, different adult activities (Barry et al., 1959).

Van Leeuwen's (1978) extension of Berry's (1976a) ecological model expands the argument so that it can accommodate other aspects of subsistence mode and variations in degree of sex differences in behavior. Thus, in sedentary, high food accumulating societies not only will females be subjected to more training to be nurturant and compliant, but the degree of the difference between the sexes' training will also be high. In low food accumulating societies, such as gathering or hunting societies, there will be less division of labor by sex and little need for either sex to be trained to be compliant. Often in such societies (at least in gathering societies, if not hunting ones, as we will see shortly) the contribution of women to basic subsistence activity are integral to it. Hence, women's work is valued by the men, who are then not inclined to derogate women or to insist on subservience from them.

One of the ways in which division of labor varies across cultures is in the degree to which women contribute to subsistence (Schlegel & Barry, 1986). Their participation in such activities may be relatively low or high, depending on the activity. For example, if food is acquired by gathering, women's participation is usually high; in eleven of fourteen (79 percent) gathering societies for which ethnographic reports were coded, women were high contributors. By contrast, in only two of sixteen (13 percent) hunting societies did women make a high contribution. Women were more apt to contribute relatively highly to subsistence where the main activity was either gathering or agriculture (other than intensive agriculture), and less highly where the activity was animal husbandry, intensive agriculture, fishing, or hunting (Schlegel & Barry, 1986, p. 144).

Does the variation in the subsistence role played by women have any consequences? Schlegel and Barry (1986) found that two sets of cultural features, adaptive and attitudinal, were associated with a female contribution to subsistence. Where women played a relatively large subsistence role, the features of polygyny, exogamy, brideprice, birth control, and work orientation training for girls prevailed. And under these same conditions (high contribution by females to subsistence), females were relatively highly valued, allowed freedoms, and were generally less likely to be perceived as objects for male sexual and reproductive needs.

What we have seen in this discussion is that females do indeed behave differently from males; we will examine these differences more closely in the next chapter. It seems clear that these gender differences are strongly influenced by cultural factors, operating through socialization practices and reflective of ecological factors. Both the consistencies in the cross-cultural data and the variations from society to society help us to understand how cultural practices have been defined differently for the two sexes, and how individuals come to behave in accord with them.

## Parental ethnotheories

There are many ethnosciences such as ethnobotany, ethnogeology, even ethnopsychology. These are the knowledge and beliefs about a particular area of life held by a particular cultural group. Similarly, groups reveal such knowledge and beliefs about the domain of parenting, which have become known as parental belief systems or **parental ethnotheories** (Harkness & Super, 1995; Sigel, McGillicuddy-DeLisi, & Goodnow, 1992). These are the beliefs, values, and practices of parents and other child caretakers regarding the proper way to raise a child, and include such common practices as the provision of affection and warmth, timetables for feeding and elimination, and even for development itself (e.g., when a child should walk, talk, ride a bicycle, choose friends). These beliefs and practices constitute the processes of enculturation and socialization which, as we have seen, have been studied for some time. The advantage of this newer concept is that it links this earlier literature on "child rearing" practices more closely to the ecological and cultural contexts in which they arise.

One example of differences in ideas about socialization is a study by Tobin, Wu and Davidson (1989) in which videotapes of children in pre-schools in Japan and in the USA were shown to teachers from both countries. US teachers commented on the large number of children (about thirty) under the responsibility of a Japanese teacher. But Japanese teachers, in turn, judged the much smaller group size preferred in the USA as less appropriate for the children to learn to interact with others. Teachers also had ideas about the reasons why children misbehaved (and the proper way of dealing with this), based on their own cultural preconceptions. Thus, Japanese teachers would tend to speculate that something went wrong in the development of the dependency relation with the mother, while US teachers would make more references to factors inherent in the individual child.

Harkness and Super and colleagues (Super et al., 1996) have studied cross-cultural differences in the regulation of sleeping patterns of young children. Parental ethnotheories play a strong role in the extent to which even young babies are left to themselves between feeding times (as in the Netherlands [Rebelsky, 1967]) or taken from their cribs when showing signs of distress (as in the USA). Harkness and Super with their colleagues have studied samples of young children (between six months and four years and six months of age) and their parents in semi-urban settings in the Netherlands and the USA, using interviews and direct observations. For the Dutch parents imposing regularity in sleeping patterns was an important issue. If children were not getting enough sleep they were believed to become fussy; moreover, young children needed sleep for their growth and development. In fact, such ideas are also emphasized in the Dutch health care system. In the USA regular sleeping patterns are seen as something the child will acquire with increasing age, but these are, by and large, not seen as something that can be induced. From diaries kept by parents it emerged that the Dutch children got more sleep during their early years. Direct observations showed that, while awake, Dutch children were more often in a state of "quiet arousal," while the US children were more often in a state of "active alertness." Super and his colleagues suggest that this may reflect the fact that US mothers talk to their children more frequently and touch them more. Dutch parental ethnotheory has it that even young children should be left to themselves; they need to organize their own behavior and keep themselves busy; this is part of a cultural expectation pattern, that the children should become "independent."

On the basis of a review of the literature Willemsen and Van de Vijver (1997) noted that Western parents tended to indicate a lower age of mastery of various skills than non-Western parents. They analyzed three possible explanations for this finding on the basis of interviews with Dutch mothers, Turkish migrant mothers living in the Netherlands, and Zambian mothers. For each of eighty-seven skills mothers indicated the age at which they would be acquired (estimates varied from less than one year to about nine years of age). Six different domains of skills were distinguished: physical, perceptual, cognitive, intra-individual, inter-individual, and social. Support was found for the first hypothesized explanation, namely that differences would vary across domains. Differences in age at which mothers expected physical skills to be present on average were very small. For social skills (like being helpful in the family, playing with siblings, and remembering the names of aunts and uncles) the Zambian mothers reported a much higher age of mastery than the two other samples, with the Turkish-Dutch mothers giving somewhat higher ages than the Dutch. For the other four domains the same pattern was found: the differences between samples were smaller than for the social domain. The second possible explanation examined by Willemsen and Van de Vijver was that cross-cultural differences would increase with the children's age of mastery. In fact, they found a curvilinear relationship: there was an increase until the age of five, but for skills mastered by children at a later age the differences between the three samples decreased. The third possible explanation was that specific context variables could explain the differences. Combining the effects of employment status of the mother, her education, and number of children and their ages, about one-third of the cross-cultural variance could be accounted for. Level of education and the number of children were the most effective predictors: higher educated mothers mentioned lower ages of mastery, and mothers with many children indicated higher ages.

These few examples of studies illustrate how different aspects of development come together in the notion of parental ethnotheories. First, the parents are observers of their own children and those in their social environment. Second, parents likely reflect the standards and expectations of the cultural environment they live in, not only in their treatment of children, but also in their perceptions. Third, parents and other caretakers will influence the development of children through socialization practices that reflect their beliefs. A further finding is that parents often do not realize the ways through which, and the extent to which, they steer children in a certain direction. In more recent research on learning it has been argued that cultural transmission takes place in interactional settings where the parent provides "guided participation" (Rogoff, 1990), but also that the child participates actively (Lave & Wenger, 1991). A more extensive review of these issues can be found in Segall et al. (1999), and in box 2.1.

## Box 2.1  Cultural learning

The developing individual also engages in a process of learning. This requires a capacity to learn culture that is uniquely human (Tomasello, Kruger, & Ratner, 1993). Social learning takes place when a person's learning is enhanced by the social situation (Bandura, 1977). But for social learning (as for learning in general), "[t]he actual learning processes are wholly individual in the sense that what is learned is through the youngster's direct interaction with the physical environment" (Tomasello et al. 1993, p. 496). This form of learning corresponds to that which is not mediated by cultural transmission, as shown on the top line of fig. 1.1. In contrast, cultural learning is not learning "*from* another, but *through* another" person (p. 496), and requires the ability to take the perspective of that other person. In culture learning "the learner must internalize into its own repertoire, not just knowledge of the activity being performed by another person, but also something of the social interaction itself" (p. 496). It is this form of learning that is one of the key components of cultural transmission (in fig. 1.1), and of the three forms proposed in fig. 2.1.

According to Tomasello et al., culture learning is "simply a special manifestation of basic processes of learning" (p. 496), including imitative, instructed, and collaborative forms of learning. These three processes appear sequentially, at different ages: nine months, four years and six years respectively. Over the lifespan, and over generations, what is learned accumulates (providing cultural stability), and modifications are made, which also accumulate (providing for cultural change).

## Adolescence

Is adolescence a biologically or a socially determined life stage? Cross-cultural research, particularly by anthropologists, has regularly contributed to this debate, starting with the now controversial descriptions of carefree adolescence on Samoa (Mead, 1928; Freeman, 1983). Whether Margaret Mead was right or wrong in this particular case, the anthropological evidence from all over the world (called hologeistic studies [Schlegel & Barry, 1991]) clearly shows that, while adolescence is everywhere a time for learning new social roles, with attendant psychological tensions, it is not the period of storm and stress claimed by Western developmental and clinical psychologists throughout most of the twentieth century. Adolescence is normally relatively brief, about two years for girls and two to four years for boys, longer when more training for adult roles is needed. In some cases, such as in rural India where children have to fulfill adult tasks from a very early age, not as much time and attention can be spent on adolescence as the Western world, and more affluent urban Indians, define it (Saraswathi, 1999).

Dasen (1999, 2000) has reviewed the cross-cultural literature on adolescence, drawing attention to three methodological approaches: (1) hologeistic studies; (2) ethnographic fieldwork in several societies coordinated by Whiting and Whiting (1988) in the Adolescents in a Changing World study; (3) clinical and developmental psychologists' reports from various non-Western countries. In attempting to define which social conditions were providing the smoothest transition from childhood to adulthood, Dasen attributed adolescent stress mainly to rapid social change, with family continuity and integrity being one of the buffer variables. Other reviews of adolescence in a cross-cultural perspective have been provided by Gibbons (2000) and by Sabatier (1999), who deals mainly with large-scale cross-national studies and research on adolescents in migrant groups of multicultural societies. Like Petersen (1988), who dealt with adolescence in mainstream developmental psychology, Sabatier provides a "debunking of myths" concerning migrant adolescents: contrary to popular belief, these adolescents are, as a rule, not particularly prone to mental illness, have positive self-esteem, and are motivated to be successful in school and in learning a trade. According to the author, the idea that acculturation reinforces the generation gap is another myth that has been overturned, or at least qualified, by recent research findings.

## Moral development

One frequently studied area of development in cross-cultural psychology is that of morality. Rooted in the general stage theory of development of Piaget (1972), and its application to morality (Piaget, 1965), cross-cultural interest in **moral development** was stimulated by the work of Kohlberg (1981, 1984), who proposed that there were three major levels of moral reasoning: pre-conventional, conventional, and post-conventional, with each level divided into two stages. At the pre-conventional level, moral conduct is in the interest of individuals themselves, or in the interest of relatives; reasons for doing right are the avoidance of punishment and the principle of fairness in an exchange. At the conventional level, concern about loyalty and about the welfare of other persons and society at large are given as reasons to justify one's actions. At the post-conventional level, actions are based on ethical principles to which individuals have committed themselves, and that serve as absolute standards, even taking priority over the laws of society that may violate these principles.

Research in this tradition has been based on the method of the structured interview. The subject is presented with a set of hypothetical moral dilemmas and is asked a set of detailed questions as to what course of action should be followed with each dilemma and for what reason. The text of one of these dilemmas reads as follows (Kohlberg, 1984, p. 640):

> In Europe a woman was near death from a special kind of cancer. There was one drug that the doctors thought might save her. It was a form of radium that a druggist in the same town had recently discovered. The drug was expensive

to make, but the druggist was charging ten times what the drug cost him to make. He paid $400 for the radium and charged $4,000 for a small dose of the drug. The sick woman's husband, Heinz, went to everyone he knew to borrow the money and tried every legal means, but he could only get together about $2,000, which is half of what it cost. He told the druggist that his wife was dying, and asked him to sell it cheaper or to let him pay later. But the druggist said, "No, I discovered the drug and I'm going to make money from it." So, having tried every legal means, Heinz gets desperate and considers breaking into the man's store to steal the drug for his wife.

Kohlberg proposed that the development of moral reasoning would follow the same invariant sequence in all cultures and lead toward the same ultimate level of development, representing universal ethical principles. However, he accepted that the rate of development and the highest level reached could show differences. Kohlberg's claims have been tested in a fairly large number of cross-cultural studies. In one review, Snarey (1985) included forty-five studies from twenty-seven cultural groups. He found considerable support for the invariance of the sequence postulated by Kohlberg. The first two levels have been identified in a wide range of societies. As far as the highest level of moral reasoning is concerned, no evidence was found for the presence of post-conventional stages in any of the eight "folk tribal or village societies" where data had been collected. Thus, post-conventional moral reasoning would seem to be characteristic of complex urban societies (non-Western as well as Western). However, even in urban samples, the typical level is that of conventional reasoning, rather than post-conventional.

Other evidence exists that suggests differences in moral reasoning across cultures. For example, Edwards (1986) believes that cultural groups can be expected to differ in the modal stage or level of moral reasoning because of differences in values and social organization. On the other hand, Snarey (1985, p. 228) contends that every culture is capable of supporting post-conventional reasoning, while other authors have suggested that the higher stages are not separate developmental stages. Eckensberger and Reinshagen (1980) have proposed that the last stage merely represents an extension of earlier stages from individual persons to the social system as a whole. Kohlberg (Kohlberg, Levine, & Hewer, 1983) accepted many of these criticisms, and modified his theory in an attempt to accommodate them.

However, cross-cultural researchers (e.g., Ma, 1988, 1989; Miller, Bersoff, & Harwood, 1990; Shweder, Mahapatra, & Miller, 1990) have subsequently raised substantial criticisms, even of this reformulation. For example, Shweder et al. (1990, p. 75) have proposed the existence of "alternative postconventional moralities" based upon conceptions of natural law and justice, rather than on individualism, secularism, and social contract, and possibly modeled on the family as a moral institution. A moral order does not need to have a "rights-based" orientation, like that postulated by Kohlberg; it can also have a "duty-based" orientation. Morality is acquired by children through the transmission of moral evaluations and judgments by parents and other authorities. Shweder and colleagues compared judgments in an urban community in the USA and a traditional group in Orissa, India, on social prescriptions like whether a widow should eat fish. They argued that the trans-gression of the widow in traditional India is seen as a moral transgression and that people tend to invest their practices with moral force. Thus different cultures have different moralities.

Turiel (1983, 1998) maintains that a distinction should be made between moral principles and conventions (in the sense of rules or practices). He discusses extensive empirical evidence that children at a young age already understand this distinction and can make judgments in terms of such principles as social sharing and fair distribution. At the same time, judgment processes can be affected by various reasoning processes, not only moral but also societal and psychological (referring to self). The outcome of a judgment process then depends on which of these processes prevails in a certain instance. We would like to add another complicating factor, namely the status of moral principles as rooted in religion. Especially in fundamentalist religious belief systems formulations of moral (and other) principles tend to be seen as ordained by God (or given by "nature"), which gives them an indisputable authority.

The work of Miller et al. (1990), also in India, has examined the hypothesis of "moral" behavior as the acceptance of social responsibilities toward persons in need. Earlier studies by Miller and her colleagues had suggested that Indians' judg-ments reflected a moral code that tended to give priority to social duties, while the judgments of Americans reflected a moral code that tended to give priority to individual rights. But Miller found similarities in Indian and American views about social responsibilities when serious (e.g., life-threatening) situations were being judged. However, there were substantial cultural differences in the scope of social responsibilities that were considered to be moral in character, and in the criteria that were used in judging whether such issues constituted moral obligations; Indians maintained a broad view, and emphasized need more than Americans did.

Based on his own work in Hong Kong, and on other cross-cultural evidence, Ma (1988) has proposed a revised theory of moral development rooted in Kohlberg's original theory, but extended to include Chinese perspectives, such as the "golden mean" (behaving in the way that the majority of people in society do) and "good will" (the virtue of complying with nature). An empirical examination of some of these ideas with samples from Hong Kong, and elsewhere in the People's Repub-lic of China, and in England, revealed that the two Chinese samples showed a stronger tendency to perform altruistic acts toward others, and to abide by the law, than did the English sample. "In general, the Chinese emphasize *Ch'ing* (human affection, or sentiment) more than *Li* (reason, rationality), and they value filial piety, group solidarity, collectivism and humanity" (Ma, 1989, p. 172). It is evident that a more detailed examination of specific cultural features, and some variations in findings in these studies in India and China, have required a reconceptualization of what constitutes moral development, particularly at the highest level of post-conventional morality.

In an evaluation of the area, Eckensberger and Zimba (1997) also have ad-dressed the claim by Kohlberg that the levels and stages formulated in his theory were universal. To assess whether they were "universal," Kohlberg proposed three different criteria: the first was whether the stages could be identified (empirically) in all cultures; the second was whether the same "operations" applied to all human beings; and the third was whether all people acted in a specific way in similar situations. With these distinctions in mind, Eckensberger and Zimba (1997) assert that "universality" does not mean that morality is completely invariant or shows identical manifestations in all cultures (a view consistent with the use of this term in this textbook). Rather, levels and stages in various cultures reveal "local adaptations in the sense that they are obviously sufficient and adequate for the solution of relevant conflicts" (p. 308).

Taking this meaning of universality, Eckensberger and Zimba (1997) consider five aspects of Kohlberg's theory. First is the "homogeneity of stages," which refers to the consistency of evidence within each stage. They conclude that cross-cultural data on this issue are rare, but that inconsistencies are more often found by researchers who are not part of Kohlberg's research group. Second is the "invariance of the stages" across cultures: do they appear in the same sequence over time in all cultures? There is evidence that in 85 percent of cross-cultural studies there is a positive correlation between age and stage, indicating a fairly high level of stage invariance. However, the best answer to this question would be longitudinal studies in a variety of cultures, and these are rare. Third, and at the core of the universality issue, is the "existence of all stages" across cultures. Eckensberger and Zimba conclude that over the mid-range (upper stage of level 1 and level 2) there is moderate support, but that level 3 appears only sporadically, especially in developing countries. Fourth, as noted earlier, each of the three main levels was divided by Kohlberg into two substages, with one expected to appear before the other. Cross-cultural evidence suggests that this expectation is supported in the few longitudinal studies that are available. Finally, the issue of "gender differences" has been a concern since Gilligan (1982) criticized Kohlberg's theory as being "justice-oriented" (presumably favoring males) and ignoring a morality of "responsibility and care" (presumably a female orientation). Across cultures, however, there is minimal evidence of gender differences along these lines, although these two aspects of moral reasoning appear to be present in all cultures.

Overall, what can be concluded about the universality of Kohlberg's stage theory of moral development? Considering the existence of levels and stages, Eckensberger and Zimba (1997, p. 327) state that "there is much material that supports the claim of universal developmental trends." From a quantitative point of view, stages in the middle range seem to exist transculturally, but from a qualitative point of view, doubts are articulated by some researchers. Many of these qualitative variations are culturally specific or relative and come from research in Asia. These include concepts that translate as "respect for older people," "obligation," "filial piety," "harmony," and "non-violence." Just as for the "culture-bound syndromes" in mental illness (see ch. 16), these culture-specific moral principles may represent some common underlying aspects, possibly a more "duty-bound" orientation.

## Conceptualizations of development

In an earlier section we alluded briefly to theories of ontogenetic development, contrasting maturational and learning theories. It should be noted that neither kind of theory attributes much significance to cultural factors. In maturational theories development tends to be seen as the realization of a more or less fixed biological program. For learning theorists the environment is very important, but in a mechanistic fashion. The adult organism is more or less the sum of all learning experiences. In this section we examine in more detail conceptualizations of ontogenetic development that are explicitly informed by culture.

### Is childhood a cultural notion?

Ideas about children and development are found everywhere and, as we have seen in the section on parental ethnotheories, such ideas can differ across cultures. Also within Western societies views about what children are like and how they should behave have changed over time. Kessen (1979) has referred to the American child as "a cultural invention," quoting sources in which, for example, the obedience of American children is emphasized and American parents are admonished not to play with their children. Kessen goes so far as to question whether there is a "fundamental nature" to the child. Ariès (1960) has questioned the existence in medieval western Europe of the emotional ties in the nuclear family that are so characteristic of the family as it is now known in these societies. Descent and arranged marriages were central rather than the romantic love relationship that forms the basis of partnerships today. Ariès based his ideas on historical accounts in which he noted the absence of expressions of emotions with regard to children. However, other authors have quoted numerous sources which mention such expressions and which give a quite different picture, suggesting that emotional bonds between parents and children did exist (e.g., Peeters, 1988). This suggests that it is meaningful to assume that there exist fundamental ways in which children are the same universally, also in how they interact with adults and how adults interact with them.

### Culture as context for development

The environment of the child is not homogeneous. In Bronfenbrenner's (1979) ecological approach a distinction is made between various environmental layers that are closer to the child or more remote to its direct experiences. These layers can be depicted as concentric circles surrounding the child. The closest circle is called the microsystem by Bronfenbrenner; it includes the settings to which the child has direct exposure, like his or her own family and the school or day care center. Then follows the exosystem, consisting of aspects of the environment that influence the child, although they are not part of direct experience (e.g., the workplace of the parents). Finally, there is the macrosystem, which is the larger cultural setting including, for example, the health and education system. The various layers interact with each other in providing the context in which a child develops.

The importance of the broader context tends to be emphasized particularly by authors from outside the Euroamerican region. Nsamenang (1992) writes about the factors that have shaped the social history of larger parts of Africa. He refers to the colonial history that led to a derogation of African traditions and religious practices, but also points to the continuation of many beliefs and customs that shape child care and the role and obligations of children. Nsamenang describes, for example, how conceptions of stages of development are not limited to the current lifespan, but extend into the spiritual realm of the ancestors, a psychological reality that is also prominent in other areas of the world, for example in Hinduism (Saraswathi, 1999). Many children in the majority world grow up under conditions of poverty and social disruption, including war (Aptekar & Stöcklin, 1997). Authors like Nsamenang (1992), Zimba (in press), and Sinha (1997) plead for a psychology that addresses the everyday reality of the developmental context and its consequences for these children. It should be clear that such consequences are not limited to the social domain; they equally lead to stunted growth and cognitive retardation. For example, Griesel, Richter and Belciug (1990) found that there was a gap in cerebral maturity, as assessed by EEG characteristics, between poorly nourished black urban children and children with normal growth in South Africa. The gap was present already with six- to eight-year-olds, but increased for older children. Corresponding differences were found between these groups of children for measures of cognitive performance.

The concept of cultural transmission appears in fig. 1.1 as a key intermediary between context (including ecology and culture) on the one hand, and human behavior on the other; and we have presented evidence in this chapter that the process is linked to the economic and other activities that are characteristic of a society. So it is natural that ecological thinking should have influenced theoretical concepts of individual development. In particular, the concept of **developmental niche** (Super & Harkness, 1986) has emphasized that all development takes place in a particular cultural context, paralleling the widely used notion of ecological niche that refers to the habitat occupied by a particular species.

As expanded by Super and Harkness (1997), the concept of the developmental niche is a system that links the development of a child with three features of its cultural environment: the physical and social settings (e.g., the people and social interactions, the dangers and opportunities of everyday life); the prevailing customs about child care (e.g., the cultural norms, practices, and institutions); and caretaker psychology (e.g., the beliefs, values, affective orientations, and practices of parents – see the section on "parental ethnotheories"). These three subsystems surround the developing child, and promote, nurture, and constrain its development. They have a number of characteristics: they are embedded in a larger ecosystem; they usually operate together, providing a coherent niche, but can also present inconsistencies to the child. Moreover, there is mutual adaptation (interaction) between the child and each subsystem, so that the child influences, as well as being influenced by, each subsystem.

## Continuing development

At virtually the same time as the rise in cross-cultural studies of development, there has been a dramatic increase in interest in "lifespan" development that covers not only the period from birth to maturity, but continues through maturity to eventual demise (Baltes, Lindenberger, & Staudinger, 1998). While these two trends have not converged into extensive empirical work, there is substantial theoretical interest in examining the role of cultural factors in lifespan development (Baltes, 1997; Valsiner & Lawrence, 1997). The views of one of the leaders in the study of lifespan development may serve to illustrate the emergent field. Baltes (1997) has proposed a framework in which biological and cultural factors play distinct roles in lifespan changes. He advances three principles that define the dynamics between biology and culture across the lifespan.

First, he considers that "evolutionary selection benefits decrease with age." In specific terms, "the human genome in older ages is predicted to contain an increasingly larger number of deleterious genes and dysfunctional gene expressions than in younger years" (p. 367). In other words, there is a decline in biologically rooted functioning over the lifespan (starting around the age of thirty years). This is so because biological evolution cannot operate on the later stages of life, since parents have their children mostly before the age of forty. This makes such dysfunctioning thereafter of minimal relevance for biological selection and transmission.

This biological decline takes place simultaneously with an increase in the "need or demand for culture," including the "entirety of psychological, social, material and symbolic (knowledge-based) resources that humans have generated over the millennia, and which, as they are transmitted across generations, make human development possible" (p. 368). In other words, there is an increase in culturally rooted functioning over the lifespan. However, there is a third principle, a countervailing decrease in the "efficiency of culture," in which "the relative power (effectiveness) of psychological, social, material and cultural interventions wanes" (p. 368). In other words, people are less able to make good use of these cultural supports – older adults take more time and practice, and need more cognitive support, to attain the same learning gains.

The application of these three principles has led Baltes to propose a dual-process model of lifespan development. For example, in the area of cognition, there is a decline in the "cognitive mechanics" (reflecting a person's biological "hardware") with age, as evidenced by speed and accuracy of information processing; but there is a stable level of "cognitive pragmatics" (reflecting the culture-based "software") over the later years, due to the countervailing principles of need for culture and effectiveness of culture. This is evidenced, by the presence of stable reading, writing, language, and professional skills, and knowledge about oneself, others, and the conduct of one's life.

## Cultural mediation

There is probably no developmental theory in which the role of culture is more explicit and encompassing than that of Vygotsky (1978; Wertsch & Tulviste, 1992; Segall et al., 1999). He placed great emphasis on the typically human aspects of behavior and how these come about, in the course of history at the societal level, and ontogenetically at the individual level. There is an internal reconstruction of external operations, making *intra*-individual processes that are initially *inter*-individual.

> Every function in the child's cultural development appears twice: first, on the social level, and later, on the individual level; first, *between* people (*interpsychological*) and then inside the child (*intrapsychological*) ... All the higher functions originate as actual relations between human individuals. (Vygotsky, 1978, p. 57; italics in the original)

This quotation makes clear that the origins of individual mental functioning are social. A human individual can only acquire higher mental functions that are already there in the sociocultural context. Hence, human behavior can be qualified as "culturally mediated."

Originally cultural mediation was thought to have a tremendously broad scope. For example, Luria (1971, 1976) studied syllogistic thinking among groups in Uzbekistan, some illiterate and some living on collective farms with (limited) formal education. From their poor performance he concluded that the illiterates did not possess a faculty for abstract thinking, while those with some education apparently had acquired such a faculty. Later it was demonstrated (e.g., Cole, 1996) that the differences between literates and illiterates were not nearly as dramatic as Luria thought. The main difference appeared to be whether syllogisms were solved by the exclusive use of information contained in the premises given by the researcher, or whether respondents also made use of their prior empirical knowledge (Scribner, 1979). The frequent mentioning by Uzbek respondents that they "did not know" the answer to simple syllogisms probably pointed to their lack of first-hand experience with matters that Luria asked about (Cole, 1992a, 1996; Tulviste, 1991; see also Segall et al., 1999).

Despite his criticisms of the broad sweep of earlier authors, Cole (1992a, 1996) maintains a position of cultural mediation. In his view the biological organism and the environment do not interact directly (as suggested notably by Piaget), but through a third mediating factor, namely culture. In a schematic representation Cole (1992a) not only makes the classic distinction between organism and environment, he makes a further, equally basic, distinction between the natural environment and culture. For Cole, development is a concept with many levels or timescales: a physical scale, a phylogenetic scale, a culture-historical scale (in which social traditions come about and disappear), an ontogenetic scale, and what he calls a microgenetic scale. The last entails the here-and-now of human experience. The interactions between these various levels are essential for an understanding of ontogenetic development. In Cole's view stages of ontogenetic development are not just there in individual children, but they emerge in complex interactions over time. An example is the empirical work in which Cole (1996) has studied how children acquire cognitive skills through computer-based activities in a setting with rich opportunities for written and oral communication.

## Evolutionary approaches

The nature–nurture controversy has been mainly concerned with how much of observable behavior can be explained by biological factors and how much by environmental influences. Already in 1958 Anastasi pointed out that a more pertinent question may be how nature and nurture relate to each other. As we shall see in ch. 12, biological theories about social behavior as advanced in sociobiology and ethology (i.e., the biological study of behavior) are beginning to lead to a theoretical understanding of how such relationships might be conceptualized. In psychology this has led to the development of evolutionary psychology (see ch. 10).

Within the evolutionary tradition there are more deterministic lines of thinking, represented, for example, by Tooby and Cosmides (1992). These authors postulate that the behavior repertoire is an expression of phylogenetically evolved modules. Such modules are the direct outcome of adaptation processes in a Darwinian sense in which the success of reproductive strategies is the central parameter. In ch. 10 we discuss these issues further. Experiments with young children have demonstrated competencies much earlier than expected by Piaget. Work on cognition with children of a few months has shown that in certain instances they distinguish already between events that are physically possible and events that are impossible (Baillargeon, 1995, 1998). This suggests a model of development in which children are born with a few general functions that guide their representations of the external world. In the course of development these are refined more and more through actual experiences.[4]

In the domain of social behavior there are also theoretical approaches in which reproductive outcomes are seen as the outcome of *interactional* processes between an organism with genetically given capacities for development and actual environmental experiences. In cross-cultural developmental psychology such interactions can be studied by linking differences in conditions in early life with differences in characteristic behavior patterns later in life (Keller, 1997). This kind of thinking is exemplified in a study by Belsky, Steinberg, and Draper (1991), who relate factors in the early environment of

---

[4] Research like that of Baillargeon (1995, 1998) implies that there is more continuity in development than Piaget believed to be the case. At the same time, experimental research also has begun to produce rather direct evidence of sudden shifts in developmental patterns that are akin to stages. However, these sudden shifts pertain to specific behaviors rather than to broad domains (like Piaget's stages) (e.g., Thelen, 1995; Wimmers, Savelsbergh, Van der Kamp, & Hartelman, 1998; Wimmers, Savelsbergh, Beek, & Hopkins, 1998).

the child to later sexual and reproductive behavior. They draw a contrast between families with limited resources, insecure attachment patterns, and stress,
and families where there is warmth and security. In the former kind of family there are tendencies for girls to reach sexual maturity at an earlier age, and
for both girls and boys to engage earlier in sexual activity. Later in life this
pattern is continued and leads to less stable pair bonding (higher rate of di-
vorce) and less parental investment, creating an insecure social environment
for the children of the next generation. Support for these results has been found
in other studies (Chasiotis, 1999). These are sweeping claims for at least two
reasons. First, intergenerational patterns as proposed by Belsky et al. have been
noted before, but were ascribed to social environmental factors that continue
across generations; Lewis (1966) spoke about "a culture of poverty" in explaining such patterns. Second, the findings by Belsky et al. imply that social
factors influence biological processes such as sexual maturation and the onset of menstruation. However, whereas in earlier times such influences were
thought to be incompatible with biological principles, it is now recognized
that processes of physical development may indeed be affected by social conditions (Gottlieb, 1998; Gottlieb, Wahlsten, & Lickliter, 1998). It will probably take a few decades of research before the validity of these interactionist
evolutionary approaches can be properly evaluated. In the meantime it is clear
that the systematic variation provided by differences in cultural conditions is
an important feature of research along these lines that can advance some of
the most basic questions of ontogenetic development (Keller & Greenfield,
2000).

## Conclusions

In this chapter we have examined the questions of *how* the background
context of a population becomes incorporated into the behavior of an individual,
and *when* this happens over the course of individual development.

We have argued that all four process variables distinguished in fig. 1.1 are
responsible for transmission from context to person, but we have emphasized forms
of cultural transmission and learning during early life, and acculturation that continues (for some) over the lifespan. We have identified the various routes that cultural transmission can take (vertical, horizontal, oblique) in all cultures, noting
that the relative emphasis on each can vary from culture to culture. Similarly, the
style (ranging from compliance to assertion) varies from culture to culture, and
can be seen as a cultural adaptation to ecological factors (particularly those of a
subsistence economy).

In our treatment of these issues, a number of theoretical and methodological
issues have been identified. First is the initial interpretation at face value of cross-
cultural differences in scores on psychological instruments that have been constructed within one particular cultural context and then used in another. Early

studies tended to overestimate cross-cultural differences and to overgeneralize the psychological implications. Such methodological and theoretical problems of interpretation of data are a recurrent theme in this book. A second major theme is the nature of the interactions between genetic predispositions and cultural or ecological variables; to a large extent this is unknown territory where it would be premature to make strong statements. One possible conclusion is that infants everywhere are set on their life course with much the same apparatus and much the same set of possibilities. Through cultural variations in socialization and infant care practices, some psychological variations begin to appear that can be understood within a framework such as that of fig. 1.1.

## Key terms

acculturation

attachment

biological or genetic transmission

child training

cultural transmission

developmental niche

enculturation

equivalence

gender

Human Relations Area Files (HRAF)

majority world

moral development

ontogenetic development

parental ethnotheories (also called parental beliefs, implicit developmental theories)

socialization

## Further reading

Bornstein, M. H. (Ed.) (1995). *Handbook of parenting* (4 vols.). Mahwah, NJ: Erlbaum. A broad set of chapters on many aspects of how parents bring up their children, including cross-cultural research.

Bril, B., & Lehalle, H. (1988). *Le développement psychologique: est-il universel? Approches interculturelles* [Psychological development: is it universal? Intercultural approches]. Paris: Presses Universitaires de France. A textbook on cross-cultural human development providing access to French-language research in cross-cultural psychology.

Cole, M., & Cole, S. R. (1996). *The development of children* (3rd ed.). New York: Freeman. An introductory text on developmental psychology paying ample attention to the relationship of child and cultural context.

Gardiner, H., Mutter, J., & Kosmitzki, C. (1997). *Lives across cultures: Cross-cultural human development.* Boston, MA: Allyn and Bacon. This introductory text is easy to read; it gives students a feel for what cross-cultural differences imply.

Kagitcibasi, C. (1996). *Family and human development across cultures: A view from the other side.* Hillsdale, NJ: Lawrence Erlbaum. An integration of ideas and findings in child development and societal development, from the perspective of the "majority world."

Munroe, R. L., & Munroe, R. H. (1994b). *Cross-cultural human development* (2nd ed.). Prospect Heights, IL: Waveland Press. A textbook, written jointly by a psychologist and cultural anthropologist, covering issues of human development at the intersection of the two disciplines.

Nsamenang, B. (1992). *Human development in cultural context: A third world perspective.* Beverly Hills, CA: Sage. A presentation and critique of developmental psychology from an African ecological and cultural perspective.

# 3   Social behavior

**CHAPTER OUTLINE**

*Sociocultural context*
*Conformity*
*Values*
*Individualism and collectivism*
*Social cognition*
*Gender behavior*
*Conclusions*
*Key terms*
*Further reading*

This chapter considers the domain of social behavior and how it relates to the general cultural context in which it takes place. We begin with a brief consideration of what social behavior is, and of some of the issues in cross-cultural psychology that attend its investigation. We then turn to a review of some features of the sociocultural system that sociologists and anthropologists consider to be important dimensions of sociocultural variation in human groups. The main sections of the chapter contain a review of research in selected areas of social behavior that have been studied cross-culturally. The section on sociocultural context begins with a brief discussion of the universalist and indigenous positions on cross-cultural variation in social behavior. Thereafter some key concepts are presented and defined. In the section on conformity we examine evidence that in certain societies individuals will follow the prevailing group norm more than others. This is followed by a major section on values, an area of research that is particularly active in cross-cultural research. One value dimension is highlighted in a separate section, namely the dimension of individualism–collectivism that received much attention in cross-cultural social psychology during the 1990s. In the section on social cognition the emphasis is on attribution, which is the tendency to explain human behavior in terms of reasons that are located either in the person or in the environment. In the section on gender behavior we briefly consider various themes in cross-cultural research: how men and women are viewed in various societies; patterns in the selection of (marriage) partners; opinions on how men and women ought to behave; and what the research record tells us about actual differences between men and women in some psychological characteristics.

One other area of social behavior, that of ethnic attitudes and prejudice within plural societies, will be considered later, in ch. 13.

## Sociocultural context

In ch. 1, we argued that *all* human behavior is cultural to some extent. This is because the human species is fundamentally a social one (Hoorens & Poortinga, 2000). Our intimate and prolonged interpersonal relations promote the development of shared meanings, and the creation of institutions and artifacts. To understand our social nature, and how it is organized, we need to examine some basic features of society. The opening focus of this chapter is on the pattern of similarities and differences across cultures in social behavior. On the one hand, social behaviors are obviously linked to the particular sociocultural context in which they develop; for example, greeting procedures (bowing, handshaking, or kissing) vary widely from culture to culture, and these are clear-cut examples of the influence of cultural transmission on our social behavior. On the other hand, greeting takes place in all cultures, suggesting the presence of some fundamental communality in the very essence of social behavior. Therefore one could make the universalist working assumption that many (perhaps most) kinds of social behaviors occur in all cultures, but that they get done in very different ways, depending on local cultural circumstances.

Much of the existing literature on social psychology that is currently available is culture bound; it has developed mostly in one society (the United States), which took "for its themes of research, and for the contents of its theories, the issues of *its own* society" (Moscovici, 1972, p. 19). This culture-bound nature of extant social psychology became a widely accepted viewpoint (e.g., Berry, 1978; Bond, 1988; Jahoda, 1979, 1986). An empirical demonstration of the cultural limits of social psychology has been provided by Amir and Sharon (1987), who attempted to replicate, in Israel, six studies that were reported in one year in an American social psychology journal. Of several hypotheses that were retested, by and large half did not replicate, while in addition some "new" significant results were found. At a theoretical level, Berry (1974a) has pointed out the inappropriateness of importing some American social-psychological concepts into Canada (such as studying French Canadian–English Canadian relations using an implicit model derived from African American–White American research). If there are difficulties in transporting theories, methods, and findings from the United States to Israel and Canada, how much more likely are there to be problems when larger cultural contrasts are involved?

One solution is to create indigenous social psychologies (Kim & Berry, 1993; Sinha, 1997). These attempt to develop social psychologies that are appropriate to a particular society or region (e.g., Berry & Wilde, 1972, for Canada; and Hewstone, Stroebe, & Stephenson, 1996, for Europe). Such activity follows the proposal of Moscovici (1972): "the social psychology that we ought to create must have an origin in our own reality" (p. 23). This corresponds to the second goal of cross-cultural psychology; as outlined in ch. 1, the intention is to explore other cultural systems to discover new social behavioral phenomena that correspond to the local sociocultural reality. However, if we do this, we are likely to end up with a proliferation of "multiple social psychologies" (Doise, 1982; Jahoda, 1986), each one corresponding to its own sociocultural context. An obvious advantage of these multiple social psychologies is that they are likely to match the indigenous realities that nurtured them. An equally obvious disadvantage is that such proliferation might lead to the fragmentation of the discipline. However, they are necessary for the discovery of the possible underlying principles and common dimensions of social behavior, which is the pursuit of the third goal of cross-cultural psychology (universals), using the comparative method (Berry & Kim, 1993; Berry, 2000a). There is little doubt, in the view of many cross-cultural social psychologists (e.g., Faucheux, 1976; Jahoda, 1979; Pepitone, 1976; Triandis, 1978) that these basic universal principles exist in most domains of social behavior (see box 3.1). Put another way, the universalist working assumption with which we started this discussion appears to be widely shared in contemporary cross-cultural psychology. However, *how* to discover these universal principles while exploring all the local indigenous social psychologies remains the core problem facing cross-cultural social psychologists. We will return to the theoretical aspects of this issue in ch. 12. Here we deal with two important dimensions of cultural variation found across cultures: role diversity and role obligation.

In every social system individuals occupy *positions* for which certain behaviors are expected; these behaviors are called *roles*. Each role occupant is the object of *sanctions* that exert social influence, even pressure, to behave according to social *norms* or standards. (Readers who are unfamiliar with these terms may wish to consult any introductory sociology text, or ch. 2 of Segall et al., 1999.) The four emphasized terms constitute some essential conceptual building blocks that enable us to understand the flow from background contexts, to cultural adaptation, to transmission, and eventually to social behavior as presented in fig. 1.1.

These elements of a social system are not random, but are organized or structured by each cultural group. Such structures are considered in this text to be influenced by the ecological context and subject to further change stemming from the sociopolitical context (see ch. 1). Two key features of social structures are that they are differentiated and stratified. By the first term is meant that societies make distinctions among roles; some societies make few, while others make many. For example, in a relatively undifferentiated social structure positions and roles may be limited to a few basic familial, social, and economic ones (such as parent–child, hunter–food preparer). In contrast, in a relatively more differentiated society there are many more positions and roles to be found in particular domains, such as king–aristocracy–citizen–slave, corporate owner–manager–worker–retiree, or pope–cardinal–bishop–priest–layperson. In the former there is minimal role diversity, while in the latter there is more.

## Box 3.1 Universals in social behavior

Aberle and his colleagues (1950) have proposed a set of functional prerequisites of society, defined as "the things that must get done in any society
if it is to continue as a going concern." These are of interest because they
probably qualify as universals, those activities (in one form or another) being found in every culture. There are nine of these:

1 Provision of adequate relationships with the environment (both physical
  and social): this is needed to maintain a sufficient population to "carry"
  the society and culture.
2 The differentiation and assignment of roles: in any group different things
  need to get done, and people have to somehow be assigned these roles
  (e.g., by heredity, or by achievement).
3 Communication: all groups need to have a shared, learned, and symbolic
  mode of communication in order to maintain information flow and coordination within the group.
4 Shared cognitive orientation: beliefs, knowledge, and rules of logical thinking need to be held in common for people in a society to work together in
  mutual comprehension.
5 Shared articulated set of goals: similarly, the directions for common striving need to be shared, in order to avoid individuals pulling in conflicting
  directions.
6 Normative regulation of means to these goals: rules governing how these
  goals might be achieved need to be stated and accepted by the population.
  If material acquisition is a general goal for most people, murder and theft
  are not likely to be accepted as a means to this goal, whereas production,
  hard work, and trading may be.
7 Regulation of affective expression: similarly, emotions and feelings need
  to be brought under normative control. Expressions of love and hate, for
  example, cannot be given free rein without serious disruptive consequences
  within the group.
8 Socialization: all new members must learn about the central and important features of group life. The way of life of the group needs to be communicated, learned, and to some extent, accepted by all individuals.
9 Control of disruptive behavior: if socialization and normative regulation
  fail, there needs to be some "back-up" so that the group can require appropriate and acceptable behavior of its members. In the end, behavioral
  correction or even permanent removal (by incarceration or execution) may
  be required.

A universal model of social relations has been proposed by Fiske (1991), in
which it is claimed that "just four elementary relational structures are sufficient to describe an enormous spectrum of forms of human social relations,

**Box 3.1 (continued)**

as well as social motives and emotions, intuitive social thought and moral judgement." These are:

1 Communal sharing: where people are merged, boundaries of individual selves are indistinct, people attend to group membership and have a sense of common identity, solidarity, unity, and belonging; they think of themselves as being all the same in some significant respect, not as individuals, but as "we" (cf. collectivism; see later).
2 Authority ranking: where inequality and hierarchy prevail, highly ranked persons control people, things, and resources (including knowledge), frequently take the initiative, and have the right to choose and exercise preference (cf. high social stratification).
3 Equality matching: where there are egalitarian relations among peers; people are separate but equal, engaging in turn-taking, reciprocity, and balanced relationships (cf. low social stratification).
4 Market pricing: where relationships are mediated by values determined by a "market" system, individuals interact with others just when and as they decide that it is rational to do so in terms of these values, and actions are evaluated according to the rates at which they can be exchanged for other commodities.

In the view of Fiske (1991, p. 25),

these models are *fundamental*, in that they are in some sense the lowest or most basic level "grammars" for social relations. My hypothesis is that these models are *general*, giving order to most forms of social interaction, thought, and affect. They are *elementary*, in the sense that they are the basic constituents for all higher order social forms. My hypothesis is that they are also *universal*, being the basis for social relations among all people in all cultures (allowing for an enormous amount of culture-specific elaboration, embellishment, and inhibition) and the essential foundation for cross-cultural understanding and intercultural engagement.

Fiske (1993) has provided empirical support for these four relational categories, using people's strategies for dealing with social errors.

These differentiated positions and roles may be organized in a hierarchy or not; when they are placed in a vertical status structure, the social system is said to be stratified. A number of cross-cultural analyses of stratification are available (e.g., Murdock, 1967; Pelto, 1968). Murdock was concerned with the presence of class distinctions (e.g., hereditary aristocracy, wealth distinctions). At one end (the unstratified) there are few such status distinctions, while at the other (the stratified), there may be numerous class or status distinctions (e.g., royalty, aristocracy, gentry, citizens, slaves). The analysis by Pelto (1968) of these and similar distinctions led him to place societies on a dimension called **"tight–loose."** In the stratified and tight societies the pressures to carry out one's roles leads to a high level of role obligation, while in less tight societies, there is much less pressure to oblige.

These two dimensions of cultural variation appear in a number of empirical and conceptual studies. For example, Lomax and Berkowitz (1972) factor-analyzed numerous cultural variables and found two dimensions, which they termed differentiation and integration. More recently (Berry, 1994), the concepts of societal size and societal conformity have been proposed to relate to a number of social behaviors, such as values and conformity. Of particular importance is that these two dimensions are closely related to some basic features of ecological systems. For example, in the work of McNett (1970), nomadic hunting and gathering societies tend to have less role diversity and role obligation, while sedentary agricultural societies typically have more diversity and obligation. In urban, industrialized societies, many studies have suggested an even higher level of diversity, but lower levels of role obligation (Lomax & Berkowitz, 1972; Boldt, 1978). These two cultural dimensions are thus clearly related to the ecological context and to the differences in cultural transmission that were introduced in ch. 2.

Keeping these central dimensions of the social and cultural context in mind, we now turn to a survey of studies in selected domains of social behavior, many of which appear to be related to variations in ecology, culture, and cultural transmission.

## Conformity

The degree to which individuals will characteristically go along with the prevailing group norm has long been a topic of interest in social psychology. As we have seen above, there are general expectations in all societies that members will conform to societal norms; without some degree of **conformity**, it is quite likely that social cohesiveness would be so minimal that the group could not continue to function as a group (one of the functional prerequisites in box 3.1). However, as we have seen in the discussion of cultural transmission (in ch. 2), there appears to be variation across cultures in the degree to which individuals are raised or trained to be independent and self- (as opposed to group-)reliant. It is thus plausible to expect a pattern of co-variation between where a society is located on the compliance–assertion dimension of socialization and the typical degree of individual conformity to the group's norms.

As we have also seen, there are some ecological, demographic, and social variables that tend to go along with compliance–assertion in socialization, and which may further encourage conformity; the size of the group, and the degree of social stratification, may "bear down" on the individual more when the group is large and highly stratified. We can thus identify a package of influences that suggest that conformity may vary across cultures: there is likely to be relatively more individual conformity in societies that emphasize compliance training (i.e., densely populated and highly stratified societies), and relatively less in societies that stress assertion training (i.e., sparse and unstratified societies). As we shall see, some evidence is available to support this expectation.

Researchers studying conformity have usually investigated the tendency of individuals to be influenced by what they believe to be the judgments of a group, even when those judgments conflict with the evidence of the individuals' own perceptions. This phenomenon was first demonstrated by Asch (1956), in studies where participants were presented with a line judgment task, and had to say which of three lines of differing length were the same length as a standard comparison line. Faced with this task, participants conformed with unanimous, but obviously incorrect, judgments of line lengths about one-third of the time. Such incorrect judgments were obtained from confederates of the experimenter who had been instructed to deliberately give the incorrect answer. Many studies have been done since, mainly with university students in Western countries using Asch-type procedures, and have both replicated and extended these findings.

Cross-cultural studies have also been conducted with Asch-type materials, and have been reviewed by Bond and Smith (1996). They sought to establish whether conformity was evident in all cultures, and whether certain features of cultures might be related to variations in degree of conformity. To begin, they distinguished between studies carried out with people in subsistence economies, and those done in industrialized societies. In the first group are studies carried out by Berry (1967, 1979), who proposed that conformity was likely to be found across cultures, but would vary according to ecological and cultural factors. Specifically, he predicted that hunting-based peoples, with loose forms of social organization (low societal conformity) and socialization for assertion, would exhibit lower levels of conformity than those in agricultural societies, with tighter social organization and socialization for compliance. He examined this relationship across seventeen samples from ten different cultures. An Asch-type task of independence versus conformity was developed for cross-cultural use, in which the community norm was communicated to the participants by the local research assistant.[1] The mean scores for each of the seventeen samples were then related to a sample's position on an ecocultural index (ranging from hunting–loose–assertion to agriculture–tight–compliance), resulting in a correlation of +.70 across the seventeen samples, and of +.51 across the 780 individuals in the study.

This study suggests quite strongly that in "loose" societies, where there is child training for assertion, there will be relatively independent performance on an Asch-type task, while training for compliance in "tight" societies is associated with greater conformity. As Barry et al. (1959) predicted, socialization practices in subsistence societies relate to adult behavior; in this case, there is a clear theoretical and empirical link between how a society characteristically socializes its children along the compliance–assertion dimension and the typical score obtained by a sample from that society on a conformity task.

---

[1] In these studies it was not possible to have the "group norm" develop and be shared by experimental confederates (as was done by Asch, 1956). Among people in a village, such a deception would become known, and its effects would diminish.

In the second (and largest) group of studies, Bond and Smith (1996) examined conformity research results in industrial societies. They found again that conformity was present in all studies, but that the degree of conformity varied with aspects of culture, and generally was related to tightness, just as in subsistence societies. However, instead of linking conformity back to ecology, social structure, and socialization (measured at the cultural group level), they sought to relate variations in conformity to a set of values obtained in previous cross-cultural surveys of individuals, whose scores were then aggregated to give a country-level score. While the topic of values follows in the next section, for now we can think of them as desired ways of living that are generally shared by a group of people. Bond and Smith (1996) found that conformity was higher in societies that held values of conservatism, collectivism, and a preference for status ascription, while it was lower in societies valuing autonomy, individualism, and status achievement. In these studies, two psychological variables were being related to each other (conformity and values), while in the earlier studies a set of ecocultural variables was being related to conformity. It is possible that both conformity and these collectivist values are related because they both are situated in a broader ecocultural context that promotes them as a consistent and functional response to living in tight societies (Berry, 1994).

## Values

The study of societal values, as characteristics of populations, has a long history in sociology and anthropology (e.g., Kluckhohn & Strodtbeck, 1961). The study of individual values has a similarly long history in psychology (e.g., Allport, Vernon, & Lindzey, 1960). The cross-cultural study of both societal and individual values, however, is relatively recent (e.g., Feather, 1975; Hofstede, 1980; Smith & Schwartz, 1997).

In both disciplines **values** are inferred constructs, whether held collectively by societies or individually by persons. In an early definition, the term "values" refers to a conception held by an individual, or collectively by members of a group, of that which is desirable, and which influences the selection of both means and ends of action from among available alternatives (Kluckhohn, 1951, p. 395). This complex definition has been simplified by Hofstede: values are "a broad tendency to prefer certain states of affairs over others" (Hofstede, 1980, p. 19). Values are usually considered to be more general in character than attitudes, but less general than ideologies (such as political systems). They appear to be relatively stable features of individuals and societies, and hence correspond in this regard to personality traits and cultural characteristics.

In anthropology and sociology values became included as one aspect of a culture or society; they appear in definitions of culture, and often appear in field-based descriptions of particular societies and cultures. Soon, such single culture studies gave way to comparative survey studies, the most renowned being that of F. Kluckhohn and Strodtbeck (1961) based on a classification of values earlier proposed by C. Kluckhohn (1951); the general scheme is presented in box 3.2.

## Box 3.2  Variations in value orientations

The empirical study of values was greatly advanced by the research of Florence Kluckhohn and Fred Strodtbeck (1961) with samples of individuals from rural communities in the USA. Drawing samples from five different cultural groups (Texan, Mormon, Hispanic, Zuni, and Navaho), they presented a series of short stories with alternative outcomes to respondents who indicated their own preferred outcome. By aggregating responses to statements embodying these alternatives, Kluckhohn and Strodtbeck were able to present a general statement about preferred value orientations in each particular cultural group. This method contrasts sharply with the earlier anthropological approach of discerning value preferences from natural cultural indicators (such as myths or political institutions). Their classification of value orientations used five dimensions:

1 "Man–nature orientation" concerns the relation of humans to their natural environment. There are three alternatives: human mastery over nature, human subjugation to nature, and human harmony with nature.
2 "Time orientation" concerns an individual's orientation to the past, the present, or the future.
3 "Activity orientation" concerns a preference for being, becoming, or doing; essentially these represent the enjoyment of a person's current existence, of changing to a new existence, or of activity without any change.
4 "Relational orientation" concerns the human relation with others, and emphasizes individualism, collateral relations (preference for others in extended group), or lineal relations (ordered succession within the group).
5 "Nature of man" is judged to be good, bad, or neither on one dimension, and mutable or immutable on another dimension.

Short stories that posed a problem were presented to respondents, who were asked to indicate which alternate solution to the problem was the best; answers were scored as indicative of one of the values on one of the five dimensions. Results indicated that it was possible to measure cultural value orientations through the use of individual responses. Moreover, systematic differences appeared across cultures: Mormons and Texans were higher on doing than the other groups; Hispanics were present- and being-oriented, and valued human subjugation to nature more than others; the Zuni preferred doing and a mastery over nature, while the Navaho preferred the present in time orientation, and the harmony with nature relationship rather than mastery. These now-classic findings showed that some general characterizations of cultural groups were possible using standard values measures. However, in some respects, these characterizations approach the overgeneralizations that were so problematic for the culture and personality school (as noted in ch. 1, and to be discussed in more detail in ch. 9).

Perhaps the best-known and most widely used approach to studying values in psychology is that of Rokeach (1973). Drawing upon the distinction by Kluckhohn (1951), Rokeach developed two sets of values, namely terminal values which were defined as idealized end states of existence, and instrumental values which were defined as idealized modes of behavior used to attain the end states. Rokeach identified eighteen values of each kind, and his instrument (the Rokeach Value Survey) requires respondents to rank order the values within each set of eighteen. For example, included in the list of terminal values are goals of "equality," "freedom," "happiness," "salvation," and "self-respect"; in the instrumental values are such behaviors as being "courageous," "honest," "polite," and "responsible."

More recently, work by Schwartz (1994; Schwartz & Bilsky, 1990; Schwartz & Sagiv, 1995) has extended the Rokeach tradition. In an extensive research project samples of students and samples of teachers in each of fifty-four societies were administered a scale with fifty-six items that had to be rated on a seven-point scale. Considerable effort went into the translation of these items. Moreover, local terms in other languages were sometimes included in the scale, but this did not lead to the discovery of value domains that were not present in the original (Western) scale. From this data set ten individual value types emerged. These are shown in fig. 3.1. According to Schwartz these ten types can best be

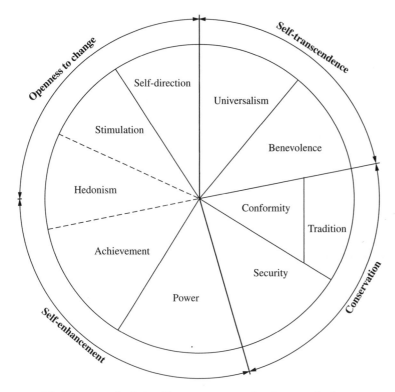

**3.1** Structure of relationships among ten national types of values
     From Schwartz & Sagiv, 1995

represented in two dimensions, and depicted in the form of a circle. The validity of this configuration has been confirmed by independent analysis on the Schwartz data set (Fontaine, 1999).

There has been considerable debate about whether more basic dimensions can be identified that underlie the ten value types, and how these dimensions cut across fig. 3.1. It has been suggested by Schwartz and Sagiv (1995) that there are two dimensions that organize the ten value types into clusters situated at either end of the two dimensions: these dimensions are self-enhancement (power, achievement, hedonism) versus self-transcendence (universalism, benevolence); and conservatism (conformity, security, tradition) versus openness to change (self-direction, stimulation). These two dimensions (and ten values) are considered by Schwartz to represent universal aspects of human existence, which are rooted in basic individual needs (biological, interpersonal, sociocultural).

As noted during the discussion of conformity, individual scores can be aggregated over individuals within a group (culture or country) to yield a score that is thought to be characteristic of the group. (This procedure has methodological and theoretical implications that will be discussed in chs. 11 and 12.) Schwartz (1994) has carried out such an aggregation, and he obtained seven country-level values: conservatism, affective autonomy, intellectual autonomy, hierarchy, egalitarian commitment, mastery, and harmony. These seven culture-level values were further analyzed, and yielded clusters at either end of three bipolar dimensions: conservatism versus autonomy; hierarchy versus egalitarianism; and mastery versus harmony. (Note that the two forms of autonomy in the list of seven values are put together in one cluster, now termed autonomy.) These three dimensions each deal with three basic concerns of all societies: the first is how individuals relate to their group (whether they are embedded or independent); the second is how people consider the welfare of others (whether relationships are vertically or horizontally structured); and the third is the relationship of people to their natural and social world (whether they dominate and exploit it, or live with it).

Further analysis (Georgas, Van de Vijver, & Berry, 2000) has shown that only two bipolar dimensions may be present: autonomy and egalitarianism (combined) versus conservatism; and hierarchy and mastery (combined) versus harmony. These two dimensions were termed autonomy and hierarchy. Note that these two value dimensions at the group level were generated by analyses of individual responses to value statements. However, they correspond clearly to findings in the anthropological literature. In particular, they resemble some of the "functional prerequisites" and "relational structures" presented in box 3.1, and two of the "value orientations" (relational orientation and man–nature orientation) presented in box 3.2. There is thus some degree of convergence among these various studies regarding the fundamental dimensions of human values across cultures, which may constitute universals.

Further evidence for these basic dimensions has been provided by a study of over 8,000 company managers in forty-three countries (Smith, Dugan, &

Trompenaars, 1996). They began with three value measures, one each for universalistic versus particularistic obligations to people; achievement versus ascription, as ways of getting things done; and individualism versus collectivism, as ways of organizing relationships in work settings. Analyses revealed the presence of two main dimensions, plus a third weaker one. Focussing on the first two dimensions, they proposed the names of conservatism versus egalitarian commitment (combining values of ascription and particularism versus achievement and universalism), and utilitarian involvement versus loyal involvement (mainly represented by values of individualism versus collectivism). Once again, two major value dimensions have been found, and once again they resemble the hierarchy and autonomy dimensions found previously. These findings further suggest the presence of universals (see also Smith & Schwartz, 1997, p. 103).

Before accepting this possibility, however, it is important to note that in all of this work, the question of cultural relevance arises: to what extent do the Rokeach values match those that are of concern to people in their daily lives in these various cultures? There is also the question of the meaning of these terms (whether translated or not): do individuals from different cultures interpret the value terms in exactly the same way (Peng, Nisbett, & Wong, 1997)? These methodological issues will be considered in more formal terms later (in ch. 11), but in the meantime they can be considered as limitations, both to understanding value preferences in any particular culture, and to comparing value preferences across cultures.

Another tradition, based in sociology and political science, is the World Values Survey. This has been carried out three times since 1981; it has sampled values from individuals in sixty-five countries containing over 75 percent of the world population (Inglehart & Baker, 2000). Using a wide range of items, Inglehart and Baker found two basic value dimensions, which they labeled traditional versus secular-rational, and survival versus self-expression. The first dimension is characterized by values that emphasize obedience rather than independence when raising children (cf. the compliance–assertion dimension discussed in ch. 2) as well as respect for authority. The second dimension is characterized by values that emphasize economic and physical security over quality of life. While these two dimensions are the result of national-level factor analyses, the same two dimensions also appear at the individual level of analysis.

When country scores are plotted on these two dimensions, a number of broad geographical clusters are revealed. For example, north-west Europe is high on both secular and self-expressive values, while ex-Communist (east) Europe is high on secular, but low on self-expressive values. English-speaking countries are intermediate on secular and high on self-expressive values. South Asia and Africa are low on both values, while Latin America is low on secular and intermediate on self-expressive values.

When these country clusters are plotted in relation to gross national product (GNP), a clear relationship appears: low GNP countries are low on both secular and self-expressive values, while high GNP countries are high on both. The issue of whether these values are precursors for, or alternatively the result of, national development, will be addressed in ch. 17.

Most of the large-scale studies of values were stimulated by Hofstede's gigantic project (1980, 1983a,b, 1991). For many years Hofstede worked for a major international corporation, and was able to administer over 116,000 questionnaires (in 1968 and in 1972) to employees in fifty different countries and of sixty-six different nationalities. Three main factors were distinguished and four "country scores" were calculated by aggregating the individual scores within each country. Although the statistical analyses pointed to three factors, according to Hofstede four dimensions made more sense psychologically. The four dimensions were the following:

1 power distance: the extent to which there is inequality (a pecking order) between supervisors and subordinates in an organization;
2 uncertainty avoidance: the lack of tolerance for ambiguity, and the need for formal rules;
3 individualism: a concern for oneself as opposed to concern for the collectivity to which one belongs;
4 masculinity: the extent of emphasis on work goals (earnings, advancement) and assertiveness, as opposed to interpersonal goals (friendly atmosphere, getting along with the boss) and nurturance. The first set of values is thought to be associated with males, the second more with females.

In fig. 3.2 a plot of the country scores on two of these value dimensions (power distance and individualism) reveals a number of "country clusters": in the lower right quadrant is the "Latin cluster" (large power distance/high individualism), termed "dependent individualism" by Hofstede (1980, p. 221); the opposite pattern, called "independent collectivism" is exhibited for Israel and Austria; most of the Third World countries are located in the upper right quadrant (a kind of "dependent collectivism"); and most Western industrialized nations are in the lower left quadrant ("independent individualism"). The figure also reveals a clear negative correlation between the two value dimensions ($r = -.67$), and both are correlated with economic development indicators, such as GNP ($r = -.65$ with power distance; $r = +.82$ with individualism). In fact, the first dimension (i.e., the dimension that explains the largest proportion of the cross-cultural variation) in all the studies mentioned in this section is closely associated with GNP, a point to which we shall return in the next section. Hofstede's study on work values is presented here to provide a basic introduction; its relevance to the cross-cultural study of organizations will be discussed in ch. 14.

As we have seen, Hofstede's work has led to a blossoming of research on values both within and across cultures. In particular, research on the individualism dimension has become very active, mainly influenced by Triandis (1988, 1995), and we now turn to this.

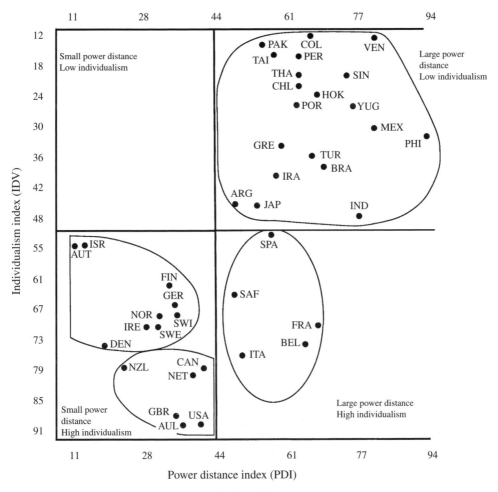

**3.2** Positions of forty countries on the power distance and individualism scales
From Hofstede 1980

## Individualism and collectivism

This value dimension has been examined more thoroughly than any other topic in contemporary cross-cultural psychology. Indeed, it has come to dominate many fields, from social, developmental, and personality psychology to political science and management (see Kagitcibasi, 1997a; Kim et al., 1994a; Triandis, 1995 for overviews). The literature is so vast that it is only possible to deal with some key issues here. Fortunately, the groundwork for our discussion has been established by the earlier examination of values, where a dimension that resembles individualism–collectivism (hereafter I–C) appears in virtually every study[2]. Also, some of the more recent refinements have linked the dimension to the second basic value dimension of hierarchy (vertical versus horizontal relationships within a society; Triandis & Gelfand, 1998). Rather than review the hundreds of specific findings in this area, the presentation here will deal with three basic issues: the nature of I–C; the dimensionality of I–C; and its possible origins in ecological and cultural contexts.

We have already seen that the defining difference between **individualism** and **collectivism** is a primary concern for oneself in contrast to a concern for the groups(s) to which one belongs. However, it is to be expected that in a broad concept finer distinctions can be made, and these have been elaborated by many researchers. For example, Triandis (1995) proposes that there are four defining attributes: (1) the definition of the self as personal or collective, independent or interdependent; (2) personal goals having priority over group goals (or vice versa); (3) emphasis on exchange rather than on communal relationships; and (4) the relative importance of personal attitudes versus social norms in a person's behavior.

Other characterizations of I–C proposed by Triandis and colleagues include self-reliance, competition, emotional distance from in-groups, and hedonism (for individualism), and interdependence, family integrity, and sociability (for collectivism). To illustrate the range of content, and a way of measuring I–C, box 3.3 provides an example of one scale (Hui & Yee, 1994). It should be apparent by now that the construct of I–C is very wide ranging, multifaceted, and possibly "over-extended" (Kagitcibasi, 1997a), to the point that it has become a catchall to explain a very large number of psychological differences across cultures.

In a conceptual analysis of I–C, Kagitcibasi (1997a) distinguishes two ways to think of the dimension: normative and relational. Normative I–C represents the view that "individual interests are to be subordinated to group interests" (Kagitcibasi, 1997a, p. 34), while relational I–C is more concerned with "interpersonal distance versus embeddedness" (p. 36). The distinction is necessary, since "[c]losely-knit relatedness or separateness can exist within both hierarchical and egalitarian groups" (p. 36). Once again, two value dimensions (I–C and hierarchy) appear to be present, and probably entwined.

While there is substantial empirical evidence to support any number of conceptualizations of I–C, varying from simple demonstrations of differences in value scales across cultures to complex factor-analytic studies (see Kim et al., 1994; Triandis, 1995), there are relatively few critical tests of the construct (Fijneman, Willemsen, & Poortinga, 1996; Van den Heuvel & Poortinga, 1999). One study that was designed to evaluate some of the more widely accepted aspects of I–C (Fijneman et al., 1996) began by noting that "Individualism–collectivism emerges

---

[2] The original conceptualization of individualism and collectivism was to see them as polar opposites on a single dimension. As we note later, more recent research has suggested that there may be two independent dimensions. Our use of I–C reflects the earlier conceptualization, which is (still) the most common.

## Box 3.3 Individualism and collectivism

Hofstede (1980) found his dimension of individualism–collectivism, using very few items in his country-level factor analyses. These items were later found not to be particularly useful to place either individuals or work organizations on the dimension (Hofstede & Spangenberg, 1987), and so a number of researchers have developed individual-level scales for use with individuals. Some items from a scale by Hui and Yee (1994) will serve to illustrate the quality of this domain.

They began with the view that I–C is a bipolar and unidimensional construct, and that the target or object would be important in a person's response. Initially, six targets were included in the set of items (spouse, parents, kin, neighbors, friends, and co-workers). However, only five factors were found, and furthermore, these were reducible to two (higher-order) factors: "in-group solidarity" included items referring to people in the nuclear family (parents and spouse) and those who could be freely chosen in relationships; and "social obligation" included items referring to other kin and neighbors.

### In-group solidarity
Teenagers should listen to their parents' advice on dating. (C)
I would not share my ideas and newly acquired knowledge with my
   parents. (I)
The decision of where one is to work should be jointly made with one's
   spouse. (C)
Even if the child won the Nobel prize, the parents should not feel honored
   in any way. (I)
I like to live close to my good friends. (C)
To go on a trip with friends makes one less free and mobile; as a result
   there is less fun. (I)

### Social obligation
I can count on my relatives for help if I find myself in any kind of trouble.
   (C)
Each family has its own problems unique to itself. It does not help to tell
   relatives about one's problems. (I)
I enjoy meeting and talking to my neighbors every day. (C)
I am not interested in knowing what my neighbors are really like. (I)

from the literature as a high-level psychological concept . . . that explains cross-cultural differences in behavior over a wide range of situations" (p. 383), and criticized such high-level concepts on historical, methodological, and theoretical grounds. These authors carried out an experimental study to test some predictions about differences in behavior between societies previously characterized as collectivist or individualist (Hong Kong, Turkey, Greece, USA, the Netherlands).

Specifically, they argued that I–C theory predicts that people in individualistic societies should be less willing to contribute resources to others in their group (inputs). However, Fijneman et al. proposed that if this was the case, such a difference would be matched by lower expectations of receiving from others (outputs). Moreover, they predicted that both level of input and of output would vary in all countries by the degree of emotional closeness between a person and various social categories (e.g., father, sister, cousin, close friend, neighbor, an unknown person). Findings revealed remarkable similarities in patterns of inputs and outputs over social categories in all six countries. In addition, in all these countries both input and output ratings varied across the social categories with degree of emotional closeness in similar ways. Thus, they demonstrated that emotional closeness to specific social others explained differences in inputs and outputs, rather than being due to the more general variable of I–C.

Another line of critical research (Realo, Allik, & Vadi, 1997) was also concerned with analyzing the high level of generality of the I–C construct. The authors focussed their study on collectivism, noting that scales purporting to measure collectivism obtained different scores depending on the target group (e.g., spouse, parents, friends), a point similar to the critique made by Fijneman et al. (1996). However, in this study, rather than measuring predictions from I–C theory, they measured the construct itself. They began with the view that collectivism is a superordinate construct within which there are a number of subordinate forms. They developed a thirty-nine-item scale for use with varied samples in Estonia. Factor analyses revealed three factors, one each concerned with collectivism in the family, in peers, and in society; they also found an overall factor, one that incorporated all three specific factors. The authors concluded that "I–C cannot be defined as a single internally homogeneous concept, but is instead composed of several interrelated, yet ultimately distinguishable, subtypes of I-C" (Allik & Realo, 1996, p. 110).

In an examination of these three specific, and the overall collectivism, scores in various subsamples, it was found that the scores varied significantly: for example, servicemen were higher than others on peer collectivism, housewives higher than others in family collectivism, and inhabitants of an isolated island higher than others on societal collectivism. The authors concluded that how collectivistic people are depends on the kind of collectivism, and on their particular life circumstances.

## Dimensionality

As we have just seen, the I–C construct may not be unitary, in the sense that there is only one way to be collectivist. Another issue in this area is whether individualism and collectivism are polar opposites on a single dimension, or two independent dimensions. If the latter is the case, then a person could be high or low on both, or high and low on one or the other. Initially (Hofstede, 1980), evidence suggested that there was a single I–C dimension, with I and C being opposites. However, more recent evidence (e.g., Rhee, Uleman & Lee, 1996;

Triandis, 1993) portrays them as being both conceptually and empirically independent. For example, Triandis (1993, p. 162) argued that individualism and collectivism "can coexist and are simply emphasized more or less in each culture, depending on the situation." Furthermore, a number of studies have indicated that individualism and collectivism are not just opposites, but are conceptually and empirically independent.

In one of the clearest demonstrations of this difference Kashima et al. (1995) found that there were three quite distinct dimensions. In a study in Australia, Japan, Korea, and the USA (Hawaii and Illinois) individualism and collectivism were empirically separable from each other (and also from a construct of "relations," that is concerned with emotional ties to others). (This study was also interested in gender differences on these three dimensions, an issue that will be addressed later in this chapter.) A second demonstration of the distinction between I and C (Rhee et al., 1996), with samples of Koreans, Asian Americans, and European Americans, used a variety of I–C items available in the literature. Their study sought answers to two questions. Are I and C bipolar opposites on a single dimension? And does it matter which group is referenced in the item (kin or others) as the in-group? They tested a number of models with factor analysis, and concluded that "collectivism and individualism are best conceived of as two dimensions, and that their relationship depends on the ingroup referents" (p. 1048). More generally, they concluded that

> currently available measures of collectivism and individualism should not be treated as either equivalent or adequate . . . there is an urgent need for scales that measure collectivism and individualism as separate dimensions, and that do so with regard to specific referent ingroups at the individual level. (p. 1050)

Moreover, the addition of the dimension of hierarchy to the conception of I–C (e.g., Triandis & Gelfand, 1998) enhances the multidimensionality of the concept. These authors found four distinct factors in an I–C scale, one each for horizontal individualism (e.g., "I'd rather depend on myself than on others"), vertical individualism (e.g., "It is important that I do my job better than others"), horizontal collectivism (e.g., "If a co-worker gets a prize, I would feel proud"), and vertical collectivism (e.g., "It is important that I respect the decisions made by my groups"). There were negative or weak positive correlations between the horizontal and vertical aspects of both individualism and collectivism. It was concluded that the horizontal and vertical forms of I and C are distinguishable, and of sufficient importance to conceptualize and measure them separately in future studies.

## Origins

In the work of Hofstede (1980), the relationship between a country's individualism score and its GNP was substantial (+.82), suggesting that affluence may bring about individualism. However, the temporal direction of such a relationship is not known: is the presence of individualist values a prerequisite for affluence, or does affluence result in the rise of individualism? More practically, do societies that are low on individualism have to change their values in order to become more economically developed? This practical issue will be taken up later in the discussion of societal development (ch. 17). In the meantime, we need to remember that if individualism and collectivism are not polar opposites, and individuals (and societies) can be high on both individualism and collectivism, then such questions may not be phrased appropriately.

Rather than one variable influencing the other, of course, it is possible that both come about as a result of other features of a society. Taking an ecocultural perspective, Berry (1994) has suggested that individualism and collectivism are each related to separate aspects of the ecosystem: individualism to the sheer size and complexity of the social system (larger, more complex societies being more individualist); and collectivism to the social tightness or conformity pressures placed on individuals by their society (tighter more stratified societies being more collectivist).

Another, more worrisome, interpretation is that individualist and collectivist societies differ in respect to response styles, or response sets. It is well known that tendencies such as social desirability (giving socially favorable and normatively required answers), acquiescence (agreeing rather than disagreeing with statements), or extremity set (giving more extreme answers) can influence the scores on personality questionnaires and attitude scales. In consumer surveys with nationally representative samples from various European countries Van Herk (2000) has found that (more collectivist) southern European, especially Greek, samples scored consistently higher on rating scales than (more individualist) Western European samples. This was independent of whether the survey questions pertained to items used in cooking, various aspects of shaving, or to values. In a meta-analysis of studies with the Eysenck Personality Questionnaire (EPQ) Van Hemert, Van der Vijver, Poortinga, & Georgas (in press) found a correlation of $r = -.70$ across countries between the EPQ lie scale and GNP, suggesting that in Western countries the norm of giving socially positive responses perhaps has become more relaxed. When these findings are combined with the overwhelming evidence of a high positive correlation between GNP and scores on I–C scales, an alternative interpretation suggests itself, namely that the higher scores on I–C scales may be due (in part) to reponse tendencies that may have little to do with cross-cultural differences in values. If one examines the items of the I–C scale presented in box 3.3, a positive reponse to the items marked "C" appears to be more socially desirable than a positive response to the items marked "I."

## Evaluation

The area of I–C is so vast and fast growing that this brief overview cannot give a proper account of it. Nor is it possible to provide a single evaluation of the field. However, we would like to examine four fundamental problems with contemporary I–C research. First, the cultural level is rarely investigated separately from the individual responses obtained from participants. Typically a country is simply declared to be more or less individualist or collectivist (sometimes on the basis of thirty-year-old Hofstede data, sometimes on the basis of stereotypical beliefs). Or, else the individual-level data are aggregated to yield a population-level characterization, leading to problems of circularity.

Second, the original conceptualization of I–C as a single dimension, with two clusters as polar opposites, can no longer be sustained. We have seen that there are now at least four ways to cut the dimension (in addition to the statistical evidence that one dimension is not an adequate description of the findings) namely the normative–relational forms (Kagitcibasi); the kin–non-kin in-group forms (Rhee et al.); the horizontal and vertical forms (Triandis); and the broader reference group forms (Realo et al.). Moreover, there is no empirical evidence to be found in the literature that these numerous aspects of I–C (components, domains, dimensions) actually interrelate to form a coherent construct. We are left asking what the utility is of the I–C construct when it has become so fragmented.

Third, the range of cultures included in many of the recent studies is limited. Although the Hofstede, Schwartz, and Trompenaars surveys cover many countries, they are primarily from urban regions of some continents, and do not sample rural or subsistence-level populations (which are still the majority of the world's peoples). Moreover, the more focussed studies rely on only a few countries, often using student samples; and these studies typically compare one or two East Asian societies with one Western society (the USA). What is required is a broader sampling of cultural settings in order to ensure that the individual-level I–C is widely present, and in order to search for the broadest culture-level contexts of these values.

Finally, there is the possibility mentioned previously that I–C first and foremost is a correlate of economic wealth or GNP, not so much because of differences between rich and poor societies in basic value orientations, but because of some other correlate, possibly related to education or response styles on questionnaires.

In summary, the danger exists that this promising line of research will not be well served or enriched by studies that uncritically accept some countries as individualist and other countries as collectivist, and that subsequently explain any observed difference in terms of the I–C dimension. Such circular explanations will not lead anywhere. As with all research topics, I–C theory, and cross-cultural psychology in general, will profit more from investigations that provide a critical examination of this conceptualization and its empirical corollaries.

## Social cognition

Within social psychology, there has been a dramatic increase in the study of how individuals perceive and interpret their social world, an area now known as social cognition. Given that such interpretations are bound to be embedded in a person's culture, it has been suggested that a more appropriate name might be sociocultural cognition (Semin & Zwier, 1997). (In ch. 5 we will examine the domain of cognition in non-social areas.) As with the field of social cognition generally, most of the cross-cultural research is focussed on the process of **attribution.**

This term refers to the way in which individuals think about the causes of their own, or other people's, behavior. In broad outline, attribution studies grew out of research on locus of control (Rotter, 1966); people can attribute behaviors to internal causes (i.e., to their own actions and dispositions), or to external causes (i.e., not to themselves but to others or to fate), and do so along a single control dimension ranging from internal to external. There is a frequently observed preference for attributions to internal dispositions, especially when it comes to the behavior of others, that has become known as the "fundamental attribution error," and has for a long time been thought by psychologists to be present in all cultures (Choi, Nisbett, & Norenzayan, 1999). However, longstanding anthropological evidence (reviewed by them and by Morris and Peng, 1994), raised doubts about this assumption of universality: ethnographic accounts (in Asia and Aboriginal North America) revealed a preference for contextual or situational attributions.

A second pattern (the "ultimate attribution error"; Ross, 1977; Pettigrew, 1979) involves the distinction between positively and negatively valued behaviors and between in-group and out-group: when attributing causes for negative behavior, the tendency is to make more dispositional attributions for the out-group's actions, while making more situational attributions for the in-group (and the opposite for positive behaviors). This, too, has also been portrayed as culturally universal. However, both of these "errors" may vary cross-culturally.

One study (Morris & Peng, 1994, p. 952) sought evidence to support the view that dispositionalism "reflects an implicit theory about social behavior that is more widespread in individualist cultures than in collectivist cultures." The authors studied Chinese and American attributions of cause using both physical and social stimuli, predicting (and finding) that with physical events (e.g., animated balls colliding) there were no cultural differences, but with social stimuli (e.g., attributions for actions of a mass murderer), Americans attributed more dispositional, and Chinese more situational, reasons for the murderer's actions. Going further, they also examined the pattern when the in-group/out-group distinction was made (the "ultimate attribution error"). They predicted that American participants would give more weight to personal dispositions than to situational pressures when the murderer was an out-group member, but that Chinese participants would not make any differential attribution on the basis of the group to which the murderer belonged. Their results provided only partial support for this prediction; however, the main expectation was supported:

> Chinese people represent behavior as situationally caused, and Americans represent it as dispositionally caused . . . Chinese subjects simulated that the person would have taken a less bloody course of action in different situations, whereas Americans simulated that the person's murderous disposition would have inexorably expressed itself, regardless of changes in the situation. (pp. 964–5)

Choi et al. (1999) concluded that both dispositional and situational attributions were present across cultures, but were used differentially. In particular, Western (European) peoples prefer to make dispositional attributions, while East Asian peoples prefer situational (contextual) ones when interpreting human behavior. They believe that this is because "East Asians have a more holistic notion of the person in which the boundary between the person and the situation is rather porous and ill defined" (p. 57). (This view will be considered in ch. 4, in the discussion of self.) Once again, we see support for universalism; the basic psychological process of attributon is present across cultures, but it is developed and used differently, according to some features of the cultural context.

Some such features were investigated in a series of cross-cultural studies of expected reactions to norm violations between members of contrasting groups in a society (DeRidder & Tripathi, 1992). Two pairs of groups involved were from India, and two pairs from the Netherlands. In both countries one pair consisted of managers and subordinates, while the other pair was a local ethnic contrast (Hindus and Muslims in India, and Turkish migrants and Dutch autochthonous inhabitants in the Netherlands). Respondents were asked for the expected reaction in their own group to various norm violations (like jumping a queue, ridiculing the other's religion, swindling an insurance company, using company petrol, etc.) by members of the other group, as well as for the expected reaction to such violations if committed by their own group. In order to explain anticipated differences, data were also collected on four context variables: (1) the perceived power of the own group, (2) the societal position of own group versus the other other group, (3) the degree of identification with own group, and (4) attitudes towards the other group. The most important result of these studies was that differences in economic and social power between the two groups in a pair, rather than the psychological variables of identity and attitude, explained differences in reactions to norm violations. Apparently, respondents assessed their situation in realistic terms: they were aware of their position in society *vis-à-vis* others and this influenced their reactions.

## Gender behavior

There has been a rapidly developing interest in the relationship between gender and behavior (e.g., Brettell & Sargent, 1993). Can cross-cultural studies contribute to our understanding of this issue? In ch. 2 we considered the question of how boys and girls are socialized differently in various cultures, and noted that girls generally are socialized more toward compliance (nurturance, responsibility, and obedience), while boys are raised more for assertion (independence, self-reliance, and achievement). We also noted that these differential socialization patterns are themselves related to some other cultural factors (such as social stratification) and ecological factors (such as subsistence economy and population density). In this section we raise the question of whether there are any social and psychological consequences of this differential treatment and experiences of boys and girls.

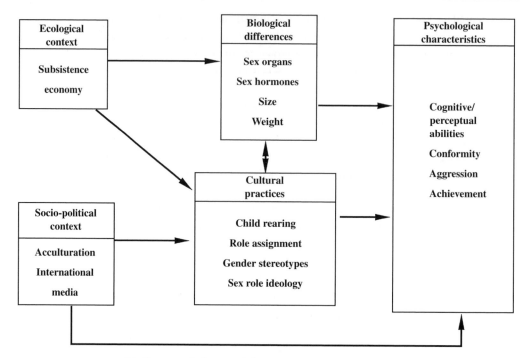

**3.3** Framework for examining relationships among contextual variables
and gender differences in behavior

A framework is presented in fig. 3.3 that draws our attention to how some of
these elements may be related. This figure is an elaboration of the biological,
cultural, and transmission variables (of fig. 1.1) that are relevant to differential
gender behavior. As in the case of the overall framework, this figure is very much
interactive, with all the main features potentially influencing all others. It is thus
somewhat arbitrary where we start our examination. However, since in psychology we are interested primarily in explaining individual behavior, we will enter
the framework at the point of an individual's birth.

At birth, a neonate has a sex, but no **gender.** At birth one's biological sex can
usually be decided on the basis of physical anatomical evidence; but culturally
rooted experiences, feelings, and behaviors that are associated by adults with this
biological distinction are a major influence on how individuals see their gender.
Much of the evidence we will review about how males and females differ, and how
they are similar, will be interpreted as a cultural construction on a biological foundation, rather than as a biological given. This is not to deny a role for biological
differences between males and females, but merely to understand that they are the
starting point, rather than the whole story (Archer, 1996; Eagly & Wood, 1999).

Biologically males and females have different sex organs and sex hormones;
there are also differences in average size and weight. However, on the basis of
these, all the extant collective images, including values, cultural beliefs (stereotypes), and expectations (ideology) swing into action, leading to male–female

differences in socialization and role differentiation and assignment, and eventually to differences in a number of psychological characteristics (abilities, aggression, etc.). While all societies build upon these early sex differences, the core question to be addressed in this section is whether societies vary widely, or are rather similar, in what they do to these initial biological differences. We will also be taking into account the increasing acculturative influences being placed on most cultures (mainly by external telecommunications media) that are likely to be changing stereotypes, ideologies, and practices in other cultures.

## Gender stereotypes

Widely shared beliefs within a society about what males and females are generally like have been studied for decades in Western societies. A common finding is that these stereotypes of males and females are very different from one another, with males usually viewed as dominant, independent, and adventurous and females as emotional, submissive, and weak. Only recently have studies examined whether distinctions are made in other cultures between male and female stereotypes, and what these beliefs are like.

The central cross-cultural study to be considered is that of Williams and Best (1990a), who posed their questions to samples in twenty-seven countries (three in Africa, ten in Europe, six in Asia, two in North America and six in South America). With the help of colleagues in these countries, the researchers obtained the views of university students (a total of 2,800 persons, ranging between 52 to 120 respondents per country, and usually close to an equal number of males and females) on a 300-item adjective check list (ACL) describing psychological characteristics of persons. The original ACL is an English-language rating task developed by Gough and Heilbrun (1965). For the cross-cultural survey, translations were made where required, usually employing forward and back translation procedures advocated by Brislin (1980).

The task for respondents was to decide for each adjective whether it was more frequently associated with men rather than women, or more frequently associated with women than men. Participants were reminded that they were being asked to serve as an observer and reporter of the characteristics generally said to be associated with men and women in their culture, and not being asked whether they believed that it was true that men and women differed in these ways, or whether they approved of the assignment of different characteristics to men and women. The task was a "forced choice" for respondents; characteristics had to be judged as being associated more with males or females, rather than equally associated. While instructions were designed to require such a dichotomous choice and to discourage "equal" answers, in fact when respondents found it impossible to make such a choice, a "cannot say" response was accepted by the researchers.

Results indicated a large-scale difference in the views about what males and females were like in all countries, and a broad consensus across countries (see box 3.4). This degree of consensus was so large that it may be appropriate to suggest that the researchers had found psychological universals when it comes to **gender stereotypes.** However, before such a conclusion is accepted, some further dimensions of the study need to be considered.

---

### Box 3.4 Characteristics associated with males and females in twenty-five countries

In the large cross-cultural study by Williams and Best (1990a) forty-nine adjectives were consensually assigned to males and twenty-five to females. Consensus was defined as having two-thirds of respondents make an assignment within a country sample, and the cross-cultural agreement was defined as having at least nineteen of twenty-five countries meet this degree of consensus. The adjectives were:

#### Male-associated items ($N = 49$)

| | | |
|---|---|---|
| Active (23) | Energetic (22) | Realistic (20) |
| Adventurous (25) | Enterprising (24) | Reckless (20) |
| Aggressive (24) | Forceful (25) | Robust (24) |
| Ambitious (22) | Hardheaded (21) | Rude (23) |
| Arrogant (20) | Hardhearted (21) | Self-confident (21) |
| Assertive (20) | Humorous (19) | Serious (20) |
| Autocratic (24) | Independent (25) | Severe (23) |
| Boastful (19) | Ingenious (19) | Stern (24) |
| Clear-thinking (21) | Having initiative (21) | Stolid (20) |
| Coarse (21) | Inventive (22) | Strong (25) |
| Confident (19) | Lazy (21) | Unemotional (23) |
| Courageous (23) | Logical (22) | Unkind (19) |
| Cruel (21) | Loud (21) | Wise (23) |
| Daring (24) | Masculine (25) | |
| Determined (21) | Obnoxious (19) | |
| Disorderly (21) | Opportunistic (20) | |
| Dominant (25) | Progressive (23) | |
| Egotistical (21) | Rational (20) | |

#### Female-associated items ($N = 25$)

| | | |
|---|---|---|
| Affected (20) | Fearful (23) | Sexy (22) |
| Affectionate (24) | Feminine (24) | Shy (19) |
| Anxious (19) | Gentle (21) | Softhearted (23) |
| Attractive (23) | Kind (19) | Submissive (25) |
| Charming (20) | Meek (19) | Superstitious (25) |
| Curious (21) | Mild (21) | Talkative (20) |
| Dependent (23) | Pleasant (19) | Weak (23) |
| Dreamy (24) | Sensitive (24) | |
| Emotional (23) | Sentimental (25) | |

Beyond this apparently universally shared description of males and females, Williams and Best (1990a) carried out a factor analysis of the adjectives assigned to each category in order to discover the underlying meanings of the set of adjectives consensually used to describe men and women in the various countries. In keeping with previous studies of this type, they found three factors which they called favorability, activity, and strength.

The first represents an overall evaluation of males and females varying from negative to positive across all countries (cf. an attitude), and across all countries there was little overall mean difference on this dimension; male favorability was 505 while female favorability was 498, scores that were just slightly above and below the standardized mid-point of 500. However, there were some clear cross-cultural differences on this dimension: the male stereotype was most favorable in Japan, Nigeria, and South Africa; the female stereotype was most favorable in Italy and Peru.

The second dimension represents a judgment about how action-oriented males and females are thought to be. In this case overall mean activity scores differed substantially (males scoring 545 and females 462), and there was a non-overlapping distribution: the countries in which females were considered most active (Japan and United States) were lower than the two countries in which males were considered most passive (France and India).

Similarly, on the third dimension of strength there was a large overall mean difference (males at 541, females at 459). And once again there was no overlap in the distributions: the two highest ratings of females on strength (in Italy and the USA) were lower than the two lowest ratings of males on strength (in Venezuela and the USA).

In summary, while males and females were described in different terms within every culture, they were also described in very similar terms across cultures. And while in terms of favorability they were evaluated on average equally, they were judged on average rather differently on the other two dimensions, with males seen as more active and stronger. Some variations between cultures occurred on all three dimensions, but these variations were rather limited when viewed in the context of overall similarity.

How can we account for this pattern of results? One possibility is that all cultures follow the sequence outlined in fig. 3.3: original biological differences have given rise over time to cultural practices, differential male–female task assignment and socialization that actually make males and females everywhere psychologically different; gender stereotypes are thus merely an accurate perception of these differences. But such a sequence can be also turned around: a sex role ideology (see next section) that specifies how males and females should be may lead to differential cultural and socialization practices and to distorted perceptions of what males and females are like. Thus, bias in perception may be sufficient to generate the findings obtained, and even to enhance any underlying biological differences.

Finally, we need to consider a third alternative: that some combination of acculturation influences and choice of samples may have contributed to the dramatic similarity in gender stereotype descriptions. University students share much in common worldwide: age, high educational attainment, and exposure to international media images of males and females. In other words, university students all over participate to a large extent in an international "youth culture" that may override more traditional, locally rooted cultural phenomena. Only a repeat study, with samples that do not have so much in common, will really help us assess this possible explanation. However, some data from Williams and Best's own study suggest that this third alternative may not be particularly potent. They also examined the gender stereotypes of children in twenty-four countries, in two age categories (five to six and eight to nine years). Once again, their evidence indicated substantial cross-cultural similarity in male and female stereotypical descriptions, and these were virtually identical to those obtained in the adult samples. The question obviously arises of whether it really is possible that children as young as five or six years have everywhere been exposed to an international "children's culture" that has propagated these gender stereotypes. The likely answer is "no," leaving us with the conclusion that these children have acquired the cross-culturally common perceptions of men and women from enculturation and socialization into their own societies.

## Mate selection

Given the near universal nature of gender stereotypes, is it possible that some of these attributed characteristics are widely sought after when selecting mates? This question was studied by Buss and colleagues (1989, 1990). Using a questionnaire with around 10,000 respondents in thirty-seven countries, Buss first asked them to rate each of eighteen characteristics (on a four-point scale) as important or desirable in choosing a mate. A second instrument requested the same respondents to rank thirteen characteristics for their desirability in choosing a mate.

Although cultures varied in their overall responses (along two dimensions, traditional versus modern and high versus low value on education), there was widespread agreement in preferences. Cross-sample correlations were +.78 for ratings on the first set of scales, and +.74 for rankings. Moreover, both males and females chose the same qualities in the first four places: being kind and understanding, intelligent, having an exciting personality, and being healthy. This basic gender similarity is evidenced by the averaged male–female correlation across all the samples of +.87.

However, within this overall similarity, both gender and cultural differences were observed. The main gender difference was for females to value potential earnings more highly than males, and for males to value physical appearance more highly than females. The cultural differences were widespread, with chastity showing the largest cross-cultural variance (this being valued less in northern Europe than in Asia). There were also differences on being a good housekeeper and a desire for home and children. The general conclusion of Buss et al. (p. 45) was that "despite these cultural and sexual variations, there were strong similarities among cultures and between sexes on the preference ordering of mate selection. This implies a degree of psychological unity, or species-typicality of humans that transcends geographical, racial, political, ethnic and sexual diversity." Once again, this pattern corresponds to a universalist view.

## Gender role ideology

While gender stereotypes are the consensual beliefs that are held about the characteristics of males and females, **gender role ideology** is a normative belief about what males and females should be like, or should do (Adler, 1993). In a second major cross-cultural study using the ACL, Williams and Best (1990b) examined how individuals believed themselves to be (actual self), how they would like to be (ideal self), and how males and females should be. For this last variable they used a sex role ideology scale (SRI) developed by Kalin and Tilby (1978) with scores ranging between "traditional" and "egalitarian."[3]

As in their other study, university student samples were obtained with the help of colleagues, who administered the ACL and SRI instruments. This time, fourteen countries were included (five from Asia, five from Europe, two from North America, and one each from Africa and South America), and approximately fifty male and fifty female respondents participated in each country (total $N = 1,563$). Translations were employed where appropriate, and data were collected and analyzed by Williams and Best.

Results showed little variation across cultures in the ACL ratings by males and females, on either actual or ideal self. However, rather large differences appeared on the SRI instrument (see box 3.5). In general, the more egalitarian scores were obtained in countries with relatively high socioeconomic development, a high proportion of Protestant Christians (and a low proportion of Muslims), a high percentage of women employed outside the home and studying at the university level, and a high country score on the Hofstede value dimension of individualism. It should be noted that all these variables are also positively related with the economic wealth of countries or GNP. Unlike the first study, where gender stereotypes were more similar, this study showed a rather large variation in gender role ideology.

## Psychological characteristics

In the previous chapter we encountered evidence for differential child rearing practices and role assignment for boys and girls, and differential role activity for men and women; in this chapter we have discovered variations in gender differences in stereotypes and ideology. On the bases of these factors (identified in fig. 3.2), can we predict differences in psychological characteristics between men and

---

[3] The term "egalitarian" is employed by us to refer to the pole opposite "traditional." Kalin and Tilby (1978) used the term "feminist," while Williams and Best (1990) used the term "modern" for this pole. We avoid the term "modern" in this text, since it is used elsewhere (ch. 17) to refer to a broader set of attitudes related to social change.

## Box 3.5  Gender role ideology in fourteen countries

In a second cross-cultural study, Williams and Best (1990b) examined the views of males and females in fourteen countries about how males and females should be and should act, using the sex role ideology (SRI) scale of Kalin and Tilby (1978). Sample items representing the traditional ideology are:

When a man and woman live together she should do the housework and
      he should do the heavier chores.
A woman should be careful how she looks, for it influences what people
      think of her husband.
The first duty of a woman with young children is to home and family.

For the "egalitarian" ideology sample items were:

A woman should have exactly the same freedom of action as a man.
Marriage should not interfere with a woman's career any more than it
      does with a man's.
Women should be allowed the same sexual freedom as men.

The scores obtained by men and women on a seven-point scale in each country varied rather widely:

| Country | Males | Females | |
|---|---|---|---|
| 1.  Netherlands | 5.47 | 5.72 | (more |
| 2.  Germany | 5.35 | 5.62 | "egalitarian") |
| 3.  Finland | 5.30 | 5.69 | |
| 4.  England | 4.73 | 5.15 | |
| 5.  Italy | 4.54 | 4.90 | |
| 6.  Venezuela | 4.51 | 4.90 | |
| 7.  United States | 4.05 | 4.66 | |
| 8.  Canada | 4.09 | 4.54 | |
| 9.  Singapore | 3.61 | 4.39 | |
| 10.  Malaysia | 4.05 | 4.01 | |
| 11.  Japan | 3.70 | 4.01 | |
| 12.  India | 3.81 | 3.88 | |
| 13.  Pakistan | 3.34 | 3.30 | (more |
| 14.  Nigeria | 3.11 | 3.39 | "traditional") |

In every case (except two which were not significant, Malaysia and Pakistan) males scored more toward the "traditional" end, and females more toward the "egalitarian" end of the scale. However, significant differences in the views of male and female respondents were limited to nine items (three "egalitarian" items on which women agreed more than men, and six "traditional" items on which men agreed more than women).

women? And can we discover how these differences may themselves be differentially related to ecological and cultural factors? We attempt to answer these two questions with respect to three behavioral domains: perceptual-cognitive abilities, conformity, and aggression.

In chs. 5 and 8 we will examine a variety of perceptual and cognitive abilities in some detail; here we are concerned only with the issues of sex differences and the possibility that the magnitude of any sex differences may be related to ecological and cultural factors. We highlight two studies, one (Berry, 1976b) that examines the issues within a single research program, and the other (Born, Bleichrodt, & Van der Flier, 1987) that provides a meta-analysis across many research studies.

It has been a common claim that on spatial tasks (and those tasks that have a spatial component) males tend to perform better than females (e.g., Maccoby & Jacklin, 1974). However, it has been reported (Berry, 1966; MacArthur, 1967) that this difference does not appear to be present in Inuit (Eskimo) samples in the Canadian Arctic. The interpretation offered by Berry (1966) was that spatial abilities were highly adaptive for both males and females in Inuit society, and both boys and girls had ample training and experiences that promoted the acquisition of spatial ability. In a study of sex differences on Kohs blocks (a task requiring the visual analysis of a geometric design, and the construction of the design by rotating and placing blocks) in a set of seventeen societies correlations between sex and test score varied widely from +.35 to −.51. (A positive sign, in this analysis, means a higher male score, a negative sign a higher female score.) When these correlation coefficients are ranked from most positive to most negative and then related to an "ecocultural index" (which takes into account subsistence economy, settlement pattern, population density, social tightness, and socialization practices) a clear pattern emerges: male superiority on this task exists in relatively tight, sedentary, agricultural societies, but is absent or even reversed in relatively loose, nomadic, hunting and gathering societies. Parallel analyses with two other spatial perceptual tasks (across only eight samples) showed a similar pattern. We take this to indicate that sex differences on spatial tasks are neither uniform nor inevitable. Since they are present in relatively tight societies, but not in looser societies, there is an interaction between gender differences and ecological and cultural factors that, as we have seen in the previous chapter, underlies differential male/female socialization and role assignment. Alternatively, one may argue that there is no specific socialization for performance on spatial tasks and that the observed differences between men and women are inborn. For example, Kimura (1999) has interpreted this set of findings in terms of biological adaptation to ecological context: those with poor spatial abilities are likely to die in hunting societies, and their genes thus be eliminated.

In a meta-analysis incorporating the results of many research studies, Born et al. (1987) noted that typically in the Western literature there were no overall sex differences in general intelligence, but that differences were present in various subtests: females tended to perform better than males on verbal tasks, including verbal fluency, and on memory and perceptual speed tasks; males tended to obtain higher scores on numerical tasks and a variety of other perceptual tasks, including closure, spatial orientation, and spatial visualization.

Their cross-cultural analysis drew together a massive literature, but it was really a cross-continent or cross-region analysis, since they used geographical areas as categories in their analysis rather than cultures; they also lumped all "minorities" together, ignoring cultural variation within that category. These problems make it difficult to understand the results obtained: in general, sex differences were smallest in "minorities," greatest in "African" and "Asian" samples. On specific tests, sex differences were greatest (males superior to females) on spatial orientation (in "Africa" and "Asia"), and on spatial visualization (in Western samples). As we have noted, it is not at all clear how "culture" might be involved to explain these patterns, since no particular cultural variables were identified in the review. Nevertheless, the Born et al. (1987) study confirms that there are differences in cognitive test scores between males and females, and that the patterns of difference are variable across cultures.

We earlier noted a variation across cultures in the degree to which individuals vary in their responses on conformity tasks. In the Western literature there is some evidence that females may be more susceptible to conformity pressures than males, but this has been the subject of heated controversy (e.g., Eagly, 1978). Once again, it is possible that the cross-cultural examination may put the issue in perspective. Using the same samples referred to in the earlier discussion of conformity in this chapter (Berry, 1979), and employing the same strategy as that used by Berry (1976b) to examine gender differences in spatial ability, a clear pattern emerged. Across the seventeen samples, greatest sex differences (females more conforming than males) were present in the tighter samples, and fewer (sometimes even a reversal) in the looser samples. The overall correlation between magnitude of gender difference and the "ecocultural index" was +.78. Thus, once again we find that the presence and magnitude of a gender difference in a psychological characteristic is variable across cultures, and predictable from a knowledge of male–female differences in child rearing, role allocation, and degree of social stratification (in which women tend to occupy the lower ranks in society).

One of the best-documented gender differences in behavior is that, on the average, males (particularly adolescents) quite consistently commit more acts of **aggression** than do females (Segall, Ember, & Ember, 1997). In industrialized nations in Europe, North America, and beyond, they account for a disproportionate number of violent crimes (Naroll, 1983; Goldstein, 1983), and equally so in non-industrial societies (Bacon, Child, & Barry, 1963). A thorough analysis of studies relating to gender, culture, and aggression was provided in Segall et al. (1999). This analysis considered several alternative explanations for the sex difference in aggression (and, by implication, for aggression itself). Here is a summary of this analysis.

Since it is the behavior of male adolescents that we are trying to explain, need we consider anything other than the high concentration of circulating testosterone that characterizes the physiological status of male adolescents? Evidence that testosterone levels are linked with dominance striving is available (Mazur, 1985), but more for primates like baboons than for humans, who often express dominance striving in ways that do not inflict harm on others or, in other words, non-aggressively. There is also evidence that testosterone levels are linked to antisocial behavior in delinquent populations (Dabbs & Morris, 1990). One student of aggression who places considerable weight on the role of sex-linked hormones notes, however, that while the human organism is "already primed for the sex difference, cultures can dampen or exaggerate it" (Konner, 1988, p. 34).

Surely the potential to act aggressively is present in human beings, but the degree to which the expression of aggression is tolerated (or even encouraged) is influenced by the sociocultural environment. In this sense aggressive behavior is a product of cultural influences, acting largely through culturally mediated childhood experiences. If males and females have different experiences that impact on their tendencies to behave aggressively, then knowing what those experiences are is necessary in any attempt to understand aggression. One class of such experiences is the well-known set of differences between the sexes in inculcation of aggression. Barry et al. (1976) found a sex difference in deliberate teaching and encouragement of aggression to children on the average over a sample of nearly 150 societies. If it were generally true that in most societies boys received more inculcation of aggression than girls, we would have a simple, strictly cultural answer to the question of why there was a sex difference in aggression. But it is not the case. The average difference found by Barry et al. was produced by relatively few societies in which the sex difference in inculcation was very large. Indeed, in only 20 percent of all cases was there a significant difference. So, other factors than inculcation differences or hormonal differences, separately or in combination, must be implicated.

In this model, then, aggression is seen partly as gender-marking behavior. In Segall et al. (1999), one may find additional examples of cultural factors. The analysis begins with the universally present division of labor by sex and the fact that a very salient feature of this is the nearly universal tendency of child rearing to be a predominantly, if not exclusively, female role. From this there is derived a mechanism whereby in many societies, especially those with very distinct divisions of labor that result in low male salience during early childhood, young boys develop a cross-sex identity which later is corrected either by severe male initiation ceremonies for adolescent males (Whiting, Kluckhohn, & Anthony, 1958), or by individual efforts by males to assert their manliness (a phenomenon dubbed "compensatory machoism"). In this model, then, aggression is seen partly as gender-marking behavior. In Segall et al. (1999) one may also find additional examples of cultural factors that currently exist to differentially set the stage for the many different forms of aggressive behavior that continue to plague humankind.

## Conclusions

Social behavior is often thought to be the most likely area in which to find substantial influence on human characteristics from cultural factors. However, as this chapter has shown, there is evidence for widespread cross-cultural similarity, as well as difference in the social behaviors reviewed.

While conformity and gender role ideology are clearly patterned according to cultural factors, other aspects of social behavior (such as gender stereotypes and mate selection) are not. Both social and biological factors have pan-human features, and can contribute to cross-cultural similiarity. These, along with some basic psychological processes (such as the perception and categorization of social stimuli), clearly attenuate the possibility of cultural variation in social behavior. We agree with Aberle et al. (1950) that the cross-cultural coordination of social relationships is possible only when such shared characteristics are present. Nevertheless, cultural factors do play variations on these common underlying processes, producing support for the assumption of many observers that social behavior is where cultural variation is most widespread.

Beyond this pattern of variation, rooted in substantial underlying similarity, we have found that the study of some social behaviors has been carried out in a limited number of cultures. The largest empirical basis refers to the contrast between a few East Asian societies, and one Western society. While this can be considered a strength, it is also a weakness: since we now know a lot about social behavior in a few more cultures, we risk misjudging this to be valid for all cultures (just as previously psychology considered Western-based findings to apply to all cultural groups). There is an urgent need to investigate social behavior in more representative samples of cultures.

Most of the social behaviors studied still derive from the interests of Western psychologists, using concepts rooted in Western thinking about human behavior. There is a need for more indigenous approaches to these, and other, social behaviors, before we can say that the area as a whole is well understood.

### Key terms

| | |
|---|---|
| aggression | gender stereotypes |
| attribution | individualism and collectivism |
| conformity | tight–loose |
| gender | values |
| gender role ideology | |

### Further reading

Best, D. L., & Williams, J. (1997). Sex, gender and culture. In J. W. Berry, M. H. Segall, & C. Kagitcibasi (Eds.), *Social behavior and applications* (pp. 163–212). Vol. III of *Handbook of cross-cultural psychology* (2nd ed.). Boston, MA: Allyn & Bacon. A review chapter presenting knowledge about how cultural factors influence gender, and in turn contribute to similarities and differences in gender-related behaviors.

Fiske, A. P., Kitayama, S., Markus, H., & Nisbett, R. (1998). The cultural matrix of social psychology. In D. Gilbert, S. Fiske, & G. Lindzey (Eds.), *Handbook of social psychology* (pp. 915–81). New York: McGraw-Hill. A review chapter, from a social psychological perspective, of selected areas of social behavior.

Kagitcibasi, C. (1997). Individualism and collectivism. In J. W. Berry, M. H. Segall, & C. Kagitcibasi (Eds.), *Social behavior and applications* (pp. 1–49). Vol. III of *Handbook of cross-cultural psychology* (2nd ed.). Boston, MA: Allyn & Bacon. A critical overview of the origins and more recent thinking and research on this central topic.

Smith, P. B., & Bond, M. H. (1998). *Social psychology across cultures* (2nd ed.). Hemel Hempstead: Harvester/Wheatsheaf. A comprehensive and integrative textbook dealing with a wide range of social behaviors from the perspective of cross-cultural psychology.

Triandis, H. C. (1994). *Culture and social behavior*. New York: McGraw-Hill. A comprehensive textbook of studies of social behavior by one of the pioneers of cross-cultural psychology.

# 4 Personality

Personality research is concerned with behavior that is typical of a person and distinguishes that person from others. Personality in this sense is the outcome of a lifelong process of interaction between an organism and its ecocultural and sociocultural environment. The effects of these external factors make it likely that there are systematic differences in the person-typical behavior of people who have been brought up in different cultures. Thus, it is not surprising that many traditions in personality research have been extended cross-culturally.

A dominant theme in personality research concerns the question of how person-typical behavior can be explained in terms of more permanent psychological dispositions, and what could be the nature of such dispositions. A global distinction can be made between psychodynamic theories, trait theories, and social-cognitive theories. The psychodynamic tradition which has the oldest and widest roots will be discussed in the chapter on cultural approaches (ch. 9). Most research in this tradition, which goes by the name of psychological anthropology (formerly called culture-and-personality), has been carried out by cultural anthropologists.

In this chapter we first discuss research on relatively stable characteristics, referred to as personality traits. In trait theories the emphasis is on individual dispositions that are consistent across time and situations. Some important traditions of research are discussed, and attention is paid to influences of "cultural bias" that endanger a valid interpretation of cross-cultural differences in scores on a large variety of instruments. The second section deals with conceptions of the self, that is the way in which a person perceives and experiences himself or herself. Self-concepts are said to differ between various cultural contexts, especially between societies that were characterized as individualist and collectivist in the

## Box 4.1 Ashanti names and personality

According to Jahoda (1954), among the Ashanti a child is given the name of the day on which it was born. The name refers to the *kra*, the soul of the day. Among boys (no such ideas appeared to exist about girls) the *kra* implies a disposition towards certain behavior. Those born on Monday are supposed to be quiet and peaceful. Boys called "Wednesday" are held to be quick-tempered and aggressive. An analysis by Jahoda of delinquency records in a juvenile court indicated a significantly lower number than expected of convictions among youngsters called "Monday." There was also some evidence that those called Wednesday were more likely to be convicted of crimes against the person of others (e.g., fighting, assault). Although relationships were weak and replication of the study might have been desirable to further establish the validity of the results, Jahoda's conclusion stands that the "correspondence appears too striking to be easily dismissed." A further question is, then, how these findings have to be interpreted: are they a reflection of social stereotypes and prejudices that focus attention on the (expected) misdemeanors of certain youngsters more than of others, or are these social expectations somehow internalized by youngsters, forming their personalities?

previous chapter. The next section discusses non-Western concepts of personality; some concepts and theories are presented that are rooted in non-Western traditions. These examples are from Senegal, from Japan, and from India. Finally we look briefly at altered states of consciousness that appear to be important to many non-Western cultures and usually have quite a different meaning than in industrial urban societies.

Before continuing we would like to call attention to box 4.1, about a possible relationship among the Ashanti between a man's name and his tendency towards criminal behavior. It is an example of one of the myriad and often unexpected interconnections between personality and sociocultural environment. The box can serve as a warning that, despite the large number of existing theories, our understanding of the relationship between the behavior of a person and the cultural environment remains limited and tentative.

## Traits across cultures

In the field of personality research there are various terms, such as motive, trait, and temperament, that refer to enduring characteristics of a person. These concepts imply consistency over time and situations in the behavior pattern of an individual. The presumed origin of consistency is not always the same. Temperament, for example, refers more to the biological basis of behavior, while motives and traits can be associated with influences of the social environment. However the alleged consistency has come about, it is thought to reflect a psychological disposition in the person that becomes expressed in a wide range of actions.

In this section we emphasize **personality traits**. Fiske (1971, p. 299) has defined a trait as "a lasting characteristic attributed to persons in varying amounts of strength." A large number of trait names can be found in the literature; examples are dominance, sociability, and persistence. In principle it should be possible to arrive at a comprehensive set of traits which together cover all major aspects of individual-characteristic behavior. This goal has been pursued particularly by Cattell (1965). The uniqueness of a person in this tradition is represented by a specific mixture of the various traits. Inasmuch as persons in a particular cultural group share certain influences with each other, but not with persons in other social environments, it is to be expected that there will be differences in modal personality across cultures. This means that there should be cross-cultural differences in the degree to which the average person from a culture possesses a certain trait.

Personality traits are usually measured by means of self-report personality questionnaires (for specific traits) or personality inventories (omnibus instruments covering a range of traits), yielding a score on each trait. The most important empirical support for the validity of traits in these self-report instruments has been obtained from factor-analytic studies. With this statistical technique the information contained in a set of items can be reduced to a limited number of common factors or dimensions. Each factor is taken to represent an underlying psychological trait.

## Interpreting score differences

When interpreting cross-cultural differences in distributions of scores a researcher has to choose between various possibilities:

1  An observed cross-cultural difference in mean score is an adequate reflection of a difference in the underlying trait that presumably has been measured.
2  A difference is due to errors in translation, a culture-bound specific meaning of some of the items, or other aspects that have little to do with the trait.
3  Personality traits are not the same across cultures.

If the first of these three applies, cross-cultural differences in score distributions can be interpreted at face value. The third possibility implies that different sets of traits have to be postulated in different cultures. A further consequence is that any cross-cultural comparison is out of the question; one cannot compare apples with oranges. The second option is the most fuzzy; the scope for interpretation depends on how, and how much, of the cross-cultural variation is a reflection of non-trait-related aspects.

The researcher who has administered a questionnaire to two or more cultural samples has to decide which of the three explanations to choose. Psychometric procedures that can help to improve such a decision will be discussed in ch. 11. Here we merely note that there are numerous non-trait-related aspects that can affect scores on any kind of psychological measurement (e.g., Van de Vijver & Tanzer, 1997). Such unintended and unwanted sources of cross-cultural variance are referred to as "cultural bias"; they lead to "inequivalence" or "incomparability" of scores. Different forms of **equivalence** have been distinguished by Van de Vijver & Leung (1997a, 1997b):

1 Structural or functional equivalence, i.e., a test measures the same trait (or set of traits) cross-culturally, but not necessarily on the same quantitative scale. (One can think of the Fahrenheit and Celsius scales for temperature.)
2 Metric or measurement unit equivalence, i.e., differences between scores obtained under different conditions have the same meaning across cultures. (The same temperature leads to different readings on the Celsius scale and the Kelvin scale, but if the temperature changes, the values on both scales go up or down equally much. It is said that the metric of the scale is the same.)
3 Scale equivalence or full score equivalence, i.e., scores have the same meaning cross-culturally and can be interpreted in the same way. (All measurements are on the Celsius scale.)

There are various psychometric conditions that presumably are satisfied by equivalent scores, but not by inequivalent scores. For example, structural equivalence can be examined by means of correlational techniques like factor analysis. If factor structures of the items of an instrument are the same, this is an indication that the same traits are measured; if the factor structures differ across cultures it has to be concluded that the instrument does not measure identical traits. The latter finding rules out any meaningful cross-cultural comparison; this would amount to comparing apples with oranges. For the other forms of equivalence it is often examined whether patterns of item responses are similar cross-culturally. More information on analysis of item bias can be found in ch. 11. Here we wish to note that it is particularly difficult to identify sources of bias that have a similar effect on all items of a questionnaire. Such threats to full score equivalence are response styles, like social desirability and acquiescence to which we have already referred in ch. 3.

## Eysenck's personality scales

One of the more frequently used self-report personality instruments for cross-cultural comparison studies is the Eysenck Personality Questionnaire (Eysenck & Eysenck, 1975). The EPQ was developed from earlier scales such as the Maudsley Personality Inventory (MPI) and the Eysenck Personality Inventory (EPI). In a cross-cultural analysis by Barrett, Petrides, Eysenck, and Eysenck (1998) data collected in thirty-four countries were included.

In the EPQ four personality dimensions are distinguished: psychoticism, extraversion, neuroticism, and social desirability. These factors have emerged from research conducted by H. J. Eysenck and his associates over a period of some forty years. According to Eysenck there is substantial evidence that the first three of these factors have a biological substratum and form temperament dimensions.

**Neuroticism** or emotionality represents a dimension ranging from instability, with "moody" and "touchy" as characteristic features, to stability, characterized by an even temper and leadership. **Extraversion** stands for a dimension from sociable and outgoing or extraverted behavior, to quiet and passive or introverted behavior. The third dimension, psychoticism, has tough-mindedness and tender-mindedness as its opposite poles. This dimension is a later addition to Eysenck's theory and conceptually somewhat less developed. Social desirability refers to the tendency to give responses that are socially acceptable and respectable. This tendency has been mentioned as the most important determinant of responses in self-report personality tests (Edwards, 1970).

The first objective of cross-cultural studies with the EPQ is to show whether the same four factors emerge in a factor analysis that were originally identified in the UK. When this is found to be the case, a second and third objective can be pursued, namely the computation of local norms and the interpretation of quantitative cross-cultural differences in the scores on the four personality scales formed by the four factors. In a typical study, the English-language items will be carefully translated and then back translated. The contents of the item will be adapted if the original meaning is not preserved with literal translation, but this usually is required for only a few items. It is safe to say that by and large the same set of items has been used in the different cultures.

Barrett et al. (1998) have demonstrated that on average the factor similarity of the other thirty-three countries in their data set was closely similar to the structure in the UK, at least for extraversion and neuroticism. For psychoticism and for social desirability the average indices of factor similarity stay just below the value of .90 that is often used as a rule of thumb criterion for essential similarity of factors. The analysis by Barrett et al. testifies to the similarity of dimensions of personality originally observed in the UK, at least across the range of literate societies where the EPQ has been administered. Other authors have related cross-cultural differences in mean scores on each of the four dimensions to various social and political antecedents and to climatic factors. For example, high stress is thought to lead to high neuroticism. Political and economic instability, war and military occupation and a hot climate are considered to be stressful. In industrially advanced Western countries neuroticism scores tend to be low; Arab countries show high scores.

Positive evidence on structural equivalence is a necessary condition for a meaningful comparison of differences in mean scores, but it is not a sufficient condition, since sources of bias that affect the level of scores cannot be ruled out. Drastic changes in the loadings of individual items are found occasionally (e.g., Eysenck & Eysenck, 1983, p. 43). Some of these changes can be attributed to translation errors; others are explained in terms of cultural differences. For example, an item concerning the locking of doors was found not to load on the psychoticism scale in Greece, apparently because people leave their windows open, which makes locking the doors rather pointless. A shift in the meaning of an item can lead to substantial changes in the relative frequency of endorsement, even with only small effects on factor structure. If such shifts happen for only a few items a significant cross-cultural difference is a likely outcome. In short, even high similarities in factors do not guarantee full score equivalence.

## Temperament

The EPQ was based on a theory about important personality dimensions that had roots in earlier work on temperament (e.g., Eysenck, 1967). In fact, Eysenck, like some other European personality psychologists, did not distinguish between temperament and core dimensions of personality. The concept of **temperament**, more than that of personality traits, refers to a biological basis of inter-individual differences. For example, on the basis of observations on individual differences in the conditioning of dogs Pavlov defined central nervous system properties which regulate the generation of excitatory and inhibitory processes in reaction to stimuli. Especially the property of "strength of nervous system excitation," or "arousability" (Gray, 1964, 1981) has been the subject of extensive research. A strong nervous system implies a high tolerance to strong and repetitive stimuli coupled with high absolute sensory thresholds; the opposite, a weak nervous system, is characterized by high sensitivity to weak stimuli, manifest in low sensory thresholds and relatively fast responses.

Some, small-scale, studies of temperament with infants have suggested that East Asian (Japanese and Chinese) babies are less excitable and easier to calm when upset than American babies (of European descent). In one study Lewis, Ramsay, and Kawakami (1993) observed reactions of Japanese and American infants to an inoculation. On average the American babies showed a more intense reaction in crying and other signs of discomfort. However, measurements of cortisol level (a hormone that is excreted more under conditions of stress) showed a more intense reaction among the Japanese infants. The interpretation of this reversal in pattern between overt behavior and biochemical reactions is not clear, but the discrepancy can serve as a warning that inferences about temperament as an inborn characteristic on the basis of cross-cultural differences in social behavior patterns are not straightforward, even in young infants.

A series of cross-cultural studies with adults has been conducted with the Pavlovian Temperament Survey (PTS). The construction of this survey was guided by the idea that temperament dimensions should be universal across cultures, in spite of the culturally specific behaviors in which these dimensions might become manifest (Strelau, Angleitner, & Newberry, 1999). This implies that the same temperament dimensions should be found everywhere. The PTS is meant to assess three dimensions, strength of excitation, strength of inhibition, and mobility, which have been derived from the work of Pavlov and his followers. Each dimension is supposed to consist of a number of components that also are assumed to be universal. To represent the entire domain various items were generated for each component. An important feature of the PTS is that culture-specific inventories can be constructed by selecting items from this common pool. In a data set spanning fifteen countries three dimensions that appeared to be similar were found in all countries, with only partly overlapping sets of items. The differences between samples in mean scores were small for one scale (strength of excitation), but were more sizeable for the remaining two scales. Strelau et al. (1999, p. 32) suggest these differences "may be the result of differences in the cultural backgrounds represented by the fifteen samples, but may also represent methodological shortcomings, for example, in the representativeness of samples."

The previous sentence could raise the question of whether only the same configuration of trait dimensions is expected everywhere, or whether traits should also be equally distributed in all cultural populations (making differences in mean scores a matter of cultural bias). Elsewhere Strelau (1998) has ruled out the latter alternative, arguing that most researchers accept that temperament traits serve adaptive functions and that depending on interactions with the environment different developmental outcomes will occur. However, theories that postulate specific differences in interaction patterns between temperament and cultural context have not been formulated in temperament studies.

Moreover, if the biological basis of temperament is taken seriously, it is not immediately evident why there should be cross-cultural differences in distributions of temperament levels. Inasmuch as cultural contexts generally allow for unstunted ontogenetic development and cannot tamper with inborn characteristics, equal mean scores on temperament scales within cultures can be reasonably expected. Measured differences would then indeed be due to bias. Taking this line of argument Poortinga (1993) engaged in an explicit search for equal score levels in basic personality variables related to strength of nervous system excitation that would be minimally affected by cultural bias. Data were collected, mostly in the form of psychophysiological recordings during simple auditory and motor tasks, with samples as far apart as Indian university students, illiterate members of a "tribal" community in India, Dutch university students, and Dutch military conscripts. Variables included reactions in skin conductance to the presentation of simple tones (in more technical terms, habituation of the orienting reflex or investigatory reflex), differences in potentials in the EEG evoked by louder and softer tones, and differences in reaction times to louder and softer stimuli. In the majority of the scores for nervous system strength no cultural differences in mean levels were observed. It was concluded that with the elimination of situation and task-specific sources of variance, cross-cultural uniformity in score distributions on basic personality dimensions becomes more evident.

## "Big five" dimensions

The five-factor model (FFM) has become the most popular model of trait dimensions. The main postulate is that five dimensions are needed, not more and not less, to adequately map the domain of personality. The five dimensions (also called the **"big five"**) tend to be seen as enduring dispositions, as likely to be biologically anchored (e.g., Costa & McCrae, 1994; McCrae & Costa, 1996) and as evolved in the human species over time (MacDonald, 1998). The evidence for a biological basis is mainly derived from twin studies; as we shall see in ch. 10, identical twins who share the same genetic material are very similar in respect of scores on personality variables. However, direct evidence linking personality dimensions to genes is still largely lacking. In other words, biological research cannot tell us (yet) whether one or the other personality theory is more adequate in terms of underlying fuctions.

The five factors were postulated because they were the only ones found recurrently on reanalysis of numerous data sets on all kinds of personality inventories in the USA (Norman, 1963). Within each factor different subfactors or facets have been distinguished, but these will not be mentioned here. The five factors are generally labeled as follows:

extraversion, with sociability, seeking stimulating social environments, and outgoingness as some of the important characteristics;

agreeableness, with compassion, sensitivity, gentleness, and warmth; agreeable persons are good to have around;

conscientiousness, with persistence, goal-directed behavior, dependency, and self-discipline;

neuroticism, with emotional instability, anxiety, and hostility; the neurotic person is tense, while the emotionally stable person is secure and relaxed;

openness to experience (earlier called culture), with curiosity, imaginativeness, and sophistication.

The inventory used most frequently to assess the big five dimensions called the NEO-PI-R (Costa & McCrae, 1992) was developed in the USA. This inventory has been translated into a large number of languages.

Cross-cultural research has been conducted mainly to establish the universal validity of the FFM. If the five dimensions represent basic tendencies of human functioning they should be replicated everywhere; if they are characteristic adaptations of Americans in the USA to their context, different cultures and languages should lead to different trait constellations (McCrae, Costa, del Pilar, Holland, & Parker, 1998). In various studies factor structures similar to those in the USA have been found in countries as far apart as France and the Philippines (e.g., McCrae et al., 1998; McCrae, 2000).

Since the NEO-PI-R is an inventory that has been constructed in the USA, it is still possible that aspects of personality that are more prominent in other cultural contexts have been omitted. In some countries personality inventories have been constructed on the basis of locally generated item pools, without reference to existing instruments. Factor structures derived from such instruments do not always correspond to the big five (e.g., Guanzon-Lapeña, Church, Carlota, & Kagitbak, 1998), but this is not very informative by itself, unless a common structure has actually been sought; after all, even in a single population different inventories often do not show the same set of factors. The possible convergence of factors was examined in studies with Chinese respondents reported by Cheung and Leung (1998). In separate studies four or five of the big five factors were found to be replicated, but also an additional factor was identified consistently, labeled Chinese tradition. "Harmony" and "relationship orientation" were important aspects of this factor. Filial piety, which is much emphasized in Chinese society, was significantly predicted by scales for harmony and social relationships even after controlling for the effects of the big five factors (Zhang & Bond, 1997, cited by Cheung & Leung, 1998). This indicates that a culture-specific factor beyond the big five can have some relevance. On the other hand, Cheung and Leung also raise the question of whether the tradition factor is unique to Chinese culture, or whether it represents a universal domain that can help to understand interpersonal aspects of personality functioning that have been inadvertently omitted from an inventory like the NEO-PI-R. On the basis of a number of studies in the Philippines that were initiated from an indigenous approach, Guanzon-Lapeña et al. (1998) concluded that (1) each of the big five domains was represented in Philippine instruments, that (2) no indigenous dimensions were found that could not be subsumed under some big five dimension, and that (3) there were cross-cultural differences in the flavor or focus of dimensions considered salient in the Philippine context.

The latter conclusion clearly suggests that cross-cultural differences should exist in profiles of facet (or subscale) scores for the NEO-PI-R. Such differences were found, for example, by McCrae, Yik, Trapnell, Bond, & Paulhus (1998), who worked with Chinese in Hong Kong and (descendants) of Chinese migrants of different duration of stay in Canada. These authors point out that there is a strong temptation to make quantitative comparisons of score levels, once satisfactory structural equivalence has been established, but that such findings may be misleading because of social norms and other method artifacts that obscure true levels of traits. McCrae et al. did find some differences in the extraversion factor between the Canadian and Hong Kong samples, regardless of country of birth of respondents, but were reluctant to interpret these, since enduring influences of Chinese norms of restraint acquired early in life could not be ruled out.

The questionnaires that led to the identification of the big five factors in the USA in part were derived from the collection of personality descriptive terms in American English. This lexical approach is based on the assumption that aspects of personality that are considered important in a particular culture will have been encoded in the language. In a recent review Saucier and Goldberg (2001) summarize the results of studies in English and twelve other languages in which local personality terms, mainly collected from dictionaries, formed the starting material. In most studies inspection of factor content showed a reasonably good replicability of all big five factors across Germanic languages. With other languages (e.g., Eastern European and Korean) support was more loose, or even problematic. However, more congruence was obtained as less stringent criteria for similarity were imposed, and when three instead of five factors were postulated. Precise congruence coefficients have been reported by De Raad, Perugini, Hrebícková, & Szarota (1998).When comparing Dutch, German, Hungarian, Italian,

Czech, and Polish structures based on the best marker terms for each of the big five factors, these coefficients on average stayed well below the value of .90 that usually is considered the lower limit for factorial similarity. Although one cannot conclude that the non-congruent portion of the variance in lexical studies should be attributed to culture-specific factors, it is also clear that there is some variance that cannot (yet) be accounted for by common factors as postulated in the FFM.

## Other trait traditions

Traditionally cross-cultural research on traits tended to be centered around certain instruments (Guthrie & Lonner, 1986). Apart from studies with the Eysenck scales and the big five, traditions have developed, for example, around the Minnesota Multiphasic Personality Inventory (MMPI; cf. Butcher & Pancheri, 1976) and its second edition, the MMPI-2 (Butcher, 1996); Spielberger's State-Trait Anxiety Inventory (STAI, Spielberger, Gorsuch, & Lushene, 1970); the Sixteen Personality Factors (Cattell, Eber, & Tatsuoka, 1970); Rotter's Internal–External Control scale (Rotter, 1966) and Gough's adjective checklist (ACL; Gough & Heilbrun, 1983).[1] Paunonen and Ashton (1998) have reviewed cross-cultural studies for some of these instrument-oriented traditions. Replicable factor structures were found across cultures in most cases, though it has to be mentioned again that criteria for similarity in many studies tend to be vague and not well defined, making it difficult to assess precisely the balance between similarities and differences.

Both the MMPI and the MMPI-2 have been used on a large scale in the diagnosis of personality and abnormal behavior virtually across the globe. Butcher, Lim, and Nezami (1998) reported that the MMPI-2 was (officially) available in twenty-two languages with a number of other adaptations in progress. Typically checks are carried out on translation equivalence by administering two-language versions to groups of bilingual subjects. Also factor analyses have been conducted in a number of countries on the ten clinical scales of the MMPI-2 and rendered a similar set of factors as found in the USA. But similarity in the profiles of scores also are apparent. According to Butcher et al. (1998, p. 196), "[m]ost of the researchers who have collected new norms (e.g., in Holland, France, Italy, Israel, Mexico, Chile) have found that the raw scores generally fall very close to the US norm statistically."

The ACL consists of 300 adjectives that are descriptive of persons and together presumably cover more or less the entire domain of personality. For the ACL, it has been claimed on theoretical grounds that the various scales have universal validity. This inventory has been used by Williams and Best (1990) for their studies on gender stereotypes (cf. ch. 3). In a later study Williams, Satterwhite, and

---

[1] It may be noted that all these instruments were originally written in English, and that with one exception (Eysenck's EPQ) they were constructed in the USA.

Saiz (1998) collected ratings of the "psychological importance" of each of the 300 items. According to the instruction to subjects this is the importance "in providing information as to what a person is really like" (p. 54). The assumption is that more important traits tell us more about a person than less important traits. The ratings were obtained from samples of students in twenty widely dispersed countries. Most analyses were carried out with country-level scores obtained by averaging the ratings of individual subjects within a sample. A second set of ratings asking for the favorability (Osgood's evaluation dimension, cf. ch. 7) of each of the ACL items was collected in ten countries. The cross-culturally most consistent patterns were found for the favorability ratings. Correlations between pairs of countries had a median value of .82. Apparently, capable, cheerful, and civilized people are liked everywhere, and the arrogant, bitter, and boastful are liked nowhere.

For the ratings of psychological importance the correlations between countries had a median value of .50. A distinction was found between two clusters of countries, (those generally viewed as individualist and as collectivist societies) in their relationship between favorability and psychological importance of the items. In the collectivist cluster the relationship was linear, in the other cluster it followed a U-curve. Favorable traits tended to be rated higher than unfavorable ones, but while some of the unfavorable items were rated as quite important in individualist countries, this was not the case in collectivist countries. In other words, in the one group of countries unfavorable traits like dominant and distrustful were rated as being quite important, while in the other cluster they were rated as unimportant.

Williams et al. (1998) interpreted their findings in terms of differences in value orientations. This interpretation fits other studies in which individualist samples provided more trait-oriented responses than collectivist samples. This difference in "traitedness" has been emphasized, among others, by Church (2000), who sees it as an important outcome variable of the interaction between cultural context and, probably, heritable traits. However, favorability is close to social desirability, a response style mentioned above. The correlation between a country's mean favorability score and its socioeconomic index had a high negative value. In this line of reasoning, the differences in favorability could be seen as reflecting, perhaps in part, cross-cultural differences in a response tendency towards answering in terms of social norms and expectations (cf. Poortinga & Van de Vijver, 2000).

## National character

The approaches mentioned so far have in common that traits are identified at the level of individuals. One can also imagine sociocultural influences that differ from culture to culture, but show little variation within cultures. This means that there also could be traits defined at the level of cultural populations (see ch. 9). An example of a traditional trait approach is the research by Peabody (1967, 1985). He drew a sharp distinction between national stereotypes (often considered to be irrational and incorrect) and national character (considered to be valid descriptions of a population) and defined as "modal psychological characteristics of members of a nationality" (Peabody, 1985, p. 8). To identify national characteristics Peabody asked judges (usually students) to rate trait-descriptive adjectives about people in various nations, including their own. In order to distinguish between the evaluative and the descriptive aspects in the ratings of the judges Peabody used an elegant method. He worked with pairs of adjectives with an opposite meaning, using two pairs for each trait. Of the two adjectives with a factually similar meaning one had a positive and the other a negative connotation. An example is thrifty (+) and stingy (−) versus generous (+) and extravagant (−). Combinations of ratings on the four adjectives were used by Peabody to separate the effects of likes and dislikes of the judges from effects due to their factual opinion. For example, if a rater was of the opinion that the Scots were likeable but not exactly big spenders he would tend to rate them higher on thrifty than on stingy. In the case of dislike this pattern would be reversed. Peabody collected data mainly in Western countries. He found two major dimensions on which nations differ, viz. tight versus loose (Pelto, 1968; cf. ch. 3), and assertive versus unassertive. In his opinion the data provided by the raters fitted with descriptions found in other sources, such as the anthropological and the historical literature on various nations.

Objections have been raised about the validity of national characteristics and judges' opinions about them. It has been argued that ratings reflect ethnocentric attitudes, that nations change, and that judges rarely have extensive first-hand experience with other countries. Peabody (1985) has discussed these objections and concluded that by and large they had to be rejected for lack of any supporting evidence. However, in our opinion the case for national characteristics has not been clearly established. In particular, we do not believe that the second-hand knowledge of students about other nations can be a valid basis for scientific knowledge. Peabody argues that virtually everything we know is acquired from others and that we do not even know that the world is round on the basis of our own experience. Of course, there is much substance to this argument, but only if we have no reason to doubt what we are told. It is clear from Peabody's own discussion that the validity of national characteristics has been seriously questioned, and that there is an inherent danger of stereotyping when we ascribe more of a certain trait to a certain nation (cf. Brewer & Campbell, 1976; Segall et al., 1999; and the discussion of stereotypes in ch. 13). At the very least, it seems undesirable to rely on the evaluations of judges who lack extensive first-hand knowledge to decide the issue.

## Beyond traits?

Can all the different trait theories be valid simultaneously? If personality is looked upon as a big round cake, it is possible that various traditions cut this cake a bit differently, and that in the long run a common structure can be agreed upon. This is likely to be the case if trait dimensions can be anchored in biological functions, like hormone excretions and nervous system properties (Costa & McCrae, 1994). However, this assumes that there is an identical cake to begin with, in other words that the make-up of what we call personality is indeed universal. In the following section we shall discuss cross-cultural research in which this basic assumption is questioned. Here we mention some other criticisms that have been raised against the notion of personality traits.

If individual behavior can be described as a function of stable traits, future behavior should be predictable on the basis of trait scores. Empirical research has mostly shown disappointing results for trait theorists. Mischel (1968, 1973) has criticized the trait approach because of the low validity of predictions. He argued that behavior to a large extent was determined by the situation in which persons find themselves, rather than by internal psychological dispositions which differed from person to person. Between this situationism and the trait approach one finds a tradition of interactionism (e.g., Magnusson & Endler, 1977) in which the interaction between person and situation (some persons show behavior consistency in some situations) is emphasized. In another move away from earlier approaches traits have been considered as prototypes, i.e., normative cognitive schemata for organizing information (Cantor & Mischel, 1977, 1979). A prototype functions as a cognitive standard. We form ourselves an idea of what a dominant person or a sociable person is like. New information is then assimilated to form an impression coherent with an already existing prototype.

The idea that traits do not reflect stable dispositions, but are merely convenient labels to reduce the information about other persons to manageable proportions, finds support in the research indicating that we attribute stable traits mainly to other persons (see ch. 3), while for our own behavior we tend to refer more to situational determinants or to our intentions (Jones & Nisbett, 1972). In short, personality traits, like stereotypes about national characteristics, should then be seen as having their origin more in the eye of the beholder than in the consistency of behavior patterns of persons.

## Effects of the environment

Finally, it should also be noted here that there are approaches in which personality is seen more as a reflection of how individuals experience their own environments, notably the ecological aspects. One concept is quality of life, which we will discuss in ch. 16, because it is mainly related to health. Another concept is subjective well-being (SWB; see ch. 16), which refers to a broad category of evaluations about life satisfaction, both in general, and in specific domains, like work, family, health, etc. SWB is predicted consistently by personality factors, including temperamental predispositions (Diener, Suh, Lucas, & Smith, 1999). There are also limited effects of factors like income and education at the individual level. Across countries national wealth has been found to be strongly correlated with SWB, and also individualism, human rights, and social equality (Diener, Diener, & Diener, 1995). The authors conclude that "efficacy in terms of meeting one's needs, and an ability to pursue one's goals may be important factors in achieving SWB" (p. 863). In this study individualism predicted SWB, even when effects of economic wealth were controlled, suggesting that feelings of autonomy may be universally important.

An extensive tradition of cross-cultural research exists in respect of **locus of control**, as developed by Rotter (1954, 1966). The concept derives from a theory of social learning in which reinforcement occupies a central position. It is believed that an individual's learning history can lead to generalized expectancies about reinforcement. One can see a (positive or negative) reward either as dependent upon one's own behavior or as contingent upon forces beyond one's control. In other words, the locus of control can be perceived as internal or external to oneself. Success in life can be due to "skill" or to "chance" and so can failure. Many events that happen in persons' lives can be taken by them as their own responsibility or as beyond their control. The most important instrument is Rotter's I–E Scale (1966). This consists of twenty-three items that offer a choice between an internal and an external option. Rotter concluded on the basis of factor analysis that the scale represents a single dimension. Hence, it should be possible to express locus of control in a single score that indicates the balance between externality and internality in a person.

One concern is whether locus of control can be generalized over various domains of behavior or whether distinctions have to be made between various reinforcement areas. In the case of specificity each domain would need to be assessed separately and a single score per person would be inadequate. In cross-cultural comparison this would imply that a single measurement may result in a rather inadequate representation of differences between cultural groups. Another question is whether the external agents can be taken together or whether a distinction is needed between, for example, fate or luck (chance) and other persons who can exert control over an individual (powerful others). These and other problems of interest for the analysis of cross-cultural differences have been reviewed by Dyal (1984).

Within the USA, where by far the largest body of cross-culturally relevant research has been conducted, it has been repeatedly found that African Americans are more external than European Americans (Dyal, 1984). Low socioeconomic status tends to go together with external control, but the black–white difference remains when socioeconomic differences have been controlled for. In the case of other groups in the USA, such as Hispanics, the results vary and depend on the level of education and socioeconomic status of the samples tested. These results are generally consistent with the explanation that the locus of control scores correspond with the actual degree of control that people can exert on the course of their own lives in the real world.

Differences between European countries and between Europe and the USA tend to be small. In contrast, there are consistent differences between Americans and East Asians; the Japanese in particular score relatively high on externality and low on internality. In the Sahel region of Africa extreme environmental degradation, against which local people can hardly take action, was found to be associated with a more external locus of control (Van Haaften & Van den Vijver, 1999).

In general locus of control represents a behavior tendency that seems to fit reasonable expectations of individuals belonging to certain groups, given their actual living conditions. Locus of control has been related to an array of other variables. One of the most consistent findings is a positive correlation between internal control and (academic) achievement. However, there are serious problems of construct equivalence and validity. The single dimension postulated by Rotter often could not be replicated, also not with other instruments. More common has been the finding that there are two factors, pointing to personal control and sociopolitical control as separate aspects, although for non-Western rural groups even more fuzzy solutions have been reported (Dyal, 1984; Smith, Trompenaars, & Dugan; 1995; Van Haaften & Van de Vijver, 1996). In a study with sometimes small samples of managers from forty-three countries, Smith et al. (1995) found three dimensions, which referred to personal control (and discounting political efficacy), individual autonomy (at the cost of social aspects) and luck. The first dimension is close to Rotter's original concept, but the additional dimensions suggest that the scale might be contaminated by other concepts beyond the one Rotter intended.[2]

The locus of control concept is theoretically rooted in social learning theories. It allows a far more explicit role for cultural context in the making of personality than the trait theories discussed earlier in this chapter. In a sense it can be seen as a precursor to social-cognitive perspectives in which the person is seen as a product of the interactions between organism and social environment (e.g., Cervone & Shoda, 1999). Cross-cultural research that has emerged from this perspective is discussed in the next section.

## Self in social context

The notion of a person as a bounded individual has been central to the discipline of psychology. Indeed, it is the description and understanding of the unique individual that has been at the core of personality psychology. Despite this established position, the possibility that person and selfhood are cultural constructions, and hence likely to vary cross-culturally, has become an issue in theoretical and empirical research only fairly recently. One central question was posed by Shweder and Bourne (1984): "Does the concept of person vary cross-culturally?" Their answer, based upon research with Indians in the state of Orissa, is that persons are believed to be altered by the social relations into which they enter and are described not so much in terms of enduring traits, but in terms of these social relationships. The links between this conception of the person and the dimension of individualism and collectivism (discussed in ch. 3) are quite apparent.

---

[2] Smith et al. used multidimensional scaling rather than factor analysis, but this should have no major effects on the dimensional structure.

A wide-ranging examination of this issue has been reported in Marsella, De Vos, and Hsu (1985) for both Western and Asian cultures. Rooted in anthropological explorations of personhood (e.g., Burridge, 1979; Carrithers, Collins, & Lukes, 1985) and of interdisciplinary considerations of self (e.g., Miller, 1988) research on the self has made attempts to bridge personality and social psychology (e.g., Yang & Bond, 1990). Triandis (1989) examined three aspects of self (private, public, and collective) as they were exhibited over three dimensions of cultural variation (individualism–collectivism, tightness–looseness, and cultural complexity). His review of a wide range of literature led him to conclude that the more individualistic the culture, the more frequent was the "sampling" of the private self and the less frequent was the sampling of the collective self. (By "sampling" Triandis means attending to self-relevant information.) Societal tightness was also linked to high sampling of the collective self, while the more complex the culture, the more frequent was the sampling of the private and public self. Child rearing and other ecological and cultural factors are proposed to account for these patterns, although they remain largely unspecified.

Kagitcibasi (1990, 1996) has differentiated between a relational self and a separated self. The relational self develops in societies with a "family model of emotional and material interdependence." Such societies have typically a traditional agricultural subsistence economy with a collectivisit life style; members of a family have to rely on each other in case of sickness and to have old age security. A separated self is found in individualistic Western urban environments with a "family model of independence." Members of a family can live separated from each other without serious consequences for their well-being. Kagitcibasi distinguished a third category of self, that develops in a "family model of emotional interdependence." This kind of self is called an "autonomous-related self"; it is found particularly in urban areas of collectivist countries. Depite growing material independence, and socialization towards more autonomy, emotional interdependencies between members of the family continue. Kagitcibasi believes that the main direction of development in the world is towards this third model, allowing for relatedness as well as autonomy in a person's interactions with society at large.

A twofold distinction between an **independent self** and an **interdependent self** has been advocated by Markus and Kitayama (1991). They postulate that people in various cultures have strikingly different construals of the self. These different construals have consequences for how persons experience themselves and others, and for cognition, emotion, and motivation. Generally the Western conception of self is of an individual who is separate, autonomous, and atomized (made up of a set of discrete traits, abilities, values, and motives), seeking separateness and independence from others. In contrast, in Eastern cultures relatedness, connectedness, and interdependence are sought, rooted in a concept of the self not as a discrete entity, but as inherently linked to others. The person is only made "whole" when situated in his or her place in a social unit. The independent construal of the self further implies that persons see themselves as unique, promote their own goals, and seek self-expression. Persons with an interdependent construal of the self seek to belong and fit in, to promote others' goals, and to occupy their proper place. In later publications the same distinction has been elaborated, both theoretically and empirically.

For example, Kitayama, Markus, Matsumoto, and Norasakkunit (1997, p. 1247) present a collective constructionist theory of the self in which it is stated that "many psychological tendencies and processes simultaneously result from and support a collective process through which the views of the self are inscribed and embodied in the very ways in which social acts and situations are defined and experienced in each cultural context." The notion of joint psychological processes is rather old, especially under the label "collective representations" (e.g., Jahoda, 1982), but has not gained much foothold, because no appropriate mechanisms could be specified. Social representations can also have a different meaning that has been fairly widely researched in the school of Moscovici (e.g., 1982). This school emphasizes shared meanings within and differences in meanings and perceptions between cultural groups. However, Kitayama et al. go much further by specifying differences in psychological processes, rather than differences in social perceptions.

When reading the Markus and Kitayama (1991) article one is struck by the dichotomies that are drawn between the psychological functioning of individuals in various societies, especially Japan and the USA. The article has been cited many times, and usually with approval. However, part of the evidence presented consists of descriptions of illustrative incidents occurring in one society for which it is difficult to establish whether or not they are absent in another society. Moreover, the interpretation of differences may also be criticized. One of the studies referred to by Markus and Kitayama was reported by Cousins (1989). He administered the twenty statements test where respondents are asked to reply twenty times to the question: "Who am I?" American students included more trait descriptions in their answers, and Japanese students more specific behaviors. A modified version was also administered in which students were asked to describe themselves in specific situations. Under this condition Japanese students gave more trait-like descriptions of themselves. Markus and Kitayama accept Cousins's interpretation that this pattern reflects the independence of the Americans. A scale developed by Kitayama to assess independence and interdependence was administered by Van den Heuvel and Poortinga (1999) to Greek students of rural and urban background and to Dutch students. The Dutch students, who usually are classified as more individualistic and independent, obtained a significantly lower score for interdependent construal of the self, which appears to be in line with Markus and Kitayama's argument. However, parts of the scale were also administered in a different format, not asking for ratings of the self in general, but in relationship to specified social categories, like parents, children, friends, etc. Now the pattern of findings was quite reversed; the Greek rural sample had a higher mean for independence and the Dutch sample for interdependence. Combining these results with those of Cousins, it could be argued that the more Western subjects apparently stated that they were more independent, but that they would act more in an interdependent fashion when at home or in school, as well as with respect to their parents and friends, etc. Thus, the question needs to be raised what independence and interdependence of self mean in practice.

In a critical examination Matsumoto (1999) seriously questions the major premise underlying Markus and Kitayama's analysis, namely that Japan is a more collectivist and the USA a more individualist society. Among eighteen studies that formally tested for differences between Japan and the USA on individualism–collectivism only one provided support, and seventeen provided little or no support for the common belief that the Japanese hold more collectivist values. In a similar review of fifteen studies Takano and Osaka (1999) reached the same conclusion. Moreover, according to Matsumoto, studies that have investigated differences in self-construals between Japanese and USA samples often have not found the expected effects. Thus, neither the presumed relationship between the I–C dimension and self-construal, nor the cross-cultural differences in self-construal have been clearly established.

Despite these criticisms, in our view some of the empirical studies of Markus and Kitayama and their colleagues have shown important results that need explanation. For example, Kitayama et al. (1997) asked Japanese and USA students to rate the impact of a large number of events on their self-esteem (*jison-shin* for the Japanese). Situation descriptions had been generated that were seen as relevant for the enhancement or the decrease of self-esteem in a separate study by similar samples of students. American respondents imagined that they would experience more increase in self-esteem to positive situations than decrease in self-esteem to negative situations. This effect was stronger for situation descriptions generated in the USA than for descriptions that came from Japan. On the other hand, Japanese respondents reported that they would experience more reduction in self-esteem in negative situations than enhancement of self-esteem if they experienced positive situations. The differences were quite substantial, suggesting a robust difference in self-criticism and self-enhancement between the two societies. In the light of criticisms like those of Matsumoto it might be argued that the differences were merely a matter of expression; Japanese people know that they have to act in a modest way about success and be self-critical. In other words the differences could be a matter of impression management or public display rules.

Kitayama et al. (1997) recognized this alternative interpretation and proceeded with a second study in which other samples of Japanese and USA students were asked to make the same ratings, but this time not with respect to the effect on their own self-esteem, but with respect to the effect on the self-esteem of a typical student. "We assumed that because the respondents were asked to estimate the true feelings (i.e., changes in self-esteem) of the typical student, they would not filter their responses through any cultural rules of public display that might exist" (p. 1256). Very similar results as in the previous study were obtained under these instructions, which was a reason for the authors to argue that the answer pattern was not a matter of display rules, but of true experiences of the self. Of course, there are other ways in which these findings can be explained. For example, the changes in instructions might not have worked in the way the authors assumed. Perhaps we do not well recognize the social deception of others and tend to accept displays as true expressions and thus ascribe psychological functioning according to social norms to others.

There was also at least one puzzling finding. In the first study a third sample was included, consisting of Japanese people who were temporarily studying at a university in the USA. They indicated that they would experience more increase in self-esteem in positive situations, than decrease in self-esteem in negative situations, for situations generated in the USA. Only for situations generated in Japan was the reverse tendency found, consistent with the results of the Japanese sample living in Japan. In our opinion, such a rapid acculturation effect is difficult to reconcile with basic differences in self.

In summary, trait theorists claim empirical support for their views and so do social cognitivists. Going back to an earlier metaphor, this is not a matter of cutting a cake differently; the question is whether the cake is made of the same ingredients. Although the debate on whether the psyche is better defined as individual or as social underlies many of the contrasts that differentiate culture-comparative and culturalist approaches in contemporary cross-cultural psychology, it is seen by many as a rather fruitless dichotomy (cf. Kagitcibasi & Poortinga, 2000). In ch. 2 we saw that theoretical positions were being defined that seek to transcend this dichotomy. In ch. 12 we shall further elaborate on this issue.

## Conceptions of the person

Psychological concepts and theories are being contributed by scientists from many cultures. Those proposed from non-Western societies are often referred to as **indigenous personality concepts**. This term is somewhat a misnomer (see ch. 17). As we have seen already, it can be argued that most personality theories in psychology are the product of a scientific tradition that is indigenous to Western industrial-urban cultures. Many studies by non-Western psychologists have built on to this tradition (cf. Blowers & Turtle, 1987). However, there are also personality theories based on non-Western traditions of reflection on human existence. We shall mention some of these, constructed by authors writing on the culture in which they were brought up. There are unmistakably Western influences, but also authentic insights not easily achieved by outsiders (cf. Sinha, 1997).

### African personality

During colonial times, the descriptions of African personality made by Western psychiatrists were largely marked by prejudices and stereotypes. An upsurge in the 1960s and 1970s of writings by African authors claiming a separate identity

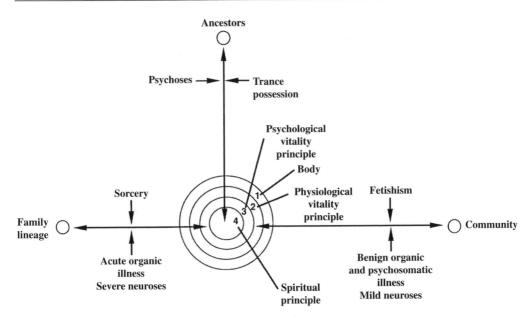

**4.1** Model of African personality according to Sow
From Sow 1977, 1978

for African people can be seen at least in part as a reaction against the generally negative picture prevalent in colonial times.

In contrast, the work of the Senegalese psychiatrist Sow (1977, 1978) provides an extensive theory of the African personality and psychopathology. A schematic representation of the person as conceptualized in Africa is found in fig. 4.1. The outer layer is the body, the corporal envelope of the person. Next comes a principle of vitality that is found in man and animals. This can be more or less equated with physiological functioning. The third layer represents another principle of vitality, but is found only in humans; it stands for human psychological existence not shared with other species. The inner layer is the spiritual principle, which never perishes. It can leave the body during sleep and during trance states and leaves definitively upon death. The spiritual principle does not give life to the body; it has an existence of its own, belonging to the sphere of the ancestors and representing that sphere in each person.

The concentric layers of the personality are in constant relationship with the person's environment. Sow describes three reference axes concerning the relations of a person with the outside world. The first axis links the world of the ancestors to the spiritual principle, passing through the other three layers. The second axis connects the psychological vitality principle to the person's extended family, understood as the lineage to which the person belongs. The third axis connects the wider community to the person, passing through the body envelope to the physiological principle of vitality. These axes represent relations that are usually in a state of equilibrium.

According to Sow the traditional African interpretation of illness and mental disorders, and their treatments, can be understood in terms of this indigenous personality theory. A disorder occurs when the equilibrium is disturbed on one or the other of the axes; diagnosis consists of discovering which axis has been disturbed, and therapy will attempt to re-establish the equilibrium. Note that in African tradition illness always has an external cause; it is not due to intrapsychic phenomena in the person's history, but to aggressive interference from outside.

If there is a rupture of the equilibrium on the first axis (linking the spiritual principle to the ancestral pole), serious chronic psychotic states may occur, but this cannot lead to death since the spiritual principle cannot be destroyed. The disturbance is due to spirits who are transmitting messages from the ancestors. A state of trance as a psychotherapeutic technique, during which the person is possessed by one of these spirits, can serve to re-establish the relations with ancestral tradition. Therefore, possession trance can have important psychotherapeutic effects.

A rupture of the equilibrium on the second axis (linking the psychological vitality principle to the family lineage) leads to organic illness, acute anxiety states, severe neuroses, and wasting away. This is likely to be a very serious illness, which can lead to death through the destruction of the vitality principle. It is due to sorcery and can only be cured through sorcery. A disequilibrium with the third, community, pole leads to more benign organic and psychosomatic illnesses as well as neurotic states. This is due to aggressions from enemies and can be cured through fetishism. As a general rule, healing requires the resolution of conflict (with the community, family, or ancestors) and the consequent restitution of equilibrium.

We have given here only a simplified account of this personality theory; for example, the model takes a slightly different form in matrilineal and patrilineal societies. In Sow's conception the supernatural, for example in sorcery, has to be understood in its cultural meaning, replete with symbolic interpretations. At the same time, Sow's writings use the language of Western psychiatry.

The importance of symbolism is emphasized by others who write on Africa, like Jahoda (1982; cf. Cissé, 1973) in his reference to the very complex personality conceptions of the Bambara in Mali. They distinguish sixty elements in the person that form pairs, each having one male and one female element. Examples are thought and reflection, speech and authority, future and destiny, and first name and family name. Jahoda sees some similarities with psychology as it is known in the West, but also important differences. Bambara psychology forms part of a worldview in which relationships between various elements are established by symbolism rather than by analytic procedures.

Nsamenang (2001) also points out that modern views in psychology about the individual as autonomous differ from the African conception in which the person coexists with the community, with the world of spirits, and with the ecological environment. The existence of an indestructible vital force which continues to exist in the world of spirits after death is emphasized in Africa (Nsamenang, 1992).

Personhood is a manifestation of this vital force through a body. Respect for the person becomes manifest, for example, in the importance attached to greetings; the amount of time spent is not a waste of time and effort, but reflects the social value attached to the greeting; the high value of greetings implies a high regard for persons. Nsamenang (1992, p. 75) further describes how in Africa "a man is not a man on his own," but is rooted in the community in which and for which he exists. The importance of the community is reflected in the saying "Seek the good of the community, and you seek your own good; seek your own good and you seek your own destruction." In Nsamenang's view the primacy of kinship relations will remain paramount, until alternative systems of social security can replace extended family networks.

## *Amae* in Japan

*Amae*, pronounced ah-mah-eh, has gained prominence in the writings of the psychiatrist Doi (1973) as a core concept for understanding the Japanese. *Amae* is described as a form of passive love or dependence that finds its origin in the relationship of the infant with its mother. The desire for contact with the mother is universal in young children and plays a role also in the forming of new relationships among adults. *Amae* is more prominent with the Japanese than with people in other cultures. Doi finds it significant that the Japanese language has a word for *amae* and that there are a fair number of terms that are related to *amae*. In Doi's view culture and language are closely interconnected.

He ascribes to the *amae* mentality of the Japanese many and far-reaching implications. The seeking of the other person's indulgence that comes together with passive love and dependency leads to a blurring of the sharp distinction, found in the West, between the person (as expressed in the concept of self) and the social group. As such it bears on the collectivist attitudes allegedly prevalent in Japanese society. Mental health problems manifest in psychosomatic symptoms and feelings of fear and apprehension can have their origins in concealed *amae* (see ch. 16). The patient is in a state of mind where he cannot impose on the indulgence of others. In a person suffering from illusions of persecution and grandeur "*amae* has seldom acted as an intermediary via which he could experience empathy with others. His pursuit of *amae* tends to become self-centered, and he seeks fulfillment by becoming one with some object or other that he has fixed on by himself" (Doi, 1973, p. 132). In an analysis of the social upheavals in Japan, in particular the student unrest, during the late 1960s and early 1970s, Doi points out that more modern times are permeated with *amae* and that everyone has become more childish. There has been a loss of boundaries between generations; *amae* has become a common element of adult-like child and child-like adult behavior.

It may be noted that Doi's conception has been questioned on important points by others within as well as outside Japan. For example, Kumagai and Kumagai (1986) have emphasized that *amae* as a feeling of love is expressed in patterns of interaction that alternate between give and take, or between self-distancing and self-assertive stances. According to Ikebe (1999) observations of specific behavior suggest that *amae* has aspects of both dependency and attachment, with aspects of regression to refuse the reality of separation and to acquire emotional and physical comforts from the target of affection. Such formulations suggest similarities with psychological mechanisms found elsewhere.

## Indian conceptions

According to Paranjpe (1984, pp. 235 ff.) the concept of *jiva* is similar to that of personality. "The *jiva* represents everything concerning an individual, including all his experiences and actions throughout his life cycle." Five concentric layers are distinguished. The outermost is the body. The next is called the "breath of life"; it refers to physiological processes such as breathing. The third layer involves sensation and the "mind" that coordinates the sensory functions. Here egoistic feelings are placed that have to do with "me" and "mine." The fourth layer represents the intellect and the cognitive aspects of the person, including self-image and self-representation. The fifth and most inner layer of the *jiva* is the seat of experience of bliss.

Paranjpe (1984, 1998) sees many similarities with Western conceptions such as those of James and Erikson, but notes an important difference. In distinction of the *jiva* there is a "real self" or *Atman,* that is the permanent unchanging basis of life. Paranjpe (1984, p. 268) quotes the ancient Indian philosopher Sankara on this point.

> There is something within us which is always the substrate of the conscious feeling of "I". . . This inner Self (*antar-Atman*) is an eternal principle, which is always One and involves an integral experience of bliss . . . The *Atman* can be realized by means of a controlled mind.

To achieve the state of bliss one has to acquire a certain state of consciousness.

We have summarized Paranjpe's description of only one school of thinking (Vedanta), but other ancient Indian scholars agree that there are different states of consciousness, including Patanjahli, who described yoga, the system of meditation that nowadays has many adherents outside of India. It is seen as highly desirable to attain the most superior state of consciousness. Restraint and control of the mind to keep it steadily on one object, withdrawing the senses from objects of pleasure, and enduring hardship are means toward this desirable condition.

To reach the ultimate principle of consciousness, the ultimate reality, transcending space and time, is a long and difficult process. Should the complete state of detachment and inner quietness be reached, then one's body becomes merely incidental (like one's shirt) and there is a change to fearlessness, concern for fellow beings, and equanimity. Ordinarily people have a low impulse control which implies that they cannot detach themselves from the always present stimuli and the vicissitudes of life. It will be clear that those trained in detachment will be far less subject to the stresses and strains of life.

On the basis of these considerations Naidu (1983; Pande & Naidu, 1992) has taken *anasakti* or non-detachment as the basis of a research program on stress. Contrary to Western psychology, where control over the outcome of one's actions is seen as desirable, the ancient Hindu scriptures value detachment from the possible consequences of one's actions. Western studies are on involuntary loss of control, and this can lead to helplessness and depression. Detachment amounts to voluntarily giving up control and is assumed to have a positive effect on mental health. The methods used to assess and validate the notion of *anasakti* are much the same as those used in Western psychometrics. This makes the approach one of the few attempts to translate directly an indigenous notion of a philosophical and religious nature into a personality index that can be studied experimentally.

## Altered states of consciousness

The generic name for phenomena that include mystic experiences, meditation, hypnosis, trance, and possession is **altered states of consciousness** (ASC) (cf. Ward, 1989). In the Protestant tradition of the Christian religion and among agnostic scientists ASC had a strong flavor of abnormality. Today the practicing of yoga or other imported forms of meditation has become fairly common, and some form of trance is apparent in techno music. The use of mild psychoactive substances such as marihuana is widespread. The use of such substances goes back to prehistoric times and excepting incidences of misuse apparently has been integrated in the life of the groups who for a long time have been familiar with their effects.

Four criteria distinguish ASC from other states of consciousness (i.e., sleep, dreaming, and wakefulness). The most important is introspection, self-reports of persons, makes clear that they have experienced a temporary state that they perceive to be different from the usual state of consciousness. During ASC sensations, cognitive processes, and emotions are changed.

Observations by outsiders of the behavior persons display during ASC form the second criterion for identification. Unusual patterns of motor behavior and facial expression often make it immediately obvious to the observer that a person is in an unusual state. Combining these two criteria, the following are characteristic for ASC in distinction from a "normal" state of consciousness: (1) alteration in thinking, (2) disturbance of time sense, (3) loss of control, (4) change in emotional expression, (5) change of body image, (6) perceptual distortions, (7) change in meaning or significance (heightened significance to subjective experience), (8) sense of the ineffable, (9) feelings of rejuvenation, (10) hyper-suggestibility (Ludwig, 1969).

Induction is the third criterion. Classifications of ASC states tend to be based on the various means of induction (Dittrich, Von Arx, & Staub, 1985). The three most important techniques are the use of hallucinogens, reduction of environmental stimulation, and its opposite, sensory bombardment and physical strain. The intake of hallucinogens is nowadays the most widely known method of induction due to the popularization of certain psychoactive drugs. Reduction of environmental stimulation is the basic induction technique for meditation. Stimulus deprivation can be self-imposed by shutting off external events and by inner-directed concentration. In other instances physical isolation and loneliness are important factors in bringing on an ASC. Overstimulation also can take different forms. Sometimes light but rhythmic stimulation leads to the desired effect, sometimes a bombardment with varying stimuli (clapping, dancing, singing) is used. Physical exertion leading to exhaustion, hunger, and thirst, and sometimes even self-mutilation are applied to facilitate the onset of ASC.

The fourth criterion for identification are characteristics in psychophysiological measures during an ASC experience. Studies have been conducted with practitioners of yoga and Zen meditation. The abundance of high amplitude alpha waves in the EEG is a finding reported by several investigators. Other remarkable results have been obtained, but they tend not to be consistent across studies. Anand, Chhina, and Singh (1961) found with two yogis that their alpha activity could not be blocked by external stimulation. They could keep their hands submerged in ice-cold water for three-quarters of an hour and still show persistent alpha activity with high amplitude.

Kasamatsu and Hirai (1966) observed onset of alpha activity within fifty seconds after the beginning of Zen meditation in their sample of forty-eight Buddhist priests and trainees. This happened despite the fact that the subjects were meditating with their eyes open, while normally abundant alpha waves can only be recorded when subjects have their eyes closed. Another finding was that alpha blocking did occur in response to an outside stimulus (contrary to the findings of Anand et al., 1961), but that there was no habituation with repeated presentation of the same stimulus. Such a habituation effect was to be expected and it was actually observed in a sample of control subjects. More research is needed to decide whether differences such as between the two studies mentioned are a function of differences between the two forms of meditation, or whether some artifact of method was involved.

ASC is a widespread phenomenon. In a survey by Bourguignon and Evascu (1977) some institutionalized form of ASC could be identified in a large majority of all the societies sampled. Institutionalization implies a religious, medical, or other social function and presupposes certain specified conditions and persons (e.g., medicine men or shamans).

An important question concerning ASC is whether there are differences in incidence and in the type of ASC found in a society that can be explained in terms of cultural variables. Bourguignon (1976, 1979) attaches importance to a distinction between trance or visionary trance and possession trance. A person in trance may be experiencing hallucinations. Quite often these take the form of an interaction with spirits, whereby the spirit or soul of the person in trance may even have left the body and gone somewhere else. The experience must be remembered in order to pass it on to others (for example, clients seeking advice from the spirits), or to use it for curing purposes.

The possessed becomes another being, namely the spirit that has taken over the body. The possessed often will not remember what happened during the episode of possession; others will have to be present to hear what the spirits are communicating. Bourguignon sees trance as an experience and possession as a performance that requires an audience. Possession is usually brought on by drumming and dancing, trance by fasting, sensory deprivation, and drugs.

Bourguignon has found certain regularities between the type of ASC, i.e., trance or trance possession, and cultural variables. Although there are many exceptions, trance is more typical of men, possession of women. Among hunter-gatherers trance is more common; in more complex societies possession is the more frequently occurring form. There are also differences between major cultural regions. Among the original inhabitants of America the use of psychoactive plants leading to trance was widely practiced. In Africa possession is more frequent. A number of explanations have been suggested for these variations. For example, the inferior position of women among agriculturalists has been mentioned as a possible cause for the higher frequency of possession trance. ASC would then be used for self-serving purposes, making the spirits express the wishes of the possessed. The manipulation of social control and political power by shamans and priests has been mentioned by several authors (e.g., Dobkin de Rios, 1989).

The effect of cultural variables has also been discussed by Wallace (1959). There are quite remarkable differences between North American Indians using peyote for religious rituals and European Americans. The Indians reported feelings of reverence and relief from physical ailments. In the European Americans the drug had a wide range of effects on mood, from agitated depression to euphoria. They showed a breakdown in social inhibitions, a shift in behavior not observed in the Indians. The changes in perception were threatening to the European American subjects who had all manner of experiences. The Indians reported visions that were in accordance with their religious beliefs and fitted their expectations about what would happen. Apparently, cultural expectations and knowledge are important determinants of subjective (experiential) and objective (observable) aspects of behavior (cf. also Ludwig, 1969; Peters & Price-Williams, 1983).

There has been a tendency to argue that the varied ASCs described in the literature are expressions of the same underlying processes. This point has been made by Peters and Price-Williams (1983) from a phenomenological perspective. In their opinion a search for meaning and insight is fundamental to all the different cultural manifestations of ASC. A somatic basis for the unity of altered states exists according to some authors in a common neurophysiological state characterized by parasympathetic dominance in the EEG (e.g., Mandell, 1980;

## Box 4.2 Some illustrations of ASC

The following example of possession has been taken from observations made by Figge (1973, pp. 29–30) among the Umbanda, a religious group in Brazil. After initial preparations such as singing and praying the mediums start dancing accompanied by drums and clapping. Spirits are invoked to "incorporate." After a while it is usually the leader of the cult group who starts writhing his upper body,

the singing becomes more intense, bystanders call greetings. When the movements stop there stands for all the believers on the place of the person an "incorporated spirit." He looks around with bloodshot eyes, greets sacred spots in the room and seniors of the group with shouts and gestures.

Ornaments which belong to the spirit are handed to him and he reinforces his presence by making his mark with chalk on the floor. Usually other mediums follow and also fall into trance. "They stand around mumbling or walk shakily up and down with small steps as animals in cages." Helpers and mediums who are not possessed receive blessings and instructions. They also can give assistance when the spirit moves out and the body of the medium is in danger of falling. "During the sessions that can last up to about 6 hours many of the mediums incorporate several of their spirits; others do not at all become possessed." Onlookers are usually present because they want to approach the spirits, to receive magical treatment, medical herbs, etc.

During the session, spirits disappear on their own, or are demanded to do so in appropriate songs. A similar intermediate condition occurs as at the beginning of the "possession" and the mediums come to themselves. Usually they have recovered so far after a few minutes that they can take their place among the other mediums, without receiving further attention. As a rule the "head spirit" of the occasion is the last to go. The session is closed with prayers.

As an illustration of trance we can refer to our own observations in 1966 among a band of Bushmen in the Ghanzi area of Botswana. Trance is rather common among Bushmen men (Lee & DeVore, 1976). The main means of induction is intensive dancing for a long period of time. The women and children sit around a small fire singing and clapping. The men are moving around this circle with rhythmic, staccato (abrupt) movements. The onset of trance is gradual; the dancing of the trancer becomes irregular and he may be moving out of the circle of dancing men. The trance session which usually takes place during a night with full moon and is arranged in advance, has a medical purpose. The person in trance who is profusely sweating and makes an uncoordinated impression strokes and rubs the ailing part of a patient's body, moving away from time to time grunting and shaking his hands (probably to throw away the agent of the illness). Because of the lack of coordination the trancer can fall down, even into the fire. There is no reflexlike withdrawal and unless others help him very quickly the trancer can suffer severe burning. The day after the event the trancer is tired and worn out.

Winkelman, 1986). As long as there is a good deal of uncertainty on the encephalic origin of EEG wave patterns precise psychophysiological theories can only be tentative.

## Conclusions

There are many traditions in cross-cultural psychology emphasizing personality differences that should be consistent over a wide range of situations. In the first part of this chapter we have reviewed relevant evidence. The similarities in basic trait dimensions, however defined, provide a common psychological basis that underlies differences in overt culture-characteristic behavior patterns of individuals.

In the second part of the chapter we have presented the work of authors who argue that there are essential differences in personality make-up across cultures, or even that what is called personality in Western psychology in essence is a cultural characteristic. Also a few conceptions of personality and personality traits originating from non-Western traditions have been discussed.

In the final section we have drawn attention to ASC, which by and large have negative mental health connotations within industrialized countries, but are often institutionalized in the religious and social practices within more traditional societies.

### Key terms

altered states of consciousness (ASC)    indigenous personality concepts
"big five" dimensions                    locus of control
equivalence                              neuroticism
extraversion                             personality traits
independent self and interdependent self  temperament

### Further reading

Church, A. T. (Ed.) (2001). Special issue on personality and culture. *Journal of Personality*, 69, 787–1060.
Church, A. T., & Lonner, W. J. (Eds.) (1998). Personality and its measurement in cross-cultural perspective. *Journal of Cross-Cultural Psychology*, 29, 5–270.
McCrae, R. R. (Ed.) (2000). Personality traits and culture: New perspectives on some classical issues. *American Behavioral Scientist*, 44, 7–157.

The further readings that we suggest for this chapter are three collections of articles that together provide a broad overview of cross-cultural studies of personality.

# 5   Cognition

In this chapter, we shift our focus from those domains of behavior that are primarily social to those that are cognitive. We present four perspectives on cognition, beginning with a set of conceptualizations that involve a unitary view of cognition. This is captured in the notion of general intelligence. We deal with various aspects, including the use of tests to assess cognitive abilities across cultural groups. The next section briefly reviews the position of Piaget, called genetic epistemology, in which different cognitive structures are distinguished but differentiated by age rather than culture. In the third section we present cognitive styles, which are fairly general tendencies to think about how to deal with the world, but are tuned to the cognitive demands of the environment. The fourth conceptualization is referred to as contextualized cognition; in these approaches cognitions are seen as task specific and embedded in sociocultural contexts (e.g., the study of specific abilities demonstrated in carrying out specific tasks).

Cognition is an area of cross-cultural research that has a history of strong controversies. Differences between cultural groups in average levels of performance on cognitive tests have been interpreted in dramatically different ways. There are authors who see such differences as a more or less direct reflection of variation in inborn competencies. At the group level such interpretations tend to invoke the notion of "race"; differences in performance as assessed by intelligence batteries (i.e., differences in IQ) are ascribed to "racial" differences in cognitive aptitude. However, it is a more common viewpoint that cognitive processes are embedded in culture. Cultural groups have different ability patterns, rooted in ecological demands as well as sociocultural patterns. From this perspective cross-cultural differences in the organization of cognitive activities, and hence qualitatively different intelligences, are anticipated. The question of how large differences in intelligence are does not even make sense any more, once it is accepted that cognition is a culture-specific domain of psychological functioning.

In view of these controversies it may be important that we outline briefly our own viewpoint in advance. There are two major themes. First, we continue the universalist approach, seeking cognitive variations that are associated with specific cultural practices, while also seeking underlying similarities that are rooted in pan-human cognitive processes. This approach requires us to consider a very wide range of studies, from those that are absolutist (viewing cognitive abilities and processes as essentially untouched by culture) to those that are relativist (viewing cognitive life as locally defined and constructed, and postulating the existence of cognitive activity that is unique to a particular culture). The universalist perspective, once again, takes up the middle ground: we consider that basic cognitive processes are shared, species-wide, features of all people, everywhere. Culture influences the development, content, and use of these processes, but does not alter them in a fundamental way.

Second, we continue to provide data in support of the argument that human behavior in general is adaptive to context, using the ecocultural framework. This position with respect to cognition has been expressed in "the law of cultural differentiation" (Irvine & Berry, 1988), and was first articulated by Ferguson (1956): "cultural factors prescribe what shall be learned and at what age; consequently different cultural environments lead to the development of different patterns of ability" (p. 121).

## General intelligence

In this first section we look at traditions of thinking and research that in one way or another take a unitary view of cognitive functioning and see general intelligence as a coherent characteristic of an individual person.

### The notion of *g*

In contrast to notions about cognition that we shall discuss later in this chapter, **general intelligence** is largely based on psychometric evidence, particularly the consistent finding of positive correlations between results obtained with tests for different cognitive abilities. Spearman (1927) explained this phenomenon by postulating a general intelligence factor, which he referred to as *g* and which represents what all (valid) cognitive tests assess in common. He saw g very much as an inborn capacity. Other researchers, like Thurstone (1938), found specific, uncorrelated factors, which were seen as incompatible with the notion of a general intelligence factor. However, it can be argued that this difference is a matter of the factor-analytic techniques applied to the data (e.g., Gustafsson, 1984). A way to organize the enormous amount of available information has been presented by Carroll (1993). On the basis of 460 data sets obtained between 1927 and 1987 he proposed a hierarchical model with three strata. Stratum I includes narrow, specific abilities; stratum II includes group factors that are common to subsets of tests; and stratum III consists of a single general intelligence factor. Thus, psychometrically the notion of $g$ or general intelligence does appear to make sense.

The extent to which a test measures $g$ is usually represented by its loading on the first principal component or factor of the intertest correlation matrix. This loading has been found to increase as a function of the complexity of tests, with tests of abstract thinking having highest $g$ loadings. Spearman (1927) had already observed that tests with a higher $g$ loading tended to reveal larger performance differences between groups. Elaborating on these observations, Jensen (1985) formulated "Spearman's hypothesis," which predicts larger performance differences between "racial groups"[1] in the USA on tests with a higher $g$-loading (i.e., tests which presumably form purer measures of intellectual capacity). Most empirical studies on this hypothesis have been carried out in the USA with persons designated, respectively, as African Americans and European Americans. Jensen (1985, 1998) found a substantial relationship between $g$-loadings of tests and average differences in scores between these two conventional categories. On tests of abstract thinking the mean score difference is in the order of one standard deviation. Jensen interprets this as evidence for clear differences in the intellectual capacity of the two groups. Because these differences often have been interpreted as racial, the psychometric approach to cognitive competence has become controversial (e.g., Neisser et al., 1996; Sternberg & Grigorenko, 1997a).

Empirical evidence from the USA points to an interpretation that challenges Jensen's (1985, 1998). For example, when Humphreys (1985) analyzed data from the Project Talent Data Bank with more than 100,000 test takers on a large set of cognitive tests, he found that loadings of $g$ correlated .17 with "race" and .86 with socioeconomic status differences. Scores were analyzed for participants of low and high socioeconomic status and for African Americans and European Americans separately. Performance differences were attributed to adverse environmental factors (low socioeconomic status [SES]) which affect all individuals to the same extent, irrespective of "race."

To examine the controversy on group differences on $g$ in the light of cross-cultural evidence, we first have to establish what, from the psychometric perspective, actually is measured cross-culturally by intelligence tests. Vernon (1969) proposed a hierarchical model that incorporates $g$ and other named factors at varying levels of increased specificity. In his empirical examinations he claimed to find support for this model. Irvine (1979), in a comprehensive overview of early cross-cultural studies, including many conducted in Africa, also found evidence for $g$ as well as for more specialized factors, such as reasoning, verbal,

---

[1] The term "racial" is placed in quotation marks, because of the highly problematic nature of categorizations of human groups in such terms (see discussion in ch. 10).

figural, mathematical, and conceptual reasoning. These analyses fit the distinctions of Carroll (1993). All in all, this evidence suggests that intelligence tests show similar structures in Western and non-Western countries. In the course of this chapter we shall come across other evidence that is in agreement with this interpretation.

The next question is whether the differences in levels of scores indeed reflect differences in some inborn capacity. To identify what basic underlying feature of an individual's cognitive life is responsible for the communality reflected by $g$, Vernon (1979) called upon Hebb's (1949) distinction between "intelligence A" and "intelligence B": the former is the genetic equipment and potentiality of the individual, while the latter is the result of its development through interaction with one's cultural environment (cf. the genotype–phenotype distinction in genetics, see ch. 10).

However, Vernon went further, introducing the notion of "intelligence C" to refer to the performance of an individual on an intelligence test. This distinction between intelligence B and C allows another role for culture, since the developed intelligence (B) may or may not be properly sampled or assessed by the test, yielding a performance (C) that may not represent adequately even the phenotype. In the previous chapter we have referred to unwanted sources of variance, leading to inequivalence of test scores, as cultural bias. Numerous cultural factors (such as language, item content, motivation, and speed) may contribute to bias. Thus, testers merely obtain data that speak directly to "intelligence C." Only by drawing inferences from data can researchers say something about "intelligence B." It should be clear that biased tests and observations will lead to wrong interpretations. This holds even more when inferences are extended to the remote concept of "intelligence A."

One difficulty is that psychometricians often have taken a rather narrow view of the equivalence of cognitive tests. Analyses of cultural bias have been mainly directed at item bias (Berk, 1982; Holland & Wainer, 1993). As we shall see in ch. 11, with these procedures each item is examined to see whether test takers with the same test score have an equal probability of solving the item correctly. Items that are relatively more difficult for one group than for another group can be identified in this way. Evidence points to limited effects of item bias (Jensen, 1980). However, the items of a test are only compared with each other in analyses of item bias. Unfortunately studies are largely absent in which a broader perspective on equivalence is taken, also recognizing the need for analyses directed at other forms of inequivalence. Particularly, forms of analysis are needed that can help to identify sources of bias that affect all or most of the items of a test to a similar extent (Van de Vijver & Leung, 1997b; see ch. 11).

More or less the same limitations apply to analyses in the USA that have been directed at the "fairness" of tests for different groups. Fairness is evaluated in terms of some standard or criterion predicted by a test and shared by various groups (e.g., success at school or in employment). A test is fair if test takers with identical criterion scores also had identical test scores. However, criteria of fairness tend to share many cultural characteristics with intelligence tests; notably they both presume knowledge and verbal skills learned at (a good) school. This is why psychometricians like Messick (1995) have been pleading for a much broader definition for the validity of tests, including societal consequences as well as psychometric aspects.

## Psychometric evidence beyond *g*

There are other ways of looking at the antecedents of cross-cultural differences in scores on cognitive tests than in terms of g. Flynn (1987, 1999) collected archival data on intelligence test scores from fourteen (mainly Western) countries. Some data sets were from military draft registrants and were based on the same test that had been administered for many years. Other data sets came from standardization samples to (re)norm a test. The military data included virtually all young men in a country, since entire age cohorts were examined for fitness to do military service. Increases in IQ over time were found in all countries, with a median value of 15 IQ points (or 1 standard deviation) in a single generation (since 1950). Flynn (1987) suggested that IQ tests do not measure intelligence as a general capacity, but have only a weak link to it. Most likely unidentified factors that have to do with education play a role. Flynn's results are informative for cross-cultural research because they show that average performance on IQ tests in a population is far from stable and can change fairly dramatically in a relatively short time.

Another example is a study by Van de Vijver (in press) on inductive reasoning in Zambia, Turkey, and the Netherlands (including native Dutch and Turkish migrant samples) with children in the last two grades of primary school and the first two grades of secondary school. Van de Vijver administered multiple choice tests to assess inductive reasoning as well as tests that assessed different components of inductive reasoning, namely classification, rule generation, and rule testing (cf. Sternberg, 1977). Moreover, he used two kinds of tasks, one based on letters, the other figural. In the construction of the tasks a facet design was used (Cantor, 1985), allowing systematic combinations of elements that increased or decreased the difficulty of items. Facets for the letter tasks included, for example, the presence (versus absence) of vowels, identical letters, and sequential position in the alphabet. With techniques for item analysis and multivariate analysis Van de Vijver found that all facets played a role everywhere and that they contributed to a similar extent to the difficulty of the tasks in each of the cultural samples. For the eight tests it was also established that the components contributed to the task difficulty in a more or less similar fashion. Van de Vijver concluded that the findings supported the structural equivalence (cf. chs. 4 and 11) of the tests. This implies that inductive reasoning and its various component processes are shared among the cultural populations concerned. Further analyses showed that quantitative differences in mean score levels could not be interpreted at face value (statistical conditions for measurement of unit equivalence, one of three conditions of equivalence defined in ch. 4, were not fully met). Van de Vijver concluded that the strong findings on structural equivalence made it realistic to assume that inductive reasoning is an aspect of cognition with largely identical components in schooled populations, at least by the end of primary school.

A view on the nature of group differences in test performance can also be obtained from comparative studies across a wider range of cultural populations. In a meta-analysis of studies of cognitive test performance Van de Vijver (1997) collected and analyzed 197 separate studies that used a variety of cognitive ability tests (mainly those that purported to measure general intelligence). One question explored was the relationship between education and performance, using an index (called affluence) based on educational expenditure (money spent per capita per year) and the GNP of a country. He found a positive relationship of affluence with performance differences of cultural groups, and also with the number of years of schooling. Van de Vijver concluded that "national differences in affluence are related to differences in mental test performance because they are a proxy for educational differences and (somewhat fortuitously) identify sources of bias in the measures " (p. 697). Thus the relationship between cognitive test performance and schooling may have two bases: performance may actually be enhanced by educational experience; and the relationship may be an artifact of the test content, being similar to school materials. This conclusion is in agreement with other findings on the relationship between schooling and cognitive test performance discussed in Segall et al. (1999).

Cultural variation has been studied in international cross-cultural comparisons of intelligence as well as in intranational (cross-ethnocultural group) comparisons. This distinction was made by Van de Vijver in his meta-analysis, allowing him to observe differences in results between these two different types of culture-comparative studies. For example, effect sizes (the magnitude of group differences) were greater for international than for intranational studies, possibly due to acculturation effects of living together in a common society, with a more or less common schooling system. Moreover, characteristics of the tests (e.g., Western versus local tests, complexity of the stimulus materials, and of the required response) were more powerful predictors of differences in intranational studies, while ecocultural characteristics of the groups (affluence) were more predictive of international test performance differences. He concluded that "even cognitively simple tasks have characteristics that give rise to cross-national performance differences. It could be speculated that these include familiarity with stimuli, response procedures and testing situations in general" (p. 697). Further support for an interpretation in terms of cultural bias derives from his finding that Western tasks revealed larger cross-cultural differences than locally developed non-Western tasks.

The findings by Van de Vijver (1997) support another basic objection against "racial" interpretations. Group differences in inborn capacities can only be inferred if the quality of the environment, insofar as it is conducive to intellectual development, has been similar. As we shall see in ch. 10, it is widely accepted that individual differences in general intelligence and cognitive abilities have to do with genetic factors (Ceci & Williams, 1999; Sternberg & Grigorenko, 1997a). But this is very different from claiming that group differences are due (at least in part) to "race." Leading behavior geneticists like Plomin and De Fries (1998, p. 69) have emphasized this: "We cannot emphasize too much that genetic effects do not imply genetic determinism, nor do they constrain environmental interventions." Cognitive developmental processes are likely to reflect interactions between organism and environment, making inferences about the initial state of one of the components rather speculative (cf. ch. 2). It is difficult to maintain that the social economic conditions of African Americans in the USA are not disadvantageous compared to those of European Americans. One book that took a different view and led to some furore in the USA is discussed in box 5-1.

## Box 5.1 The Bell Curve

This is the main title of a book by Herrnstein and Murray (1994) on the distribution of intelligence in the total population of the USA. The subtitle is "Intelligence and class structure in American life." The basic tenet of the argument by Herrnstein and Murray is that in contemporary American society IQ is the main factor required for success in life; it is thus very important where you find yourself in the bell-shaped population distribution on intelligence. Based on their IQ scores disproportionally many members of some groups, notably African Americans, are at the lower end of the bell curve. Because of the unchangeable character of intelligence Herrnstein and Murray argue that intervention is not going to make much difference and that large intervention programs are therefore not a sound social investment.

Apart from other criticisms (e.g., Fraser, 1995) this position is incompatible with much of the cross-cultural evidence reviewed in this section on at least three counts:

1 In *The Bell Curve* IQ mistakenly refers to a general capacity, "a measure of a person's capacity for complex mental work" (p. 4). Moreover, IQ is "substantially heritable" (pp. 10, 23), it is "stable across much of a person's life" (p. 23), and IQ tests are not "demonstrably biased" (p. 23). From the perspective outlined in the present book "intelligence C" is misrepresented as "intelligence A" (see discussion on Vernon, 1979), the view on bias is narrow and does not take into account a broader cross-cultural view (see discussion of Van de Vijver and Leung, 1997), and the assumption of the constancy of group differences is indefensible (see the discussion of Flynn, 1987).

2 The effectiveness of intervention programs is dismissed. This point is supported by Herrnstein and Murray mainly with data from the famous Head Start program for which great success at the cost of limited effort was claimed initially, but disappointing results were obtained later. From the intervention literature we know that the amount of effort has to be commensurate to the amount of change in behavior that one desires, and that

## Box 5.1  (continued)

programs have to be directed at the context as well as at the individual if success is to be achieved (Eldering & Leseman, 1999; Kagitcibasi, 1996). Once a child has fallen behind, it requires much effort to compensate.

3   In their distinctions between groups Herrnstein and Murray refer to "race"; they presume breeding populations (cf. ch. 10) that are different in intellectual endowment. However, "black" and "white" are rather arbitrarily categorized in the USA, because of the non-dichotomous, clinal, phenotypical traits (e.g., skin color) not to mention the extensive mixing of various populations. And ethnicity is heavily confounded with the educational and economic variables (the myth of equal opportunity). Moreover, the cognitive capacities on which African Americans and European Americans supposedly differ are of such a recent origin (think of the "underdevelopment" in medieval times in Europe, often referred to as the "dark ages") that genetic change cannot be the explanation. The social connotations of ethnicity are linked to inborn capacities without adequate evidence. For example, controlling for IQ diminishes black–white differences in unemployment (p. 328). However, controlling for IQ does not mean controlling for "intelligence A" (see above). Similar arguments pertain to the relationship between IQ and other social factors (pp. 319–31). One example is the observed relationship between IQ and the probability of unmarried motherhood (found more frequently with African Americans). The relationship is valid, but any inference to intelligence made by Herrnstein and Murray is unsubstantiated. There was an increase of unmarried mothers between the 1960s and 1990s in all groups in the USA; does this mean that the intelligence in all groups has actually gone down in that period?

In short, there are relationships between IQ and all kinds of economic and social factors. The causal direction of such relationships is often unclear.

## Problems in ability testing

In an article with the expressive title "You can't take it with you: Why ability assessments do not cross cultures" Greenfield (1997a) has argued that tests presuppose all kinds of conventions and values that are shared by a test taker and the test administrator, but that are unlikely to apply in other societies. She rightly rejects culture-blind comparison of test scores, as if cognitive tests measured the same abilities and measured them on identical scales in all cultures, so that a given score had the same meaning everywhere (see ch. 11). While much ability testing across cultures has ignored these issues, and sometimes continues to do so, there are also cross-cultural studies that have taken them seriously.

The **transfer of tests** for use with another cultural population according to Poortinga and Van der Flier (1988) presupposes an answer to three questions. The first is whether the behavior domain (ability, trait) sampled by the items has at least approximately the same meaning; for example, there is no point in administering an arithmetic test requiring formal operations with digits to unschooled subjects. The second question is whether the ability or trait measured plays approximately the same role in the organization of behavior of members of the new culture as in the original culture. As we have seen earlier on in this chapter and in ch. 4, this can be investigated by psychometric analyses of structural equivalence. The third question is whether a score in a quantitative sense has the same meaning for test takers independent of their cultural background (full score equivalence, see ch. 4). Only if the latter is the case can the original norms be applied to all test takers. Unless the repertoire of behavior in the culture of origin and the target culture is very similar, new norms will certainly be needed. Otherwise the use of a foreign test with the original norms will lead to serious errors of interpretation; objections like those voiced by Greenfield (1997a) then certainly apply.

Cross-cultural ability testing usually implies one of the following: (1) an existing procedure is used for a different country than that for which it was originally designed; (2) test takers within a single country differ from each other in ethnic or cultural background, or (3) test takers currently living in different countries take part in the same assessment procedure. In all three situations there is transfer of tests across cultures. Major reasons for test administration include the assessment of individuals for educational or job selection, or for clinical diagnosis. Sometimes such test use can be competitive (e.g., in selection), but often this is not the case. It is clearly the responsibility of test users and test authors not to just assume but to demonstrate the "transferability" of tests (see also box 5.2).

Testing programs, notably for educational and personnel selection, have taken two forms: the transfer of existing (Western) tests with translation and adaptation of content insofar as this is needed, and the construction of new tests that are suitable for the target population. An example of the latter is the General Adaptability Battery (Biesheuvel, 1954) and its revision, the Classification Test Battery (Grant, 1970). These test batteries were designed for non-literate and semi-literate subjects. The instruction took place by means of a silent film. For many years they played an important role in the selection and placement of personnel in southern and eastern Africa. Examples of tests for educational selection can be found in the work of Drenth and colleagues (Bali, Drenth, Van der Flier, & Young, 1984; Drenth, Van der Flier, & Omari, 1983). The rationale for the use of these tests in East Africa and elsewhere was to provide information on a broader range of mental abilities than school achievement data, and to compensate for unevenness in school quality.

Transfer of existing tests, mostly originating from the USA or the UK, is very common. Important test batteries like the Wechsler Adult Intelligence Scales (WAIS) and Wechsler Intelligence Scales for Children (WISC) have been translated and adapted in numerous countries all over the world. Transfer can have important advantages. If a test can be demonstrated to be (approximately)

## Box 5.2 Standards for the translation and adaptation of tests

A set of guidelines for the translation and adaptation of tests has been developed by an international working group under the auspices of the International Test Commission (Hambleton, 1994; Van de Vijver & Hambleton, 1996). The twenty-two guidelines listed by Hambleton cover four domains:

1 Context, i.e., principles of multicultural and multilingual studies. An example is: "Effects of cultural differences which are not relevant or important to the main purposes of the study should be minimized to the extent possible."
2 Construction, i.e., good practices for developing tests. An example is "Instrument developers/publishers should insure that the translation/adaptation process takes full account of linguistic and cultural differences among the populations for whom the translated/adapted versions of the instrument are intended."
3 Test administration, i.e., issues of familiarity with item and response format and administration conditions. An example is "Instrument administration instructions should be in the source and target languages to minimize the influence of unwanted sources of variation across populations."
4 Documentation/score interpretation, of which an example is "Score differences among samples of populations administered the instrument should NOT be taken at face value [emphasis in the original]. The researcher has the responsibility to substantiate the differences with other empirical evidence."

structurally equivalent, it is a reasonable expectation that the findings on construct validity that have accumulated in the country of origin will also hold. Sometimes a test is merely translated with hardly any standardization, but on other occasions great effort is spent on adaptation, including the writing and trying out of new items, the construction of new norms, and the examination of validity (e.g., Vander Steene et al., 1986).

So far less effort tends to be spent on the standardization of tests for various groups in culturally diverse societies. Particularly in western European countries that have become multicultural in recent decades and face an urgent need for integration, there is now a realization that proper adaptation of tests is required (e.g., Bleichrodt & Van de Vijver, 2001). Another form of international testing mainly in the cognitive domain are large-scale comparative international projects on school achievement. Most comparisons derived from these projects deal with quality of school education, rather than level of intelligence of the pupils. In fact, they are only meaningful if it is assumed that pupils everywhere have a similar capacity to learn.

The use of tests across cultures still meets with suspicion, and not without reason. There is a long history of culture-comparative test use in which low scores were interpreted in terms of some deficit. On the other hand, one has to realize that assessments of persons are made anyway, with or without tests (APA, 1992). Psychometric tests offer the advantage that the assessment process, insofar as it makes use of tests administered under controlled conditions, is accessible for systematic analysis and scrutiny. Tests can be criticized precisely because (unlike interviews and other more subjective procedures) they form a public part of assessment.

## Other approaches to general intelligence

As we have seen, there is wide disagreement about the interpretation of cross-cultural differences in test scores among researchers with a psychometric orientation. Others who agree on the notion of intelligence as a useful summary label of the level of cognitive performance of individuals, go a step further and argue that intelligence as measured by (Western) tests provides a highly biased account of what it means to be intelligent in other societies. Often such arguments refer to unschooled populations. A review of local conceptualizations of intelligence, for example in various regions of Africa, can be found in Segall et al. (1999). Here we refer to some additional research.

In sharp contrast to the absolutist tradition of racial interpretations is one that is rooted in the perspective of indigenous cognition (Berry, Irvine, & Hunt, 1988), which assumes universal characteristics of cognitive functioning, but attempts to understand variations in the cognitive life of cultural groups from their own context. This approach owes much to the broad tradition of ethnoscience (see ch. 9). One study of how a particular cultural group defines intelligence is presented in box 5.3. It should be clear from this study that it would be very difficult to assess the Cree concept of intelligence with standard IQ tests, and that if Cree intelligence were measured with Cree tests, it would be difficult to make comparisons between it and the intelligence of other groups who did not share the Cree concept of intelligence.

The psychometric approach as a whole is rich in data and poor in theories. If test performances are generally related to each other (the basis of the IQ score), and if there is a unitary cognitive capacity that is considered to underlie these performances, what factors are usually identified by intelligence theorists as being responsible for this capacity? As we shall see later, for some the speed and efficiency of one's neural network is the key variable (Eysenck, 1988; Vernon, 1987). Others emphasize a range of cultural experiences, sometimes packaged as the concept of "cultural advantage–disadvantage."

McShane and Berry (1988) have critically reviewed a number of these deficit models of explanation for cultural differences in cognitive test performance. In addition to the genetic and physiological deficits proposed in the literature, they identified individual deprivation (poverty, poor nutrition, and health), cultural disorganization (a group-level version of deprivation, in which whole cultural groups experience the deculturation and marginalization that will be discussed in ch. 13),

## Box 5.3  Diverse conceptions of intelligence

Ethnoscience is concerned with people's conceptions and understanding of various phenomena; ethnopsychology is one branch, concerned with people's knowledge about human behavior; one specific domain is people's understanding of cognitive competence ("intelligence") in their culture (e.g., Stern, 1999). Studies of this domain have been reviewed by Berry (1984b) and by Ruzgis (1994), who concluded that there were many alternative views about human competence, often contrasting those views that were narrowly cognitive, with those that incorporated social and moral competencies.

One study was done by Berry and Bennett (1992) among the Cree people of Northern Canada. The community educational council had sought an answer to the questions: "Toward what goals should we be educating our children, and how can we achieve this?" They knew that the Eurocanadian educational system was not working well for them and wanted to consider a Cree alternative, aided by two researchers already working in their community.

In this study both ethnographic and psychometric procedures were used to uncover what the Cree understand by notions such as "intelligent," "smart," "clever," "able," and "competent." The first stage was to elicit Cree concepts for these and similar terms, and to seek both linguistic and contextual elaborations of them. They collected a list of twenty words dealing with cognitive competence through a series of very loosely structured interviews conducted with key informants in the Cree community of Big Trout Lake. This part of the research was broadly ethnographic.

The twenty words were written out in the Cree syllabic script on cards. The cards were given to sixty participants, all of whom were able to read syllabics. They were asked to put the cards into piles on the basis of similarity of meaning. Multidimensional scaling revealed two dimensions (see fig. 5.1). Reading from left to right (on the horizontal axis) there is a movement from negative to positive evaluation, with the possible inclusion of a moral dimension as well. That is to say, words on the left side of the figure are not only disliked (stupidity and craziness are not positively valued) but they are probably considered to be morally reprehensible as well (viz. "cunning" and "backwards knowledge").

The vertical dimension is more difficult to label. At one extreme are two words for "mentally tough" in the sense of brave, of having courage or fortitude. At the other extreme are "religious" and "understands new things." This dimension may have something to do with openness or sensitivity. The paucity of words in the lower half of the diagram makes it difficult to be more specific.

Looking further at fig. 5.1, there is a cluster of words on the right side and slightly above center (i.e. both sensitive and morally good) containing the words rendered in English as "wise," "respects," "respectful," "listens,"

**Box 5.3 (continued)**

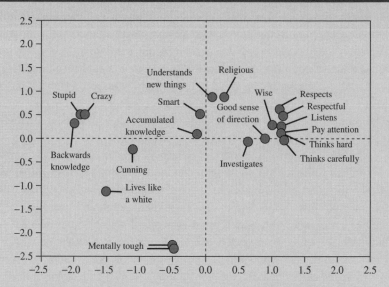

**5.1** Two dimensions of cognitive competence among the Cree
From Berry & Bennett, 1992

"pays attention," "thinks hard," and "thinks carefully." This cluster constitutes the core meaning of "thinking well" among the Cree.

It is interesting to note that the word most directly opposite the core cluster, the word which is therefore most distant from it on both dimensions (i.e. insensitive and morally bad) is rendered as "lives like a white," in the sense of behaving, thinking, and comporting oneself like a white person. It is tempting to regard this as something like the Cree version of being a "Klutz" (particularly since clumsy boorishness features in so many stories of white men in the bush), and has some quite derogatory overtones. Its very position on the diagram should alert us to look for meanings of negative moral content and insensitivity. Its closeness to words like "cunning," "stupid," "crazy," and "backwards knowledge" (wisdom turned to the service of disruption and disharmony) underlines this view. All of the words in this cluster need some elaboration as most have a distinctly Cree flavor and do not translate easily into English.

"Respect, respectful" – The idea of respect centers around knowledge of and personal engagement with people, animals, objects (both man-made and natural), the Creator, the land, and so on. Discussions of respect, and disrespect, invariably shade off into areas which English designates with words or phrases such as "understanding," "deep knowledge," "enjoyment," "enthusiasm," "self-control," and "following advice." Such respect for others in one's environment is a central value among many hunting and gathering peoples.

## Box 5.3 (continued)

"Paying attention" – The Cree term rendered as "pays attention" was just as often translated as "discipline" or "self-control." This notion of discipline lacks the European nuances of coercion, force, obligation, or social duty, all of which reflect the idea of power exercised between persons of unequal status. The Cree are not saying that individuals have a moral duty to listen to others and carry out what they say. They are telling us that listening to others is smart.

A study like this one leaves us with the question of how would it be possible to decide whether the Cree were more or less intelligent than some other cultural group (particularly urban, Western societies), when their vision of the competent person is so different. From the indigenous perspective, this question is quite absurd.

and disruption (or uprooting, leading to maladjustment and loss of coping skills). In contrast to these deficit explanations, a number of difference models were identified which do not share the negative value-laden character of the deficit models. Instead, it is assumed that processes and levels of competence are widely shared across cultural groups; performance differences arise because of cultural or other differences in the way these underlying qualities are expressed. This difference class of explanation is consistent with the universalist perspective.

## Information processing

Models of **information processing** are based on the idea that cognitive tasks can be decomposed into elementary information-processing components (Sternberg, 1969). Thus, tasks are described in terms of cognitive elements or steps that occur sequentially in problem solving. Such stages include an encoding phase, an inference phase, a mapping phase, and a response phase. With an increase in complexity of mental processes, more components are added and thus more time should be required to perform the task.

For reaction time tasks with a single stimulus, mean response times are about the same in unschooled as in literate populations (Jensen, 1982, 1985; Poortinga, 1971). This supports the notion that there is cross-cultural invariance of information processing at an elementary level. On slightly more complex tasks, namely choice reaction time tasks in which respondents have to indicate which one of a set of stimuli is presented, cross-cultural differences have been reported, for example in South Africa (Jensen, 1982, 1985; Poortinga, 1971; Verster, 1991). With increasing complexity these differences increase (e.g., Verster, 1991). Patterning of response times tends to be similar; with an increase in the number of stimuli in a set the reaction time increases as a logarithmic function of the number of stimuli in the set, a relationship known as Hick's law (1952). Training on a task will shorten the response time.

Reaction times for simple tasks have been found to be negatively correlated with IQ scores, although these correlations are not high. As tasks become more complex the correlations increase somewhat, up to values of −.30 or −.40 (e.g., Jensen, 1982). This makes it plausible that speed is a component of intelligence, and this idea has been incorporated in various theories (cf. Vernon, 1987). However, another factor that can explain such differences is prior exposure or experience (Poortinga, 1985a; Posner, 1978). Familiarity is not only important for the stimulus materials, but also for the response procedures. For example, Deregowski and Serpell (1971) asked schoolchildren from Scotland and Zambia to sort models, colored photographs, or black and white photographs of cars and animals. In the sorting of the models no differences were found between the groups, but the Zambian children were slower in the sorting of pictures.

The influence of stimulus familiarity on cross-cultural differences in reaction time tasks was tested explicitly in an experiment of Sonke, Poortinga, and De Kuijer (1999). Three visual tasks, consisting of simple geometric figures of varying cognitive complexity, were administered to Iranian and Dutch samples on three successive days. The influence of experience was investigated in two ways, by training one of the tasks and by administering an isomorphic task with easily distinguishable Arabic letters as stimuli, which were more familiar for the Iranian group. The patterns of results over tasks and over days were similar for the two groups, with the Dutch respondents reacting somewhat faster on all three tasks with geometric stimuli. For the Arabic letters the reverse was found; on this task the Iranian participants responded faster. The results are presented in fig. 5.2. The figure also shows that there was improvement with practice, but that an asymptotic value was reached for none of the tasks. This study clearly demonstrates the

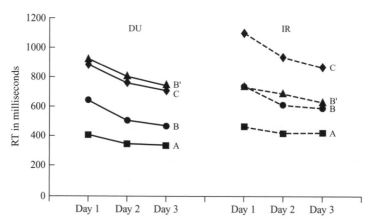

**5.2** Reaction time tasks (in milliseconds) for Iranians (IR) and
Dutch (DU) respondents on four tasks during three days

A: choice RT task with three black and one white (target) square.

B: four target figures had to be memorized from a set of sixteen; in each trial a
target was presented among three non-targets.

B′: identical to task B, but with Arabic letters instead of geometric figures.

C: the one given figure out of four had to be chosen that was complementary in
terms of black and white surface to a given standard.

From Sonke, Poortinga, & De Kuijer, 1999

similarity of cognitive processing, at least for simple tasks. Perhaps more important, it shows how difficult it is to make cross-cultural comparisons in terms of score levels, because even on tasks with a low level of stimulus complexity performance across cultures can be affected by differences in stimulus familiarity.

## Cultural factors in memory

Cross-cultural research on memory has been reviewed by Wagner (1981, 1993). Following common models he made a distinction between two major aspects, structural features and control processes. The structural features include a short-term memory store, and a long-term store. The former has a limited capacity for information, while the capacity of the latter is virtually unlimited. Forgetting is a structural characteristic of memory, although rates of forgetting are much higher for the short-term than for the long-term store. Control processes are strategies that people employ in the acquisition of information (e.g., rehearsal, clustering of items that belong together) and in retrieval. In Western studies it is usually found that stimuli which somehow belong together are remembered in clusters. Also, stimuli at the beginning of a series are recalled better (primacy effect), because subjects apply rote learning during stimulus presentation. In addition, recall tends to be better for the last stimuli in a series, the so-called recency effect.

It appears that structural features of memory become fixed rather early in life. The increase in performance on both recall and recognition tasks which has been found between approximately four and fourteen years of age has to be attributed to the development of better control strategies.

According to Wagner structural features of memory do not appear to be much affected by cultural factors. The short-term storage capacity seems to have similar limits everywhere and forgetting rates also are relatively invariant. Control processes are more culture specific.

Empirical research on which these conclusions are based includes a number of studies by Cole and his associates (e.g., Cole, Gay, Glick, & Sharp, 1971; Cole & Scribner, 1974). In experiments on recall with series of words which were presented five times, Kpelle subjects showed a very low rate of improvement over successive presentations compared to subjects from the USA. The Kpelle did not seem to apply rote learning, demonstrated by the fact that the serial position of a word in a sequence of stimuli did not have a noticeable effect on the rate of recall. The results of the Kpelle also showed limited clustering in responses when stimuli with related meanings (for example, plate, calabash, pot, pan, and cup [cf.; Cole et al., 1971, p. 69]) were included in a series. In further experiments it was found that a few years of schooling did not have much effect, but that longer schooling did lead to an increase in performance. For illiterate subjects a higher rate of recall was observed when they could be brought to apply clustering to the task. This happened spontaneously when the recall task was embedded in a story.

In two experiments with various groups of subjects in Morocco the findings on the Kpelle were further extended by Wagner (1978a, 1978b). Wagner found that schooling, and to a lesser extent urbanization, led to better recall scores. The primacy effect, which suggests task rehearsal during the administration of the task, was evident for older schoolchildren.

In other research the effect of schooling on recall was confirmed. Jahoda (1981) derived stimuli from an indigenous game in Ghana that makes high demands on memory, rather than a type of task that is reminiscent of the school setting. He still found that schooled subjects obtained better scores. Rogoff and Waddell (1982) emphasized that the type of task is important. In their opinion Western (schooled) subjects perform better on isolated stimuli that are not organized in a meaningful context. In a small study where children had to place objects in a panoramic scene at the same location they had occupied previously, Mayan children from Guatemala did not obtain lower scores than children in the USA.

Memory has also been implicated in the explanation of the large differences in mathematical skills between, on the one hand, Chinese and Japanese, and on the other hand, US children, identified by Stevenson and his colleagues (e.g., Stigler & Perry, 1990; Stevenson, & Stigler, 1992). The greater amount of time spent on mathematics was likely to be the most important factor. Miller and Stigler (1987) suggested that the structure of number words in most Asian languages, such as "ten one" instead of eleven, makes counting easier. Stigler, Lee, and Stevenson (1986) also found that young Chinese children could recall a larger number of digits. The explanation is that there are differences in the time required to pronounce number words in the languages involved. Hoosain and Salili (1988) reported a faster articulation rate for digits in Chinese than in English, and an even slower rate in Welsh. Such differences have to do with the word length of number words. A clear relationship between the mean number of syllables per numeral on the one hand, and the speed at which digits can be read, as well as the number that can be remembered (digit span) on the other hand, has been found by Naveh-Benjamin and Ayres (1986) in a comparative study of English-, Spanish-, Hebrew-, and Arabic-speaking samples.

These findings can be explained by Baddeley's (1986) "articulatory loop hypothesis." This theory postulates a short-term memory storage capacity with a duration of maximally two seconds. Thereafter the memory trace needs to be refreshed. Memory span has been found to be larger for short than for long words. Moreover, fast readers, who can rehearse more words in a given time, also have a higher memory span. Thus, in terms of Baddeley's theory short numbers, like in Chinese, offer a mnemonic advantage.

Information processing models discussed in the previous subsection, and even more a precise theory like Baddeley's articulatory hypothesis, seem to offer starting points for precise explanations of cross-cultural performance differences in terms of concrete aspects of culture. In ch. 12 we will come back to this point when we discuss various levels of interpretation of cross-cultural differences.

## Genetic epistemology

Like the approach of general intelligence, the theoretical contribution of Jean Piaget, known as **genetic epistemology,** posits coherence among cognitive performances when various tasks are presented to an individual. However, in contrast to much work on general intelligence, four sequential stages are proposed (each with its own underlying cognitive structure) appearing one after the other as a child develops (Piaget, 1972). The first of these intelligencies (sensorimotor) has already been mentioned in ch. 2, and the cross-cultural evidence for the theory has been treated extensively by Segall et al. (1999). Hence, in this chapter we present only a brief summary of the basic ideas, followed by a consideration of later developments in the approach (called "neo-Piagetian").

In the course of ontogenetic development, a child is considered to pass through four stages in the fixed sequence: sensorimotor, pre-operational, concrete-operational, and formal-operational. At each stage, a "cognitive structure" appears, incorporating the previous structures. The two processes by which these changes take place are "assimilation" (the integration of new external elements), and "accommodation" (the adaptation of internal structures to external novelty).

In the sensorimotor stage (up to two years of age) the child deals with reality in basic ways through its sensory and motor activity. At the concrete-operational stage (starting in Western industrialized settings at around six or seven years and continuing until around puberty) the child is able to perform the well-known "conservation" tasks, implying the "reversibility" of thought. In between these two stages (two to six years) is the pre-operational stage, during which the child begins to organize its world of ideas. With the formal-operational stage (after puberty) comes the capacity to carry out hypothetico-deductive reasoning and scientific thinking. While the performance of various tasks within a stage is thought to be related to each other, there is, nevertheless, some temporal sequencing (called "horizontal decalages" by Piaget) of performances, with conservation of quantity usually appearing before weight, and weight before volume, for example.

With respect to factors that are antecedent to cognitive development, Piaget (1966/1974, 1972) proposed four categories. First, biological factors lie at the root of the maturation of the nervous system, and are unrelated (in Piaget's view) to social or cultural factors. Second are equilibration factors, involving the autoregulation that develops as the biological organism interacts with its physical environment; for Piaget, this factor also probably has little to do with one's social environment. Third are social factors that are common to all societies (cf. Aberle's "functional prerequisites of society" discussed in ch. 3). While these do involve the social environment, for Piaget they are not likely to be cross-culturally variable. Fourth are the cultural transmission factors that are highly variable across cultures, including education, customs, and institutions.

The cross-cultural enterprise in Piagetian research has been rich and controversial; it has also been reviewed repeatedly (see Dasen, 1972; Dasen & Heron,

1981; Segall et al. 1999). Our interest here will be mainly in the epistemological shifts that have occurred in cross-cultural Piagetian psychology. We will, in particular, point out some of the advantages that the so-called "neo-Piagetian" theories have over the more orthodox versions of Piaget's theory, when it comes to taking cultural diversity into account.

Despite its reference to a single theory, and most often to a set of more or less standardized tasks, Piagetian psychology grew from a homogeneous to a heterogeneous research venture. The "orthodox" tradition tended to follow an absolutist orientation, taking the sequence of stages and the definition of the end state of development as the same everywhere and paying little attention to the cultural validity of the assessment contexts. Piaget himself posited the invariance of the stages, even though he paid lip-service (Piaget, 1966/1974) to the need for empirical, cross-cultural tests. In his view any human environment provides the stimulation needed by the individual to move from one stage to the next. In orthodox Piagetian theory, no attempt is usually made to account for social or cultural differences. The theory deals with an "epistemic" subject that has no counterpart in a "real" child. The stages are defined by unitary structures that lead to the expectation of overarching "developmental levels," not unlike "general intelligence."

Such an absolutist Piagetian approach has been criticized repeatedly, notably because the interpretation of cultural differences in terms of a standard developmental sequence may easily lead to value judgments in terms of "retardation" or "deficit" against an ethnocentric, middle-class Western norm (Cole & Scribner, 1977). However, Dasen, Berry, and Witkin (1979) have argued that it is not necessary to link developmental sequences to value judgments if an ecocultural framework is used as a guiding paradigm, since each adaptive context sets its own standards for development.

Cross-cultural research using the ecocultural paradigm has led to the conclusion that ecological and cultural factors do not influence the sequence of stages, but that they do influence the rate at which they are attained. Cultural differences are expected to occur at the performance (surface) level for concepts that are culturally valued (i.e., are needed for adaptation in a particular ecocultural setting) and also at the competence (deep) level for concepts that are not valued. Research using training techniques (e.g., Dasen, Ngini, & Lavallée, 1979) has shown that the asymptote in the development curves (the apparent leveling off in the attainment for some concrete-operational concepts) is usually a performance phenomenon that disappears in many cases after repeated testing and after a small number of training sessions. In short, with Piagetian tasks, the inference from performance to competence is as difficult to ascertain as with other tests.

The link between the ecocultural contexts and the developmental (performance) outcomes is established using the concepts of enculturation and socialization practices during infancy and childhood. Dasen (1984) has paid some attention to the developmental niche of concrete operational thought. The relationships between operational development and locally valued aptitudes have been studied among the Baoulé of Côte d'Ivoire in terms of the parental ethnotheory of intelligence (Dasen et al., 1985), and Dasen (1988) has used behavior observations to document the relevant learning contexts. Other work along this paradigm is Saxe's (1981; Saxe & Moylan, 1982) research on the development of number and measurement concepts among the Oksapmin of Papua New Guinea, that integrates Piagetian theory with a local number system and counting practice using body parts (see ch. 9 for more details on such a system). Occasionally, an extreme culturally relativistic approach has been advocated for cross-cultural Piagetian research (e.g., Greenfield, 1976), but no convincing empirical work has been carried out using this approach. Furthermore, while cultural validation is obviously necessary, a totally relativist strategy precludes the search for commonality (cf. ch. 2). Cognitive development, according to the existing data, is neither exactly the same everywhere nor totally culture specific.

By the end of the 1970s, a revival of structuralist approaches had occurred, trying to integrate both structural and contextual aspects. The new models looked for structural invariants accounting for developmental changes, or for commonalities across situations, while insisting on the necessity to take situational variables into account. These so-called neo-Piagetian theories have been developed by a number of authors, including Case (1985, 1992; Case & Griffin, 1990), Demetriou (Demetriou, Shayer, & Efklides, 1992; Demetriou & Efklides 1994), Fischer (e.g., Fischer, Knight, & Van Parys, 1993), and Pascual-Leone (1980, 1984).

Neo-Piagetian models combine a Piagetian qualitative-structuralist framework (the existence of qualitatively different stages) with functional approaches; they draw heavily on Piaget's description of development, while refining it (by describing more stages and substages), but most of them reject the use of general logical structures such as those favored by Piaget. Some of the theories import contributions from information processing approaches, such as the necessity of task analyses and the concept of attentional capacity (or working memory). The latter plays an important role in most neo-Piagetian theories, and corresponds to the quantitative aspects of individual development. Attentional capacity refers to the number of units of information that a subject can process simultaneously. For Case (1985) this quantitative mechanism is seen as coexisting with qualitative changes, whereas for Pascual-Leone (1980), "M-power" (the chronological increment in the number of elements that can be integrated) is seen as sufficient to account for the qualitative changes. Dasen and de Ribaupierre (1987) have examined these neo-Piagetian theories in terms of their potential for taking cultural and individual differences into account, and have found them to be potentially more apt than Piaget's original theory to do this. They summarized the advantages under the following six points (p. 826):

1 The structural invariants that are defined are independent of Western logic.
2 Models can be applied to various domains, choosing culturally valued ones; these include social cognition, moral development, and emotions.

3 Therefore new, culturally appropriate tasks can be devised, or spontaneous behaviour can be observed in naturalistic settings.

4 The models link structural and functional aspects, and introduce a clearer distinction between deep and surface phenomena.

5 There is a convergence between the sociohistorical school (see ch. 2) and
genetic epistemology: social factors are acknowledged in the process of stage
transition.

6 They allow for domain specificity.

Dasen and de Ribaupierre (1987, p. 827) also noted that

> none of the neo-Piagetian models has as yet gone through a complete replica-
> tion in a non-western culture ... Cross-cultural psychology in its "theory-testing"
> role has an important contribution to make; however, it regularly lags behind
> mainstream "laboratory" psychology by some years. In the case of neo-Piagetian
> theories, this lag may have been increased by the jargon and technicalities of
> the models, and the difficulty of choosing among them."

Unfortunately, the same can be said today. Even smaller scale cross-cultural projects based on neo-Piagetian theories are few and far between (but see Fiati, 1992).
This is certainly an area of great potential for future cross-cultural research.

## Theories of mind and metacognition

As an outgrowth of genetic epistemology, the attention of many developmental psychologists, starting with Flavell (1974; Flavell, Zhang, Zou, Dong, & Qi,
1983) and together with primatologists (Premack & Woodruff, 1978), has turned
to the study of **theories of mind**, that is the tendency to impute mental states
to oneself and to others. One draws on theories of mind to understand other
people's behaviors and psychological states, and by projecting oneself on to
others. Although Semin and Zwier (1997) do not include the topic in their coverage of cross-cultural aspects of social cognition, theories of mind are akin to
attributional processes.

There are indications that, whereas chimpanzees have little mental insight
(Tomasello, 1999; Tomasello et al., 1993), the basic processes of theories of mind
are universal in human infants (see Lillard, 1998). Studies with young children give
mixed results. According to Flavell et al. (1983), Chinese children showed an ability to distinguish appearance and reality at about the same age as American children. However, Chen and Lin (1994) did not replicate the anticipated change
between three- and four-year-old Chinese children in Beijing. They attributed this
to Chinese child rearing practices "with their emphasis on morality and control,
external sanctions on action rather than on mentalistic analysis" (p. 43).

A majority of Baka pygmy children could understand false beliefs by age five
years, at about the same age as American and European children (Avis & Harris,
1991). In this study, they were invited to move some food from its container to a
hiding place in the absence of the adult preparing the food; they correctly predicted

that the adult would approach the original but now empty container, would feel happy rather than sad before lifting its cover, and surprised and sad rather than happy after discovering the disappearance of the food. However, some of the six-year-old Baka children gave incorrect answers, and the authors were left to speculate about their understanding of the task.

Cultural differences in the rate of development of theories of mind were reported by Wahi and Johri (1994), who tested Indian children in two groups, affluent and deprived, on mental–real distinctions (whether a real and a thought-about object could be seen). While most children made the distinction correctly by age seven to eight, the speed at which children in India did so was slower than that reported in the West, and there was a significant difference between rich and poor children at age five to six years.

Vinden (1996) used the standard "surprising objects" (e.g. a sponge that looks like a rock) and "deceptive container" (e.g. a matchbox full of pebbles) tasks with thirty-four Junín Quechua children living in a remote area of Peru, aged four to eight years. A majority of the children demonstrated an understanding of the appearance–reality distinction, but performed poorly on questions that tested their understanding of representational change ("Before you touched the object, what did you think it was?") and false belief ("If another child just looks at the object, what would he think it is?"). The author attributed this to the absence of explicit mental vocabulary in the Quechua language, and she left it open whether "the children have in fact developed a metarepresentational ability, but are unable to apply it to the domain of intentional behavior because their language contains so little of the language of thought" (p. 1715). In another study involving 143 Mofu children in Cameroon, 119 Tolai and 50 Tainae children of Papua New Guinea, and 45 Western children attending a school in that country, Vinden (1999) found that almost all children from non-Western cultures had difficulty predicting an emotion based on a false belief. In conclusion, the author states that

> in some cultures one simply may not discuss emotions, or emotions may be thought to arise from external sources. The kinds of questions asked in Western culture may therefore not be appropriate to explore the understanding of the relationship between false belief and emotion in other cultures. (p. 46)

It seems that the predominance of evidence has been shifting from presumed universality to cultural differences, whether only in rate of development (Wahi & Johri, 1994), or even in the type of thinking (Vinden, 1999). We clearly need more research in this area, but whether the basic processes turn out to be universal or not, there is the additional puzzle that, according to ethnographic records, adults' theories of mind, or what Lillard (1998) calls "ethnopsychologies," vary a great deal from culture to culture. Lillard summarizes "four basic types of variation in folk psychological thinking" (p. 23), namely (1) differential attraction to magic; (2) different conceptual distinctions regarding thoughts and feelings, sensory inputs, and the links between body and mind; (3) denying negative emotions; (4) different values regarding knowing minds, rational thought versus feelings, and science versus spirituality. As children become adults, they come to accept these different ethnopsychologies, yet little is known about the cognitive processes that this entails. In other words, there is a big gap between the psychological studies that attempt to assess specific thinking processes in children, and the ethnographic descriptions of ethnopsychologies such as those reviewed by Lillard, reminding us of the distinction between individual processes and collective representations pointed out by Harris and Heelas (1979).

Another area of research on cognitive development started by Flavell (1976), that has become important in recent years, particularly in educational psychology, is metacognition. It refers to "knowledge about, and awareness of, one's own capabilities and cognitive plans vis-à-vis the task" (Davidson & Freebody, 1988, p. 21). **Metacognition** includes knowledge of cognition, in which Schraw (1989) and Schraw and Moshmann (1995) distinguish between declarative knowledge (about oneself as a learner and the factors that influence one's performance), procedural knowledge (about the execution of skills) and conditional knowledge (about when and why to apply cognitive actions), and control processes such as planning, monitoring, and evaluation. These authors further distinguish three levels of representation:

1 cognitive level: tacit (without any explicit awareness), domain specific, with limited transfer;
2 metacognitive level: informal, fragmentary, some across-domain transfer;
3 conceptual level: formal (explicit and integrated) mental models and theories, broad transfer.

According to Schraw (1989), metacognition is acquired through autonomous learning, peer-regulated learning, and direct learning, the latter two mainly in schools, and "clearly, all three are necessary to develop Level 2 and Level 3 knowledge" (p. 100).

We could possibly draw an analogy between Schraw's third level and Piaget's formal operations, Western-type schooling at secondary level being necessary but not sufficient for their attainment (Dasen & Heron, 1981). Whether the metacognitive level is also dependent on schooling is still open to discussion, and to cross-cultural testing.

There certainly are metacognitive skills developed outside of school. Davidson and Freebody (1988), for example, argue that there are socioeconomic and ethnic differences in the metacognitive knowledge children bring to school (linked, for example, to the degree of reading in the home), and this is in turn linked to success in school. Australian Aboriginal teacher trainees were found to possess metacognitive knowledge about indigenous story telling, but this knowledge seemed to be situation specific, and difficult to transfer to school tasks.

Cultural differences in metacognition have been reported by Carr, Kurtz, Schneider, Turner, and Borkowski (1989) between German and American students, presumably in relation to different teaching styles both at home and in school. This and other cross-cultural studies, often related to reading and other school-related activities, are reviewed by Davidson (1994), who regrets that

> there is still a general lack of knowledge about the extent to which people engage in metacognitive thinking and the nature of that thinking in everyday-life settings and on everyday-life tasks, particularly if the cultural contexts of those settings and tasks are different from that of classrooms (p. 2)

In this respect, research on metacognition could link up with the topic of everyday cognition (Segall et al., 1999; Schliemann, Carraher, & Ceci, 1997), in which there is some cross-cultural information, for example on planning skills (Gauvain, 2001; Strohschneider & Güss, 1998; Tanon, 1994).

## Cognitive styles

In contrast to the general intelligence and genetic epistemology approaches, **cognitive styles** refer more to "how" (stylistic) rather than "how much" (ability) aspects of a person's cognitive life. The position taken in this section is that a middle ground has to be found between those who relate all cognitive performance to a single underlying trait ("general intelligence") and those who distinguish a myriad of task-specific skills that do not generalize to other tasks (see next section on contextualized cognition). Cognitive abilities and styles are then seen as ways for a cultural group and its members to deal effectively with problems encountered in daily living. Interest in cognitive styles has varied over the past few decades, but it has recently become the focus of more attention (Sternberg & Grigorenko, 1997b), because it provides an alternative way to view individual and group differences in cognitive activity. And, when combined with an ecocultural approach (as is often done in its cross-cultural use) a less controversial, more value neutral, position is facilitated (Witkin & Berry, 1975; Berry, 1976a, 2000b).

The cross-cultural approach to cognitive style begins with an attempt to understand how particular cognitive performances might be important in particular ecological and cultural contexts, drawing upon the proposal by Ferguson (1956), noted earlier, that different cultural environments lead to the development of different patterns of ability. In the cognitive-styles approaches, there is an interest in an "ecological analysis" (Berry, 1980a) of the demands of the situation, posing the two questions of what has to get done in order to survive (termed "ecological demands") and what the cultural practices are that lead to the development of the required cognitive performances (termed "cultural supports") (Berry, 1966). The cognitive styles approach searches for the patterns of cognitive activity, based on the universalist assumption that the underlying processes are common to all groups, but that their differential development and use will lead to different patterns of ability.

The most influential conceptualization of cognitive style has been that of Witkin (Witkin, Dyk, Paterson, Goodenough, & Karp, 1962) who developed the dimension of the field-dependent/field-independent (FDI) cognitive style. Witkin's starting point was a concern with perceptual and orientation abilities in air pilot trainees, but he soon noticed that a number of abilities were related to each other in a way that evidenced a "pattern" (in the Ferguson sense). However, the construct that best explained this pattern was far less comprehensive than that of general intelligence: it was the tendency to rely primarily on internal (as opposed to external) frames of reference when orienting oneself in space. Subsequent studies extended this pattern of co-variation to include cognitive and social behaviors. At one end of the FDI dimension are those (the relatively field independent) who rely on bodily cues within themselves, and are generally less oriented toward social engagement with others; at the other end are those (the relatively field dependent) who rely more on external visual cues, and are more socially oriented and competent; as for any psychological dimension, few individuals fall at the extreme ends, most fall in the broad middle range of the dimension.

The FDI cognitive style is referred to by Witkin, Goodenough, and Oltman (1979, p. 1138) as "extent of autonomous functioning." The notion of cognitive style itself refers to a self-consistent manner (or "style") of dealing with the environment. In the case of FDI the construct refers to the extent to which an individual typically relies upon or accepts the physical or social environment as given, in contrast to working on it, for example by analyzing or restructuring it. As the name suggests, those who tend to accept or rely upon the external environment are relatively more field dependent, while those who tend to work on it are relatively more field independent. The construct is a dimension, the poles of which are defined by the two terms; individuals have a characteristic "place" on this dimension, reflecting their usual degree of autonomy. However, individuals are not "fixed" into their usual place. Overall, the FDI cognitive style is a pervasive dimension of individual functioning, showing itself in the perceptual, intellectual, personality, and social domains, and it tends to be stable over time and across situations. It "involves individual differences in process rather than content variables; that is to say, it refers to individual differences in the 'how' rather than the 'what' of behavior."

Much of the cross-cultural use of the FDI construct has been carried out in relation to the ecocultural framework (fig. 1.1). Early studies (e.g., Berry, 1966; Dawson, 1967) employed a rudimentary version of the emerging framework (mainly the ecology and socialization components). Later studies (e.g., Berry, 1976a; Berry et al., 1986; Mishra, Sinha, & Berry, 1996) have used the full ecocultural framework. Work up until the mid-1970s has been reviewed by Witkin and Berry (1975), while later work has been reviewed by Berry (1991). Only a summary of the evidence can be provided here.

The ecocultural framework has some obvious relevance for the theory of psychological differentiation. This relationship between the framework and the

| Antecendent | Prediction of cognitive sytle | |
| variable | Field independence | Field dependence |
| --- | --- | --- |
| Subsistence pattern | Hunting, Gathering | Agriculture |
| Settlement pattern | Nomadic | Sedentary |
| Population density | Low | High |
| Family type | Nuclear | Extended |
| Social/political stratification | Loose | Tight |
| Socialization | Assertion | Compliance |
| Western education | High | Low |
| Wage employment | High | Low |

**5.3** Relationships between ecological, cultural, and acculturation
variables and cognitive style

theory is most succinctly presented in fig. 5-3, which illustrates the major
ecological, cultural, and acculturational variables, along with their expected
relationships with the FDI cognitive style.

It would be expected that nomadic hunters and gatherers, who are relatively
loose in social structure and who emphasize assertion in socialization, would be
likely to be relatively field independent; in contrast, sedentary agriculturalists,
who are tight in social structure and who emphasize compliance in socialization,
are likely to be relatively field dependent. Furthermore, those undergoing acculturation, particularly those with higher Western schooling, are likely to be more
field independent than those with less such experience.

In the literature reviewed by Witkin and Berry (1975), correlations were found
to be significant among tests representing the perceptual domain, but this was
not always the case, particularly in Africa. Less consistency appeared in the literature between the perceptual and other domains.

With respect to gender differences, there was a variable but interpretable
pattern. An early "anthropological veto" was provided by Berry (1966) and replicated by MacArthur (1967), demonstrating that the usually found gender difference (females relatively more field dependent than males) did not appear in a
variety of Inuit and North American Indian samples. This was interpreted as an
outcome of the relatively similar socialization and other ecological and cultural
experiences of boys and girls in these hunter-gatherer societies. In most such
societies a relatively field-independent cognitive style was judged to be highly
adaptive for both males and females in individual economic roles, in family life,
and in hunting and gathering activity more generally. In contrast, in tighter and
more structured societies (such as those found among agricultural peoples) the
usual gender differences were typically in evidence.

One of the clear theoretical points of contact between Witkin's theory and the
ecocultural framework is that the description of characteristic family and socialization practices (leading to variation in cognitive style development) matches the
descriptions of these practices as they vary across cultures from an emphasis on

assertion to one on compliance (Barry et al., 1959). The conclusion was drawn from a review of over a dozen studies within and across cultures that the socialization of cognitive style as proposed by the theory was generally supported.

Turning to other cultural factors, within which these family practices are set, Witkin and Berry (1975, p. 46) concluded that

> a relatively field-dependent cognitive style ... is likely to be prevalent in social settings characterized by insistence on adherence to authority both in society and in the family, by the use of strict or even harsh socialization practices to enforce this conformance, and by tight social organization. In contrast, a relatively field-independent cognitive style ... is likely to be prevalent in social settings which are more encouraging of autonomous functioning, which are more lenient in their child-rearing practices, and which are loose in their social organization.

Ecological factors, within which both cultural and family practices are set, focused on variations in cognitive style across groups that engage with their environment differentially (e.g., nomadic hunting and gathering societies, versus sedentary agricultural ones). This ecological perspective provided the broadest context for examining the origin of differences in cognitive style. Witkin and Berry (1975, pp. 61–2) concluded that "individuals from hunting-based samples tend to be more field-independent on tasks of perceptual differentiation, while those from agriculture-based samples tend to be relatively field-dependent. There may also be a congruent difference in degree of personal autonomy."

The last major section of their review was concerned with adaptation and change, particularly in relation to acculturation (contact with other societies, primarily through formal schooling and the experience of industrialization). Virtually all of the studies reviewed provided evidence for increased field independence with acculturation experience. However, it was unclear whether such experiences fundamentally alter the cognitive style of individuals, or whether they alter the approach to the test materials, through greater familiarity and practice in acquiring "test taking tricks." This finding is similar to that in the first two approaches to cognition: acculturation, particularly schooling, has a profound influence on a person's cognitive life.

Since 1975, cross-cultural empirical work has continued on the theory. By far the largest program of cross-cultural research was conducted by Durganand Sinha and his colleagues in India. Generally, Sinha adopted the ecocultural framework and sought out populations in India with whom he could test and extend predictions from the model. In a first study, Sinha (1979) worked with two subgroups of the Birhor, one of which remained nomadic hunter-gatherers, the other of which had made the transition to being sedentary agriculturalists. A third group, of longstanding agriculturalists (the Oraon), was also included. Predictions were that, with the expected variations in socialization practices (but no variation in acculturation), mean scores would vary according to ecological engagement. Samples of boys and girls of age eight to ten years from each of the three groups were administered an embedded figures task in which a simple figure had to be found in a complex background (i.e., by "disembedding"). Results showed a significant group effect, and Sinha interpreted this finding as support both for his hypothesis, and for the ecocultural framework.

More recently, three indigenous groups ("tribals" or *adivasi*) in the state of Bihar have been studied by Mishra et al. (1996). Two groups were selected to represent a contrast between a nomadic hunting-gathering group and a sedentary agricultural group, while a third group consisted of former hunters who had recently settled as agriculturalists. Using a variety of tests (both "cognitive style," such as embedded figures, and "cognitive ability," such as pictorial interpretation), predictions were made regarding group differences due to ecological and acculturation contexts. Overall, the expected differences were found: hunting peoples were relatively more field independent than the agricultural peoples, and those with high "contact acculturation" were so as well. Moreover, acculturation impacted ability test performance; for these ability tests, acculturative influences were stronger than those stemming from ecocultural context differences. However, the acculturation effects were not as important among the nomadic hunter-gatherer group.

A second program of research attempted to disentangle some of the hypothesized antecedents to cognitive-style development. Up until the 1980s most studies involving ecological contrasts compared the cognitive style of indigenous North American hunter-gatherers to that of African agriculturalists. Two replications were needed, one of agricultural North American Indians and one of hunting and gathering Africans. The first study (Lonner & Sharp, 1983) showed that indigenous agricultural peoples (Yucatecan Maya) tended to be field-dependent relative to the hunting and gathering peoples in the literature, thus providing one of the two critical test cases. The second was a study of cognitive style in Africa (Berry et al., 1986) comparing an African Pygmy hunter-gatherer sample (Biaka) with a sample of agriculturalist villagers (Bagandu) living in the same geographical region as the Biaka. The differences between the two groups were more limited than anticipated, perhaps because the Biaka are employed for a couple of months each year as agricultural laborers, while the villagers do some trapping and hunting. In other words, the contrasts between the two groups in their interactions with the ecological environment were not nearly as strong as the terms "hunter-gatherers" and "agriculturalists" implied. Some findings showed that there was a difference between the two cultural groups on an African embedded figures test, designed to fit the local context, but only when differences in acculturation were taken into account. This was taken as evidence for the joint importance of both variables, as predicted from the ecocultural framework.

Other cognitive styles have been proposed (e.g., Ji, Peng, & Nisbett, 2000), but few have been studied cross-culturally. One related approach to "ways of thinking" is presented in box 5.4.

Cross-cultural research on cognitive style has diminished in recent years, but it remains a viable alternative way of understanding how cognitive activity is related to ecocultural and acculturation contexts (Berry, 2000). It also serves as a useful way to conceptualize individual differences (Sternberg & Grigorenko, 1997b), particularly for those seeking a less quantitative, more qualitative, way of understanding both individual and group differences.

## Box 5.4 Two ways of thinking?

Research with respondents in which differences in performance are related to ways of thinking characteristic for various cultures has been reported by Peng and Nisbett (1999). They distinguish between differentiation in thinking (i.e., comparison of opposites and the selection of one as the correct position), and dialectical thinking (i.e., seeking reconciliation between opposites). In a series of experiments they found that Chinese students demonstrated relatively more preference for dialectical solutions when confronted with social conflict situations or logically contradictory information. American students were more inclined to polarize conflicting perspectives and to choose one alternative as correct. For example, Americans expressed somewhat less preference for dialectical proverbs in Yiddish, and gave higher plausibility ratings to their preferred alternative in the case of contradictory reports of research findings. In the latter case Chinese students were more inclined to give some credit to both reports.

Peng and Nisbett see their results as a reflection of two different cognitive traditions of East and West. Drawing on other sources of evidence, including ethnographic and philosophical work they extend their findings to differences in the history of science. They conclude "We believe that dialectical versus nondialectical reasoning will turn out to be only one of a set of interrelated cognitive differences between Asians and Westerners" (p. 750).

This conclusion has been challenged. Chan (2000, p. 1064) has argued that the distinctions between forms of thinking cannot be maintained in the light of the literature on formal logic. He states: "I am compelled to reject two key assertions made by Peng and Nisbett (1999): the first asserting that Chinese dialectical thinking and the laws of formal logic are incongruent, and the second asserting that there are two distinct arguments (logical vs 'dialectical')." Ho (2000) asserted that in addition the interpretation of the empirical results can be questioned. In his opinion it might be better to see as "conciliatory" the reactions that Peng and Nisbett called "dialectical." Thus Ho suggests an interpretation of the differences in terms of social factors rather than cognitive processes. Moreover, we would like to point out that there was considerable overlap in the distributions of responses of American and Chinese students, suggesting that many Chinese students have answered in the "American" way and many American students in the "Chinese" way.

## Contextualized cognition

In contrast to the first two approaches, others (notably cultural psychologists, such as Michael Cole and his colleagues) have criticized grand theories that attempt to link all cognitive performances together with a presumed underlying general cognitive processor. Instead, in a series of monographs (Cole, 1975, 1992a, 1992b, 1996; Cole et al., 1971; LCHC, 1982, 1983; Scribner & Cole, 1981), they outlined a theory and methodology that attempted to account for specific cognitive performances in terms of particular features of the cultural context, and the use of specific cognitive operations; hence the name of **contextualized cognition**. Much of this work has been stimulated by the sociocultural or sociohistorical tradition (Cole, 1988; Vygotsky, 1978; Luria, 1974), and has links with research on "everyday cognition" (Schliemann et al., 1997).

In their 1971 monograph, Cole and his colleagues proposed that "people will be good at doing the things that are important to them, and that they have occasion to do often" (p. xi), and concluded their volume with the proposition that "cultural differences in cognition reside more in the situations to which particular cognitive processes are applied, than in the existence of a process in one cultural group and its absence in another" (p. 233). Their context-specific approach is characterized as a "formulation that retains the basic eco-cultural framework, but rejects the central processor assumption as the organizing metaphor for culture's effect on cognition" (LCHC, 1982, p. 674).

> Instead of the universal laws of mind that control development "from above," the context-specific approach seeks to understand how cognitive achievements, which are initially context-specific, come to exert more general control over people's behavior as they grow older. The context-specific approach to culture and cognitive development takes "development within domains of activity" as its starting point; it looks for processes operating in the interactions between people within a particular setting as the proximal cause of the increasingly general cognitive competence. (LCHC, 1983, p. 299)

To substantiate their approach, Cole and his colleagues have produced a large volume of empirical studies and literature reviews (see Cole, 1992a, 1992b, 1996). Their early studies (e.g., Cole et al., 1971), were carried out among Kpelle schoolchildren and adults in Liberia, and American subjects in the USA in a set of projects concerned with mathematics learning, quantitative behavior, and some more complex cognitive activities (classification, memory, and logical thinking). Their general conclusion from these, and many similar studies, is that much Kpelle cognitive behavior is "context-bound," and that it is not possible to generalize cognitive performances produced in one context to other contexts. In later writings (LCHC, 1982, 1983), they claim support for their position by critically reviewing the work of other researchers in such areas as infant development, perceptual skills, communication, classification, and memory. More recently, Cole (1992a, 1992b, 1996) has emphasized the concept of "modularity," which refers to the domain-specific nature of psychological processes as they have developed in the course of human phylogenetic history (Fodor, 1983).

In Cole's theory of cultural-historical psychology "modularity and cultural context contribute jointly to the development of mind" (1996, p. 198). As far as the conceptualization of culture is concerned, Cole's work has been influenced by Vygotsky and his school, where ontogenetic development is seen as culturally mediated (cf. ch. 2). An important difference between Cole and orthodox Vygotskian thinking lies in the level of generality of cross-cultural differences (see ch. 2).

Perhaps the major contribution to cross-cultural psychology from Cole's school has been the work challenging the views of Luria and others (e.g., Goody & Watt, 1968) that literacy has served as a "watershed" in the course of human history, that preliterates cannot, while literates can, carry out certain abstract cognitive operations (Scribner & Cole, 1981). Among the Vai people (also of Liberia), Scribner and Cole were able to find samples of persons who were illiterate as well as samples literate in various scripts, namely in a local Vai script, in Arabic taught to those who attended the Quran school, or in English taught in Western-style schools. This eliminated the usual confounding between schooling and literacy as contributors to cognitive test performance.

Using a battery of tasks, covering a wide range of cognitive activity (e.g., memory, logical reasoning) Scribner and Cole sought to challenge the idea that literacy transforms the intellect in a general way. They found that there were general performance effects of Western-style schooling, but not of other forms of literacy. However, there were some specific test performances that were related to particular features of the Vai script and of the education in Arabic. They concluded with respect to the Vai script that:

> Instead of generalized changes in cognitive ability, we found localized changes in cognitive skills manifested in relatively esoteric experimental settings. Instead of qualitative changes in a person's orientation to language, we found differences in selected features of speech and communication ... our studies among the Vai provide the first direct evidence that literacy makes some difference to some skills in some contexts. (Scribner & Cole, 1981, p. 234)

In interpreting their results, they noted that Vai literacy is "restricted," in the sense that not many people know and use it, and those who do use it for only limited purposes: "Vai script literacy is not essential either to maintain or to elaborate customary ways of life ... At best, Vai script literacy can be said to engage individuals with familiar topics" (p. 238) rather than opening up new experiences.

Thus, one possible reason for a lack of a general change in intellectual life is the rather limited role that literacy plays in Vai society. A study among the Cree of Northern Ontario carried out by Berry and Bennett (1989) is relevant to this problem. Once again, literacy is present in a form (a syllabic script) that is not associated with formal schooling. Most Cree are functionally literate in the script; it is less restricted than among the Vai since it is very widely used by many people, and for many purposes. However, it is restricted in the broader cultural senses noted by Scribner and Cole (above). The results of this study also found no evidence for a general cognitive enhancement (assessed by an elaborated version of Raven's Progressive Matrices), but some evidence for abilities that involved the same mental operations (rotation and spatial tasks) that are important in using this particular script. Thus, also in this study on the effects of literacy there was no evidence that a major shift in ways of thinking had taken place. The "watershed" view of the role of literacy in the course of human history thus has to be rejected, at least with respect to its effects on individual thought; however, the social and cultural consequences of literacy are not addressed by these studies.

Cole and his colleagues have not typically posed the question of intertest relations of their data; this issue has not been of central importance to their research goals. Instead they have typically considered the influence of one single cultural experience on one cognitive performance. The problem with considering culture as a set of discrete situation-linked experiences has been identified by Jahoda (1980) in an early review of their approach. For Jahoda, it

> appears to require extremely exhaustive, and in practice almost endless exploration of quite specific pieces of behavior, with no guarantee of a decisive outcome. This might not be necessary, if there were a workable "theory of situations" at our disposal, but as Cole admits, there is none ... (Jahoda, 1980, p. 126).

However, Cole (e.g., 1992a, 1992b) does appear to subscribe to the view that cultural experiences are intertwined, rather than being a discrete set of situations: "the real stuff of culture is believed to reside in the interaction among elements; the independent variables are not independent" (LCHC, 1982, p. 645).

In the end, then, there may be an evolving rapprochement between Cole and those who seek some degree of generalization from culture–cognition research. Cole remains convinced of his early assertion, namely that non-performance on a particular cognitive task should not be generalized either to an expectation of non-performance on other tasks, or to the absence of the necessary underlying cognitive process or operator. Such a viewpoint is quite compatible with a universalist approach.

## Conclusions

It is clear from the material in this chapter that ecological and cultural factors affect human cognition. It is equally clear that such effects cannot be explored in relation to naive questions about which groups are smarter than others. Rather, some important distinctions between cognitive process, competence, and performance reveal the complexity of the relationships. Theoretical differences between four major schools of thought have drawn attention to the various ways in which these cognitive distinctions can be employed in empirical research.

We have first examined what cross-cultural differences could be like if intelligence were analyzed from the perspective of a unitary information processing organism. In the next two sections approaches were discussed in which cognitive functioning cannot be understood without interaction between the organism and the cultural environment. However, in Piaget's epistemology and Witkin's style dimension, the nature of the cognitive process can still be defined independently of culture. This principle is given up in contextualized approaches in which cognitive processes themselves are seen as a function of participation in cultural-historical processes. Thus, theories differ particularly in the relative emphasis on more general and more context-specific views on differences in performance on cognitive tasks. How to balance or integrate these views remains a difficult question.

No simple summary or conclusion is possible in the face of such diversity. Our own reading of this varied set of ideas and data is that the main characteristics of cognitive functions and processes appear to be common to all human beings, as universally shared properties of our intellectual life. Cognitive competencies are developed according to some common rules, but can result in highly varied performances that are responsive to ecological contexts, and to cultural norms and social situations encountered both during socialization and at the time of testing.

## Key terms

cognitive styles

contextualized cognition

*g*

general intelligence

genetic epistemology

information processing

metacognition

theories of mind

transfer of tests

## Further reading

Mishra, R. C. (1997). Cognition and cognitive development. In J. W. Berry, P. R. Dasen, & T. S. Saraswathi (Eds.), *Basic processes and human development* (pp. 143–76). Vol. II of *Handbook of cross-cultural psychology* (2nd ed.). Boston, MA: Allyn & Bacon. A review chapter that examines both cognitive development and performance in relation to cultural contexts in which they take place.

Neisser, U. et al. (1996). Intelligence: Knowns and unknowns. *American Psychologist, 51*, 77–101. A portrayal of issues and findings about the concept of intelligence, with only limited attention to cultural factors.

Sternberg, R. & Grigorenko, E. (Eds.) (1997b). *Intelligence, heredity and environment*. New York: Cambridge University Press. A book of original papers examining conceptual and empirical links between genetics, culture, and intelligence.

Van de Vijver, F. J. R. (1997). Meta-analysis of cross-cultural comparisons of cognitive test performance. *Journal of Cross-Cultural Psychology, 28*, 678-709. A comprehensive examination of many studies of cognitive abilities across cultures.

# 6   Language

Compared to that of other species, human speech is a highly differentiated faculty, enabling us to communicate complex information in an efficient way
through language. There are many aspects to the psychological study of language,
including its production and understanding (listening, articulation, memorization),
and the use of indirect means of communication through writing and reading. In
this chapter we deal with a selection of issues that are particularly relevant to
cross-cultural psychology. In the first brief section we discuss language development. We then turn to a central issue in the study of the relationship between behavior and culture, namely the relationship between language and thought
processes. In research on linguistic relativity the question is to what extent speaking a particular language influences one's thinking. We discuss two topics on which
much of the discussion about linguistic relativity has been focussed, namely perception and categorization of colors, and orientation in space. The third section is
on culture-comparative research that has not only identified differences, but also
universals in language. Finally, we elaborate on a more specific issue. In the section on bilingualism we discuss consequences of the learning and use of more
than a single language, highly relevant for ethnocultural and immigrant groups.

## Language development

Language develops with the ontogenesis of the child. Babies cannot
speak when they are born. When growing up children first acquire the sounds of
their language, then words, and thereafter sentences.

The smallest identifiable units of speech are called phonemes. For example, the words "bad" and "sad" are distinguished by their initial phonemes, indicated as "b" and "s." Many studies have been carried out with phonemes that differ on a single phonetic dimension, such as (in English) "b," "d," and "g." Speakers of a particular language usually have no difficulty in making the correct identifications of phonemes that occur in their language. We shall not concern ourselves with vowels, but for consonants the boundaries of **phoneme categories** tend to be very sharp. When pairs of artificially produced sounds belonging to different categories are presented, discrimination is nearly perfect. However, with sounds acoustically equally different, but falling within the same phonemic category, discrimination is hardly better than chance (Strange & Jenkins, 1978).

There are differences between languages in the set of phonemes that are used. Well-known examples include the "l" and "r," two sounds in English that are not distinguished in Japanese, and an aspirated "b" in Arabic that does not occur in English. When artificially produced sounds are presented respondents will categorize them in accordance with the categories of their own language. Abrahamson and Lisker (1970, mentioned in Strange & Jenkins, 1978) found, for example, that respondents from the USA used two categories ("d," "t") where Thai respondents used three ("d," "t," and an aspirated "t"). Miyawaki et al. (1975) demonstrated that respondents from the USA could discriminate well between stimuli like "la" and "ra," while Japanese hardly did better than chance.

Evidence suggests that infants already differentiate between phonemic categories before they produce articulated speech. They even appear to distinguish categories that are not found in the adult language of their environment (e.g., Eimas, 1975). The facility to make phonemic distinctions that are never used disappears in the course of development. When learning a second language later in life the discrimination of category boundaries that do not coincide with one's own language can be a difficult process. This is illustrated by Goto (1971), who recorded English words with "l" and "r" (e.g., lead and read). Japanese discriminated poorly between "l" and "r." Even when listening to recordings of word productions that they had spoken themselves, they could not make accurate discriminations.

From about six months of age infants start to produce speech-like sounds that are known as babbling; these sounds already appear to differ slightly between languages (see Harley, 1995). At around one year of age children start to use words (i.e., speech productions that consistently refer to the same object or action) and the set of sounds that they use becomes much more restricted; differences between languages are now much in evidence. From then on there is a tremendous acceleration in language development reaching a maximum of up to ten new words learned per day (Levelt, 2000). The next big step in language development is the combining of words into sentences following grammatical and syntactical rules. The child begins with two-word sentences and gradually the average length of utterances increases. Cross-linguistic differences in grammatical complexity have been demonstrated to affect somewhat the age of acquisition. For example, McCarthy and Prince (1990, mentioned in Harley, 1995) mentioned that markings

of plurality, which are complex in Arabic, are acquired by children at a somewhat later age than in English, where the plural is relatively simple.

To become fluent a child has to master other aspects of communication, such
as prosodics (e.g., tonal patterns in speech), pragmatics (e.g., turn taking, greetings; cf. ch. 15), and patterns of gesticulation. In literate societies there is the additional task of learning to read and write. Again different skills are sometimes
required, especially for languages that are written in different ways (e.g., Altarriba, 1993). In alphabetic languages the way a word is written tends to correspond
to the sounds (phonemes) and children tend to be aware of this (phonological
awareness). However, in traditional Chinese, characters correspond to syllables
or words. Holm and Dodd (1996) reported a study with students learning English as a second language in Australia. With a variety of tasks they found that
students from Hong Kong displayed less awareness of the correspondence between sounds and letters than students from the People's Republic of China (PRC)
and Vietnam. The students from Hong Kong had learned the traditional Chinese
characters; the PRC students had learned to write in pinyin, a phonemic representation of Chinese in roman letters, and roman characters are also used in
writing in Vietnamese. Similarly, Huang and Hanley (1994) found with primary
school children in Hong Kong, Taiwan, and the UK that performance on a phonological awareness task was more closely related to learning to read English than
Chinese, while learning to read Chinese was more related to visual skills.

## Linguistic relativity

Thinking and language are experienced as being intimately connected.
It is difficult to imagine how we could think at all, if we had no language in
which to think (Hunt & Agnoli, 1991). Therefore, it is not surprising that the
question has been raised whether people who speak different languages also will
think in different ways. This has led to the notion of **linguistic relativity**, which
implies a relationship between characteristics of a language and the thoughts that
will be found in a culture where that language is spoken. The notion has a long
history, but today it is usually referred to as the "Sapir–Whorf hypothesis," after
the linguist Whorf, and the anthropologist Sapir.

In Whorf's view (1956, p. 212)

> the background linguistic system (in other words, the grammar) of each lan-
> guage is not merely a reproducing instrument for voicing ideas but rather is itself
> a shaper of ideas, the program and guide for the individual's mental activity, for
> his analysis of impressions, for his synthesis of his mental stock-of-trade.

From this passage it is quite clear that language is seen not only as a means to
communicate ideas and thoughts, but as intrinsic to their formation.

Whorf based his theory of linguistic relativity on a comparison of standard
average European (SAE) with Native American languages. Between the European
languages such as English, French, and Italian, Whorf saw much commonality;

hence the term SAE. Major differences are seen when one compares European languages with languages from other families. An example is the sense of time among the Hopi Indians. Whorf (1956, p. 57) argued that a Hopi-speaking person has no general notion of time as "a smooth flowing continuum in which everything in the universe proceeds at an equal rate, out of a future, through a present, into a past." The reason is that the Hopi language contains no words or grammatical constructions to refer to time, either explicitly or implicitly. In Whorf's opinion this shows that just as there can be other geometric systems next to the Euclidean, it is possible to have valid descriptions of the world in which our familiar concepts of space and time do not occur.

The Hopi language and culture have a metaphysics which differs from that of English and only can be described properly in the Hopi language. However, an approximate description in English is possible, according to Whorf. The major distinction in Hopi is not between past, present, and future, but between the manifested, or the objective, and the unmanifest, or the subjective. The manifest comprises everything that is accessible to the senses, i.e., the physical world of the past and the present. The unmanifest includes the future, but also everything that exists in the mind (the Hopi would say the heart) and the realm of religion and magic. To the unmanifest belong desire and purpose. The term also implies that which is in the process of becoming manifest. As such it pertains to part of what in English is the present time. In the Hopi verb there is a form that refers to the emergence of manifestation, like going-to-sleep. However, most of what in English is the present time belongs to the realm of the manifest and is not distinguishable in Hopi from the past.

The SAE notion of time also emerges in the use of plurality and numbers. In English one can as easily speak about ten days as about ten men. Whorf has pointed out that ten men can be perceived as a group. Ten days cannot be experienced objectively; we can only experience today. A group of days is a mental construction. It is a linguistic usage that is patterned on the outer world.

> Concepts of time lose contact with the subjective experience of "becoming later" and are objectified as counted QUANTITIES, especially as lengths, made up of units as a length can be visibly marked off into inches. A "length of time" is envisioned as a row of similar units, like a row of bottles . . . (Whorf, 1956, pp. 139–40)

In Hopi there are no imaginary plurals. The expression "ten days" will not be found. Rather reference will be made to the day that is reached after the number of ten days has passed. Staying for ten days will be expressed as staying until the eleventh day. Length of time is regarded by the Hopi as "a relation between two events in lateness. Instead of our linguistically promoted objectification of that datum of consciousness we call 'time', the Hopi language has not laid down any pattern that would cloak the subjective 'becoming later' that is the essence of time."

The example shows that Whorf extended the principle of linguistic relativity to the level of grammatical characteristics of a language and that he saw these as cultural themes, shared by the speakers of the language. The evidence on which these interpretations are based was rather anecdotal. It has certainly not been demonstrated by Whorf that the Hopi cannot discriminate between past, present, and future in much the same way as SAE speakers. Among others, Lenneberg (1953) has criticized Whorf's method of translation which led to such strong inferences about cross-cultural differences in thinking.

Later attempts were made to better specify the nature of linguistic relativity. An important distinction is that between the lexical or semantic level, and the level of grammar or syntax (e.g., Fishman, 1960). Another distinction can be made between the influence of language on perception and cognition and its influence on verbal communication.

There have been a large number of reports on grammatical aspects of language, especially in the anthropological literature, in which various differences between two languages have been linked to a difference between the speakers of those languages in other behavior patterns. With few exceptions these links have been made post hoc. Since any two cultures differ in many respects, non-linguistic differences may have nothing to do with linguistic factors; they can be due to some other cultural variable (see ch. 11). Hence unambiguous evidence is needed to validate such interpretations.

One of the few experimental studies into linguistic relativity of grammar was carried out by Carroll and Casagrande (1958). They used a feature of the (Native American) Navajo language in which the conjugation of the verb differs according to whether the form or some other feature of an object is referred to. They hypothesized that the concept of form would develop early among Navajo-speaking children. Carroll and Casagrande found that Navajo-speaking children more than English-speaking children from Navajo origin would use form rather than color as a basis for the classification of objects. However, this support for the Whorf hypothesis lost much of its meaning when a control group of Anglo-American children showed an even stronger tendency to classify objects in the way hypothesized for the Navajo-speaking respondents.

Another study (Bloom, 1981) focussed on a particular difference between English and Chinese. English has a conditional construction to indicate that a statement is counterfactual. The sentence: "If I knew French, I could read the work of Voltaire," implies that the speaker does *not* know French. The listener deduces that the premise is false and that the meaning of the sentence is counterfactual. Chinese does not have such a conditional mode of expression. If the listener has no advance information the sentence has to be preceded by an explicit negation. For example: "I do not know French; if I knew French, I could read Voltaire." According to Bloom the absence of a counterfactual marker negatively affects the ability of speakers of Chinese to think counterfactually.

He presented Chinese and English-speaking respondents with a story in which counterfactual implications were mentioned following a false premise. The counterfactuals were presented in a conditional form in the English version, but not, of course, in the Chinese version. Bloom found substantial differences when he asked whether the counterfactual events had actually occurred. The percentage of counterfactual responses varied from 6 percent to 63 percent among samples of Chinese students in Taiwan and Hong Kong, depending on the wording of the stories and level of education of the respondents. For samples from the USA the percentage hardly varied, from 96 percent to 98 percent. In Bloom's (1981, p. 29) opinion the differences in linguistic form "may well be highly responsible for important differences in the way English speakers, as opposed to Chinese speakers, categorize and operate cognitively with the world."

Au's (1983, 1984) results from similar experiments were in direct contradiction to those obtained by Bloom. She hardly found any differences between speakers of English and Chinese. More evidence was reported by Liu (1985), working with Chinese speakers who had minimal exposure to English. Using respondents in various school grades and various presentations she concluded that education level, the presentation, and the content of the story were crucial variables for the level of performance. But she found no cross-cultural effects of linguistic markers of counterfactuality.

Another study in which two levels of counterfactuality could be manipulated within a single language is reported in box 6-1. The results show that grammatical construction influences the meaning of a sentence, but there is no evidence of more general effects.

In summary, at the grammatical level evidence on the Sapir–Whorf hypothesis is negative. At least for the time being the hypothesis can be shelved that the grammatical structure of a language has substantial effects on thinking.

Of course, this does not tell us much about the semantic level. Language in the form of labeling influences the organization and recall of representations in memory (e.g. Santa & Baker, 1975). There are numerous examples which demonstrate non-correspondence of denotative word meaning across languages. The Inuit have several words for the semantic category that in SAE languages is represented by the single word "snow." On the other hand, the Aztecs have only one word where SAE languages use cold, snow, and ice. This leads to two expectations. First, the availability of words for certain categories presumably makes it easier to discriminate certain nuances in the outer world. Second, the availability of more words within a certain category should lead to greater ease of communication. If words are taken as codes, a larger number of words for a given range of phenomena implies a more accurate codability of these phenomena.

Thus, the linguistic relativity hypothesis requires an answer to questions such as the following. Do the Inuit perceive more varieties of snow than speakers of SAE languages? And do Africans speaking Bantu languages in which there are few words for geometric forms, like triangle and square, experience special difficulties with mathematics (Du Toit, 1968)? Or does such absence merely reflect different interests of people in their interactions with the environment in which they live? Can we communicate within the realm of shared experiences a particular state of affairs with a string of words if no single label is available?

## Box 6.1  Counterfactuality in northern Sotho

Vorster and Schuring (1989) presented a story with counterfactual statements
to South African respondents from three languages, namely English, Afrikaans,
and Sepedi, or northern Sotho. Samples consisted of school children from grades
three, five, and seven. Vorster and Schuring made use of a feature of the Sepedi
language, namely that there are two modes of expressing counterfactuality, of
which the one is stronger than the other. It is also noteworthy that these authors
asked questions about factual as well as counterfactual statements in the stimulus
story. They argued that group differences in responses could not be ascribed
to the effects of counterfactuality, if it had not been shown that similar
differences were absent for factual statements.

The results are summarized in fig. 6.1. They show that the percentage of
correct responses to factual items was very high even for the youngest children. Counterfactual statements led to large percentages of wrong answers,
especially with younger children. The crucial finding is that with the less strong
counterfactual cueing the Sepedi-speaking children show a similar pattern of
results to the children from Afrikaans- and English-speaking backgrounds,

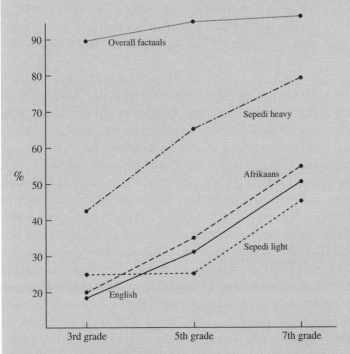

**6.1**  Percentage of correct responses to questions on factual statements (over all
respondents) and on counterfactual statements (for four samples separately)
From Vorster & Schuring, 1989

**Box 6.1 (continued)**

while with the stronger cues the percentages of correct responses are much higher for the Sepedi. The differences in reactions by these Sotho-speaking respondents to the two versions of the same story indicate that the way in which counterfactuality is formulated in a specific instance should be seen as the determining factor, rather than a general mode of thinking. This is clearly not compatible with the Whorfian hypothesis.

## Coding and categorization of colors

Color is a physical quality of objects as well as an impression or sensation of the human observer. On the one hand each color can be defined unambiguously in terms of physical qualities, notably the dominant wavelength (hue). On the other hand one can ask respondents to name colors, to remember colors, to provide **color categorizations,** and so on. The physical measurements can then be related to the psychological reports. As we shall see in this section, this does not mean that such relationships are unproblematic. In early studies color terms were taken as indices of what people in a particular culture were thought to perceive. Later on sets of chips came into use in which the whole range of visible colors was represented. Most familiar is the Munsell system, in which colors are mapped according to three parameters, namely hue, saturation, and brightness (or gray value).

The history of cross-cultural research on the perception of colors is usually taken to start with the work of the British politician Gladstone published in the middle of the nineteenth century. He called attention to certain oddities in the poetry of Homer, such as the absence of words for brown and blue, which he attributed to a limited differentiation in color vision among the ancient Greeks. Somewhat later Geiger (1880) extended this idea of differential sensitivity from early history to modern times. Originally only black and red were distinguished, later came yellow and green, and finally blue. Geiger obtained the evidence for his thesis from old literary sources, such as Homer and the Germanic epic poems.

Magnus (1880) was the first to report on an empirical investigation with contemporary data. He collected information from colonial foreign residents in a number of countries, using a questionnaire as well as chips of different colors. The objective was to establish the range of color vision of "uncivilized" peoples as well as the verbal expressions for various colors. Thus, a distinction was made between physiological and linguistic issues. So far Magnus had believed that evidence on color vision could be derived from the study of color names. Against his own expectations he found that the range of perceivable colors was invariant across cultures. He also established that color perception and color naming do not always correspond. In many languages words for certain colors were lacking. This concerned colors with a short wavelength (green, blue, violet), rather than long wavelength colors (red, yellow). In particular, the absence of separate words for green and blue was found frequently, while there was always a term for red.

Because of this consistency in the pattern of findings, Magnus kept on looking for some physiological explanation. Through the spectrum from violet to red he suggested an increase in vividness of the colors. The less vivid colors would be less salient to non-Europeans and for that reason less likely be identified with a separate term. Rivers (1901) took up the study of color vision and color naming during a famous expedition to the Torres Straits (cf. ch. 8). He found a frequent confusion between green and blue and between saturated blue and dark or dull colors. Also, his respondents detected a faint red more readily than a faint blue, taking the thresholds of Europeans as a standard. To account for his findings Rivers suggested that genetic differences in pigmentation play a role. Short wave colors are absorbed to a greater extent by pigment in the retina and dark-skinned people have more of this pigmentation.

Interest in the work on color perception of these nineteenth-century cross-culturalists soon dwindled. Only in part had this an empirical reason. Titchener (1916, cf. Lloyd, 1977) replicated some of Rivers's research with students in the USA and showed that they also had a relative insensitivity to blue when tested under similar conditions of illumination as used by Rivers. The findings on physiological differences fell into disregard, mainly under the influence of cultural and linguistic relativity.

To test Whorf's hypothesis the domain of color is excellently suited, because any color can be unambiguously defined in terms of objective physical measurements. The mediation of language in color naming was advocated among others by Ray (1952), who concluded from his own studies with Native Americans that each culture has divided the visible spectrum into units on a physically quite arbitrary basis. He rejected even the famous confusion between blue and green, and attributed it to a greater rather than a lower subtlety in classification. Where Western cultures use only blue and green, he found a three-way division elsewhere. The middle region is then not identified as blue-green but as a separate color. However, there has been no further empirical validation of Ray's observations.

A new line of research was started by Brown and Lenneberg (1954) with the introduction of the term codability. This was a composite measure of agreement in (1) the naming of a color chip, (2) the length of the name, and (3) the response latency in naming. It was expected that more codable colors would be better remembered and more easily identified in a recognition task. Some positive results were found in the USA, but the research was not replicated elsewhere. Lantz and Stefflre (1964) suggested another measure, namely communication accuracy. They asked listeners to identify a certain chip in an array of colors on the basis of color terms that were presented to them. Some terms were found to lead to more accurate identification than other terms. When used in a recognition experiment the more accurately communicable terms also were better recognized. Thus, this work showed an influence of language on communication and memory.

The linguistic relativity hypothesis was radically challenged in a book by Berlin and Kay (1969), with the title *Basic color terms: Their universality and evolution*. These authors asked bilingual respondents resident in the area of San Francisco to generate **basic color terms** in their mother tongue. A basic term had four main characteristics: (1) it was monoleximic, i.e. the meaning could not be derived from the meaning of its parts, as in lemon-colored; (2) the color it signified was not included in another color term (e.g., scarlet is a kind of red); (3) its usage should not be restricted to certain classes of objects; and (4) it had to be psychologically salient. This was evaluated with several indices, such as stability of reference across informants and occasions of usage.

After a listing of basic color terms had been obtained a respondent was given a panel with 329 differently colored chips from the Munsell system and asked to indicate for each term that had been previously generated: (1) all those chips that would be called "x"; (2) the best, most typical example of "x" in the Munsell display. It is important to note that the respondents worked with terms that they had generated themselves. The experimenter had no idea which shade of color was signified by a particular term.

The results of respondents from twenty languages are summarized in fig. 6.2. The map shows that the most typical, or focal, chips for basic colors are neatly clustered. Apart from clusters for black and white with terms in all twenty languages, there is also a word in all these languages for the area that is called red in English. Then the number decreases to nineteen for green, eighteen for yellow, sixteen for blue, fifteen for brown and purple, fourteen for grey, and eleven for pink and orange. Large parts of the diagram remain outside the areas covered by the basic color terms. Hence, it is justifiable to speak about focal colors. Berlin and Kay (1969, p. 10) concluded that "color categorization is not random and the foci of basic color terms are similar in all languages."

Many cultures do not have names for all the eleven basic colors in English. The second important finding by Berlin and Kay was a strong relationship between the number of basic color terms in a language and the subset of focal colors for which there is a basic term. They claimed that the focal colors become encoded in the history of a language in a (largely) fixed order. The sequence of stages is summarized in fig. 6.3. In the most elementary stage there are two terms, one for white, encoding also for light and warm colors (e.g., yellow) and one for black that includes dark and cool colors (e.g., blue). In the second stage a separate term for red and warm colors emerges. From the third stage onwards the order is not precisely fixed. It is possible that either green or blue (together called "grue") is the next term, but one also finds that a term for yellow is found in a language, but not for grue. It can be seen from the figure that pink, orange, grey, and purple are added to a language in the last stage.

For Berlin and Kay the various stages are steps in the evolution of languages. To support their evolutionary scheme they drew on a large number of reports in the (mainly ethnographic) literature. There were a few color vocabularies that did

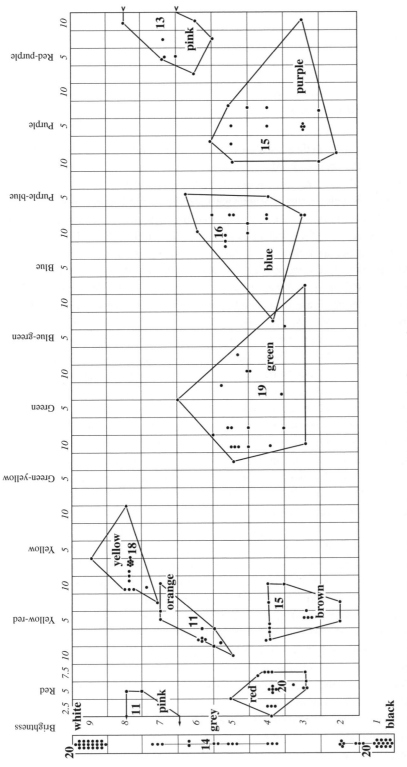

**6.2** Clusters of dots representing foci (averaged over subjects) in each of twenty languages

The number in each cluster indicates the number of languages that had a basic term for the color concerned (numbers in the margins refer to the Munsell color system)

From Berlin & Kay, 1969

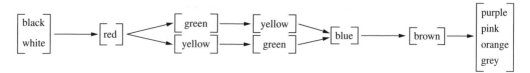

**6.3** The sequence in which terms for focal colors emerge in the history of languages
After Berlin & Kay 1969

not readily fit, but in their view the available information showed a striking agreement with the proposed order.

Berlin and Kay's research was criticized on a number of points. Their definition of basic color terms is somewhat fuzzy, although it seemed to work quite well. More serious was the objection that the respondents from San Francisco had all been living for a longer or shorter period in the USA. The body of empirical evidence as well as the theoretical basis has been much extended since 1969. In more recent work also somewhat more complicated schemes than the one presented in fig. 6.3 have been presented (e.g., Berlin & Berlin, 1975). In addition, theories were formulated about the neurophysiological basis of color perception (e.g., Kay & McDaniel, 1978). At the same time, many of the categorizations derived for specific terms in specific groups by Berlin and Kay were questioned by cultural anthropologists, who also argued that in this line of work the functional and social meaning of colors, for example in relations to rituals, is ignored (e.g., Sahlins, 1976).

In experimental research Heider (also publishing as Rosch; 1972, 1977) established that focal colors had a higher codability, in the sense that they were named more rapidly and were given shorter names than non-focal colors by respondents from twenty-three languages. She then tested the hypothesis that focal colors would also have a higher codability than non-focal colors, even for those focal colors for which there was no basic term in a respondent's language. She studied the Dani, a group in Papua New Guinea with only two basic color terms (i.e., a language at the first stage in the Berlin and Kay sequence). When the Dani were shown color chips they did indeed recognize focal colors better than non-focal colors after a thirty-second interval (as did American students). In a second study with the Dani, eight focal colors and eight non-focal colors were all paired with a separate response word. The number of trials it took a respondent to learn the correct response for each stimulus was the dependent variable. It was found that the focal colors required significantly fewer trials than the non-focal colors. In Rosch's view the results should be explained with reference to physiological factors underlying color vision, rather than linguistic factors. She concluded (1972, p. 20) that "far from being a domain well suited to the study of the effects of language on thought, the color space would seem a prime example of the influence of underlying perceptual-cognitive factors on the formation and reference of linguistic categories."

More direct evidence on the role of possible physiological factors in the linguistic categorization of colors was reported by Bornstein (1973). He related the wavelength of the focal colors found by Berlin and Kay (cf. fig. 6.2) to the spectral sensitivity of four types of cells found in the brain of Macaque monkeys. These cells were found to be sensitive for wavelengths corresponding to red, yellow, green, and blue respectively. In a further study (Bornstein, Kessen, & Weiskopf, 1976) the technique of stimulus habituation was used with four-month-old babies, using red, yellow, green, and blue stimuli. The authors hypothesized that when the same stimulus was presented repeatedly looking time would decrease. At the presentation of a different stimulus there would be a dishabituation effect that was stronger as the new stimulus was more dissimilar. All stimulus changes in this experiment were identical in one respect; the size of the change, measured in wavelength, was always equal. However, with some of the changes the new stimulus remained within the same color category as the original stimulus (e.g., both would be designated as red by an adult observer), while with other changes the new stimulus would be classified in another color category (e.g., a shift from red to yellow). It was found that the infants indeed reacted more to the new stimulus when the latter type of change occurred. This indicated that the categories and boundaries between categories for babies long before the onset of speech are much the same as those for adults. In the debate on the primacy of language versus perception in color identification, this quite convincingly suggested the primacy of perception.

In the 1980s it was generally accepted, certainly among psychologists, that categorizations of colors as represented by monoleximic color names are not randomly distributed in the spectrum of visible colors and reflect to some extent universal principles of perception. But the issue was not really settled. Three kinds of counterarguments were raised. First, instances of color terms continued to be reported that were said not to fit the scheme of Berlin and Kay (e.g., Wierzbicka, 1996). Such findings were mainly based on ad hoc reports of informants about the meaning of certain terms in certain languages, rather than on systematic exploration of the entire color domain. Therefore, they have failed to convince researchers with more universalist views (see Hardin & Maffi, 1997).

The second argument concerned the salience of color. Whereas it had been argued before that color was less salient in pre-industrial societies, it was now argued by some of the leading critics that color may not be a perceptual category at all in some societies (Saunders, 1992; Saunders & Van Brakel, 1997). This implies that color is not a universal aspect of perception, but would have to be seen as a cultural construction. On the basis of interviews with members of the Kwakiutl group on the Pacific coast in Canada and a reinterpretation of anthropological records, Saunders (1992) suggested that current color words in the Kwakiutl language did not refer to color before American Indian cultures came into contact with Western colonizers. However, for this reinterpretation only very tentative evidence is supplied. Moreover, this contention is hardly supported by findings in the ethnographic record on other societies.

The third argument is that neurophysiological processes linking perception to color naming remain largely unknown. The pathways from retina to cortex appear to carry an intricate mixture of information on form, luminosity, texture, etc., but no specific cells for specific colors have been identified. This makes any interpretation which assumes universal mechanisms a matter of speculation according to Saunders and Van Brakel (1997). Their analysis undoubtedly exposed the fact that the neurological basis of color categories could be taken for granted too easily. However, Saunders and Van Brakel failed to come up with an alternative theory, let alone alternative data, that explained the occurrence of color categories in human societies everywhere. In other words, the conclusion by Bornstein (1997, p. 181) "to see colors is to categorize the spectrum into hues" seems to be unaffected.

As far as the universality of specific basic color categories is concerned, some of the experimental evidence still stands, especially that infants already perceive major color categories (Bornstein et al., 1976; Bornstein, 1997). However, Heider's (Rosch [Heider], 1972) findings, indicating that focal colors in English could be identified by the Dani even in the absence of color words, were largely not replicated in a series of studies comparing Berinmo in Papua New Guinea with British respondents. Roberson, Davies, and Davidoff (2000) worked with Munsell color chips, as Heider had done. They found five monoleximic color terms for the Berinmo, including *nol*, a term more or less covering green, blue, and purple. In a memory task there was more resemblance between Berinmo patterns of color naming and memory than between Berinmo and British memory patterns. Roberson et al. also found that paired associates learning of words and color chips was not faster for (English) focal as opposed to non-focal chips. Again, Heider's results with the Dani were not replicated. The research with the Berinmo was extended with similarity judgments and learning of categories with the English blue–green and the Berinmo *nol–wor* distinction (*wor* corresponds to yellow, orange, and brown). It turned out that performance was better for distinctions made in the respondents' own language than for distinctions according to the categories proposed by Berlin and Kay.

It should be noted that the findings of Roberson et al. are somewhat more complicated than has been reported here. For example, in one memory task a Berinmo sample showed a better performance for (English) focal than for non-focal chips. Since the Berinmos gave also more incorrect answers on focal chips Roberson et al. explain this as an artifact of response bias. However, the reason for the higher salience of the focal colors is perhaps a better discriminability; focal colors may stand out more than non-focal color chips, which is precisely why researchers like Heider would expect a better memory for focal chips.[1] Nevertheless, one can

---

[1] The color chips in the Munsell system were prepared so that there was equal distance between them on physical characteristics. Some authors have suggested that chips should be selected for equal discriminability, making the focal chips more difficult to recognize. It can be argued that this amounts to the introduction of an unnatural bias against focal chips (cf. Lucy & Shweder, 1979; Poortinga & Van de Vijver, 1997; Roberson et al., 2000).

agree with Roberson et al. (2000, p. 394) that they demonstrated quite unambiguously a broad effect of language on color categorization: "the results uphold the view that the structure of linguistic categories distorts perception by stretching perceptual distances at category boundaries."

Any precise conclusion based on the evidence seems premature. Maps of color words collected in the World Color Survey (e.g., Kay, Berlin, Maffi, & Merrifield, 1997) continue to give the impression that there are similarities in the distribution of terms across the visible space of colors. On the other hand, the similarities are probably not as strong as was once believed. More recent evidence has shifted the balance towards a larger effect of linguistic and cultural context on color categorization than suggested by the earlier findings from Berlin and Kay (1969) and Heider (Rosch [Heider] 1972).

## Spatial orientation

Another behavioral domain that has been studied fairly extensively is **spatial orientation**. It is evident that humans, like other species, are equipped for this purpose with an elaborate biological apparatus, including vision, binaural hearing, and the vestibular system. The question is to what extent this leads to universally uniform notions about natural space and spatial orientation. According to Levinson (1998), extensive research in non-Western societies has shown that such notions can differ in fundamental ways from those of Western societies and that this difference arises from spatial terminology in the language. In Indo-European languages like English the location of objects in the horizontal plane is given from an ego-referenced orientation. For example, English speakers may say "the table is to the right side of the chair"; if they then move to another position around the same display, they would say "the table is to the left of the chair." In some other languages, the preference is to use absolute or geocentric spatial coordinates that stay the same independent of the position of the observer. For example, the direction of the rising and declining sun, and directions on the compass derived from magnetic north provide coordinates that are independent of the position of the observer.

Levinson and his colleagues devised a number of tasks designed to ascertain which system of encoding, relative or absolute, informants are using when confronted with a spatial display they were asked to memorize. One such task made use of identical cards, each with a red square and a blue square. Two cards were placed on a table so that the blue square was to the left on one, and to the right on the other card. A respondent was to remember one of the cards, say blue to the right/to the south. The respondent was then led to another room, presented with a similar pair of cards on a table, but rotated 180°, and asked to point out the card previously chosen. Indo-European speakers tended to choose the card with the squares in the same position from the observer's perspective (e.g., blue to the right), while speakers of languages in which a geocentric system was favored predominantly selected the card with the squares in the same compass direction (e.g., blue to the south).

One of the groups of Australian Aborigines that Levinson and his colleagues found to work with absolute coordinates are the speakers of the Guugu-Yimithirr language. There is no exclusive use of absolute spatial coordinates in this language. Words like "here" and "there" and "come" and "go," are used with an ego orientation. On the other hand, the left–right distinction, so common in English, appears to be absent (Haviland, 1998).

In Bali, Wassmann and Dasen (1998; Dasen, 1998) found a similar situation. The left–right distinction exists in the Balinese language, but is used only to designate objects in contact with the body. Otherwise, objects are located by using a geocentric system based on the main axis up/down (to the mountain/to the sea) and two quadrants more or less orthogonal to this axis (in the south of Bali, this corresponds to sunrise/sunset, but the coordinate system turns as one moves around the island). Many aspects of Balinese life are organized according to this orientation system: the way villages and temples are laid out, the architecture of the compounds, the customary orientation for sleeping, as well as symbolic aspects (each direction is associated with a particular god) and very practical ones (e.g. "Go fetch my shoes that are in the uphill room in the downhill corner"). When spatial language was elicited from adults, the absolute reference system was clearly predominant, and only 3 percent of egocentric descriptors (left/right, in front, behind) were given.

Using two tasks devised by Levinson and colleagues (similar to the one described above), it was found that on one of the tasks, easy to encode in language, young children (aged four to nine years) systematically used absolute (geocentric) encoding, as did 80 percent of older children (eleven to fifteen years) and adults. On another, more visual task, there was an even split between absolute and relative encoding. The impression gained from these results was that the Balinese, whether children or adults, preferentially use an absolute encoding, in accordance with the predominant orientation system in their language and culture. Depending on task demands, relative encoding was also available, and there seemed to be a slight developmental shift from absolute to relative encoding (which, if replicated, would represent a reversal of the standard sequence described by developmental psychologists).

Dasen, Mishra, and Niraula (2000) pursuing this research in India and Nepal with schooled and unschooled children aged four to fourteen years, chose various settings (a village in the Ganges plain, one in the Nepalese mountains, and a city), and found that spatial language varied markedly according to ecology. Encoding of spatial arrays was again found to be task dependent, with a marked predominance of absolute encoding on one of the tasks; but this was quite independent of the language used by the respondents to describe the task (absolute language could be used to explain a relative encoding, and vice versa). No significant relationship was found between absolute or relative encoding and the performance on Piagetian tasks of spatial cognitive development. Overall, the results did not support the hypothesis of linguistic relativism.

Bowerman (1996) has addressed semantic categories referring to positions of objects in relation to each other, like "on," "in," "up," and "under." For example, in English a cookie is *on* the table, but *in* the bowl. The question is to what extent such locative categories are a matter of language, rather than of perceptual mechanisms. There is little doubt that children know about space, even before they master locative prepositions. But Bowerman shows with examples from various languages that prepositions often are not translation equivalent, and sometimes even do not make sense. Thus, in Finnish one says something akin to the English: "The handle is in (rather than on) the pan and the band aid is in (rather than on) the leg." A step further away from English is Tzeltal, a Mayan language, where the equivalent of the prepositions on and in (as in x is "on" the table or "in" the bowl) is not expressed, but locations are expressed with verbs that are differentiated according to the shape of objects. Thus, for a bowl on the table the verb *pachal* is used, and for a small ball the verb *wolol*. In Korean different verbs are used for putting on clothes on different parts of the body (e.g., *ipta* for the trunk, and *sinta* for the feet).[2]

Numerous examples in this section seem to show that at the lexical level of expression in one language may facilitate the processing of certain information in ways that are less available in another language. In the words of Hunt and Agnoli (1991, p. 387) "different languages pose different challenges for cognition and provide differential support for cognition."

According to Gumperz and Levinson (1996) research has led to an intermediate position in which linguistic and cultural differences are considered within the context of universal features, shared by all languages and cultures. But Lucy (1997, p. 308) warns that the broadening of research to underlying processes "should not be allowed to obscure the central reality and significance of structural differences in meaning between languages." And Levinson (1998, p. 14) infers the following about relative (ego-oriented) and absolute spatial orientation.

> A relative system fits with a culture that promotes individual perspective, that is preoccupied with viewpoint-dependent order – as enshrined for example in domestic architecture or writing systems, symbolisms of left and right, or ceremonial arrangements of chattels. An absolute system permits abstraction away from individual perspective, allowing individuals to become mere points in a landscape ... No doubt these associations are too simplistic to fully capture the ranges of use of either kind of system, but up to a point they seem to match the characteristics of the societies that utilize them.

In our view such an interpretation is not supported by the empirical evidence. It is not disputed that differences between languages do have effects. Slobin, who has reported extensively on comparative studies of language (Slobin, 1985–97)

---

[2] Bowerman could perhaps have found a similar effect in a language much closer to English, namely Dutch where one *zet op* (places on) a hat, *doet om* (puts around) a shawl, and *trekt aan* (pulls on) trousers and shoes.

## Box 6.2 A test of the effects of grammatical differences in event order expressions

Bohnemeyer (1998) analyzed Yukatek Maya, a language spoken in Yucatan. There are very few ways in which temporality, or the order of events, can be expressed grammatically in this language (for example, modes of the verb like the perfect or future in English are absent). In order to investigate possible consequences for communication Bohnemeyer designed an experiment for which the basic elements were video recordings of scenes like drinking a coke, or making a stack of books until the stack collapsed. Pairs of scenes like this were combined so that they presented one sequential scene to a viewer. Moreover, various combinations of pairs of basic elements were prepared, differing in temporal order of events (i.e., the stack of books could fall *before* or *after* the drinking of the coke). Yukatek and German participants were given the task of identifying which scene had been shown to one of them. The participants worked in pairs; one was shown the target video (i.e., the video to be identified). The other was shown two videos differing in order of events, described the difference between the two videos, was allowed to ask a single yes–no question to the first respondent, and from the answer had to infer which of the two videos had been shown to this person.

Despite the differences between their languages, the German pairs of participants and the Yukatek Mayan pairs failed in their cooperative task at nearly the same rate (13 percent and 15 percent of the cases, respectively). As expected the German participants made ample use of event order expressions in their language (in 92 percent of relevant expressions), while the Yukatek Mayan speakers hardly did so (in only 1 percent). The latter participants made more frequent use of "phasal operators," like "start," "continue," "end," etc. In summary, there was no evidence that the absence of expressions of event order in grammar made the distinction of temporality of events for the Yulatek Mayan speakers more difficult.

has suggested that when acquiring a language speakers are guided by the grammatical distinctions of that language in their attention to various aspects of events that they experience (Slobin, 1996). The evidence on spatial orientation and language seems compatible with this viewpoint. Hunt and Agnoli (1991) point out that the Whorfian hypothesis is ultimately about how language influences the schemata that we use to order non-linguistic experiences. However, neither their review nor the research discussed in this section has led to a single case that in our reading unambiguously shows language-based differences in perceptual or cognitive functioning beyond a small domain directly pertinent to the observed differences in language. It is unfortunate that there is hardly any research in which broader consequences of linguistic differences have been demonstrated rather than inferred (see box 6.2 for an example).

## Universals in language

The Sapir–Whorf hypothesis reflects the position that language determines cognition. There are other positions. Piaget (1975) sees language development as a concomitant of the cognitive structures of sensorimotor intelligence. In this sense cognitive development is considered to be a necessary condition for language. However, cognitive development can take place, at least to a certain extent, independent of the availability of language. Research with deaf children has shown this quite clearly (e.g., Lenneberg, 1967; Eibl-Eibesfeldt, 1979 ). Thus, a genetic basis for human language has been assumed, which should show up as **universals in language**. In a classic work on the biological foundations of language Lenneberg (1967) has argued that the processes by which language (including its structural properties) is realized are innate. Perhaps the most powerful evidence is that deaf children bring language-like structure into their gestures. Goldin-Meadow and Mylander (1998) found that deaf children in both the USA and China used strings of gestures to communicate messages, whereas hearing children and adults tend to use single gestures. These authors concluded that the structural similarities in the children's gestures were striking, despite large variations in environmental conditions, and therefore were likely to be innate.

In line with Lenneberg's ideas Chomsky (e.g. 1965, 1980) suggested that there is a universal grammar to which any human language conforms. This grammar corresponds with the nature and scope of human cognitive functioning. According to Chomsky there is an innate organization, a "language acquisition device," that determines the potential for language. At birth the mind is equipped with a mental representation of the universal grammar. Essential in Chomsky's writings is a distinction between the surface structure of a sentence and the deep structure. The surface structure (i.e., the sentence as it appears), can be changed through a series of transformations to the deep structure (i.e., the meaning of the sentence). More recently (Chomsky, 2000) has confirmed his position that the faculty of language can be regarded as a "language organ," in the same sense as the visual system or the immune system. This faculty is genetically based and the initial state is common to the species. This language acquisition device "takes experience as 'input' and gives the language as an 'output'" (Chomsky, 2000, p. 4). Both input and output are open to examination and form the observational basis for inferences about qualities of the language organ. Thus, Chomsky's approach amounts mainly to an analysis of grammatical features of languages.

The properties of the language acquisition device should be reflected in all human languages. However, so far the grammatical analysis of sentences has not resulted in extensive demonstration of universal characteristics. Few cross-cultural studies have been conducted aiming to test this theory. Rather, the available evidence is mostly based on detailed rational analyses of abstract structures (such as the deep syntactic structure) in one language. Universal properties of languages that have been postulated were mainly derived from descriptive surveys of grammatical and other characteristics of languages, and from experimental research on language-related psychological features.

There has been a fairly extensive amount of culture-comparative research on other aspects of psycholinguistics, ranging from directly observable phonological variables, via word order in sentences, to semantic meaning. Sometimes data have been collected in a wide range of cultures. Much of the descriptive research has been inspired by Greenberg (1963, 1978). As in most other fields it is possible to emphasize cross-cultural similarities as well as variations. For example, the word order object–subject–verb has not been observed in any single language, suggesting constraints on word order. Also, all languages have nouns and verbs, but adjectives as they are known in English apparently are not found everywhere (e.g., Hopper & Thompson, 1984). Intonation is a universal feature of speech, with a high pitch indicating that the speaker is placing emphasis. Also, toward the end of a discourse there tends to be a lowering of pitch (Bolinger, 1978). On the other hand, there are tone languages in which the semantic meaning of words can be dependent on the level of pitch at which phonemes are pronounced. In Papiamento, a language spoken in the Caribbean, *pàpá* (low–high) means daddy and *pápà* (high–low) means porridge. Tonality is widely spread; it is found in many African languages as well as in America and in Asia (e.g. Chinese languages). Although the number of tone levels usually is two, up to five distinctive levels have been found (Maddieson, 1978).

Far-reaching implications for cognitive functioning have been ascribed to tonality (e.g., Wober, 1975). There have even been claims that tonal and non-tonal language speakers differ in the neurological processing of information (Fromkin, 1978). Verbal information tends to be processed more in the left hemisphere; processing of non-verbal information, including emotional aspects of speech, is more located in the right hemisphere (e.g. Bradshaw & Nettleton, 1981). However, contrary to some earlier reports, Van Lancker and Fromkin (1973) found among Thai-speaking respondents a left hemisphere dominance for tone words. This is an indication that semantic aspects of tonality are processed as verbal information. A replication showed similar results for English-speaking respondents (Van Lancker & Fromkin, 1978).

Further negative evidence for the hypothesis that tonality has broad effects on cognition comes from an extensive study by Joe (1991). With tonal (Papiamento) and non-tonal (Creole English) speaking children from the Caribbean she found that the Papiamento children could better discriminate between tonal and non-tonal words, also in a foreign language (Mandarin Chinese). In a series of other perceptual and cognitive tasks there was only some indication of a better pitch discrimination with sequences of pure tones. On all the other tasks, including paired associates learning and sensitivity for emotional cues in spoken stories, no effect of tonality emerged. Also no evidence was found of differences in hemispheric preference with a series of dichotic listening tests.[3] Thus, except for the understanding of tonal words there appeared to be little connection between tonality and cognitive functioning.

In addition to structural (e.g., word order) and prosodic (e.g., intonation) aspects of language there is semantic meaning. An important research tradition is that of Osgood; he has drawn on the work of Greenberg (1963), as well as his own research on affective meaning that will be discussed in ch. 7. Among the features presumably shared by all languages Osgood (1980) postulated the principle of affective polarity. He found three factors of affective meaning, namely evaluation, potency, and activation, each with a positive and a negative pole. Affectively negative words will be "marked" more often and positive words will be "unmarked" more often. The marking of a word implies extension with an affix. A clear example in English is the prefix "un" as in *un*happy, or *un*fair. In all thirty language communities studied by Osgood and his colleagues (Osgood, May, & Miron, 1975) adjectives with a positive meaning, particularly on the evaluation dimension, were also used more frequently and over a wider range of situations than adjectives with a negative meaning.

Apparently, positive words are also easier to process cognitively. This was demonstrated for English and Chinese by Osgood and Hoosain (Osgood, 1980). When respondents were asked to respond "positive" to positive words and "negative" to words with a negative affective meaning, response times (measured with a voice-key) tended to be longer for negative words. Another study by Osgood (1979) concerns the use of "and" or "but" in various languages. He argued that the polarity of positive and negative is a basic characteristic of human cognition, already expressed in the ancient Chinese principles of *yang* and *yin*. Osgood anticipated that respondents, when asked to connect two adjectives with either "and" or "but," would use "and" for adjectives with an affectively congruent meaning. When the meaning of two adjectives was affectively incongruent, they should use "but." For example, we tend to speak about noble *and* sincere, beautiful *but* nasty, happy *but* sad, and so forth. From his project on affective meaning, mentioned above, Osgood could calculate for various languages a similarity index between pairs of adjectives. Thereafter the correlation was computed between this similarity index and the frequency of using "and" as a connective between two adjectives. The average of this correlation for twelve languages, including among others American English, Finnish, Turkish, and Japanese was $r = .67$, pointing to a universal presence of the cognitive properties involved.

A universalist approach to research in psycholinguistics is not limited to finding similarities; one can also study differences, mainly as a function of unequal

---

[3] Hemispheric dominance or lateralization can be assessed by means of dichotic listening procedures in which separate stimuli are presented simultaneously to the right ear and to the left ear. When respondents reproduce better the stimuli presented at their left ear this is an indication of right hemisphere dominance; with better reproduction of stimuli to the left ear there is right hemisphere dominance.

antecedent conditions that speakers of a language have been exposed to. In fact, we have given relevant examples already earlier in this chapter. For example, if speakers of Japanese have difficulty distinguishing the English spoken words "lead" and "read," this is a reflection of differences in antecedent experiences. Other phonological features that affect processing of speech have to do with the segmentation of words. Sentences come to a listener as a string of sounds in which (contrary to subjective experience) separate words are not clearly demarcated. It has been demonstrated that there are differences between speakers of various languages in the use of information that can help to recognize separate words in a stream of spoken sounds. In languages like Italian and French where there are many open syllables (consonant–vowel) segmentation is more syllable based, while in languages like English and Dutch where syllables tend to be more complex (e.g., consonants–vowel–consonants, as in the word "strength") listeners make more use of emphasis or stress. In Japanese there is a *mora,* which is a subsyllabic unit, consisting of a small vocalic and/or nasal sound; these *morae* rather than syllables appear to be the unit of segmentation. There is evidence that listening patterns of the first language persist and lead to errors of understanding of languages learned later in life (Otake, Itatano, Cutler, & Mehler, 1993; Vroomen, Van Zon, & De Gelder, 1996; see Van Zon, 1997, for a summary).

All in all, the available evidence in experimental psycholinguistics indicates that language as an instrument for thinking has many cross-culturally invariant properties. As humans we may not all be sharing the same thoughts, but our respective languages do not seem to predestine us much to different kinds of thinking.

## Bilingualism

Up until now in this chapter, language has been discussed mainly with respect to a person's mother tongue (i.e., the language a person first learnt and still understands/speaks). This language is usually the dominant one in use in the culture in which individuals have been enculturated. However, most people in the world learn and speak more than one language; estimates range from between two and five languages typically known per person (Baker & Prys, 1998; Romaine, 1989). Hence, bilingualism (even multilingualism) is the norm, rather than being the exception. Given this fact, we need to consider the phenomenon of **bilingualism** if we are to understand language behavior fully. We also need to consider the cultural contexts in which bilingualism flourishes; this is typically in culturally plural societies, where the process of acculturation is underway (see ch. 13).

Bilingualism has been viewed in various ways (see Mohanty & Perregaux, 1997 for a review). Some are interested in the development of the phenomenon (as a process of second language acquisition); others are more concerned with the outcome (competence in formal language or cognitive tests, or in carrying out daily activities); and others focus on the social aspects (cultural identity and intercultural relations). Because the linguistic situation is becoming more and more complex in most societies, there is also a strong interest among educational researchers in devising plurilinguistic teaching methods (Billiez, 1998; Perregaux, 2000). Despite these differing approaches, the core of bilingualism has been defined by Mohanty and Perregaux (1997, p. 229) as "the ability of persons or communities to meet ... the communicative demands of the self or the society in two or more languages in interaction with the speakers of any or all of these languages." Core issues in bilingualism are its nature, its assessment, and its consequences (both cognitive and social).

A now widely accepted view about bilingualism is that it is not the sum of two monolingualisms, but is a "unique and specific linguistic configuration" (Grosjean, 1982, p. 471). This view holds that a bilingual person is likely to have variable competencies in different domains of life, and that these will change over time and across contexts. From this perspective, the assessment of bilingual competence should not be made using two monolingual tests and their respective norms, but by more holistic estimates of overall bilingual competence. The former approach frequently leads to the negative characterization of bilinguals as "double semilinguals," while the latter approach is a more valid reflection of bilinguals as having a complex and composite linguistic system. Several studies have tried to understand the complexity of cognitive and emotional development when plurilingualism emerges over the lifespan, using the linguistic biographies both of authors and of common people (Deprez, 1994; Green, 1987; Leconte, 1997).

The cognitive and social consequences of bilingualism have been studied extensively. A key research program in dealing with both these issues is that of W. E. Lambert (1967, 1977, 1980). Early studies of the academic, intellectual, and social achievements of bilingual children generally showed that they were "behind in school, retarded in measured intelligence and socially adrift" when compared to monolingual children (Lambert, 1977, p. 15). However, Lambert observed that these comparisons did not control for social class or educational opportunities, and when these factors were controlled in his own studies, bilingual children were ahead on both verbal and non-verbal measures of intelligence (Peal & Lambert, 1962; Lambert & Anisfeld, 1969).

Since then, this picture has been broadened to include bilingual children from Singapore, Sweden, Switzerland, South Africa, and Israel, in addition to the original samples from Montreal. In particular, bilingual children (even when matched on IQ) appeared to be advanced in cognitive flexibility, divergent thinking, and creativity, possibly resulting from the perspective gained from knowing and using a whole new set of linguistic signs and categories (see Segalowitz, 1980 for a review). More recent research has proposed the concept of "metalinguistic awareness," which refers to a sensitivity to language, its rules, and its appropriate use. Studies have shown that bilingual children are more proficient in detecting ambiguity in sentences, have greater sensitivity to intonation (Mohanty, 1994), and a greater facility in the detection of phonemic units of non-words (Perregaux, 1994) than monolingual children. Other studies suggest that these metalinguistic abilities of bilinguals enable them to be even better at learning yet other languages (Thomas, 1988).

Such studies, Lambert (1977) has noted, all involve bilingualism in two languages that are socially valued in their particular context; that is, the learning of the second language is not likely to threaten the survival of the first language. This situation has been termed additive bilingualism by Lambert, in contrast to a subtractive bilingualism where learning a second language often implies a loss of the mother tongue (because of national linguistic or educational policies). It is an important research question to discover whether the positive cognitive consequences of bilingualism are also evident in subtractive situations.

The social consequences of bilingualism, particularly effects on personal identity, have also been examined. In a parallel series of studies in the USA (Louisiana) and Canada (Quebec), Lambert and his colleagues (Gardner & Lambert, 1972) noted wide individual differences in the identities of bilingual children: some identified with one or the other language group, some with both, and some with neither. This pattern corresponds rather closely to the four acculturation strategies (to be described in ch. 13). Mohanty (1994) has examined this correspondence further, and has concluded that the metalinguistic attributes of bilinguals may be particularly advantageous in societies that support additive forms of bilingualism (i.e., integrationist societies), and less so in subtractive situations (i.e., assimilationist societies).

Because so much of the work on these language issues has been conducted in Western societies, it is essential for cross-cultural psychologists to examine them in the other plural societies in the world. The legacy of the colonial era has yielded many nation states (e.g., Nigeria, India) where numerous indigenous languages exist and are used regionally, while one or more national languages (sometimes including that of the former colonial power) are being advocated. As we have argued throughout this book, it is inappropriate to attempt to generalize these (mainly) Western findings to other societies, and would be foolhardy to develop educational or other programs on their basis.

## Conclusions

There is no aspect of overt behavior in which human groups differ more than in the languages they speak. However, by itself this does not have any more far-reaching implications, since there are hardly any connections between the phonemic features of words and their meanings. Frequently occurring notions may be coded in shorter words, but this is about the only regularity. In this chapter we first saw how different languages are acquired through similar steps in ontogenetic development, with cultural differentiation in the use of sounds starting already at an early age.

We then explored the perceptual and cognitive consequences of lexical and grammatical differences, concentrating on two domains where objective reality can be matched with subjective experience and expression, namely color naming and the use of spatial coordinates. The exploration of the literature for evidence of linguistic relativity was followed by a similar exploration of evidence for similarities that could qualify as universal properties of human language. No attempts were made to integrate the two bodies of evidence; for the time being they seem quite far apart.

A somewhat more specific topic was discussed in the last section of the chapter, namely bilingualism and the acquisition of a second language.

## Key terms

basic color terms                    phoneme category
bilingualism                         spatial orientation
color categorization                 universals in language
linguistic relativity

## Further reading

Altarriba, J. (Ed.) (1993). *Cognition and culture: A cross-cultural approach to cognitive psychology*. Amsterdam: North Holland. A series of chapters that deal with issues of cross-cultural cognition and language (also mentioned with the previous chapter).

Gumperz, J. J., & Levinson, S. C. (1996). Introduction: Linguistic relativity re-examined. In J. J. Gumperz & S. C. Levinson (Eds.), *Rethinking linguistic relativity* (pp. 1–18). Cambridge: Cambridge University Press. This introduction provides a relativist view on language and how it influences behavior.

Hardin, C. L., & Maffi, L. (Eds.) (1997). *Colour categories in thought and language.* Cambridge: Cambridge University Press. The chapters of this book examine the evidence on universals in color naming, mostly from a universalist and sometimes from a relativist perspective.

Mohanty, A., & Perregaux, C. (1997). Language acquisition and bilingualism. In J. W. Berry, P. R. Dasen, & T. S. Saraswathi (Eds.), *Basic processes and human development* (pp. 217–53). Vol. II of *Handbook of cross-cultural psychology* (2nd ed.). Boston, MA: Allyn and Bacon. This review chapter critically appraises and integrates research from Europe, Asia, and the Americas, dealing with language and bilingual development.

Slobin, D. I. (Ed.) (1985–97). *The cross-linguistic study of language acquisition* (5 vols.). Mahwah, NJ: Erlbaum. These are five volumes of studies with contributions mainly by linguists, analyzing a variety of languages on a number of grammatical and other linguistic features.

# 7    Emotion

Research on emotions has become increasingly popular in the past few decades. Everyone knows what emotions are; we experience them within ourselves and sense them in others. However, concepts of emotions and theoretical approaches in psychology vary widely (e.g., Ekman & Davidson, 1994). In cross-cultural studies the most central question is how to find a balance between emotions as psychological states that presumably are invariant across cultures, and emotions as social constructions that differ in essential ways across cultures. This theme guides most of the discussion in the chapter. However, we start with a section called "understanding 'others'." It gives an account of a classic research project by Osgood and colleagues demonstrating that dimensions of affective meaning are cross-culturally quite similar and that common concepts also tend to have the same affective meaning. In our view the findings make clear how it is possible that stories and movies originating from one culture more often than not are understood elsewhere.

In the second section we present research aimed at distinguishing a set of universal basic emotions. The evidence derives mainly from culture-comparative studies showing evidence of cross-cultural similarities in the expression of emotions in the face, in the voice, and in gestures. In the next section an opposite viewpoint is presented, suggesting that emotions are cultural states, implying that they are primarily social or cognitive constructions and that elsewhere there are emotions that "we" do not experience, and that "we" may have emotions that are not found in other cultures. Here the evidence comes mainly from ethnographic accounts and linguistic analysis. The last section presents the componential approach to emotions. This approach combines aspects of the two previous perspectives. It emphasizes that an emotion is not so much a singular state of the organism, but is made up of a sequence of processes or components, like, for example, the appraisal of the situation and the tendency to act in a certain way. Across cultures there can be similarities and differences in each of the components.

There is an important prior point to note. Claims to the effect that cross-culturally an emotion (or emotion component) is "similar," or to the effect that an emotion is "different," often are not stated precisely. There is an absence of precise criteria or standards in terms of which it can be decided that an emotion is different, that it is similar, or even identical. Take the following imaginary example. Suppose a young boy has gone with his friend to some forbidden place. He denies having gone there, but is caught lying about this by his father. The father is angry, which becomes manifest in the boy being scolded and given a punishment. It is quite likely that this event could be observed in two societies culturally quite far apart. Can we conclude that the expressions and actions of the two fathers point to there being an emotion of anger that is similar if not identical? A more detailed narrative undoubtedly would show up some differences. In the one case the father's anger may be more a matter of concern about the moral character of the son, in the other case more about the challenge to the father's own authority, or because of danger to the son. Can we then conclude that the anger of the two fathers is *not* the same?

When formulated in this way the question of whether psychological processes can be cross-culturally identical can never be answered unambiguously. If processes and behavior manifestations are seen as closely connected, a difference in manifestation implies a difference in process and it becomes impossible to demonstrate cross-cultural invariance of emotions. On the other hand, if one takes a less detailed perspective and abstracts more from concrete reactions in specific situations, general characteristics are likely to emerge more clearly. One obvious solution is to consider the two opposing viewpoints as complementary. However, unless this complementarity is formulated in an explicit way that is accessible to critical examination, this solution becomes an unacceptably vague compromise (cf. ch. 12).

## Understanding "others"

In this section we formulate a tentative answer to the question of why human beings, even from very different cultures, often make sense of each other's behavior. We do this with reference to a "classic" empirical research project conducted by Charles Osgood (1977; Osgood et al. 1975). The project stems from a research tradition in which the central theme is how members of various cultural groups experience themselves and their social environment. A distinction can be made between objective and subjective aspects of culture (Herskovits, 1948). The objective aspects are reflected in indicators about climatic conditions, number of years of schooling, national product, etc. Subjective indices reflect how members of a culture view themselves and how they evaluate their way of life. This reflects their **subjective culture**.

In the analysis of subjective culture people are asked how they perceive themselves and how they see others. Triandis and Vassiliou (1972) found that Greeks tend to describe themselves as *philotimous*. As much as 74 percent of a sample of respondents used this term in self-description. There is no direct English equivalent of the concept of *philotimo*. Triandis and Vassiliou (1972, pp. 308–9) write: "A person who has this characteristic is polite, virtuous, reliable, proud, has a 'good soul', behaves correctly, meets his obligations, does his duty, is truthful, generous, self-sacrificing, tactful, respectful, and grateful." They summarize by stating that a person who is *philotimous* "behaves towards members of his ingroup the way they expect him to behave."

Apparently Triandis and Vassiliou are of the opinion that they can communicate the meaning of the Greek concept to their (mainly) American and west European readers. The question can be asked whether this is indeed possible. Does the description capture all essential aspects of *philotimo* as experienced by the Greeks or is there still something important missing? If the former alternative is correct, a second question can be asked, namely what the implications are of the emphasis on *philotimo* in Greece.

Words not only have a denotative, but also a connotative meaning. A word points to a certain referent; it has a designative or referential meaning, that is called denotative. In addition a word has an emotional and metaphoric tone; this is called the connotative meaning. The terms objective meaning and subjective meaning capture more or less the same contrast. The semantic differential technique (Osgood, Suci, & Tannenbaum, 1957) is a method for describing the connotative meaning of words. A respondent is given a word that has to be rated on a number of seven-point scales. The poles of each scale are marked by a pair of contrasting adjectives, for example good versus bad, light versus dark, or quick versus slow. From factor analyses in the USA it emerged that the ratings on all kinds of words could be represented by three factors that were labeled evaluation (good–bad), potency (strong–weak), and activity (active–passive). These three factors together defined a three-dimensional space of **affective meaning**. The affective meaning of any word can be identified in terms of its position in this three-dimensional space. For example, the word "kind" has a high positive value on the evaluation factor, a medium value on potency, and a low value on activity.

In a project that lasted more than fifteen years data were collected with the semantic differential technique in thirty communities (Osgood et al., 1975; Osgood, 1977). In each one hundred nouns were used as the concepts to be rated. These included "house," "fruit," "cloud," "hunger," "freedom," "money," and "policeman." These presumably culture-common notions were first used to elicit in each culture a large number of adjectives associated with these nouns. In a computer analysis fifty bipolar pairs of adjectives were selected from the data set in each culture. It may be noted that these scales were chosen by means of a computational procedure in which the meaning of the adjectives did not play any role; these adjectives were not even translated into English.

The hundred nouns were then rated in each culture by one hundred teenage boys on each of the fifty bipolar scales. These results were analyzed for the thirty cultures together in what is called a pan-cultural factor analysis. The three-dimensional structure described earlier emerged very clearly. For each of the three dimensions bipolar pairs of adjectives with a high loading could be found in each of the thirty cultures. On translation of these adjectives into English it was evident that there was a high similarity in meaning. Consequently, it could be concluded that the three dimensions had similar meaning across all thirty populations.

For more practical use of the semantic differential technique a short form was developed for each culture consisting of the four local scales with the highest loadings on each of the three factors, evaluation, potency, and activity. This short form with twelve bipolar rating scales was prepared for large-scale application in each of the thirty cultures.

The short forms were used in each culture to rate 620 concepts. These data form the basis of the famous Atlas of Affective Meaning (Osgood et al., 1975). Chunks of data from the atlas have been used to identify universals (non-chance trends across all societies), sub-universals (clusters of societies sharing certain patterns of deviations), and uniquenesses (deviations of individual societies from universal trends). In respect of color words, which we mentioned in ch. 6, it was found universally, for example, that "brightness" is more positively evaluated than "darkness," but that "darkness" is higher on potency. "Red" is less positively evaluated than "blue," but it is higher on activity.

Among the culturally unique features is a relatively high positive evaluation of "being aggressive" in the USA. Osgood gives as a reason that in the USA aggression also implies being competitive in sports and at school and that it does not so much imply an intent to cause injury to others, the more common meaning elsewhere. Other examples include a unique meaning of the color black among Indian students in Delhi. Black showed unusually low potency and high activity. By local informants the high activity was ascribed to the association of black with the god Krishna and with hair, and the low potency to the lower status of a dark skin. It is well recognized that uniquenesses may reflect method artifacts and that the interpretations can only be tentative until supported by other evidence. The emphasis in the atlas is on the universal rather than on the specific.

The research by Osgood and his colleagues provides some means to answer the two questions asked earlier in this section. These results are suggestive of a common structure of affective meaning. This implies that differences in traits, such as the emphasis on *philotimo* among the Greeks, should indeed be communicable to members of other cultures. Of course, we cannot be perfectly sure that Triandis and Vassiliou have indeed rendered correctly the meaning of *philotimo* for their readers. However, the research by Osgood and his associates indicates that at least this should be possible in principle.

Inasmuch as "culture" can be identified with subjective culture the semantic differential technique can be used to assess the distance between populations defined in cultural terms. It seems intuitively likely that the distance in cultural matters between cultures A and B will not be equal to that between A and C, and A and D and so on. If cross-cultural differences are large, ratings on denotatively identical concepts can be expected to show larger connotative discrepancies than when such differences are small.

Still, it is difficult to know what the implications are of the emphasis among the Greeks on the concept of *philotimo*. As we saw, in the Atlas uniquenesses have also been identified. The concept of *philotimo* can be seen as representing a location in an affective meaning space for which in English there is no specific word. Triandis and Vassiliou mention that *philotimo* is a rather central concept for people in Greece. For example, a *philotimous* young man in traditional Greek society will not marry before he has earned the dowry that is needed for his sister's marriage. It is likely that Greeks will often refer to *philotimo* as the reason for an action. In other societies an obligation in respect of the marriage of one's sister may not exist. However, there will be other obligations, or in a more general sense, other prescriptive norms for social behavior. The reasons given for such obligatory acts presumably will include concepts such as doing one's duty, truthfulness, respect, and other terms from the list that we quoted earlier from Triandis and Vassiliou. Thus, the area in semantic space covered in the Greek language by *philotimo* is represented by other terms in other languages. At the same time, more interpretive methods may also reveal a specific usage of the word *philotimo* that readers of the description by Triandis and Vassiliou in other cultures would never think of. The three dimensions of Osgood are not exhaustive and do not capture all possible shades of meaning.

In other words, the implications of the emphasis of the Greeks on *philotimo* for their actual behavior in distinction to non-Greeks cannot be established from the analysis of subjective meaning alone. Our second question is unanswerable without additional information. Examples of studies are available where findings with the semantic differential technique are placed in a broader context (Triandis, 1972; Osgood et al. 1975), but these additional data do not match the semantic differential ratings in extent and quality.

Considering the evidence we are inclined to conclude that the study of subjective culture has pointed to common elements in the experiences of humans independent of their cultural background. However, some reservation has to be expressed as Osgood's work was limited to young students in all cultures investigated, thus systematically excluding all illiterate populations.

## Universality of emotions

There is a range of theories in biology and the neurosciences about the evolutionary history of emotions and their location in brain structures (e.g., Gazzaniga, 1995; McNaughton, 1989). In psychology there is a long tradition of research in which psychophysiological processes and other bodily events, like facial expressions, have been investigated as concomitants of internal states experienced as emotions. The nature of the relationships between self-reports of feeling states and underlying processes is not very clear, and many researchers would seem to agree that the biological basis of commonly distinguished separate emotions like happiness, anger, fear, and sadness has not been clearly established (Cacioppo & Tassinary, 1990). However, quite apart from their validity the theories do reflect a fairly common belief that emotions are associated with biological processes characteristic of the human species. Thus, it is not surprising that there is also cross-cultural research pursuing universalities in emotional life. The most extensive topic of study has been the facial expression of emotions.

## Recognition of facial expression

Modern studies of the expression of emotions go back to Darwin (1872/1998). He saw the universal occurrence of the same facial expressions as important evidence that emotions are innate. From a survey among British residents in various countries Darwin acquired information which he saw as a validation of his viewpoint. Ekman (e.g., 1973; see also Darwin, 1998) has pointed out that Darwin's criterion of universality of emotional expression does not provide a sufficient proof for the biological inheritance of emotions. Early experiences common to all humans in infancy and childhood form an alternative explanation.

When the biological basis of behavior was challenged by social scientists in the first half of the twentieth century, Darwin's results were also questioned and the point of view became popular that there were major cultural differences in emotional expressions. According to authors like Klineberg (1940) and Birdwhistell (1970) these differences mean that human emotional expression is acquired in the process of socialization, at least to a considerable extent. Impressive illustrations have been quoted: the widow of a Samurai fighter who died in combat, supposedly would be proud and smile rather than be sad. Ekman (e.g., 1998) has reviewed the evidence favoring culture-specific views. He found that such results, like those of Darwin, rested on casual observations and anecdotal data.

The best-known studies that systematically probe the question of cross-cultural invariance of facial expression are those conducted by Ekman among the Fore in East New Guinea. Ekman (1980) has published a series of photographs that show a similar range of emotional expressions as are found in the industrialized countries. Although subjectively convincing, this does not constitute strong scientific evidence. Ekman and his team also conducted two types of experiments. In one type they presented the respondents with three photographs of people each displaying a different emotion, and asked them to indicate the person to whom something had happened (e.g., whose child had died). In the other type of experiment respondents were asked to make the face they would show when they were happy to see their friends, angry enough to fight, etc. These facial expressions were photographed and later on analyzed to determine whether the same emotion-specific muscular patterns in the face could be found as previously established for Western respondents.

In contrast to previous studies the photographs displaying an emotion had been selected on the basis of a theory, developed by Tomkins (1962, 1963), that suggested links between central nervous system activity and contractions of the facial muscles. Ekman and Friesen (1969) suspected that most facial expressions reflect a blending of more than a single emotion. A postulate following from their theory was that there is a characteristic pattern of the facial muscles for each so-called basic emotion. On this basis they selected photographs that showed one of six unblended emotions: happiness, sadness, anger, fear, surprise, and disgust. Later on a further muscular pattern was distinguished and a seventh expression, contempt, was added to the set of **basic emotions** (Ekman & Friesen, 1986).

The first substantive cross-cultural evidence was obtained when respondents in five societies (Argentina, Brazil, Chile, Japan, USA) were shown photographs displaying the six emotions. Terms for these emotions were given as response alternatives with each stimulus. The overall rate of correct identification was quite high and, most important, no significant difference between cultures was found when the results for the six emotions were combined (Ekman & Friesen, 1969).

Although this pleaded strongly against culture specificity, there was still a possibility that the emotional content of photographs from the USA could be recognized in other countries because of people's previous exposure to American movies and other cultural products. To rule out the alternative explanation of cultural diffusion (cf. ch. 11), the research was extended to groups isolated from Western visual materials and Western persons, like the Fore. Leaving out a confusion between fear and surprise, the percentage of agreement between the Fore and Western respondents on the meaning of (Western) facial expressions was as high as 80 percent for a sample of adults and 90 percent for children (Ekman & Friesen, 1971). In the reverse case where filmed emotions of the Fore were shown to American students similar results were obtained, again with a confusion between fear and surprise.

The results of Ekman and his associates do not stand alone. Their work was replicated among the Dani, a group living in the mountains of West Irian (West New Guinea). The results again showed that the basic facial expressions of emotion were interpreted in a similar way as in the industrialized urban world. Independent studies by other researchers, like Izard (1971), have also provided results that were compatible with the findings of the Ekman group. Several attempts have been made to elaborate on aspects of the research procedure. The main reason for such attempts is that despite the overall similarities the recognition rate of facial stimuli tends to be lower as respondents have less previous contact with Western culture. In the research among the Fore the rates of agreement were mostly of the same order of size as in the earlier study by Ekman and Friesen with respondents from six countries, but the task had been simplified from a six-choice to three-choice format.

The obvious question is to what extent the lower recognition rates reflect artifacts of the test method (e.g., cultural idiosyncrasies in the stimuli) and to what extent they reflect effects of cultural factors on emotions. Studies designed to probe this problem (e.g., Boucher & Carlson, 1980; Ducci, Arcuri, Georgis, & Sinseshaw,

1982) did not lead to unambivalent results. There appeared to be at least *some* cultural variation in the ease of recognition of specific emotions. On the other hand, Ekman and colleagues (Ekman et al., 1987) in a ten-culture study (with countries as far apart as Estonia, Turkey, and Japan) demonstrated that blended (or mixed) emotion expressions also are recognized across cultures.

A comparison between the Asian and Western samples of the intensity ratings for the stimulus faces (that were all Caucasian) showed lower intensity ratings for the Asian respondents. Therefore, Ekman et al. suggested that possibly less intense emotions are attributed to expressions on foreign faces. In later studies differences in intensity ratings have been attributed to differences in the perception of emotion expressions. Broad cultural dimensions have been proposed as an explanation, in particular individualism–collectivism. For example, Matsumoto (1992), using Japanese and American faces with samples from Japan and the USA, found lower ratings of intensity to negative emotions in the Japanese sample. He suggested that in Japan, as a relatively collectivist country, the display of negative emotions is discouraged, and hence their recognition is lower, since negative emotions are disruptive of social relations. In the USA, an individualist country, more open expression of these emotions is tolerated and this leads to better recognition. Needless to say that this interpretation presumes the validity of the individualism–collectivism difference between the two countries that later on was questioned by Matsumoto (1999; cf. ch. 4).

In the early 1990s the universality of facial expressions for basic emotions had become widely accepted and much of the debate had shifted toward the implications of universal facial expressions. However, a major challenge was issued by Russell (1994) in an article of which the summary started with the telling sentence: "Emotions are universally recognized from facial expressions–or so it has been claimed" (p. 102). Russell presented a number of criticisms of Ekman's findings. Among other things he argued that the notion of universality tends to be rather imprecise, and thus also what constitutes evidence of universality. Moreover, a distinction needs to be made between the occurrence of facial muscle movements per se, their representation of emotions, and the attribution of emotional meaning by observers. Russell also questioned the strength of the empirical results on several counts. Most studies were conducted with students and in literate societies, limiting cultural variation, and allowing the possibility of cultural diffusion. And most studies used a method of presenting stimuli without context (i.e., staged facial expressions) and a limited range of response alternatives (namely a set of terms representing the six or seven basic emotions) in a forced-choice format.

Russell (1994) noted that in studies with a free choice of reactions a broad range of terms and descriptive sentences tended to be used by respondents for one and the same stimulus face. In such studies rates of recognition were lower than with the response format used by Ekman and colleagues, unless very broad clusters of terms were scored as evidence of recognition of one and the same emotion. For example, does "frustration," as an answer to a stimulus meant to represent anger, form a positive or a negative recognition score? Russell argues that still less consistency of recognition is found in results obtained in groups with little exposure to Western influences. In discussing Ekman's original studies he finds only clear support for the recognition of happiness and concludes that the "pattern of results for the Fore is not easy to reconcile with the original hypothesis" (p. 129).

In Russell's view research with photographs tells us little about the facial expressions that occur naturally in a society, with what frequency, and in which situational contexts. He is quite willing to concede that a null hypothesis to the effect there is no cross-cultural agreement whatsoever has to be rejected, but this is about as far as the evidence goes. It cannot be ruled out that the categorization of emotions varies among languages (and even among individual persons). Moreover, there is substantial evidence for dimensional rather than categorical distinctions, with two or three dimensions similar to those of Osgood mentioned earlier in this chapter (cf. Russell, 1991). Although the opinions on emotions found in other cultures cannot be assumed to be better than our own, we need to study these cultures to find out more about our beliefs. Going even a step further Russell ends his article with the comment: "We might more usefully gather the beliefs of different cultures rather than evaluate them" (p. 138).

In a reaction Izard (1994) points out that the evidence for inborn facial expressions being linked to emotions goes much beyond the language-dependent data that Russell made the target of his comments. Izard argues that Darwin proposed a testable hypothesis to the effect that human emotions and their facial expressions have an evolutionary-biological origin. This "innateness–universality hypothesis" was not directly addressed by Russell's criticisms, which concerned only the universality of semantic attributions to facial expressions. Izard mentioned evidence from studies with infants at pre-verbal ages in which consistent and recognizable facial expressions were found across cultures. However, he also defended the semantic attribution hypothesis, arguing, among other things, that emotion recognition is a much easier task than emotion labeling and that this may well explain the lower rate of correct identifications with a free-response format. Also, translation inequivalence can play a role. Izard concluded that it remains most plausible that there is a limited set of emotion expressions which is innate and universal.

A rather sharp rebuttal to Russell came from Ekman (1994), who basically upheld his own position. One of his main points is that universality does not require perfect agreement in judgments, but only an amount of agreement that is statistically significant. Ekman (1994, p. 270) writes: "A reader of [Russell's] article might not know that our view of emotional expression was, from the outset, not absolutist" (see ch. 12 for a similar concern). In fact, the theory was named a neurocultural theory, emphasizing two sets of determinants of facial expressions, one responsible for universals, the other for cultural differences. It is to be expected that the matching of words to emotions would be inherently imperfect. In addition, cultures are likely to verbally label emotions in different ways, including references to emotion antecedents, consequences, sensations, etc. Ekman spends most of his article showing that the cross-cultural agreements were much more substantial than acknowledged by Russell, including the findings from pre-literate societies. In a final reply Russell (1995) conceded some minor points, but, not surprisingly, the major differences of opinion remained substantially unchanged.

Direct relationships between facial expressions and autonomic nervous system activity for separate emotions have been examined in a study by Levenson, Ekman, Heider, and Friesen (1992) among the Minangkabau on Sumatra, where the display of negative emotions like anger is frowned upon. Levenson and his colleagues asked respondents to voluntarily contract facial muscles (e.g., "pull your lower lip down"; "wrinkle your nose"). In this way prototypical facial configurations were made up, corresponding to happiness, sadness, disgust, fear, and anger. When a configuration was considered sufficiently accurate, the respondent was asked to hold it for about ten seconds. Psychophysiological variables, like heart rate, skin conductance, and respiration were recorded. Afterwards, the respondent was asked whether any emotion had been experienced during the facial configuration. Although the configurations were not very precise, patterns of emotion-specific physiological reactions were observed that resembled some-what results found in the USA. Levenson et al. emphasize that these patterns oc-curred also for anger, despite the strong disapproval among the Minangkabau of its expression. However, unlike findings from the USA, self-reports of associated emotions experienced during the staging of the facial configurations were at less than chance levels. The authors intrerpret this as evidence for cultural learning about which internal states are labeled as "emotions." An alternative interpreta-tion is perhaps that this dissociation between psychophysiological events and experienced state further weakens the findings of this interesting study.

Challenges to the universalist position of Ekman have led to further research. In one study Haidt and Keltner (1999) presented posed pictures of fourteen facial ex-pressions to respondents in the USA and India. The expressions included Ekman's seven basic emotions as well as some other emotions, like shame, embarrassment, and compassion. Respondents were asked for free responses and were also pre-sented the photographs in a forced-response format including a "none-of-the-above" alternative. Moreover, they were asked for contextual information, i.e., what hap-pened to the person in the photograph. Although differences in method did matter, the results showed that the earlier findings of Ekman could not be ascribed to method artifacts. Six of his seven basic emotions were among the seven best-recognized photographs. At the same time, there were several cross-cultural dif-ferences in rate of recognition. However, these were difficult to explain, and may have been due in part to less adequately controlled aspects of method.

The extension of the set of emotions in this study draws attention to a major issue, namely the number of basic emotions and the criteria for demarcation, (i.e., how to differentiate emotions from each other). Ekman's position is clear; the presence or absence of a characteristic facial expression is the main criterion. This means that social emotions like shame and guilt, or love, which are seen by others as basic emotions, for example by Izard (1977), are subsumed as blends under the recognized basic emotions, or have to be excluded from the domain of emotions. The complexity of the demarcation problem does not diminish when more basic emotions and/or other methods of assessment are allowed. For example, there is extensive research with questionnaires in which the distinction of shame, guilt, and embarrassment is the main focus of attention (Tangney, 1990; 1992), and where researchers struggle with similar problems.

## Recognition of vocal expression

Research on cross-cultural recognition of emotional intonation in the voice has shown similar results to those obtained for facial expression. Albas, McCluskey, and Albas (1976) collected speech samples meant to express happiness, sadness, love, and anger from English- and Cree-speaking Canadian respondents. These expressions were made semantically unintelligible by means of an electronic filtering procedure that left the emotional intonation intact. Respondents from both language groups recognized the emotions intended by the speakers far beyond chance level, but the performance was better in the own language than in the other language. In another study McCluskey, Albas, Niemi, Cuevas, and Ferrer (1975) made a comparison between Mexican and Canadian children (six to eleven years of age). With a similar procedure they found that the Mexican children did better than the Canadian respondents also on the identification of Canadian English expressions, a finding which was tentatively ascribed to a greater importance of intonation in Mexican speech.

Van Bezooijen, Otto and Heenan (1983) tried to explain why the vocal expression of certain emotions appears to be recognized more easily than that of others. They made a comparison between Dutch, Taiwanese, and Japanese respondents, using a single brief phrase in Dutch that had been expressed by different speakers in nine different emotional tones (i.e., disgust, surprise, shame, joy, fear, contempt, sadness, anger, as well as a neutral tone of voice). With one exception all emotions were recognized at better than chance level by all three groups, but the scores of the Dutch respondents were much higher, suggesting a fair amount of information loss due to cultural and/or linguistic differences between the three samples. On the basis of an analysis of the rate of confusion between the various emotions Van Bezooijen et al. suggested that emotions were more difficult to distinguish when they reflected a more similar level of activation or arousal. Activation level was found to be more important for recognition than the evaluation dimension (i.e., positive and negative emotions). In a scaling analysis the distance between, for example, the passive emotions of shame and sadness and that between the active emotions of joy and anger turned out to be small, while the distance between shame and anger was much larger. This is in line with the general literature on the recognition of vocal expression of emotion (e.g., Scherer, 1981).

## Display rules

As mentioned before, emphasis on the universality of emotions never meant that there would be no cross-cultural differences in manifestations of emotions, for example in the frequency and intensity with which emotions are expressed. Ekman (1973, p. 176) has introduced the notion of **display rules**, "norms regarding the expected management of facial appearance." Within each culture there are rules about what face to put on at certain occasions, and whether one should or should not show certain emotions (e.g., as noted earlier, the widow of a Samurai fighter may smile when feeling grief). The cultural rules prescribe in this case the emotional expression that should be simulated. There are few controlled experiments in which the suppression or production of expressions in social situations has been demonstrated. An exception is a study by Ekman and Friesen (Ekman, 1973).

Japanese and USA students were shown stressful films in isolation and in the presence of an experimenter. Without the respondents' awareness the emotional expressions on the face were recorded in both conditions. Highly similar expressions were found in reaction to the same movie episodes when the respondents were alone. However, in the presence of the other person the Japanese respondents showed far fewer negative facial expressions than the Americans. Needless to say, this result fits the existing notions in the West about the impassive Japanese.

Some more recent studies have also reported differences in display rules. For example, Matsumoto and Hearn (1991, reported in Matsumoto, 1996) asked respondents in the USA, Hungary, and Poland to rate how appropriate expression of each of six basic emotions would be in each of three situations: (1) by yourself, (2) in the company of in-group members like friends and family, and (3) with "outsiders," for example in public. The east Europeans, more than the Americans, reported that it was less appropriate to display negative emotions in in-groups and more appropriate to display positive emotions. It should be noted that the notion of display rules is suggestive of cross-culturally similar underlying emotions, with differences in the promotion or inhibition of their expression. Researchers who assume essential cross-cultural differences in emotions, discussed in the following sections, are less inclined to use this notion.

## Non-verbal communication

Emotions serve communicative functions in social interaction. According to Fridlund (1997) facial expressions have evolved in the evolutionary history of the human species for this purpose. According to Frijda (1986, p. 60) it is an open question whether emotional expressions have evolved phylogenetically for the purpose of communication; they may have come about for quite different reasons (see also ch. 10). Nevertheless, emotional expresssions can often serve communication and they can be produced with that intention. There are also other channels of non-verbal communication, some of which will be mentioned here. For a general overview of this literature we refer to Argyle (1988). In this section we are particularly interested in the question of to what extent these other channels of communication confirm the impression of basic similarities across cultures that has emerged from the study of facial and vocal expressions.

A well-studied form of non-verbal communication are gestures. This interest has cross-cultural roots. In earlier times explorers often managed to acquire goods and even engaged in some kind of bargaining with people with whom they did not share any common language. Many modern day tourists have similar experiences. In the eighteenth and nineteenth centuries the idea of gestures as a universal, be it rudimentary, form of language gained some popularity (e.g., Kendon, 1984). However, identity of the meaning of gestures as a general rule cannot be maintained. Morris, Collett, Marsh, and O'Shaughnessy (1979) found that common well-defined gestures can have a different meaning in various regions of Europe; and even within countries they are not always used with the same meaning.

Most gestures are not made to communicate a message. Ekman and his coworkers (e.g., Ekman, 1982; Ekman & Friesen, 1969) have distinguished various categories of gestures, such as adaptors (or body manipulators), regulators, illustrators, and emblems. Adaptors, like scratching one's nose, have developed from movements connected with bodily needs or interpersonal contacts. In the course of development they can become fragmented and lose their function. Scratching one's nose when deep in thought can be a remnant of nose picking. Regulators are head and arm gestures or body postures that play a role in taking turns of listening and speaking in the conversation between two or more interactants. Illustrators are directly tied to speech; they serve to underline or depict what is being said and are related to features of the language. Emblems have a cognitive meaning by themselves that is usually familiar to members of a culture. They are meant to communicate this meaning and usually there is a verbal equivalent; the research by Morris et al. (1979) was based on emblems.

Presumably all these types of gestures are shaped in the process of socialization and enculturation. Child training includes the modification of adaptors, especially those that are considered improper in the presence of others. Regulators are made without explicit awareness, but according to Ekman and Friesen can become a source of misunderstanding between persons from different cultures.

On the other hand, even in respect of emblems there is cross-cultural commonality. Many emblems can be understood even when the perceiver has no knowledge of the culture of the sender. Argyle (1988) argues that some of the more common gestures, such as the shrug, may well be innate; others may be common because they follow from the nature of physical space. The arm gesture "come to me" is likely to be understood worldwide. But a fist with an outstretched finger to indicate a gun presumes knowledge of a cultural product not found everywhere and offers no basis for recognition for someone who has no prior knowledge of guns. Ekman and Friesen (1969) have made a distinction between referential emblems, where the distance between the form of a gesture and the referent (what is being depicted) is small, and conventional emblems, where this difference is large and dependent on prior cultural knowledge. Poortinga, Schoots, and Van de Koppel (1993) found that Dutch students could not only give the meaning of referential emblems generated by persons from China and Kurdistan, but also reported that most of these gestures were present in their own culture.

This suggests that there is a repertoire of referential emblems common to at least a broad range of cultures. However, the rate of recognition for conventional emblems varied; a few, like some emblems depicting a Chinese character for a numeral, were interpreted correctly below chance level in a multiple-choice test.

However, the importance of cross-cultural differences may well lie mainly in the frequency of usage of gestures of various types, or (analogous with facial expression) in the display rules concerning the use of gestures. Italians tend to give an excited impression to visitors from more northern countries presumably because of their more lively movement patterns. Efron (1941/1972) compared gestures of Italian and east European Jewish immigrants in New York and found differences in gesturing style. Among other things quite different illustrators were used. A comparative study of Italians and British showed that the presence of gestures with the verbal description of complex geometrical shapes aided the Italians in the accuracy of understanding, but hardly made any difference to the British respondents (Graham & Argyle, 1975).

Somewhat related to gestures are body position and personal space. Most of the research is of a less recent date and has been summarized by Altman and Chemers (1980). The notion of personal space is based on the idea that every person is surrounded by a private sphere. When somebody comes and stands too close to us this is experienced as an intrusion. The anthropologist Hall (1966), who was the first to draw attention to cross-cultural differences in personal space, noted that Arabs, southern Europeans, and Latin Americans stand close together when talking. They tend to touch each other and even breathe in each other's faces, while people of northern European descent keep a much larger physical distance. Subsequent research has only led to a very partial corroboration of Hall's dimension of high-contact and low-contact cultures. Intracultural variations due to social class and situational factors obscure the original dimension. For example, Sussman and Rosenfeld (1982) found that Japanese students in the USA were seated further apart than students from Venezuela when talking in their own languages. When speaking English this difference disappeared and students from both countries sat at a similar distance as observed for students from the USA. This suggests that the differences are not very deep seated, but amount to cultural practices that are subject to acculturation.

## Emotions as cultural states

A well-known study rejecting the notion that human emotional experiencing is basically the same across cultures is an ethnographic analysis by Lutz (1988) of the emotional life of the Ifaluk who live on an atoll in the South Pacific. She set out to contrast cultural assumptions found in Western thinking about emotions with those found in another society. She argues: "This book attempts to demonstrate how emotional meaning is fundamentally structured by particular cultural systems and particular social and material environments. The claim is made that emotional experience is not precultural but *preeminently* cultural" (p. 5, italics in the original). Indigenous models about self and social interaction should be used to understand emotion terms. Lutz concentrates her analysis on two emotions that in her opinion are not found in the USA: namely *fago* (an amalgam of what in English is expressed as compassion, love, and sadness) and *song* (translated as "justifiable anger"). Like anger, "*song* is considered an unpleasant emotion that is experienced in a situation of perceived injury to self or to another" (p. 156). Unlike anger *song* is not so much about what is personally disliked as about what is socially condemned. There are other words that refer to forms of anger, but these are clearly distinguishable from "the anger which is a righteous indignation, or justifiable anger (*song*), and it is only this anger which is morally approved" (p. 157).

One might ask the question whether Lutz's account of Ifaluk emotional life is accurately perceived by her and made understandable to a Western reader. Since replication studies in ethnography have shown poor consistency (e.g., Kloos, 1988), such a question is legitimate (cf. also Russell, 1991). If we assume that Lutz presents a more or less accurate picture of what *song* means the next question is whether this emotional state is indeed unknown in the USA or other Western countries. The description of *song* could be said to be reminiscent of the indignation shown by a trade union leader in front of a TV camera who strongly condemns an unacceptably low salary offer by management and makes clear that such an offer is morally and socially unacceptable.

Rather than presenting such an impressionistic argument one might examine systematically whether in the USA one can find distinctions similar to those made by the Ifaluk, or elsewhere. Such a study was carried out by Frank, Harvey, and Verdun (2000). Following descriptions of five forms of shame in China by Bedford (1994), these authors wrote different scenarios that captured the distinctions and they prepared scales (e.g., feeling helpless, disgraced myself, wishing to hide) on which these scenarios had to be rated. Results of USA students showed that the original grouping could be largely recovered, suggesting that Americans can also recognize varieties of shame distinguished by Chinese. Frank et al. emphasized that their findings do not reflect possible differences in the importance of these varieties of shame in everyday life.

Emphasis on the **social construction of emotions** as a rule does not imply a complete denial of biological aspects. According to Averill (1980) theories that appear as incompatible merely address different aspects of the same phenomena. At the same time, he argues that emotions are not biological givens, but social constructions. For Averill an emotion is a transitory social role; for such a role the relevant rules in the form of norms and expectations regarding social behavior are given. Emotion-specific meanings are attributed to events and these meanings are likely to differ across cultures. The main route of research is the ethnographic description (cf. Heelas, 1986).

A central point in such descriptions is the meaning of specific emotion terms that are not easily translated into another language, and that are seen as shaped by the specific cultural context in which they occur. *Song* is such an emotion term. Another example is the term *liget* among the Ilongots in the Philippines that has been de-scribed by Rosaldo (1980). *Liget* is a form of anger, but also covers feelings of grief; it is associated with the practice of headhunting. Sometimes there are more words for a part of the emotional domain that is covered by a single term in English. A well-known example are several words in Javanese for each of which the closest translation would be "shame" in English (Geertz, 1961). In other instances there appears to be no word even for some basic emotion as distinguished by Ekman; for example, a word for sadness seems to be absent on Tahiti (Levy, 1984).

A summary table with about twenty cases where a word for a basic emotion appears to be missing in some language is presented by Russell (1991). A high emphasis on a particular emotion according to Levy amounts to an elaborate cognitive structure and a differentiated set of terms; this is called "hyper"cogni-tion (i.e., overrecognized). Similarly low salience could lead to "hypo"cognized (i.e., underrecognized) emotions for which few words should be expected. A somewhat similar suggestion has been made by Markus and Kitayama (1994) with the notion of "core cultural ideas," that is, key cultural ideas in which members of a specific culture are socialized and which are important for the way they view themselves and the world. It may be noted that such distinctions are reminiscent of the Sapir–Whorf hypothesis discussed in the previous chapter.

A researcher who gives a central role to language is Wierzbicka (1994, 1998, 1999). Since translations of words in languages are bound to be distorted, we need to make use of a metalanguage derived from cross-linguistic research. There are words in any language that are not found in other languages, but there are also words that have corresponding meanings in every language. These refer to universal human concepts and form the basis for a "non-arbitrary and nonethnocentric meta-language" (1999, p. 36). This shared core is represented in conceptual primitives and lexical universals. Some of these primitives refer to emotions. Thus, in general the universality of emotions is not questioned, but they need to be conceptualized in certain themes which are linked to cognitive scenarios underlying the emotion concepts of a group. Semantic analysis must make a distinction between context-independent invariants and contextual interpretations. For example, a smile has the invariant core meaning of "I feel something good now."

In respect of emotion universals Wierzbicka (1999) makes several assumptions among which are the following. All languages have a word for "feel" and some feelings can be described as good and others as bad. There are facial expressions that in all groups are linked with either good or bad feelings. All languages have words linking feelings with certain thoughts, for example "the thought that something bad can happen to me," which is overlapping with the English word "afraid," and the thought "I want to do something," which comes close to the word "angry." Moreover, cognitive scenarios of emotions tend to point to social and moral issues, and to interpersonal interactions. These few comments should suffice to illustrate that the essence of emotions is located in thinking and language.

In studies of the meaning of emotion words in specific languages, Wierzbicka (e.g., 1998), presents elaborate descriptions of cultural embeddedness and specificity of meaning. An example is the meaning of the word *Angst* (anxiety) in German which differs from the word *Furcht* (fear). Contrary to *Furcht,* that has an object (being afraid of something), *Angst* is fear without an object to be afraid of; it is a frequently used and salient term in German, and represents a basic emotion of which the roots are said to go back to the writings of the sixteenth-century theologian Martin Luther who, like many of his contemporaries, was struggling with the uncertainties of life and of life after death.

Not everybody may be convinced that cultural elucidations as mentioned justify the conclusion that *Angst* in Germany is a cultural creation differing in essential ways from anxiety as a basic emotion in other societies. It certainly has not been demonstrated in a systematic way by comparing feeling states of Germans with those of other language groups. The main issue has been expressed by Frijda, Markam, Sato, and Wiers (1995) as follows: "One can assume that there exist words ('emotion words') that dictate the way things are seen; or one can assume that there exist things ('emotions') that are given names and thus have words assigned to them." One might say that authors like Ekman want to use cross-cultural evidence to validate distinctions between basic emotions believed to be rooted in internal bodily states. Authors like Lutz (1988) and Wierzbicka (1999) see the essence of human emotions not in inherent characteristics of the human organism, but in cultural processes of social construction, language, and cognition.

## Componential approaches

A synthetic approach in which emotions are no longer considered as unitary entities, but as consisting of multiple **emotion components,** has gained much ground in the 1990s. This approach emphasizes that cross-culturally emotions can be simultaneously similar in some respects and different in other respects. It has been developed in the context of the cognitive tradition in psychology (Frijda, 1986) and has evolved towards seeing an emotion as a process in which several aspects can be distinguished. Much of the relevant cross-cultural information can be found in two reviews by Mesquita and Frijda (1992) and by Mesquita, Frijda, and Scherer (1997). Components include antecedent events (conditions or situations that elicit an emotion), appraisal (evaluation of a situation in terms of a respondent's well-being or the satisfaction of goals), subjective feelings, physiological reaction patterns (cf. Levenson et al., 1992), action readiness (behavior impulses for certain kinds of action), behavioral expression (like facial expressions), and regulation (inhibition and control over expression).

In the following subsections we shall present some illustrations of studies of these components. However, it should be noted that the demarcation between the various components is often not very clear. In general, the overlap between the various components and the strong relationships between, for example, appraisals and action tendencies (cf. Frijda, Kuipers, & Ter Schure, 1986) points to coherence of an emotion process and imposes limits on componential diversity.

## Antecedents to emotions

Systematic research into the **antecedents of emotions** has been conducted by Boucher. The largest of these studies (Brandt & Boucher, 1985) was based on samples of respondents from Korea, Samoa, and the USA. A large pool of narratives was collected asking informants to write stories about events causing one of six emotions, anger, disgust, fear, happiness, sadness, and surprise. A selection of these stories was translated and stripped of specific cultural referents and of all emotion terms. A set of 144 stories was presented to respondents from the three countries. The respondents indicated in each case which of the six emotions the person in the story had experienced. Substantial overall agreement was found in the assignment of emotions to stories between cultures as well as within cultures. Contrary to expectation, respondents did *not* do better overall on stories from their own cultures. This result suggests that antecedent events to emotions by and large are quite similar for people in different cultures. Also findings on patterns of crying and the antecedents to crying behavior suggest cross-cultural similarities (Becht, Poortinga, & Vingerhoets, 2001).

Cross-cultural differences in antecedents have been mainly related to different interpretations of situations and culture-specific beliefs. Such specific interpretations are non-trivial according to Mesquita et al. (1997) when they lead to differences in subsequent emotional responses. As an example they mention situations that have characteristics associated with the supernatural in some cultures, but not elsewhere.

## Appraisal

When a person is confronted with a situation, there is a rapid and automatic **appraisal**. This offers "the clue for understanding the conditions for the elicitation of different emotions, as well as for understanding what makes one emotion different from another" (Frijda, 1993, p. 225). A limited set of dimensions have been commonly found, including attention to change or novelty, pleasantness versus unpleasantness, certainty versus uncertainty, a sense of control, and agency (i.e., whether the situation is due to oneself, someone else, or a non-human agent). Emotions, such as happiness and fear, differ in terms of characteristic patterns on these appraisal dimensions.

In a series of studies initiated by Scherer (Scherer, Wallbott, & Summerfield, 1986; Scherer, Wallbott, Matsumoto, & Kudoh, 1988) an open-ended questionnaire was used to ask about an event in a respondent's life that related to one of four emotions (joy, sadness, anger, fear). In addition to emotional feeling per se questions addressed appraisal and reactions. Few differences were found between European countries. Between the USA, Europe, and Japan there were major differences in the relative importance of eliciting situations. It was also found that the American respondents reported higher, and the Japanese respondents lower, emotional reactivity than the Europeans.

Scherer and his colleagues (Scherer et al., 1988) quite readily made quantitative comparisons between various cultures. They write, for example,

> The lower fear intensities in Japan might be due to the fact that the fear of crime, which seems to lead to fairly high fear intensities, is less pronounced there and that there might still be more of a feeling of being safe in a network of social support. It is difficult to see why American respondents report higher intensities throughout, particularly for joy and anger. These findings may be attributable to either a higher emotionality or emotional responsivity on the part of the American respondents. (Scherer et al., 1988, p. 21)

However, before accepting such interpretations at face value, one would have liked to see that obvious threats to cross-cultural equivalence (see chs. 4 and 11), due for example to response styles, had been ruled out.

In a later project with respondents from thirty-seven countries items for appraisal were included (Scherer, 1997a). This time precoded response scales were presented for items on appraisal derived from a theory developed by Scherer (1986). Respondents were again asked to think back about an emotional experience (joy, anger, fear, sadness, disgust, shame, and guilt) and then given questions on whether they expected the event to happen, whether it was pleasant, whether it obstructed their goals, etc. Scherer (1997a, 1997b) found that the various emotions showed strong differences in appraisal patterns, supporting the conclusion that each of the basic emotions examined in the study universally has the same appraisal profile. Substantial differences between countries were also found, indicating that certain appraisal dimensions appear to be more prominent in certain countries.

The largest differences were found for an item asking whether the event, if caused by a person, would be considered improper or immoral. The next largest difference was found for an item asking for the unjustness or unfairness of the event. Appraisals of events by respondents in Africa tended to be high on immorality and unfairness, while in Latin America ratings tended to be low on immorality. The interpretation of country differences is hampered by the fact that respondents selected emotional events from their own experiences; this may have led to systematic differences on any aspect except the targeted emotion. While we agree with Scherer that the data support both universality and cultural specificity in the emotion process, the former aspect is rather striking in view of the fact that the emotion label was the only restriction in the self-selection of experienced events by the respondents. Mesquita et al. (1997) rightly point out that the similarities in appraisal dimensions which are at a high level of generality may obscure more specific concerns, like the concern for honor that has been found to be prevalent in Mediterranean countries (Abu-Lughod, 1986).

## Other components

In the thirty-seven-country study just mentioned, respondents were also asked questions on other components of emotional experience, including motor expression, physiological symptoms, and subjective feelings (Scherer & Wallbott, 1994). The design of the study allowed for an estimation of the size of (1) differences between emotions, (2) differences between countries, and (3) the interaction between countries and emotions. Substantial differences were found between the emotions. Differences between countries were clearly less large, and the interactions between countries and emotions were still smaller. The latter finding can be interpreted as an indication of the consistency of the patterns of differences between countries and between emotions. Scherer and Wallbott (1994, p. 310) interpret their results "as supporting theories that postulate both a high degree of universality of differential emotion patterning and important cultural differences in emotion elicitation, regulation, symbolic representation, and social sharing."

The componential approach to emotions can be seen as an attempt to free emotions research from the constraints of a focus on a small set of basic emotions pursued with a limited set of methods, to a much broader perspective with emphasis on the influence of concrete cultural settings in molding emotional life (Mesquita et al., 1997). Conceptually this enrichment is mainly reflected in the differentiation of various components. Of course, current listings of components need not be definite. We have already noted the close relationships between various components, and there are perhaps some other components that should be added. An example is the social sharing of emotions, the communication with others about emotion events. There are distinct patterns in prevalence and preference of communication with others belonging to social categories like parents, partners, friends, etc. (Rimé, Mesquita, Philippot, & Boca, 1991; Rimé, Philippot, Boca, & Mesquita, 1992). More unitary conceptualizations of emotions, have also been broadened by categorizations according to dimensions (e.g., Russell, 1991) or prototypes (e.g., Fehr & Russell, 1984; Shaver, Wu, & Schwartz, 1992). According to prototype theory there exists a level of categorization with an optimal trade-off between inclusiveness and informativeness, called the basic level (Rosch, 1978). In cross-cultural studies on the cognitive structure of emotions, two high-order clusters, distinguishing positive versus negative emotions, tend to emerge. At a somewhat lower level of inclusiveness four basic emotion categories have been identified, corresponding to anger, fear, sadness, and positive emotion (Shaver et al., 1992).

Methodologically there is a tendency not to provide single emotion terms to respondents, but more elaborate descriptions with more contextual information, including sequential aspects of an emotion event. Such scenarios are referred to as "emotion scripts" (e.g., Fischer, 1991). Needless to say, scripts allow for more subtle distinctions than generalized representations of emotions in one-word or one-sentence items.

Of course, an important question is the extent to which these broader approaches have led to new insights about the relationship between culture and emotions. A definite answer is difficult to give. In fact, we do not even have a good idea about the extent to which there are cross-cultural differences that generalize beyond narrow categories of culturally specific situations. Mesquita et al. (1997) claim that substantial cross-cultural differences have been found for various components. However, in their review there is also evidence of a great deal of similarity. To connect these two findings research is needed that allows the simultaneous estimation of similarities and differences. Such an attempt is discussed in box 7-1.

## Box 7.1  Can a universalist approach be compatible with cultural specificity?

Wierzbicka (1999, p. 25) wrote the following:

Ekman (1993: 384) has claimed that "no one to date has obtained strong evidence of cross-cultural disagreement about the interpretation of fear, anger, disgust, sadness, or enjoyment expressions". But how *could* anyone obtain such evidence if the key interpretive categories "fear", "anger", "enjoyment", etc. are taken for granted from the outset and built into the research project itself? [italics in the original]

In previous chapters we have argued that culture-comparative research presumes that equivalence of data, in one form or the other, is feasible. Valid comparison is impossible unless somehow a common scale can be defined. We agree with Wierzbicka that the use of concepts, stimuli, and response scales by Western theorists implies the danger of cultural imposition. On the other hand, studies depending on data from only one society do not allow for comparison either, making claims to the effect that things are different elsewhere gratuitous.

Fontaine, Poortinga, Setiadi, and Markam (in press) tried to bridge this gap in a series of studies on the cognitive structure of emotions in Indonesia and the Netherlands. In such research cognitive representations of emotional experience are derived through multivariate statistical analysis from ratings of similarities and differences in the meaning of emotion words (e.g., Shaver, Schwartz, Kirson, & O'Connor, 1987; Shaver et al., 1992). In a first study Fontaine et al. collected a broad array of emotion words separately in the two countries. Ratings were then obtained from local university students as to what extent each of these words was prototypical for an emotion. Terms with high scores clearly belonged to the emotion domain, terms with low scores did not. The most prototypical terms in Indonesia were (translated into English) happiness, love, hate, joy, and sadness; in the Netherlands joy, anger, sadness, and rage. The 120 terms with the highest prototypicality ratings in each country were selected for further use.

In a second study another sample of students in each of the two countries carried out a similarity sorting task on the 120 terms. They were asked to put terms (printed on little cards) with a similar meaning together in the same category, and those with different meanings in separate categories, making as few or many categories as they wished. Statistical analysis on the matrix of similarity ratings (i.e., how often each term was placed in the same category as another term) showed a good fit for a three-dimensional structure in both countries, explaining 90 percent of the total variance in Indonesia and 88 percent in the Netherlands. The three dimensions could be labeled as pleasantness or evaluation (separating positive from negative emotion terms), dominance or potency (separating anger terms from fear and sadness terms), and arousal or activation (separating sadness from fear and anger terms).

## Box 7.1 (continued)

Such a structure, replicating the three dimensions of Osgood has been found also by other researchers (Russell, 1983, 1991).

It may be noted that so far the researchers had worked with locally selected emotion terms, and without imposing any criteria on correspondence of terms or categories. In the third study Fontaine et al. (in press) tried to establish a connection between the two sets of terms. Using nine independent sources, like dictionaries and bilinguals, two terms were considered language equivalent if literally the same translation was made in at least five of the nine sources. Despite this strict criterion that ruled out the inclusion of synonyms and near synonyms, fifty pairs of terms were found to be acceptable. Although cognitive equivalence is often assumed for translation-equivalent terms, it is quite possible that terms that consistently are translated in a certain way still have a different meaning; translation equivalence does not necessarily imply cognitive equivalence (e.g., Russell, 1991). A case in point, the word *malu* in Indonesian appears to refer to both shame and embarrassment in English. Fontaine et al. argued that cognitively equivalent pairs should be close together in a common dimensional space, something unlikely to be found for pairs of terms with cognitively different meanings. Analysis showed again a three-dimensional space in which of the fifty pairs of translation-equivalent terms, forty-two pairs were also found to be close together, thus meeting the criterion for cognitive equivalence.

All the terms were then entered into an analysis in which the equivalent terms had the same position for the two groups and in which no constraints were imposed on the other terms. Thus, the forty-two cognitively equivalent pairs were each represented by a single point in the emotion space. The remaining seventy-eight Indonesian terms and seventy-eight Dutch terms were represented by separate points. This common solution accounted for 87 percent of the variance in the Indonesian and Dutch sample, which was only slightly less than the 90 percent and 88 percent respectively for the two specific configurations mentioned above. Thus, imposing a common structure hardly twisted the cognitive representation of emotional experiences in either of the two samples. Of course, structural equivalence as demonstrated in this study does not say much about the frequency with which an emotion is felt, the situations in which it is felt, the way it is enacted, etc. However, it was shown that when an emotion is experienced it is in important respects likely to be quite similar for the groups studied, i.e., Indonesian and Dutch students, which culturally are supposed to be quite far apart.

Two pairs of emotions for which linguistic equivalence but not cognitive equivalence was found, namely shame and guilt, were further analyzed. Ratings on the distance of shame and guilt to other emotion terms were collected. These ratings showed that both pairs of emotion terms share a negative meaning in

### Box 7.1 (continued)

the two cultures. Within this common pattern the most notable difference was that shame and guilt in Indonesia were somewhat less distant from fear and more distant from anger than in the Netherlands. The (small) shift of guilt in the direction of fear was in line with other findings from Indonesia (Heider, 1991).

In their conclusion Fontaine at al. argue that their combined culture-specific and culture-comparative approach offered a way to identify cultural specificity in the emotion terms for guilt and shame based on an empirically identified common standard without falling into the trap of cultural imposition. At the same time it has to be noted that Ekman's claim quoted at the beginning of this box was not invalidated by the findings, despite avoidance of cultural impositions in the research design.

## Conclusions

In this chapter we reviewed evidence that points to considerable invariance in emotions across cultures, supporting the view that emotions are biologically rooted. We then discussed approaches in which emotions are seen as having a cultural identity, rooted in cognitive and social processes. Finally we examined a more differentiated view in which it should be possible to accommodate both the biological and the cultural orientations. The main theme of the discussion coincides with a major theme of this book, namely the relative extent to which there is universality and culture specificity in human psychological functioning.

An absolutist position axiomatically asserts pan-cultural invariance of emotions. The role of cross-cultural emotions research is limited to helping identify the true set of basic emotions. Interpretations of differences never go beyond rules of expression and situations with a specific cultural meaning. Such an approach carries a risk of cultural sterility by declaring a priori all differences to be incidental. Equally fruitless is an axiomatic position in which emotions have to be different. When Kitayama and Markus (1994, p. 1) state: "Specifically, we wish to establish that emotion can be fruitfully conceptualized as being social in nature or, in Lutz's (1988) words, as being 'anything but natural,'" the question has to be asked whether this is an expression of an article of faith or a summary of a research agenda. Componential approaches allow a more differentiated view and as such may be seen to strike a better balance.

There is perhaps no body of empirical evidence that fits more comfortably into a universalist perspective than the accumulated cross-cultural research on emotions. On the one hand, distinctions between major emotions as they have emerged in systematic Western psychological research, by and large have been replicated in all studies that allowed comparison of data. On the other hand, the manifestation of emotions has contextual aspects, for example in terms of the rules and norms for emotion expression. A major question for future research remains to what extent differences in manifestations do indeed reflect differences in emotional experiences, whether defined in terms of underlying psychophysiological states, or in terms of other component processes.

## Key terms

| | |
|---|---|
| affective meaning | components (of emotions) |
| antecedents of emotions | display rules |
| appraisal | social construction of emotions |
| basic emotions | subjective culture |

## Further reading

Darwin, C. (1872/1998). *The expression of the emotions in man and animal* (3rd ed.). London: Harper and Collins. Darwin's classic account of universality in emotional expression of the human face (with a foreword and conclusion by Paul Ekman).

Ekman, P. (Ed.) (1982). *Emotion in the human face* (2nd ed.). Cambridge, Cambridge University Press. A comprehensive overview of the early studies and findings on the universality of emotions in the human face.

Mesquita, B., & Frijda, N. H. (1992). Cultural variations in emotions: A review. *Psychological Bulletin, 112*, 179–204. A review article that seeks to establish a balance between universalist and relativist views on emotions.

Mesquita, B., Frijda, N. H., & Scherer, K. R. (1997). Culture and emotion. In J. W. Berry, P. R. Dasen, & T. S. Saraswathi (Eds.), *Basic processes and human development* (pp. 255–97). Vol. II of *Handbook of cross-cultural psychology* (2nd ed.). Boston, MA: Allyn and Bacon. This chapter extends the information of Mesquita and Frijda (1992).

Russell, J. A. (1991). Culture and the categorisation of emotions. *Psychological Bulletin, 110*, 426–50. A discussion on how emotions are the same and how they are different, drawing on a wide range of literature.

# 8 Perception

Conventional wisdom would have it that cross-cultural differences in perception are of minor significance. The universal similarity in the anatomy and the physiology of the sensory organs and the nervous system makes it likely that sensory impressions and their transmission through the perceptual apparatus are invariant across cultures.

The first section of this chapter gives a brief review of historical roots of contempary cross-cultural research in this domain. This is followed by a section on studies of sensory functions ranging from sensory acuity to information transmission. Then we turn to perception in a more strict sense. When contrasted with sensation, perception implies stimulus selection and other forms of active engagement of the organism. Extensive research, mainly in the 1960s and 1970s, concerns the perception of patterns and pictures. We will examine cross-cultural differences in the perception of simple figures, including visual illusions, and in the perception of depth with two-dimensional depictions of three-dimensional objects and scenes. The fourth section deals with the well-established finding that face recognition of members of other groups is more difficult than recognition of own-goup members. Finally we have included a section on esthetics, with emphasis on perceptual aspects of appreciation.

Most of the discussion in this chapter is on the visual modality. In this respect we merely follow the literature, where a similar emphasis is found.

## Historical roots

Many psychologists consider W. H. R. Rivers (1864–1922) as one of the founding fathers of cross-cultural psychology. His main work (Rivers, 1901) was based on data collected with Torres Strait Islanders. The Torres Strait is located between New Guinea and Australia. Rivers took part in the famous Cambridge Anthropological Expedition organized by the anthropologist A. C. Haddon. The main body of data was gathered during a period of four months by Rivers and some students on Murray Island. Measurements were taken on visual acuity, color vision, color blindness, after images, contrast, visual illusions, auditory acuity, rhythm, smell and taste, tactile acuity, weight discrimination, reaction times to visual and auditory stimuli, estimates of time intervals, memory, muscular power, motor accuracy, and a number of similar topics. The data were organized around three main subjects: visual acuity, perception, and visual/spatial perception. Here we shall concern ourselves mainly with the first topic.

In many respects Rivers's study could be called exemplary even today, although the data analysis pre-dated the development of most statistical analyses now employed routinely. In his report Rivers shows great concern for issues of method. He worried whether a task was properly understood and tried out different methods to find out which one worked most satisfactorily. His report is especially readable because the quantitative data are backed up by different kinds of contextual evidence, mainly obtained from observation. For example, in his analysis of vision Rivers not only studied color naming and the sensitivity for different colors, he also asked for preferences and even took note of the colors of the scarfs that people would wear on Sundays in church.

Rivers had an open eye for possible alternative explanations. When discussing the then popular notion of the extraordinary visual acuity of non-Europeans, he distinguished between the power of resolution of the eye as a physiological instrument, powers of observation, and familiarity with the surroundings. Data on visual acuity were mainly collected with Snellen's E-chart. This E-figure is placed with the opening in one of four different positions; the correct one has to be indicated by the respondent. A poster with Snellen figures in decreasing sizes was used by Rivers, who further manipulated the difficulty of the task by varying the distance between the poster and the respondent. Rivers examined the eyes of his respondents for defects and diseases. He measured visual acuity with and without correcting lenses for deficient eyesight.

Rivers found the visual acuity of the Torres Strait Islanders to be in no way extraordinary. He analyzed the available literature, which already was quite extensive at the beginning of the twentieth century. However, studies were lacking in methodological rigor and many observations were casual. On the basis of his own work and what information he had gained from other sources Rivers concluded "that the visual acuity of savage and half-civilized people, though superior to that of the normal European, is not so in any marked degree" (1901, p. 42). Rivers discussed at length differences that he attributed to accurate observation of the "savages" and their attention to minute details. He was of the opinion that "the predominant attention to objects of sense [is] a distinct hindrance to higher mental development . . . If too much energy is expended on the sensory foundations, it is natural that the intellectual superstructure should suffer" (pp. 44–5). This complementary relationship between the sensory and the intellectual domain is repeatedly mentioned. In our opinion it shows that despite the openness of mind which is so manifest in his writings, even Rivers was deeply influenced by the ethnocentric ideas prevalent in his time.

The work of Rivers did not mark the beginning of a continuous research tradition in cross-cultural psychology. In the miscellaneous studies on perception that were published between 1910 and 1950, the now discredited notion of "race" remained the dominant explanation of differences, but often without gross implications of inferiority. An example is the work of Thouless (1933) and Beveridge (1935, 1940) on constancies, or phenomenal regression. From most angles of vision the projection of a circular disc on the retina of an observer forms an ellipse. When asked what they see respondents tend to draw an ellipse that is between the form of the actual retinal projection and a full circle (the phenomenon). This regression toward the phenomenon can be observed not only for form, but also for size, brightness, and so forth. For example, when a grey paper is illuminated at a higher intensity so that it reflects more light than a white paper, it may not appear lighter to the respondent who "knows" that it is grey.

Thouless found that a small sample of Indian students, compared to Scots, showed a greater tendency to phenomenal regression for two tasks (relative size of two discs, and circular versus ellipsoid form of a disc). He related this finding to Indian art where, in the absence of perspective, objects are drawn as they are, rather than as they present themselves to the observer. In Thouless's opinion the simplest explanation for this finding is that there are differences in how people perceive. These differences make Indian artists, compared to Europeans, see objects in a manner that is further removed from what would be expected according to the principles of perspective. Beveridge (1935) found a greater tendency to phenomenal regression among West African college students than among British students for shape and size. In a later study (Beveridge, 1940) he extended the range of tasks and concluded that Africans were probably less affected by visual cues than Europeans.

The suspicion that preconceived ideas about the mental status of various so-called races affected the outcome of research is strenghtened when the work of Oliver is considered. He took an almost modern position on racial comparisons of intelligence test scores, arguing for the incorporation of indigenous elements in test items and the recognition of difficulties of language and instruction (Oliver, 1934). In a study with the Seashore test for musical abilities he found that West African students, compared with American students of a similar level of schooling, acquired higher scores for loudness discrimination, tone duration discrimination, and identification of rhythm, but lower scores for pitch dicrimination, discrimination of timbre, and tonal memory. Oliver (1932) noted that the tests for timbre and tonal memory were the only two that correlated with intelligence, presumably because the instructions were difficult to understand.

Recapitulating this section, it can be stated that in the past perceptual and sensory processes were seen as important indices of complex mental functioning. Depending on the prior beliefs of an author, cross-cultural differences were seen either as the outcome of cultural experiences or of "racial" inheritance. In the following sections we shall explore more recent notions.

## Sensory functions

There are four classes of cross-cultural explanations of cross-cultural differences in reactions to simple **sensory stimuli,** namely (1) conditions in the physical environment that affect the sensory apparatus directly, (2) environmental conditions that affect the sensory apparatus indirectly, (3) genetic factors, and (4) cultural differences in the interaction with the environment.

An example of the direct effect of physical conditions can be found in Reuning and Wortley (1973). They reported a better auditory acuity in the higher frequency ranges (up to 8,000 Hz) for Kalahari Bushmen than the reference values given for Denmark and for the USA. The differences were more striking for older respondents, suggesting that in the Kalahari desert there is less hearing loss with increasing age. Reuning and Wortley emphasized that other factors, such as for example diet, can provide alternative explanations. Still, they were inclined to see the low levels of ambient noise in the Kalahari as the critical factor, citing findings by other authors on slow deterioration of hearing in non-industrial societies. It may be pointed out in passing that Wortley and Humphriss (1971) did not find Bushmen to have a better visual acuity (although they needed correcting lenses less often) than urbanized groups in southern Africa.

An indirect effect of an environmental factor, namely poor nutrition, was suspected when black recruits to the South African mining industry were found to have a slower dark adaptation than white South Africans (Wyndham, 1975). It was thought that deficiencies in the diet could have led to a low level of vitamin A. (A low level of this vitamin leads to insufficient functioning of the rods in the retina that are used for vision under conditions of low illumination.) When a change in diet did not lead to the expected improvement, it was suggested that many of the mineworkers might suffer from subclinical forms of liver ailments (cirrhosis), which, in turn, were associated with a high incidence of nutritional dieases in early childhood. This example is informative as it mentions both major factors that are nowadays seen as causal to cultural differences in sensation or motor performance, namely nutritional deficiencies and diseases. It is understood that certain diseases can have a debilitating effect on behavior, even if there are no clear signs of clinical symptoms. This was demonstrated for psychomotor ablities as well as cognitive abilities in research on the effects of endemic goiter (Bleichrodt, Drenth, & Querido, 1980). Goiter is an enlargement of the thyroid gland that is caused by iodine deficiency. It is associated with cretinism, a syndrome characterized by mental deficiency and neurological abnormalities. Bleichrodt and colleagues found in Indonesia as well as in Spain that not visibly afflicted children in iodine-deficient areas obtained on average much lower scores on certain tests than children from neighboring areas where the water contained sufficient iodine.

It has been established that some genetic traits occur with different frequencies in various populations. Most famous is the difference in the incidence of red–green color blindness. It was already known in the time of Rivers (1901) that the frequency of red-green color blindness was much lower in some non-European groups than in some European groups. Within an evolution-theoretical framework this has been attributed to the disadvantages that color-blind people have when hunting and gathering is the main means of subsistence (cf. Post, 1962, 1971). In ch. 10 we shall come back to this point. Another example is the inability to taste substances that contain phenylthiocarbamide or another thiocarbamide group. About 30 percent of Europeans are "taste blind" for these bitter tasting substances. Africans and Native Americans are populations that have only a few percent non-tasters (Kalmus, 1969; Doty, 1986). A further illustration of differential sensitivity for the effects of certain chemical compounds is the "alcoholic flush," a reddening of the face, that is common among east Asian people after the consumption of only a few alcoholic drinks (Wolff, 1972, 1973), but is rarely found in people of European descent.

Socialization and enculturation practices are generally seen as the main antecedents of differences in sensory sensitivity and discrimination. Of the differences in sensation that have been reported in the literature many have to do with a socially conditioned preference or dislike for stimuli, rather than with the capacity for discrimination or with tolerance thresholds. For example, Kuwano, Namba, and Schick (1986) have argued that small differences in the evaluation of loudness of neighborhood noise between Japan, Great Britain, and West Germany should be interpreted with reference to sociocultural factors (how much you tolerate) rather than in terms of sensory impact or another perceptual variable. Several differences in preference or hedonistic value of sensory stimuli have also been found in studies on taste. For example, Chinese respondents rated sucrose at low concentrations as more pleasant than European American respondents in the USA (Bertino, Beauchamp, & Jen, 1983). A stronger preference of African Americans for sweet foods has also been reported. The role of experience is quite obvious here, since sucrose preference can be manipulated by dietary exposure. Also, it has been demonstrated in conditioning experiments that a more or less neutral taste becomes more appreciated when it is coupled with a well-liked flavor (cf. Doty, 1986, for a review).

An important question is whether observed differences in sensory functions stand in themselves or whether they have wider ramifications. It is an important scientific premise that complex behavior is an assembly of more elementary abilities and skills. Children learn to pay attention to certain stimuli and to acquire certain preferences, but do these in turn in turn lead to the development of more complex abilities?

In this context we can refer to the belief, widespread in pre-independence Africa, that Africans generally excelled in auditory tasks while Europeans were more oriented to visual stimuli. This view, which was expressed by well-known cross-cultural psychologists such as Biesheuvel (1943) and Ombrédane (1954), is an example of a "compensation hypothesis." In the previous section we mentioned that even Rivers was of the opinion that paying much attention to sensory stimuli would be to the detriment of intellectual development. More recent formulations of compensation hypotheses have been less encompassing; they concerned the balance between various modalities. In the 1960s McLuhan (1971) emphasized the dominance of the visual modality in Western people and Wober (1966) coined the term "sensotypes" to indicate differences between cultural groups in the relative importance of one sensory modality over the others.

A good theoretical account of the cultural antecedents that could have led to the relative predominance of auditory perception in Africans was never given. Also, empirical evidence on the salience of auditory or kinesthetic cues for Africans is very limited. Wober administered field-dependence tests (cf. ch. 5) with stimuli for different senses to Nigerian respondents and compared the patterns of scores with those reported in the literature on respondents from the USA. He found relatively high scores for proprioceptive cues, but the results have been questioned for reasons of method (cf. Deregowski, 1980b). Poortinga (1971, 1972) conducted a series of experiments on information transmission with corresponding auditory and visual stimuli. Black and white South African students served as respondents. In one of the experiments they made judgments on the brightness of a white spot and on the loudness of a pure tone. With these two scales no evidence was found in support of a relative superiority of the black students in auditory judgments. In another experiment the choice reaction time (CRT) to visual and auditory stimuli was used to assess the rate of information transmission for both senses. Even after fairly extensive practice, the CRTs of the white students remained faster. However, the difference was of approximately the same size for the two kinds of stimuli, so that also this experiment failed to support the notion of relative differences between the various senses in information transmission. Since the 1970s notions such as sensotype or relative auditory versus visual predominance have largely disappeared from the cross-cultural literature on perception.

Cross-cultural studies with simple sensory stimuli have fallen far behind in the general growth of the field since the 1950s. In a bibliography with 3,122 entries on Africa south of the Sahara, covering the period from 1960 to 1975, Andor (1983) listed only nine studies on the sensory bases of perception. This probably more than anything else reflects the contemporary belief that sensory differences are only of minor significance. Following the traditions of the field we have mainly been dealing with differences in this section. The overall impression one gains from the accumulated literature is that cross-cultural differences in the sensory impact of stimuli are exceptional rather than the rule and that if they do occur a variable outside the perceptual system should be sought for explanation.

In the remainder of this chapter we shall pay attention to perceptual variables. Traditionally, sensation implies a more passive role for the organism as a recipient for stimuli, whereas perception presumes an active engagement on the part of the organism in the selection and organization of stimuli.

## Perception of patterns and pictures

The drawing in fig. 8.1 is taken from a study on pictorial recognition among a remote group in Ethiopia, the Mekan or Me'en, who, at the time, had little previous exposure to pictorial representations (Deregowski, Muldrow, & Muldrow, 1972). With few exceptions they identified a leopard, but only after some time and not without effort. In the process of examination some respondents would go beyond visual inspection; they would touch the cloth on which the pictures were painted and sometimes even smell it. These results were in line with various miscellaneous reports to the effect that the perception of clear representational pictures and even (black and white) photographs is not always immediate in cultures without a pictorial tradition.

Not only lack of recognition, but also the possibility of culturally idiosyncratic depiction can lead to difficulties in understanding. Winter (1963) asked black South African industrial workers what they saw on a series of safety posters. There were many instances where the intention of the artist was not understood, because symbolic meanings (such as a red star to indicate that someone had been hit) were misinterpreted. The number of misinterpretations was much lower for urban than for rural respondents and also decreased as a function of the number of years of schooling of the respondents. A striking example of the kind of discrepancy between intended and perceived message occurred in a scene where a person was holding out a hand to receive something. This was often seen as an act of giving. Winter could relate this to the African custom of accepting with two cupped hands and giving with one hand.

These two examples bear on an important controversy. Some researchers in perception are of the opinion that all portrayal makes use of arbitrary codes

**8.1** One of the stimuli used in a recognition task by Deregowski et al. (1972). The original figure was much larger (50 by 100 cm) and drawn on coarse cloth

(Gombrich, 1977). Pictures are non-arbitrary mainly because of cultural traditions about how to represent an object or scene. Codes are conventions that members of particular cultures learn and adhere to even when they are not aware of this. An opposite viewpoint is emphasized by Gibson (e.g., 1966), who argued that a picture could represent an object or scene because it contained information for any perceiver that was similar to information from the real environment.

## Simple patterns and figures

Pictures such as that of the leopard in fig. 8.1 are fairly complex and involve culturally rooted artistic styles. Therefore, it may be useful to look at simpler figures.

First of all there are data which show cultural differences in the susceptibility of two-dimensional, geometric **visual illusions**. For an overview we refer to Segall et al. (1999). A summary of the findings is presented in box 8.1. Although the effects of physiological factors on illusions cannot be ruled out, long-term exposure to environmental conditions, summarized in the concept of carpenteredness, seems

### Box 8.1 Susceptibility to visual illusions

An extensive body of cross-cultural research on visual illusions was triggered by the landmark study of Segall et al. (1966). This study had its origin in a difference of opinion between the anthropologist Melville Herskovits and the psychologist Donald Campbell, both of whom were Segall's mentors. Herskovits, whose ideas about cultural relativism implied almost unlimited flexibility of the human organism, believed that even such basic experiences as the perception of the length of line segments would be influenced by cultural factors. Campbell thought this view required empirical testing. When they re-analyzed Rivers's data from the Torres Straits expedition, referred to above, several differences reported by Rivers for some visual illusions turned out to be statistically significant. But they found Rivers's explanation of differences unsatisfactory, and generated their own interpretations, rooted in the work of Brunswik (1956). He believed that repeated experience with certain perceptual cues would affect how they were perceived. This is expressed in the notion of ecological cue validity. Illusions occur when previously learned interpretations of cues are misapplied because of unusual or misleading characteristics of stimuli.

Three hypotheses were generated for the empirical research:

1 The carpentered world hypothesis. This postulates a learned tendency among those raised in an environment shaped by carpenters (rectangular furniture, houses, and street patterns) to interpret non-rectangular figures as representations of rectangular figures seen in perspective. If the hypothesis is correct, people in industrial urban environments should be more susceptible to illusions such as the Müller–Lyer and the Sander parallelogram.

**Box 8.1  (continued)**

2  The foreshortening hypothesis. This pertains to lines extending in space away from the viewer. In pictorial representations these appear as vertical lines. People living in environments with wide vistas have learned that vertical lines on the retina represent long distances. They should be more susceptible to the horizontal–vertical illusion than people living in an enclosed environment, such as a rain forest.

3  The sophistication hypothesis. Learning to interpret patterns and pictures should enhance geometric illusions that are presented two-dimensionally. Exposure to pictorial materials makes people more susceptible to visual illusions.

It may be noted that according to these hypotheses the illusion effect arises because of a 3D perceptual interpretation of 2D figures. This suggests close links between figural depth perception and susceptibility for illusions (cf. Deregowski, 1980a, 1980b).

Fourteen non-Western and three Western samples were tested by Segall et al. (1966) with a series of stimuli for each of the six illusions presented in fig. 8.2. The reasons for selecting the first four illusions have been indicated already. The fifth figure is a modified Ponzo illusion. It was expected that in more carpentered societies the perception of the figure would be toward orthogonal angles and parallel lines. This would lead to a correlation in susceptibility between this illusion and the Müller–Lyer and the Sander. The last figure, the Poggendorf, has been included for the sake of completeness. Segall et al. did not find reliable data for this illusion, partly because of instructional difficulties.

On both the Müller–Lyer and the Sander parallelogram the Western samples were more illusion prone than any of the non-Western samples. Samples drawn from regions with open vistas were more susceptible for the two versions of the horizontal–vertical illusion than samples from regions where such vistas were rare. Also compatible with the second hypothesis was the finding that on the whole non-Western respondents were more prone to the horizontal–vertical illusion than Western respondents. The patterning of the findings with non-Western respondents being more susceptible to some, but less to other, illusions rules out an explanation in terms of an overall factor, such as test sophistication. All in all, the results were clearly in support of the hypotheses.

The version of the Ponzo illusion used by Segall et al. showed only weak effects. In subsequent cross-cultural studies with the original Ponzo illusion (where the highest of the two horizontal line segments does not intersect one of the two other lines) clearer illusion effects were obtained. Susceptibility for the Ponzo illusion was shown to be influenced by enrichment of the context. Brislin and Keating (1976) even worked with a 3D version constructed from wooden planks and placed at a larger distance (approximately 10 meters) from the respondent. They found that respondents from the USA were more prone to this version of the illusion than respondents from Pacific islands.

**Box 8.1 (continued)**

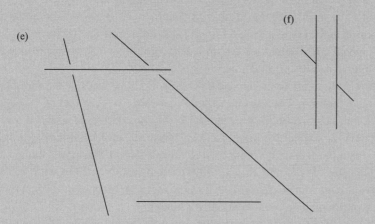

**8.2** Visual illusions used by Segall, Campbell, and Herskovits (1966). The respective patterns are (a) Sander parallelogram, (b) Müller–Lyer illusion, (c) and (d) two versions of the horizontal–vertical illusion, (e) modified form of the Ponzo illusion and (f) Poggendorff illusion

## Box 8.1  (continued)

Numerous other factors have been examined in further research, such as enrichment of the context (Leibowitz, Brislin, Perlmulter, & Hennessey, 1969; Brislin, 1974), effects of attention (Davis & Carlson, 1970), training in drawing (Jahoda & Stacey, 1970), and skin color. The latter variable served as an index of pigmentation of the retina and for some time provided a challenge to the environmental interpretation of the data given by Segall et al. as well as most other cross-cultural researchers.

The implication of retinal pigmentation rested on a series of findings. Pollack (1963) established that at older ages the ability for contour detection decreases. Pollack and Silvar (1967) found a (negative) correlation between contour detection and susceptibility for the Müller–Lyer illusion. They also found correlations between skin color and both retinal pigmentation and contour detection (Silvar & Pollack, 1967). Since most non-Western samples in the study of Segall et al. came from Africa, an explanation in physiological and genetic terms could not be ruled out, at least for one illusion.

Initial empirical support for the retinal pigmentation hypothesis came from studies by Berry (1971) and Jahoda (1971). The latter tested respondents' illusion susceptibility for the Müller–Lyer with blue and red stimuli. Pigmentation affects the transmission of blue light more than red light. Jahoda found no difference for Scottish students with presumably low pigmentation under the two conditions, but a sample of Malawian students with high pigmentation was indeed significantly less susceptible to the blue stimuli. However, soon the tide turned. In an extended replication Jahoda (1975) found no further support for the retinal pigmentation hypothesis. In other studies skin color was varied in a constant environment (Armstrong, Rubin, Stewart, & Kuntner, 1970), or the environmental carpenterdness was varied, keeping skin color constant (Stewart, 1973). The results were clearly more in line with the environmental than with the physiological explanation.

Not all the data fitted the carpentered world hypothesis or the foreshortening hypothesis. The most important discrepancy was the finding by Segall et al. that the susceptibility for nearly all illusions decreased with age, while the ever increasing exposure to the environment would lead one to expect the opposite, at least for the Müller–Lyer and related illusions. Among others Wagner (1977) and Brislin (1974) found results, mainly with various forms of the Ponzo illusion, that were more ambiguous and sometimes showed an increase of susceptibility with age.

Although the effects of cultural variables on the perception of visual illusions are still a matter of some debate, the hypotheses mentioned at the beginning of this box are by and large supported by the available evidence, as shown in a review by Deregowski (1989).

to account for most of the cross-cultural differences that were reported by Segall, Campbell, and Herskovits (1966). It may be important to note explicitly that all populations are at least to some degree susceptible to all illusions which have been explored in cross-cultural comparisons. Another example is provided by a series of studies on symmetry by means of a symmetry completion test designed by Hector (1958). In the most extensively used version of this test each item consists of a drawing of three narrow rectangles, two grey and one black. The respondent is given a black oblong of the same size as the rectangles. This has to be placed in such a position on the paper that it forms with the three rectangles already there a symmetrical pattern. Two forms of symmetry have been used, namely bilateral or mirror symmetry, and rotational or centric symmetry. A figure is rotationally symmetric if it is the same after rotation (in this case over 180 degrees). An example of both kinds of item is given in fig. 8.3.

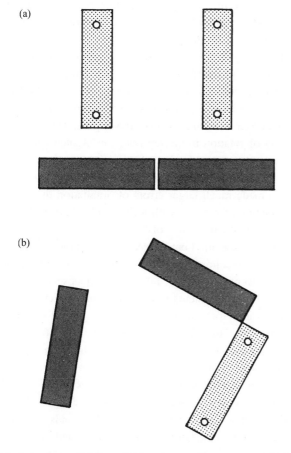

**8.3** A (completed) bilateral (a) and a rotation symmetry (b) item
   Respondents indicate an answer by making a mark with a pencil in two small
   holes indicated by small circles on the oblong figure and the matched figure
   After the symmetry completion test, NIPR, Johannesburg

Reuning and his associates administered this test to various non-literate groups, including Bushmen in the Kalahari desert. It was found that the idea of bilateral symmetry was easily grasped. According to Reuning and Wortley (1973, p. 58) "it was one of our greatest surprises to see how easy the Bushmen found it to deal with these unfamiliar patterns. Even the least intelligent from them could find the solutions to a few items, the majority to about half and some bright ones to nearly all of them." Even the part of the test for rotational symmetry led to some fairly high scores, despite difficulties in explaining and demonstrating this form of symmetry with adequate administration procedures.

Analyses of incorrect answers on the symmetry completion items made by the Bushmen and several other groups in southern Africa have shown that most errors can be classified in two categories (cf. Deregowski, 1980a for a summary). The first is a lack of accuracy in placing the oblong precisely in the right position. The second category consists of errors that lead to regular patterns, but not in accordance with the required principle of symmetry. Instead of bilateral symmetry often translational symmetry was found. (In this case the two halves of a pattern are identical, but they do not form mirror images.)

The non-random character of erroneous responses can in itself be a topic of investigation. This can be illustrated with research on changes in orientation between the original and the copy that respondents provide when asked to redraw or reconstruct patterns. Especially respondents with a low level of schooling tend to produce patterns that differ in orientation from the original. Deregowski (1972, 1977) found that errors of rotation in the reproduction of such patterns have a tendency toward stability. A pattern is stable when one of the edges is parallel to the edge of the table at which a respondent is seated. Also Jahoda (1978) found that children in Ghana made much larger errors of orientation than children in Scotland in the reproduction of patterns with Kohs blocks. Part of this could be related to the culturally shaped meaning of "sameness." When asked whether two patterns, identical in composition but different in orientation, were the same or different, Ghanaian schoolchildren far more often than children in Scotland would respond that they were the "same." Jahoda further observed that Ghanaian respondents who had been instructed to pay attention to orientation and did so during initial trials, would lapse into neglecting this aspect of the task during the course of the experiment. He comments (Jahoda, 1978, p. 56), "The disposition to respond in this manner appears strongly established in some respondents, but readily susceptible to situational modification in others."

Another experiment in which cross-cultural differences were found in the way information is handled has been reported by Cole, Gay, and Glick (1968). They presented arrays of dots with a brief exposure time (0.25 seconds) to Kpelle children in Liberia and to children in the USA. The respondents had to assess in each stimulus the number of dots. This varied from three to ten. The experimental variable was a distinction between stimuli with a random array of dots and stimuli in which the dots formed a pattern. Cole et al. found that the American children did better on the ordered arrays than on the random patterns. For the Kpelle hardly any difference was observed between the two kinds of stimuli. Apparently the two groups differed in the extent to which they made use of the structural information that was present in the patterned stimuli.

Only a few studies on cross-cultural differences in the perception of simple patterns have been presented. Various antecedent factors have been mentioned in explanation; they all emphasize specific experiences (or a lack of certain experiences), but do so retrospectively. This kind of explanation does not allow us to predict with much accuracy whether a certain task will be easy or difficult for a certain group. Reuning and his associates were surprised to find that the Bushmen could deal with symmetry so well, but the finding by Jahoda that Ghanaian children tended to neglect orientation despite elaborate instructions is similarly surprising. Apparently, the effects of cultural conditions, even on simple perceptual tasks, are far from clear.

## Depth perception

The systematic study of **depth cues in pictures** was initiated in South Africa by Hudson (1960, 1967). Two stimuli of the set he used are shown in fig. 8.4. Hudson wanted to include the depth cues of object size, object superimposition, and perspective in the pictures. Respondents were asked first to identify the man, the antelope, etc., to make sure that the elements in the picture were recognized. Thereafter they were asked what the man was doing and whether the antelope or the elephant was closer to him. If there was an answer to the effect that the man was aiming the spear at the antelope or that the antelope was nearer to the man than the elephant, this was classified as a three-dimensional (3D) interpretation. Other answers (that the elephant was aimed at, or was nearer to the man) were taken as evidence of a 2D interpretation.

Hudson's test was administered to various groups in South Africa that differed in education and cultural background. School-going respondents predominantly gave 3D answers, the others responded almost entirely two-dimensionally. Hudson's method was criticized on a number of points, but in essence his results were confirmed by later research; the ability to interpret Western-style pictorial

**8.4** Two of Hudson's (1960) pictures

materials increases as a function of acculturation and school education (Duncan, Gourlay, & Hudson, 1973).

Potentially the most critical objection is that a 3D answer can be derived analytically, by considering that the elephant is much smaller than the antelope and thus has to be further away. Deregowski and Byth (1970) investigated this possibility with Pandora's box (Gregory, 1966), an apparatus that allows the respondent to adjust a light spot according to the distance between himself and an object in any selected part of a figure. Support was found for the hypothesis that 3D responders more than 2D responders saw the man, the antelope, and the elephant in different planes. At the same time, not all 3D responses coincided with differential settings. This means that verbal reponses have to be treated with some suspicion. There have been other criticisms of Hudson's work (e.g., Hagen & Jones, 1978; Jahoda & McGurk, 1974a). A considerable amount of research was carried out, mainly in the late 1960s and 1970s, to expand on Hudson's work.

The most important development has been the design of alternative methods to measure depth perception in pictorial representations. Deregowski (1980a) has made extensive usage of methods in which respondents have to construct a 3D model after a 2D drawing. In one of these tasks respondents were asked to build, with sticks and small balls of plasticine, models of abstract geometrical drawings. An example of a stimulus is shown in fig. 8.5(a). In another task drawings of assemblies of cubes (cf. fig. 8.5(b)) had to be copied with real blocks. Maybe the most interesting, because of its simplicity, is an experiment with a pair of wooden callipers. The respondent has to set the callipers at the same angle as that shown in simple drawings of the kind presented in fig. 8.5(c) and (d). The right-hand figure can be perceived as a rectangular object photographed at an obtuse angle. If it is seen as such the perceived angle should not be the same as for the flat figure but more rectangular. If no depth is perceived in the right-hand figure, the respondent can be expected to set the callipers at the same angle for both figures.

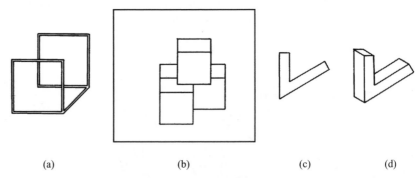

(a)                    (b)                    (c)          (d)

**8.5** Stimuli for two construction tasks (a) and (b) and the calipers task (c)
     After Deregowski, 1986; Dziurawiec & Deregowski, 1986; Deregowski &
     Bentley, 1986

A comparison between Hudson's stimuli and items as given in fig. 8.5(a) showed that Zambian domestic servants and schoolchildren produced more 3D responses on the latter (Deregowski, 1968). Thus, the responses of the respondents were shown to vary with the nature of the task. It may seem somewhat counterintuitive that performance should be better on the abstract figures than on Hudson's pictures which are closer to the recognizable environment. However, it is in line with theoretical ideas, mentioned in box 8.1, that the effect of illusions such as the Müller–Lyer has to be explained as a consequence of a 3D interpretation by the perceiver. It is also consistent with findings on the callipers task. A discrepancy was observed between settings for the two kinds of stimuli, which showed that most respondents in a sample of Bushmen settlers in Namibia were influenced by the depth cues. The proportion of 3D responders was higher than anticipated on the basis of previous findings with the Hudson pictures (Deregowski & Bentley, 1986).

Jahoda and McGurk (e.g., 1974b; McGurk & Jahoda, 1975) used a test in which elevation (i.e., the position of a figure, higher or lower in the picture) formed the most important depth cue. They relied on non-verbal responses, asking their respondents to place models of human figures on a response board in similar positions as these figures occupied in the stimulus pictures. Even young children (four years old) showed evidence of depth perception. Children in various cultures, including Ghana, Hong Kong, and Zimbabwe, with hardly any exception gave responses that demonstrated the effect of elevation and some other depth cues. Jahoda and McGurk argued that Hudson's test procedure tended to overemphasize the difficulties of perceiving depth in pictures, particularly by African respondents.

There are two depth cues that deserve special attention. The first is the gradient of texture. When one is looking along a brick wall details of separate bricks can be seen in the foreground. As the distance to the observer increases fewer and fewer details of texture can be perceived – hence the term "gradient of texture." This is a powerful depth cue in photographs, but one that is absent from virtually all stimulus sets used in cross-cultural studies. This is one reason why these stimuli are lacking in important information and to the first-time observer may display unusual qualities.

The second cue is linear perspective. In many pictures, including some of Hudson's, a horizon is drawn on which all lines converge that represent parallel lines from real space. It has been a point of considerable debate whether this depth cue, that has an evident impact on the perception of depth for Western respondents, should be seen as a cultural **convention**. One of the arguments for the conventional character of this cue is the existence of many art traditions in which linear perspective does not occur. In fact, it became only commonly used in Europe during the Renaissance. In addition, linear perspective in drawings does not correspond as closely to reality as is often thought. Parallel lines converge at infinity, but the horizon of our visual field is never at infinity. Standing on a railway the tracks may be seen to come closer together at a large distance, but they do not visibly converge into a single point. On the other hand, it can be argued that drawings based on the prescripts of linear perspective better resemble the optic array of real space than drawings constructed following other principles. In other words, linear perspective is not a convention in the sense of an entirely arbitrary agreement. As a rule it leads to more realistic representation than other conventions (Hagen & Jones, 1978).

Deregowski and Parker (1994) moved a step forward by differentiating between conditions where the convergent perspective represents the experiences of observers more adequately, and conditions where a divergent perspective is seen as more adequate. A divergent perspective, where parallel lines diverge with increasing pictorial depth, is found frequently in Byzantine art. The task used by Deregowski and Parker required the adjustment of a 3D array so that it appeared as a cube. When the array was placed straight in front of respondents, the adjustments were in agreement with a convergent perspective. However, when the array was shifted sideways so that it was no longer in front of the respondent, adjustments were according to a Byzantine divergent perspective. It is unclear why a particular art tradition has developed to emphasize certain modes of representation. However, findings like these show how at first sight quite radically different modes on closer examination provide evidence of close relationships in terms of the underlying perceptual mechanisms (Russell, Deregowski, & Kinnear, 1997).

In his analyses of pictorial perception Deregowski (1980a, 1980b, 1989) has made a distinction between epitomic and eidolic perception. Certain pictures can be recognized to represent an object without evoking an illusion of depth. Such pictures, of which silhouettes are the best illustrations, Deregowski calls epitomic. There are also pictures that evoke a notion of depth. Deregowski then speaks about eidolic pictures. Some pictures have eidolic qualities when they cannot even be associated with an object. Impossible figures such as the two-pronged trident in fig. 8.6 are the clearest examples. The eidolic character of this picture is so strong that it evokes the impression of an object which cannot exist in most adult Western respondents, though the 3D character is not perceived universally (e.g., Deregowski & Bentley, 1987). We are aware of epitomic cues; clouds are perceived to form epitomic pictures, such as a face or an animal. We are usually not aware of eidolic cues; we accept those as they appear. The link between visual illusions and depth perception, mentioned in box 8.1, is a plausible one if we

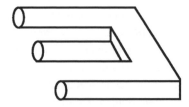

**8.6** The "two-pronged" trident
Deregowski & Bentley, 1987

accept that visual illusion figures have some eidolic quality. Deregowski has suggested that on a dimension from epitomic to eidolic the pictures by Hudson are more to the epitomic side and tasks such as those used by Jahoda and McGurk as well as the callipers are more to the eidolic side. This would be the reason why there were more 3D responders on the latter tasks than found by Hudson.

The epitomic–eidolic distinction is also an important one insofar as it reminds us that the perception of figures should not be seen as a unitary psychological process. Together with Serpell (Serpell & Deregowski, 1980) Deregowski has arrived at a conception in which picture perception is considered as a set of skills. A skilled perceiver can deal with a wide variety of cues and use those cues which are appropriate in a given situation. Basic is the recognition by the perceiver that a situation requires the application of certain skills. This means that one has to learn to treat pictures as a representation of real space. As mentioned before, the Mekan had some initial difficulty with this. Another skill is to know how to interpret impoverished cues. Apparently Western respondents have learned to interpret linear perspective cues as drawn in some of Hudson's pictures.

The term "skill" is used in different ways. On the one hand it refers to such general phenomena that it almost borders on the term "perceptual mechanism." On the other hand knowledge of specific symbols (such as multiple depictions in cartoons for representing movements) is also called a skill. This raises the question of whether the various skills stand by themselves or whether they are hierarchically organized in some way.

Theorizing about pictorial perception as a set of skills makes clear that cultures can differ in the cues which are used and/or the relative importance attached to each of them. It is assumed that culturally specific conditions will determine how skills will develop. In this respect an approach postulating a set of skills does justice to the variations in cross-cultural differences in responses to pictures that from a Western point of view contain similar depth cues. However, this kind of theorizing fails to go much beyond the observation of a given state of affairs.

When summarizing the evidence, the empirical findings allow a quite clear conclusion. There is little doubt that schoolchildren everywhere in the world easily recognize photographs of common objects and clear representational drawings. Relatively simple pictorial material has been shown to be educationally effective in countries ranging from Scotland to India and Ghana (Jahoda et al. 1976). Perceptual difficulties arise most often with pictorially unsophisticated persons and with technically advanced and complex patterns, especially in combination. The intepretation of schematic technical drawings is the most obvious case in point (e.g., Sinaiko, 1975; Dziurawiec & Deregowski, 1986).

The theoretical findings can be evaluated in two somewhat contrasting ways. On the one hand, one can emphasize that important insights into the difficulties of pictorial communication have been gained in a few decades of fairly intensive research. On the other hand, it can be argued that an integrated theoretical approach which specifies how perceptual mechanisms and environmental experience interact is still beyond our reach. Nor are we sure in what direction to proceed. A key issue concerns the extent to which conventions of depiction are arbitrary. If certain conventions more than others lead to representations which closely simulate real space, then cross-cultural research can help us to discover principles of perception.

## Face recognition

People from groups with different facial features from our own group tend to look more alike to us; we also better remember faces of individuals from our own ethnic group (Malpass, 1996). In the USA, where a number of studies have focussed on the recognition of African Americans by European Americans, and vice versa, this **cross-ethnicity effect** is known as the "cross-race effect" or "own-race bias." Wherever the phenomenon has been investigated, it has been found, although research has been conducted in only a limited number of countries (Meissner & Brigham, 2001).

Differential recognition is usually established in experiments where respondents are shown, one at a time, a series of photographs of own-group members and persons belonging to some other ethnic group. After some time these photographs (or part of them) are presented again together with photographs not shown before (distractors). The respondents have to indicate for each photograph whether or not they saw a picture of that person before. One early experiment by Malpass and Kravitz (1969) used a yes/no recognition task and established a differential recognition effect quite clearly. There have been a number of variations on this basic study. Obvious factors influencing this effect are the delay time between presentation and recognition, and the presentation time of the stimulus faces. Other parameters include the awareness or non-awareness of the respondents that they are taking part in a recognition experiment when first looking at the photographs, and whether the same photographs are presented of the target persons at the recognition task or different photographs. In order to systematically vary features sometimes representations have been developed with facial composite construction kits, a kind of device that is often used by the police to draw up a picture of a suspect on the basis of information of eye-witnesses.

It has become quite common to analyse the results in terms of a signal detection model (Swets, 1964) in which a distinction is made between two parameters, namely sensitivity and criterion bias. In this kind of model four categories of answers are distinguished: (1) the correct identification of a face seen before (yes–yes); (2) the correct identification of a face not seen before (no–no); (3) the incorrect identification of a face seen before (no–yes); and (4) the incorrect identification of a face not seen before (yes–no). Sensitivity refers to the proportions of correct and incorrect answers. Criterion bias can refer to a tendency of a respondent not to identify a face shown before (resulting in false negatives), or a tendency to "recognize" faces not shown before (false positives). The latter happens more frequently.

It may seem an intuitively plausible explanation that the lower recognition of other ethnic groups reflects stereotypes or negative attitudes towards these groups. However, such social psychological explanations have found little support in experimental findings; rather it appears that perceptual mechanisms are involved. Such mechanisms are postulated in the "contact hypothesis" (see ch. 13). In its simplest form this hypothesis states that correct recognition is a function of frequency of contact. This variable on its own does not seem to have an important role in diminishing differences between own-group and out-group recognition rates. However, when combined with quality of contact such an effect can be demonstrated (cf. Sporer, 2001). Thus, Li, Dunning, and Malpass (1998) found that European Americans who were ardent basketball fans had better recognition of African American faces than non-fans. This effect was expected by the authors as basketball in the USA has a large number of African American players, and fans have considerable experience identifying individual players.

The contact hypothesis can be seen as an instance of perceptual learning models that form the most widely accepted family of theories on the in-group versus out-group difference in recognition. According to Gibson (1966), perceptual skills involve learning to differentiate between task-relevant and task-irrelevant cues. In the course of time we learn the perceptual dimensions that are best used for discriminating faces. Inasmuch as physiognomic features and configurational properties (e.g., positioning of features) vary in different ways across groups, we gain more experience with the more salient dimensions for distinguishing own-group faces and relatively less with the dimensions of other groups. It is known that descriptions of own-group faces and those of other ethnic groups differ in terms of the categories used (Ellis, Deregowski, & Shephard, 1975).

Various forms of perceptual learning theory presume that faces are stored in some hypothetical space in which relevant features (or composites of features) form the dimensions (e.g., Valentine, 1991; Valentine & Endo, 1992). Out-group faces then become better separated in this space with increasing experience; presumably more similar appearing out-group faces should be located closer together in the perceptual space than the more differentiated own-group faces. Despite considerable support (e.g., Sporer, 2001) this theorizing has been challenged by MacLin, Malpass, and Honaker (2001). With a construction kit the latter authors prepared faces that were ethnically ambiguous. This can be done by taking the average of each typical feature of two ethnic groups (in this case Hispanic American and African American). The ambiguous faces were provided with an "ethnic marker," namely a Hispanic American hair style, or an African American hair style. Hispanic American respondents classified about two-thirds of these faces with the ethnic group suggested by hair style, while they classified the remaining one-third in various ethnicities, including Amerindian and Euroamerican. Thus, the authors obtained faces with identical physiognomic features (except hair style), that consequently should be equally distinguishable. However, when a recognition task with these faces was carried out by Hispanic American students, the faces with the Hispanic American hair style were better recognized.

According to MacLin et al. it appears that the ethnic marker drives the categorization which takes place according to ethnicity and that the recognition is influenced by this perceptual categorization, rather than by higher perceived similarity due to lesser experience with out-group faces. The authors argue that if indeed the differential recognition effect starts already with the encoding of the stimuli in memory, it may be difficult to change this effect by increasing awareness of its existence.

In a meta-analysis, in which the majority of the studies came from African American and European American ethnic contrasts, Meissner and Brigham (2001) found that respondents were 1.4 times more likely to identify correctly a previously seen face of the in-group than a face from an out-group. Moreover, respondents were 1.6 times more likely to incorrectly identify a not previously presented face as seen before (false positives). As far as criterion bias is concerned the effects were smaller, but there was a tendency toward a less strict criterion for out-group faces than for in-group faces. Of course, it is difficult to generalize these findings to eye-witness identification in real life. However, taken at face value the differences are so large that eye-witness evidence in judicial courts by members of one ethnic group involving other groups can be taken to result in (unintended) discrimination, especially in view of the weight attributed by juries to evidence given by eye-witnesses of a crime (Malpass, 1996).

## Psychological esthetics

Looking at works of art leads to two perplexing findings. The first is the tremendous variation in conventions and styles of expression. The second is the flexibility of the human perceptual mechanisms in coping with this range in variation. Consider how little formal similarity there is between Bushman rock paintings, the stylized drawings in classical Egypt, post-Renaissance landscapes from the Dutch school, and Japanese landscapes painted in the traditional style, just to mention a few of the major styles in pictorial art.

We have seen that conventions play a certain role in perception, especially of depth cues. They certainly are important in the making of art, witness the large variation in styles. If conventions play a dominant role in appreciation there is no reason to expect much agreement between respondents from different cultures. A few comparative studies of esthetic preferences have been reported that support this expectation. For example, Lawlor (1955) showed eight designs from West Africa to respondents from that region and to British respondents, asking them to indicate which two they liked best and which two they liked least. There was considerable agreement between the respondents within each sample, but the preferences of the two groups were quite distinct. Lawlor concluded that there was little evidence for a general factor that depended on the designs. Rather the cultural background of the judges was the important determinant of agreement in ratings.

Still, the weight of the evidence is that there is at least a moderate agreement in esthetic preferences between cultures. Morris (1956) found positive correlations between rankings of Western paintings by students from China, India, and the USA, although the correlation between the two Asian samples was much higher than the correlation of either of these two groups with the Americans. Research along similar lines was carried out by Child and his co-workers (e.g., Child, 1969). It included evaluations of art objects from Congo, Japan, Fiji, and the USA. Positive and sometimes substantial correlations in appreciation were found between local artists and American experts. Child often worked with artists because he believed that becoming an artist was a matter of certain personality characteristics regardless of culture. In an analysis of a collection of decorative band patterns from a broad variety of cultures Hardonk (1999) found regularities like relative simplicity, ease of design, and compactness, all of which suggested limited cultural determination.

Theory-guided research was initiated by Berlyne (1960, 1971). He postulated psychological determinants of esthetic appreciation which were independent of artistic style. Berlyne related appreciation to certain stimulus characteristics, referred to as **collative variables**. He saw esthetic appreciation as a special instance of curiosity, or stimulus-seeking behavior. There is a close relationship with a complex of psychophysiological events known as the orientiation reaction (e.g., Kimmel, Van Olst, & Orlebeke, 1979). Stimulus seeking is intrinsically motivated behavior. Certain stimuli are sought because the activity of dealing with them is satisfying or pleasurable in its own right. Strictly speaking, Berlyne's theory deals with motivation as well as with perception. As we shall see just now, an analysis of the informational content of stimuli forms the major concern of research in this tradition. As such it can be seen as a natural extension of research in perception.

The stimulus characteristics that evoke curiosity and appreciation include novelty, uncertainty or ambiguity, incongruity, and complexity. These are formal or structural properties that can be defined independent of a particular art style. This does not mean that the reactions of respondents from different cultures to a given stimulus should be the same. For example, what constitutes a novel stimulus in one setting may be highly familiar somewhere else. The relationship between collative variables and curiosity is often curvilinear. This implies that a moderately complex or incongruous stimulus will evoke the strongest reaction.

Berlyne and his colleagues (Berlyne, 1975; Berlyne, Robbins, & Thompson, 1974) used pairs of patterns that differed in complexity in various ways. The number of elements could differ, the shape of a depicted pattern could be regular or irregular, the patterns could be symmetrical or asymmetrical, and so on. Measurements included the looking time for a stimulus, paired comparisons for pleasingness, and ratings of the separate stimuli on seven-point rating scales for attractiveness and some other dimensions. Data were collected in Uganda among urban, semi-urban, and rural respondents, in Canada among students, and in India among students and villagers. Berlyne (1980) emphasized that the results showed impressive similarities across cultures. Looking times increased with complexity, the numbers of respondents preferring the same stimulus in a pair correlated positively across all six samples, and factor analyses of ratings also showed similarities across cultures.

Bragg and Crozier (1974) obtained ratings on various scales for a set of sound patterns in which the informational complexity was varied systematically. The tones of which the patterns consisted were sine waves (pure tones) differing in frequency, loudness, and duration. Small samples from Canada, India, Japan, and the Ivory Coast were tested. Graphs for ratings such as complexity and pleasingness of the various stimuli showed a large degree of similarity across cultures.

Poortinga and Foden (1975) used visual stimuli in a comparative analysis of curiosity in black and white South African students. They collected four kinds of data; these included measurements of collative variables (incongruity, ambiguity, complexity, and novelty), self-reports on stimulus seeking behavior, psychophysiological indices of arousal, and intelligence tests. These measurements were administered twice to control for effects of unfamiliarity with the experimental situation and the various tasks. As it turned out some of the precautions had been unnecessary. There was hardly any session effect. There were a few differences in the psychophysiological indices, but these were not related to the scores on the various collative variables. The correlations of the intelligence tests with the collative variables were very low. Consequently, it could be ruled out with reasonable confidence that the scores on the collative variables would be determined by unfamiliarity with the situation, arousal, or factors related to intelligence.

Two measurements of complexity in this project may be used to illustrate the experimental analysis of esthetic preferences a bit further. One task consisted of non-representational stimuli, namely symmetrical patterns of line segments, generated by a computer at eight different levels of complexity (cf. fig. 8.7). In each trial two patterns differing in complexity were projected for three seconds. Respondents

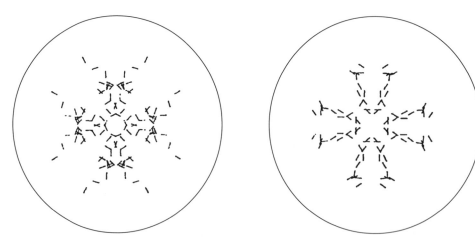

**8.7** Two stimuli from a non-representational complexity task
The original stimuli were white on a black background
After Poortinga & Foden, 1975

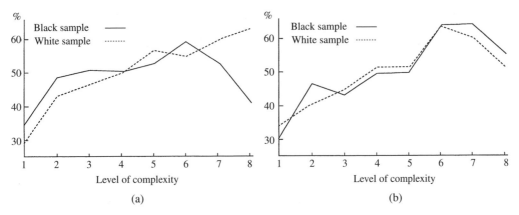

**8.8** Preference for stimuli at different levels of complexity on a non-representational (a) and a representational complexity (b) task
Poortinga & Foden, 1975

indicated which one of the two they wished to see for a second time, and the selected pattern was then projected for a further three seconds. The percentages of choices for the stimuli at each level of complexity are presented in fig. 8.8(a). The curve for the black group was clearly curvilinear, while for the white sample there was no peak probably because the level of complexity had not been extended far enough for these respondents. This was confirmed in further analyses in which curves for subsamples from both groups with similar levels of preference for the more complex patterns were found to be almost identical over the whole range of stimulus complexity.

The second measure of complexity was based on existing visual art expressions from six different cultural traditions, varying from Bushmen rock paintings to abstract modern art. Negative slides in black and white were prepared so that the complexity of the original was retained, but much of the colour, tone, and shading was eliminated. To establish the complexity level of the stimuli, ratings by judges from both cultural populations were obtained for slides from each art tradition separately and in combination. This task was administered the same way as the other complexity test. The relative preference of the samples for each level of complexity is presented in fig. 8.8(b). The similarity of the graphs is striking.

For the discrepancy between the results of the two tests Poortinga and Foden did not offer any interpretation. They merely noted that such discrepancies show that a quantitative cross-cultural difference in scores on any single variable has to be interpreted very cautiously.

The score distributions of the two groups in Poortinga and Foden's study generally showed a remarkable degree of overlap for the self-report questionnaires as well as the collative variables. The mean of the black sample, averaged over all collative variables, was only 0.30 standard deviation units below that of the white sample. This value dropped to 0.15 standard deviation units when the task with the most atypical results, the test with the non-representational stimuli, was left out.

The research on collative variables suggests that underneath the different conventions about esthetic expression there appear to be universal psychological mechanisms in the perception and appreciation of visual stimuli. However, collative variables are not the only determinants of esthetic preferences. In their review Russell, Deregowski, & Kinnear (1997) have pointed to some other factors, including ecological variables that relate to the actual environment in which people live. Unfortunately, research on such factors so far has been limited.

## Conclusions

It is obvious from this overview that not all perceptual variables are equally likely to show cross-cultural differences. On tasks for basic sensory functions, such as perceptual constancies and stimulus discrimination on psychophysical scales, an approximately equal level of performance is to be expected for all cultural groups.

At a higher level of stimulus complexity the pattern of findings changes. Object recognition in clear representational pictures does not create many problems anywhere in the world, provided the perceiver has had at least some exposure to pictorial materials. Depth cues are readily experienced in certain kinds of pictures such as geometric patterns, but contrary to intuitive expectation, culture-specific conventions can play a dominant role in the perception of depth in simple schematic drawings, like Hudson's test.

Perceptual habits that are transferred from real space to pattern perception have been cited as antecedents of cross-cultural differences in the susceptibility for certain visual illusions. Some of these illusions are pictorially very simple, consisting only of a few line segments. On the other hand, seemingly difficult perceptual notions such as symmetry appear to be readily grasped by a Bushmen group where pictorial representation was largely absent.

As the discrepancy between real space and pictorial representation becomes larger cross-cultural differences increase. However, research on esthetic appreciation has shown that common mechanisms appear to lie underneath the conventions of various artistic traditions. As more emphasis is placed on these common mechanisms, the explanation of cross-cultural differences in perception is shifting to conventions in the sense of cultural agreements which have a certain arbitrariness. Most conventions are limited to fairly specific classes of stimuli. They are not compatible with broad generalizations as have been made in the past, for example in the formulation of compensation hypotheses. However, it would be a mistake to think that an emphasis on conventions means that cross-cultural differences are trivial. If their number is large enough together they can have a profound influence on the repertoire of behavior. Maybe this is the most important lesson that cross-cultual psychologists can learn from variations in artistic styles. Such styles appear to be rather arbitrary from the viewpoint of basic perception, but sometimes they have retained distinctive style characteristics for centuries.

## Key terms

collative variables
convention
cross-ethnicity effect (in face recognition)

depth cues in pictures
sensory stimuli
visual illusions


## Further reading

Deregowski, J. B. (1980a). *Illusions, patterns and pictures: A cross-cultural perspective.* London: Academic Press. This book provides a thorough overview of cross-cultural research on perception.

Deregowski, J. B. (1989). Real space and represented space: Cross-cultural perspectives. *Behavioral and Brain Sciences, 12,* 51–119. A review article that is followed by peer discussion.

Meissner, C. A., & Brigham, J. C. (2001). Thirty years of investigating the own-race bias in memory for faces: A meta-analytic review. *Psychology, Public Policy and Law* 7, 3–35. An overview of research on face recognition across ethnic groups.

Russell, P. A., Deregowski, J. B., & Kinnear, P. R. (1997). Perception and aesthetics. In J. W. Berry, P. R. Dasen, & T. S. Saraswathi (Eds.), *Basic processes and human development* (pp. 107–42). Vol. II of *Handbook of cross-cultural psychology* (2nd ed.). Boston, MA: Allyn and Bacon. The authors review evidence on most topics in cross-cultural perception research, with the exception of face recognition.

**II**

# Pursuing relationships between behavior and culture: research strategies

# 9   Approaches from cultural anthropology

In earlier chapters we have frequently used the term "culture" as if it needed no lengthy discussion. In ch. 1, however, we did indicate that we would use the term to refer to the "shared way of life of a group of people." In this chapter we first examine various conceptions of culture in more detail. We then consider some aspects of ethnography, including ethnographic fieldwork and the use of ethnographic archives. We then turn to a consideration of two domains of anthropological research that are related to cross-cultural psychology: psychological anthropology, and cognitive anthropology.

The relationships between anthropology and psychology have been thoroughly examined by Jahoda (1982); his book should be read by those wanting an in-depth treatment of these issues. In this chapter we attend mainly to those features of the anthropological tradition that have had a direct bearing on the development and conduct of cross-cultural psychology, including various conceptions of culture, and the practice of ethnography. However, we do not attempt to portray the field of **anthropology** as a whole. Those seeking an overview of the field should consult a recent textbook (e.g. Ember & Ember, 1998) or a chapter by Munroe and Munroe (1997).

## Conceptions of culture

While the term **culture** first appeared in an English dictionary in the 1920s (Kroeber, 1949), the first use in an anthropological work was by Tylor (1871), who defined culture as "that complex whole which includes knowledge, belief, art, morals, laws, customs and any other capabilities and habits acquired by man as a member of society."

Two rather short, but now widely used definitions were later proposed: Linton (1936, p. 78) suggested that culture means "the total social heredity of mankind," and Herskovits (1948, p. 17) that "Culture is the man-made part of the human environment." In contrast to these concise definitions we also have lengthy listings of what is included in culture. One of these is by Wissler (1923), who included speech, material traits, art, knowledge, religion, society, property, government, and war. This list is similar to the general categories that are used in the Human Relations Area Files (HRAF) that will be presented later in this chapter (see box 9.1).

In a classic survey of many definitions, Kroeber and Kluckhohn (1952) suggested that six major classes of definition of culture were to be found in the anthropological literature:

1 Descriptive definitions are those that attempt to list any and all aspects of human life and activity thought by the writer to be an example of what is meant by "culture." Both Tylor's and Wissler's definitions are of this type. To Kroeber and Kluckhohn, descriptive definitions tend to emphasize the view of "culture as a comprehensive totality" (p. 85).

2 Historical definitions, as in Linton's, tend to emphasize the accumulation of tradition over time, rather than enumerating the totality or range of cultural phenomena. The term "heritage" is frequently used in these definitions (also the term "heredity"), but the context clearly indicates that no biological factors are thought to be involved in the accumulation.

3 Normative definitions emphasize the shared rules which govern the activity of a group of people. Unlike the descriptive and historical definitions, where the cultural life being referred to is clearly observable, normative definitions require us to dig into the overt activity and to try to discover what lies behind it. Later in this chapter we will refer to this distinction using the terms explicit and implicit culture.

4 Psychological definitions emphasize a variety of psychological features, including notions such as adjustment, problem-solving, learning, and habits. For example, culture is learned, and the result of this learning is the establishment of habits in a particular group. This category is rather broad, and includes both implied (e.g., attitudes) and observable (e.g., habits) cultural phenomena. A consideration of "culture as a psychological construct" will be presented later in ch. 12. For the time being it is useful to note that some cross-cultural psychologists assert that cultures can be studied and described on the basis of psychological data collected from samples of individuals, and then aggregated to the level of their group (e.g., in ch. 3, where individual value preferences are used to characterize a whole culture or nation). The most explicit statement of this belief has been by Triandis (1996), who uses the notion of cultural syndrome to refer to "a pattern of shared attitudes, beliefs, categorizations,

self-definitions, norms, role definition and values that is organized around a theme" (p. 408). He argues that cultures can be studied and understood using both anthropological methods at the cultural level, and that "we can also use data from the individual level . . . The cultural and individual difference analyses are complementary and allow us to describe cultures" (p. 412).

5 Structural definitions emphasize the pattern or organization of culture. This view is related to the first (descriptive) category, in that the overall or total picture is emphasized. However, structural definitions again require going beyond the overt features in order to discover the arrangements that exist. The central view is that culture is not a mere list or hodge-podge of customs, but forms an integrated pattern of interrelated features.

6 Genetic definitions emphasize the origin, or genesis of culture (not genetic in the biological sense). Within this category there are three main answers given: culture arises as adaptive to the habitat of a group, out of social interaction, and out of a creative process (both individual and interactive) that is a characteristic of the human species. Note that the ecocultural framework used in this text generally corresponds to this definition of culture. It adopts the view that culture is adaptive to both the natural habitat and to sociopolitical contexts (the first two origins), and that the third origin (creative processes) is represented as feedback from human accomplishments to other features of the framework. This dynamic, interactive view of how populations relate to their ecosystem treats culture not as a stable end product, but as part of a constantly changing system, both adapting to, and impacting on, its habitat (Kottak, 1999).

Concluding their review with a definition of their own, Kroeber and Kluckhohn (1952, p. 181) proposed that:

> Culture consists of patterns, explicit and implicit, of and for behavior acquired and transmitted by symbols, constituting the distinctive achievements of human groups, including their embodiments in artifacts; the essential core of culture consists of traditional (i.e., historically derived and selected) ideas and especially their attached values; cultural systems may on the one hand be considered as products of action, on the other as conditioning elements of further action.

In this definition, despite the many specific conceptions, there is an explicit acceptance that culture is comprised of both concrete, observable activities and artifacts, and of underlying symbols, values, and meanings. For a long time the first set of characteristics was the main focus of anthropology, and this influenced how cross-cultural psychologists drew the concept into their work. In essence, culture was seen as being "out there" and concrete, having an objective reality and a large degree of permanence. The second set of characteristics, which are largely "in here" (inside people, or between individuals during interactions) and more changeable, was less influential.

However, in the 1970s, a move was afoot to emphasize the second more symbolic view, in which culture was to be found within and between individuals in their shared meanings and practices. Culture was no longer considered to be only or primarily an objective context for human development and action, but as more subjective, with "culture in the mind of the people" as "an historically transmitted pattern of meanings embodied in symbols" (Geertz, 1973, p. 89), and as "a conceptual structure or system of ideas" (Geertz, 1984, p. 8). This newer approach has given rise to a more cognitive emphasis in anthropology (e.g. Romney & Moore, 1998, p. 315). They boldly assert that "the locus of culture . . . resides in the minds of members of the culture." This conception is now broadly adopted by those who identify with "cultural psychology" (e.g. Cole, 1996; Shweder, 1990). While for them the pendulum has swung away from viewing culture as "out there" to being "in here," it is important to note that Geertz (1973, p. 12) argued against the "cognitive fallacy" that "culture consists of mental phenomena." As D'Andrade (1995, p. 246) has pointed out:

> It is probably the case that the mainstream of anthropology was more or less convinced by Geertz's arguments; it was felt without much explicit discussion that there is something public about culture, and that placing meaning too deeply in the mind would lead to imperialist claims by psychologists!

These changes in how culture is conceptualized (often linked to postmodernism) have created a crisis for many anthropologists, to the point where the very legitimacy of the concept has been questioned (e.g., Abu-Lughod, 1991), while others have defended it (e.g., Bennett, 1999; Brumann, 1999; Munroe & Munroe, 1997). The arguments advanced against the current usefulness of the concept are many: it is too static, and cannot deal with the obvious changes underway worldwide; it ignores individual agency in the construction of daily cultural interactions; it places boundaries around phenomena that exhibit continuous variation, etc. These can all be recognized as part of the deconstructionist or postmodernist challenges to positivist and empirical science. Many similar ideas have been advanced within psychology, and are part of the culturalists' challenge to cultural comparativists (see ch. 12). Fish (2000) and Greenfield (2000) have presented contrasting perspectives on how this postmodernist challenge impacts on our understanding of culture–behavior relationships.

In defence of the concept of culture, those who reject the social (de)constructionist ideology point out that there is a set of phenomena that despite their changeability and almost infinite variability continue to be recognizable characteristics (both behavioral and symbolic) of human populations (Shweder, 2000). As phrased by Bennett (1999, pp. 954–5):

> Although the concept received bad press, and is a no-word in contemporary cultural anthropology, it remains on the whole the most profitable general way of handling multidimensional behavioral data. Whether we admit it or not, we are all still functionalists ... Classic anthropology's concern for objectivity was not such a bad thing.

Munroe and Munroe (1997) also accept the concept of culture as a set of knowable regularities that characterize human groups. Similar to the universalist position adopted in this text, they argued that "universals, generalizations and similarities across cultures could be expected due to our single-species heritage and the necessity of adapting to environmental constraints" (p. 174). And addressing the constructionist exclusive focus on variability, rather than the commonalities, Munroe and Munroe (1997, p. 176) consider this to be a "one-sided, and misleading view, in fact a half-truth." We will return to these arguments in chs. 11 and 12, where the debate in psychology (see also Hermans & Kempen, 1998; Tweed, Conway, & Ryder, 1999) is taken up.

In this text, we adopt the views that "culture" is still a useful notion, and employ the concept as if it has some objective existence that can be used to characterize the relatively stable "way of life of a group of people." We also take the view (see ch. 12) that such an objective and stable quality of a group can both influence, and be influenced by, individuals and their actions. As we have argued:

> To the cross-cultural psychologist, cultures are seen as products of past human behavior and as shapers of future human behavior. Thus, humans are producers of culture and, at the same time, our behavior is influenced by it. We have produced social environments that continually serve to bring about continuities and changes in lifestyles over time and uniformities and diversities in lifestyles over space. How human beings modify culture and how our cultures modify us is what cross-cultural psychology is all about. (Segall et al., 1999, p. 23)

Since the term "culture" is now part of our daily vocabulary, it is useful to briefly consider how it differs in anthropology and cross-cultural psychology from these colloquial uses. First, it is not restricted to "high culture," referring only to painting, classical music, etc., but to *all* such products of human life, ranging from comic books and pop music to those products normally preserved in museums and performed in concert halls or opera houses. Second, culture is not "civilization"; *all* human groups possess culture, including those ethnocentrically referred to as being "civilized" and "primitive." Most anthropologists (as well as cross-cultural psychologists) avoid the terms civilized and primitive because they are value judgments about the quality of culture (see section below on cultural evolution). Third, culture is not the same as society, although the two terms are closely linked. One definition of society refers to "an organized collectivity of interacting people whose activities become centered around a set of common goals, and who tend to share common beliefs, attitudes and modes of action" (Krech, Crutchfield, & Ballachey, 1962, p. 308). From this definition we can see that a society is composed of people, while culture is the way of life they hold in common. This distinction between culture and society is often blurred; even in the literature of cross-cultural psychology, writers occasionally slip and use "culture" when they mean "society."

In ch. 1 we considered the idea that different disciplines employ different levels of analysis, and do so legitimately without having to protect themselves from reductionistic attacks from more basic disciplines. In anthropology, the concept of culture is clearly a group-level or collective phenomenon. Just as clearly, though, biological and psychological variables may be related to cultural variables, and from time to time there have been attempts to use them to explain cultural phenomena.

One protection against this reductionism has been proposed by Kroeber (1917), who argued that culture is superorganic, "super" meaning above and beyond, and "organic" referring to its individual biological and psychological bases. Two arguments were presented by Kroeber for the independent existence of culture, at its own level. First, particular individuals come and go, but cultures remain more or less stable. This is a remarkable phenomenon; despite a large turnover in membership with each new generation, cultures and their institutions remain relatively unchanged. Thus, a culture does not depend on particular individuals for its existence, but has a life of its own at the collective level of the group. The second argument is that no single individual "possesses" all of the "culture" of the group to which he or she belongs; the culture as a whole is carried by the collectivity and, indeed, is likely to be beyond the biological or psychological capacity (to know or to do) of any single person in the group. For example, no single person knows all the laws, political institutions, and economic structures that constitute even this limited sector of his or her culture.

For both these reasons, Kroeber considers that cultural phenomena are collective phenomena, above and beyond the individual person, and hence his term "superorganic". This position is an important one for cross-cultural psychology since it permits us to employ the group–individual distinction in attempting to link the two, and possibly to trace the influence of cultural factors on individual psychological phenomena. Whether "culture" can constitute the "independent variable" in such studies is a matter of debate, and will be addressed in ch. 12 in the section on culture as a psychological concept.

In the comprehensive definition of culture offered by Kroeber and Kluckhohn, the terms explicit and implicit were used to qualify the term culture. The distinction between explicit and implicit culture is similar to one which is well known to psychologists, namely between observable behavior and (presumably) underlying psychological functions and processes. Some cultural phenomena are overt, readily observable, and fairly concrete; these are the day-to-day customs, practices, and usages that can be gauged by virtually any observer, whether an insider (member of the culture) or an outsider. These phenomena correspond, in psychology, to the overt behaviors that are the basic data for all psychologists (and which usually constitute the only acceptable data for stringent behaviorists). Explicit culture, then, is the set of observable acts and products regularly found in a group.

In contrast, implicit culture refers to the organizing principles that are inferred to lie behind these regularities, on the basis of consistent patterns of explicit culture. This corresponds, in psychology, to the inferred traits or characteristics of individuals that we postulate to account for behavioral consistency. Whether implicit culture and traits actually exist in their own right or only exist in the cognitive life of observers is an epistemological and methodological question of long standing. Inferred characteristics cannot be observed directly by an outsider (anthropologist or psychologist) and often cannot even be articulated by the persons exhibiting these regularities. Grammar that controls speech, rules of address that regulate interaction, and norms that guide proper conduct, are all examples of implicit culture; so, too, are the fundamental features of social structure, myth, and ritual, all of which result from cognitive activity (inference, comparison, generalization) on the part of those seeking to discover the meaning behind cultural regularity.

## Cultural evolution

The dimension of cultural variation underlying the "civilized"–"primitive" distinction is essentially one of **cultural evolution**: historically, cultural groups have appeared in an identifiable sequence from small hunting and gathering bands, through societies based on plant and animal domestication (agricultural and pastoral peoples) to industrial and now post-industrial societies (see e.g., Lomax & Berkowitz, 1972). In the past it was thought by many (and it is probably still thought by most people living in Western industrial societies) that this historical sequence somehow displayed "progress" (see analyses and criticisms by Preiswerk & Perrot, 1978). There is sometimes thought to be a parallel between biological evolution (from amebas to mankind; see ch. 10) and cultural evolution (from hunters to industrial societies), a sequence termed "social Darwinism." Critics (Nisbet, 1971; Poggie & Lynch, 1974; Sahlins & Service, 1960) reject the idea that, over time, there has been "improvement" (in some absolute sense) in the quality of culture. This rejection is based upon the belief that such judgments do not have any scientific basis, and must inevitably rest on personal preferences about what is "good" and what is "bad" in human existence. In this book, we also reject such absolute notions of progress and improvement in culture over time.

In an attack on this general position, Sahlins and Service (1960) have made an important distinction between specific evolution and general evolution. In the former, cultural diversity and change appear, often in adaptation to new ecological (both physical and social) conditions. In the latter, general evolution "generates progress; higher forms arise from and surpass lower forms" (1960, pp. 12–13). We accept the first view of evolution (diversity through adaptive modification), while not accepting the second (progress and higher forms resulting from change). The reason for this position is that there is ample objective evidence for ecologically induced change, but there are only subjective value judgments to provide a basis for claiming one adaptation to be better than another. As Sahlins and Service (1960, p. 15) have phrased it: "adaptive improvement is relative to the adaptive problem; it is so to be judged and explained. In the specific context each adapted population is adequate, indeed superior, in its own incomparable way." Not everyone, however, accepts this judgment. Hallpike (1986), for example, has argued that modification through adaptation is not the whole of the story. There is indeed a "directional process" (p. 375) at work that actually leads change toward a more advanced state. Despite this alternative view, we espouse, in this book, a basically functionalist perspective, in which culture and behavior are considered to be an adaptation to ecological and sociopolitical factors.

## Cultural relativism

The opposite position to that of "social Darwinism" is **cultural relativism**, first introduced by Boas (1911) and elaborated by Herskovits (1948). As introduced to cross-cultural psychology by Segall et al. (1966), p. 17):

> the ethnographer attempts to describe the behavior of the people he studies without the evaluation that his own culture would ethnocentrically dictate. He attempts to see the culture in terms of its own evaluative system. He tries to remain aware of the fact that his judgements are based upon this own experience and reflect his own deep-seated enculturation to a limited and specific culture. He reminds himself that his original culture provides no Olympian vantage from which to view objectively any other culture.

This position of cultural relativism provides a non-ethnocentric stance from which to view cultural and psychological diversity. It can range from a general awareness of the problems inherent in ethnocentric thinking about differences, through to a "radical cultural relativism" (Berry, 1972). This more extreme position has been advocated for some topics in cross-cultural psychology where the social and political consequences of scientific ethnocentrism can be harmful. In particular, in the areas of cognition and development, scientific errors due to ethnocentrism (generalizations such as "they have lower intelligence" or "they are less morally developed" can have important consequences for large numbers of people). Here, the "radical" position is to avoid comparisons completely (rather than by just tempering them with our awareness of the problems of ethnocentrism) until thorough local analyses have been carried out. In this way, scientific caution is maximized, and potential error and harm can be minimized. We will return to the issue of relativism in ch. 12 when we consider the advantages and disadvantages of this stance, and of some alternatives to it (the absolutist and universalist positions).

## Cultural universals

One of the more subtle features of cross-cultural psychology is the balance sought between seeking to understand the local phenomena, while at the same time attempting to develop pan-human generalizations (cf. the second and third goals of the field that we proposed in ch. 1). The position of cultural relativism assists us in the first endeavour, while the existence of **cultural universals** provides a basis for the second. Similar to the claim of Aberle et al. (1950) that there are certain functional prerequisites for a society (see box 3.1), is the position that there are certain common features to all cultures: these are basic qualities of culture, and consist of those phenomena that one can expect to find in any and every culture. In turn, activities that all peoples engage in (even though obviously carried out in very different ways) are the basis for claims about uniformities in psychological functioning. In other words, cultural universals reflect psychological universals.

These cultural universals may be derived theoretically or generated empirically (Lonner, 1980). For example, Malinowski (1944) posited a set of universal aspects of culture based upon a set of (universal) basic biological needs. With the biological need for reproduction there comes the cultural response of kinship systems; with a need for health, there comes a system of hygiene, and so on. However, these have been termed "fake universals" by Lonner (1980) and described as "vague tautologies and forceless banalities" by Geertz (1965, p. 103). The claim that families and socialization practices exist in all societies does not take us very far, except to alert us to the fundamental role of such institutions in genetic and cultural transmission.

More concrete and useful for psychological research are listings based on a wide range of work in many cultures. Such elaborated lists do more than provide a "handy checklist"; they provide a comprehensive set of descriptive categories that may form the basis for comparative work. One candidate for use as a comparative tool is the set of categories developed by Murdock (1949) and used in the HRAF which will be discussed later in this chapter (box 9.1).

## Ethnography

Anthropologists have a long experience of working in virtually all of the world's cultures. The legacy of this tradition resides in thousands of published volumes of "fieldwork" in particular cultures. These ethnographic reports are a rich source of information, and serve as an important foundation for cross-cultural psychology. Two other scientific activities are based on this ethnographic foundation: ethnology and archives.

In the field of ethnology, researchers attempt to understand the patterns, institutions, dynamics, and changes of cultures. This search for the larger picture requires the use of ethnographic reports from numerous cultures, comparing them and drawing out similarities and differences. In so doing, ethnologists work with original ethnographic materials (sometimes their own, sometimes those of others), seeking what may lie behind, or account for, the ethnographic variation. In a sense, while ethnography remains descriptive of explicit culture, ethnology becomes interpretive, using scientific inferences to comprehend implicit culture (using a term introduced earlier). In practice, however, most anthropologists do not maintain such a strict distinction between doing ethnography and ethnology.

In the case of archives, research is conducted using a vast array of ethnographic reports, sometimes organized into a systematic framework that is amenable to comparative and statistical use.

## Ethnographic fieldwork

Cross-cultural psychologists will inevitably need to have a good grasp of how to conduct ethnographic work in the field. Longstanding problems, such as how to enter the field, and how to carry out ethnographic research, have been major issues for anthropology, and much has been written to assist the fieldworker (e.g., the classic *Notes and Queries* of the Royal Anthropological Institute, 1951). Other problems, such as interviewing and testing, reside in the psychological tradition, while still others, such as sampling and the use of observational techniques, belong to both disciplines. Two discussions of these issues, written expressly for cross-cultural psychologists, can be found in Goodenough (1980) and in Munroe and Munroe (1986).

The first approach to, and contact with, a cultural group or community can be the single most important act in a program of research; how can it be done with sensitivity and without major gaffes? In a discussion of the problem (Cohen, 1970), experienced fieldworkers concluded that there was no single best approach to the field, each situation requiring attention to local standards, and some degree of self-knowledge on the part of the researcher. Indeed, the fieldworker as a sojourner experiences acculturation, and may also experience acculturative stress (see ch. 13) in which self-doubt, loss of motivation, depression, and other problems may become great enough to hinder the work.

Perhaps the most effective and ethical way to enter the field is to establish a collaborative relationship with a colleague in another culture. However, much of the early anthropogical research was "extractive" (Gasché, 1992) rather than collaborative: the anthroplogist returned home with information and artifacts, much as a geologist would return with mineral specimens, and hence became identified as part of the colonial enterprise. Nowadays many anthropologists join forces with informants to look at the question together. In this way local knowledge and acceptance may be acquired easily and quickly. It is also probable that research questions that are important to the population are addressed, and that results obtained can be made relevant to local problems. We have already noted the methodological advantages of such an arrangement in ch. 1, where the elimination of ethnocentrism was established as a goal for cross-cultural psychology.

While a complete ethnographic study is probably not necessary (and likely to be beyond the capabilities of a psychologist), there is, nevertheless, the need to verify the information contained in a previous ethnography of the people involved in the study. To do this, we need to have some familiarity with ethnographic methods. Full treatments of this topic can be found in Alasuutari (1995), Bernard (1998), and Naroll and Cohen (1970). We focus here on some broad, but central, questions that need to be considered when learning to do cross-cultural psychology in the field (see also Lonner & Berry, 1986a).

First, some basic features of the culture need to be examined, in order to understand the general context in which one's research participants developed, and now carry out their lives. The list of features studied by most anthropologists, of what constitutes a culture, has been presented earlier. Foremost on these lists is the language, and this is often the best place to begin learning about another culture; it not only provides cultural knowledge in its own right, but it also provides a vehicle to learn about most other aspects of culture.

While field anthropologists usually acquire a functional fluency in the local language, cross-cultural psychologists rarely do. Herein lies a major difference and a major problem. Anthropologists learn the local language because it is an important part of the culture-to-be-understood; cross-cultural psychologists do not because their research question (unless it is in psycholinguistics) may have little to do with language. However, it can be argued that psychological understanding is so subtle, so dependent on interpersonal communication, that local language learning should be a primary, preliminary objective also for cross-cultural psychologists.

An alternative to this rarely achieved goal is to rely on others as vehicles for understanding; this can be done by way of bilingual assistants, or by collaborating with bilingual co-researchers. The use of local research assistants, with whom one shares a common language, is probably the most frequently employed alternative. The researcher can locate, hire, and train members of the community who then serve as linguistic informants, translators of research instruments and instructions, and act as research assistants during the course of data collection (see Brislin, 1980, 1986). Care should be taken both in deciding whom to hire (taking local advice into account, in addition to one's own impressions), and in training (not to bias the data collection in favour of one's hypothesis). Indeed, it is an interesting question whether to reveal or disguise one's research theory or hypothesis. By disguising it, the risk of bias may be reduced, but the assistant (like the curious subject) may spend much of the time attempting to guess the hypothesis. By revealing it, the risk of bias may be increased ("giving the researcher what he wants"). However, a full sharing of the research hypothesis with one's assistants may very much improve one's understanding of the issue in local terms, and the degree of rapport and trust in the working relationship.

Other cultural variables that are implicated in the research framework need to be examined. For example, economy, material goods, social stratification, political organization, religion, and myth may play a role in one's research. The most commonly used approaches to obtaining such information in field anthropology are by intensive interaction with key informants and by the use of observational techniques.

Key informants have a central role in anthropological research because of the presumed normative nature of most aspects of culture. That is, culture is thought to be a widely shared phenomenon, and hence any (or a few) individuals should be able to give a detailed account of their own culture. Extensive, followed by intensive questioning, checking, and rechecking of previously obtained information, and trying out one's formulations for comment from informants, all contribute to the growing body of knowledge about the cultural group. Over time, with the help of only a few individuals, a comprehensive picture can be built up.

Observations made of daily life also serve to check on the information gained from key informants, and as a way of verifying one's own formulations about the culture (Bochner, 1986; Longabaugh, 1980; Munroe & Munroe, 1994). Discrepancies will be encountered (between formulations and observations), and a return to one's key informants will be required to help sort them out. Hence, there is often an iterative process, moving back and forth between asking informants and direct observations, until one is satisfied that the cultural variables of interest are adequately understood.

However, even this process does not guarantee the validity of ethnographic observations and interpretations. For example, in what has become known as the "Mead and Freeman controversy" (see section on "Psychological anthropology"), dramatically different accounts of the same culture have been presented.

## Ethnographic archives

By far the most frequently used **ethnographic archive** in cross-cultural psychology is the vast set of materials known as the **Human Relations Area Files (HRAF)**. If one wanted to locate a set of cultures for a comparative project that met certain criteria, it would be a long and difficult task to wade through hundreds of ethnographic reports searching for specific groups that would serve this purpose. Fortunately, a good deal of the ethnographic literature has been organized (assembled, categorized, and coded) into these files (see Ember and Ember, 1988 for a practical guide; and the HRAF to the web page [http://www.yale.edu/hraf/home.htm]).

The HRAF were started in 1936, and are based upon two classifications, namely of societies and of topics, that were thought to be applicable worldwide (Moore, 1971). One is the *Outline of world cultures* (Murdock, 1975, 5th ed.) and the other is the *Outline of cultural materials* (Murdock, Ford, & Hudson, 1971, 4th ed.). The first of these (*Outline of world cultures*) is a comprehensive listing of many of the world's cultural (including ethnic and political) units, and this constitutes the population from which researchers may identify and sample cultures. A related inventory of societies is the *Ethnographic atlas* (Murdock, 1967) which includes 863 societies, arranged into six "culture areas" (sub-Saharan Africa, circum-Mediterranean, east Eurasia, Oceania, North America and South America). Another listing of societies contains the standard probability sample (Murdock & White, 1969) selected to provide a representative set of 60 independent societies (arranged in eight culture areas) for use in the search for patterns of correlations among characteristics across cultures.

The *Outline of cultural materials* contains seventy-nine topics that are considered to be a universal set of categories to be found in all cultural groups. These have been arranged into eight broad categories by Barry (1980). Box 9.1 provides a selection of these topics.

## Box 9.1 Cultural topics contained in "Outline of cultural materials"

In Murdock et al.'s *Outline of cultural materials* variations in cultural practices around the world are placed in seventy-nine categories; these in turn are organized into eight major sections. It is interesting to compare these aspects of culture to those in Wissler's earlier definition.

Some of the seventy-nine cultural categories of Murdock, as arranged by Barry (1980), are:

**I General characteristics**
Methodology
Geography
Human biology
Behavior processes and personality
Demography
History and culture
Change
Language
Communication

**II Food and clothing**
Food quest
Food processing
Food consumption
Drink, drugs, and indulgence
Clothing
Adornment

**III Housing and technology**
Exploitative activities
Processing of basic materials
Building and construction
Structures
Settlements
Energy and power
Machines

**IV Economy and transport**
Property
Exchange
Marketing
Finance
Labour
Business and industrial organization
Travel and transportation

**Box 9.1 (continued)**

**V Individual and family activities**
Living standards and routines
Recreation
Fine arts
Entertainment
Social stratification
Interpersonal relations
Marriage
Family
Kinship

**VI Community and government**
Community
Territorial organization
State
Government activities
Political and sanctions
Law
Offenses and sanctions
Justice
War

**VII Welfare, religion, and science**
Social problems
Health and welfare
Sickness
Death
Religious beliefs
Ecclesiastical organization
Numbers and measures
Ideas about nature and man

**VIII Sex and the life cycle**
Sex
Reproduction
Infancy and childhood
Socialization
Education
Adolescence, adulthood, old age

Thus, there are two major dimensions cross-cutting each other: a universe of cultures, and a universe of cultural characteristics. With this massive archive, virtually any feature of a society can be sought and found by the researcher. For example, one can search for a subset of all cultures in a particular part of the world and count the proportion of cultures in these regions that have hunting, as opposed to agriculture, as their basic economic activity. Given the availability of geographical information (on latitude, altitude, temperature, and rainfall) for these cultures one could then ask the question: "Is basic economic activity distributed in a way that is predictable from geographical information?" Prior to the availability of the HRAF, researchers interested in these ecological questions (such as Kroeber, 1939) had to go to numerous original sources for their information.

Actual uses of the HRAF have largely been to discover patterns of regular associations (correlations) between two sets of cultural variables across cultures. This **"holocultural"** or "hologeistic" approach incorporates the "whole-world" range of data and findings (Naroll, 1970a). We have seen one specific example in the search for a relationship between socialization practices and subsistence economy (reported in ch. 2). For ease of use many numerical codes have been produced so that each researcher does not have to convert verbal descriptions of a custom (such as child rearing) to a digit each time a category of cultural activity is employed. A massive set of codes is available in both the *Ethnographic atlas* (Murdock, 1967) and in the survey *A cross-cultural summary* (Textor, 1967). More specialized codes continue to be produced (Barry & Schlegel, 1980), and many are now available in computerized form.

A number of problems have attended the use of the HRAF, leading to many criticisms and and equally attempts to deal with them (Naroll, Michik, & Naroll, 1980). We examine briefly here some of these problems and the solutions proposed within anthropology; further consideration from the point of view of cross-cultural psychology will be given in ch. 11. A basic problem is to define what a cultural group is exactly–what are its limits and boundaries, and who is a member? Naroll (1970b) has proposed the notion of "cultunit" (short for "culture bearing unit"), which is a term for a defined group that exhibits a specific culture (see ch. 11).

A second issue in the statistical use of cultunits is the question of their independence. This issue has been termed Galton's problem (see Naroll, 1970c), and it has been a substantial thorn in the side of those who wish to use correlational analyses in holocultural studies. The essence of the problem is the diffusion of cultural traits from one cultunit to another; the presence of a particular practice in adjacent cultunits may be due to borrowing, and not to independent development. Thus, for example, the correlation across twenty cultunits between the emphasis on compliance in socialization and reliance on agriculture for subsistence might be due to one society establishing such a link and then sharing it with other societies. Since correlations of this sort require independence of cases, the apparent linking of these two factors in the twenty cultunits might represent only a single case diffused, rather than twenty independent cases. The solution that has been proposed by Naroll (1970c) is the "double language boundary"; two cultunits may be considered to be independent of each other for statistical purposes if there are at least two language borders between any two cultunits in the study. The standard cross-cultural sample (mentioned earlier) was chosen, in part, to meet this independence requirement.

A third problem is that the quality of the data is extremely variable in the HRAF. Some were collected by explorers and merchants, some by military invaders and missionaries, and some by anthropologists. While it would be tempting to claim the greatest data accuracy and quality for those trained to be objective fieldworkers, this may not necessarily by the case. To evaluate this problem, and to control for it, Naroll (1962) has introduced a procedure called "data quality control," in which one "assumes that there is variation in the degree of accuracy of holocultural data, and that this variation is related to characteristics of the data generation process" (Naroll et al., 1980, p. 497). For example, whether the report is from a person who knew the language or not may be correlated with variations in reported cognitive ability, or missionary status may be correlated with reported religious beliefs. Five control factors have proven to be valuable in assessing data quality: length of fieldwork; knowledge of language; description of current life as observed versus remembered life as recalled by elders; number of data sources and cross-checks employed; and number of publications cited in the formal written presentation of the ethnographic account. However, data control procedures can hardly account for biases in ethnographic descriptions arising from the theoretical orientation of the ethnographer. Thus, we find, for exmple, that in early psychoanalytically inspired research, there was much emphasis on childhood variables, like weaning. One of the consequences of theoretical differences is that replication studies (i.e., two ethnographies of the same cultural group, written in different periods) usually show only poor resemblance (Kloos, 1988). Needless to say that also in psychology historical changes in theoretical orientation have led to wide variations in the aspects of behavior studied.

A final problem to be noted here is that of the categories of culture used in the HRAF. In box 9.1 there were seventy-nine categories or topics mentioned, into which all cultural data are slotted. The question is whether these categories are a perfect fit, an approximate fit, or a poor fit for the whole range of cultural data being reported from around the world. In other terms, are these really universal categories of culture, or do some cultural data become selected or distorted, in order to match such a neat conceptual scheme? Are the data within each category truly comparable (see ch. 11)? The solution proposed by Naroll et al. (1980) is to make quite explicit all of the coding rules to be employed when taking material from an ethnographic report and entering them into the HRAF. For example, is cannibalism to be understood as any eating of human flesh, or must it also be known (not accidental), customary (not one time only), and approved of (not under duress)? Similar coding rules may be generated and applied to distinguishing between such cultural practices as science, religion, magic, witchcraft, myth, and ritual. With such rules, coding errors and forced categorization may be avoided. However, numerous data that cannot be categorized may require an expansion or reorganization of the present system of categories.

While cross-cultural psychologists may wish to use the HRAF to search for systematic co-variation between population-level variables, two other uses are being suggested here. One is that an "initial reading" of a psychological theory or hypothesis (prior to the effort and expense of going to the field) may be possible using variables and data already in the HRAF; and in this way one may be able to direct one's activity more effectively toward fruitful questions when one eventually goes to the field. The second one (as we noted at the outset) is that with the help of the HRAF, specific cultures can be identified as providing particular cultural contexts and experiences which are required for a particular comparative psychological study. For example, if our interest were in the effects of variations in socialization practices, we could select a set of societies varying from the extreme assertion to the extreme compliance ends of the dimension, and then go to the field and use psychological assessment procedures with a sample of individuals to see if the expected behavioral outcomes were indeed present.

As Munroe and Munroe (1997) have noted, the two areas of cultural anthropology that are most similar to the interests of cross-cultural psychologists are psychological anthropology and cognitive anthropology. We now turn to a discussion of these two topics.

## Psychological anthropology

In ch. 1 we noted that another subdiscipline shares the interspace between psychology and anthropology: **psychological anthropology** (formerly known as "culture and personality"). As noted by Jahoda and Krewer (1997), filling the space between the two parent disciplines was of concern to many social scientists over half a century ago. It was the anthropologist Boas, who provided a psychological orientation to American anthropology (particularly to Benedict and Mead; see below). And in Europe, both the psychologist Bartlett (1937; see also Saito, 2000) and the anthropologist Malinowski (1931) sought a way to work with, and between, the two disciplines:

> Between the spheres of psychology and anthropology, there is today a No-man's-land. Whether or not this will ever be claimed a special branch of science, it must for the present be filled by workers in both fields making excursions towards the other's province. Nor should the serious worker in either field ignore or resent such excursions, for they may have much of value for him in indicating new lines of research. (Malinowski, 1931, p. xi)

Some features distinguish psychological anthropology from cross-cultural psychology: the latter is conceptually and methodologically rooted in academic psychology, while psychological anthropology is rooted primarily in anthropology and to some extent in psychoanalytic psychiatry. Those wishing to have a recent and more extensive discussion of the field of psychological anthropology are referred to Bock (1994) and Suarez-Orozco, Spindler, and Spindler (1994), and to the journal *Ethos*. The critical evaluation by Shweder (1979a, 1979b, 1980) is also useful in understanding the evolution of the field. Indeed, for some (including Shweder, 1990), the field of "cultural psychology is psychological anthropology without the premise of psychic unity" (p. 17). The relationships between cross-cultural psychology, and cultural psychology are complex, and will be examined in detail in ch. 12.

At the outset the name of the subfield needs to be explained. Originally referred to as "culture and personality," it has now become generally known as "psychological anthropology" following a proposal of Hsu (1961). The two terms will be taken as synonyms in this book. One definition of the field is that "psychological anthropology comprises all *anthropological investigations* that make systematic use of psychological concepts and methods" (Bock, 1980, p. 1). Its development "has been influenced by the interplay between *anthropological problems* and the psychological theories that were being formulated" at the time (Bock, 1980, p. xi). In these two assertions, the added emphasis draws our attention to the fundamentally anthropological nature of the field.[1] What does this mean? First, it signals that most of its practitioners are anthropologists, whose education, theoretical preferences, and methodological practices are firmly rooted in that discipline. In contrast, cross-cultural psychologists are usually rooted in psychology, with its own disciplinary biases. Second, the theoretical level of analysis remains distinctive: population-level concerns predominate in psychological anthropology (with some inferences occasionally made to individual dispositions), while individual-level issues (individual processes and inter-individual differences) predominate in cross-cultural psychology. Third, there is, as noted by Edgerton (1974), a longstanding methodological commitment to "naturalism" in anthropology and psychological anthropology, and to "experimentalism" in psychology and cross-cultural psychology. Phenomena are typically observed in the field in one case, while they are stimulated in the laboratory, or other standard situations, in the other. These characterizations are only general modal descriptions; the use of tests and interviews is not uncommon in psychological anthropology, while field observations are also employed by cross-cultural psychologists.

The origin of the field of psychological anthropology is usually traced to the simultaneous interest of anthropologists (mainly from the USA) in psychological explanations of cultural phenomena, and the availability of the Freudian theory of psychoanalysis. The major period of development was in the 1920s and

---

[1] In his 1988 text, however, Bock goes on to make the provocative statement that "all anthropology is psychological." This can be interpreted in at least two ways. One is as a form of scientific reductionism (see ch. 1) in which cultural phenomena are reducible to psychological ones. The second, more likely, explanation is that it signals a search for a rapprochement between anthropology and psychology, a goal we heartily endorse.

1930s, and the central issue was the "relationship between culture in the widest sense (including economic, sociopolitical and even ecological) and personality characteristics, as mediated by the socialization process" (Jahoda, 1980, p. 76).

Bock has distinguished four main approaches: configurationalist (1920–40) with Ruth Benedict and Margaret Mead as the main figures; basic and modal personality (1935–55) with Abram Kardiner, Ralph Linton, and Cora Dubois; national character (from 1940 on) with Clyde Kluckhohn and Alex Inkeles; and cross-cultural (from 1950 on) with John Whiting and Robert LeVine. The first three are largely concerned with single-culture analysis, while the latter approach studies relationships comparatively. For Jahoda (1980, p. 76) these two trends are easily distinguishable: "one is concerned with the analysis of the role of socialization processes and personality factors *within* a cultural group; the other concentrates on attempts to identify the general processes whereby culture shapes, and is shaped by, personality factors *across* human cultures."

The configurationalist approach derives its name from the writings of Sapir (1949) and Benedict (1932), who proposed that culture is the personality of a society: "cultures . . . are individual psychology, thrown large upon the screen, given gigantic proportions and a long time span" (Benedict, 1932, p. 24). Like personalities, cultures are complex, organized, and patterned.

In Benedict's main work (*Patterns of culture,* 1934), the influence of gestalt psychology is also apparent: patterns or forms are emphasized, and give meaning to the details that constitute them; indeed, details are often downplayed, even ignored, in her preference for understanding the overall configuration. Such an orientation led Benedict to describe and label whole cultures with diagnostic terms derived from clinical and psychoanalytic psychology. Margaret Mead is also usually identified with the configurationalist approach. Her views on the nature and origin of sexual behavior have become very well known and have tended to overshadow her early and important role in configurationalist studies. Even this work on sexual behavior (e.g., *Coming of age in Samoa*, 1928) has now been severely criticized for its ethnographic inaccuracy (Freeman, 1983).

Mead was one of the most influential of all cultural anthropologists. She was convinced that human beings were almost infinitely malleable, and much of her research was undertaken to investigate, and prove, this point. In Samoa, she found evidence for liberal attitudes towards sexual relationships, with equal rights for boys and girls. These writings were a major influence and fueled beliefs in the power of sociocultural factors at the cost of biological constraints on the development and educational potential of children. However, Freeman (1983) pointed out numerous discrepancies between Mead's description of Samoan culture generally (and Samoan female adolescents specifically) as lacking in guilt, conflict, and turmoil, and the observations of other ethnographers. Freeman's own view emphasized such Samoan cultural and psychological qualities as violence, jealousy, competitiveness, and stress, as indicated in high rates of rape, assault, and homicide. The publication of Freeman's book unleashed a storm of controversy that soon entered the realms of ideology and politics (including cultural versus bio-logical determinism, the women's movement, sexual liberation, and permissive parenting). The subjective nature of the ensuing debate has revealed, to a sub-stantial degree, the subjective nature of the anthropological enterprise itself. Most explanations of the discrepancy between the two views are based in their differ-ent a priori ideologies. Access to different sectors of Samoan culture, and their varying command of the Samoan language, appear to take second place to the preconceived explanations with which *both* researchers approached their infor-mants (see Cote, 1994, for a review and analysis of this controversy).

The basic and modal personality approach developed during a seminar at Columbia University in New York; "anthropologists 'presented' the cultures with which they were most familiar, after which psychologists 'interpreted' the data to reveal their dynamic significance" (Bock, 1980, p. 86). In their book (1945) Kardiner (a psychiatrist) and Linton (an anthropologist) worked out the concept of the basic personality structure which "places the focal point of culture inte-gration in the common denominator of the personalities of the individuals who participate in the culture" (Kardiner & Linton, 1945, pp. viii–ix). This approach asserts a causal link between personality and culture, not just a similarity or iden-tity between the two concepts (as proposed by the configurationalists). The causal chain begins with primary institutions (such as the subsistence activity, family organization, and socialization practices present in a culture), leading to the basic personality found in the culture, and then leading to the secondary institutions (such as religion, myth, and folklore) of the culture. For Kardiner and Linton, secondary institutions are to be understood as the effects of the primary institu-tions acting on the human mind; put another way, basic personality is an adap-tation to the fundamental realities of life in a particular culture.

Following the basic personality approach, DuBois (1944) proposed the notion of modal personality in which the more global notion of basic personality was replaced by a statistical one that expresses greater frequency (mode), rather than a fundamental or basic uniformity in personality. This permitted her to deal with variability in personality, and with discrepancy and incongruity between person-ality and culture. For DuBois, personality assessment was likely to give "multi-modal rather than unimodal results." Moreover, she thought it likely that only a small percentage of people in a society would belong to these modal groups.

In ch. 1 we briefly mentioned that cross-cultural and cross-national studies have been conventionally distinguished from each other by one focussing on small-scale traditional and usually non-industrial cultures, and the other on con-temporary industrialized nation states (Inkeles, 1997). So, too, in the field of psychological anthropology, we find studies of national character as a distinct approach, one that attends to the psychological qualities of present-day nation states. For example, both Clyde Kluckhohn (1957) and Ruth Benedict (1946) worked on characterizations of the Japanese. Benedict sought to explain the con-tradiction in Japanese character between restrained estheticism (seen in art and ceremony) and militarism (typified by the ideal of the Samurai warrior). A similar analysis of German national character (Fromm, 1941) during the Nazi period was rooted in the national characteristic of the "authoritarian personality" (see also Adorno et al., 1950) which was thought to be present in German society.

It should be noted that other approaches, which do not originate from psychological anthropology, fit the modal personality or national character orientation. For example, Hofstede, whose four value dimensions we mentioned in ch. 3, argues that national character traits can be revealed by survey studies of the kind he carried out and that the "mental programs of members of the same nations tend to contain a common component" (Hofstede, 1980, p. 38). This theme was carried further in his later work (Hofstede, 1991, 2001).

Finally, the cross-cultural approach to psychological anthropology emerged when attention switched from intensive examinations of single cultures and the collective personality of their members, to extensive examinations of relationships across cultures between cultural and personality variables. As we saw in ch. 2, Whiting and Child (1953) drew on psychoanalytic theory and data in the HRAF to explore the possibility that there might be systematic relationships between the ways in which children were socialized and their adult personalities. In this approach, as we have seen, correlations are sought between cultural characteristics (usually rated as present or absent for a particular culture), and some other characteristic (of the culture, or of individuals in the culture). Using these correlations, links are established between child personality and adult personality; antecedents to the former are sought in cultural characteristics (usually child training practices), and consequents of the latter are sought in cultural outcomes (cf. the secondary institutions of Kardiner).

An elaborate model has been proposed by Whiting (see box 9.2) which is similar to the ecocultural framework (fig. 1.1) that is employed in the present text. These similarities are in part due to the obvious general influence of the early culture and personality schools on contemporary cross-cultural psychologists, in part to the specific influence that Whiting has had on the field, and in part due to the similarities (both theoretical and methodological) between the cross-cultural approach in psychological anthropology and cross-cultural psychology.

We end this overview of earlier work in culture and personality with some evaluative comments and critical observations. From the point of view of cross-cultural psychologists, many would agree that the field of psychological anthropology is "untidy" (Jahoda, 1980) and "fuzzy" (Hsu, 1972). These judgments arise for a number of reasons, some theoretical, some methodological.

On the theoretical side, there is the widespread attachment to the psychoanalytic theory of Freud. Given that this theory is often judged by psychologists to be untestable, not to say unscientific, this attachment was bound to raise doubts about the scientific status of the field of psychological anthropology.

More specifically, both Bock and Shweder have presented similar criticisms, often employing similar terms. First is the issue of characterizing whole societies with a single label ("global traits" for Shweder (1979a); and the "uniformity assumption" for Bock, 1980). Psychologists usually discover distributions within

## Box 9.2 Whiting's model for psychocultural research

The model proposed by John Whiting (1974, 1994) is the most recent of a series of models that he developed to guide research into personality and its relationships to culture. The core assumption, derived from Freud's writing, was that child socialization experiences should be predictive of adult personality. To this core Kardiner added antecedent primary institutions and consequent secondary institutions in the culture. Whiting has elaborated all of these components, often renaming them as their nature became more clear or more specific. For example "primary institutions" became differentiated into a set of three interrelated contexts in Whiting's model: physical environment, social history, and cultural maintenance systems. "Child rearing" became elaborated into the child's learning environment, now including physical as well as social aspects (and resembling the developmental niche; see ch. 2). "Adult personality" became a set of more specific attributes, with a basic distinction between innate and learned outcomes, and including cognitive and motivational characteristics, in addition to those conventionally included within the notion of "personality." Finally, "secondary institutions" evolved into a large range of projective expressive systems, including subjective aspects such as beliefs and myths, as well as objective social indicators, such as crime and suicide rates.

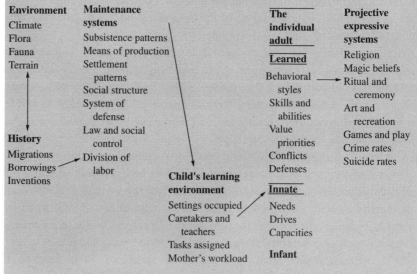

**9.1** Model for psychocultural research
From Whiting, 1974

A comparison of this model (fig. 9.1) with fig. 1.1 in this text reveals many similarities. Beyond this structural similarity, Whiting has also adopted research strategies that resemble the empirical and theoretical approaches

**Box 9.2  (continued)**

advocated in this text. As characterized by D'Andrade (1994, p. 1), "Whiting's vision involves a model of a psychological anthropology in which human biological potentials interact with culture and society, and in which research is carried out using a systematic comparative and cross-cultural methodology based on the testing of explicit stated hypotheses." Extending this view, Whiting (1994, p. 36) has strongly advocated use of the comparative method in psychological anthropology:

Another frequently made criticism of the cross-cultural method is that it takes data out of context thus distorting their meaning. This criticism rests on the assumption that each culture is unique and cannot be compared with any other. However, if scientific principles of cultural integration or culture change are to be developed, cultures must be compared. To do this, the transcultural attributes must be identified.

populations; there are variations within groups, and individual differences between persons in virtually every psychological study ever conducted. This common finding is ignored in most research in psychological anthropology, where differences within groups are ignored or minimized, and differences between groups are magnified.

Also dubious is the premise rooted in Freudian thought, that the "child is father to the man" ("search for childhood origins" for Shweder (1979a); and the "continuity assumption" of Bock (1980)). Research examining relationships between child training and childhood experiences on the one hand, and adult personality on the other, has not been so clear. As suggested by the reviews of Orlansky (1949) and Shweder (1979a), individual adult personality is not determined by individual childhood experiences. This does not undermine the claim that some aspects of behavior are influenced by characteristic socialization practices used in a particular society (as proposed and documented in ch. 2). However, whether or not such practices are predictive of broad personality traits in adults remains a question.

With respect to method, researchers in psychological anthropology have not been able to "make really independent assessments of the two major sets of variables relating to culture and to personality" (Jahoda, 1982, p. 87). This problem has arisen because ethnographic accounts are often the source for evidence regarding both cultural and personality variables. Correlational techniques, at the very least, require independence in measurement. In part, this problem is overcome by the use of personality tests by some researchers. However, most tests used by anthropologists have been projective tests, and provide scope for substantial subjective involvement of the ethnographer in their interpretation.

The "objectivity assumption" (Bock, 1980) is related to this issue: can an outsider like an anthropologist ever really take an unbiased or objective view of the personalities of other peoples? Anthropological field methods require personal immersion, whereas psychologists often distance themselves with the use of "objective" tests. There are, of course, advantages and disadvantages to both approaches, but it can be argued that systematic data collection that is repeatable by others, with culturally appropriate and standard tests, protects the researcher (and the participants!) from gross subjective assessments and interpretations.

Future directions have been suggested, for example by Jahoda (1982, p. 96), who has expressed the view that "there are extensive and important areas of behavior about which academic personality theory has little if anything to say." He refers to the study of envy as an example; while the psychological literature is virtually silent on this widely distributed psychological phenomenon, the anthropological literature is rich, and is largely based on the very methods and theories which have been so much criticized by psychologists.

A comprehensive effort to redefine the field of psychological anthropology has been made by LeVine (1982), who considers the field to encompass the "comparative study of the connections between individuals (their behavior patterns and mental functioning) and their environments (social, cultural, economic, political)" (p. 3). The scope of this field is virtually identical to the one we have taken for cross-cultural psychology in ch. 1. We will therefore examine LeVine's views in more detail to differentiate his view of psychological anthropology from our view of cross-cultural psychology.

In his definitions of the two central terms of culture and personality we find no means of distinguishing the fields. LeVine (p. 3) defines culture as "both the distinctively human forms of adaptation, and the distinctive ways in which different human populations organize their lives on earth," and personality as

> the organization in the individual of those processes that intervene between environmental conditions and behavioral response ... These processes include perception, cognition, memory, learning and the activation of emotional reactions as they are organized and regulated in the individual organism. (p. 5)

It is clear that the specific definition of culture used by LeVine resembles that employed in the present text. Moreover, his notion of personality incorporates all of the domains of psychology and hence matches in scope the concerns of cross-cultural psychology as we have identified them. Similarly, one general theoretical perspective is shared – that of culture and behavior as adaptive to ecological context LeVine (1982) is quite explicit in his acceptance of this fundamental point of view, as we are in ch. 1. However, in two other theoretical perspectives we find substantial divergence: one is LeVine's adoption and rather uncritical acceptance of the psychoanalytic theories of Freud; the other is his central concern (rooted in anthropology) for how people are similar within cultures.

More recently (LeVine, 1999, p. 15) has expanded the agenda for psychological anthropology, in an effort to revitalize the field:

> The promise of psychological anthropology resides in its roles as a bridge between social science and psychology and as a means of integrating them in theory and research. Its goals should be to rebuild anthropology on firm psychological as well as cultural foundations; to revise psychology in the light of

evidence from all parts of humanity, and to launch psychosocial research programs yielding knowledge that leads to deeper understanding and wiser policy.

Given this agenda, it remains difficult to distinguish psychological anthropology from cross-cultural psychology.

In LeVine's view, psychological anthropology lacks coherence, having no single unified theoretical framework; it lacks connection to "mainstream" cultural anthropology, existing as a segregated, even marginal, speciality; it lacks connections to academic psychology (other than psychoanalysis); and lacks engagement with major social policy issues. LeVine's final criticism of psychological anthropology is that it lacks comparative analysis; however, the comparative approach is at the very core of cross-cultural psychology. Despite these similarities, the traditions that separate the fields are strong and are likely to remain distinct ways of working in the "no-man's-land" identified by Malinowski so long ago.

## Cognitive anthropology

Another branch of anthropology that has close links with psychology is that of **cognitive anthropology**. Most broadly stated, "cognitive anthropology is the study of the relationship between human society and human thought" (D'Andrade, 1995, p. 1). More specifically, its goal is to understand how people in various cultures describe, categorize, and organize their knowledge about their natural (and supernatural) world. It shares with psychological anthropology a concern for normative knowledge, what and how people in general know, rather than for psychological processes or individual differences, and differs from the cross-cultural psychological study of cognition (reported in ch. 5) on these same dimensions.

Another name for this general area is ethnoscience (e.g., Sturtevant, 1964); it is defined as a branch of anthropology that seeks to understand the scientific knowledge of other cultures. In principle, there could be any number of branches, such as ethnobotany, even ethnopsychology (and, as we saw earlier in ch. 2, parental ethnotheories). This initial orientation has led, in psychology, to a concern with indigenous knowledge systems, including practical knowhow ("bricolage"– Lévi-Strauss, 1962; Berry & Irvine, 1986) and "everyday cognition" (Schliemann et al., 1997; Segall et al., 1999, ch. 6) and larger-scale cognitive systems ("indigenous cognition"– Berry et al., 1988). An excellent overview of the developing field has been prepared by D'Andrade (1995).

In the early studies in cognitive anthropology, a key to understanding cognition is to recognize the great importance given to language as a cultural phenomenon. As we saw earlier in this chapter, language is one constituent element of culture, and along with tool-making, may be one of the few really distinctive qualities of human culture (after all, many non-human species have social organization, territory, and even games).

Language is also readily identified with the cognitive life of the human species, since it is clearly implicated in learning, remembering, and thinking. Anthropologists interested in human cognition thus sought to gain their particular entry to cognitive phenomena by way of this particular cultural phenomenon, that of language. Historically, two main influences made this language–cognition link the focus of cognitive anthropology. First, as noted in ch. 6, Whorf (1956) argued that language categories (both words, and relations among words) serve to codify and organize the world on the one hand, and mold the cognitive life of the individual on the other. The empirical evidence for this view is slight (see ch. 6); nevertheless, the links are intuitively compelling, and were sufficient to move anthropologists in this direction. Second, formal linguistic analyses (e.g., Greenberg, 1957) provided a model method for examining categories, and the structure of categories, that was easily adopted by cognitive anthropologists. Linguistic analyses of the way people talked about a domain (e.g., kinship, animals) thus formed a basis for an analysis of their cognitive organization of the world (i.e., how they thought about the domain). This approach is concerned with collective cognition (how people in general understand their world) not with individual cognition (how persons are similar or different from each other, or the nature of the underlying cognitive processes). Indeed, Jahoda (1982, pp. 214–25) expresses a commonly held view among cross-cultural psychologists that such "collective representations" (cf. Moscovici, 1982) cannot really provide access to any individual psychological processes, be they cognitive, motivational, or attitudinal.

In this conclusion we find a correspondence with that drawn from studies in the previous section on psychological anthropology: individual differences and individual processes (the core of psychological inquiry) are simply beyond grasp when one merely has population-level data. However, this should not be a basis for dismissing the work of cognitive anthropologists; indeed, like those working in psychological anthropology, they have opened up whole new domains for inquiry by cross-cultural psychologists, and have provided a language-based method for studying individual behavior.

The view that the language of a group is an important way to understand the cognitive life of a people found an early expression in the "componential analysis" (Goodenough, 1956), especially in the study of kinship terms (e.g., Romney & D'Andrade, 1964). Also called "feature analysis," the process begins with a selection of a cultural domain, such as family relationships, and the elicitation of terms employed to refer to various members. For example, in English, both gender and the generation distinction are made (e.g., grandmother, grandfather, mother, father, daughter, son) as well as the lateral distinctions (e.g., sister, brother); but for some terms gender is not distinguished (cousin), and nor is whether the relationship is by common descent ("blood") or by marriage (e.g., uncle, aunt). In contrast, other languages make more distinctions (e.g., whether the cousin is male or female; whether the aunt is by blood or by marriage), and are more inclusive (e.g., uncle can include all adult males that are close to one's parents). Componential analysis has been applied to many other domains, such as "things to eat," or "animals," and even to abstract domains, such as "character traits," and "intelligence" (cf., the study of Cree competence in box 5-3). In the view of D'Andrade (1995, p. 3), componential analysis was important, because it showed "how to investigate cultural systems of meaning," revealing "native categories that are derived from an emic analysis of discriminating things in their world, rather than imposing categories from the outside."

More recent approaches have shifted away from a focus on language to a concern with actual behavior (Gatewood, 1985). In the terms of Dougherty and Keller (1982), there is less interest in "taxonomy," and more in "taskonomy," that is, individual differences in how people actually use the cultural knowledge have become the object of study. One example of the convergence between anthropological and psychological approaches is the work of Wassmann and Dasen (1994a, 1994b) who studied number systems and classification rules among the Yupno people of New Guinea. This interdisciplinary collaboration (between an anthropologist and a psychologist) produced evidence for the general (cultural-level) way of counting and classifying objects, and for some individual differences (psychological-level) in how people actually go about these cognitive activities.

Their approach is to gain the advantages of viewing a phenomenon through the use of multiple methods (Wassmann & Dasen, 1994b): first, they interview key informants to obtain an understanding at the cultural (or normative) level; second, they make observations of daily behaviors that are in the behavior domain of interest (e.g., counting or sorting); and third, they develop tasks, and ask participants to carry them out, so that individual differences and underlying processes may be discovered. The first is an ethnographic study, the third is a psychological study, and the second represents a technique shared by the two disciplines.

In the first study, Wassmann and Dasen (1994a) noted that the Yupno start counting on the left hand, folding down each finger in turn from the little finger to the thumb; distinct number words exist for 1, 2 and 3; number 4 is "2 and 2," and 5 is called "the finger with which one peels bamboo shoots," namely the thumb; the sum is indicated by showing the closed fist, and saying "one hand." Numbers 6 to 10 are counted in the same way on the left hand, and 11 to 20 on the feet. For numbers 21 to 33, symmetrical body parts are designated two by two, intermixed, to mark each group of five (and number 33), with parts on the central body line. Once the last body part (the penis, called "the mad thing") is reached, the sum is expressed as "one man dead." The process can be repeated on a second person if there is a need to count beyond 33.

Beyond this general (ethnographic) description, the authors were interested in various psychological issues, such as gender and age differences. However, it proved impossible to study women, because Yupno women are not supposed to know the number system and therefore refuse to answer any questions. Nor was it practicable to study children and younger men, because the former only use the decimal system taught in school, and the latter use the traditional system only up to 20, as is done on the coast of New Guinea, where many of them had been working. Any attempts to carry out developmental studies were therefore impossible, showing the limits of psychological research in some field situations.

One most interesting finding, however, emerged from the psychologist's insistence on asking several older men to demonstrate the counting with the number system: although four of them used the system as described above, ending with 33, one of them produced a system ending with 30, two with 32 and one with 37. With one exception (a man starting from bottom up), counting always ended on the penis, but the number of intermediate body parts could vary. This revealed a property of the counting system, namely that it is done in face-to-face situations where variations in the numbering can be taken into consideration.

In their second study, Wassmann and Dasen (1994b) found that the Yupno have a conventional cultural way of classifying objects, based on the distinction between "hot" and "cold" (with an intermediate "cool" category). All Yupno know about this distinction, and are thought to know which objects belong in which category. All objects (gardens, animals, people, etc.) are always in one of these three states. "Hot" and "cold" are undesirable states: "hot" is dangerous because it cannot be controlled; "cold" is undesirable because it produces immobility and speechlessness; only "cool" is good, and most objects are usually in this state. These states are changeable only by specialists (sorcerers) who know how and are paid to change them: objects can be "heated up" (to protect them from intruders) or "cooled down" (to make objects invisible). Other widespread beliefs about the nature and functions of these categories are documented, all of which show their central position in everyday Yupno life. In addition, one sorcerer described how he was able to "cool down" an object and situation, although the researchers were not able to actually observe the process, because such activities are secret.

Wassmann and Dasen (1994b) made extensive observations on how the Yupno classify objects, and how the taxonomy they provide through interviews does not necessarily fit with daily practices. To examine this issue, a third study was carried out with sorting tasks. Local objects were selected that could be clearly classified as "hot" or "cold," but could also be sorted by other means (e.g., color, shape). Using a classical sorting method, participants were shown the objects in random order, asked to name them, and then to put the objects together that "belonged together." They could make as many groupings as they wished, and were then asked to explain the basis for their sortings. Six groups of participants were studied: sorcerers, older men (not sorcerers), women, younger men, children with, and children without schooling ($n = 5$ in each group).

Results showed that only the sorcerers used the "hot–cold distinction . . . explicitly and spontaneously" (p. 32). The older men sorted objects to some extent, but only implicitly, according to the hot–cold distinction; the women made functional sorts, linked to their daily activities; and younger participants mainly sorted by color (rarely by form). Wassmann and Dasen conclude that the cultural-level distinction between hot and cold is used explicitly only by those for whom it is of daily relevance. Moreover, it is used only rarely, if at all, by others in the Yupno culture for whom it is available, but "hidden, present only at some deep level" (p. 35), or no longer relevant at all.

## Conclusions

Other than psychology, it is clear that the most important parent discipline of cross-cultural psychology is cultural anthropology. The central concepts of culture, of relativism, and of universalism have been contributed by anthropology; so, too, have the methods used in field settings. While these notions and practices have had to be translated from the language of the collective to that of the individual, the task for cross-cultural psychology has been informed in many ways by this pioneering work in anthropology.

Despite this assistance, occupying the middle ground between the population and the individual has not been all that easy for cross-cultural psychology. The study of the individual in context (particularly the concern with individual differences) has meant some distancing from, even some conflicts with, our anthropological ancestor.

Similarly, a concern for the cultural context has distanced us from our more experimentally oriented psychological parents. It should be clear, however, that cross-cultural psychology has been informed in major ways by the anthropological traditions, only a portion of which we have been able to present in this chapter.

## Key terms

| | |
|---|---|
| anthropology | culture |
| cognitive anthropology | ethnographic archives |
| cultural evolution | holocultural approach |
| cultural relativism | Human Relations Area Files (HRAF) |
| cultural universals | psychological anthropology |

## Further reading

Bock, P. (Ed.) (1994). *Handbook of psychological anthropology.* Westport, CT: Greenwood. A wide-ranging treatment of topics in this anthropological approach to studying relationships between culture and behavior.

D'Andrade, R. G. (1995). *The development of cognitive anthropology.* Cambridge: Cambridge University Press. A comprehensive and critical examination of the origins, and contemporary anthropological research on cognition.

Ember, M., & Ember, C. (1998). *Cultural anthropology* (9th ed.). New York: Prentice-Hall. A widely read comprehensive textbook of general anthropology that serves as an introduction to the field.

Munroe, R. L., & Munroe, R. M. (1997). A comparative anthropological perspective. In J. W. Berry, Y. H. Poortinga, & J. Pandey (Eds.), *Theory and method* (pp. 171–213). Vol. I of *Handbook of cross-cultural psychology* (2nd ed.). Boston, MA: Allyn and Bacon. A thoughtful overview of what comparative research in anthropology can contribute to cross-cultural psychology.

Schwartz, T., White, G., & Lutz, C. (Eds.) (1992). *New directions in psychological anthropology*. New York: Cambridge University Press. A collection of original essays that has contributed to rethinking how anthropologists approach the study of culture–behavior relationships.

# 10 Biology and culture

Within cross-cultural psychology biological bases of behavior are seldom emphasized. The focus is usually on the sociocultural environment and how it interacts with behavior. This may lead to an unbalanced view of reality. In the ecocultural framework presented in fig. 1.1 we have included biological adaptation and genetic transmission among the concepts that have to be taken into consideration in cross-cultural psychology. For the understanding of behavior, its similarities as well as its cultural variations, the study of the biological basis is as essential as the analysis of sociocultural context. In fact, the two are intricately related.

In the first section of this chapter we give a brief overview of some core concepts of evolution theory. The subject area of the second section is behavior genetics. The third section deals with ethology, that is the study of animal behavior. When the methods and theories of ethology are extended to the human species we speak about human ethology, or sociobiology. The fourth and last section of this chapter is devoted to models of cultural transmission which have been developed from a biological perspective in analogy with models of genetic transmission.

## Evolution and adaptation

The theory of evolution, formulated originally by Charles Darwin in the nineteenth century and further developed in the course of over one hundred years, is central to the biological sciences, including their perspective on behavior. Of the core concepts in the theory there are two which are of particular interest in the present context, namely that species change over time and that natural selection is the key to such change.

Essential for the theory of evolution is the diversity between the individual organisms within a single species. In most species parents produce a large number of offspring. Many of these fail to reach maturity and to procreate in turn. If for some reason a certain heritable trait enhances the probability of survival and reproduction, the frequency of this trait in the population will increase over successive generations. Individual organisms possessing this trait are then said to have a higher **fitness**, than individuals without the trait. Over many generations such a differential rate of reproduction leads to systematic changes in a population. This is **natural selection**, which Darwin saw as a causal process under the influence of environmental factors. At the time of Darwin the reasons for individual variation were not well understood, although it was known from the breeding of domestic animals and plants that systematic changes in morphological or behavioral traits could be brought about. Through the mating of individuals with desired characteristics a breeder could increase the probability that these characteristics would also be found in subsequent generations. It was only much later, after the discovery of DNA, that these observations could be accounted for in terms of genetic principles.

Artificial selection practiced by breeders serves a purpose. The presence or absence of a purpose or goal in evolution has been vigorously debated for many decades. At the present time most biologists share Darwin's opinion that changes in species can be seen as the outcome of interactions between organisms and their environments. We shall briefly describe how these mechanisms of change operate. Since a proper understanding requires some knowledge of genetics, a brief summary of a few basic principles is given in box 10-1.

The law of Hardy-Weinberg, mentioned in box 10-1, states that in a static environment, the relative frequencies of existing alleles do not change over generations. How, then, do changes in species come about? First of all, new alleles emerge from time to time. This can happen under the influence of external factors which influence the genetic material; nuclear radiation and certain chemicals are known causal agents. New alleles can also be formed without any known external determinant being present. In the complex process of DNA synthesis during sexual reproduction an occasional replication error occurs. Changes in the genetic material lead to so-called mutations. These are relatively rare and most mutants are not viable. However, the actual occurrence of an event is not only a function of its probability, but also of the number of times it potentially can happen. In rapidly reproducing micro-organisms mutations provide a realistic prospect for change (cf. the various strains of the influenza virus). In higher organisms with a longer lifecycle other factors are likely to have a more appreciable effect on the rate of change.

These factors include natural selection, migration, assortative mating, and chance fluctuations. The Hardy-Weinberg law presupposes an infinite population

## Box 10.1  Genetics

The account given here is based on the human species, but is, with some variations, valid for all species that multiply through sexual reproduction (cf. Mange & Mange, 1999; Snustad & Simmons, 1997). The genetic material consists of DNA molecules which form long double strands made up of pairs of nucleotides. Each nucleotide contains a base. This base occurs in only four forms, often indicated with the letters A, T, C, and G. Various sequences in which the ACTG groups occur correspond (in triplets) with the structure of amino acids. Through a kind of copying process amino acids originate from the DNA. Long strings of amino acids form polypeptides which, as enzymes, have an effect on specific biochemical reactions.

A **gene** is a DNA segment that can be recognized by its specific function; the gene is the functional unit of genetic material. Each gene has a certain place (locus) within a chromosome. Of a single gene (identified by locus and function) often more than one variation is found. These variations, which are called **alleles**, form the most important basis for individual variation within a species.

The chromosomes in which the genetic material is contained form long coiled strings of DNA. In humans there are twenty-three pairs of chromosomes, together forming the genome, and by common convention numbered from 1 to 23. In the process of cell division the chromosomes replicate so that each cell of an organism contains all the genetic material. There is one important exception, namely in sexual reproduction. In the process by which reproductive cells (gametes) are formed, the chromosomes are reduced to half the original number. There is an extra division in which only one of each pair of chromosomes is transmitted to each gamete. With fertilization the chromosomes of two gametes, one from the father and one from the mother, combine to form a new cell with a complete set of chromosomes.[1]

The chromosomes of a pair closely resemble each other, with one exception. Males have an X- and a Y-chromosome, females two X-chromosomes. This determines biological sex differences. The other chromosomes in a pair show, in the normal case, only small differences. They are homozygous for a particular gene when the alleles at a certain locus are identical; they are heterozygous when unlike alleles of that gene are present in the two chromosomes of a pair. In the case of heterozygosity the one allele can suppress

---

[1] The mother exclusively contributes some other genetic materials to the mitochondrion, an organelle in the ovum and other cells that are needed for metabolic processes providing energy for the cell. It is through the analysis of group differences in mitochondrial DNA that the relationships between human groups in various parts of the world have been traced. Most results point to a common "mother" (often called mother Eve) living in Africa between 100,000 and 40,000 years ago (Cann, Stoneking, & Wilson, 1987; Ingman, Kaessmann, Pääbo, & Gullensten, 2000).

## Box 10.1 (continued)

the other; the dominant, but not the recessive, allele finds its expression in the phenotype of the organism. Alternatively, the two chromosomes can also both contribute to the results of the genetic process of production of amino acids. This leads to some combination of the expression which the two alleles have separately. A distinction is often made between genotype, the genetic constitution of an organism, and the phenotype, the characteristics of the organism as they can be observed.

The chromosomes contain an enormous amount of information; there are approximately six billion (milliards) of base units. They form genes of varying length, usually extending over thousands of base pairs. There would be enough material for a few million genes, but only a small percentage of all DNA forms part of the genetic code that is expressed. Estimates of the number of genes in the human species have been as high as 100,000. More recently the estimate has been reduced to around 30,000. For many of the genetic loci there exists more than one allele. This gives an indication of the genetic variability present in the human species. Through sexual reproduction each organism acquires a specific combination of the total pool of genetic material available in the species. Only monozygotic (identical) twins are genetically identical.

Nevertheless, in an environment which remains constant, existing genetic variation within a species by itself does not lead to change. Variation follows the law of Hardy-Weinberg, which states that the ratio between different alleles of the same gene remains constant over generations. If at a certain time there are two alleles of a gene with the relative frequencies of $p_1$ and $p_2$, then the same values will be found for $p_1$ and $p_2$ at any later point in time, if other factors remain constant. The conservation of gene frequencies results in a genetically stable population.

with random mating patterns and a constant environment. In reality mating populations can be quite small, for example because they are geographically isolated. Random fluctuations in the distributions of alleles will occur in all breeding populations. This genetic drift is negligible in large populations, but not in small groups. A single individual among the founding parents of a group of settlers can sometimes have an appreciable effect on the frequency of a certain characteristic in the descendants many generations later. This also makes clear why migration, with the consequent introduction of different alleles in a breeding population, can have quite remarkable effects.

Non-random or assortative mating patterns are very much in evidence among humans, where the choice of a marriage partner is often governed by social rules. In certain societies marriages between blood relatives are encouraged and even customary; this can even give rise to inbreeding.[2] In other societies such close-relative marriages are frowned upon and even prohibited.

Another factor in assortative mating is the selection of partners on the basis of similarity in psychological characteristics. In many contemporary societies level of education, which is associated with intelligence, is important for partner choice. If intelligence has a heritable component, the expected variation in intelligence is larger in a population with than in a population without partner choice on the basis of intelligence. In itself this does not lead to any change in the population as a whole. Only when there is a correlation between level of intelligence and number of offspring can assortative mating have a long-term effect on a population as a whole. Few if any of such effects are known in humans (e.g., Cavalli-Sforza & Bodmer, 1971).

Disturbance of the Hardy-Weinberg equilibrium can also take place when the condition of a constant environment is violated. Certain changes in the environment can lead to differential reproduction of a given genotype. As mentioned, this is the principle of natural selection. Selection effects have actually been demonstrated in experiments and field studies. Well known are the studies in which it was shown that in certain species of moth the most frequently found color can change from light to dark under the influence of industrial pollution. One moth in Great Britain, that was almost invariably light in pre-industrial times, is now predominantly dark colored in smoke- and soot-covered industrial areas. A possible explanation is that moths which blend with their environment are less conspicuous for predators and hence have a higher survival and reproduction rate. This explanation was validated in a study in which both dark and light moths (with markings to distinguish them from non-experimental animals) were released in both light and dark environments. When the surviving moths were trapped again later on, a differential survival rate in each of the two environments was found in favor of the moths with the matching color (Kettlewell, 1959). In the human species a selective mechanism is known that has caused a high incidence of sickle-cell anemia in some populations. This is described in box 10-2.

## Adaptation

When there is a change in a population through natural selection in reaction to demands of the environment this is called an **adaptation**. The concept of adaptation used to have wide usage in biology, but nowadays can be found more

---

[2] Many deleterious, but recessive, alleles exist with low frequency in a population. Two relatives have far more genes in common than two randomly selected individuals. Hence, there is a larger probability that a certain deleterious recessive allele will be transmitted by both parents (and thus express itself) when they are relatives than when they are not relatives. The resulting higher probability of a genetic defect leads to what is called inbreeding.

## Box 10.2 Sickle-cell anemia

Sickle-cell anemia is a genetically transmitted defect in which the hemoglobin (red blood) corpuscles are easily deformed from round to sickle-shaped. It leads to a severe form of anemia and patients usually do not continue to live until they have children. The condition is caused by a single nucleotide which occurs in two forms, called "S" and "s." There are three ways in which these two alleles can be combined in the genetic material of an individual. The two chromosomes of the relevant pair both can be "S," both be "s," or one can be "s" while the other is "S." The (homozygotic) carriers of s–s suffer from sickle-cell anemia. S–S homozygotes are normal, and the heterozygotic carriers of S–s tend to suffer from a mild form of anemia (e.g., Mange & Mange, 1999).

The striking feature about sickle-cell anemia is its very unequal distribution in the world. In equatorial Africa frequencies of up to 35 percent of (mostly heterozygotic) carriers of "s" have been observed in certain populations. The incidence is much lower in northern and southern Africa. The "s" allele is also found around the Mediterranean and in certain aboriginal groups in India. In the North European populations it is virtually absent. Given the low rate of reproduction of the s–s homozygotes it is incomprehensible at first sight that the incidence of the "s" allele can be so high.

What is the reason for this unequal distribution? Vogel and Motulsky (1979) listed three possible explanations.

1 The mutation rate may be different for some external reason (e.g. climate), or due to some other internal genetic factor.
2 Chance fluctuations (genetic drift) have played a role.
3 There is some selective advantage to sickle-cell anemia in areas where it is found frequently.

The size of the populations makes it highly unlikely that the differences in incidence can be due to random error and for this reason the second possibility has to be rejected.

The first alternative has been investigated. For example, in theoretical studies the rate of mutation needed to maintain the high frequencies actually found in certain areas was calculated. Also, the rate of inheritance was studied empirically by comparing children with their mother. On both counts it could be ruled out that mutations formed a feasible explanation.

A selective advantage for the S–s heterozygote was indeed found after it was noted that there was a coincidence between the presence of sickle-cell anemia and malignant forms of malaria. In a number of studies, which we will not review here, support for a causal relationship was found. The most important evidence was that the incidence of malaria infections is higher in young children who are S–S homozygotes than in heterozygotes. A ratio of

## Box 10.2 (continued)

2.17 between these two categories has been reported (Allison, 1964, quoted by Vogel & Motulsky, 1979). Given the overall high mortality of children due to malaria, this provides a sufficient selective advantage to maintain a high frequency of the "s" allele despite the mortality of the s–s homozygotes. Thus, the high incidence of sickle-cell anemia in equatorial Africa and some other regions of the world very likely reflects a genetic adaptation to long-term conditions in the environment.

frequently in psychological and anthropological writings, as we have seen in ch. 9. Broadly speaking, adaptation refers in the social sciences to changes which take place during the lifetime of an organism in response to environmental demands (e.g., Relethford, 1997). In evolutionary biology the term refers to the adjustment of a population to an environment. However, the conclusion that a certain change is the result of an adaptive process tends to be made afterwards; it is a post hoc inference. Such inferences are risky, because alternative explanations are easily overlooked. Similarly risky are post hoc inferences about cultural influences on behavior. Therefore, we shall discuss the analysis of biological adaptation in some detail, following a classical exposition by Lewontin (1978).

First, the environment that imposes the demands leading to adaptation has to be defined. But this can only be done with reference to the way of life of an organism. Each species occupies an ecological niche in the environment. This niche defines the way of life of the species in the total environment: how the organisms of that species cope with the prevailing temperature, how they move around in the environment, what food they use and how they collect it, and so on. Since the world can be broken up in many different ways it is easy to define an ecological niche. If an (almost) infinite number of alternatives is available, it becomes trivially easy for a species to find a niche. Thus the concept of adaptation, which implies adaptation to a particular niche, may not have much explanatory value.

Second, organisms are not passively shaped by their environment; they interact with it. For example, the soil can change because of the excreta that are deposited; and insects contribute to the fertilization of plants from which they draw honey and thus help in ensuring a future food supply. It can be said that an organism contributes to establishing its own ecological niche through the way it interacts with the environment. This would mean that all organisms always are already adapted. So there would be no scope for evolutionary change.

To cut through this dilemma one can take as a starting point for analysis a species as it exists in a particular ecological niche at a particular time. Over a large time period the environment is not constant and the ecological niche will change. If the species is not to die out something has to happen. From this perspective adaptation is the process of keeping up with the changing environment. This is expressed in the notion of environmental tracking. Subpopulations of the same species can come to face different environmental challenges, depending on the geographical location where they live, and can differentially evolve into new species.

This still does not solve the problem of post hoc interpretation, unless a precise functional relationship can be specified between a well-defined property of the environment and an equally well-defined property of an organism. But this is not easy either. For example, in humans the chin protrudes much further than in primates. Articulated speech is facilitated by the form of the chin, suggestive of an adaptational change leading to better communication. Attempts to explain the larger chin as an evolutionary change failed until it was realized that it is not the chin that has grown larger. Taking the primates as a standard, the part of the human jaw where the teeth are set is small in relation to the bony part of the jaw. Compared to primates humans appear to have less protruding teeth rather than a more protruding chin. A functional relationship can only be specified when both in the organism and in the environment a functional unit of analysis can be defined. It has emerged that the protruding chin is not such a functional unit. Presumably it is merely a byproduct of some other evolutionary change.

The difference between two alleles often is not restricted to a single effect on the phenotype. A gene can have various effects on the development of an organism. This is called **pleiotropy**. In a process of natural selection where an evolutionary change takes place in a gene, all effects of that gene will become manifest (directly or indirectly) in the phenotype. This implies, for example, that human speech, a main condition for the development of culture, biologically may have to be explained as coincidental to the functionally unrelated adaptive process of recession of the teeth, rather than as an adaptation in its own right.

So far we have indicated a number of traps that we can fall into when inferring an adaptive process based on the principle of natural selection. The question of how such an inference can be more validly made still remains to be answered. Lewontin (1978) refers to the analysis of the adaptive value of a characteristic as an engineering analysis of organism and environment. This is a procedure in which a particular idea is tested in a number of coherent ways. If none of the expectations has to be rejected, more and more confirmatory evidence for that idea is collected. This research strategy is in fact the same as the internal and external validation of theories used by social scientists. The systematic analysis of the various possible explanations for the high incidence of sickle-cell anemia mentioned in box 10-2 provides an example of this approach.

The notion of pleiotropy affects the principle that each feature, in the behavioral as well as the physical phenotype, must be the adaptive outcome of a selection-driven process. This principle was further challenged by Gould and Lewontin (1979) when they introduced the term "spandrels" in this connection. Spandrels are the spaces between the shoulders of adjoining arches as found in buildings, like gothic church windows or old stone bridges. They have no structural function in the construction and could be left empty, but usually they are filled up, often with sculptures. In a similar sense certain adaptive biological changes may have created spaces for additional functions beyond those that led to these changes initially. Moreover, Gould (1991) has suggested that apart from adaptations there can also be *exaptations*; these are features that now enhance fitness, but originally came about for another function. For Gould the complex brain is a feature of the human organism that has opened up a large scope for what we commonly call culture, including religion, art, and technology, for which it hardly can have been developed originally. It should be noted that Gould's views are contested, especially in evolutionary psychology (Buss, Haselton, Shackelford, Bleske, & Wakefield, 1998), a school of thought to which we shall return later in this chapter.

## Human "races"

Biological mechanisms of change and human migrations over many thousands of years are responsible for the emergence of the physical differences between human groups traditionally living in different parts of the world. The resulting phenotypical differences have led to the notion of **human "races."** Behavioral and social scientists often refuse to recognize "race" as a valid concept (see Segall et al., 1999). Biologists more often tend to argue that differences in environmental conditions, such as climate and geographical separation with limited possibilities for interbreeding, have led to some systematic genetic divergence. Skin color is easily the most distinguishable characteristic on which human groups differ genetically. It is controlled by a number of genes. Possibly dark pigmentation has had a selective advantage against sunburn in tropical areas. More likely, there have been changes in the direction of a light skin in areas with little sunshine (e.g., Vogel & Motulsky, 1979). Sunlight is needed for the synthesis of vitamin D which prevents rickets (a bone disease). Other visible traits on which there are are traditional differences include body height, the shape of the nose, hair color, and the implantation of the hair. Also in terms of the distributions of various blood groups there are small but noticeable differences in distributions between geographical groups (Cavalli-Sforza & Bodmer, 1971; Cavalli-Sforza, Menozzi, & Piazza, 1994). However, it has long been recognized that geographical differences are small compared to the genetic diversity within groups (e.g., Lewontin, 1972), a state of affairs confirmed by more recent findings (see box 10-3).

## Box 10.3 Race, racism and the human genome project

"From a genetic perspective, all humans are ... Africans, either residing in Africa or in recent exile." This is a conclusion drawn by Pääbo (2001, p. 1219) on the basis of evidence about human genetic diversity which shows that the gene pool in Africa shows more variation than that found in other regions.

This assertion contrasts with conventional wisdom about human diversity. In ch. 5 we already emphasized how "race" has been used as an explanation for visible physical and behavioral differences that distinguish certain categories of persons from other categories. In such "explanations" "racial" category labels vary greatly from society to society, and even differ over time in a single society. Nevertheless, socially constructed racial categories continue to be virtually reified; they are still widely thought to be biologically determined and, to a large extent, fixed.

In the USA, for example, most people are identified (and indentify themselves) as either "white" or "non-white," with the latter category broken down into a dazzling array of group labels, reflecting skin color, place of recent ancestral origin, parental language, religious identity of parents, or whatever determinant matters socially. Thus, persons carry category labels such as "black" or "African American," "Hispanic" (some of whom a recent USA census schema suggests are "black" while others are "white"), "Native American," and "Asians," to generate an incomplete list. For most Americans, including the government officals who designed and administered the census form, these categories constitute "races." According to Fish (2000, p. 559), the white–black classification in popular use in the USA "would force the great majority of Brazilian subjects into 'racial' classifications that they would view as inaccurate," although racial distinctions also exist in this Brazil. To cite just one more case, in Australia, the aboriginal peoples are frequently referred to as "Blacks" by many Australians of European origin, who think themselves as "Whites."

The common thread in such conceptions is the doctrine of "races" itself. However, it is quite clear (e.g., Cavalli-Sforza et al., 1994; Fish, 1997; Langaney, Hubert van Blyenburgh, & Sanchez-Mazas, 1992; Montagu, 1997; Segall, 1999; Segall et al., 1999) that "race" as a categorial concept has only the appearance of a property of nature. While physical anthropology initially had only a few external markers to go by (e.g., skin and eye color, type of hair), the introduction of blood groups started to change the picture: the four main blood types, although somewhat unevenly distributed across the continents, exist everywhere. If you had to get a blood transfusion, there is almost as good a likelihood that you could get it safely from someone on a different continent than from your neighbor. As more markers have become available, individuality as the basis for human diversity has only become stronger (cf., Langaney et al., 1992; Segall, 1999; Segall et al., 1999).

**Box 10.3 (continued)**

This has been confirmed by research on the human genome. Considering how our view of ourselves is impacted by the human genome findings, Pääbo (2001) underscores how similar humans are to each other. What is called "race" reflects only traits that have a continuous distribution across all regions of the worlds and that are determined by only a small proportion of the total number of genes.

Still, what people *believe* to be true about "race" matters; racial beliefs have often sustained racism, the manifestations of which range from polite tolerance through mutual avoidance to genocide (see discussion of prejudice in ch. 13). Examples abound from ancient through contemporary history, nearly everywhere in the world, enough of them to fill this entire book. Our daily newspapers review country by country not only in Australia, Brazil, or the USA, but also in other parts of the world, including Europe, numerous incidents of xenophobic hatred in connection with access to economic resources, political power, and even sports like soccer (which, ironically, are often promoted, because they are supposed to foster understanding). Of course, dispelling the notion of "race" would not by itself put an end to racism. But the truth about "race" needs to be inserted into the efforts to combat the racism that has permeated intergoup relations for so long. That truth, confirmed by the human genome project, is that our species comprises only one "race". . . the human race.

## Behavior genetics

In genetics a distinction is made between morphological, physiological, and behavioral traits; the study of the latter traits is called **behavior genetics**. The search for direct links between phenotype and genotype has been most successful at the morphological level, that is, the level of physical characteristics. The heritable basis of certain morphological traits in the pea plant was clearly established in the famous experiments of Mendel in the middle of the nineteenth century. Genetic mechanisms for behavioral traits have been more resistant to analysis. Most of the evidence in behavior genetics derives from experimental studies of individual differences in non-human species. Nowadays the effects of separate genes more and more are analyzed using genetic manipulation (i.e., artificially induced mutations). Most of the available evidence is difficult to transpose to behavior, and especially human behavior, where cultural influences play a particularly important role.

Environmental variables exert a limited effect on the expression of traits encoded by a single genetic feature, such as eye color. Simply stated, there are no influences in the natural environment which will change the color of someone's eyes from brown to blue or vice versa. Hence, the range of modifiability of this trait is small. With respect to many other traits, the amount of co-variation with environmental factors is much larger. We shall not attempt to explain the genetic basis for environmentally controlled modifiability (about which knowledge is still very incomplete anyway), but mention just one aspect. A distinction can be made between *structural* and *regulatory* mechanisms. Structural genes control the structure of polypeptides (cf. box 10-1). The rate of expression of a structural gene (that is, how much of an enzyme is produced) is controlled by regulatory genes. A regulatory gene need not be limited in its effects to one or more structural genes, but can also trigger other regulatory genes. In this way complex sequential biochemical events can come about, such as the hormonal changes in puberty or during pregnancy. The interaction between various processes is not only genetically determined. There is increasing evidence that environmental events can influence regulatory processes in an organism (cf. Gottlieb, 1998).

The impact of gene action on behavior is direct, broad, and unmistakable in the case of certain malfunctions. Examples are Down's syndrome (or mongolism, also called trisomy-21 after the fact that instead of two there are three number 21 chromosomes) and phenylketonuria (caused by the absence of or inactivity of one particular enzyme that is needed for the metabolism of an amino acid found in milk). Among the diseases in which some genetic predisposition is strongly suspected, but not (yet?) clearly demonstrated at the level of genes or chromosomes, are the major mental disorders schizophrenia and depression. Their genetic basis has been mainly inferred from family and twin studies (Plomin, DeFries, McClearn, & Rutter, 1997). In the context of this book it is significant that all major mental disorders appear to occur universally, although it cannot be excluded that there are cross-cultural differences in the rates of incidence and in symptoms of manifestation. In ch. 16 we shall come back to this point.

## Personality

Is genetic variation also relevant to variations in typical human behavior, or is "normal" behavior more or less exclusively a function of environmental variables? Behavior genetics research on personality traits and cognitive abilities is relevant to this question.

In the older literature the term "temperament" used to be associated with the heritable components of personality. In early conceptions such as that of Heymans (1932; Van der Werff, 1985) temperament referred to a dominant mode of reacting which was characteristic of a person across a large range of situations. After a period in which environmental explanations dominated in psychology, research on temperament has started to gain more attention (Strelau, 1998) and also in traditions emphasizing personality dimensions, like the Big Five, the interest in biological explanations of individual differences has been increasing, as we have seen in ch. 4. Much of this research is focussed on heritability estimates, i.e., the proportion of the total variance that can be attributed to genetic factors. The personality dimension for which most heritability estimates have been obtained is probably that of extraversion–introversion, with average her-itability estimates in twin studies of about .50. For other dimensions, including the other Big Five dimensions, values vary mostly between .30 and .50 (e.g., Fuller & Thompson, 1978; Plomin et al., 1997; Bouchard, McGue, Hur, & Horn, 1998).[3]

In typical studies the genetic component of the total variance is inferred from differences in correlations between scores of individuals who are genetically more related and individuals who share fewer genes. Often studied are differences in heritability between monozygotic (identical) and dizygotic (non-identical) twins and between twins reared together and reared apart (in cases of adoption), but other family relationships are also examined. For example, Loehlin (1992) calculated heritability coefficients for extraversion of .51 in a sample of identical twins reared together, .16 in a sample of parents and their own children, and only .01 in a sample of parents and their adopted children.

The latter value points to a negligible effect of the environment in which children grow up. Some research on behavior genetics has strongly questioned popular beliefs that children from the same family act alike because they grew up in the same environment. In fact, for many traits there are salient environmental effects *not* shared with family members (called "non-shared environment" by Plomin & Daniels, 1987). Why individuals react in different ways to the same environment is not very clear, but it seems likely that in part these differences may be genetically mediated (Plomin et al., 1997). In other words, individual differences in reactions to the same environment can be brought about by genetic differences.

There are several difficulties with research in behavior genetics. For example, adoption studies generally tend to result in lower heritability estimates than twin studies. More important, there is no personality trait which is controlled by a single gene and for which a pattern of inheritance can be found following simple Mendelian principles in the same way as for some physical traits like eye color. To meet such objections the methodology of research in behavior genetics has been much advanced in the 1980s and 1990s. More sophisticated approaches have been developed that allow, for example, for co-variation between various genes (e.g., Riemann & De Raad, 1998). Behavior geneticists have begun to study differences in phenotypic traits as a function of variations in alleles of more genes simultaneously, allowing for multiple genes and interactions to contribute to psychological dimensions (Plomin & Caspi, 1998; Plomin et al., 1997).

## Intelligence

Estimates of the heritability of intelligence (also called $g$, as we saw in ch. 5) usually are higher than those for personality traits; in adolescents and adults they

---

[3] Heritability is often expressed as an index: $h^2$ is an estimate of the ratio between genetic variance and total (phenotypic) variance. It can range in value from 0.00 (all variance is environmental) to 1.00 (all variance is genetic). Estimates of $h^2$ can be derived from correlations in test scores between relatives.

reach values in the order of .75. Genetic effects tend to increase with age, reaching similar values as for body height, a highly heritable characteristic. For example, when the performance on intelligence tests of young adopted children is correlated with that of the non-adopted children in the same families, substantial effects of family environment are found. At the time of adolescence this correlation has virtually disappeared. Apparently, children become more independent of their family environment when growing up and pursue more those intellectual experiences that fit their propensities (e.g., Loehlin, Horn, & Willerman, 1989; Plomin et al., 1997).

So far we have dealt with individual differences. However, there is a long history in psychology in which the heritability of intelligence has been taken as evidence that differences in cognitive test scores between populations must also have a genetic basis (e.g., Rushton, 1988). In ch. 5 we have already mentioned important arguments against this position. Here we like to add two comments that derive from research in genetics.

First, there is no logical basis for inferences about intergroup variation on the basis of intragroup variation. Even if within all human groups a large proportion of individual differences has to be accounted for in genetic terms, this does not imply that an observed difference between groups also has a genetic basis. The underlying argument has been presented many times, among others by Furby (1973). She gives the imaginary example of a population in which there exist individual genetic differences for height. The phenotypic height is affected by the daily consumption of milk. For each glass of milk per day a quantity $c$ is added to a person's stature. Suppose that different groups from this population are exposed to environments characterized by different quantities of milk. Between-group differences in height will then be entirely determined by the drinking of more or less milk, while the within-group variance is entirely determined by genetic factors. It is easy to see that in this example the mean height of two groups drinking one and two glasses of milk respectively will differ by a quantity $c$.

The example of body height is not entirely arbitrary. It is known, mainly from military archives in which the height of all army conscripts was recorded, that over the last century the average height of youngsters in west European countries has increased by about 10 centimeters. Improvements in the diet are a major reason, but other environmental factors should not be excluded. In ch. 5 we have seen that on the basis of similar archival data on intelligence test scores, an increase of fifteen to twenty IQ points in a single generation (since 1950) has been computed for Western countries by Flynn (1987). From our discussion on genetics it is obvious that such rapid changes cannot possibly be due to evolutionary genetic forces – environmental factors have to be far more important. The apparent scope for change in IQ test scores indicates that these tests cannot possibly render a precise estimate of intelligence as a stable psychological characteristic of a human population.

Our second comment has to do with the notion of environment. In behavior genetics variation in the environment is one of the key parameters. However, environment as it is operationalized in studies with twins and in adoption studies represents only a limited proportion of the total variation that we find in a society. For example, adoptions often take place within families, and twins reared apart frequently are brought up by the sister of the mother or another relative. When we consider behavior genetics in a cross-cultural perspective, an even broader range of environments has to be considered. Bronfenbrenner and Ceci (1994; see also Ceci, Rosenblum, De Bruyn, & Lee, 1997) have made a distinction between actualized genetic potential and non-actualized potential. Actualized potential is observed as outcome, but the non-actualized potential cannot be known. Heritability as observed is exclusively a function of the former of the two factors. If gene–environment interactions are important, the range of environmental variation somehow is part of any equation in which heritability coefficients are computed. This variation tends to be defined poorly; even within societies definitions hardly include differences in economic wealth, ethnic discrimination, and similar factors (Ogbu, 1978).

For more precise and less controversial evidence of heritability at the population level we have to look at other phenomena than personality traits and cognitive abilities. An example of interactions between environmental conditions and genetic disposition is that of cross-cultural differences in lactose tolerance, discussed in box 10-4. Another example is population differences in the incidence of color blindness (e.g., Post, 1962, 1971). There is ample evidence that in hunter-gatherer populations the frequency of red–green color blindness is not more than 2 percent as opposed

## Box 10.4 Differences in tolerance for lactose

Lactose is the most important carbohydrate in milk. It cannot be absorbed in the intestine, but needs to be split in two molecules by the enzyme lactase. In newborns the (very rare) absence of the enzyme is lethal unless special food can be provided. Until fairly recently it was considered normal by Western medicine that in older children and adults the activity of lactase was maintained. We now know that this is the rule among west Europeans and their descendants in other countries. In many other populations the continuation of lactase excretion in older children and adults is virtually absent, leading to lactose intolerance. Lactose intolerance is manifested by diarrhea, abdominal pain, and flatulence after consumption of, let us say, half a liter of cow's milk. This holds for many East Asian groups, Melanesians, Native Americans and for most Africans. Groups of nomadic pastoralists in Africa, such as the Fulani, form a notable exception with high prevalence of lactose tolerance. In southern Europe and in certain regions of India intermediate values (from 30 percent to 70 percent) are found (see Dobzhansky, Ayala, Stebbins, & Valentine, 1977 or Vogel & Motulsky, 1979 for further references).

Although there is no perfect correlation the relationship between lactose tolerance in adults and animal husbandry is striking. Two explanations have been suggested, one cultural, and the other referring to physical qualities of

### Box 10.4 (continued)

the environment (Flatz & Rotthauwe, 1977). In the cultural explanation it is postulated that the consumption of milk, because of its nutritional value in proteins, should give a selection advantage. Once there were a few individuals who can tolerate milk, this trait could slowly spread through the population over a large number of generations. The fact that there are cattle farming populations with a low frequency of tolerance weakens this hypothesis. In addition, when milk has fermented it is low in lactose content and is digestible in the absence of lactase in the consumer's intestinal tract.

The second hypothesis postulates an advantage of lactose tolerance in areas with relatively little ultraviolet sunlight, such as northern Europe. Sunlight plays a role in the production of vitamin D which is needed for calcium metabolism. A too low level of vitamin D leads to rickets, a bone disease. It has been suggested that lactose is an alternative substance to vitamin D in the metabolism of calcium. Another version of this hypothesis bears on the direct absorption of vitamin D contained in milk and milk products.

Whatever the precise explanation, lactose intolerance explains why milk is considered repulsive by adults in many countries. Sometimes it is considered good for children and by extension for other weak and sickly persons, but not for strong and healthy people. Obviously such opinions have a much more valid basis than originally thought in Western folklore and medicine.

Of more interest to us are possible wider ramifications. To what extent has the intolerance for fresh milk been a barrier against the development of animal husbandry in various societies? The form of economic subsistence influences major cultural variables in a number of ways, as we have seen in chs. 2 and 9. Thus, variations in the digestion of milk may well have been a factor in the shaping of cultures, even if it is not clear at this stage how this biological mechanism has actually operated.

to about 5 percent in groups which in time and mode of subsistence are furthest removed from a hunting existence. This form of color blindness is usually linked to the Y-chromosome and is far more prevalent in men than in women. The most suggestive explanation is that hunter-gatherers are more dependent for their survival on accurate color vision (spotting of game or snakes) than agriculturalists and people living in industrialized societies. The higher survival rate of color-blind mutants in agricultural societies would then be the most likely genetic mechanism.

The evidence in an example like red–green color blindness differs substantially from the evidence in complex psychological traits, like intelligence. First, color blindness is a dichotomous trait for which heritability pathways can be traced precisely. Secondly, color blindness can be assessed unambiguously and is not affected by socialization or gene–environment interactions during the course of development. This allows for a plausible causal inference from the morphological phenotype to an underlying genetic mechanism. On the other hand, with complex traits we know that assessment procedures (and even the definition of concepts) are culture dependent (see ch. 11) and that their ontogenetic development more than likely is influenced by interactions with the social environment. Such factors obscure possible causal relationships between phenotype and genotype and make it almost impossible to draw valid inferences about genetic differences between populations.

However, the fact that we cannot interpret group differences in test performance in genetic terms does not imply that personality traits and intelligence are mere environmental or cultural products. Quite the contrary; the available evidence in our view only allows one conclusion, namely that genes count (see Sternberg & Grigorenko, 1997a for a review of various positions). Such a position has theoretical consequences for cross-cultural psychology (cf. Hunt, 1997). It means that the pursuit of a universalist perspective, developing theories and investigating how phenotypically personality and cognition are actualized in various cultural environments, is more fruitful than a relativist perspective in which typically human functions are seen as inherently cultural (cf. ch. 12).

## Ethology

**Ethology** is the study by biologists of animal behavior in natural environments. Characteristic of this branch of the biological sciences are elaborate and detailed field studies of animals in their natural habitat. The resulting descriptive accounts form the basis for theoretical explanations which are further developed along three lines of inquiry: through additional observations, through experiments to test specific hypotheses, and through the comparison of findings across species. It is particularly in respect of this last strategy that biologists claim to have an advantage over psychologists who tend to keep their research restricted to a single species and thus are not able to cross-validate their conceptualizations in a broader biological framework. In this section we shall first briefly examine what the ethological approach can contribute, and then move to the application of ethological approaches to humans. Among the topics frequently studied by ethologists are courtship behavior, territoriality, care for offspring, strategies for predator evasion, efficiency in foraging, communication (e.g., acquiring species-specific song in birds), and social organization as found in bees and ants.

The early ethologists were struck by regular patterns in much of the behavior of animals. Often one can observe behavior sequences consisting of a number of distinguishable acts. Once such a sequence is set in motion, it cannot be interrupted and then continued; after interruption it has to be started again from the beginning. Hence the notion was proposed of fixed action patterns. These patterns are triggered by specific stimuli, which act as releasers of an available behavior process. Another important notion was that of imprinting. It was observed that young birds tend to react to the first moving object they see after hatching as they normally respond to their parents. For example, animal keepers in zoos have found themselves in the position of substitute parents. They are then followed by young birds in the same way as these chicks normally follow the mother hen. At adult age such animals have been known to make sexual advances to members of the substitute human parent species, rather than to their own species. For this reason Lorenz postulated critical periods in the process of development. What an animal acquired during such a period was considered fixed and irreversible. A sharp distinction was made between instinct and learning. This divide also marked more or less the boundary between ethology and psychology from the 1930s until the 1970s. The term instinct referred to genetically inherited and thus pre-programmed and rather immutable behavior. At that time psychology was dominated by behaviorally inspired learning theories. It was believed by many that through classical conditioning in the tradition of Pavlov and operant conditioning as developed by Skinner, virtually any reaction an animal was capable of making could be linked to any stimulus that an animal could perceive.

This conclusion proved to be premature. Rats can be conditioned easily to avoid foods which later make them ill if these foods have a certain taste, but conditioning is difficult if the consumption of these foods is accompanied by electric shock to their feet (Garcia & Koelling, 1966). Conversely, rats have great difficulty in learning to jump for food, but can be taught easily to jump for shock avoidance. Visual cues have also been found to be ineffective in rats for learning food avoidance. For other species, such as monkeys, visual cues are quite effective in avoidance learning of toxic foods. Apparently, cues are most effective when they match the natural lifestyle of a species (e.g., Gould & Marler, 1987). Some ethologists had already argued earlier that the learning abilities of animals were greatly dependent on context. There are predispositions for certain stimulus–response associations and a reward which will reinforce a certain response may not work well for other responses.

The distinction between learning and instinct has also become more blurred because ethologists withdrew somewhat from the earlier position of Lorenz on imprinting as a special kind of learning dependent on "critical" periods. They now tend to speak about "sensitive" periods instead. Genetic factors will facilitate or constrain the learning of certain associations in a relative rather than in an absolute sense. These factors are not necessarily constant; they can cause different effects during various phases of individual development (Archer, 1992; Hinde, 1982). The animal is seen as innately equipped to learn what it needs in the particular ecological niche it occupies. At the same time "instinctive" responses cannot develop without environmental influences, making an ecological approach to behavior necessary. It requires only a small step to argue that learning in the human species, with its own evolutionary history and adapted to its own particular niche, is subject to the same considerations. Moreover, ethologists have asked the question of whether culture is so exclusively human as often thought (see box 10-5).

## Box 10.5 Emergence of culture in chimpanzees

Ethologists have made extensive observational studies of groups of great apes, especially chimpanzees, sometimes following them for many years. Most widely known is the work of Goodall (1986), but there are a number of similar field sites. Whiten et al. (1999) drew up an initial listing ($n = 65$) of behaviors reported in the literature for chimpanzees. All of these behaviors were assessed by directors of several field sites as to whether or not they had been observed in local groups of chimpanzees. Six categories were used, namely customary, habitual, present, absent, absent with ecological explanation, absent possibly because of inadequate observation, answer uncertain.

Thirty-nine behaviors were found that were absent at some sites, but customary or habitual elsewhere, including some shared between two or more communities. These patterns were especially concerned with sexual advances, grooming, and the use of tools. The patterns resembled those of human societies, in which differences between cultures are constituted by a multiplicity of variations in technology and social customs.

We can mention as examples field observations reported by one of these researchers. Boesch (1991, 1993, 1995) has suggested that mother chimpanzees influence the development of nut cracking in their infants through stimulation, facilitation, and active teaching. Certain contexts may favor teaching with regard to tool use in opening nuts. This can lead to the acceleration of behavior in an inexperienced individual. Eating of leaves of two species of plants was observed for the first time in a group, then spread rapidly within the community. Boesch proposed that there was cultural transmission. Observations by Russon (in press) have shown how young orangutans who grew up in captivity and then were released initially may not know how to obtain certain foods that are difficult to handle (e.g., because of spines), but later have learnt this from contacts with other individuals possessing the relevant skills.

Is the term "culture" appropriate in view of such behavior patterns? An answer to this question depends ultimately on the defining criteria of the concept. It is quite possible to make a list of criteria that excludes all species except humans (cf. McGrew, 1992; Segall et al., 1999). However, Whiten and colleagues, who have long and first-hand field experience, are clearly inclined to attribute elementary forms of culture at least to chimpanzees.

## Human ethology

The extension of ethological methods and theories to the human species is sometimes referred to as **human ethology**. In their quest for a variety of evidence ethologists more than psychologists are combining results from different disciplines.

Almost inherent to this strategy is the danger of overinterpreting the findings from other research areas than the one or two in which one has first-hand experience.

The scope of human ethology has been outlined by Eibl-Eibesfeldt (1979, 1989). Central to his approach is the biological heritage of human behavior. He writes:

> the comparative approach is a basic source of information, but it has been crit- icized for making too much of "similarities". Yet if we compare the structure or the behavior of animals and man, we do indeed encounter striking similarity. In greeting rituals, for example, weapons are turned away in a conspicuous fash- ion to indicate peaceful intent. Boobies [a small sea bird] sky point with their beaks, the Masai thrusts his spear into the ground, and in our culture we salute state visitors with twenty-one averted guns. Similarities of this kind call for an explanation. They can be accidental, but most of the time they are not, being due to similar selective pressures that have shaped behavior during phylogenetic and cultural evolution alike, or else to a common heritage resulting from a shared ancestor. (1979, p. 2)

Only in a footnote does Eibl-Eibesfeldt add to these statements a small reser- vation about cultural traditions that can be passed on through human communi- cation and may not have evolved independently in different cultures. He continues by drawing a distinction between homologies and analogies. Similarities geneti- cally transmitted from common ancestors are called homologies. In Eibl- Eibesfeldt's opinion we can confidently infer that most behavior patterns which we share with the great apes are homologies. Analogies are similarities between species in morphological or behavioral traits which have arisen in response to sim- ilar environmental demands. The eye of an octopus which is anatomically re- markably similar to the human eye obviously also has the same function. There are also functional similarities in behavior, the cross-species comparison of which can be helpful for the explanation of human behavior.

After mentioning evidence of animal behavior Eibl-Eibesfeldt (1979) discusses evidence from humans to show that phylogenetic adaptation has also pre- programmed their behavior to a significant extent. One of the sources of evidence is cross-cultural research. Reference is made to the extensive recordings on film of unstaged social interactions which he and his collaborators have made in a num- ber of mainly traditional cultures.[4] The films revealed a large number of universal patterns. An example is the kiss which is universally found as a sign of affection to children. It has derived from mouth-to-mouth feeding and is linked to similar behavior in non-human primates. Another example is the display of "coyness," which is clearly recognized independent of the culture where it has been filmed.

---

[4] When subjects know that they are being filmed they tend to start acting. In order to obtain un- staged recordings Eibl-Eibesfeldt and his team made use of a lens with a mirror device so that what happened in front of the camera was not being filmed, but events to one side at an angle of 90 de- grees. Reuning (personal communication to one of the authors), who is an expert on the Bushmen, has questioned who is being tricked by this device; persons who are not familiar with movie cam- eras and who will watch the filmer rather than the device, or investigators who underestimate the social skills of illiterate peoples?

There are also differences between cultures, for example in the non-verbal communication of expressing "no." In most cultures people shake their head. Other gestures are used, for example by the Greeks who throw back their head and turn it sideways, and by the Ayoreo Indians who wrinkle their nose (as if smelling something bad) and pout. According to Eibl-Eibesfeldt all these patterns are found universally and all express some denial or rejection. Apparently, it is possible that one of these patterns becomes the standard convention in a group instead of the more common horizontal head shake which seems emotionally the most neutral to express a factual "no."

Eibl-Eibesfeldt also finds important basic similarities in the structure of rituals, i.e. complex behavior patterns with a symbolic nature (cf. also Eibl-Eibesfeldt, 1989). He argues that in a friendly encounter there are universally three phases, each with a specific function. The first or opening phase is characterized by a mixture of aggressive displays and appeasement. As an illustration is mentioned a Yanomami Indian going to another village who will perform an aggressive display dance, but will be accompanied by a child waving green leaves.

> The Yanomami salutation is certainly a culturally specific ritual. We in the West do not perform war dances on such an occasion. But consideration of the more general principles expressed does reveal comparable displays in our way of saluting. A visitor of state, for example, is greeted by a welcoming cannonade, and in addition is received by a child with a bouquet of flowers. In the most diverse salutations we discover the same principle ... So, too, in our culture the handshake – and squeeze – are partly display and partly challenge, mitigated by smiling, nodding, and embracing. (1979, p. 21)

Eibl-Eibesfeldt goes so far as to suggest that bodily characteristics have evolved to serve as releasing signals. It was noted already by Lorenz that babies possess certain qualities which make them look "cute" and which solicit caretaking and affective responses. Among other things he mentioned the relatively large head, the rounded body shape, and the round protruding cheeks. The latter are sometimes said to have a function in sucking, but this is not clear. Eibl-Eibesfeldt (1975) argued: "Such an additional function is feasible, of course, but we notice that monkeys and other mammals can get along without this formation. This argues for a specifically human organ that evolved in the service of signaling" (p. 490).

Eibl-Eibesfeldt (1979, 1989) concludes that there is a universal "grammar" of human social behavior. Genetic mechanisms are presumed to underlie what many consider to be qualities which are acquired in the process of socialization. Even symbolic behavior is reduced to inborn behavior patterns. In contrast, most students of culture tend to argue that the validity of such claims cannot be demonstrated by such vague similarities as mentioned in the last couple of paragraphs. The examples show that Eibl-Eibesfeldt is not very sensitive to the warnings by Gould and Lewontin, mentioned earlier in this chapter, that certain changes may not be adaptations, but may have come about as a byproduct of other changes.

For example, dominance of the male sex in the human species could easily be seen as a homology because of similar patterns in related species, especially the chimpanzees with whom we appear to share more than 99 percent of our genes. However, matters are not that easy since we know that the bonobo or dwarf chimpanzee, which is a species that is phylogenetically equally closely related to humans as the chimpanzee, shows far less male dominance and displays (in human terms) a sexually very promiscuous life style (De Waal, 1988, 1995). Moreover, if the range of modifiability of human behavior is so large that a short handshake, or even a verbal greeting, can have the same meaning as an elaborate dance display, there is an important difference between human behavior and the fixed action patterns which ethologists have observed in animal behavior.

## Sociobiology

Human ethology as presented here can be seen as the European counterpart of the American school of **sociobiology**. Although the adherents of both traditions will point out certain differences, these are small from the perspective of the present book. Sociobiology took off after Edward O. Wilson (1975) published a book with this term in the title. The book contained a powerful attempt to explain social behavior, including that of the human species, within an evolutionary framework. Central to the sociobiological doctrine is the axiom that the behavior of an individual organism is geared towards maximizing its inclusive fitness. Unlike the traditional notion of fitness mentioned in the first section, inclusive fitness is not limited to an organism's own offspring, but is extended to encompass other relatives with whom genes are also shared, be it to a lesser extent. An organism without own children can be biologically successful when it has many nephews and other relatives with whom it shares part of its own genes. To promote the interests of its kin is in the evolutionary interest of the organism.

Classical evolution theory had been unable to account for altruistic behavior, except when it promotes the interests of direct descendants. Not only among humans, but also in other species, one can frequently observe behaviors that seem incompatible with self-interest. Clear examples are found among insects such as bees and ants, where workers who do not produce their own offspring devote their entire lives to the care of other members of the society. Hamilton (1964) demonstrated that the behavior of worker bees can be understood as self-serving, given the principle of inclusive fitness. In insect societies in which the kind of altruism mentioned is found among workers, the genome of females tends to be quite different from that of males. Females (including workers and queens) are diploid; they receive a double set of genes, just like, for example, human beings. One set comes from the father and one from the mother. Males are haploid, they only get one set of genes, from the mother. A queen bee can lay unfertilized and fertilized eggs. The unfertilized eggs develop into males and the fertilized eggs into females. This implies that "sisters" have three-quarters of their genes in common; they share the entire genotype of their (homozygous) father and they share, on average, half of the genes they receive from their mother. Under these conditions "sisters" share even more genes than mothers and daughters, namely three-quarters as against a half.

Hamilton argued that worker bees may increase their own inclusive fitness more by looking after their sisters than by caring for own offspring. This argument is strengthened by the role of male bees who do not take part in the caretaking activities of the workers, do nothing to gather their own food, and almost live as parasites in the community. In evolution theory the key to the differences in behavior between workers and males is the genetic relationship which between brothers and sisters is much lower than between sisters.

Wilson had no hesitation in extending sociobiological arguments to the human species. In the last chapter of his book dealing with the human species, he argued that from an outsider's perspective "the humanities and social sciences shrink to specialized branches of biology; history, biography, and fiction are the research protocols of human ethology; and anthropology and sociology together constitute the sociobiology of a single primate species" (Wilson, 1975, p. 547).

Wilson's book triggered a large amount of research on the question of whether human cultural patterns could be reduced to evolutionary principles. The criterion for a biological origin is that a phenomenon occurs in a preponderance of human societies. Examples are male dominance, sexual taboos, and extended socialization of children. An area of particularly intensive study, and speculation, has been that of human sexuality (e.g., Alcock, 1984; Daly & Wilson, 1983). Men and women differ systematically in their desire for sexual variety, with men being clearly more adulterous. Men are also more jealous about the promiscuity of their partners than are women. These patterns fit different strategies for reproductive success, characteristic of the male and female sex not only among humans but in most species, at least of mammals.

A woman can have only a limited number of offspring, given the energy, resources, and time she has to invest in each child during pregnancy and lactation. Pair bonding is in her interest so that her partner can help provide for her and her offspring. One mate should be enough to provide her with the maximal number of children she can have. The human male, like the male sex in most species, has a large capacity for reproduction. To achieve a large number of biological descendants the man's best strategy is to inseminate as many females as possible and to fight for his chances if necessary. However, there are factors which reduce the success of this strategy. For example, the period of receptivity in the female menstrual cycle is not noticeable among humans, as it is among most other species. Allegedly, this is an adaptation with an advantage for the female; her escort has to stay with her for a longer period if he wants to make sure that she will bear his child (Alcock, 1984). Alternatively, females among our hominid ancestors who made themselves sexually available were more successful in obtaining meat from the hunters when hunting became a predominantly male activity (Symons, 1979).

Sociobiologists have no argument with the major findings of psychology and cultural anthropology. Learning mechanisms, for example, whether they are based on conditioning or imitation, can easily be incorporated in a genetic framework. Principles of learning can be seen as adaptations to certain ecological demands that have developed in the process of evolution. For the sociobiologists differences between cultural groups are merely variations on a common theme. The genetic constraints on human behavior allow only a small margin for cultural differences. To many social scientists this kind of reduction is unpermitted and unforgivable. What to biologists like Wilson is merely a small margin for them is an area governed by its own unreducible principles. As Sahlins (1977) has stated: "Within the void left by biology lies the whole of anthropology."

## Evolutionary psychology

The evolutionary thinking of ethology and sociobiology is at the basis of **evolutionary psychology**. One landmark study by Buss (1989; Buss et al., 1990) on preferred characteristics of mates in thirty-seven countries has already been referred to in ch. 3. Here we can mention that Buss was looking for, and found, differences between the preferences of young men and women along the lines of the differential reproductive strategies as just described. The results showed that both men and women highly value mutual attraction and love, a dependable character, and an understanding and intelligent partner. However, the young women in this study expressed relatively somewhat more interest in good financial prospects and good earning capacity (i.e., partners capable of looking well after them and their offspring), while the young men gave relatively higher ratings to good looks and physical attractiveness (presumably a good appearance reflects health and the capacity to bear children). Another line of research is on differences between men and women in the preferred age of a partner and the changes in this preference over the lifespan (Kenrick & Keefe, 1992). A large number of sources (such as advertisements for partners, and archives) in a range of societies show a similar pattern. During adolescence men tend to be slightly younger than women in a partnership, but this age difference soon reverses and with increasing age women tend to marry men who more and more are older than themselves. An obvious evolutionary explanation is that men, who continue to be fertile much longer than women, have a phylogenetically evolved strategy to prefer partners who can have children.

It is a basic assumption in evolutionary psychology that all human psychological functions ranging from ethnocentrism (e.g., Reynolds, Falger, & Vine, 1987) to esthetics (Dissanayake, 1992) have to be considered in the light of reproductive fitness. According to Tooby and Cosmides (1992) such functions reflect design features of the human mind that have been shaped by evolutionary processes. In the process of selection those features are retained that are functional as opposed to dysfunctional (i.e., less successful in reproduction). Thus, separate successful features are linked together in the reproduction process and in this way a coherent overall design has emerged. There are likely to be a large number of complex evolved psychological mechanisms that are domain specific. Results like those of Garcia and Koelling (1966), mentioned earlier, are seen as evidence of such specificity, and also the fact that one finds phobias for snakes, heights or open spaces, which have always been part of the human environment, but never for electricity sockets, which have been in existence for a few generations only.

The notion of functions has been described for ethology by Tinbergen (1963), who proposed four criteria for a behavior pattern to be part of the adaptive equipment of a species: (1) its mechanism or cause; (2) its evolutionary history; (3) its ontogenetic development; and (4) the function it supposedly serves. Thus, in an examination of evolutionary studies a major question is whether sufficient evidence exists for the validity of functional explanations. The objection has been raised that findings like those of Buss and of Kenrick can also be explained in terms of traditional cultural patterns that have created distinctions between men and women (Eagly & Wood, 1999). The question of how these differences are patterned in various societies requires psychological and anthropological explanation. At the same time it is difficult to decide how far objections such as those by Eagly and Wood are to the point, because they address current practices, while evolutionary psychologists seek to address the possible psychobiological roots of such practices.

The notion of the biological givenness of functional entities, also called modules, is also questioned in evolutionary theories emphasizing interactions between organism and environment. According to such interactionist theories reproductive strategies can be modified by factors in the environment of the organism. In ch. 2 we mentioned the assertion by Belsky et al. (1991) that insecure patterns of attachment in infancy lead to an early onset of puberty and sexual partnerships. Similar relationships between early childhood experiences and the onset of puberty have been reported in other studies (cf. Keller, 1997). In interactionist approaches genetic mechanisms are capabilities that can be evoked and shaped by specific environmental conditions.

It seems meaningful to distinguish three orientations. The first is a kind of biomechanistic approach in which features of human behavior (modules) are explained as the outcomes of phylogenetic adaptation processes. Tooby and Cosmides (1992) and Buss (1995; Buss et al., 1998) are representative of this approach. The second orientation is more interactionist; environmental factors foster a specific developmental outcome that is drawn from an array of predispositions (see Keller, 1997). The third position emphasizes far less constrained evolutionary pathways. In this position formulated by Gould and Lewontin (1979) there is also a much wider scope for cultural adaptations. At the same time, because there are fewer constraints, it is a position for which it is difficult to find unambiguous supportive evidence.

## Models of cultural transmission

In the first section of this chapter we described how genetic information is transmitted from generation to generation. In subsequent sections we have discussed various fields of research in which analysis is focussed on the genetic underpinnings of human psychological functioning. Earlier in the book, in ch. 2, we discussed the psychological transmission of information between members of a cultural group in the socialization process, which does not necessarily require a genetic relationship. Biologists have developed formal models in which the transmission of both genetic and cultural information is dealt with. The distinction between vertical, oblique, and horizontal transmission (cf. Cavalli-Sforza & Feldman, 1981), mentioned in ch. 2, is an example. Cavalli-Sforza and Feldman have described mathematical models of the non-genetic transmission of aspects of culture. One of the areas which they discuss is the diffusion of innovations, for which similar mathematical models can be fitted as for the spread through a population of an advantageous biological mutation. The scope of most models goes beyond mere description. They are intended to give biological and cultural phenomena a place within a single explanatory framework.

One early attempt to construct models of cultural transmission meeting this requirement was by Lumsden and Wilson (1981). They postulated the notion of a "culturegen" which forms the basic unit of culture. A culturegen is a more or less homogeneous set of artifacts, behaviors, or mentifacts (Lumsden and Wilson's term) that are related. Transmission takes place via epigenetic rules. Epigenesis is the process of interaction between genes and the environment. Any regularity in development which gives direction to behavior forms an epigenetic rule. Examples in Lumsden and Wilson's book include principles of perceptual information transmission and incest taboos. However, they go further:

> Human beings are thought [by cultural anthropologists] to pursue their own interest and that of their society on the basis of a very few simple structural biological needs by means of numerous, arbitrary, and often elaborate culturally acquired behaviors. In contrast to this conventional view, our interpretation of the evidence from cognitive and developmental psychology indicates the presence of epigenetic rules that have sufficiently great specificity to channel the acquisition of rules of inference and decision to a substantial degree. The process of mental canalization in turn shapes the trajectories of cultural evolution. (Lumsden & Wilson, 1981, p. 56)

These few sentences in no way do justice to the sophisticated arguments presented by Lumsden and Wilson. However, they are sufficient to indicate the kind of concepts, analogous to those found in genetics, in terms of which cultural transmission is described.

Apart from attempts to incorporate cultural and biological transmission within a single framework, one also finds theories that draw distinctions between mechanisms of biological and cultural transmission. None of the authors questions the evolutionary basis of cultural variation and cultural change, but some accept, contrary to orthodox sociobiologists and evolutionary psychologists, that other mechanisms have to be postulated in addition to the natural selection of alternative alleles in the genetic constitution.

One well-known example is the **dual inheritance model** of Boyd and Richerson (1985). In addition to the genetic inheritance system that has been described in the first section of this chapter they postulate a cultural inheritance system that is based on social learning. What an individual has learnt during his or her lifetime is not transmitted genetically; only the capacity for learning, which is part of the genotype, is passed on to his or her offspring and remains in the population. However, during a lifetime a person can pass on cultural information to other members of the group. This information can stay in the possession of the group from generation to generation. The transmission of cultural information has "population-level consequences" according to Boyd and Richerson (1985, p. 4).

The cultural and genetic inheritance systems differ among other things in the nature of parenthood. Cultural traits can be transmitted by "cultural parents" who may well be different from the biological parents, as in oblique transmission. Also, in the cultural inheritance system, specific experiences gained during an individual's lifetime can be transmitted to that individual's cultural offspring and become part of the inheritance of the group. This is in contrast to genetic transmission, which can only have an effect through a differential rate of reproduction.

The close correspondence between biological and cultural transmission in the theorizing of Boyd and Richerson is especially evident in the mechanisms that they postulate for explaining cultural change. Apart from "mutations" (i.e., error rates due to imperfect memory) and chance variations due to selective retention of information in certain groups, an important place is attributed to social learning and systematic biases in the transmission of information. Social learning is distinguished from individual learning. The latter is based on trial-and-error or conditioning principles. Boyd and Richerson believe that a large cultural repertoire cannot be acquired only by socially controlled conditioning of youngsters. This process would be too uneconomic. They attach great importance to Bandura's (1977) social learning theory, in which imitation of behaviors that only have been observed is seen as a sufficient condition for learning. Social learning by observation and imitation leads to cultural stability of behavior patterns. Individual learning, shaped by specific environmental conditions, leads to change.

Boyd and Richerson (1985) have constructed models of cultural transmission analogous to models of genetic transmission. The relative incidence of individual and social learning is one of the parameters in these models. The consequences of a change in this parameter, for example on the rate of responsiveness to changes in the environment, can be calculated. The models are further elaborated through the inclusion of the concept of transmission bias. An individual within a culture is exposed to different variants of the available cultural repertoire.

In a static culture the relative frequency of the variants presumably would remain constant (in accordance with the Hardy-Weinberg law). But Boyd and Richerson assume that the available options can be evaluated and the most adaptive variant selected. This is illustrated with the example of a child learning to play table tennis and observing that there are two ways to hold the bat, the "racquet" grip and the "pencil" grip. No bias occurs when the child chooses randomly one player as a role model, but there are other possibilities. After some practice the child can choose the grip with which the best results are obtained. If it takes too much practice to find this out, another option is to use the most successful player as a model. Still another option is to simply follow the majority in one's choice.

This last strategy, a conformist one, is linked by Boyd and Richerson to altruism, or cooperation, and to ethnocentrism. The conformist strategy, which makes people follow the most popular variant in a group, leads to a decrease in cultural variation within groups relative to between-group variation. Even though cooperation with group members rather than the pursuit of self-interest can be disadvantageous to the individual (and thus should have disappeared in the process of evolution according to traditional evolution theory), the lower fitness of cooperators within groups can have been offset by a higher survival rate of groups with a high frequency of cooperators. If this is the case, and Boyd and Richerson specify relevant conditions within their models, a high frequency of cooperators is maintained more or less indefinitely. At the same time, the conformist bias can only have this effect if the cooperative behavior is restricted to a limited group. One kind of group which seems to meet the requirement of the models is the cultural group with the associated characteristics of ethnocentrism, including cooperative behavior towards members of the in-group and uncooperative behavior towards the out-group.

Complexities are added if a further diversification of levels or modes of transmission is introduced (e.g., Durham, 1982; Plotkin & Odling-Smee, 1981). The role of culture as environmental context has been further elaborated by Laland, Odling-Smee, and Feldman (2000). In line with traditional evolutionary theory they recognize that a species through interactions with the environment modifies its environment, a process called niche construction. However, Laland et al. go further. In human populations niche construction is not only a genotypical characteristic of the species. Two other kinds of processes are involved, namely ontogenetic processes of information acquisition (e.g., learning to read and write) and cultural processes. From this perspective farming with cattle for milk (niche construction) could be at the basis of the genetic change towards tolerance for lactose, as discussed in box 10.4.

Another model is that of Hinde (1987). He argues that interactions between individuals evolve into relationships when there is a series of such interactions over time. In turn these relationships are located within larger networks of groups and ultimately society. According to Hinde each of these levels of social complexity has properties that are not found at the lower levels; in addition, levels mutually influence each other. For each level there are relationships with the ecological and sociocultural context. For example, a fear of snakes is part of the human biological heritage; it is influenced by social experience, and plays a role at the cultural level through symbolic qualities attached to snakes (Hinde, 1992). Thus, the genetic influences on human behavior may not be very straightforward, and these influences may dissipate when social and cultural aspects of human functioning are considered.

The most diversified conceptualization of organism–environment relationships is due to Campbell (1974; cf. Overman, 1988). In his theory of evolutionary epistemology a series of levels is distinguished, including among others genetic adaptation, observational learning and imitation, cultural accumulation and science. All of these levels function according to the same evolutionary principles of selection and adaptation. In selection processes poorly adapted entities gradually disappear and well-adapted entities remain. However, evolutionary epistemology is perhaps better qualified as a philosophical system than as a framework for empirical research.

The main problem with the more complex models discussed in this section is that they lack the theoretical strength of traditional evolutionary biology. The definition of higher levels and the specification of relationships between them becomes increasingly fuzzy as one moves from more biological to more cultural phenomena. From the perspective of cross-cultural psychology it can be argued that ethology and evolutionary psychology, with their emphasis on invariant, genetically based aspects of human psychological functioning, provide minimum estimates of the effects of cultural conditions. Culture-comparative research, if it extends over a sufficient range of cultural populations, tends to lead to maximum estimates of cultural variation. The variety of available models can be seen as evidence that interactions between nature and nurture are difficult to trace. However, this is clearly more so in monocultural than in cross-cultural approaches. We expect that culture-comparative research will increasingly become the testing ground of models and theories as mentioned in this section.

## Conclusions

In this chapter we have first outlined the mechanisms of genetic transmission which provide the foundation for biological thinking about human behavior. We then discussed behavior genetics, which seeks to discover the genetic underpinnings of cognitive and personality traits by comparing pairs of individuals who share more genetic material with pairs who share less genetic material. Thereafter we shifted the focus to evolutionary theories of human social behavior. We finished with a brief outline of some models that make distinctions between genetic transmission and other modes of transmission.

Perhaps we should add explicitly what biological thinking as presented in this chapter is *not* about. It is *not* about genes as a deterministic force that preempt moral choices. It is also *not* about the explanation of behavior differences between cultural groups. And it is *not* about the dichotomy between nature and nurture, which is a false dichotomy. Biologically speaking we cannot really go against our genes, but the observable behavior repertoire is the outcome of a range of possible responses. The fascinating question is what the space is in which humans can operate and build culture.

The human species is morphologically and physiologically quite similar to other species, but the extensive facility for culture provides for a psychologically unique position. The facilities for conscious reflection and the formulation of long-term goals and plans that can be reached along a variety of routes adds a dimension to human behavior not found to the same extent in other species. This can be seen as a dimension of opportunities or affordances (see ch. 12). To define this space more insight into cross-cultural variations and uniformities of behavior is needed than is presently available. It seems obvious to us that cross-cultural research will have to make a contribution to the further accumulation of such knowledge. At the same time the chapter is meant to provide a warning; we should be careful not to fall into the dogmatic and ideological traps either of those biomechanistic evolutionists who are inclined to see any coincidence as a causal relationship, or of those environmentalistically minded social scientists who cling to the view that the biological basis is largely irrelevant to the study of what is typically human in behavior.

Finally, inasmuch as it makes sense to accept sociocultural evolution as a relevant determinant of cultures that we find today, an important warning is issued by Campbell (1975) which we can ignore only at great future cost. Campbell has argued that in an evolutionary framework cultural inheritance has to be regarded as adaptive. For this reason it has to be treated with respect. He pleads that when we come across puzzling and incomprehensible features of a culture, including our own, we should diligently search for ways in which it may make adaptive sense.

## Key terms

adaptation (biological)  fitness
adaptation (social)  gene
allele  human ethology
behavior genetics  natural selection
dual inheritance model  pleiotropy
ethology  sociobiology
evolutionary psychology

## Further reading

Buss, D. M. (1995). Evolutionary psychology: A new paradigm for psychological science. *Psychological Inquiry*, *6*, 1-30. Buss gives an account, followed by contributions of discussants, of evolutionary psychology as a paradigm for psychology.

Eibl-Eibesfeldt, I. (1989). *Human ethology.* New York: Aldine de Gruyter. A voluminous book, in which the author gives an overview of the subject area with many illustrations of uniformities in behavior patterns across cultures.

Keller, H. (1997). Evolutionary approaches. In J. W. Berry, Y. H. Poortinga, & J. Pandey (Eds.), *Theory and method* (pp. 215–55). Vol. I of *Handbook of cross-cultural psychology* (2nd ed.) Boston, MA: Allyn and Bacon. The chapter provides an overview of evolutionary thinking in developmental psychology.

Laland, K. N., Odling-Smee, J., & Feldman, M. W. (2000). Niche construction, biological evolution, and cultural change. *Behavioral and Brain Sciences, 23,* 131–75. This article provides an illustration of the kind of model that emerges when the role of the ecological and sociocultural environment is emphasized more than in traditional evolutionary approaches.

Plomin, R., DeFries, J. C., McClearn, G. E., & Rutter, M. (1997). *Behavioral genetics* (3rd ed.). New York: Freeman. These authors give a very readable overview of the field of behavior genetics.

# 11 Methodological concerns

This chapter will consider some of the more prominent methodological concerns in cross-cultural research. As noted in ch. 1, there is much more to a cross-cultural study than collecting data in two countries and comparing the results. In fact, Campbell long ago warned against the uninterpretability of two-group comparisons. In other chapters we have seen that differences in test scores may not reflect differences in the traits supposedly measured. Here the design of cross-cultural studies and the interpretation of data will be more fully explored. We shall see that we have to guard carefully against alternative explanations and against the effects of cultural bias in research methods.

The chapter begins with a section on qualitative research. This approach has captured the attention of many cross-cultural psychologists who for a long time have felt that their research questions did not fit in the restraining mold of traditional quantitative methodology. Thereafter we turn to quantitative methods. The second section discusses the design of culture-comparative studies, including controls to rule out alternative explanations, and problems of sampling. The third section, psychological data in cultural context, addresses some consequences of the fact that in cross-cultural psychology we deal simultaneously with individual-level (the traditional emphasis of psychology) and population-level data. In the fourth section we deal with a main issue of cross-cultural data analysis, namely the analysis of equivalence or comparability; this is the question of whether or not results of tests, or other measures, obtained in different cultures can be interpreted the same way. This section reviews some of the numerous ways of protecting interpretations against the inadvertent effects of cultural bias. In the last section on the classification of inferences, the interpretation of results is discussed. We argue that some inferences stay much closer to the data than others and are more open to analysis of equivalence.

## Qualitative methodology

Debates on methodology have taken place ever since psychology emerged as a distinguishable science. In Germany, which in many respects was the cradle of experimental psychology in the early twentieth century, also research methods rooted in phenomenology were developed and kept an important place until the 1950s. Behaviorism, first in the USA and later in Europe, was a reaction to these "subjective" approaches. A more "objective" experimental orientation was sought because researchers objected to the speculative nature of subjective interpretations. The elaborate constructions in psychoanalysis about what happens in the unconscious are a case in point. However, many psychologists also started to feel uneasy with behaviorism in which there was emphasis on stimuli and responses (the so-called S–R paradigm), but in which theoretical concepts referring to processes within the person (the S–O–R paradigm) were considered untestable and outside the reach of scientific analysis.

Arguments in the debate may have changed over time, but many of the earlier controversies continue. These are indicated with various pairs of terms, like ideographic versus nomothetic, subjective versus objective, and **qualitative methodology** versus **quantitative methodology**. Cross-cultural psychology is particularly sensitive to this debate, since here we find both cultural research, where qualitative approaches dominate, and culture-comparative traditions, where quantitative methods prevail. This is not surprising since qualitative methods have been, and continue to be, prominent in cultural anthropology. In our opinion, the differences in emphasis are real, but it is most unfortunate that the two categories tend to be treated as mutually exclusive rather than compatible. Much of the controversy arises from the fact that opinion leaders in both traditions tend to consider their own methodology superior per se, rather than just different in scope.

According to Denzin and Lincoln (2000b, p. 8):

> The word *qualitative* implies an emphasis on the qualities of entities and on processes and meanings that are not experimentally examined or measured (if measured at all) in terms of quantity, amount, intensity, or frequency. Qualitative researchers stress the socially constructed nature of reality, the intimate relationship between the researcher and what is studied, and the situational constraints that shape inquiry. Such researchers emphasize the value-laden nature of inquiry. They seek answers to questions that stress *how* social experience is created and given meaning. [italics in the original]

Creswell (1998, p. 15) speaks about qualitative research as:

> an inquiry process of understanding based on distinct methodological traditions of inquiry that explore a social or human problem. The researcher builds a complex, holistic picture, analyzes words, reports detailed views of informants, and conducts the study in a natural setting.

The methodological traditions that Creswell refers to are related to the disciplines that frequently use these methods. In cultural anthropology (see ch. 9) the main method is ethnography (Hammersley, 1992). This qualitative tradition is one of the foundations of cross-cultural psychological research. The goal of ethnography is to make sense out of the narrations of informants and one's own observations in terms of a system of meanings or values. In history an important method is the biography through which the researcher tries to reconstruct events and their background. In sociology the researcher, if following qualitative rather than quantitative approaches, is seeking grounded theory via an inductive process starting with the analysis of single cases and the subsequent development of progressively more abstract categories (Charmaz, 1995). In psychology qualitative methods include unstructured interviews, focus groups, and non-scheduled observations, as well as interpretive assessment methods where not rule-bound scoring methods, but the insight of the psychologist into the meaning of the respondent's reactions is central (Smith, Harré, & Van Langenhove, 1995). The major methods of qualitative research, according to Silverman (1993), include observation, analysis of text and documents, interviews, and recordings with transcripts; and often these methods are used in combination.

In the citation Creswell mentions natural settings as typical for qualitative research. It should be obvious that much of cross-cultural research *is* qualitative in this sense, and in our view *has to be* qualitative. Moreover, there is no incompatibility between the methods of data collection mentioned by Creswell and Silverman and quantitative research methodology.

However, if we look at the quotation from Denzin and Lincoln it is clear that the definition of qualitative methodology can also go much further. Experiment and measurement are de-emphasized; reality is portrayed as subjective, and the person of the researcher, including the values he or she represents, are made part of the research process. Moreover, the focus is on the construction of meaning rather than on the explanation of behavior or underlying psychological processes. The quotation addresses the nature of inquiry in qualitative research, which is partly a methodological, and partly a meta-methodological, concern, as well as the philosophical question of the nature of reality. In box 11-1 these issues are discussed somewhat further.

The main controversy between methodological orientations regards the issue of **validity**. To many authors on qualitative and quantitative methodology alike, it is a primary task of researchers to demonstrate that their findings, and thus the methods through which they were collected, have validity. According to Cook and Campbell (1979, p. 37) the concepts of validity and invalidity "refer to the best available approximation to the truth or falsity of propositions, including propositions about cause." They add that validity is always approximate, since there are no absolute scientific truths (see box 11-1). Various forms of validity have been distinguished and there are many sources of evidence. We shall not discuss these here.[1]

---

[1] There is an important point to note, namely that in empirical science knowledge cannot be applied, for example in interventions and support programs, unless there is a basis for believing that such knowledge is valid. In this sense validity is a key concept also when it comes to the accountability of scientists towards society.

## Box 11.1  Four paradigms

Lincoln and Guba (2000, see also Guba & Lincoln, 1994) describe four world-views or **paradigms**, reflecting philosophical positions that are distinguishable in terms of ontology (the nature of existence), epistemology (the nature of knowing), and methodology. These four paradigms are called positivism, post-positivism, critical theory, and constructivism. The constructivist paradigm is relativistic; reality is socially constructed, and the results of research are created through hermeneutical and dialectical methods in the process of research. In critical theory reality is seen as historically grown, but for all practical purposes social structures and psychological traits are "out there." In this family of critical theory emphasis is on the epistemological position that methods and knowledge are subjective and value bound. The first paradigm, positivism, reflects the belief that reality is out there and that through a process of experimental verification research will enable us to find out the true state of reality.

The second paradigm, post-positivism, that Lincoln and Guba mention remains the leading paradigm in psychology today. It assumes a reality out there of which our knowledge will always be imperfect, but we can differentiate more incorrect views from less incorrect views through systematic inquiry. Such inquiry should be based on the epistemological principle of refutation or falsification, developed by Karl Popper (1959). In his opinion it is beyond scientific research to establish a universally valid empirical truth. The statement that "All ravens are black" can never be the result of observation, since we can never observe all ravens, including future ones. Therefore, the statement can never be completely verified. However, it can be falsified; the statement is demonstrably wrong the moment we observe a non-black raven. According to Popper scientific research proceeds by a process of progressively ruling out incorrect theories through critical experimentation.

A practical difficulty with Popper's position has been identified by Lakatos (e.g., 1974) who pointed out that debates in science often are on the merits of methods and procedures. For example, Galileo's views were challenged by the clergy of his time because they refused to accept that his observations could be valid. These were made with a lens, a mere piece of glass, that could not possibly yield observations superior to those of the human eye created by God. Similar kinds of arguments have been raised in cross-cultural psychology in respect of the use of Western concepts and methods in other cultures.

A more principled critique of Popper came from Kuhn (1962), who gave a historical description of changes in scientific worldviews. He showed that evidence that falsifies hypotheses often is ignored; paradigmatic views and major theories tend to be adapted in order to accommodate new evidence,

## Box 11.1 (continued)

but scientists tend to resist rejection of their theories (beliefs) because of negative results.

However, these criticisms of Popper do not so much address the epistemological principle of falsifiability as the historical reality of fallible scientists who hang on to their preferred theories. Undoubtedly such subjective preferences affect the selection and interpretation of empirical evidence. The question is whether or not these limitations make it necessary to accept relativistic and value-laden epistemological positions. The perspective taken in this book is that scientific theories can be demonstrated to be wrong on the basis of empirical evidence, and that good research exposes one's preferred theory to falsification. Criticisms as mentioned make clear why scientific research is difficult, not that the epistemological principle of falsifiability is incorrect. In short, Kuhn being right does not make Popper wrong.

However, in postmodernist and constructivist approaches the search for validity of methods and findings is rejected by some as a misguided objective. For example, Gergen and Gergen (2000) argue that our understanding of accounts of the world does not come from the world, but from the tradition of cultural practices in which we have grown up. "The pursuit of general laws, the capacity of science to produce accurate portrayals of its subject matter, the possibility of scientific progression toward objective truth, and the right to claims of scientific expertise are all undermined" (p. 1026). Gergen and Gergen are among those researchers who seek other ways of inquiry that converge on discourse and rhetoric about the situatedness of research and seeking multiple opinions (cf. also other chapters in Denzin & Lincoln, 2000a). Extreme relativism of this kind is not productive in empirical sciences (Poortinga, 1992a); it has been qualified as a "flight from science and reason" (Gross, Levitt, & Lewis, 1996) and it has been shown to be incapable of exposing even hoax arguments (cf. Sokal, 1996a, 1996b).

In the present book we advocate that complementarity should be sought between qualitative and quantitative research methods. This can be done in two ways. First, theoretical distinctions can be made between domains of inquiry more suited to one kind of methodology and domains more suited to another kind. We shall return to this point in the next chapter, where we discuss theoretical issues on the relationship between behavior and culture. Second, one can draw a distinction between the formulation of a theory or interpretation, and the examination of scientific statements with a view to establishing whether they are valid or invalid. An analogous pair of terms is that of scientific discovery and justification. A third pair, perhaps the most widely known, is exploration and verification (including falsification), the two parts of the empirical cycle. Both aspects of scientific inquiry are equally real, and equally needed. However, it appears that qualitative methodology is more oriented toward discovery, and quantitative methodology towards justification. But this distinction is not acceptable to many qualitative researchers (for example, Erlandson, Harris, Skipper, & Allen, 1993).

## Emic and etic orientations

One early attempt in cross-cultural psychology to address many of the issues raised in the previous section is captured in the distinction between **emic** and **etic approaches**. These terms were coined by Pike (1967) in analogy with phonetics and phonemics. In the field of linguistics phonetics refers to the study of general aspects of vocal sounds and sound production; phonemics is the study of the sounds used in a particular language. Berry (1969) has summarized Pike's comments on the emic–etic distinction as it applies in cross-cultural psychology. This summary is presented in table 11.1.

Many qualitative researchers argue that behavior in its full complexity can only be understood within the context of the culture in which it occurs. In the emic approach an attempt is made to look at phenomena and their interrelationships (structure) through the eyes of the people native to a particular culture, avoiding the imposition of a priori notions and ideas from one's own culture on the people studied. This point of view finds its origin in cultural anthropology where, via the method of participant observation, the researcher tries to look at the norms, values, motives, and customs of the members of a particular community in their own terms.

The danger of an etic approach is that the concepts and notions of researchers are rooted in and influenced by their cultural background. They are working with "imposed" etics (Berry, 1969, p. 124), or "pseudo" etics (Triandis, Malpass, & Davidson, 1972, p. 6). The goal of empirical analysis is to progressively change the "imposed" etics to match the emic viewpoint of the culture studied. This should lead eventually to the formulation of "derived" etics which are valid cross-culturally.

More extensive listings of distinctive features between emic and etic have appeared in the literature (Pelto & Pelto, 1981; Ekstrand & Ekstrand, 1986), which further subdivide the contrasts listed in table 11.1. On the other hand, the emic–etic distinction has also been criticized, notably by Jahoda (1977, 1983). In cultural anthropology, where they originated, Jahoda notes that the terms etic and emic are

**Table 11.1** The emic and etic approaches

| Emic approach | Etic approach |
| --- | --- |
| Studies behavior from within the system | Studies behavior from a position outside the system |
| Examines only one culture | Examines many cultures, comparing them |
| Structure discovered by the analyst | Structure created by the analyst |
| Criteria are relative to internal characteristics | Criteria are considered absolute or universal |

From Berry, 1969

used at the level of cultural systems; they are research orientations. In cross-cultural psychology, interest is primarily focussed on the measurement of variables and the analysis of relationships between variables. To label research orientations with the same term as one used for types of variables may be confusing.

The literature is not very informative when one is looking for empirical procedures to separate the emic from the etic. Berry (1969, 1989; see also Segall et al., 1999) has suggested an iterative approach. Researchers will typically start with an imposed etic. They will scrutinize their conceptions and methods for culture appropriateness in an emic phase. Insofar as the search leads to similarities, derived etics will be identified in terms of which valid comparisons can be made, at least across the cultures concerned. Extension of the research can ultimately lead to so much evidence that it can be reasonably concluded that a psychological characteristic is universally present. At the same time, emic explorations within cultural settings should allow the identification of what is culture specific in psychological functioning (Berry, 1999b).

In discussions of the emic–etic distinction, the shortcomings and pitfalls of the traditional psychometric and experimental methods are emphasized, but research projects are still guided by the principles of the experimental paradigm, to be described later in this chapter. This means that researchers tend to make a distinction between independent and dependent variables, and that they favor the use of standardized methods (so that studies can be replicated) when testing hypotheses.

In cultural approaches the emic–etic distinction sometimes is rejected as essentially insufficient. The types of problem that lend themselves to experimental and psychometric analysis are often seen as trivial for the analysis of behavior in context. Instead, authors in cultural psychology recommend descriptive and interpretive methods that find their roots in the culture that is being studied (i.e., what we call here an emic approach).

## Qualitative approaches in cross-cultural psychology

As mentioned above, the distinction between qualitative and quantitative research in cross-cultural psychology has much overlap with that between culturalist and culture-comparative perspectives (e.g., Greenfield, 1997a; Ratner, 1997; Valsiner, 1987). Methodologically cultural psychology can perhaps be summarized in three points: First, the appropriate level of analysis is the cultural system in which the behavior occurs, rather than the level of separate variables. The ethnographic literature abounds with examples showing that the meaning of behavior patterns is dependent on the rules and customs of the society in which it is observed. It is obvious that experiments and measurement by means of standardized tests and questionnaires hardly have a place in such approaches. Behavior is usually described and interpreted on the basis of observations in natural settings and records of historical antecedents. Thus, Paranjpe's (1984, 1998) presentation of Indian personality (see ch. 4) is informed primarily by Hindu ancient scriptures that continue to play a role in contemporary Indian society.

Second, there is an emphasis on processes of individual development and change in interaction with the cultural environment. These dynamic aspects require longitudinal observation studies of interactions between the individual and the environment. Moreover, it is claimed that the dynamics of development cannot be captured in experiments, which essentially assume a static relationship between independent and dependent variables. In studies of development, as discussed in ch. 2, development is often inferred from differences in scores; it is not directly observed. A more direct approach where researchers try to stay close to the observations has been illustrated by Rogoff, Mistry, Göncü, & Mosier (1993). In their study of guided participation they present data from narratives and narrative case descriptions, and provide close analyses of the meaning of events, as well as graphs and statistics. They wrote: "Our analysis was a process of abstraction from contextually rich ethnographic analyses of the data from each family to a systematic examination of the generality and variations in patterns appearing in the 14 families of the four cultural communities" (p. 33). In a review of methods for cultural psychology, Greenfield (1997a) has emphasized the monitoring of events in context, allowing for the observation of developmental change. She stressed the importance of analysis of culture as an ongoing process, drawing on information from members of the community that was being studied. One method that Greenfield recommends is the use of video recording; it provides a good access to ongoing behavior.

The third point is that in cultural psychology there is limited place for comparison of data, since the meaning of behavior, including behavior solicited by psychological instruments, is seen as relative to the cultural context. This implies that cultural psychologists often reject the use in other societies of methods and instruments originating from Western settings (e.g., Greenfield, 1997b). However, on this point the contrast is not clear as researchers with a culturalist view sometimes report quantitative comparisons of scores (e.g., Shweder et al., 1990; Kitayama et al., 1997; see ch. 4).

Earlier on we introduced validity as a touchstone for meaningful scientific inquiry. Jahoda (e.g., 1990b), who has argued in favor of the analysis of behavior as it functions in a cultural system, has given examples showing how ethnographers go through a process of postulating hypotheses on the basis of certain field observations and then testing these by checking whether other observations fit. Although these validation procedures are post hoc, they reflect a serious concern for validity. This concern is also found in concepts like "transparency" and "credibility"; the researcher has to report how an interpretation was arrived at (Guba & Lincoln, 1994).

Greenfield (1997b) has emphasized three forms of validity as particularly relevant for cultural psychology. The first is interpretive validity (cf. Maxwell, 1992), which is concerned with communication between researcher and the target group. Interpretive validity implies "(1) understanding the communicational and epistemological presuppositions of our subjects, and (2) making sure that all data collection procedures conform to these presuppositions" (p. 316). The second form is ecological validity, which addresses the question of to what extent the data solicited by a research procedure have relevance outside the research context. Greenfield argues that ecological validity is ensured when studying naturally occurring rather than laboratory behavior. However, it is not quite clear how on the basis of ecological validity, the validity of the interpretations of data can be substantiated (or falsfied). The third form of validity is theoretical validity, reflecting concerns of what in quantitative research traditions is called construct validity.

Validity remains an Achilles heel of much qualitative research, also in cultural psychology. With most of the several forms of validity that have been distinguished (cf. Denzin & Lincoln, 2000a) the correctness of an interpretation of data is beyond empirical scrutiny by others. Unless a permanent record is kept, non-standardized methods of data collection cannot be replicated and checked for errors of assessment and interpretation. By virtue of the absence of standardized and replicable methods, the entire research process (selection of events, assessment, and interpretation) to an important extent becomes concentrated in the person of the researcher. The history of psychology makes sufficiently clear that this is a questionable kind of practice (cf. Poortinga, 1997).

## Designing culture-comparative studies

The quantitative tradition in cross-cultural psychology tends to follow the canons of experimental methodology and psychometrics, as found in most areas of psychology. According to Van de Vijver and Leung (1997a) four common types of culture-comparative studies can be distinguished. These are presented in table 11.2.

In the table the first distinction is between exploratory research and hypothesis testing. Exploratory studies are conducted when researchers have few ideas about what they can expect to find. As we shall see later in this chapter, there are all kinds of factors leading to differences between cultural groups that are unrelated to the research question. This makes exploratory research vulnerable to erroneous interpretation and for this reason we shall concentrate on hypothesis testing in this section. The second distinction in table 11.2 is between studies that consider contextual factors, and those that do not. The design of the former

**Table 11.2** Four common types of cross-cultural studies

| Consideration of contextual factors | Orientation | |
| --- | --- | --- |
|  | Hypothesis testing | Exploration |
| No | Generalizability | Psychological differences |
| Yes | Theory driven | External validation |

From Van de Vijver & Leung, 1997a

kind of study can be called culture informed; in the latter kind cultural factors may be referred to in the interpretation of differences, but this can only happen in an ad hoc fashion.

In external validation studies, variables from the cultural context are brought into a study at the design stage. Observed differences on a variable of interest can then be explained in terms of such variables. In theory-driven studies the explanatory variables are part of the theoretical framework that is examined. Cultural populations can be selected beforehand and specific hypotheses formulated. This is the kind of study that probably will most advance our knowledge, since more than in the other kinds, alternative explanations are ruled out. In generalizability studies the researcher is interested in the question of whether findings obtained in one cultural setting can be replicated elsewhere. Replicated findings are usually interpreted as support for the validity of instruments and/or theory. However, when cross-cultural differences are observed, these can only be interpreted post hoc. This is also the case with studies of psychological differences, the most common type in the cross-cultural literature, according to Van de Vijver and Leung. Here the researcher administers one or more instruments in different cultures to explore similarities and differences. Needless to say, findings from such studies are vulnerable to erroneous interpretation.

A hypothesis-testing study is based on theoretical conceptions. To test a hypothesis derived from the theory, a study is designed for which data have to be collected in various cultures. In the following chapter we shall discuss how in such studies "culture" amounts to some sort of "treatment" or "condition," in the sense of an experiment (Strodtbeck, 1964).

The leading research design in psychological research continues to be the controlled experiment; however, it is seldom available to cross-cultural researchers. This is unfortunate, because the results of a well-designed experiment are less open to alternative interpretations than those obtained with other forms of scientific inquiry. In the experimental paradigm a distinction is made between the independent variable (denoting a set of stimulus conditions or treatments) and the dependent variable (describing a set of behaviors or responses). An experiment is meant to investigate the antecedent–consequent relationship between these two variables.

In a well-designed experiment the researcher has control over the treatments administered to the subjects in the various experimental conditions, as well as over ambient variables. In addition, the researcher can assign subjects at random to the various conditions so that any prior differences between them which may affect their responses are randomly distributed across conditions. However, for many studies in real-life situations, intact groups are used that differ from each other in many ways. Each variable that potentially has an effect on the dependent variable has to be taken into account in the explanation of the observed differences; otherwise it leaves room for an alternative explanation of the differences (Campbell, 1969; Cook & Campbell, 1979).

**Table 11.3** Control over treatment conditions and the assignment of respondents

| Control over subject allocation | Control over treatment (Control over treatment and *most* ambient events) | Control over treatment and *few* ambient events | No control of treatment or ambient events (Selection of populations) | (Ad hoc choice of populations) |
|---|---|---|---|---|
| Random assignment of subjects to treatments | True experiment | | | |
| Group membership, *weak* effects on exchangeability | | Quasi-experiment | | |
| Group membership, *strong* effects on exchangeability | | | Cross-cultural comparative study | Cross-cultural studies with post-test only |

After Malpass & Poortinga, 1986

In cross-cultural research it is difficult to rule out all plausible alternative explanations. There are two considerations: the allocation of subjects, and the lack of experimental control over cultural conditions that are taken as independent variables. Much of our argument is summarized in table 11.3. Down the vertical axis three categories of subject allocation are indicated. On the horizontal axis there are four categories that differ in the degree of control by the researcher over the actual treatment and over confounding variables.

In a laboratory experiment subjects are allocated at random to experimental conditions. It is a plausible assumption that if the subjects had been allocated differently, this would not have changed the results. Furthermore, the researcher ensures that there are no known factors on which those assigned to the various conditions differ systematically.

In studies with already existing groups of subjects the allocation of subjects is not strictly random. Such studies of non-equivalent groups are referred to as quasi-experiments. Consider an educational research project where different teaching methods are administered to school classes with a view to comparing the effectiveness of these methods. On some variables there will be systematic differences between schools, for example in the competence of the teaching staff and the average socioeconomic status of pupils. However, the set of variables on which differences will occur is limited. A researcher would not be concerned if some children moved from one school to another prior to the start of the study.

In the case of cultural populations the set of variables on which subjects differ is immense and the differences may also be larger than within a single society. Socialization practices, availability of words for certain concepts, education, religious beliefs, and access to mass communication media, are only some of the many variables that can differ between groups. The impact on design becomes evident when one tries to imagine subject exchange between cultures; this would defeat the purpose of the study, since subjects are inherently linked to one culture.

Another feature which distinguishes an experiment from a non-experimental study is the control by the experimenter over the treatment conditions. In the laboratory researchers define the treatment, although even their control over ambient variables, like the motivation of participants, is imperfect. In field testing, for example of educational programs, the lack of precision in control tends to be greater, especially when the treatment extends over weeks or even months. In addition to the treatment, pupils undergo many other experiences that can affect their performance. However, within the limitations of administration accuracy the researcher still has control over the treatment as such.

Direct control over treatment is usually not available in cross-cultural research. Cultural factors extend their influence over a long period of time. The effect of a postulated cultural factor is typically inferred post hoc on the basis of ethnographic descriptions. Cross-cultural researchers have to be aware of this when interpreting their findings.

In the cross-cultural literature some powerful psychological influences have been identified, each of which has an effect on a broad range of measurements. The most important is school education, Western style. It forms part of a complex of which literacy, test-taking experience, urbanization, economic wealth, and acculturation all form part. These variables are largely subsumed in the sociopolitical context of the ecocultural framework (fig. 1.1). It is hard even to imagine a psychological measurement unaffected by such variables.

## Controls

The absence of direct control through manipulation of treatment, and through subject allocation, does not mean that valid explanation is out of reach; it is only more difficult to achieve than in other areas of psychology. We shall briefly mention four kinds of measure for reducing plausible alternative explanations of differences between cultural groups (cf. also Malpass & Poortinga, 1986; Van de Vijver & Leung, 1997a, 1997b).

The cultural populations should be selected a priori on the basis of ethnographic descriptions, and not because the samples happen to available. It is in post-test-only designs (Cook & Campbell, 1979) that vulnerability to incorrect interpretation is unacceptably high. It is only within the context of a theory that differences between cultural groups on some dependent variable can be predicted from their position on an independent variable (Malpass, 1977). When groups are included for reasons other than their position on the independent variable, the most important form of experimental control in a comparative study is lost. Many studies of ethnic or minority groups are a case in point. In this kind of research, the selection of a minority and the majority within a society is confounded. Differences between these groups can be ascribed to factors in the minority, the majority, or the interaction between the two.

A second strategy for eliminating competing alternatives is available if the dependent variable can be expressed as a function of two, or more, separate measures. An example is the score that can be obtained by taking the difference between two measurements. For example, Cole et al. (1968) studied visual information processing among Kpelle and North American respondents (see ch. 8). It was found that the Kpelle did less well in estimating the number of dots in a tachistoscopically presented display than subjects from the USA. This finding is of little interest by itself, since many explanations can be thought of which have nothing to do with the processing of visual information. Cole and his colleagues also established that the intercultural differences were larger when the dots formed regular patterns than when they were randomly scattered. Of many uncontrolled variables (like motivation of the subjects, comprehension of the task, etc.), it can be reasonably assumed that they had an equal effect in the two experimental conditions. Therefore, it is a plausible conclusion that the American respondents made more use of the organization of dots in the stimulus displays, a finding that probably has educational relevance.

A third form of control open to the cross-cultural researcher is the elimination of effects of irrelevant variables through statistical analysis (e.g., by means of analysis of co-variance or regression techniques). Although some alternative explanations can be ruled out, statistical control remains a poor alternative to experimental control (Cook & Campbell, 1979). Of course, the elimination of a particular explanation through statistical analysis requires that relevant information is available. This means that the variables that can provide this information have to be included in the design of a study.

The fourth type of control involves the extension of the database from which an interpretation is derived. An important strategy is to use more than one method of measurement. One can have more confidence in a finding if it is established not only with one method (most often a self-report questionnaire), but also with other methods. The distinction between convergent and discriminant validity (Campbell & Fiske, 1959) is relevant here. Evidence about validity can be obtained from relationships between variables that are expected on theoretical and/or empirical grounds; this is convergent validation. Evidence can also be derived from the absence of relationships between variables for which no relationship is expected; this is discriminant validation. For example, in ch. 5 we mentioned research by Scribner and Cole (1981), who found a relationship between schooling and abstract thinking among the Vai, but failed to find a relationship between literacy and abstract thinking. The second finding can be seen as a case of discriminant validity; it provided negative evidence for the belief that literacy is the major factor in abstract thinking. It may be added that Scribner and Cole chose to do their research among the Vai because of the presence of different forms of literacy and schooling. Such a separation of variables that in most societies are closely linked (most children learn to read and write at school) is called unconfounding.

## Sampling

Three levels of sampling will be distinguished. First a choice has to be made regarding which cultural populations are to be included in a study. Then the question arises of whether or not the selection can be restricted to certain subgroups within each culture. Finally, it has to be decided how individuals are to be selected within each culture or group (cf. Lonner & Berry, 1986b; Van de Vijver & Leung, 1997b).

There are two acceptable strategies for the selection of cultures in comparative studies. Most common is the choice of only a few cultures clearly differing on some variable that provides a contrast of interest to the cross-cultural psychologist. This amounts to theory-guided selection. The second and less common strategy is to draw a sample of cultures that can be considered representative of all the cultures in the world. It is not an acceptable strategy to select a few countries on the basis of chance meetings at a conference with colleagues who are willing to collect data, or on the basis of one's interest in visiting a particular country. Data collection should be dictated by a theoretically interesting contrast between the cultures concerned, rather than by mere opportunity.

This means that cultures should be selected which differ on the postulated independent variable that is the focus of research. The initial selection has to be made on the basis of available information, for example from the ethnographic literature (cf. ch. 9). It is recommended that a check be carried out on whether the presumed differences on the independent variable indeed are present. This was done by Segall et al. (1966), who in their study on visual illusions (cf. ch. 8) included a questionnaire with items on environmental features. It was to be completed by local researchers for the group in which they collected the data.

Sometimes a culture is included in a study to serve as a reference standard. If the researchers take their own culture as a reference they can check whether the results (levels and patterns of scores) conform to prior expectations. This is particularly useful when newly constructed methods are used. If the findings in a familiar culture do not fit expectations, the validity of the results in other cultures is all the more questionable.

Additional cultures can be included in a study to obtain a better distribution over the range of an independent variable; this is the technique of stratified sampling (e.g., Kish, 1965). With an extension of the number of cultures, sooner or later the strategy of drawing a sample at random from all the cultures in the world has to be considered. The size of such a sample depends on the degree of accuracy required, but for most variables it should certainly not contain fewer than twenty or twenty-five cases.[2] For Osgood's Atlas of Affective Meaning (see ch. 7) data

---

[2] A general rule cannot be given. The accuracy of results is dependent on how reliably societies can be distinguished from each other on the variable concerned (see Cohen (1988) for further information).

were collected in thirty countries, but this did not form a random sample of the world's cultures. For one thing, the respondents all had to be literate. This is also true for the sampling in other large-scale psychological studies that have been reported, for example, by Hofstede (1980) on work-related values, and by Schwartz (1994) on values, mentioned in ch. 3. In cultural anthropology there are a large number of hologeistic studies; these are studies with samples from cultures all over the world, including non-literate societies. They are based on available descriptions, mainly from the HRAF mentioned in chs. 2 and 9.

There are two aspects of sampling that have received far more attention in anthropology than in cross-cultural psychology. The first is known as Galton's problem (Naroll, 1970c; Naroll et al., 1980). It has to do with the spreading of cultural characteristics through contacts between groups. If two cultures have a similar score on a variable, this may be due to the exchange of knowledge and artifacts through contact and communication (called diffusion). As we have seen in ch. 9, Naroll has suggested ways to avoid this problem that are based on the assumption that similarities between neighboring groups are more likely to reflect diffusion than are similarities between groups living at a large geographical distance from each other. After all, probability of diffusion over great distances is less than between neighbors.

The second problem is at what level cultures should be defined. At the most general level Murdock (1967) distinguished six cultural areas: sub-Saharan Africa, Asia, Australasia, circum-Mediterranean, North America, and South America. On many dimensions of interest to psychologists (e.g., literacy, socialization practices, collectivism) the range of variation within these cultural areas is about as large as the variation between these areas. Therefore, selection of a sample stratified according to areas (e.g., picking an equal number of cultures from each) serves a useful purpose in only a limited number of instances.

At a somewhat less general level societies are (too) often confounded with nation states. In articles published in the *Journal of Cross-Cultural Psychology* and the *International Journal of Psychology*, "culture" quite typically coincides with "country." In cultural anthropology this is considered an unacceptable practice (Naroll, 1970b). The definition of a culture, more properly named a "culture-bearing unit" (or "cultunit"), has to coincide with the level at which a variable is operating. If political organization is of interest, the nation state is the appropriate unit of selection. But in a study of the psychological effects of tonality in language the unit of selection should be the language group (cf. ch. 6). Child rearing practices usually will have to be defined on smaller culture-bearing units, as there can be large differences within a country, for example between urban and rural groups. The underlying principles can be summarized in two points. First, the definition of a culture-bearing unit depends on the nature of the independent variable studied. Second, culture-bearing units have to be selected to cover adequately the range of variation on this variable.

The relative lack of concern among cross-cultural psychologists for a precise definition of culture-bearing units can also have implications for the selection of (sub)groups within these units. It is usually a fallacy to assume homogeneity within cultures with respect to the factors studied. Most, if not all, psychological variables show systematic variation between the members of a culture-bearing unit. This implies that there are virtually always groups which are distinguishable in terms of high and low scores. Therefore, the size of a cross-cultural difference will depend directly on the selection of particular groups.

It is almost impossible to select a group in one culture so that it will precisely match a group in another culture. Strong warnings have been issued against the use of matched samples in culture-comparative studies (Draguns, 1982; Lonner & Berry, 1986b). The crux of the objections is that matching on one variable almost without exception leads to mismatching on other variables. Suppose a researcher would like samples of Americans and Africans matched on education. Educated Africans are more likely than the average citizen of their country to have a high income and a high social status, while they may be less likely to value traditional norms and customs.

In a representative sample each member of the population of interest has an equal probability of selection. This requires random selection of individuals. The samples used in cross-cultural research seldom, if ever, even get close to meeting this requirement. It depends on the distributions of relevant variables in the populations to be investigated whether deviations from a random selection procedure have serious effects on the outcome of a study. Again, the sampling procedure is rather immaterial when individual differences (within-group variance) are small compared to the differences between cultures (between-group variance). But for many psychological variables, the former clearly exceed the latter (e.g. Poortinga & Van Hemert, 2001).

The following conclusions emerge from this discussion. First, cross-cultural researchers should be careful not to generalize their results to large cultural populations of which the subjects tested are not selected by some random procedure. As far as we can see, the use of smaller, more precisely defined, culture-bearing units will lead to more precision both methodologically and theoretically. A consequence of this recommendation is the need for a fairly detailed description of the populations in all comparative studies. Second, the requirement for random selection of individuals within the population of interest applies in cross-cultural psychology just as much as in other areas of psychology.

## Psychological data in cultural context

In earlier chapters we have come across studies at the individual level (using psychological tests and behavioral observations), as well as population-level research (with data from the HRAF and field ethnography). In this section we shall discuss how these two levels can be brought together (see Berry, 1980b).

Traditionally, much of the discipline of psychology has attempted to comprehend behavior as a function of stimuli impinging upon an individual. The approach of ecological psychology (e.g., Barker, 1969, 1978; Brunswik, 1957) has noted that the stimuli usually employed in psychology represent only a very narrow range of all possible stimuli, and that they tend to be artificial in character. As a result, ecological psychology has emphasized the need to study behavior in more naturalistic contexts. Similarly, as we have mentioned frequently, cross-cultural psychology proposes that we should be attending to broad ranges of *contexts* drawn from a cross-section of cultures.

First, at a high level of generality there is the *ecological context,* or the "natural-cultural habitat" of Brunswik (1957), or the "pre-perceptual world" of Barker (1969). It consists of all the relatively stable and permanent characteristics of the population that provide the context for activity. In terms of fig. 1.1, it includes the population-level variables identified in the ecological context, the sociopolitical context, and the general cultural adaptations made by a group. The ecological context serves as the basis for the emergence of customs of a population; these are the complex, sometimes longstanding, shared behavior patterns that gradually have evolved in response to ecological demands.

Nested in this ecological context are two levels of what Lewin (1936) has referred to as the "life space" or "psychological world" of the individual. The first, the *experiential context*, is that pattern of recurrent experiences that provides a basis for individual learning and development; it is essentially the set of independent variables that cross-cultural psychology tries to spot as being operative for individuals in a particular habitat during the development of behavioral characteristics. These variables include such day-to-day experiences as child rearing practices, occupational training, and education. Individual consequences of the experiential context are reflected in the behavior repertoire, the relatively stable complex of behaviors that individuals have learned over time in the recurrent experiential or learning context. Included are the skills and traits and attitudes which have been nurtured in particular roles, or acquired by specific training or education, whether formal or informal. The other aspect of the psychological world is the *situational context*, the limited set of environmental circumstances (the "setting" of Barker, 1969) which may be observed to account for the performance of particular behaviors at a given time and place. Particular settings lead to particular actions, i.e., the behaviors that appear in response to immediate stimulation or experience.

Finally, a fourth level, namely the *assessment context*, represents those environmental characteristics, such as test items or stimulus conditions, that are designed by the psychologist to elicit a particular response or test score. The assessment context may or may not be nested in the first three contexts; the degree to which it is nested can be said to represent the ecological validity of the task. In research studies, the assessment context usually is reflected in scores derived from the behaviors that are observed, measured, and recorded during psychological assessment (such as experiments, interviews, or testing). If the assessment context is part of the other contexts, then the data will be representative of the repertoire of the organism, and the customs of the population. It is difficult for experimental approaches to contribute to an understanding of relationships at the various levels while collecting data almost exclusively in an assessment context. The qualitative methods of cultural psychology emphasize and allow more flexibility in this respect. Cross-cultural psychology usually attempts to work at all four levels, thereby linking data obtained from individuals to the various contexts in which they occur.

Thus, a frequent goal of cross-cultural research is to explain individual-level differences between cultures on some dependent variable in terms of context variables, which are population-level variables. An approach for analyzing the effects of context variables on outcome variables has been described by Poortinga and Van de Vijver (1987). They see a cross-cultural study as successful when all differences between cultures on an outcome variable have been explained in terms of context variables. Their analysis includes a dependent variable, samples of data from two or more cultures, and one or more context variables (measured at the individual or the population level).

The analysis starts with determining whether there is a significant difference between cultures on the outcome (dependent) variable. If this is the case, the next step in the analysis establishes how much of this between-culture variance can be explained by each of the available context variables. More and more of the variance is "peeled off," until ideally no difference between the cultures is left to be explained. The goal of the analysis is to split the total effect of "culture" on the dependent variable into components that can be accounted for by more specific context variables.[3]

When using population-level variables to explain individual differences, it is an assumption of such a procedure that variables assess the same traits at the two levels; in other words that variables at the two levels are equivalent. The need to distinguish between population and individual differences has been recognized for a long time, among others by Leung and Bond (1989) and by Hofstede (1980). The use of data collected at one level to explain phenomena at another level can lead to errors or fallacies in interpretation. A distinction can be made between aggregation errors (due to applying individual data at the population level) and disaggregation errors (due to applying population-level data to individuals). An example of disaggregation is the inapplicability of a population statistic, like the percentage of pregnancies in a population, to individual women. An example of an aggregation error is the explanation of population differences in intelligence in similar terms as individual differences. We can refer to the example of Furby mentioned in ch. 10, illustrating how differences in food intake could lead to population differences in body height quite apart from genetic factors that may be determining individual differences in height.

In summary, researchers should employ methods that will give them access to both population-level and individual-level information that is sufficiently rich to

---

[3] Statistically the analysis takes the form of a stepwise multiple regression analysis, or an analysis of covariance. Poortinga and Van de Vijver (1987) point out that context variables have to be carefully chosen; they should not be in any way confounded with the outcome variable, and they should be measured at least at an ordinal-, and preferably at an interval-scale level.

provide a full interpretation of their results. All too often in cross-cultural psychology we find studies that leap from a very limited knowledge of the ecological or so-ciopolitical context (for example "they are herders," or "they are immigrants") to an explanation of the data obtained from an experiment or test.

## Analysis of equivalence

"For a specific observation a belch is a belch and nepotism is nepotism. But within an inferential framework, a belch is an 'insult' or a 'compliment' and nepotism is 'corruption' or 'responsibility'." This comment from Przeworksi and Teune (1970, p. 92) puts in a nutshell the view that the meaning of behavior is dependent on the cultural context in which it occurs. This is not only true for behavior as observed by ethnographers, but also for reactions elicited with inter-views (whether open or standardized), focus groups, questionnaires, and psycho-metric tests. When scores on an instrument cannot be interpreted in the same way (for example, in predicting a criterion or measuring an outcome) and thus do not have the same psychological meaning in different cultural contexts, they are called non-comparable, inequivalent, or culturally biased. In this section we shall de-scribe some psychometric approaches to analyzing whether or not data can be taken as meeting conditions of **equivalence**. In box 11-2 an outline is given of the rationale underlying much of this presentation.

Concern about the equivalence of data should begin right at the start of a cross-cultural research project. In a set of guidelines on the cross-cultural adaptation of educational and psychological tests, mentioned in ch. 5, it is recommended that the development of instruments should be carried out with participants of all cultural populations involved in a study (Hambleton, 1994; Van de Vijver & Hambleton, 1996). However, in most culture-comparative research use is made of existing in-struments. It is this more common situation that we shall further examine.

### Analysis of stimulus content

A first step in an analysis of equivalence is to look at the content of the stimuli (or items) in an instrument. A close scrutiny of each stimulus is necessary to iden-tify possible peculiarities in meaning, or other reasons why that stimulus might be inappropriate in a particular culture and should not be used. There are two kinds of methods, namely judgmental methods and methods for translation equivalence.

In judgmental methods experts are asked to give an opinion about the content of stimuli. Usually they evaluate for each stimulus whether or not it belongs to the domain of behavior of interest, and whether or not it presupposes specific knowl-edge or experiences more readily available in one of the groups to be compared.

For a proper evaluation, the judges should have an intimate knowledge of the cultures in a comparative study, as well as of the theory and notions behind an instrument. Judgmental methods have been mainly employed in the USA to trace

## Box 11.2  A definition of cultural bias

In a cross-cultural comparison of psychological data one can distinguish three aspects: (1) the groups of persons, A and B, to be compared, (2) a psychological concept C (e.g., a trait or behavioral domain) to which the comparison pertains, and (3) data on a variable D from both groups. A comparison of the data can be misleading for two reasons. First, the concept C may not be invariant for the groups A and B. A non-psychological example is that, if C corresponds to weight in group A and to length in group B, a comparison of measures from A and B makes logically no sense. Something like this can happen when a test of arithmetic with verbally formulated items creates problems of language, for example for migrant children.

Second, the relationship of observed score variable D in the two groups, D(a) and D(b), with the scale of concept C may not be identical. An example is measurements in degrees Centigrade and degrees Fahrenheit that are not related to the concept of temperature in the same way; comparison on the basis of temperature measured in Celsius for A and in Fahrenheit for B obviously would be misleading.

It is important to note that in this argument a measurement scale or observed score variable ($^\circ$F or $^\circ$C) is sharply distinguished from the underlying concept (temperature). Inferences are made in terms of the concept, thus the concept scale is the actual comparison scale. Differences in scores for two groups A and B are of little relevance per se; it is the inferences or interpretations that matter. With this in mind the following definition of cultural bias can be formulated.

Data are biased or inequivalent when differences in observed scores between populations are not matched by corresponding differences on the scale of comparison (Poortinga, 1989, p. 738; Poortinga, 1995).

The consequence of this definition is that bias is not taken as a quality of an instrument per se, but as a quality of the inferences or interpretations derived from cross-cultural differences in scores.

In psychology the concept of interest usually is a non-observable or hypothetical construct. The scale of such a construct is unknown and one may just as well use the observed scores of one of the groups to represent the underlying construct. Analysis of equivalence then centers around the question of whether or not the scales of observed variables are invariant across cultural populations. Analysis of this question is possible by analyzing relationships between the data sets from the cultural populations involved in a study.

items in educational achievement and intellectual ability tests that are biased against women or ethnocultural groups. A review can be found in Tittle (1982; cf. also Van Leest, 1997). Although judges can have fairly strong opinions as to which items are biased, these ideas quite often are not confirmed by empirical findings; it has proven difficult to predict on which items a certain group will show a relatively low performance level. In cross-cultural studies it is often not easy to find qualified judges; the least that can be done to identify inappropriate stimuli is to consult with colleagues in cultures involved in a project.

There is a need for a careful check on translation equivalence whenever verbal stimuli or instructions are used cross-culturally (Brislin, 1976, 1980, 1986). Usually researchers are satisfied that translation equivalence has been attained when, after translation from the original language in the target language followed by independent back translation, the original wording is reproduced more or less precisely. The procedure requires that translators are available who are fluent in both the original language and the target language. The forward translation and back translation procedure sometimes has to be repeated by an independent team before the original version is reproduced with sufficient precision. Brislin has pointed out that it is often necessary to change the original stimulus, because it is found to be simply untranslatable. He recommends that the original and the modified version in the source language both be administered to a group of subjects to check whether the changes have had any systematic effect on the scores.

The process of translation is closely linked to what Werner and Campbell (1970) have called "decentering." Since an instrument is developed within a particular cultural context it will contain certain features characteristic of that culture which have little to do with the trait that is being assessed. Such features have to be avoided in cross-cultural comparison, with the consequence that the original instrument also has to be modified. This may imply that not only a change in wording, but also a change in stimulus content, is needed. Thus we have to reckon with the possibility that what is referred to in a stimulus does not exist at all in some other culture. Elimination of the stimulus concerned is then the only solution. If this happens for more than an occasional stimulus, cultural decentering raises a more fundamental question, namely whether the non-equivalence of stimuli points to the cross-cultural non-identity of the trait being measured by the instrument. We shall come back to this point.

Another difficulty the researcher has to face in establishing linguistic equivalence is that bilinguals when filling out a questionnaire in a certain language adapt their answers somewhat according to the stereotypes which they hold about the culture concerned (e.g., Bond, 1983). Brislin (e.g., 1986) has pointed out that for the assessment of translation equivalence, monolinguals as well as bilinguals are needed; the latter usually form a subgroup that is not representative of the total population.

## Psychometric analyses

The psychometric analysis of equivalence of data sets obtained from samples of different cultural populations is based on presumed order or structure. For example, items in an attitude questionnaire can be ordered from highly positive to highly negative; items in an ability test range from easy to difficult. For equivalent or comparable scores it is reasonable to expect that cross-culturally the same order of item difficulty or preference will be observed. Similarly, it is to be expected that correlations between variables in one culture should also be found in other cultures if an instrument addresses the same trait. This kind of consideration can lead to the formulation of conditions which should be met by equivalent data, but are unlikely to be satisfied by inequivalent data. Van de Vijver and Leung (1997a, 1997b) have proposed a distinction between three levels of equivalence which we follow here (see also ch. 4).

## Levels of equivalence

The first question to be answered is whether an instrument reflects the same underlying concept or construct across cultures. For example, there is evidence that in African conceptions of intelligence social aspects are important, but these are hardly covered by (Western) intelligence batteries that focus on analytic cognitive abilities (Segall et al., 1999). Similarly, Ho (1996) has argued that the concept of "filial piety," associated with being a good son or daughter for one's parents, covers a much broader range of behavior in China than in Western countries. In both these examples there is a concept that is not quite the same cross-culturally, and thus there can be no common scale, ruling out the possibility of any meaningful comparative measurement. However, more often than not the researcher will be faced with a situation where it is unclear whether or not a concept is the same, and whether an instrument measures this concept in the cultural populations involved in a study. The researcher can then use correlational techniques to examine the interrelationships of the items (or subtests) of an instrument in the various cultures. It is a condition for structural equivalence that the patterns of correlations between items are the same cross-culturally.

Such correlational patterns are usually investigated by means of factor analysis. An exploratory factor analysis in each cultural sample followed by rotation toward a common factor structure is the most time-honored procedure. Factorial agreement can be expressed in various indices of which Tucker's phi is found most often in the literature. There is some disagreement how high the value of this index should be to accept that factors are similar or identical, but a lower limit of .90 is often mentioned for the acceptance of factors as similar (e.g., Van de Vijver & Poortinga, 1994).

Invariance or similarity of factor structures at the individual level and at the population level can be examined as a condition for equivalence at these two levels of aggregation. Expanding on multilevel techniques developed in the field of educational psychology (e.g., Muthén, 1991), Van de Vijver and Poortinga (in press) have described a procedure based on exploratory factor analysis. In an illustration of the procedure with the postmaterialism scale of the World Values Survey (Inglehart, 1997; see ch. 3) they could show that it was doubtful whether postmaterialism had the same meaning at the two levels. A restriction of this analysis is that a fairly large number of cultural populations, each with a sample of fair size, are needed for stable outcomes.

The correlation coefficient provides information on the structural or qualitative aspects of the meaning of scores (Is the same concept or dimension being measured?), rather than on the quantitative aspects (Is the measurement in identical scale units?). Hence, similarity in correlation values leaves open the possibility that there are quantitative differences in scores that are not related to the target concept of a measurement instrument (cf. box 9-2). This becomes obvious when one considers the following. If a constant is added to all the scores on a variable, the correlation of that variable with other variables does not change in value. Similarly, if a biasing effect influences all scores in one group but not in other groups, this will not change the value of correlations. In short, the similarity across cultures in the correlations between tests is insufficient to guarantee meaningful comparison of quantitative differences in scores.

There is measurement unit equivalence when the metric of a scale (i.e., the unit of measurement) is the same across groups. If this condition of equivalence is met, quantitative differences between patterns of scores (for example those obtained at various points in time, or for various subscales) can be compared cross-culturally. For example, we have seen earlier on that scores on questionnaires can be differentially affected by response sets cross-culturally, but it may not be unreasonable to assume that such effects will be the same when a questionnaire is administered at various occasions (e.g., before and after a certain intervention).

Full score equivalence has been reached when both the origin (usually the zero point) and the metric of a variable are identical across cultural groups. Quantitative differences on a single score variable can only be interpreted meaningfully when this condition has been satisfied. We shall see later that this form of equivalence is difficult to establish in many cross-cultural studies, definitely when broad concepts such as personality traits or cognitive abilities are being assessed.

The latter two forms of equivalence are both concerned with quantitative aspects of scores. There are various analysis techniques, like regression analysis and analysis of variance, in which conditions can be stipulated to address both these aspects, sometimes even in a single analysis procedure. For example, unequal linear regression functions of test and criterion scores in two cultural groups can be taken as evidence against full score equivalence (level parameter) or measurement unit equivalence (slope). In analysis of variance designs a significant item by culture interaction effect makes full score equivalence questionable.

Structural and metric aspects of bias analysis can be combined when techniques for structural equation modeling are applied, such as LISREL (Jöreskog & Sörbom, 1999). An elegant feature of these techniques is that an ordered set of conditions can be tested, imposing increasingly less strict constraints on equivalence (e.g., Byrne & Campbell, 1999; Little, 1997; Marsh & Byrne, 1993).

## Sources of cultural bias

A lack of equivalence can be due to a host of reasons, which are referred to with the generic term of **cultural bias**. The effects of a biasing factor can be limited to a single item or a few items (e.g., translation errors). This is called item bias or differential item functioning (DIF). The effects can influence also the responses on most or all items, leading to method bias. Finally, bias can pertain to the operationalization or definition of a concept; this is referred to as concept bias or construct bias. An overview of various sources of bias is presented in table 11.4. More extensive overviews can be found in Van de Vijver and Tanzer (1997) and Van de Vijver and Leung (1997b).

It is clear that there is a correspondence between levels of equivalence and sources of bias. This is most evident at the level of concept bias, with factors like unequal notions about concepts, which lead to systematic differences in concept representation across cultures. The consequences for equivalence are least clear in the case of item bias. If only a single item or a few items show evidence of bias, they can be eliminated and this improves the equivalence of scores. However, evidence of item bias or stimulus bias can also be taken as an indication that an instrument does not represent precisely identical traits.

The notion of item bias is immediately clear if one thinks of an example. An item asking for the name of the capital of a country should be much easier

**Table 11.4** An overview of three types of bias and their possible sources

| Kind of bias | Source |
|---|---|
| Construct | Incomplete overlap of definitions of the construct across cultures |
| | Differential appropriateness of item content (e.g., skills do not belong to the repertoire of either cultural group) |
| | Poor sampling of all relevant behaviors (e. g., short instruments covering broad constructs) |
| | Incomplete coverage of the psychological construct |
| Method | Differential social desirability |
| | Differential response styles such as extremity scoring and acquiescence |
| | Differential stimulus familiarity |
| | Lack of comparability of samples (e. g., differences in educational background, age, or gender composition) |
| | Differences in physical testing conditions |
| | Differential familiarity with response procedures |
| | Tester effects |
| | Communication problems between subject and tester in either cultural group |
| Item | Poor item translation |
| | Inadequate item formulation (e. g., complex wording) |
| | One or a few items may invoke additional traits or abilities |
| | Incidental differences in appropriateness of the item content (e. g., topic of item of educational test not in curriculum in one cultural group) |

From Van de Vijver & Poortinga, 1997

for nationals of that country than in other countries. However, item bias can also be the consequence of subtle differences in shades of meaning (Ellis, 1989; Ellis, Becker, & Kimmel, 1993). An item is identified as biased if test takers with the same score on the instrument but belonging to different populations do not have the same probability of giving a certain answer (e.g. "yes" answer, correct answer) for the item (Shepard, Camilli, & Averill, 1981). Thus, the test score variable on the instrument as a whole is used as the standard to evaluate each separate item. Some simple bias indices have been proposed, like the correlation between the difficulty levels of ability test items in two cultures, or between the levels of endorsement of questionnaire items. Another index of item bias is the interaction between items and culture in an analysis of variance.

Psychometrically more sophisticated techniques are based on item response theory (Hambleton, Swaminathan, & Rogers, 1991) or loglinear models (Van der Flier, Mellenbergh, Adèr, & Wijn, 1984). A popular technique for analyzing bias in dichotomous items (e.g., yes–no; right–wrong) is the Mantel–Haenszel procedure (Holland & Wainer, 1993). For items with a graded response scale better use is made of the available information if an analysis of variance is carried out with item score as the dependent variable and score level on the instrument and culture as independent variables. (For overviews of procedures see Van de Vijver & Leung, 1997b; Van de Vijver & Poortinga, 1991.)

It is important to note that analysis techniques as mentioned examine relationships between items within an instrument. With these techniques for internal bias analysis, it is quite possible that method bias (affecting all or most items in an instrument) remains undetected. For the analysis of method bias external standards or criteria are needed. In culture-comparative studies where relevant common criterion variables are hard to find, the analysis of method bias requires considerable effort, because usually extensive additional data have to be obtained. For example, in ch. 5 we have seen that it is difficult to rule out effects of stimulus familiarity as a source of cross-cultural differences in cognitive performance. In table 11.4 sources of method bias are the most numerous. This may reflect the importance of this category of bias that has largely been ignored in cross-cultural research. The main measure against effects of method bias is the standardization of data so that the score distributions in each sample has a mean of 0.0 and a standard deviation of 1.0 (e.g., Leung & Bond, 1989) prior to further analysis. One can then still investigate structural aspects and relative differences between item scores (or subscale scores). However, the precise consequences of such (non-linear) transformations are not always clear (Van de Vijver & Leung, 1997b). In box 11-3 we illustrate how effects of bias that go unnoticed can distort the meaning of cross-cultural differences in score.

Finally, it should be noted that although identification of bias is likely to preempt planned comparisons, the information gathered in the course of bias analysis can also lead to further ideas about the nature of cross-cultural differences.

## Box 11.3  The questionable null hypothesis

In an experimental study, the research hypothesis is accepted when the null hypothesis can be rejected with a certain level of confidence. When testing the null hypothesis two errors can be made. A type I error occurs when the null hypothesis is wrongly rejected. There is no difference between conditions, but the outcome of the test leads the researcher to believe there is. A type II error is made when the null hypothesis is actually false, but not rejected (e.g., Hays, 1988). For the ideal experiment the probability of both types of error can be estimated. The accuracy of a statistical test of the null hypothesis can be improved by increasing the sample size or by replication studies. In other words, the margin of error can be reduced by investing more effort. However, if a difference between groups is due to some other factor than the target trait of a measurement, extension of the database does not lead to a more accurate assessment of the probability of a valid intergroup difference, but to an increased confidence in the erroneous rejection of the null hypothesis.

This is illustrated in figure 11.1. The vertical axis gives the probability that a statistically significant difference (alpha < .05) is found. On the horizontal axis the sample size is given. The broken line gives the probability of a type I error in unbiased data; it is independent of the sample size. The solid lines show that the probability of a significant difference is higher when a "bias" component is added to the scores of one of two groups with an otherwise equal score distribution. The magnitude of the bias is expressed in standard deviation units (i.e., 1/16 sd, 1/8 sd, and 1/4 sd). It is evident that the probability of

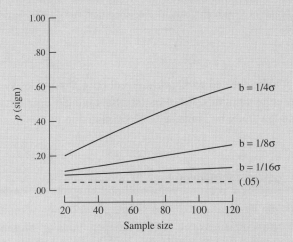

**11.1**  The relationship between sample size and the probability ($p$) that a significant a difference (alpha < .05) will be found resulting from a bias effect (b)
After Malpass & Poortinga, 1986

## Box 11.3 (continued)

a significant difference between the means of the two groups increases with the sample size, as well as with the magnitude of the bias effect.

The thrust of the argument is that the null hypothesis is a fairly meaningless proposition unless the presence of even a small amount of bias can be ruled out with confidence. The implications have been formulated by Malpass and Poortinga (1986, pp. 51–2) as follows:

In view of the high a *priori* probability of ambient factors contributing to the observed differences, the likelihood of erroneous inference is so high that in general the results of cross-cultural comparative studies cannot be taken seriously if alternative explanations are not explicitly considered and, preferably, excluded on the basis of empirical evidence. We feel strongly about this point since it can be argued that the high probability of finding differences in the long run will tend to have cumulative effects on our insights about the impact of cultural variation on behavior.

Another tendency of researchers may strengthen this effect, namely the interpretation of statistically significant differences as "meaningful" or "big." Next to the statistical significance of a difference it is commendable to report what proportion of the total variance is explained by it. In culture-comparative research a convenient way of showing the importance of a difference is the non-overlap in distributions of scores of cultural samples. We do well to heed the warning of Cohen (1988, 1994):

All psychologists know that *statistically significant* does not mean plain-English significant, but if one reads the literature, often one discovers that a finding reported in the results section studded with asterisks implicitly becomes in the discussion section highly significant, or very highly significant, important, big. (1994, p. 1001)

Cultural bias is not to be equated with measurement error, it provides systematic information about cross-cultural differences (see for example Poortinga & Van der Flier, 1988 and the study by Fontaine et al. discussed in box 7-1).

## Classification of inferences

In this section we shall introduce a simple classification scheme that is meant to facilitate distinctions between various interpretations or **inferences** derived from a cross-cultural data set (cf. Poortinga & Malpass, 1986). The point of departure is that a psychological instrument usually is meant to represent a much larger set of stimuli than those it actually contains. The test stimuli form a sample from this larger set, which one can refer to as a domain of behavior. Interest is not in the test scores per se, but in the domain of behavior to which they are generalized in the interpretation. In other words, an inference or interpretation based on test scores can be seen as a generalization to some domain (cf. Cronbach, Gleser, Nanda, & Rajaratnam, 1972).[4]

Two distinctions can now be made. The first distinction is between cross-culturally identical and non-identical domains. For example, the lexicon (i.e., all the words in a language) is a domain which differs from language to language. This is also the case for subdomains, like the set of color names in different languages. Similarly, it seems likely that the set of situations that provoke anxiety is partly different from culture to culture and thus does not form an identical domain. In contrast, examples of identical domains are the tones in the pitch scale (expressed in hertz) and the colors defined by wavelength of the light. Note that the latter examples are defined in terms of physical scales. It follows from earlier dicussion in this chapter that domains have to be identical, or at least approximately identical, across cultures for meaningful comparison.

The second distinction has to do with the extent of empirical control over the validity of inferences derived from cross-cultural differences. Imagine a continuum; at one end are placed generalizations that are fully accessible to empirical control, and at the other end are generalizations that are hardly open to control. To illustrate the continuum we shall describe three **levels of inference** or generalization, corresponding to a low, a medium, and a high level of inference.

First, we have low-level inferences. Here measurement instruments can be considered as direct samples from domains. Inferences are generalizations to domains of which all the elements, at least in principle, can be listed. An instrument can be constructed by selecting a sample of stimuli from the appropriate set of elements. An example is an arithmetic test for young children consisting of items representing the major operations of addition and subtraction with one-digit numbers. Another example is an attitude scale for intergroup relations in which all important areas of contact, such as intermarriage, social contacts, and commercial relations are included. Thus, a characteristic of low-level inferences is that they are limited to a domain from which the instrument concerned contains a more or less representative sample of all the relevant stimuli. A comparison is valid if the instrument on which a comparison is based is truly representative of the domain of generalization.

In practice, a comparison should be carried out with an eye open for effects of item bias or method bias that led to inequivalence of scores. However, with methods discussed in the previous section, checks on equivalence should usually make it possible to decide with sufficient accuracy whether or not scores have the same meaning cross-culturally.

The second level concerns medium-level inferences; here measurements provide indices of domains. These concern generalizations to domains defined in terms of

---

[4] Cronbach et al. (1972) speak about a universe; we use the term domain of behavior to avoid errors between "universe" and "universal."

unobservable psychological traits of individuals, like cognitive abilities, personality traits, or moral values, which are assumed to underlay certain behaviors. Theoretical and empirical relationships, as established in validation research, determine the range of behaviors of a domain at this level. For this type of inference instruments are not constructed with a view to obtaining a representative sample of all possible elements. Rather, stimuli are selected which supposedly capture the essence of a trait or ability. A test of spatial relations may consist only of items in which the test taker has to reconstruct 3D figures from 2D projections. The mental manipulations needed for correct solutions are seen as the essential core of spatial ability. At this medium level of inference a measurement can be said to serve as an index of the domain of generalization.

At this level of generalization it is usually difficult to decide unambiguously whether domains of behavior are identical across cultures. Can we expect that the spatial orientation of Bushmen or Inuit hunters is adequately represented by a spatial relations test as mentioned (see ch. 5)? And does the cultural construction of the emotional meaning of events lead to different emotions, or is this more a matter of display rules (see ch. 7)? These examples illustrate that scores on instruments using expressions of emotion to assess an underlying emotional state or figural depictions to assess spatial insight may not be psychometrically equivalent. In our view cross-cultural psychologists should be extremely careful in the interpretation of score-level differences in trait and ability scores, especially when dealing with data from populations with large differences in observable behavior repertoires.

The third category can be called high-level inferences. Interpretations are in terms of large and fuzzy domains, which can be qualified as unconstrained domains. High-level inferences involve generalizations to domains that cannot be properly defined in terms of measurement procedures. In this third category it is not clear whether or not instruments provide valid indices of the domain of interest. In fact, the domain of interest is often not even defined when research starts. When observed cross-cultural differences are explained post hoc without clear evidence for the choice of particular concept, the interpretation can be said to be in terms of an unconstrained domain.

Examples of high-level concepts are "intelligence A," "adaptation," and "adaptability." The difficulties with intelligence A (ch. 5) and adaptation (ch. 10) have been discussed previously. The concept of adaptability (i.e., the capacity of a population to cope with the demands of a changing environment) was introduced by Biesheuvel (1972) to replace the concept of intelligence. A difficulty is that adaptability is contingent upon different environmental requirements in each group. How are we to establish that one group has adapted better psychologically to its environment than a second group to another environment? For any answer to a general question like this some evidence can be mustered, but it is hard to be sure about its validity; one can certainly not falsify such a notion. Thus, generalizations of this kind seem somewhat gratuitous; they go beyond what can be reasonably inferred on the basis of psychological data.

## Conclusions

    In this chapter we first looked at qualitative approaches to cross-cultural psychology, which are shared with cultural anthropology. These are necessary at least in exploratory phases of cross-cultural research. Such approaches can lead to novel insights, but tend to be weak when it comes to validity, as there are few agreed upon procedures to validate (or refute) interpretations. Thereafter we turned to quantitative approaches that are rooted in the experimental traditions of psychology. We described the difficulties and the scope for (quasi-)experiments in culture-comparative studies, and also noted weaknesses in these approaches because of insufficient attention to alternative interpretations. A special feature of cross-cultural research was elucidated, namely that it often has to deal simultaneously with population-level and individual-level data.

    The analysis of cross-cultural data was discussed in the second half of the chapter. The analysis of equivalence was here the central concern. Reference was made to numerous sources of cultural bias. The last section of the chapter dealt with the interpretation of cross-cultural data. We focussed the discussion on standardized instruments. Unlike non-standardized methods, these offer researchers the possibility of carrying out checks on cross-cultural equivalence. In the 1990s a trend started towards considering more explicitly cross-cultural similarities in addition to differences. Only by finding out how human beings are alike as well as how they are different can we work towards a full account of human psychological functioning (e.g., Poortinga, 1998).

    In the final analysis, the methodological problems of cross-cultural psychology do not differ in principle from those of general psychology. If there are more alternative explanations that need to be controlled, this means that the difficulties are greater. However, by using a wide range of methods and by taking context variables into account, the degree of accuracy that is required for a valid interpretation of important cross-cultural differences ultimately should be within our reach.

### Key terms

| | |
|---|---|
| cultural bias | levels of inference |
| emic approach | paradigm |
| equivalence | qualitative methodology |
| etic approach | quantitative methodology |
| inference | validity |

### Further reading

Cook, T. D., & Campbell, D. T. (1979). *Quasi-experimentation: Design and analysis issues for field settings.* Boston, MA: Houghton Mifflin. Although published quite some time ago, this book provides a good insight into the methdology and pitfalls of quasi-experimental research.

Greenfield, P. M. (1997b). Culture as process: Empirical methods for cultural psychology. In J. W. Berry, Y. H. Poortinga, & J. Pandey (Eds.), *Theory and method* (pp. 301–46). Vol. I of *Handbook of cross-cultural psychology* (2nd ed.). Boston, MA: Allyn & Bacon. This chapter gives an overview of methodology in cultural psychology; emphasis is placed on qualitative methods, and the study of ongoing processes in cultures.

Van de Vijver, F. J. R., & Leung, K. (1997a). *Methods and data analysis for cross-cultural research*. Newbury Park, CA: Sage. This book gives a fairly complete account of the essentials of methodology and analysis in culture-comparative research. A shorter text covering many of the same materials is Van de Vijver and Leung (1997b).

# 12 Theoretical issues in cross-cultural psychology

"Culture" and "behavior" are somewhat abstract and diffuse concepts that are not accessible for scientific analysis without further specification. The process of specification is guided by the theoretical and metatheoretical orientations of researchers and becomes also manifest in the methods and research questions that are selected. As we have seen in previous chapters, there is no common approach in cross-cultural psychology; however, there is a common sphere of interest, namely the relationships between culture and human behavior. The major issues of debate can be traced far back in history, as demonstrated by Jahoda (1990a) and Jahoda and Krewer (1997). In this chapter we review major perspectives on behavior–culture relationships as they have emerged in cross-cultural psychology since it became a recognizable subdiscipline in the mid-twentieth century.

In the first section on inferred antecedents of behavior we take up again two major distinctions in interpretations, namely those between genetic transmission and cultural transmission (see chs. 2, 9, and 10), and between various levels of inferences or generalizations (see ch. 11). In the second section we link three major categories of interpretations that are developed in the first section to three general orientations in the ways cross-cultural psychologists approach the issue of human variation: absolutism, relativism, and universalism. The third section contains a discussion of conceptualizations of culture–behavior relationships and how these are variously employed by cross-cultural psychologists of different schools. In the final section we discuss whether there are ways of bridging the gaps between the various conceptualizations.

During the last fifty years we think that much progress has been made in the understanding and explanation of cultural influences on behavior. Nevertheless, a critical attitude about the validity of our present insights remains as necessary as ever. To invoke such an attitude, box 12.1 portrays some earlier preferred explanations for behavioral differences across cultures.

## Box 12.1 Climate, race, and culture as explanatory concepts

In a review article on "the nature and amount of race differences" the psychologist C. W. Mann (1940) argued as follows:

In some respects the quest for a solution has resembled the classic game of "passing the buck." During the early part of the Nineteenth Century, clergymen and others, impressed by the obvious differences in the physical appearances and in the customs of races and feeling the need for a justification of slavery as a social institution, rationalized that these differences were innate and produced indubitable evidence in favor of the superiority of the white race. (Mann, 1940, p. 366)

According to Mann the theologians passed the buck to social philosophers and anthropologists. The former soon produced additional armchair evidence for white superiority, while the latter adhered more to the principle of the "psychic unity of mankind." However, researchers in these fields soon turned their attention to societal problems, and passed the buck of the problematic mental differences to the psychologists. "Showing little reluctance," Mann (1940, p. 367) wrote, "the psychologists took up the problem and either because they were less astute or more tenacious have stayed with it ever since ... The literature of the last 30 years is full of the results of comparative tests of racial differences." This literature, in fact, has extended over the the whole of the twentieth century.

Mann could have gone further back in history to show that preconceptions about human differences can mold "scientific" arguments. Boorstin (1985) relates that in 1550 the Habsburg emperor Charles V announced a special congregation in Valladolid on the question whether the Indians in America were or were not inferior to the Spaniards. Despite lengthy sessions and arguments no vote was taken on the issue. However, this probably did not matter too much as the conclusion was reached "that expeditions of conquest were desirable on condition that they be entrusted to captains zealous in the service of God and the king who would act as a good example to the Indians and not for the gold" (Boorstin, 1985, p. 634). Boorstin adds that Philip II, who succeeded Charles V, banned the word "conquest" which in future had to be replaced by "pacification."

In the eighteenth century, during the Enlightenment, a quite different explanation was in vogue. Rather than involving personal qualities as a reason for cultural differences, reference was made to the external condition of climate (Glacken, 1967). It was argued that the temperate climates of the

## Box 12.1 (continued)

Middle East and Western Europe were more conducive to attaining a high level of civilization than the tropical areas, where the heat would stifle human effort, or than the cold regions.

Since 1940 when Mann wrote his review, psychologists have begun to change the locus of the interpretation of perceived differences in cognition, or other behaviors, by naming "culture" rather than "race" as the presumed antecedent factor.

Many behavior differences between major population groups in the world may, at face value, fit quite well an interpretation in terms of either climate or "race." For example, the correlation between the distance of nation states to the equator and per capita income is approximately .70. Does this justify a climatic interpretation? A contrast between north and south that is correlated with climate is also likely to correlate with skin color. Does this justify a "racial" interpretation?

The largely mythical explanations in terms of climate and race could become popular because of an insufficient distinction between co-variations which were coincidental, and co-variations which reflected a causal or functional relationship. For all we know, the examples we give here may well refer to coincidences. For cohesive explanation, theories are needed which cover a wide range of phenomena, but allow strict tests of postulated relationships. Such theories are not available. This means that high-order concepts such as climate and race, but also culture, can only serve as labels that indicate a general orientation. However, more specific concepts are needed for scientifically acceptable explanation. This does not make the choice between the three general labels a trivial matter. Each has its own connotative meaning and because of the social implications as well as its utility in psychology, we consider the notion of culture a better starting point on the road to the explanation of differences than either climate or race.

The lesson to be learned from this box is that climate and race functioned in many respects as justifications of ethnocentric prior beliefs. In the future, will the contemporary emphasis on culture and cultural differences in behavior also be seen as ethnocentrism in disguise? The philosophers and theologians in Valladolid did not have to settle the question of the equality or inferiority of the Indians, as long as the "pacification" of America was not impeded. Could it be that the behavioral and social scientists of today need not provide answers about the nature of cross-cultural differences as long as they do not create impediments for economic expansion that helps to maintain a high standard of living in the West at the cost of environmental pollution everywhere, and for the transfer from "North" to "South" of Western-style education, which may function as a cloak for continued cultural dominance?

## Inferred antecedents

In ch. 11 various difficulties in the interpretation of cross-cultural data were discussed. We presented a categorization of inferences or generalizations that was based mainly on methodological considerations. Here we want to look at interpretations from a more theoretical perspective. In fig. 1.1 psychological outcomes were presented as the consequences of four classes of antecedent variables: ecological influences, genetic transmission, cultural transmission, and acculturation influences. These four classes of variables correspond to four classes of inferences about the antecedent conditions which may have led, directly or indirectly, to certain behaviors of persons belonging to culturally distinct groups. Two of these (ecological and acculturation influences) can be direct, and two (genetic and cultural transmission) are indirect.

The distinction between indirect and direct links from context to behavior is an essential one. It is not meaningful to study behavior as a function of genetic or cultural factors without postulating a pool of genetic information and a pool of cultural information at the population level. To illustrate: the rate of color blindness in a society is a function of the gene pool in the (breeding) population; and the custom that children live in their mother's family reflects a collective norm in the population concerned. With respect to ecological influences and acculturation, direct reference to the ecological or sociopolitical context can be quite meaningful. For example, customs of dress vary with summer and winter, and changes in behavior during acculturation can be explained in terms of the requirements of a given sociopolitical situation.

Theoretical concerns in cross-cultural psychology have been mainly with behavior outcomes that are mediated by population-level transmission processes (both cultural and genetic, in fig. 1.1) and less with outcomes that can be traced to ecological or sociopolitical contexts. Inasmuch as ecological and acculturative influences have direct effects on human behavior, population-level variables are not involved; differences result directly from actual environmental conditions. There is another reason for the theoretical emphasis on genetic and cultural transmission, namely the longstanding controversies about the relative importance of these two mechanisms that have repeatedly emerged in the course of this book.

The two population-mediated transmission mechanisms and their relationship to inferences are presented in more detail in fig. 12.1. The two axes demarcate a field in which the various inferences about the nature of behavior–culture relationships can be located. Thus, the figure builds on the distinction between genetic and cultural transmission. In the last section of the previous chapter we differentiated between three levels of inference or generalization. These also come back in this figure.

The two axes represent the two principles of **genetic transmission** and **cultural transmission,** as shown in fig. 1.1 (see also Boyd and Richerson, 1985, mentioned in ch. 10). The shaded area in the lower left corner of the field is the location of the body of information (usually a data set) from which an inference

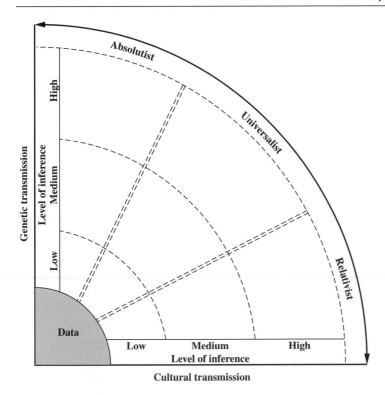

**12.1** A classification of inferences according to level of inference and
two transmission principles
After Poortinga, 1985b

is derived. The field is divided by three curved arcs (broken lines) that define the
three **levels of inference or generalization** distinguished in ch. 11: low-level
inferences to domains of which the data form a more or less representative sample;
medium-level inferences to domains for which the data have some demonstrated
validity; and high-level inferences to virtually unconstrained domains.

We have also divided fig. 12-1 into three sectors. To the sector nearest to the
vertical axis belong inferences that are defined in terms of fundamental properties
of human behavior. Where such properties are inferred, reference is made to the
biological basis of behavior, even when a precise genetic mechanism has not (yet)
been identified. To the sector nearest to the horizontal axis belong interpretations
that are defined predominantly in terms of the subjective outlook or understandings of the members of a cultural group and the way in which they organize their
world. Between these two sectors is a third kind of interpretation referring to interactions between properties mentioned for the vertical and the horizontal sector.
In this middle sector are interpretations that postulate a biological basis for behavior,
as well as cultural impact on its development and display. The three kinds of interpretation can be associated with three general orientations in cross-cultural
psychology that we have referred to with the terms absolutism, relativism, and

universalism (see ch. 1), and to which we shall return in the next section. Together the straight lines and the arcs delineate nine areas, which correspond to nine types of inferences about the nature of antecedent variables in cross-cultural studies.

In the most vertical sector of fig. 12.1 are placed inferences to psychological processes that have been acquired through genetic transmission. These by and large determine the behavioral potential of an individual. We believe that within a cultural group, differences exist between individuals with respect to (hypothetical) traits postulated in this sector. To what extent such differences exist between cultural populations is rather unclear. In an environment with heavy restrictions on the development of some traits the range of variation between individuals may well be smaller than when no restrictions are exerted, but we do not know of any examples of well-established genetically based intercultural differences in typical psychological variables. There are such differences in physical variables (e.g., skin color, lactose intolerance) and direct derivatives of physical variables (e.g., rate of red–green color blindness). As mentioned in ch. 10, red–green color blindness is a well-defined domain. Moreover, there is a direct link between color blindness and the assessment of this phenomenon by means of colored plates with figures that the color-blind person cannot perceive. Hence, we see this as a low-level inference.

Broader inferences about population differences tend to be made in some temperament theories and personality theories that postulate traits, like extraversion–introversion. We would place these at a medium level of inference. These concepts refer to domains for which the validity of cross-cultural differences is more questionable (see ch. 4), but not beyond empirical validation. Even further go generalizations from test score differences to an inborn capacity like general intelligence ($g$). We have argued (ch. 5) that this is a high-level inference beyond empirical scrutiny. It should be clear that inferences in this sector imply only a minor role for cultural context in the psychological functioning of individuals, once minimal conditions needed for unstunted development have been met.

In the most horizontal sector of fig. 12.1 belong inferences to culturally defined domains of behavior. An interpretation of behavior emphasizing cultural transmission will refer to aspects of the sociocultural context in which that behavior occurs. Low-level inferences include, for example, social representations (Moscovici, 1982; ch. 9). Medium-level inference is involved in arguments that there are differences in moral principles (not merely in moral reasoning about concrete instances) between India and Western countries, as suggested by Snarey (1985) and Shweder et al. (1990; ch. 2). We consider as high-level inferences claims to the effect that there are broad cross-cultural differences, for example in the construction of the self, as either an independent self or an interdependent self (Markus & Kitayama, 1991; see ch. 4). Supporting evidence can be found in specific instances (representing small domains), but the broad definition of such assertions makes a convincing validation extremely difficult.

Inferences in this horizontal sector are based on sociocultural and contextual antecedents, with little reference to universal properties. Insofar as each culture represents a different history and a different system of ideas and beliefs, inferences tend to imply different psychological variables and unequal relationships between such variables. There are two implications. First, inasmuch as behaviors are dependent on shared knowledge and common beliefs and attitudes, only small interindividual differences are to be expected (at least in relatively homogeneous cultures). Second, since psychological processes are seen as dependent on a specific context, substantial variation across cultures can be expected. It could be argued that all behavior is an expression of underlying (hypothetical) traits or mechanisms, but especially cultural psychologists rightly emphasize that this is not informative unless the relationship between overt action and presumed traits can be specified. Take, for example, the observation that in India many parents prefer to have a son rather than a daughter, while in France such a preference is far less evident, if it exists at all. For a difference like this there should be some reason, which makes it psychologically meaningful, but the observation contains no reference to a psychological relationship between cultural context and behavioral variables. The example can be amplified, and it will make sense psychologically when we know that in India daughters are to be given dowries and move to live with their in-laws, while sons are expected to look after their parents in old age. In France, like many Western countries, the obligations of children are less well defined and may even fall more on daughters than on sons. This additional information leads to a shift in the interpretation. We can understand both the Indian and the French attitudes as well as the differences between them from a more general principle, for example that behavior tends to be self-serving. However, by invoking such psychological principles we have moved to the middle sector of the diagram.

In the middle sector belong interpretations that see behavior as the outcome of complex interaction processes between human beings with biological features, including a propensity for what we call culture, and the ecocultural and sociocultural context they live in. Examples of low-level inferences in this sector include skills, such as those involved in depth perception of pictures (Deregowski, 1980; see ch. 8). Virtually anyone can learn these skills, but not all cultures may provide the relevant experiences. Perhaps most characteristic for this middle sector are inferences about possible cross-cultural differences in social norms, cognitive abilities, and personality traits. These concepts tend to refer to an intermediate level of generalization. High-level inferences again imply broad inclusive domains. In our view the dimension of individualism–collectivism, discussed in ch. 3, falls in this category, because, like the independence–interdependence of self, it includes many aspects of psychological functioning. However, for Triandis (e.g., 1990; Triandis, McCusker, & Hui, 1990) individualism–collectivism does not derive from cultural conceptions or meanings, but is to be explained in terms of cultural antecedents (especially economic prosperity and cultural complexity) and in turn leads to behavioral consequences (especially pursuing one's own goals or those of one's in-group).

We would to like to add two comments. First, looking back at the previous chapters, it is clear that we have been critical particularly of research traditions involving what we have called in fig. 12.1 "high-level inferences," independent of the sector in the figure. Second, it goes without saying that the categorization of inferences is based on our judgments, and that the authors to whom we refer might be inclined to argue, particularly about the examples at a high level of inference where we are hesitant about the scope for empirical validation.

## Absolutism, relativism, and universalism

The three sectors of fig. 12.1 show a fairly close correspondence with the three general orientations in cross-cultural research proposed in ch. 1. Although they have been named differently by various writers, we have identified them by the terms **relativism**, **absolutism**, and **universalism**. Each of these has been mentioned numerous times in previous chapters, but here we attempt to define and

**Table 12.1** Three orientations to cross-cultural psychology

|  | Absolutist | Universalist | Relativist |
|---|---|---|---|
| 1. *General orientation* | | | |
| (a) Factors underlying behavior | Biological | Biological and cultural | Cultural |
| (b) Role of culture in behavior variation | Limited | Substantial | Substantial |
| 2. *Theoretical perspectives* | | | |
| (a) Similarities due to | Species-wide basic processes | Species-wide basic processes | Generally unexamined |
| (b) Differences due mainly to | Non-cultural factors | Culture–organism interactions | Cultural influences |
| (c) Emics and etics | Imposed etic | Derived etic | Emic |
| (d) Context-free definition of concepts | Directly available | Difficult to achieve | Usually impossible |
| 3. *Methodological perspectives* | | | |
| (a) Context-free measurement of concepts | Usually possible | Often impossible | Impossible |
| (b) Assessment procedures | Standard instruments | Adapted instruments | Local instruments |
| (c) Comparisons | Straight-forward, frequent, evaluative | Controlled, frequent, non-evaluative | Usually avoided, non-evaluative |

elaborate them. To help our exploration of these orientations, table 12.1 outlines a number of features of the three orientations under three headings: general orientation, theoretical perspectives, and methodological perspectives.

As we noted in ch. 9, the relativist position (right-hand column of table 12.1) was first identified in anthropology by Herskovits (1948), but was based on an earlier set of ideas advanced by Boas (1911). This general orientation seeks to avoid all traces of ethnocentrism by trying to understand people "in their own terms," without imposing any value judgments, or a priori judgments of any kind. It thus seeks not just to avoid derogating other peoples (an evaluative act), but it also seeks to avoid describing, categorizing, and understanding others from an external cultural point of view (a cognitive act). "In their own terms" thus means both "in their own categories" *and* "with their own values." There is the working assumption that explanations of psychological variations across the world's peoples are to be sought in terms of cultural variation, with little recourse to other factors. Theoretically, relativists do not show much interest in the existence of similarities across cultures, except to assume a general egalitarian stance (e.g., "all people are equal"), and to explain any cultural differences that they do observe as being due to cultural contexts that influence individuals' development. Differences are typically interpreted qualitatively: for example, people differ in their form or style of intelligence, rather than in intellectual competencies. Methodologically, comparative studies are avoided, because they are considered so problematic and ethnocentric as to render valid comparison impossible. All psychological assessment should take place with procedures (tests, etc.) developed within the local culture's terms; these practices place relativists in the emic, indigenous, and cultural psychology approaches, as discussed in ch. 11.

In sharp contrast, the position of absolutism seems little concerned with the problems of ethnocentrism, or of seeing people "in their own terms." Rather, psychological phenomena are considered to be basically the same across cultures: the essential character of, for example, "intelligence," "honesty," or "depression" is assumed to be the same everywhere, and the possibility is ignored that the researchers' knowledge is rooted in their own cultural conceptions of these phenomena. Methodologically, comparisons are considered to create no essential problems, and are carried out easily and frequently, based on the use of the same instruments (presumed to have the same psychological meaning) in many cultures. These instruments are employed in a standard fashion; at most, linguistic equivalence is checked, but this is often the only nod in the direction of recognizing the possible role of cultural influences. Since instruments are likely to be biased, both procedurally and conceptually, this approach clearly leads to imposed etics as outlined in ch. 11. Theoretically, it is based on the assumption that psychologically people everywhere are pretty much alike. Where differences do occur, they are quantitative differences on the assumed underlying common construct; different people are just "less intelligent," "less honest," or "more depressed."

The position of universalism adopts the working assumptions that basic psychological processes are likely to be common features of human life everywhere, but that their manifestations are likely to be influenced by culture. That is, variations are due to culture "playing different variations on a common theme"; basic processes are essentially the same, but they are expressed in different ways. Methodologically, comparisons are employed, but cautiously, heeding the safeguards described in ch. 11; they should neither be avoided nor carried out at whim. Assessment procedures are likely to require modification. While the starting point may be some extant theory or test, one's approach to their use should be informed by local cultural knowledge.

Universally applicable concepts will have to come about by reformulation of existing concepts. Theoretically, interpretations of similarities and differences are made starting from the belief that basic psychological processes are pan-human, and that cultural factors influence their development (direction and extent), and deployment (for what purposes, and how, they are used). Thus the major questions are to what extent and in what ways cultural variables influence behavior. Quantitative interpretations can be validly made along dimensions that fall within a domain in which the phenomena of interest are similar. For example, in cultures that share the same conception, and encourage the same expression of depression, differences on a test of depression may be interpreted quantitatively. At the same time, in cultures that differ in conception and expression of depression, it may be impossible to obtain equivalent measurements. Differences that are of a qualitative nature require theoretical analysis to define a common dimension on which they can be captured as quantitative differences, before a comparison can be made.

In ch. 1 we sought to distinguish the universalist position from the absolutist one, by claiming that universalism emphasizes the role of culture in bringing about diversity, while there is virtually no role for culture in the absolutist view. Another way of phrasing this distinction is to think of absolutism as implying behavioral universalism. What we have called the universalist position places emphasis on the identity of shared basic psychological processes that are the legacy of human phylogenetic history. Hence, one can also speak about psychological universalism to describe this position (Poortinga, 1998; Poortinga et al., 1993).

Combining the outlook contained in fig. 12.1 and table 12.1 the following summary can be given. In the absolutist view a definition of psychological concepts free of cultural context effects is judged to be within reach of the researcher. Such context-free measurement requires the avoidance of pitfalls in the formulation of items and careful translation, but there are no barriers that should prove to be insurmountable. Relativists believe that there can only be context-bound definition of psychological concepts in such areas as personality, cognition, and social behavior. It follows that context-free psychological measurement should not even be attempted. In the universalistic perspective, context-free definition of psychological concepts is seen as a goal that can be approximated through the modification of culture-specific concepts. The expression of behavior in many respects is culture bound, and context-free measurement of certain kinds of variables may well be a goal that can never be fully reached.

The three positions have implications for the theoretical definition of psycho-logical concepts, as well as for the psychometric assessment of cross-cultural similarities and differences. They also have implications for the operational de-finition of **universality**. In general terms, a psychological concept, or a relation-ship between concepts, qualifies as universal if it can be validly used to describe the behavior of people in any culture. According to Triandis (1978, p. 1) it is "a psychological process or relationship which occurs in all cultures." This defini-tion is rather imprecise and will apply to almost any concept. Jahoda (1981, p. 42) suggests "invariance across both cultures and methods" as a requirement for uni-versality. This is a description that would fit an absolutist orientation, but also can be used by a relativist to indict the absolutist approach, because it imposes conditions that rarely can be met.

The difficulties in identifying universals should not be taken to imply that they do not exist. Arguments and findings to the contrary have been presented in a re-view from a comparative anthropological perspctive by Munroe and Munroe (1997). Another review is by Lonner (1980) who has noted considerable varia-tion in approaches to universals in cross-cultural psychology. In one orientation, derived from the psychometric tradition, Van de Vijver and Poortinga (1982) have elaborated on this and argued that the universality of concepts can be defined at several levels of psychometric accuracy and that more cross-cultural similarity in behavior is implied as the definition becomes more precise. Their definitions are given in terms of invariant properties of scales to qualitatively or quantita-tively express cross-cultural differences. They distinguish four levels of concepts:

1 Conceptual universals are concepts at a high level of abstraction perhaps without any reference to a measurement scale (e.g., modal personality, or adapt-ability).
2 Weak universals are concepts for which measurement procedures have been specified and for which validity has been demonstrated in each culture inves-tigated (through evidence on structural equivalence, ch. 11). Generally, a claim to this level of universality is implicitly held by most psychologists for virtu-ally all current concepts in psychology even without a much-needed analysis of their validity.
3 Strong universals are concepts that can be established with a scale that has the same metric across cultures, but a different origin (i.e., meeting conditions for metric equivalence, see ch. 11). Common patterns of findings provide relevant evidence.
4 Strict universals show the same distribution of scores in all cultures. For such universals instruments are needed that meet requirements for full score equivalence.

The important point in these distinctions is that they do away with a dichotomy between universal and culture-specific phenomena. Van de Vijver and Poortinga (1982, p. 393) argue that it seems meaningful "to consider the degree of in-variance of data across cultural groups as a function of the similarity in cultural patterns or background variables between them." This argument fits with the idea of universalism as an approach that sees invariance at various levels as a potential outcome of cross-cultural inquiry.

## Conceptualizations of behavior–culture relationships

Discussions on behavior and culture have a long history (Wandt, 1913; Jahoda & Krewer, 1997). As we have seen in ch. 1, usually two or three main perspectives are distinguished in cross-cultural psychology. When a dichotomous categorization is made, it is between relativist orientations (cultural psychology) and universalistic (culture-comparative) approaches. When three perspectives are distinguished, the categories are cultural psychology, indigenous psychologies, and culture-comparative research. Both culturalist and indigenous approaches tend to share a relativist view, and this is the reason why they are sometimes taken together. All three have been mentioned before in this book, particularly with reference to the dichotomy between relativism and universalism. Indigenous approaches will be discussed further in ch. 17. In the present section we specifically review views on behavior–culture relationships.

### Cultural psychology

**Cultural psychology** covers a range of approaches (Miller, 1997b). Perhaps the main theoretical principle is that culture and behavior are essentially inseparable, and thus cannot be studied apart from each other. "[C]ultural psychology is the study of all the things members of different communities think (know, want, feel, value) and *do* by virtue of being the kinds of beings who are the benficiaries, guardians and active perpetuators of a particular culture" [italics in original] (Shweder et al., 1998, p. 867). As noted in ch. 9, a shift in cultural anthropology from viewing culture as external context to "culture in the mind of the people" (Geertz, 1973) formed an important precursor. The focus of research is on more subjective aspects, such as the meaning that behavior has for the actor, rather than on more objective aspects of behavior, as observed and rated by experts. Three important features of cultural approaches include intentionality (or purposeful action), historicity of behavior and developmental change, and the system-like character of the behavior repertoire in a culture.

Shweder (1991, p. 97) argued that:

> the life of the psyche is the life of intentional persons, responding to, and directing their action at, their own mental objects or representations and undergoing transformation through participation in an evolving intentional world that is the product of the mental representations that make it up.

Thus, "cultural psychology is the study of intentional worlds. It is the study of personal functioning in particular intentional worlds" (Shweder, 1990, p. 3).

He emphasizes reality as subjective. "Intentional things have no 'natural' reality or identity separate from human understandings and activities" (1990, p. 2).

Historicity is reflected in the principle that behavior is mainly, or even exclusively, context dependent. The focus is on continuity and change in behavior and understanding over time, usually within a single society. For example, in social constructionism, a school of thinking that represents postmodernism in cultural psychology (Gergen, 1994; Miller, 1997b), behavior is considered as grounded in social interaction and communication, particularly linguistic communication. The world is understood as social artifacts, products of historically situated interactions between people. Analyses of rhetoric in arguments (Billig, 1987) or the use of expertise as power in social relationships (Parker & Shotter, 1990) are topics of analysis (cf. Peeters, 1996).

Coherence of a culture in a psychological sense is a basic assumption of cultural psychology which it shares with much of cultural anthropology, where it is common to speak of a "culture as a system." Things may not be interrelated in neat regular patterns, but they hang very much together. Geertz (cf. Shweder, 1984b) considered the octopus a suitable metaphor. This may be an oddly shaped organism, but it is an organism nevertheless, and as such an entirely coherent entity. In an earlier review Rohner (1984) defined culture as a symbolic meaning system, with particular emphasis on learning, with "equivalent and complementary learned meanings" transmitted from one generation to the next. Complementarity implies that not every member of a culture has to learn everything that forms part of the symbolic meaning system. But there has to be a certain sharing of meaning to maintain the system. In ch. 9 we have seen that the anthropologist Kroeber postulated culture as a superorganic entity. It was given an existence in its own right, because a culture is governed by its own laws and is not dependent on specific individuals for its continued existence. In cultural psychology the cultural system is in the minds of persons. It is not so much a matter of technology, customs, or behaviors ("explicit culture"), but is more or less exclusively defined in terms of ideas and meanings ("implicit culture"). In such an approach the study of isolated psychological variables taken from the complex fabric is considered a highly questionable practice.

## Action theory approach

Related to intentionality is the concept of action, as put forward by Eckensberger (1996, p. 76). He sees actions as "future-oriented, goal directed activities of a potentially self-reflecting agency." Eckensberger (1979) has given an early and far-ranging evaluation of psychological theorizing as it applies in cross-cultural psychology. He distinguished five paradigms, which are hierarchically ordered, a higher one being more inclusive than a lower one. Most comprehensive is the paradigm of the reflexive human being. As indicated by the name, the reflection of humans on themselves and on their own actions, goals, and intentions is

## Box 12.2  Action as behavior in context

An action, in action theory, is not a property of the individual–it is placed between the individual and the environment. Eckensberger (1987, p. 18) argues that it is

this change in the focus on the action, instead of a focus on the culture or the individual (so common in psychology), which exactly neutralizes the opposition between the individual and the culture, which connects the environment with the individual, and which therefore opens psychology as a discipline to other social sciences such as sociology and anthropology...

An example taken from Eckensberger and Meacham (1984, p. 169) may illustrate the meaning of the concept of action and show the basic concerns of the action theorists:

imagine a tree. Standing next to the tree is a man. The man has an axe. What is happening here? How can we as social scientists understand the situation? We can begin by assuming that the chopping of the tree relates to a future goal of the man, for example, so that the tree can be cut into boards to build a house. Further, we can assume that the man has considered various means by which he might chop down this tree. For example, he may have used a saw instead of an axe. After considering these and other means for chopping down the tree, the man made a free choice among these, and he chose the axe. Now the man is chopping. He may be thinking about many things ... [but when asked] he will be able to set aside his thoughts of other things, and become conscious of the fact that he is chopping down the tree ... he understands that if, as an unintended consequence of his chopping down the tree, the birds lose their home, then he would be responsible for this, for he has made the decision that he will chop down the tree.

The description contains four essential aspects of action theory:

1 the behavior is structured by some future goal;
2 there is a choice among alternative means to reach the goal;
3 the acting person can be aware of the goal and the means employed; and
4 the person can anticipate the consequences, intended as well as unintended, and will accept the responsibility for these.

The action theorist tries to cope with behavior in all its phenomenal complexity. Means and goals are hierarchically structured. Going to work is a goal, but it is also a means of earning a salary. Different stages are often distinguished in the course of an action.

The action theorist attempts to understand the structure of reasons in which the chopping of the tree takes place. Eckensberger and Meacham demonstrate how minor changes in the situation, particularly when interpersonal interactions are involved, can lead to major changes in its meaning. They also point out that a proper understanding requires knowledge about the cultural and the historical context of the action.

characteristic of theories within this paradigm. A brief discussion of what is meant by the word "action" can be found in box 12.2.

Of the various action theories particularly the one by Boesch (1976, 1980, 1991) has a strong cultural flavor. Change and development of the individual can be understood as the outcome of dialectical transactions with the physical, and especially, the social environment. We are not only shaped by our environment, but we also form it; we reflect on it and can change the course of events through our actions. Following Boesch, Eckensberger opts for the paradigm of the reflexive human being because it pertains to the understanding of the unique aspects of a behavioral event. Not only the sociocultural context of an action falls within the scope of action theories, but also the understanding of the idiosyncratic interpretation of a particular situation by a specific person. Eckensberger recommends this paradigm for the study of cultural influences on behavior, within a society as well as across societies. It places culture at the interface between person and environment; culture is an ingredient of any action by any person in any situation.

## The sociocultural school

The historical and contextual nature of behavior has been brought to psychology in a forceful manner by Vygotsky (1978). He formulated his ideas in the period shortly after the Marxist revolution in Russia but was "discovered" in the West only a few decades later. As mentioned in ch. 2, Vygotsky saw the development of what he called higher mental functions as a historical process at the level of societies. These functions, of which abstract thinking received most attention, appear first on the social level as interpsychological categories shared by members of a society. Only when they are present in a society can they be transmitted to the individual person in the course of his or her ontogenetic development. This principle of cultural mediation of psychological functioning has been received positively by educators, who according to this viewpoint very much influence the growing minds of children.

As mentioned in chs. 2 and 5 an important change was made to Vygotsky's conceptions of behavior–culture relationships by Cole (1992a, 1992b, 1996). Cultural mediation in Cole's view does not take place at the level of global mental functions that manifest themselves in broad domains of behavior. The evidence rather points to cultural mediation at the level of specific skills and metacognitions. These are acquired in specific activity settings, like the school environment or the work environment, which forms activity systems with rich and multiple kinds of interactions (e.g., Engeström, 1993).

Unlike many authors Cole does not treat culture as a given. He is concerned about its origins, postulating different timescales in human development, including phylogenetic development, and cultural historical time (see ch. 2), as well as the interactions that can take place between levels that are defined at these different timescales. For example, human activities have consequences for societal changes in historical time (and vice versa), and ultimately also for phylogenetic change.

Moreover, ontogenetic development is not a unitary event. Cole endorses the notion of modularity (Fodor, 1983), which states that psychological processes are domain specific and biologically constrained. Cole adds to this that cultural context selectively engages various modules, and that in the course of socialization cognitive processes become more and more part of culturally organized activities.

## Indigenous psychologies

As we shall see in ch. 17, the movement to create local **indigenous psychologies** in non-Western countries is a reaction to Euroamerican dominance, the most salient aspect of which is the limited attention in cross-cultural psychology to issues that are relevant to the majority world, like poverty, illiteracy, and so on. Another important argument, of concern in the present chapter, is theoretical: namely that psychology by nature is culture bound and that each cultural population needs to develop its own psychology (hence our preference for the plural – indigenous psychologies). It is easy to see that this is a relativistic viewpoint that is closer to the cultural than to the comparative perspective (cf. Hwang & Yang, 2000).

However, more than in the literature on cultural psychology, there is debate among theorists of indigenous approaches on how to balance indigenous and culture-common aspects of psychological functioning (e.g., Enriquez, 1993; Sinha, 1997; Triandis, 2000b; Yang, 2000). For example, Sinha (1997) maintains very explicitly that the two should be seen as complementary rather than antagonistic. Although the Western dominance in psychology unfortunately will continue as long as resources for research and access to publication outlets remain unequally distributed, it is of interest to ask in an analysis of behavior–culture relationships how various indigenous approaches (including the dominant Western one) can relate to each other.

Various types of research can be distinguished (Poortinga, 1997). First, there is transfer of methods. For example, Puhan (1982; Kulkarni & Puhan, 1988) has developed a "projective-inventory" technique in which the projective reactions of a respondent are given in the form of answers on inventory–type response scales (agree–disagree). This test was developed for an Indian population, but can be adapted for use elsewhere maintaining the theory and principles underlying its construction.

More difficult to transfer is knowledge derived from studies based on indigenous psychological concepts. The methodological difficulties of comparison identified in ch. 11 apply here. An example is the work by Naidu and Pande (Naidu, 1983; Pande & Naidu, 1992) on *anasakti* (non-detachment), a concept prominent in Hindu religion and ancient writings. To operationalize and validate this concept they used methods that are much the same as those found elsewhere. However, conceptually the notion is considered to be typical of Hinduism as part of a worldview in which identification with the material world is considered an impediment to self-realization. Other examples, mentioned before, include *amae* in Japan (Doi, 1973) and *philotimo* in Greece (Triandis, 1972). Studies of this kind in which indigenous notions are formally conceptualized as personality traits, social norms, values, or therapeutic principles, appear central to indigenous psychologies (Sinha, 1997; Kim & Berry, 1993). It can be argued that they are also the most fruitful, in that they most obviously extend the range of variation of psychological phenomena studied in research.

In a relativistic perspective, concepts such as *anasakti* or *philotimo* are seen as requiring culture-bound interpretation. However, we have referred before to analyses that show how such concepts are understandable as part of, and even fit into, structurally equivalent dimensional representations, for example when we discussed the "Big Five" dimensions of personality (ch. 4) and Osgood's findings on dimensions of connotative meaning (ch. 7).

A third kind of indigenous research goes beyond methods and concepts by trying to develop an entire psychology on the basis of the body of knowledge available in a cultural population. The first steps towards such a psychology in a non-Western country were made in the Philippines, with attempts to develop a local psychology on the basis of indigenous notions through the use of indigenous methods (Enriquez, 1990). Concepts as they are expressed in local language were listed and methods (*pagtatanung-tanong*, asking around) combining elements of surveying and interviewing of informants were applied. In ch. 4 we mentioned evidence showing that, despite the independence of this research from Western instruments and methods, there were important similarities with personality factors identified in the USA and Europe (Guanzon-Lapeña et al., 1998).

In our view these findings do not detract from the need to enrich a global science of psychology with local thinking about behavior and psychological functioning. At the same time, the evidence does not necessarily support the need for a relativist position. Enriquez (1993) saw indigenous psychologies as an intermediate, be it necessary, step towards a universal psychology. In his view cross-indigenous comparisons can lead to universals. A step-wise approach starting with monocultural research and moving towards an indigenously derived global psychology has been described by Yang (2000). However, questions on cultural specificity and universality and how to balance the evidence will remain a major issue in cross-cultural research for some time to come (Kagitcibasi & Poortinga, 2000).

## Culture-comparative research

Since a universalist and **culture-comparative research** perspective permeates much of this book, we shall mention here only a few salient theoretical points in which it is distinct from more relativist orientations. The search for antecedent–consequent relationships between cultural context and behavior outcomes is probably the main feature of this perspective.

Most straightforward is an approach where culture is treated as a set of conditions. A particular ecocultural and sociopolitical environment is seen as an (enormously complex) condition or treatment. Most  members of a culture have been assigned by birth to that culture, in the same sense as subjects are allocated to one condition in a laboratory experiment. However, according to Segall (1983, 1984), culture is a higher-order factor that ought not to have the status of an independent variable; it is too diffuse to be measurable. Rather, culture has to be dissected into separate contextual factors (Whiting, 1976, referred to "unpackaging" cultural variables). These include social institutions such as schools, language, rules governing interpersonal relationships, and features of the physical environment.

It is common for culture-comparative research to start with the observation of some important behavioral difference, and then try to find an antecedent variable which can explain this difference. Poortinga, Van de Vijver, Joe, and Van de Koppel (1987) have expanded on Segall's notion of culture as highly diffuse. They suggested that the analysis of cultural variables can be illustrated with the metaphor of peeling an onion. One can take off more and more layers until in the end no onion is left. In the same sense, these authors claim that a cross-cultural study has only been completely successful when all variation in behavior between cultures has been fully explained in terms of measurable variables.

In a review from a culture-comparative perspective Lonner and Adamopoulos (1997) distinguish three further approaches. Culture can also be seen as context. Rather than as an (assembly of) independent variables culture serves more as an overarching frame encompassing all kinds of interactions and relationships between variables. While views of culture as (a set of ) independent variables or as context postulate direct relationships between cultural antecedents and behavior outcomes, the two remaining conceptions attribute a secondary or indirect influence to cultural variables in explaining behavior outcomes. In one of these two conceptions culture acquires the status of a mediator variable. For example, in analyses of work-related values (Hofstede, 1980), psychological variables like merit in the work place and compliance with orders, can be said to be "affected" by the prevalence of individualism (or collectivism) in a society. Intra-individual determinants have a direct or proximal role in such analyses, while culture has a secondary status. The fourth and final role assigned to culture in the literature is, according to Lonner and Adamopoulos, that of a moderator variable; this is a variable that influences the relationship between two other variables. They give the example of Markus and Kitayama (1991; see ch. 4), for whom culture influences the emergence of particular self-systems (independent or interdependent) in a society and in this way potentially alters psychological processes.

In most culture-comparative approaches reference is made to variables rather than to systems (Jahoda, 1984). At first glance, this may seem to suggest far less coherence than in cultural approaches, but such an impression could be misleading. For example, Triandis (1996) suggests coherence or generalizability of patterns with the notion of cultural "syndromes," referring to shared attitudes, beliefs, norms, role- and self-definitions, and values of members of each culture that are organized around a theme. Moreover, as we have seen before, there is a tendency among researchers to postulate broad explanatory variables, encompassing a wide range of phenomena (high-level inferences), like individualism–collectivism, self-construals, and cognitive capacities.

Of course, human behavior hangs together, if only because of the fact that individuals as actors are physically coherent organisms. But this does not necessarily imply that differences between cultural populations in psychological functioning are also organized in a coherent fashion. Larger clusterings of differences in overt behavior can be observed in direct reactions to the ecological environment. There is hardly a psychologically meaningful cultural variable unrelated to GNP. However, as we have seen in the scheme of Lonner and Adamopoulos (1997), many psychologists emphasize the *indirect* role of culture between antecedent conditions and behavior outcomes; culture becomes *internalized* in the form of values, self-conceptions, and so on, and such interpretations imply medium-level and frequently even high-level inferences.

In this book culture and behavior have been presented as functionally adaptive to context. So far this view has often implied an interpretation of cultural and behavioral differences at a relatively high level of inference. Another way of looking at such differences that requires only low-level inferences emerges if we consider the behavior repertoire in a culture as a large number of **conventions**, cultural practices, or cultural rules. These are explicitly or implicitly accepted agreements among the members of a group as to what is appropriate in social interactions or in some field of activity, like in art (Van de Koppel & Schoots, 1986). Conventions are not trivial. They can make a certain situation very strong (Mischel, 1973) so that (almost) all members of a culture will show the same reaction, while in some other culture some other reaction is equally prevalent. But they have an aspect of arbitrariness from an outsider's perspective. Rules or conventions are not limited to overt actions, they include ways to handle problems (e.g., building stone houses and not wooden houses), and explanations of other rules (looking at someone while talking shows honesty and openness, versus not looking someone in the eye is a matter of respect; Girndt, 2000; Girndt & Poortinga, 1997).

Conventions are perhaps best equated with the words in a dictionary, because of their large numbers. This analogy is relevant in another way: when translating terms on the basis of a dictionary one is likely to go wrong on shades of meaning, and it can be said that in a similar fashion mismatches occur from one cultural repertoire to another, for example, in intercultural communication or in the translation of questionnaires. Even if we basically know certain rules of a society we are likely to err in their proper application. Just as we feel most confident and at ease with our mother tongue, we are also most at ease with our own cultural repertoire and least likely to commit errors.

As described here conventions or rules exercise a strong effect on the total behavior repertoire, because they occur in large numbers. They also lead to consistent cross-cultural differences. A society needs conventions about how to behave in certain situations, and about what is proper; social interactions would become complete chaos without rules. At the same time, there is often no psychological reason why there happens to be a certain convention in a society and not another convention. Insofar as conventions have an aspect of arbitrariness this limits the interpretation of cross-cultural differences either in terms of psychologically meaningful independent variables, or in terms of cultural system properties.

## Beyond current controversies?

There are two basic ways to handle the controversies between the culturalist and culture-comparative perspectives. One can simply declare that the other camp is wrong. In the early 1990s such a position was taken by Shweder (1990, 1991). Alternatively, one can seek a position where the concerns of both major perspectives may be accommodated. Three strategies for bridging relativism and universalism can be envisaged, namely combination, integration, and demarcation (Poortinga, 1997; Poortinga & Van Hemert, 2001).

The strategy of combination refers to a selection of elements from both perspectives. Assuming that any dichotomy is in the minds of researchers rather than in actual behavior and that neither side has an exclusive claim to validity, combination makes sense. The distinction between emic and etic is often used in this way. Unfortunately, this happens sometimes in an ad hoc fashion. Cross-cultural differences that are found in a data set are qualified as referring to emic aspects, and similarities across the samples investigated tend to be called etic. Needless to say, such a pragmatic use shortchanges the theoretical basis of the original distinction of Pike (1967) and Berry (1969). A critical testing of differences is needed.

An example of a cultural anthropologist and a psychologist carefully pooling their expertise is the research by Wassmann and Dasen (1994a, 199b) on the cognitive consequences of the Yupno numbering system (see ch. 9). They analyzed this system in terms of collective representations of informants, as well as in terms of cognitive skills on which individuals differed according to exposure and experience. A position of combination has been argued for by Berry (2000a), and by Yang (2000). Universalism as described in this chapter has features of a combinatory approach. Aspects from both sides are taken into account to develop a mid-way position (see fig. 12.1 and table 12.1). However, by postulating interactions between the human organism and the cultural context this position can be said also to seek integration.

The second strategy is the integration of contrasting methodological and theoretical concerns in one and the same study. It requires that researchers of different traditions reach fundamental agreement on theoretical issues. Looking at the long history and enduring contrasts between perspectives (Jahoda & Krewer, 1997) this does not seem to happen easily. In the available literature, it appears to us that most theoretical attempts at integration have been undertaken from, and ultimately maintain, a relativist position. This is the case with the model of the reflexive person in principle capable of acting consciously in a future-oriented (intentional) way, described by Eckensberger (1979, 1996). Another example can be found in the work of Cole (1992a, 1992b, 1996). His basic framework consists of three components of development: biological, environmental, and cultural. Cole wants to transcend the misguided debate on nature and nurture in human behavior by postulating a third entity, namely culture in the sense of historically specific features of the environment. To his end he reduces "environment" in the traditional sense to "universal features of the environment." Cole (1992a, p. 735) writes: "According to this cultural context view, the two factors *biology* and *the environment* or *the individual* and the *society* ... do not interact directly. Rather their interaction is mediated through a third factor, culture" [italics in original].

The postulate of culture as a third entity makes this a relativistic framework. The separate status for this entity makes Cole's framework less parsimonious than schemes in which there is only one major distinction, namely between organism and environment which are seen to interact in various ways. For example, in the ecocultural framework (fig. 1.1) population-mediated adaptation has similar functions as ascribed by Cole to culture. In addition, Cole takes the somewhat unusual position of restricting "environment" to universal features of the environment, but this in turn brings back the need for a universality–specificity distinction.

A third attempt at integration is an analysis by Kashima (2000). He starts from a conception in which culture is an integral part of the person. He sees an emerging consensus between what he calls the empiricist and interpretivist approaches on the following four points. First, most psychologists accept a physicalist ontology (i.e., thoughts and feelings have a physical basis), making earlier dualist conceptions of mind and body something of the past. Second, there is broad consensus on culture as a phylogenetically developed faculty of the human species, with both genetic and cultural transmission of information from one generation to the next. Third, the human mind is a product of interactions among genetic and cultural factors, woven together in a complex pattern. Fourth, the cultural context is part of the process that constitutes the human mind. Such a conception in Kashima's opinion defuses the old materialism–idealism opposition. However, emphasizing context as part of the human mind (and person) is in essence a relativistic viewpoint. It preempts the status of cultural variables as antecedent variables in a comparative (quasi-)experimental research design, because such a status presumes that culture and individual person can be defined as separate entities. It is possible to think of alternative formulations of Kashima's fourth point. A description like "the manifestation of psychological processes is influenced by cultural factors" presumably would be acceptable for universalists, but not for relativists.

The third possible strategy, demarcation, seeks to take both culture-common and culture-unique variance seriously, but explaining each in a different way. This strategy rests on the explicit recognition that the two perspectives are incompatible and, at least for the time being, will remain so. It further accepts that the concerns expressed in both relativism and universalism have to be recognized, but that the reach of either of the two as an approach to behavior–culture relationships has its limitations. This idea has been further elaborated by Poortinga (1992b, 1997). Here we follow a description by Poortinga and Soudijn (in press).

A starting point is the observation that the range of imaginable actions of a person is much larger than the observed range. One way to look at this is from a conception of constraints that apparently limit the range of alternative actions actually available to a person. On the other hand, in most situations there remain various alternative courses of action open to a person. These can be seen as affordances or opportunities. Constraints can be defined at various levels from distal to proximal; and they can be internal within the person as well as external (imposed by the environment). Affordances can be defined as the space of alternatives left by constraints at each level; thus affordances are complementary to constraints. Such distinctions are inherent in contemporary ecological thinking about organism–environment relationships, employing the notion of possibilism (see ch. 1). They can be made at several levels; in table 12.2 they are arranged from distal (far away from the behaving person) to proximal (close to the behaving person).

At the most general level the scope of human behavior is determined (and constrained) by the phylogenetic history of our species. The environment, or ecological niche, in which humans as a species function imposes constraints on adaptation outcomes. However, we have seen in ch. 10 that, according to biologists like Gould (1991), current features may not always be the direct outcome

**Table 12.2** Levels of constraints and affordances varying from distal to proximal

|  | Constraints | | Affordances |
|---|---|---|---|
|  | Internal | External |  |
| **Distal** | *Genetic transmission (species)* | | |
| \| | adaptations | ecological niche | pleiotropies and "spandrels" |
| \| | *Cultural transmission (group)* | | |
| \| | epigenetic rules | ecological context | technology |
| \| | | sociopolitical context | enabling conditions (conventions) |
| \| | *Genetic transmission (individual)* | | |
| \| | aptitudes | poor fit in cultural niche | capacities |
| \| | *Cultural transmission (individual)* | | |
| \| | enculturation (skills, beliefs, etc.) | socialization to prevailing conditions | enabling conventions (skills, beliefs, etc.) |
| \| | | | |
| **Proximal** | situation "meaning" | actual situation | perceived choices |

Adapted from Poortinga & Soudijn, in press

of selection-driven genetic transmission processes; they can also result from exaptations and spandrels (see p. 263). Gould sees the complex brain as a feature of the human organism that has opened up many affordances, like religion, art, and technology, for which it hardly can have been developed originally.

Cultural transmission at the group level can be distinguished from genetic transmission with the help of a notion like epigenetic rules (Lumsden & Wilson, 1981, ch. 10) referring to processes of interaction between genes and environment. Which cultural patterns will develop depends to a large extent on the resources that are available in a given natural environment. There are also patterns that are unlikely to develop, given adverse ecocultural or sociopolitical conditions. In this sense the environment acts as a set of constraints. At the same time, the natural environment provides affordances that have been developed in different ways by various cultural populations, and thus have resulted in different technologies and customs to deal with the environment, including the social environment.

The next row in table 12.2 addresses transmission as an individual-level phenomenon. One's genetic make-up imposes restrictions on what can be achieved, in terms of physical as well as mental dimensions. One's environment equally does not provide optimum opportunities for development (e.g., less than optimal nutrition), thus providing external constraints. On the other hand, individual capacities need not be seen only in terms of their limiting effects. One's capabilities also form the basis for the development of competencies or skills which can be employed to realize desired achievements; in this sense capabilities can also be viewed as affordances.

The final form of transmission distinguished in the table is cultural transmission at the individual level in the form of enculturation and socialization to prevailing economic conditions and sociocultural context. Enculturation usually refers to all forms of cultural learning, including imitation (cf. Segall et al., 1999). It is a limiting condition insofar as the individual manages only incompletely to learn from experience. External constraints are added by the limited range of experiences available in a given context, as well as by prevalent socialization practices. The idea of socialization as a constraining process was proposed by Child (1954), who argued that individuals are led to develop a much narrower range of behavior repertoire than the potentialities they are born with.

The last row of the table refers to concrete situations or stimuli which a person is actually facing. Insofar as a situation demands certain actions and makes other actions inappropriate (e.g., evasive action in the case of physical danger) there are external constraints. Internal constraints are present insofar as a person attributes certain meanings to a situation. At the same time, in most situations the actor can perceive alternative possible courses of action that can be conceptualized as affordances.

In psychology, the emphasis is on individual-level explanation. In cross-cultural psychology the focus is also on the interaction of individual and cultural context. Constraints can be seen as the defining characteristic of a culture, i.e., "[c]ulture becomes manifest in shared constraints that limit the behavior repertoire available to members of a certain group in a way different from individuals belonging to some other group" (Poortinga, 1992b, p. 10).

Of course, the table is only schematic. Constraints and affordances are often two sides of the same coin and to some extent a matter of perspective. Also there are interactions between the various levels in the table and within rows between constraints and affordances that can be illustrated with Super and Harkness's idea of the developmental niche (ch. 2). What matters here are the implications for the topic of discussion in this chapter. Inasmuch as shared constraints limit the range of behavior alternatives this should lead to inter-individual regularities that are open to analysis by observational, experimental, and psychometric methods. To the extent that constraints are known one should be able to predict behavior. Ecological constraints can make the development of certain technologies highly unlikely; it is difficult to imagine that any kind of agriculture could have developed in the Arctic area.

Insofar as there is freedom from constraints, future events are beyond the reach of prediction; only in retrospect can we try to make sense of the choice that actually has been made in a certain instance. One can either declare such events out of bounds for scientific analysis, or extend the range of methods to include qualitative modes of analysis, such as description and hermeneutics. Thus, the distinction between constraints and affordances outlines a complementarity between the two perspectives of universalism and relativism. Culture defined as a set of antecedent conditions is most appropriately analyzed by (quasi-)experimental methods. To the extent that there are no constraining antecedent conditions, the rules and conventions that have emerged in a certain group lend themselves to description and interpretive analysis, but escape "lawful" explanation.

Finally, if we take a step back and look at the theoretical arguments discussed in this section, two points seem to emerge. The first is that all overarching formulations explicitly incorporate the biological side of individual human behavior. At the same time, culture is a biologically rooted faculty of the human species that allows for diversity in behavior patterns. A second, widely shared characteristic is the implicit emphasis on a developmental perspective (see also Keller & Greenfield, 2000). Perhaps it is along these lines that the controversies which have such a prominent place in thinking about behavior–culture relationships can be gradually transcended.

## Conclusions

In this chapter we have tried to deal with major theoretical issues in cross-cultural psychology. We first presented a classification in which different ways of interpreting cross-cultural findings could be ordered in a meaningful way. For this purpose we used distinctions introduced before, namely between the two principles of population-mediated transmission, genetic and cultural, and between three levels of inference. We pointed out that inferences about cross-cultural differences at a high level of generalization are difficult to validate, whether they refer to genetic or to cultural processes of transmission. Three major orientations present in the classification of inferences, namely absolutism, relativism, and universalism, were further examined and we concluded that universalism appears to be the most sustainable of the three positions.

We then examined three major traditions of thinking in cross-cultural psychology: cultural psychology, indigenous psychology, and the culture-comparative research tradition. These imply important differences in perspectives that are in need of some kind of resolution. In the final section we suggested ways in which the gap between the main theoretical positions in cross-cultural psychology could perhaps be bridged, namely by combining elements from both, by integrating them, or by acknowledging that they both address valid, but separate, concerns.

## Key terms

absolutism

conventions

cultural psychology

cultural transmission

culture-comparative research

genetic transmission

indigenous psychologies

levels of inference (or generalization)

relativism

universalism

universality

## Further reading

Cole, M. (1996). *Cultural psychology: A once and future discipline.* Cambridge, MA: Belknap. A book-length discussion of cultural psychology, especially Cole's own sociocultural tradition.

Kashima, Y. (2000). Conceptions of culture and person for psychology. *Journal of Cross-Cultural Psychology, 31,* 14–32. An attempt at bridging the gap between relativist and universalist approaches.

Lonner, W. J., & Adamopoulos, J. (1997). Culture as antecedent to behavior. In J. W. Berry, Y. H. Poortinga, & J. Pandey (Eds.), *Theory and method* (pp. 43–83). Vol. I of *Handbook of cross-cultural psychology* (2nd ed.). Boston, MA: Allyn and Bacon. A chapter reviewing various theories from a universalist perspective.

Miller, J. G. (1997). Theoretical isues in cultural psychology. In J. W. Berry, Y. H. Poortinga, & J. Pandey (Eds.), *Theory and method* (pp. 85–128). Vol. I of *Handbook of cross-cultural psychology* (2nd ed.). Boston, MA: Allyn and Bacon. A review chapter presenting various relativist views.

Poortinga, Y. H. (1997). Towards convergence? In J. W. Berry, Y. H. Poortinga, & J. Pandey (Eds.), *Theory and method* (pp. 301–46). Vol. I of *Handbook of cross-cultural psychology* (2nd ed.). Boston, MA: Allyn & Bacon. An attempt to bridge relativist and universalist perspectives, but based more on the latter than on the former.

# Applying research findings across cultures

# 13 Acculturation and intercultural relations

Up until now, we have identified two approaches to understanding how culture and behavior may be related: cross-cultural and cultural psychology. Increasingly, a third perspective is coming to the fore, that of intercultural psychology, which is the focus of this chapter. In the first section, we consider how intercultural work in plural societies differs from the cross-cultural and cultural perspectives. Then we examine in much more detail a concept that derives from anthropology, and was introduced in chs. 1 and 2: **acculturation.**

How groups and individuals orient themselves to, and deal with, this process of culture contact and change constitutes the balance of this chapter. Intercultural strategies (how people try to live with the two cultures), psychological acculturation (the personal changes and stresses that people undergo), and adaptation (the long-term, relatively stable outcomes) are considered in turn. Then, drawing upon sociology and social psychology, the field of intercultural relations is outlined (particularly the work on understanding and reducing prejudice). Finally, taking concepts and evidence from political science, the attempt to deal with acculturation and other intercultural phenomena is outlined, using the idea of multiculturalism.

Intercultural psychology differs from cross-cultural and cultural psychology in a number of respects. First, cross-cultural psychology has tended to accept the prior existence of cultural systems, which are relatively bounded and stable. However, cultural changes due to the "sociopolitical context" were included in the ecocultural framework (fig. 1.1), and "culture change" was included in the definition of the field in ch. 1. In the cross-cultural approach, these serve to represent the dynamic aspects of how cultures and individuals change when they come into contact with each other. Indeed, Taft (1974) argued that an intercultural approach was an integral part of the emerging field. This position has become widely accepted, to the point where studies of culture contact and resultant acculturation are now a prominent part of the field. Thus, charges that cross-cultural psychology uses fixed cultural categories and dichotomies can be easily refuted; few people nowadays advocate that cultures are "independent, coherent and stable" (Hermans & Kempen, 1998, p. 1111), that they have fixed geographical locations, or that globalization processes are not underway. Such claims clearly do not reflect the current focus and substance of cross-cultural psychology (Phinney, 1999; Tweed et al., 1999).

Second, in the case of cultural psychology, we have seen that the focus is usually on single cultures. While they are viewed as dynamic, in the process of constant (re)construction, change is viewed as resulting from interaction between individuals within a culture, rather than from contact between cultures. Virtually no intercultural studies are represented in the body of contemporary cultural psychology.

We take the position that intercultural psychology is a fundamental part of cross-cultural psychology, and has been so from early times. One way of viewing this area is to think of it as doing cross-cultural psychology at home in culturally diverse societies, where numerous cultural groups have come to live together. This approach implies theoretical and methodological positions. First, we consider that the groups have a culture: hence we use the term "ethnocultural" rather than "minority" group. As a result, they need to be studied and interpreted using all the conceptual and methodological safeguards outlined in chs. 11 and 12. Second, since they are no longer "independent" groups, they cannot serve as unique cases in a comparative framework (cf. Galton's problem), nor can the sources of cultural influence on behavior be uniquely ascribed (cf. fig. 2.1) to one specific culture. Finally, one of the outcomes of culture contact is the emergence of new ethnocultural groups; hence the research effort required may be multiplied, since both original cultures, and the evolving culture, all need to be studied as contexts for human behavior.

In addition to this thirty-year tradition in cross-cultural psychology, the field has a number of other roots. In anthropology, work began in the 1930s on the psychological aspects of acculturation (Hallowell, 1945) among indigenous peoples in Canada. Second, there is an active interest in psychological features of immigrants in France and elsewhere in Europe as they attempt to live successfully there (Camilleri, 1991; Denoux, 1993), known as *psychologie interculturelle*.

## Plural societies

A culturally **plural society** is one in which a number of different cultural groups reside together within a shared social and political framework (Skelton & Allen, 1999). It contrasts sharply with a unicultural society that has "one culture, one people." It used to be the case that such unicultural so-cieties actually existed; however, there is no contemporary society in which one culture, one language, one religion, and one single identity characterizes the whole population. Despite this obvious fact, some people continue to think and behave as if their societies were culturally uniform (or if they are not now, they should be!). However, others know and accept that there are usu-ally many cultural groups trying to live together in their society, and that there should not be attempts to forge a single culture, a single people out of this diversity.

Two contrasting views of plural societies have been distinguished (Berry, 1998b). In one (the "mainstream-minority"), there is a "melting pot"; here the view is that of a single dominant or "mainstream" society, on the margins of which are the various "minority" groups. The usual assumption is that such groups should be absorbed into the mainstream in such a way that they essentially dis-appear. As a result, there is to be "one people, one culture, one nation," as an overriding goal. This is reminiscent of early conceptions, such as "manifest des-tiny" in the American (US) tradition in the last century. This view assumed that the whole continent of North America was destined to be peopled by one nation, speaking one language, and professing one general system of religious and political principles. It is also reminiscent of the colonial policy pursued earlier by France: "to gently polish and reclaim for humanity the savages of the world." If such incorporation is not achieved (for whatever reasons), then the groups on the margins literally become marginalized (see below). A second view is a "mul-ticultural" one, in which there is a "mosaic" of **ethnocultural groups** who retain a sense of their cultural identity, and who (on that basis) participate in a social framework that is characterized by some shared norms (legal, economic, politi-cal agreements) about how to live together, but which permits institutions to evolve in order to accommodate different cultural interests (see last section of this chapter)

What kinds of groups are there in plural societies? One answer to this question may be provided by looking at the reasons (historical or contemporary) for people of different cultural backgrounds to be living together in the same place. There are three reasons. First, groups may find themselves together either because they have sought out such an arrangement voluntarily, or alternatively because it has been forced upon them. Second, some groups have remained on home ground, while others have settled far from their ancestral territory (sedentary versus migrant). And third, some people are settled into a plural society permanently, while others are only temporary.

Some of the more common terms used to refer to constituent groups in plural societies can be defined in relation to these three reasons. Starting with the longest-term residents, *indigenous peoples* are those who have "always been there" in the sense that their roots go way back, and there is no evidence of any earlier people whose descendants are still in the population. Of course, all peo-ples have migrated from a common source population (probably in Africa) and hence indigenous peoples may more correctly be termed "early migrants." There is considerable controversy in some countries about the term "indigenous" (or "native," or "aboriginal") because of special rights that may be claimed. A similar term, used in some European countries, is "national minority," such as Basque, Breton, Catalan, Frisian, and Sami. The basic characteristic of such groups is their long-term residence in territories that were forcefully incorporated into a larger nation state; their residual lands are often reduced in size and capacity to sustain life, and they have come to be seen as just another "minority group" within the larger plural society. They are clearly "involuntary," as well as "sedentary."

Other peoples who have a long history of settlement are the descendants of earlier waves of immigrants who have settled into recognizable groups, often with a sense of their own cultural heritage (common language, identity, etc.). These ethnic groups can be found the world over, for example in French- and Spanish-origin communities in the New World, in the groups descended from indentured workers (such as Chinese, and Indian communities in the Caribbean), from those who were enslaved (such as African Americans), and in Dutch and British groups in Southern Africa, Australia, and New Zealand. Such groups may be large or small, powerful or powerless, depending on the overall history and the national context within which they live. Whatever their histories, most are now voluntary participants in the national life of their contemporary societies.

In contrast to these two sedentary constituents of plural societies, there are others who have developed in other places and have been socialized into other cultures, who migrate to take up residence (either permanently or temporarily) in another society. Among these groups are immigrants who usually move in order to achieve a better life elsewhere. For most, the "pull factors" (those that attract them to a new society) are stronger than the "push factors" (those that pressure them to leave). Hence, immigrants are generally thought of as "voluntary" members of plural societies.

While immigrants are relatively permanent participants in their new society, the group known as sojourners are there temporarily in a variety of roles, and for a set purpose (e.g., as international students, diplomats, business executives, aid workers, or guest workers). In their case, the process of becoming involved in the plural society is complicated by their knowledge that they will eventually leave, and either return home or be posted to yet another country. Thus there may be a hesitation to become fully involved, to establish close relationships, or to begin to identify with the new society. Despite their uncertain position, in some societies sojourners constitute a substantial element in the resident population (e.g., the Gulf states, Germany, Belgium) and may hold either substantial power, or be relatively powerless.

Among involuntary migrants, refugees and asylum seekers (now often called collectively "forced migrants," Ager, 1999) have the greatest hurdles to face: they frequently do not want to leave their homelands, and if they do, it is not always possible for them to be granted the right to stay and settle into the new society.

Those who arrive at the border of a country that has signed the Geneva Convention on Refugees have a right to be admitted and given sanctuary (as "asylum seekers") until their claim is adjudicated; if granted permanent admission as refugees, much of the uncertainty that surrounded their life during their flight is reduced. However, most live with the knowledge that "push factors" (rather than "pull factors") led them to flee their homeland and settle in their new society; and of course, most have experienced traumatic events, and most have lost their material possessions.

There are two reasons why these six kinds of groups were introduced, according to three factors (voluntary-involuntary; sedentary-migrant; and permanent–temporary), rather than simply listed. The most important reason is that, as groups, they carry differential size, power, rights, and resources; these factors have an important bearing on how they will engage (as groups or as individuals) in intercultural relations. A second important reason is that the attitudes, motives, values, and abilities (all psychological characteristics of individuals in these groups) are also highly variable. These factors, too, impact on how their acculturation and intercultural relations are likely to develop.

## Acculturation

As we discussed in ch. 2, there is an important distinction to be made between the processes of **enculturation** and **acculturation**. The former is the process that links developing individuals to their primary cultural contexts, while the latter is a process that individuals undergo in response to a changing cultural context. We have also noted (in ch. 11) that acculturation is one of the inferred antecedents of observed variation in behavior. Related to acculturation is the more general phenomenon of culture change (see Berry, 1980c; Segall et al., 1999, ch. 11). Acculturation is only one form of culture change, namely that due to contact with other cultures. In practice it is often difficult to separate the actual causes of change due to external forces from those due to internal forces. This is because many factors are usually operating simultaneously including contact, diffusion from other cultures and innovation from within the cultural group (Berry, 1990a).

### Cultural level

The first major study of acculturation was that of Herskovits (1938); this was followed quickly by others (e.g., Linton, 1940). Together with Redfield, they defined the concept:

> Acculturation comprehends those phenomena which result when groups of individuals having different cultures come into continuous first-hand contact, with subsequent changes in the original culture patterns of either or both groups . . . under this definition acculturation is to be distinguished from culture change, of which it is but one aspect, and assimilation, which is at times a phase of acculturation. (Redfield, Linton, & Herskovits, 1936, pp. 149–52)

In another formulation, acculturation was defined as:

> Culture change that is initiated by the conjunction of two or more autonomous cultural systems. Acculturative change may be the consequence of direct cultural transmission; it may be derived from noncultural causes, such as ecological or demographic modification induced by an impinging culture; it may be delayed, as with internal adjustments following upon the acceptance of alien traits or patterns; or it may be a reactive adaptation of traditional modes of life. (Social Science Research Council, 1954, p. 974)

In the first formulation, acculturation is seen as "one aspect" of the broader concept of culture change (that which results from intercultural contact), is considered to generate change in "either or both groups," and is distinguished from assimilation (which may be "at times a phase"). In the second, a few extra features are added, including change that is indirect (not cultural but "ecological"), delayed ("internal adjustments," presumably of both a cultural and psychological character, take time), and can be "reactive" (that is, rejecting the cultural influence, and changing toward a more "traditional" way of life, rather than inevitably toward greater similarity with the dominant culture).

## Psychological level

In cross-cultural psychology it is important to distinguish between group- and individual-levels of acculturation. Graves (1967) has coined the term **psychological acculturation** to refer to the changes that an individual experiences as a result of being in contact with other cultures, and as a result of participating in the process of acculturation that his or her cultural or ethnic group is undergoing. The distinction between group-level acculturation and psychological acculturation is important for two reasons. One is that the phenomena are different at the two levels, as we shall see later in the chapter: for example, at the population level, changes in social structure, economic base, and political organization frequently occur, while at the individual level, the changes are in such phenomena as identity, values, and attitudes. A second reason for distinguishing between the two levels is that not all acculturating individuals participate in the collective changes that are underway in their group to the same extent or in the same way. Thus, if we want to eventually understand the relationships between culture contact and psychological outcomes for individuals, we will need to assess (using separate measures) changes at the population level, and participation in these changes by individuals, and then relate both of these measures to the psychological consequences for the individual.

From the definition of acculturation presented earlier we may identify some key elements that are usually studied in cross-cultural psychology. First there needs to be contact or interaction between cultures which is continuous and first hand; this rules out short-term, accidental contact, and it rules out diffusion of single cultural practices over long distances. Second, the result is some *change* in the cultural or psychological phenomena among the people in contact, usually continuing for generations down the line. Third, taking these first two aspects together, we can distinguish between a process and a state: there is activity during and after contact which is dynamic, and there is a longer-term result of the process which may be relatively stable: this outcome may include not only changes to existing phenomena, but also some novel phenomena that are generated by the process of cultural interaction. It should be clear by now that acculturation does not inevitably lead to cultural loss or to international or domestic cultural homogeneity. While the process can be destructive (i.e. through elimination or absorption), it can also be reactive, in which individuals and groups re-establish their original cultures (by revitalization or reaffirmation of their cultures), and it can be creative, in which new cultures emerge from the interactions over time.

## General framework

A framework that outlines and links cultural and psychological acculturation, and identifies the two (or more) groups in contact is presented in fig. 13.1. This framework serves as a map of those phenomena which need to be conceptualized and measured during acculturation research. At the cultural level (on the left) we need to understand key features of the two original cultural groups (A and B) prior to their major contact, the nature of their contact relationships, and the resulting cultural changes in both groups and the emergent ethnocultural groups during the process of acculturation; this requires extensive ethnographic, community-level

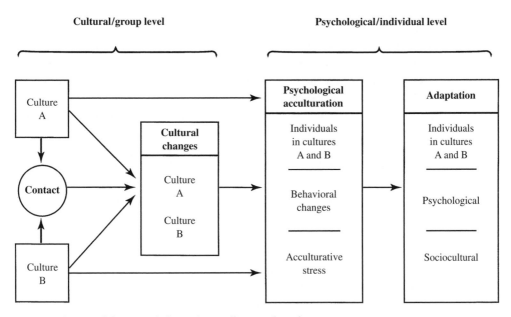

**13.1** A general framework for understanding acculturation

work. These changes can be minor or substantial, and range from being easily accomplished through to being a source of major cultural disruption.

At the individual level (on the right) we need to consider the psychological changes that individuals in all the groups undergo, and their eventual adaptation to their new situations; this requires sampling and studying individuals who are variably involved in the process of acculturation. These changes can be a set of rather easily accomplished behavioral changes (e.g., in ways of speaking, dressing, eating, and in one's cultural identity), or they can be more problematic, producing **acculturative stress** (e.g., uncertainty, anxiety, depression, even psychopathology; Al-Issa & Tousignant, 1997). **Adaptation** can be primarily internal or psychological (e.g., sense of well-being, of self-esteem) or sociocultural, linking the individual to others in the new society (e.g., competence in the activities of daily intercultural living; Searle & Ward, 1990). General overviews of this process and these specific features can be found in the literature (e.g., Berry, 1990a, 1997a; Berry & Sam, 1997; Birman, 1994; Liebkind, 2000; Ward, 1996).

In principle each culture could influence the other equally, but in practice, one tends to dominate the other, leading to a distinction between dominant and non-dominant groups. For a complete picture, mutual influence should be studied; however, for most of this chapter we will focus on the culture receiving the greater influence (e.g., the non-dominant). This is not to say that changes in the dominant culture are uninteresting or unimportant: acculturation often brings about population expansion, greater cultural diversity, attitudinal reaction (prejudice and discrimination) and policy development (for example in the area of multiculturalism; see MOST [1995]).

One result of the contact and influence is that aspects of the non-dominant groups become transformed so that cultural features are not identical to those in the original group at the time of first contact; and frequently, over time, new ethnocultural groups emerge. A parallel phenomenon is that individuals in these groups undergo psychological changes (as a result of influences from both their own changing group and from the dominant group), and with continuing contact, further psychological changes may take place.

The course of change resulting from acculturation is highly variable, and depends on many characteristics of the dominant and non-dominant groups. For both groups, it is important to know the purpose, length, permanence of contact, and the policies being pursued. Cultural and psychological characteristics of the two populations can also affect the outcome of the acculturation process. Acculturative changes, at the group level, include political, economic, demographic, and cultural changes that can vary from relatively little to substantial alterations in the way of life of both groups. While these population-level changes set the stage for individual change, we have noted previously that there are very likely to be individual differences in the psychological characteristics that a person brings to the acculturation process; and not every person will necessarily participate to the same extent in the process. Taken together, this means that we need to shift our focus away from general characterizations of acculturation phenom-ena to a concern for variation among individuals in the groups under-going acculturation.

## Intercultural strategies

Having set this general stage, we turn now to the concept of intercultural strategies, which is relevant to all components of this general framework. These strategies consist of two (usually related) components: attitudes and behaviors (that is, the preferences and actual outcomes) that are exhibited in day-to-day intercultural encounters. Of course, there is rarely a one-to-one match between what an individual prefers and seeks (attitudes) and what he or she is actually able to do (behaviors). This discrepancy is widely studied in social psychology and is usually explained as being the result of social constraints on behaviors (such as norms, opportunities, etc.). Nevertheless, there is often a significant positive correlation between attitudes and behaviors, permitting the use of an overall conception of individual strategies.

The centrality of the concept of intercultural strategies can be illustrated by reference to each component of fig. 13.1. At the cultural level, the two groups in contact (whether dominant or non-dominant) usually have some notion about what they are attempting to do (e.g., colonial policies, or motivations for migration), or what is being done to them, during the contact. Similarly, the goals of the emergent ethnocultural group will influence their strategies. At the individual level, both the behavioral changes and acculturative stress phenomena are now known to be a function, at least to some extent, of what people try to do during their acculturation; and the longer-term outcomes (both psychological and sociocultural adaptations) often correspond to the strategic goals set by the groups of which they are members.

### Acculturation strategies

As we have seen, the original definitions of acculturation foresaw that domination was not the only relationship, and that cultural and psychological homogenization would not be the only possible outcome of intercultural contact. Why not? An answer to this question lies in the observation that people hold different views about how they want to live following contact. They adopt different **acculturation strategies**; not everyone seeks out such contact, and even among those who do, not everyone seeks to change their culture and behavior to be more like the other (often dominant) group. In the 1936 statement by Redfield et al., it was noted that assimilation is not the only form of acculturation; there are other ways of going about it. Taking this assertion as a starting point, Berry (1970a; Sommerlad & Berry, 1970) first distinguished between the strategies of **assimilation** and **integration**, and later between **separation** and **marginalization** as various ways in which acculturation (both of groups and individuals) could

take place. These distinctions involved two dimensions, based on orientations towards one's own group, and those towards other groups (Berry, 1970a, 1974b,
1980a). The first dimension is rendered as a relative preference for maintaining
one's heritage culture and identity (issue 1), and the second as a relative preference for having contact with and participating in the larger society along with
other ethnocultural groups (issue 2). This formulation is presented in fig. 13-2
for both the ethnocultural groups and the larger society. As we shall see, these
strategies vary across individuals, groups, and societies; they also vary because
of the interaction between the strategies of the two groups in contact.

Orientations to two issues can vary along dimensions, represented by bipolar
arrows. Generally positive or negative views about these issues intersect to define
four strategies of intercultural relations. These strategies carry different names,
depending on which group (the dominant or non-dominant) is being considered. From the point of view of non-dominant ethnocultural groups (on the left
of fig. 13.2), when individuals do not wish to maintain their cultural identity and
seek daily interaction with other cultures, the assimilation strategy is defined. In
contrast, when individuals place a value on holding on to their original culture,
and at the same time wish to avoid interaction with others, then the separation
alternative is defined. When there is an interest in both maintaining one's original culture, while having daily interactions with other groups, integration is the
option; here, some degree of cultural integrity is maintained, while at the same
time members of an ethnocultural group seek to participate as an integral part of
the larger social network. Finally, when there is little possibility is or interest in

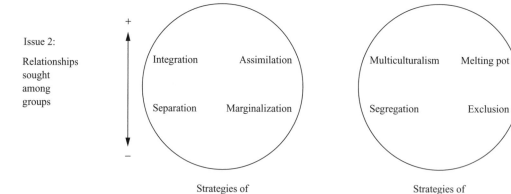

**13.2**  Acculturation strategies in ethnocultural groups and the larger society
From Berry, 2001a

cultural maintenance (often for reasons of enforced cultural loss), and little interest in having relations with others (often for reasons of exclusion or discrimination) then marginalization is defined.

This presentation assumes that non-dominant groups and their individual members have the freedom to choose how they want to engage in intercultural relations. This, of course, is not always the case (Berry, 1974b). When the dominant group enforces certain kinds of relations, or constrains the choices of non-dominant groups or individuals, then other terms need to be used. This is most clearly so in the case of integration, which can only be "freely" chosen and successfully pursued by non-dominant groups when the dominant society is open and inclusive in its orientation toward cultural diversity (Berry, 1990a). Thus a mutual accommodation is required for integration to be attained, involving the acceptance by both dominant and non-dominant groups of the right of all groups to live as culturally different peoples within the same society. This strategy requires non-dominant groups to adopt the basic values of the larger society, while at the same time the dominant group must be prepared to adapt national institutions (e.g., education, health, labor) to better meet the needs of all groups now living together in the plural society (i.e., the multicultural view of a plural society).

Obviously, the integration strategy can only be pursued in societies that are explicitly multicultural, in which certain psychological pre-conditions are established (Berry & Kalin, 1995). These pre-conditions are: the widespread acceptance of the value to a society of cultural diversity (i.e., the presence of a positive **multicultural ideology**); relatively low levels of prejudice (i.e., minimal ethnocentrism, racism, and discrimination); positive mutual attitudes among ethnocultural groups (i.e., no specific intergroup hatreds); and a sense of attachment to, or identification with, the larger society by all individuals and groups.

Just as obviously, integration (and separation) can only be pursued when sufficient numbers of one's ethnocultural group also share in the wish to maintain the group's cultural heritage. Other constraints on one's choice of acculturation strategy have also been noted. For example those whose physical features set them apart from the society of settlement (e.g., Koreans in Canada, or Turks in Germany) may experience prejudice and discrimination, and thus be reluctant to pursue assimilation in order to avoid being rejected (Berry, Kim, Power, Young, & Bujaki, 1989).

These two basic issues were initially approached from the point of view of the non-dominant ethnocultural groups only (as on the left side of fig. 13.2). However, the original definitions clearly established that both groups in contact would become acculturated. Hence, in 1974, a third dimension was added: that of the powerful role played by the dominant group in influencing the way in which mutual acculturation would take place (Berry, 1974b; 1980a). The addition of this third dimension produced a duplicate framework (right side of fig. 13.2). Assimilation, when sought by the dominant group, can be termed the "melting pot." When separation is demanded and enforced by the dominant group it is "segregation." For marginalization, when imposed by the dominant group it is a form of "exclusion" (and in its extreme form, it becomes "ethnocide"). Finally for integration, when cultural diversity is an objective of the society as a whole, it represents the strategy of mutual accommodation now widely called **multiculturalism** (see later section).

There are now hundreds of studies that have examined these acculturation strategies in non-dominant acculturating groups (see Berry & Sam, 1997, for a partial review). Usually, one scale for each of the four strategies is developed yielding a score for assimilation, integration, separation, and marginalization attitudes (e.g., Horenczyk, 1996; Van de Vijver, Helms-Lorenz, & Feltzer, 1999). Sometimes the two underlying dimensions (cultural maintenance and participation) are measured (e.g., Dona & Berry, 1994; Nguyen, Messe, & Stollack, 1999; Ryder, Alden, & Paulhus, 2000; Ward & Rana-Deuba, 1999); in a few studies, four vignettes are used, each portraying one of the four strategies (e.g., Georgas & Papastylianou, 1998). In most studies, preferences for integration are expressed over the other three strategies, with marginalization being the least preferred. One of the more common exceptions is that of Turks in Germany (Piontkowski, Florack, Hoelker, & Obdrzalek, 2000), and lower socioeconomic status Turks in Canada (Berry & Ataca, 2000), who prefer separation over integration. A similar result has been obtained for some indigenous peoples in various parts of the world (e.g., Berry, 1999a); but in other places, integration is preferred (e.g., Mishra et al., 1996).

It is important to note that when all four strategies are assessed, it possible to have independent measurement, and to obtain variable degrees of preference, for each strategy. For example, one could logically have a preference for both integration and separation, since they both involve the maintenance of one's cultural heritage and identity. Or these two strategies may be seen as opposed, on the ground that they differ on the issue of contacts with others. Moreover, while assimilation and separation differ on both issues, it is possible for these two attitudes to be positively correlated; this happens when both are rejected in favor of another strategy (such as integration). Thus all possible relationships among the four strategies are theoretically possible, and have been found empirically (Berry, 1990a). Once the four strategies are taken as the appropriate way to understand how people acculturate, it no longer makes sense to refer to the "degree" or "level" of acculturation (e.g., as in "highly acculturated"); it is possible to consider only the degree or level of support for each of the four strategies. Usually, when "level of acculturation" is used in the literature, it is intended to mean "level of assimilation" only.

Fewer studies of the **larger society** or dominant group have been carried out. One continuing program in Canada (Berry, Kalin, & Taylor, 1977; Berry, & Kalin, 1995) has employed a scale, termed "multicultural ideology," in national surveys. This scale represents integration items at its positive pole, and the other three strategies at its negative pole. Over the past twenty-five years, the preference for integration has risen from about 65 percent to about 70 percent, indicating a general and increasing acceptance of the "multicultural" model in the general population in Canada.

More recently, Bourhis and colleagues (Bourhis, Moise, Perreault, & Senecal, 1977) have presented an "interactive acculturation model" in which the "acculturation expectations" of the larger society (cf., multicultural ideology) are assessed, as well as the acculturation strategies of the various non-dominant groups. They propose the existence of varying outcomes ranging from "consensual" to "conflictual," depending on whether views match or differ.

In another approach, Horenczyk (1996) asked Russian immigrants to Israel about their perception of the "acculturation ideologies" of Israeli society (in addition to their own views). Integration was the most frequently expected way for immigrants to acculturate, followed by assimilation and separation. This pattern was interpreted as representing a major shift away from the earlier Israeli "absorption" or assimilationist ideology, and as presenting a better match with the immigrants' own acculturation strategies, which were largely integrationist.

A European study of views in the larger society (Piontkowski et al., 2000) employed samples in Germany, Switzerland, and Slovakia, using measures of the two basic issues, rather than the four attitudes. Members of non-dominant groups (Hungarians, Turks, and former Yugoslavians) living in Germany and Switzerland were also studied. Overall, integration was preferred, although the pattern varied across dominant/non-dominant pairs. For example, in dominant samples in both Germany and Switzerland, a preference for integration was followed by assimilation; however there was "remarkable support for separation and marginalization" (p. 11) among the Swiss with respect to Yugoslavians. And in Slovakia, there was roughly similar support (around 30 percent) each for integration, assimilation, and marginalization with respect to Hungarians living there. (As already noted, the non-dominant groups in this study preferred integration, with the exception of Turks in Germany, who preferred separation.) There is a very clear mismatch between these two sets of acculturation strategies, especially for Turks in Germany (integration versus separation), for Yugoslavians in Switzerland (integration versus marginalization), and for Hungarians in Slovakia (also integration versus marginalization).

## Identity strategies

A parallel approach to understanding intercultural strategies uses the concept of **cultural identity** (Aboud, 1981; Berry, 1999a; Liebkind, 1996; Phinney, 2000). This notion refers to a complex set of beliefs and attitudes that people have about themselves in relation to their culture group membership; usually these come to the fore when people are in contact with another culture, rather than when living entirely within a single culture. Two substantial conceptual schemes have been proposed to help us think about cultural identity, both from European scholars. Tajfel (1978) has developed social identity theory, and Camilleri (1991) has put forward a theory of identity strategies (*stratégies identitaires*). As we shall see, both have clear similarities to the various acculturation strategies, and both have become widely used more recently in North America (e.g., Berry, 1999a; Brewer, 1991; Kalin & Berry, 1995). Just as the notion of acculturation strategies is based on two underlying dimensions (own cultural maintenance, and involvement with other cultures), there is now a consensus that how one thinks of oneself is also constructed along two dimensions. The first is identification with one's heritage or ethnocultural group, and the second is identification with the larger or dominant society. These two aspects of cultural identity have been referred to in various ways: ethnic identity and civic identity (Kalin & Berry, 1995); heritage identity and national identity (Salazar & Salazar, 1998). Moreover (as for the acculturation dimensions) these dimensions are independent of each other (in the sense that they are not negatively correlated, or that more of one does not imply less of the other); and they are nested (in the sense that one's heritage or ethnic identity may be contained within a larger national or civic identity, so that one can be, for example, an Italian Australian).

Using these two identity dimensions, one can see clear similarities with the four acculturation strategies: when both identities are asserted, this resembles the integration strategy; when one feels neither, then there is a sense of marginalization; and when one is strongly emphasized over the other, then identities resemble either the assimilation or separation strategies. Evidence for this link is found in numerous empirical studies where both acculturation strategies and cultural identities have been assessed. For example, these two kinds of strategies have been examined together by Georgas and Papastylianou (1998) among samples of ethnic Greeks remigrating to Greece from Albania, Australia, Canada, Russia, and the USA. They found that those with a "Greek" identity were high on the assimilation strategy, those with a "mixed" (e.g., Greek Albanian) were highest on integration, and those with an "indigenous" (e.g., "Albanian") identity were highest on separation. These findings are consistent with expectations about how acculturation and identity strategies should relate to each other. Similarly, Laroche and colleagues (Laroche, Kim, Hui, & Joy, 1996; Laroche, Kim, Hui, & Tomiuk, 1998) found the expected correspondence between measures of cultural identity and acculturation strategies in studies with French Canadians.

In their work on identity strategies (e.g., Camilleri & Malewska-Peyre, 1997) a distinction is drawn between a "value identity" (what they would like to be ideally; cf. acculturation attitudes) and their "real identity" (what people are like at the present time; cf. acculturation behaviors). These two aspects of identity can be very similar, or very different (cf. discrepancy between acculturation attitudes and behaviors). In the latter case, people will usually strive to reduce the difference between the two. In situations where individuals engage in intercultural relationships, this distinction becomes more salient. This is so because non-dominant individuals (e.g., Muslim migrants in France, where most of Camilleri's work has been done) may begin to perceive a greater difference between their real selves (as rooted in their own culture), and new ideal selves that are communicated, perhaps imposed by the dominant society. For Camilleri and Malewska-Peyre (1997), such discrepancies are particularly large among immigrant adolescents, who often share the values of their peers in the dominant society, in opposition to those of their parents in the immigrant group. This frequently leads to conflict that needs to be resolved using various strategies to preserve the "coherence of identity."

One of these strategies is to maintain "simple tolerance," avoiding identity conflict by clinging to one's heritage cultural values, and ignoring or rejecting challenges to these from the dominant culture. This identity strategy resembles that of separation. A second strategy is that of "pragmatism" in the face of pressure to adapt to the dominant culture. In this case, young immigrants maintain "traditionalist" identity and behavior in their relationships with their parents (and their heritage cultural community), and a "modernist" orientation with their peers; this may also be seen as a "chameleon identity." When such a combination is possible, it resembles one form of the integration strategy. Another strategy that resembles integration is that of "conflict avoidance by complex coherence." In this case, individuals use a "strategy of maximization of advantages" in which the most advantageous aspects of each culture are selected and interwoven into their identity. If there are conflicts between the two, then substrategies (e.g., by "dissociation") are employed to achieve coherence. Of course, when one's heritage culture no longer contributes to one's sense of self, then exclusive identification with the dominant society can take place, resembling the assimilation acculturation strategy. Alternatively, when neither the heritage nor the dominant cultures are part of one's identity (which is the case frequently of young immigrants in Europe), the situation of marginalization is present.

The "social identity theory" (SIT) of Tajfel and his colleagues proposes that the concept of social identity is central to understanding intercultural relations. First, social identity is "that part of an individual's self concept which derives from his knowledge of his membership in a social group (or groups), together with the value and emotional significance attached to that membership" (Tajfel, 1978, p. 63). That is, there is both a knowledge or cognitive component that one is in a particular social category (e.g., Australian, male, worker) and an affective or evaluative component that represents a sense of attachment to that category. Empirical evidence for this conceptual distinction has been provided by Hocoy (1998) and Jasinskaja-Lahti and Liebkind (1999). In these studies, both aspects of identity were found using factor-analytic techniques with Chinese in Canada and Russians in Finland. In a national survey in Canada, Kalin and Berry (1995) found that people could readily place themselves in an ethnic category, and also provide a self-rating of strength of attachment to a number of relevant ethnic categories. While the strength rating was highest for the category in which they primarily placed themselves, high attachment ratings were exhibited for other categories as well. Thus, how people usually think of themselves (the categorical, or cognitive identity) does not have a close relationship to how strongly people feel they are attached to a number of cultural categories. This phenomenon has been described as a nesting of identities, more specific ones (e.g., a local, regional, or ethnic identity) being contained within larger (e.g., national or civic) identities.

A second aspect of SIT proposes that individuals are fundamentally motivated to achieve a positive social identity, to think well of themselves, rather than negatively. And third, this goal will prompt people to make social comparisons with other groups in order to achieve a distinct identity, as well as a positive one.

The strategies used to achieve a distinct and positive social identity have been studied extensively in the social psychology of intergroup relations (see Taylor & Moghaddam, 1994, ch. 4; and Stephan & Stephan, 1996, ch. 4, for reviews of the empirical literature). In summary, there is now evidence to support the following generalizations. Where the act of comparison yields a positive identity, people will then seek to maintain, or even extend or enhance it. Where comparison reveals an inadequate social identity (neither positive nor distinct), people will seek to change themselves or the situation in which they find themselves. Some of these changes are "individualist," in the sense that the individual "goes it alone," while others are "collectivist," in which individuals seek change along with the rest of their group.

Some of these strategies involve absorptions (cf. the assimilation strategy as outlined earlier), while others pose a direct challenge to the dominant group (cf. the separation strategy). The first obviously involves the loss of a distinctive identity, while the second seeks to reinforce it. Other strategies include a redefinition of the situation (e.g., emphasizing one's "indigenous" status, with special rights), or changing the dimension of the comparison (e.g., "we may be poorer at school, but we are much better at sports"). In these last two cases, the ideas of Tajfel and his colleagues go beyond the kinds of strategies outlined above; however, to the extent that they emphasize the qualities of one's own cultural group, they might be seen as aspects of the separation strategy.

## Psychological acculturation

One of the two dimensions underlying acculturation strategies is the degree to which groups and individuals maintain or change their customary practices and behaviors. At the group level, many terms have been used to characterize what happens following contact between a dominant and non-dominant culture. A number of very broad descriptions have been proposed, including westernization, modernization, industrialization (Berry, 1980c). However, such broad characterizations are considered to be too general to be of use to cross-cultural psychology (Kagitcibasi, 1998).

### Behavioral changes

At the individual level, virtually all aspects of a person's behavioral repertoire are candidates for change, and have been described earlier as the behavioral component of acculturation strategies. These behavioral aspects have also been referred to (in fig. 13.1) as behavioral changes. They have two components: culture shedding and culture learning (Berry, 1992). The first involves either the deliberate or accidental loss of existing cultural or behavioral features over time following contact. The second involves the deliberate or accidental acquisition of novel ways to live in the new contact setting. These two processes rarely involve the complete range of existing activities; more often they are selective, resulting in a variable pattern of maintenance and change. Moreover, as envisaged by the originators of the concept of acculturation, wholly new cultural and behavioral features are created in the crucible of contact, so that the new features appear to balance any that may be lost. This is the main reason that cultural and behavioral diversity appears not to be declining as a result of acculturation.

How are these patterns of change related to the four acculturation strategies? A straightforward case is where there is maximal culture learning (of ways to live in the new culture); this is clearly what happens when an individual pursues assimilation. As noted earlier, the actual achievement of assimilation also depends on the strategies of the larger society, and on the absence of prejudice and discrimination toward the ethnocultural groups. The opposite occurs with separation in which there is minimal culture shedding of heritage culture, combined with minimal culture learning in the new culture. Sometimes this can involve a re-learning of previously lost aspects of a person's heritage culture (as in "revitalization movements"). In the case of integration, there is moderate to substantial culture learning about how to live in the larger society, combined with minimal culture shedding; this pattern can happen where there is no inherent incompatibility between the two groups, or when the larger society does not create a situation where a person is forced to choose between cultures. Finally, in the classic situation of marginalization, there is maximal culture shedding (often demanded by the dominant group), combined with minimal culture learning (often because access to full participation and opportunity are denied due to prejudice and discrimination in the dominant society).

How are these behavioral changes related to the various aspects of culture outlined in ch. 9? The concept of **cultural distance** has been used to refer to how far apart two cultural groups are on dimensions of cultural variation. In general, it is found that the greater the differences (e.g., in language, religion), the more difficult is the process of acculturation (Ward, 1996). When cultural distance is great, behavioral changes pose a greater challenge since the amount of change required (of both groups, but usually more for the non-dominant group) is greater. When these challenges create serious threats to the individual's well-being, then the phenomenon of acculturative stress needs to be brought into the intercultural framework.

## Acculturative stress

Up until now, there has been an assumption that when groups come into contact, their cultures will change in a relatively straightforward way. Similarly, it has been implied that individuals will change easily through the processes of culture learning and culture shedding. However, this is not always (perhaps not even usually) the case. Cultures can clash, especially when the purpose of the contact is hostile; and individuals can conflict, especially when there are scarce resources. Moreover, the process of learning and shedding may involve psychological conflict, where, for example, incompatible values are held by members of the dominant and non-dominant groups.

To deal with this problem aspect of acculturation, the concept of **acculturative stress** was proposed (Berry, 1970a). Acculturative stress is a response by individuals to life events (that are rooted in intercultural contact), when they exceed the capacity of individuals to deal with them (Berry & Ataca, 2000). Frequently, these reactions include heightened levels of depression (linked to the experience of cultural loss), and of anxiety (linked to uncertainty about how one should live in the new society). This notion is broadly similar to that of culture shock (Oberg, 1960) but acculturative stress is preferred for two reasons. First, the term "shock" has pathological overtones, while the term "stress" has a theoretical basis in studies of how people deal with negative experiences (called stressors) by engaging in various coping strategies (see Lazarus & Folkman, 1984). In these studies, people are seen as potentially able to deal effectively with stressors in their lives and to achieve a variety of outcomes (adaptations) ranging from very negative through to very positive. Thus, from a stress (in contrast to a shock) perspective, acculturation experiences can be both advantageous (such as providing opportunities and interesting experiences), as well as undermining one's life chances (such as limiting opportunities and diminishing experiences that provide meaning to life).

A second reason to prefer the notion of acculturative stress is that the source of the stressful experiences lies in the interaction between cultures (hence "acculturative"), rather than in one "culture." Thus, by using the term "culture," it is possible to misidentify the root of the difficulty. True, it may sometimes lie in the dominant culture (e.g., when there is prejudice and discrimination) or in the non-dominant culture (e.g., when there is a lack of resources, such as education, to adapt to the new situation). However, even in these two examples, a case can be made that prejudice and resource shortage are essentially problems that are located in the interaction between the two cultures, rather than uniquely in one or the other.

There is a massive literature on the phenomenon of acculturative stress. A framework to help understand the various findings is presented in fig. 13.3. It elaborates some of the features of fig. 13.1, showing the processes involved, the factors affecting its course, and the eventual outcomes (adaptation). On the left are aspects of the groups in contact, and the resultant acculturation. On the right is the central flow of psychological acculturation (at the mid level) from contact experiences to eventual adaptation. Above are those pre-existing individual characteristics that influence this flow, and below are those that arise during the process of acculturation.

To expand on fig. 13.3 we consider in detail the various situational and personal factors that are widely believed to influence how people deal with psychological acculturation.

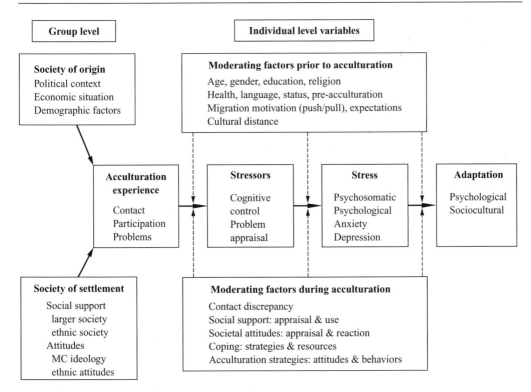

**13.3** Factors affecting acculturative stress and adaptation
From Berry, 1997a

A complete study of acculturation needs to start with a comprehensive examination of the two societal contexts: that of origin and that of settlement. In the society of origin, the cultural characteristics that accompany individuals into the acculturation process need description, in part to understand (literally) where the person is coming from, and in part to establish cultural features for comparison with the society of settlement as a basis for estimating cultural distance between the two groups in contact. The combination of political, economic, and demographic conditions being faced by individuals in their society of origin also needs to be studied as a basis for understanding the degree of voluntariness in the **migration motivation** of acculturating individuals. Arguments by Richmond (1993) suggest that migrants can be ranged on a continuum between reactive and proactive, with the former being motivated by factors that are constraining or exclusionary, and generally negative in character, while the latter are motivated by factors that are facilitating or enabling, and generally positive in character; these contrasting factors were earlier referred to as push/pull factors in migration motivation.

Of importance in the society of settlement are the general orientations of society and its members toward pluralism and attitudes toward specific groups. Some societies seek diversity and are accepting of the cultural pluralism resulting, taking steps to support the continuation of cultural diversity as a shared communal resource; this positive multicultural ideology (Berry & Kalin, 1995) corresponds to the integration strategy outlined earlier. Others seek to reduce diversity through policies and programs of assimilation, while others attempt to segregate or marginalize diverse populations in their societies. Murphy (1965) has argued that societies supportive of cultural pluralism provide a more positive settlement context for two reasons: they are less likely to enforce cultural change (assimilation) or exclusion (segregation and marginalization) on immigrants; and they are more likely to provide social support both from the institutions of the larger society (e.g., culturally sensitive health care, multicultural curricula in schools) and from the continuing and evolving ethnocultural communities that usually make up plural societies. However, even where pluralism is accepted, there are well-known variations in the relative acceptance of specific ethnocultural groups (e.g., Berry & Kalin, 1995; Hagendoorn, 1993). Those groups that are less well accepted (i.e., are the objects of negative ethnic attitudes) experience hostility, rejection, and discrimination, one factor that is predictive of poor long-term adaptation (Clark et al., 1999; Liebkind & Jasinskaja-Lahti, 2000; Noh, Beiser, Kaspar, Hau, & Rummens, 1999).

The central line in fig. 13.3 represents the five main phenomena included in the process of psychological acculturation, beginning with group acculturation and individual acculturation experience, and ending with some long-term adaptation. This process is highly variable for two main reasons. First is the operation of moderating factors that existed prior to major acculturation taking place (and hence which cannot be much changed by public policies in the society of settlement); second are those that may arise during the process of acculturation (and which are controllable, to some extent). These moderating factors are important for both groups and individuals, and can be seen as both risk factors and protective factors, depending on their degree or level.

The five main features of psychological acculturation have received many different names in both the general and acculturation literatures. However, there is broad agreement (see e.g., Aldwin, 1994; Lazarus, 1990) that the process of dealing with life events begins with some causal agent that places a load or demand on the organism. During acculturation, these demands stem from the experience of having to deal with two cultures in contact, and having to participate to various extents in both of them.

Second, individuals consider the meaning of these experiences, evaluating and appraising them as a source of difficulty (i.e., as stressors), or as benign, sometimes even as opportunities. The outcome of this appraisal is variable: when acculturation experiences are judged to pose no problem for the individual, changes are likely to be rather easy and behavioral changes will follow smoothly. When greater levels of conflict are experienced, and the experiences are judged to be problematic, but controllable and surmountable, then acculturative stress results. In this case, individuals understand that they are facing problems resulting from intercultural contact that cannot be dealt with easily or quickly.

Third, as we have noted, individuals engage in strategies that attempt to deal with the experiences that are appraised as problematic. These basic coping strategies can be understood in relation to the intercultural strategies outlined earlier. Within the general stress and adaptation approach, other strategies have been proposed, and are linked to the notion of coping. Lazarus and Folkman (1984) have identified two major functions: problem-focussed coping (attempting to change or solve the problem); and emotion-focussed coping (attempting to regulate the emotions associated with the problem). More recently, Endler and Parker (1990) have identified a third: avoidance-oriented coping. These analyses of coping may or may not be valid cross-culturally; Aldwin (1994) and Lazarus (1991) suggest that cross-cultural variations are likely to be present in these distinctions, and in which ones are preferred. One key distinction, made by Diaz-Guerrero (1979), is between active and passive coping. The former seeks to alter the situation, and hence may be similar to problem-focussed coping (and to primary control, described in ch. 1). It may have only limited success if the problem lies in the dominant society, especially if there is little interest in the dominant group in accommodating the needs of acculturating individuals. Passive coping reflects patience and self-modification, and resembles the assimilation acculturation strategy (and secondary control). These strategies are likely to be successful only if the dominant society has positive attitudes towards, and is willing to accept, members of the non-dominant groups. If attitudes are hostile, the passive coping strategies may well lead to unacceptable levels of exclusion or domination.

The fourth aspect of psychological acculturation is a complex set of immediate effects, including physiological and emotional reactions, coming closest to the notion of stress. When behavioral changes take place without difficulty, stress is likely to be minimal and personal consequences are generally positive. When acculturative problems (stressors) do arise, but have been successfully coped with, stress will be similarly low and the immediate effects positive; but when stressors are not completely surmounted, stress will be higher and the effects more negative. And when acculturative problems have been overwhelming, and have not been successfully dealt with, immediate effects will be substantially negative and stress levels debilitating, including personal crises, and commonly anxiety and depression.

The last of the five main features of psychological acculturation is the long-term adaptation that may be achieved. As we saw earlier, adaptation refers to the relatively stable changes that take place in an individual or group in response to environmental demands, and has two main facets: psychological and sociocultural (see below).

We are now in a position to consider the moderating factors that exist prior to (top of fig. 13.3) and those that arise during (bottom of fig. 13.3) the process of acculturation. Although termed "moderating" (i.e., influencing the relationship between the main events in fig. 13.3), they sometimes serve as "mediating" variables (i.e., they intervene directly between the main events). Different empirical studies assign different roles to these factors: it is not possible at this point in acculturation research to unambiguously claim them to be one or the other.

Individuals enter into the acculturation process with a number of personal characteristics of a demographic, psychological, and social nature. In particular, a person's age has a known relationship to the way acculturation will proceed. When acculturation starts early (e.g., prior to entry into primary school), the process is generally smooth (Beiser et al., 1988). The reasons for this are not clear; perhaps full enculturation into a person's primary culture is not sufficiently advanced to require much culture shedding or to create any serious culture conflict; or perhaps personal flexibility and adaptability are maximal during these early years. However, older youths do often experience problems (Aronowitz, 1992; Sam & Berry, 1995), particularly during adolescence. It is possible that conflict between the demands of parents and peers are greater at this period, or that the problems of life transitions between childhood and adulthood are compounded by cultural transitions. For example, developmental issues of identity come to the fore at this time (Phinney, 1990) and interact with questions of ethnic identity, thus multiplying the questions about who one really is. If acculturation begins in later life (e.g., on retirement, or when older parents migrate to join their adult offspring under family reunification programs) there appears to be increased risk (Beiser et al., 1988). Perhaps the same factors of length of enculturation and adaptability suggested for children are also at work here: a whole life in one cultural setting cannot easily be ignored when one is attempting to live in a new setting.

Gender has variable influence on the acculturation process. There is substantial evidence that females may be more at risk for problems than males (e.g., Beiser et al., 1988; Carballo, 1994). However, this generalization probably itself depends on the relative status and differential treatment of females in the two cultures: where there is a substantial difference, attempts by females to take on new roles available in the society of settlement may bring them into conflict with their heritage culture (e.g., Moghaddam, Ditto, & Taylor, 1990; Naidoo, 1992), placing them at risk.

Education appears as a consistent factor associated with possible adaptations: higher education is predictive of lower stress (Beiser et al., 1988; Jayasuriya et al., 1993). A number of reasons have been suggested for this relationship. First, education is a personal resource in itself: problem analysis and problem solving are usually instilled by formal education and likely contribute to better adaptation. Second, education correlates with other resources, such as income, occupational status, and support networks, all of which are themselves protective factors (see below). Third, education may attune migrants to features of the society into which they settle; it is a kind of pre-acculturation to the language, history, values, and norms of the new culture.

Related to education is one's place in the economic world. Although high status (like education) is a resource, a common experience for migrants is a combination of status loss and limited status mobility (Aycan & Berry, 1996). One's "departure status" is frequently higher than one's "entry status," since credentials (educational and work experience) are frequently devalued on arrival (Cumming, Lee, & Oreopoulos, 1989). Sometimes this is due to real differences in qualifications, but it may also be due to ignorance and/or prejudice in the society of settlement, leading to status loss, and the risk of stress. For similar reasons, the usual main goal of migration (upward status mobility) is thwarted, leading again to risk of various disorders, such as depression (Beiser, Johnson, & Turner, 1993). In a sense, these problems lie in personal qualities brought to the acculturation process, but they also reside in the interaction between the migrant and the institutions of the society of settlement: hence, problems of status loss and limited mobility can usually be addressed during the course of acculturation.

Reasons for migrating have long been studied using the concepts of push/pull motivations and expectations. As we noted earlier, Richmond (1993) has proposed that a reactive–proactive continuum of migration motivation should be employed, in which push motives (including involuntary or forced migration, and negative expectations) characterize the reactive end of the dimension, while pull motives (including voluntary migration and positive expectations) cluster at the proactive end. Such a single dimension allows for more concise conceptualization and ease of empirical analysis. Viewing previous research in this light permits some generalizations about the relationship between motives, stress and adaptation. For example, Kim (1988) found that, as usual, those with high "push" motivation had more psychological adaptation problems. However, those with high "pull" motivation had almost as great a number of problems. It appears that those who were reactive were more at risk, but so too were those who were highly proactive; it is likely that these latter migrants had extremely intense or excessively high (even unrealistic) expectations about their life in the new society, which were not met, leading to greater stress.

Cultural distance (how dissimilar the two cultures are in language, religion, etc.), too, lies not uniquely in the background of the acculturating individual but in the dissimilarity between the two cultures in contact. The general and consistent finding is that the greater the cultural differences, the less positive is the adaptation. This is the case for sojourners, and immigrants (Ward & Kennedy, 1992; Ward & Searle, 1991) and for indigenous people (Berry, 1976a). Greater cultural distance implies the need for greater culture shedding and the presence of culture conflict, leading to poorer adaptation.

Personal factors have also been shown to affect the course of acculturation. In the personality domain, a number of traits have been proposed as both risk and protective factors, including locus of control, introversion/extraversion (Ward & Kennedy, 1992), and self-efficacy (Schwarzer, Hahn, & Schröder, 1994). However, consistent findings have been rare, possibly because, once again, it is not so much the trait by itself but its "fit" with the new cultural setting that matters. Kealey (1989) has advocated such a person × situation approach to studying sojourner adaptation (cf. the interaction approach described in ch. 4).

One finding (Schmitz, 1994) among a group of immigrants to Germany, was that stress reaction styles were related to a person's preferred acculturation strategy. Using the Grossarth-Maticek, and Eysenck (1990) psycho-social stress inventory, the "approach" style was positively related to a preference for assimilation, the "avoidance" style to separation, the "flexible" style to integration, and "psychopathology" to "marginalization."

Turning to factors that arise during acculturation, it is now clear that the phase of acculturation needs to be taken into account if stress and adaptation are to be understood, i.e., how long a person has been experiencing acculturation strongly affects the kind and extent of problems. The classical description of positive adaptation in relation to time has been in terms of a U-curve: only a few problems are present early, followed by more serious problems later, and finally a more positive long-term adaptation is achieved. However, there is little empirical evidence for such a standard course, nor for a fixed time (in terms of months or years) when such variations will occur. Church (1982, p. 452) has concluded that support for the U-curve is "weak, inconclusive and overgeneralized," although there are occasional longitudinal studies suggesting fluctuations in stress over time (e.g., Beiser, 2000; Hurh & Kim, 1990; Klineberg, 1980; Ward & Kennedy, 1995; Zheng & Berry, 1991).

An alternative to a fixed, stage-like conceptualization of the relationship between length of acculturation and problems experienced is to consider the specific nature of the experiences and problems encountered as they change over time (e.g., initially learning a language, obtaining employment and housing, followed by establishing social relationships and recreational opportunities) and the relationship of such problems to the personal resources of the migrant and to opportunities in the society of settlement (Ho, 1995). This approach emphasizes the high degree of variability to be expected over the time course from initial contact through to eventual long-term adaptation.

Acculturation strategies have been shown to have substantial relationships with positive adaptation: integration is usually the most successful; marginalization is the least; and assimilation and separation strategies are intermediate. This pattern has been found in virtually every study, and is present for all types of acculturating groups (Berry & Kim, 1988; Berry & Sam, 1997). Why this should be so, however, is not clear. In one interpretation, the integration strategy incorporates many of the other protective factors: a willingness for mutual accommodation (i.e., having two social support systems); and being flexible in personality. In sharp contrast, marginalization involves rejection by the dominant society, combined with own-culture shedding (even though this may be voluntary), and separation involves rejection of the dominant culture (perhaps reciprocated by them). In the simplest version of this explanation, integration involves two positive orientations, marginalization involves two negative ones, while assimilation and separation involve one positive and one negative relationship.

Another possible reason for the finding that integration is the most adaptive strategy is that most studies of the relationship between acculturation strategies and adaptation have been carried out in multicultural societies in which there is acceptance of cultural diversity, i.e., there could be benefits to persons matching their acculturation strategies to that generally advocated and accepted in the larger society. However, in recent studies in societies that are more "melting pot" or assimilationist in orientation, the integration strategy remained the most adaptive (and marginalization was the least adaptive) strategy. For example, this was the case among Indian immigrants to the USA (Krishnan & Berry, 1992), and Third World immigrant youth in Norway (Sam & Berry, 1995). Schmitz (1992b, p. 368), working with a variety of immigrant groups in Germany, concluded that "The findings suggest that integration seems to be the most effective strategy if we take long term health and well-being as indicators."

Related to acculturation strategies are the coping strategies discussed earlier. Some empirical evidence supports the relationship between coping and acculturation strategies. For example, in the same study Schmitz (1992b) found, using the three coping styles identified by Endler and Parker (1990), that integration is positively correlated with task orientation, segregation is positively correlated with emotion and avoidance orientation, and assimilation is positively correlated with both task and emotion orientation. And, as we have just noted, these strategies were related to health outcomes for immigrants to Germany.

In the field of psychological well-being generally (see ch. 16), the variable of social support has been widely studied (Lin, Dean, & Ensel, 1986). Its role in adaptation to acculturation has also been supported (e.g., Furnham & Alibhai, 1985; Furnham & Shiekh, 1993; Jayasuriya et al., 1992; Vega & Rumbaut, 1991). For some, links to one's heritage culture (i.e., with co-nationals) are associated with lower stress (e.g., Vega, Kolody, Valle, & Weir, 1991; Ward & Kennedy, 1993); for others links to members of the society of settlement are more helpful, particularly if relationships match one's expectations (e.g., Berry & Kostovcik, 1990); but in most studies, supportive relationships with *both* cultures are most predictive of successful adaptation (Berry, Kim, Minde, & Mok, 1987; Kealey, 1989). This latter finding corresponds to observations made earlier about the advantages of the integration strategy.

It has been widely reported that the experience of prejudice and discrimination has a significant negative effect on a person's well-being (e.g., Halpern, 1993; Noh, Beiser, Kaspar, Hou, & Rummens, 1999). In groups experiencing acculturation this can be an added risk factor (Beiser et al., 1988). Murphy (1965) has argued that such prejudice is likely to be less prevalent in culturally plural societies, but it is by no means absent (e.g., Berry & Kalin, 1995). Indeed, Fernando (1993) has designated racism as the most serious problem and risk factor facing immigrants and their mental health.

## Adaptation

The last part of fig. 13.3 shows various kinds of **adaptation**. This refers to the long-term ways in which people rearrange their lives and settle down into a more-or-less satisfactory existence. It is "more-or-less" because adaptation, while a continuing process, eventually settles into outcomes that can range from being a very positive through to a very negative way of living in the new cultural setting. In this sense, adaptation refers to the relatively stable changes that take place in an individual or group in response to external demands. Moreover, adaptation may or may not improve the "fit" between individuals and their environments. It is thus not a term that necessarily implies that individuals or groups change to become more like their environment (i.e., adjustment by way of assimilation), but may involve resistance and attempts to change environments, or move away from them altogether (i.e., by separation). Adaptation can be seen as ranging from achieving "primary control" to "secondary control," as discussed previously. Moreover, adaptation is an outcome that may or may not be positive in valence (i.e., meaning only *well* adapted). Thus, long-term adaptation to acculturation is highly variable, ranging from well-to-poorly adapted, varying from a situation where individuals can manage their new lives very well, to one where they are unable to carry on in the new society.

Adaptation is also multifaceted (Altrocchi & Altrocchi, 1995). The initial distinction between psychological and sociocultural adaptation was proposed and validated by Ward and colleagues (Searle & Ward, 1990; Ward, 1996; Ward & Rana-Deuba, 1999). Psychological adaptation largely involves a person's psychological and physical well-being (Schmitz, 1992a), while sociocultural adaptation refers to how well an acculturating individual is able to manage daily life in the new cultural context.

While conceptually distinct, psychological and sociocultural adaptation are empirically related to some extent (correlations between the two measures are in the +.4 to +.5 range). However, they are also empirically distinct in the sense that they usually have different time courses and different experiential predictors. Psychological problems often increase soon after contact, followed by a general (but variable) decrease over time; sociocultural adaptation, however, typically has a linear improvement with time. Analyses of the factors affecting adaptation reveal a generally consistent pattern: good psychological adaptation is predicted by personality variables, life change events, and social support, while good sociocultural adaptation is predicted by cultural knowledge, degree of contact, and positive intergroup attitudes. Both aspects of adaptation are usually predicted by the successful pursuit of the integration acculturation strategy, and by minimal cultural distance (Ward & Kennedy, 1993; Ward, 1996). A third aspect of adaptation has been suggested, that of economic adaptation, by Aycan and Berry (1996), who showed that psychological and sociocultural adaptation were predicted by much the same set of variables as in Ward's studies, while economic adaptation was predicted by migration motivation, perception of relative deprivation, and status loss on first entry into the work world.

Research relating adaptation to acculturation strategies allows for some further generalizations (Berry, 1997a; Ward, 1996). In most cases, for all three forms of adaptation, those who pursue and accomplish integration appear to be better adapted, while those who are marginalized are least well adapted. And again, the assimilation and separation strategies are associated with intermediate adaptation outcomes. In studies of sojourners, Kealey (1989) found this pattern for international aid workers from Canada. However, Ward and Rana-Deuba (1999) found that integration predicted better psychological adaptation only; a preference for assimilation predicted better sociocultural adaptation.

## Intercultural relations

As we have just seen, acculturation involves two basic issues; the continuity or loss of culture and behavior; and the quality of contact between ethnocultural groups. In the first part of this chapter, the focus was on the former aspect; we turn now to issues of intercultural contact, and to relationships that ensue (Berry, 1990b). Considerable research has now accumulated on these issues (see Gudykunst & Bond, 1977; Pettigrew & Tropp, 2000).

### Prejudice

The central concept in this area is that of ethnic **prejudice**. While most attention has been paid to prejudice in western societies (e.g. Duckitt, 1994; Jahoda, 1999), it is probably a universal feature of intercultural relations (LeVine & Campbell, 1972). It is usually considered to have three components: cognitive (stereotypes; shared beliefs about characteristics of groups); affective (attitudes; evaluations of groups); and behavioral (discrimination; actions taken in dealing with groups). Since whole volumes have been prepared on these topics (see Brown & Gaertner, 2000; Stephan & Stephan, 1996), it is beyond the scope of this section to review all that is known about intercultural relationships.

Our intention here is simply to refer to the core concepts, and attempt to illustrate how they can be incorporated into cross-cultural psychology and applied to the understanding and resolution of problems that arise in culturally plural societies.

If we look upon **ethnic stereotypes** simply as cognitive categories which are necessary to bring order to diversity (Hamilton, 1981), then stereotypes may be useful psychological tools to have available in multicultural societies; in order to keep track of the numerous groups around them, people may develop and share these generalizations as a normal psychological process (Berry, 1970b). While earlier thought to be problematic in themselves, these acts of categorization are in essence benign; the difficulty lies in the overgeneralizations and the often negative evaluations (attitudes and discrimination) which are directed toward members of the categories. Thus, while stereotypes which are inaccurate or which carry negative evaluations are a problem, they can also make us aware of, and keep readily available, information which is important to have handy in day-to-day multicultural interactions.

These arguments have been elaborated by Taylor (1981) who has examined some of the "socially desirable" aspects of stereotyping in multicultural societies. These exist in "situations where intergroup stereotypes reflect mutual attraction, even though the members of each group maintain, through stereotypes, their own ethnic distinctiveness" (Taylor, 1981, p. 164). This situation, where a desire for positive relations *and* group distinctiveness both exist, we have identified earlier as the integration mode of relations in plural societies.

A fundamental feature of plural societies is that **ethnic attitudes** are likely to exist between in-group and out-group members. These may be relatively independent of ethnic stereotypes; one study (Gardner, Wonnacott, & Taylor, 1968) has demonstrated their factorial independence; that is, the degree of stereotyping of an ethnic group was unrelated to the evaluation (positive or negative) of that group. This finding lends support to the argument made above that ethnic stereotypes may be relatively benign in a plural society, since they are not inevitably linked to ethnic attitudes (which are often not benign).

A basic argument in our earlier discussion was that there should be consideration of reciprocal attitudes (in a two-group case) or of the matrix of ethnic attitudes among all interacting groups in a plural society, rather than a focus on just what the mainstream thinks of various minorities. The first study to take this approach was that in east Africa of Brewer and Campbell (1976), who studied 30 cultural groups' mutual attitudes. They found that pairs of groups tended to reciprocate the other group's attitude. Subsequently, Berry and Kalin (1979) drew data from a national survey in Canada (Berry et al., 1977), and extracted attitudes towards the five most numerous ethnic groups in the sample. The data in the five-by-five matrix have each group's own-group rating on the diagonal, while the two halves of the matrix contain the particular pairs of intergroup ratings. Three questions may be asked of such a matrix: first, does the ethnocentric tendency to rate one's own group relatively highly hold for all groups? Second, does the tendency to rate all other groups in a consistent hierarchy also hold? Third, is there a balanced relationship (Heider, 1958) among the mutual attitudes held by a pair of groups?

Berry and Kalin found there to be a consistent tendency toward ethnocentrism (own-group ratings always being higher than other group ratings), a high degree of commonality (a tendency to share a view of the "place" of each group in the plural society), and a moderate degree of reciprocity or balance in mutual evaluations. These findings were replicated in a second national survey in Canada (Kalin & Berry, 1996), and in Europe (Hagendoorn, 1993). From a mainstream-minority perspective we might have learned only that the dominant group is on top of the attitudinal hierarchy, and that all others (examined only in relation to them) are located somewhere lower in attitudinal space. With a full matrix, we can better appreciate the complexity of multiple intergroup attitudes in plural societies. We also may be able to advance social psychological theory in general by providing new insights into the nature of ethnocentrism, and the applicability of Heider's (1958) balance theory beyond individual relations to the realm of intergroup relations.

As we noted earlier, the acculturation attitudes of members of individuals in the dominant society can also be examined (right side of fig. 13.2). To do this we can ask a sample in the larger society to indicate how they think the acculturation of others should proceed. Thus, we may replace the items in scales designed to assess acculturation attitudes among acculturating groups so that they can be posed to these others; now the issue is whether these others think that assimilation, integration, marginalization, and segregation *should* be how acculturation should proceed (see also Bourhis et al., 1997).

A concrete outcome to these various cognitive and evaluative variables is the level of **discrimination** to be found in plural societies. Indeed, critics of multiculturalism as a general policy often claim that it has, as its real motive, the wish "to keep people in their place" by more easily identifying them as different and perhaps of lower value in society. In terms of the two issues raised in fig. 13-2, it is indeed possible that culturally distinct peoples are encouraged by a larger society to maintain their differences in order to exclude them from day-to-day participation in the economic, political, and educational life of the society. The danger has been recognized by many observers of multiculturalism, and has been identified by Jayasuriya (1984) as the possibility of one's "lifestyle" limiting one's "life chances" in Australian society.

Note that discrimination is used here to refer not only to acts of forceful exclusion (such as in segregation and marginalization), but also to forceful inclusion (as in assimilation). Only in the integration mode, when a society is open to, and accepting of, the wishes of an individual or group, and where individuals are free to choose their preferred degrees of cultural maintenance and participation in the larger society, do we consider there to be no discrimination.

There is reason to believe that external factors like discrimination are an important determinant of the position of a group in society. In research on intergroup relations in India and the Netherlands (DeRidder & Tripathi, 1992, see ch. 3), a questionnaire was used in which subjects were asked to indicate what behavior they expected in reaction to various norm violations. These researchers worked with pairs of groups that were ethnically distinct, and with pairs that were socially distinct (i.e., managers and workers in industry). Subjects indicated how their own group would react to a norm violation by the other group, as well as how the others would react to a norm violation by the subject's own group. Patterns of reactions tended to be similar across pairs of groups. In other words, if subordinates expected a stronger reaction from managers than from their own group, then managers would show a similar response pattern.

## Prejudice reduction

Applications of knowledge about prejudice are essentially devoted to its reduction (see Aboud & Levy, 1999). There are three broad approaches to this task (Amir & Ben Ari, 1998). First is the contact model, which considers that a lack of mutual contact is the cause. Second is the information model, which holds that a lack of mutual knowledge is responsible. And third is the psychodynamic model, which believes that the roots of prejudice lie in an individual's psychological problems. Reducing prejudice depends on the model adopted: improved contact, better information or alleviating the person's difficulties are taken as the basis for programs to reduce prejudice. Some programs attempt to reduce the development and operation of the three psychological components (stereotypes, attitudes, and discrimination), while others focus on changing the social context (such as public policies, and educational and work settings). By far, the largest literature has examined the role of intercultural contact in reducing prejudice, by relating this aspect of the context to levels (or changes in) prejudice. The **contact hypothesis** was first proposed by Allport (1954): under certain conditions, intergroup contact will reduce the prejudice between groups.

These conditions are that the groups in contact should have roughly equal status; that they should share some common goals; that they should be in contact voluntarily; and that there should be some support for the contact (rather than prohibiting it).

To illustrate research on this contact hypothesis, we examine a study with school students in Finland (Liebkind & McAlister, 1999). Three pairs of schools were selected, matched by percentage of foreign students (ranging from a low of 3 percent to a high of 19 percent), with one school from each pair assigned to an experimental or control condition. In the experimental condition peer "role models" were presented in news or documentary stories in which students ("peer models") tell about their own attitude change; control schools received no manipulation. Both experimental and control schools completed measures of tolerance toward foreigners, before and after the peer modeling. Results showed significant main effects for experimental groups and gender (girls more tolerant than boys), but no main effect for ethnic density of the school. These results reveal the complexity of findings typical of studies of the contact hypothesis; on the one hand, exposure (contact) through peer modeling increased tolerance; on the other hand, ethnic density in the school (potential for contact) showed no relationship with tolerance.

Hundreds of studies have now been carried out, and they have been frequently subjected to review and evaluation; the most recent and thorough is by Pettigrew and Tropp (2000), who carried out a meta-analysis of over 2,000 studies (with over 300 samples and 700 tests of the hypothesis). These studies came from many countries, across the age range (from children to older adults), and in many diverse settings (schools, work, experiments).

Their findings provide general support for the contact hypothesis. Effect sizes were highest for the 2030 studies (and only slightly lower for 313 samples and 746 tests). That is, intergroup contact does generally relate negatively to prejudice. This relationship was present in studies of both dominant and non-dominant samples; when contact was voluntary (as predicted) but also (unexpectedly) when not voluntary; across high and low contact experimental settings; across social contexts (highest for work, lowest for recreation and tourism); and across types of groups (highest for sexual orientation and for ethnic groups, lowest for the elderly). That is, support for the contact hypothesis is both robust and generalizable.

Given this broad conclusion, Pettigrew and Tropp (2000) propose that "optimal intergroup contact should be a critical component of any successful effort to reduce prejudice." They conclude with some practical implications: the conditions initially proposed by Allport should be used to structure intergroup contact situations; all components of prejudice should be addressed (stereotypes, attitudes, and discrimination); focus on contact in settings that are longer term (e.g., work rather than tourism settings); and change institutions (educational, work) and policies (housing, political) that provide for changes in all the above conditions.

## Multiculturalism

The term **multiculturalism** has been used a number of times in this chapter. In this section we consider various meanings given to the concept, and some empirical findings; we end with a discussion of their application to policy and programs in plural societies (MOST, 1995).

In fig. 13.2, multiculturalism was identified as the orientation that accepts *both* the maintenance of cultural identity and characteristics of all ethnocultural groups *and* the contact and participation of all groups in the larger plural society. This understanding of the term, linking it to the two issues involved in acculturation, was proposed (Berry, 1984a) as a way to provide a psychological basis for evaluating Canadian multiculturalism policy.

In Canada, as in most immigrant-receiving countries, early policies favored assimilation. However, this gradually changed, leading to the view that assimilation had not worked anywhere in the world, and that it was impracticable as a general policy. In 1971 the Canadian federal government announced a national multiculturalism policy, that was intended to

> break down discriminatory attitudes and cultural jealousies. National unity, if it is to mean anything in the deeply personal sense, must be founded on confidence in one's own individual identity; out of this can grow respect for that of others and a willingness to share ideas, attitudes and assumptions. A vigorous policy of multiculturalism will help create this initial confidence. It can form the base of a society which is based on fair play for all. The Government will support and encourage the various cultures and ethnic groups that give structure and vitality to our society. They will be encouraged to share their cultural expression and values with other Canadians and so contribute to a richer life for all. (Government of Canada, 1971, p. 3)

In essence the policy asserts that in Canada "although there are two official languages, there is no official culture, nor does any ethnic group take precedence over any other" (p. 1). Further, the policy asserts that the other cultural communities "are essential elements in Canada and deserve government assistance in order to contribute to regional and national life in ways that derive from their heritages, yet are distinctively Canadian."

Similar policies have been proposed in other plural societies. In Australia, early views were largely assimilationist but evolved toward integrationist views. In the early 1970s the government set the country on a multicultural course, claiming that "Australia is a multicultural society ... one of the most cosmopolitan societies on earth" (quoted by Bullivant, 1985, p. 17). Later, in 1978, a policy of multiculturalism was formally endorsed by the Australian government.

In Israel, where thousands of people have emigrated from both Western (Europe and western hemisphere) and Eastern (North Africa and Middle East) cultural traditions, and where a large Arab population was already resident, there is clearly a plural society in operation. However, a policy of westernization of Eastern Jews was proposed:

> the Israeli national leadership adopted the approach (supported by social scientists) that Middle Easterners should become Westernized through a process of resocialization ... facilitated by such factors as common Jewish nationality, religious tradition, and the relative similarity in physical appearance. Ethnic, cultural and economic differences were considered to be temporary and of only superficial importance. (Amir, 1986, p. 3).

This assimilationist policy now seems to be diminishing in force, and a "more genuine integration" is taking its place (Amir, 1986, p. 8). However, there is a clear de facto segregation between Jews and Arabs: "90% of Arab Israelis reside in separate towns and villages. Even the 10% who live in mixed cities occupy separate residential areas" (Amir, 1986, p. 11). Thus, we find a sharp contrast in policy toward different sectors of a population within a single plural society.

In Sweden, an explicit multicultural policy was adopted in 1975 with three goals: equality, freedom, and choice of partnership:

> The goal of *equality* implies continued work to give immigrants the same living standard as the rest of the population. The goal of *freedom of choice* implies that public initiatives are to be taken to assure members of ethnic and linguistic minorities domiciled in Sweden a genuine choice between retaining and developing their cultural identity and assuming a Swedish cultural identity. The goal of *partnership* implies that the different immigrant and minority groups on the one hand and the native population on the other both benefit from working together. (Lundström, 1986, p. 10)

This policy is implemented in various domains of public life, including libraries, drama, newspapers, broadcasting, and education, where many languages and cultural traditions are increasingly being represented.

Elsewhere in Europe, the recent tradition of guest workers and of immigrants from former colonies has directed the attention of many social scientists to the issue of pluralism. Most European countries have tended to favor an assimilationist orientation, and much of the research has been cast in a similar mold. However, some research has shifted more to a pluralistic point of view. For example, Van Oudenhoven and Willemsen (1989, p. 248), reviewing the evidence from intergroup relations in Europe, concluded that

> in our opinion, some form of pluralism is to be preferred over complete assimilation. One of the negative consequences of full assimilation is that a cultural vacuum among minority group members may develop. The second generation of immigrants in particular may lose their ethnic, linguistic, or religious roots, while not being rooted in a majority culture either.

This shift in research and policy has been documented by Dacyl and Westin (2000) for Europe and other regions of the world.

In many parts of the world, there is an evolving meaning for multiculturalism (Glazer, 1997), one that appears to correspond to the "integration" orientation as noted above. However, for some observers, "multiculturalism" implies primarily the maintenance of many cultures in a society, without much participation or sharing. In this meaning, multiculturalism comes closer to "separation" than to "integration," because it "carries the risk of accentuating cultural differences ... and exacerbates the 'us–them' type of thinking" (Kagitcibasi, 1997b, p. 44). For others, multiculturalism is not real integration, since it is perceived as a temporary way station on route to assimilation; this is a view taken by "threatened minorities," who consider that involvement with other (more dominant groups) will lead to loss of their culture and identity. Of course, the term can have any number of meanings; however, in most contemporary plural societies, it conveys a sense of balance, one that is at the core of integration as an intercultural strategy. As phrased by Watts and Smolicz (1997, p. 52):

> Multiculturalism presupposes the existence of an over-arching framework of shared values that acts as a linchpin in a multi-ethnic state – a framework that is flexible and responsive to the various cultures and ethnic groups that compose the nation.

Referring again to fig. 13.2, the strategies of both the ethnocultural groups and the larger society can be examined at three levels: national, institutional, and individual. Fig. 13.4 shows the three levels for each side of the intercultural relationships. On the right are the views held by the various ethnocultural groups (which usually are non-dominant in the intercultural relationship). On the left are the views held by the larger society. There are three levels, with the most encompassing (the national society or ethnocultural groups) at the top; at the bottom are the least encompassing (the individual); and in between are various social groupings (called "institutions"), which can be governmental agencies, educational or health systems, or work places.

At the first level, we can examine national policies and the stated goals of particular ethnocultural groups within the larger plural society. For example, the Canadian and Australian national policies of multiculturalism correspond to the integration strategy (Berry, 1984a) by which both heritage cultural maintenance, and full participation in the larger society by all groups, are promoted. Many ethnocultural groups also express their preferences in formal statements:

| Levels | Dominant<br>Mainstream<br>Larger society | Non-dominant<br>Minority group<br>Cultural group |
|---|---|---|
| National | National policies | Group goals |
| Institutional | Uniform<br>or plural | Diversity<br>and equity |
| Individual | Multicultural<br>ideology | Acculturation<br>strategies |

**13.4** Locus of intercultural strategies

some seek integration into the larger society (e.g., Maori in New Zealand), while some others seek separation (e.g., Scottish National Party or Parti Québécois, who seek full independence for their group). At the individual level, as we have seen, we can measure "acculturation expectations" or "multicultural ideology" in the larger society, or the "acculturation attitudes" that individuals in ethnocultural groups hold toward these four strategies. At the institutional level, competing visions rooted in these alternative intercultural strategies confront and even conflict with each other daily. Most frequently, non-dominant ethnocultural groups seek the joint goals of diversity and equity. This involves, first, the recognition of the group's cultural uniqueness and specific needs, and second, having group needs met with the same level of understanding, acceptance, and support as those of the dominant group(s). The dominant society, however, may often prefer more uniform programs and standards (based on its own cultural views) in such core institutions as education, health, justice, and defense. The goals of diversity and equity correspond closely to the integration and multiculturalism strategies (combining cultural maintenance with inclusive participation), whereas the push for uniformity resembles the assimilation and melting pot approach (see Berry, 1996c). The working out of these contrasting views finds its expression in many institutions, especially in education (see below), work (see ch. 14), and health (see ch. 16).

With the use of this framework, comparisons of intercultural strategies can be made between individuals and their groups, and between non-dominant peoples and the larger society within which they are acculturating. The ideologies and policies of the dominant group constitute an important element of intercultural relations research (see Berry et al., 1977; Bourhis et al., 1997), while preferences of non-dominant peoples are a core feature in understanding the process of acculturation in non-dominant groups (Berry, 2001a).

## Schooling

For many, the test of the integration strategy resides on the success or failure of multicultural education. Everyone agrees that one of the main functions of the school is to transmit important aspects of culture from one generation to another (Camilleri, 1986); as such, it is a central institution in the processes of social-ization and enculturation (see ch. 2). In a plural society, the questions naturally arise. *Whose* culture is to be transmitted in the schools, using *whose* language, and incorporating *whose* values, knowledge, and beliefs? Until quite recently in most countries the answer was clear; the dominant culture's interests held sway, and there was little tolerance for pluralism in a nation's classrooms.

Most plural societies are grappling with these issues, and numerous volumes have been published (e.g., Eldering & Kloprogge, 1989; Modgil, Verma, Mallick, & Modgil, 1986; Ben Ari & Rich, 1997; Ouellet, 1988; Samuda, Berry, & La-ferriere, 1984). Societies range from those that have rejected pluralistic alternatives to those that have embraced "multicultural education," and are experimenting with a variety of options (see e.g., Banks & Lynch, 1985). The key components in multicultural education are the educational system (which often reflects only the culture of the larger or dominant society), the teacher (who may or may not be culturally part of the larger society), and the student (who, in the present analysis, is culturally *not* a member of the larger society). There is a complex triangular relationship among these components (cf. Chodzinski, 1984), within which cultural similarities and differences need to be understood. The most common situation is one where the school and teacher share the her-itage of the larger society, but the student does not. However, other patterns are also evident. For example, in areas of large-scale immigration, both the teachers and students can share a particular heritage that is different from that of the school and the larger society; or there may be some individual students of the dominant society in a school where another ethnocultural heritage is dominant among teach-ers and other students.

According to one analysis (McLeod, 1984), there are three main types of mul-ticultural schooling; ethnic specific, problem oriented, and intercultural. In the first type, the cultural content (history, values, religion, language) of a particular ethnic group is emphasized by the group who operate a school for their own members, sometimes full time, but sometimes part time. Such schools have existed in most plural societies for a long time, and are not in and of themselves multicultural; in fact, they are unicultural, and provide for each group the educational services that a public school does for the majority group. But taken together the educational system in which such schools operate may be termed multicultural, since more than one cultural group is catered for by the system as a whole. Indeed, such schools may be an important first step on the road to full multicultural education, since such schools provide a vehicle for culture and language maintenance; however, they clearly do not provide a vehicle for group participation.

The problem-oriented type of education is directed toward some identified difficulty being experienced by particular groups. These include poor achievement in learning a second language (usually the dominant language), and compensatory programs for the "culturally disadvantaged." As we have seen, full participation in the national society usually requires functional fluency in the national language(s); thus, solutions to the first of these problems may be of fundamental importance. However, as we have also seen (in ch. 6), such second language acquisition should be attempted in an "additive" rather than "subtractive" way, if other problems (both cognitive and social) are to be avoided. In contrast, the second problem usually being addressed (that of "cultural disadvantage") requires a further distinction.

Sometimes it resides mainly in the historical prejudices of the dominant society. As Feuerstein (1979, p. 39) has cogently argued, this concept should only be employed when a person or group no longer has access to their own cultural traditions and supports; it should not be used when they are functioning outside the dominant culture. Put in terms of our own framework, marginalized persons and groups may be "culturally disadvantaged," and so perhaps also may those who are on the route toward assimilation (prior to full incorporation in the new culture), but not those who pursue cultural distinctiveness by separation or integration strategies. The other aspect of "cultural disadvantage" is that it is often used as a euphemistic term for "economic disadvantage," indicating unequal access to the common resources of a society (see Sinha, 1990).

The third type, which emphasizes intercultural knowledge and competence, comes closest to multicultural education in its most common usage. Here, there are educational materials that represent, if not all the world's peoples, then the major cultures, especially if they are represented in the plural society. In addition to learning about a variety of peoples, there is an emphasis on learning to live with cultural differences; the cognitive is supplemented by an emphasis on the social and affective aspects of education (McLeod, 1984).

What is common among all of these forms is an acceptance of the view that cultural variation should be represented and transmitted in the school system, in order for children to accept it in society. At the same time there is a recognition that the school should build links for the children to others, outside their own group, with whom they will eventually live and work. Thus, the hallmarks of a multicultural education are both cultural maintenance and participation; the former without the latter leads to encapsulation (of both the dominant group and the various ethnic groups), while the latter without the former leads to enforced assimilation.

Because of the central role of language in education, a great deal of research has been conducted on linguistic aspects of formal schooling in plural societies (Edwards, 1984; Baker, 2000). In addition to language being the practical vehicle for much of what transpires in the school, it also has a great political and symbolic value for its users (Laferriere, 1984). The central issue surrounds the concept of bilingual education:

bilingual education is primarily education for minority groups – either indigenous or immigrant – and, as such, it has something to do with assimilation or
non-assimilation of these groups into the larger society ... is bilingual education
to serve the cause of an enduring cultural pluralism or multiculturalism, or is it
actually to expedite the smooth assimilation of disparate groups into the mainstream? (Edwards, 1984, p. 184)

In response to this central question, two distinct forms of bilingual education
have been developed: transitional and maintenance. The first is a bridging operation, in which both the child's mother tongue and the dominant languages are
used, but with the goal of phasing out the former and replacing it with the latter, once functional competence has been developed to a level sufficient to carry
the curriculum to the child. The second form has the goal of developing fluency
in the language of the dominant society without diminishing competency in the
mother tongue.

Of particular interest is the immersion type of program for acquiring a second
language. Initiated by the work of Lambert and his colleagues (Lambert & Tucker,
1972), this approach places the child immediately and completely in the classroom where the second language only is used; the child often has no prior
exposure to, or knowledge of, that language. In Canada, these programs have
been employed mainly to provide native English speakers with French fluency,
but the system has been extended to other countries. Careful evaluation by
Lambert generally shows no lag in native language competency, or in general
academic progress; but there is a large-scale improvement in second language
competency. As Edwards (1984) points out, however, these studies have taken
place (and have been evaluated) in a particular social, cultural, and political
context, where the two languages involved both have "official" status, where the
second language (French) is usually that of the local majority, and where the
mother tongue (English) is that of the national majority.

All of these factors point to an additive form of bilingualism, with substantial
opportunity for daily use of the second language, and the possible operation of
both integrative and instrumental motives to learn the second language. Whether
the same, generally positive, outcome will be present in other sociopolitical
contexts is largely an open question. Once again, it would be unwise to pursue
immersion-type bilingual education programs without considering the potential
influence of these contextual factors.

## Conclusions

Research on the consequences of intercultural contact now forms a major
part of the field of cross-cultural psychology. Much of this work has been carried out in those countries that have been built through immigration, and have
become culturally plural as a result. Just as for all areas of cross-cultural psychology, there is an urgent need to extend these studies to other societies that

have different histories and different experiences of diversity, in order to discover which findings are culture specific and which are more general.[1]

Despite this lack of information for many societies, there is a clear trend indicating that acculturating people (individuals and groups) prefer, and adapt better, when they are attached to both their heritage culture and to the larger national society (i.e., integration).

Although some countries have adopted multicultural policies (as a counterpart to integration), there are many which continue to practice assimilation, segregation, or exclusion. Further research is required to know whether multiculturalism is always advantageous, or whether policies of cultural loss or exclusion may serve people just as well.

## Key terms

| | |
|---|---|
| acculturation | ethnocultural (ethnic) group |
| acculturation strategies | integration |
| acculturative stress | larger society |
| adaptation (to acculturation) | marginalization |
| assimilation | migration motivation |
| contact hypothesis | multicultural ideology |
| cultural distance | multiculturalism |
| cultural identity | plural society |
| discrimination | prejudice |
| ethnic attitudes | psychological acculturation |
| ethnic stereotypes | separation |

## Further reading

Berry, J. W., & Sam, D. (1997). Acculturation and adaptation. In J. W. Berry, M. H. Segall, & C. Kagitcibasi (Eds.), *Social behavior and applications* (pp. 291–326). Vol. III of *Handbook of cross-cultural psychology* (2nd ed.). Boston, MA: Allyn and Bacon. A review chapter that provides an overview of concepts and empirical findings about psychological acculturation in a variety of groups.

Gudykunst, W. & Bond, M. (1997). Intergroup relations across cultures. In J. W. Berry, M. H. Segall & C. Kagitcibasi (Eds.), *Social behavior and applications* (pp. 119–61). Vol. III of *Handbook of cross-cultural psychology* (2nd ed.). Boston, MA: Allyn & Bacon. A review chapter covering current theories about how cultural groups relate to each other, with a selection of empirical findings.

---

[1] As in the case of all research, these further studies should be comparative. An explicit framework for such comparisons has been presented by Berry et al. (1987). They propose a program of research that examines the psychological acculturation of a variety of groups (e.g., immigrants, refugees) coming from a variety of cultures (e.g., Vietnamese, Ethiopians) to a variety of settlement countries (e.g., Australia, Britain, Canada) using some standard concepts (e.g., contact indices, acculturation attitudes, and acculturative stress) and, as much as possible, standard instruments. Only within such a comparative framework will it be possible to produce valid generalizations about acculturation phenomena.

Liebkind, K. (2000). Acculturation. In R. Brown & S. Gaertner (Eds.), *Blackwell Handbook of Social Psychology*. Vol. 4. *Intergroup processes* (pp. 386–404). Oxford: Blackwell. A review chapter linking acculturation to theories and findings in social psychology, with an emphasis on European research.

Marin, G., Balls-Organista, P., & Chung, K. (Eds.) (2001). *Acculturation*. Washington, DC: APA Books. A set of original papers that provides an overview of a variety of issues in acculturation research and application.

Ward, C. (1996). Acculturation. In D. Landis & R. Bhagat (Eds.), *Handbook of intercultural training* (pp. 124–47, 2nd ed.). Newbury Park, CA: Sage. A review chapter that emphasizes sociocultural aspects of acculturation among sojourners.

# 14 Organizations and work

Cross-cultural psychologists often try to achieve a broad range of cultural variation in the phenomena they study by including in their projects groups far removed from urbanized industrial ways of life. In contrast, work and organizational psychology, or industrial psychology, has mainly focused on societies that have been industrialized or are in the process of industrialization. This stands to reason as the field's main interest is human behavior in contemporary industrial or administrative work settings. Interest in cultural factors has increased with intercultural contacts in industry, science, and technical assistance programs.

This chapter is centered around three themes where cultural differences and organizational variables intermesh. First we discuss to what extent the structure of organizations is the same everywhere, and to what extent there are systematic differences across cultures in the way organizations tend to be structured. Then we deal with management behavior, drawing attention to two aspects, leadership behavior and decision making. The third section is concerned with differences in workers' values and motives across cultures.

## Organizational structure

An important characteristic of complex organizations is the distribution of tasks. Not every employee has the same responsibilities and the same kind of work. The total body of work that has to be performed is assigned to different divisions and subdivisions. **Organizational structure** has been mainly studied from an institutional-level perspective in organizational sociology and organization science, but, as we shall see, these flow into individual-level concerns. The structure of organizations is usually represented in organizational charts. The question we pose is whether or not organizations in different countries have similar structures.

Lammers and Hickson (1979) studied cultural variation in organizational structure. They suggest three types of organizations: "Latin," "Anglo-Saxon," and "Third World." The Latin type is more of a classical bureaucracy with (among other things) a centralized structure and a large number of hierarchical levels. The Anglo-Saxon type is more flexible, with decentralization and a relatively small number of hierarchical levels as important features. This flexible type is prevalent in north-west Europe and in North America. The classical or Latin type is found in southern Europe, and also in eastern Europe. For the non-industrialized countries the traditional organization is characterized by central decision making, little formalization of rules, and paternalistic leadership. The features of the traditional organization, according to Lammers and Hickson, are also found in small firms and family businesses in west European countries. Lammers and Hickson believed that Hofstede's study (to be discussed later in this chapter) supports their categorization, although in their opinion a fourth type emerges from his results, namely an inflexible bureaucracy with strong rule orientation but limited hierarchy. Germany and Israel are among the countries where this type is found relatively frequently.

Udy (1970) has carried out one of the very few comparative studies of organizations over a wide range of pre-industrial societies. He analyzed data from 125 societies, in the HRAF (Murdock, 1975). In Udy's view there is a shift from production-determined (associated with hunter-gatherers) to socially determined (associated with agriculturalists) forms of work in pre-industrialized societies. In a production-oriented form of organized work the objectives of how and what to produce are given by the environmental setting. The buffalo hunt of some Native American groups is an example. The socially determined work context leads to a relatively stable organization that continues to exist when production does not demand it. An example is the family unit doing agricultural work. This form of organization is, according to Udy, low in effectiveness, efficiency, and innovative capacity.

Udy's study addressed the question of to what extent subsistence variables are responsible for differences in organizational types. In many respects the shifts in type coincide with shifts in industrial development. At the same time, the traditional organization that Lammers and Hickson consider characteristic of the Third World can still be found in industrial societies, for example in small agricultural communities of many regions in western Europe. As we shall see later, structural aspects of organizations are correlated with other aspects of technological development, and this makes it difficult to disentangle the various variables.

In the 1970s and early 1980s the importance of political factors was emphasized, in particular the contrast between (Marxist) socialism and capitalism. As far as industrial organizations are concerned the main distinction is between public and private ownership. The latter leads to hierarchical domination and exploitation of the workers, according to Marxist theory (see box 14.1).

## Box 14.1 The influence of the political context

The most extensive politically inspired changes in organizations have occurred in the People's Republic of China (e.g., Laaksonen, 1988). The Workers' Congress, legally established in 1950, gave the rank and file workers of
an organization some influence in management, although much of the authority remained with the members of the Communist Party.

After the Cultural Revolution of the 1960s managers and administrators
were required to do physical work for one day per week. Students and teachers, including university professors, were sent to rural areas to do manual
work. These practices may have had some advantages (managers learned to
know the work of their subordinates and communication was improved), but
they were mainly inspired by the political ideal of a more egalitarian society.
Later on technical expertise and knowledge (including academic knowledge)
became again a respected reason for social and economic (salary) inequality in the PRC. Political changes usually were followed by staff changes at
the managerial level. For example, after 1978 there was a trend towards more
influence of employees in the election of managers (Lockett, 1983).

Despite the upheavals, the Chinese economy started to develop rather well.
Laaksonen (1988, p. 233) suggests: "Perhaps, taken as a whole, the changes
after all only rubbed the surface structure of Chinese society, and the basic
structure, leaning upon the old culture, has not been destroyed too much."
The majority of the Chinese still live in rural areas, which were largely untouched by the political changes.

A major study on the distribution of power and influence in organizations
as a consequence of differences in legislation was carried out in eleven
(mainly Western) European countries and Israel by an international research
group called Industrial Democracy in Europe (IDE, 1981). The goal of this
project was to find out whether state regulations and legislation were related
to organizational structure and behavior, particularly as far as workers' participation was concerned. It was found that participation, especially at the
collective level through labor unions indeed was influenced by the extent to
which regulations concerning participation were entrenched in the law.

Individual rank and file workers were found to have little influence in the
West European democracies; most organizations in these countries could be
characterized as centralized and undemocratic. Individual employees, especially
at low levels of the hierarchy, also felt little involved with decision-making
processes in the organization. In former Yugoslavia, the only socialist state in
the IDE study, workers' influence was clearly more substantial. According to
the IDE group their results indicate that democracy in industries is influenced
by sociopolitical factors rather than by requirements of a technological or structural nature. They argued that modification of the hierarchical characteristics of
the work organization can lead to more democracy. However, this requires a
complex sequence of changes that is not easily realized.

Political variables are mentioned here because in cross-cultural comparisons of organizations they are confounded with other cultural variables like values, beliefs, and customs. This is emphasized in an orientation that has had a significant impact on the discussion of the role of cultural factors in organizations, namely the contingency approach.

Organizational theory distinguishes dimensions of organizational structure from the determinants of this structure. For example, according to Robbins (1987) there are three important dimensions: complexity, formalization, and centralization. Complexity refers to the degree of differentiation in an organization, i.e., the diversity of groups of specialists, the number of levels in the management hierarchy, and the number of different locations at which the organization is actually operating. Formalization refers to the degree of standardization in tasks, ranging from almost total absence of any rules to a high degree of programming about what to do and how to do it. Centralization refers to the concentration of decision making, which can be centered in a single point in the organization or widely dispersed.

Structure is supposed to be contingent upon variables such as the size (number of employees), technology, resources, and the history of the organization. In a broader sense contingency variables also include the environment in which the organization is functioning; environmental conditions affect the organization, but fall largely outside its sphere of control. Some aspects of the environment are directly relevant, e.g. attitudes of customers, government regulations, and prices of commodities. The broader environment of an organization also encompasses the form of government of the country, the level of education of the workforce, and even technological progress in some other part of the world, insofar as it affects the market for an organization's product. The explanatory status of contingency variables is a matter of debate. By some authors they are seen as direct determinants of structure, by others as constraints that limit the range of potential structures of an organization.[1]

One form of **contingency theory**, reminiscent of the absolutist perspective outlined in ch. 12, is the "culture-free hypothesis." This maintains that situational demands are the sole determinants of organizational change and that theories about organizations have validity independent of the culture in which an organization functions. The effects of technology are so strong that they suppress the more subtle effects of cultural variables. Consequently, the relationships between structural or contextual variables are supposed to be invariant across cultures (e.g., Miller, 1987). The optimal structure of an organization can be derived from the technological and political conditions under which it has to operate. Adaptation of a given technology will have the same structural consequences in all national

---

[1] Related to this are differences of opinion as to how important contingency variables are. For example, Robbins (1987) argues that they act as constraints which narrow decision-making choices, and emphasizes that the structure of an organization to a considerable extent is the outcome of a battle for power; those in power want a structure that allows them to keep maximal control.

settings. Countries at approximately the same level of industrial development should show strong similarities in organizations. The idea that technological development will have a homogenizing effect on organizations is known as the convergence hypothesis (e.g., Ronen, 1986). One group of researchers working in Britain, the Ashton group (Pugh & Hinings, 1976), found that changes in the number of employees influenced the structure of an organization, but that technological changes had little effect (Pheysey, 1993).

However, in some international comparative studies, with companies of similar size operating in the same branch of industry, major differences have been reported. Maurice (1979) adhered to a relativist position (cf. ch. 12), claiming that cross-national comparisons within the contingency approach are no more than extensions of studies within a single country. One might say that the convergence approach, according to Maurice's views, is based on imposed etics (cf. ch. 11). In such comparisons, Maurice argues, culture is treated merely as something accidental that happens to be as it is, but also could have been different. He maintains that culture is part of the essence of an organization, which cannot be understood separately from the culture in which it is situated.

In a comparison of the hierarchical structure of matched pairs of firms from France and Germany, two neighboring countries of similar technological advancement and political orientation, considerable differences were found in salary between employees low and high in the hierarchy. There were also differences in the number of hierarchical levels and opportunities for advancement on the basis of technical experience as opposed to formal education, with France having the more hierarchical structures. Maurice has explained these differences in terms of cultural background variables, such as the educational system and social stratification variables, which differ between France and Germany. In another study with data from Great Britain, France, and Germany, similar variations between the countries were reported (Maurice, Sorge, & Warner, 1980).

While convergence could occur at the level of organizational structure and technology (macro-level variables), individual attitudes and values (micro-level variables) might remain culturally distinct. According to Child (1981), external factors impose certain limits within which organizations develop in harmony with the culture of a country. Cultural variables can moderate the effects of an existing political and economic system as well as organizational characteristics. Thus, differences exist where contingency theory would predict uniformity. However, like the Ashton group, Child noted that the influence of situational factors on variables of organizational structure is weaker and less consistent than on process variables at the behavioral level, such as decision-making processes and managerial roles. The results with which he illustrated his argument came again from western Europe (a study with 137 executives in eighteen British and 50 executives in twenty-six German firms).

Drenth and colleagues (Drenth & Groenendijk, 1984, 1997; Drenth & Den Hartog, 1999) also questioned the convergence hypothesis that technological requirements (which lead to convergence) should have stronger effects than cultural factors. They see little reason to assume strong cultural influences on structural characteristics, because clear patterns of interrelationships between cultural variables and organizational structure have not been established. Drenth and Groenendijk argue that although cultural variables do not have much to do with how an organization is structured, they may have much to do with how it functions. With respect to a structural variable such as formalization (i.e., the presence of formal rules and procedures) there are few cultural prescriptions, but the extent to which employees adhere to the rules will differ between cultures. Similarly, in respect of centrality of decision making there can be large differences between cultures in the actual influence of lower echelons, even if structurally the decision-making power is in the hands of top executives everywhere.

Our discussion has revealed little consensus on the significance of cultural variables. Opinions differ along two main dimensions. The first concerns the contrast between institutional-level and individual-level variables. Organizational structure is primarily a concept from organizational sociology and tends to be defined at the institutional level. The cross-national typology by Lammers and Hickson (1979) is an example. Among psychologists (e.g. Drenth and Groenendijk) there is a tendency to emphasize the importance of organizational processes and individual behavior. The second dimension concerns the role of culture; two contrasting viewpoints were identified, corresponding roughly to the contrast between absolutism and relativism described in ch. 12.

This lack of consensus reflects a paucity of research on the relationship between organization-level and individual-level variables, and how the two levels interact. Some of the problems are that: the range of cultural variables is poorly defined (Aycan, 2000); technology, political conditions, and economic constraints are not properly distinguished from other cultural variables such as beliefs and values; and nation states tend to be treated as homogeneous cultures. Tayeb (1988, p. 41) has asked: "How is one to know, for instance, that the 'British' organization which is compared with, say, an Indian company, is not in fact staffed largely by immigrants from the sub-continent?" In reviews the poor conceptualization of culture has long been cited as a weakness (e.g., Bhagat & McQuaid, 1982; Ronen, 1986).

## Organizational culture

Culture is traditionally defined at the level of populations and it encompasses many spheres of life. **Organizational culture** is defined at the level of organizations. The underlying assumption is that organizations differ from each other not only on variables such as production techniques, marketing, and the attitudes of their employees, but also in respect of deep-rooted beliefs, meaning, and values. Deal and Kennedy (1982) write about the "inner values," "rituals," and "heroes" of an organization as determinants of its success. Heroes are significant figures (the company founder or other senior executives with a large influence).

The concept of organizational culture is based on the observation that organizations in some countries have a much better performance record than in others. Particularly the Japanese industries have shown a rapid rate of development from the 1950s through the 1980s. This success has been largely ascribed to social policies and management practices that supposedly find their origin in Japanese culture (e.g., Ouchi, 1981). The step from the national level to the level of separate organizations was easily made. The popularity of the concept of organizational culture largely results from best-sellers written for managers. A book by Peters and Waterman (1982) has been most influential. It contained analyses of companies in the USA with an excellent record, despite the depressed economy of the late 1970s and the early 1980s. The authors gave two reasons for this success, namely strong leadership and a complex of values that was shared by those who belonged to the organization. Peters and Waterman have been strongly criticized for the ad hoc character of their research. They never showed that the desirable features were less prominent in less excellent companies. Moreover, many of their excellent companies soon were in trouble (e.g., Calori & Sarni, 1991).

To capture the essence of an organization's culture, qualitative research methods have been prominent. An analogy with ethnographic research, including "thick description" as advocated by Geertz (1973), has been suggested repeatedly (e.g. Allaire & Firsirotu, 1984; Frost, Moore, Louis, Lundberg, & Martin, 1985). An author with a background in psychology like Schein (1985) emphasizes less tangible aspects. He distinguishes three levels: observable behaviors and artifacts; values; and, underlying the other two levels, unconscious basic assumptions about relations to the environment, and the nature of reality. These basic assumptions form the core of culture. Schein refers to the "feel" of an organization and recommends the use of more subjective methods, like interviewing, observation (without standardized schedules), and group discussion.

A limited volume of empirical research is based on more objective methods. For example, Reynolds (1986) developed a questionnaire for fourteen aspects of organizational culture described in the literature. A presumably excellent company differed from two others on only four of the fourteen dimensions. Lens and Hermans (1988) distinguished four types of organizational climate (a term with a meaning similar to organizational culture), which they saw as corresponding with four types of individual motivation. No significant correlations were found between questionnaire scores for organizational climate and motivational orientations of senior managers.

An informative study was reported by Hofstede, Neuijen, Ohayv, and Sanders (1990). Twenty organizations in Denmark and the Netherlands participated. First, interview data (guided by a checklist) were collected from key informants. Then an extensive questionnaire was administered to a stratified sample in each organization. Finally, the findings were checked in feedback discussions. Employee values were found to differ more on demographic variables (such as nationality, age, and education) than on organization membership. The main differences between organizations were found in daily practices as they were perceived by the employees. The core of an organization's culture appeared to lie more in shared daily practices than in shared values. Hofstede and his colleagues argued that cultural values were acquired fairly early in life and were difficult to change later on; in contrast, organizational practices were learned at the work place. From this study organizational culture and culture at the level of nations emerged as phenomena of a different order. Hofstede and his colleagues pointed out that the use of the same term at both levels could be misleading; still, they did not abandon the term organizational culture.

Thus, comprehensive notions of culture continue to be used. For example, a distinction is made by Van Muijen, Koopman, and De Witte (1996) between two levels of organizational culture. At the first level, visible and tangible manifestations are situated (like buildings, rules, technology, etc.). At the second level there are values and norms on which behaviors are based. An international group of experts developed a questionnaire with a descriptive part (directed at the first level) and evaluative part (with items pertaining to the second level). Data were collected from employees in many organizations in a number of (European) countries. At the level of organizations larger differences between countries were found in evaluative (values) items than in descriptive items. Also in individual-level analyses value differences between countries emerged. The questionnaire was meant for the assessment of the culture of an organization and changes in this culture. A major part of the study by Van Muijen et al. is devoted to case analyses. But little information is given about the empirical validity of such analyses.

It appears to us that caution is needed in drawing parallels between national and organizational culture. Apart from terminological confusion there is the problem whether culture at the societal level can have (approximately) the same meaning as at the level of an organization. Organizational culture is a label derived from research which initially employed mainly impressionistic and subjective methods. Results with these and other methods (questionnaires) have not led to very consistent results.

## Managerial behavior

This section deals with one of the most studied aspects of work and organizational psychology, namely leadership. We have selected two topics, leadership styles and decision making. References to other aspects can be found, for example, in Aditya, House, and Kerr (2000).

### Leadership styles

A good leader influences employees to pursue the goals of the organization, but this can be done in different ways; different **leadership styles** can be followed. In the American literature two behavior categories have emerged as typical for effective leaders. In the Ohio State, leadership studies they were called consideration and initiating structure (cf. Wexley & Yukl, 1984). Consideration has to do with the concern and support of the leader for subordinates. Initiating structure refers to the definition and structuring by leaders of the various roles and tasks to be performed by themselves and other employees. Blake and Mouton (1964) expressed these dimensions as "concern for people" and "concern for production," while Likert (1967) distinguished between "exploitative" (or authoritative) and "participative" behavior. Cross-cultural variations of these categories have been described by J. B. P. Sinha (1980, 1984a) for India and by Misumi (1985) for Japan.

Sinha has proposed the concept of the "nurturant–task leader." This management style has two components: concern for the task and a nurturant orientation towards subordinates. The nurturant–task leader creates a climate of purposiveness and maintains a high level of productivity. But he also shows care and affection for the well-being of his subordinates and is committed to their professional growth. The nurturant–task leadership style is flexible and as a subordinate needs less guidance and direction it should change to a more participative style. The personal character of the relationship with a father-like role for the leader appears to be the most outstanding feature of the nurturant–task leader. Sinha (1980, p. 63) writes that the nurturant–task leader "understands the expectations of his subordinates. He knows that they relish dependency and personalized relationship, accept his authority and look towards him for guidance and direction."

The nurturant–task leadership style is an authoritative, but not an authoritarian, style according to Sinha. He proposes a continuum from authoritarian (which often is seen as related to the task-oriented leadership style in the US literature) to participative, with nurturant–task leadership in the middle. Participative management is considered the ideal, but this can only function under certain social conditions that often are not (yet) present in India. One factor is the preference for personal over contractual relationships. Rules and regulations can be sidestepped to accommodate a friend or relative. Other examples are a dependence proneness in Indian society, a lack of team orientation, and the conspicuous use of resting time (late arrival at work and long lunches) as a sign of status. These and similar factors make an authoritative leadership style necessary.

In a series of studies in which employees of Indian organizations were interviewed extensively, Sinha identified a profile of the nurturant–task leader, distinct from both a participative and an authoritative leadership style. Evidence was found for a superior performance record of Indian managers who adhered to the nurturant style, compared to those who applied other styles. However, it should be noted that Sinha's views are not shared by all Indian researchers. Others have been arguing for the positive effects of a democratic participative leadership style (cf. Khandwalla, 1988). On the other hand, Singh and Paul (1985) argued against the task orientedness of the nurturant–task leader; the leader always has to show unconditional affection, even when subordinates are showing poor performance, in order to bring them back to the group.

Another conceptualization, this time by a Japanese author, is Misumi's (1985) PM leadership theory. He distinguishes two main functions in a group: one is contributing to the group's goal achievement and problem solving, the other is promoting the group's self-preservation and strengthening the group processes. The achievement function is called Performance or P by Misumi, and the self-preservation function is called Maintenance or M.[2] M leadership is aimed at increasing interpersonal encouragement and support, and reducing conflict and strife (which leads to disintegration of the group when unchecked). Both the P and the M function play a role in any leadership process. How these functions manifest themselves varies, among other things depending on the degree of structural differentiation in the organization. The two functions are not independent, but are interacting dimensions: the meaning of P amounts to "pressure for production" with (low) M, and to "planning" with (high) M. Misumi makes a distinction between general characteristics of leadership and specific situational expressions. This distinction pertains to both the form (morphology) and the causes (dynamics) of managerial behavior.

The theory leads to a typology with four basic types, namely PM, Pm, pM and pm leadership (a capital indicates a high value on a dimension and a small letter a low value). A finer grading is possible by a further division of the types into subtypes. The scheme has been validated not only in survey research, but also in quasi-experimental studies within organizational settings in Japan, varying from schools and government departments to industrial firms. In the latter setting the effectiveness of leadership types has been assessed in terms of external variables (such as long-term achievement, work motivation, accident rates, and turnover) as well as self-report criteria (such as satisfaction and norms for own performance). There is a consistent order in the effectiveness of the four types of leadership, namely PM, pM, Pm and pm. Only for subjects with a low task motivation has the Pm leadership style been found to be the most effective.

Misumi sees his typology as an extension of (classical) Western theories which often emphasized a single dimension and were operationalized in a standard (survey) instrument. In his opinion new measures are required for the P and M aspects for each setting in which leadership is being studied. He expects that the PM theory as such will be found to have universal validity because the morphology and dynamics of leadership elsewhere should be similar to those in Japan.

Studies that support these expectations have been summarized by Smith and Peterson (1988). Data from Britain, Hong Kong, the USA, and India show positive correlations between subordinates' ratings of their work situation and ratings on P and M scales for their supervisors. From these studies another result has emerged. In a set of questions pertaining to specific behaviors some correlated consistently with general leadership dimensions in all the countries studied, but

---

[2] Note that the Japanese researcher Misumi, though trained in the USA, postulates a dimension for the continued existence of the group, while in the Western literature the corresponding dimension emphasizes concern for the individual.

for other items the correlations differed between countries. For example, a supervisor who talks about a subordinate's personal difficulties to his colleagues is seen as inconsiderate in Britain and the US, but as considerate in Hong Kong and Japan. These results support Misumi's claim that a distinction has to made between general attributes of leadership and specific manifestations.

This was also pointed out by Heller (1985). In his opinion broad questions rather than specific ones lead to fairly clear cultural differences. Examples of general items are those used in the classical studies by Haire, Ghiselli, and Porter (1966) and by Hofstede (1980) which will be discussed later on. Reactions to items on specific aspects of day-to-day decision making used by Heller and Wilpert (1981) were found to be contingent upon situational demands rather than on cultural (national) differences between Western countries. The reason is perhaps that the items of Heller and Wilpert were more task related while those in the studies mentioned by Smith and Peterson were primarily person oriented.

Not only the actual behavior of mangers, but also the expectations and perceptions of their behavior can be a source of variance between cultures. Differences in what is seen as prototypical of good managers may affect the acceptance and effectiveness of foreign managers (Shaw, 1990). One study using data from a worldwide project (the GLOBE study cf., House et al., 1999) examined cultural variation in leadership prototypes across twenty-two European countries (Brodbeck et al., 2000). More than 6,000 middle-level managers rated 112 questionnaire items on the degree to which the trait or the behavior formulated in that item facilitated or impeded "outstanding" leadership. From earlier research, including samples from outside Europe, twenty-one consistent leadership prototypicality scales had been derived, like "visionary," "inspirational," "diplomatic," "autocratic," and "human orientation."

Leadership prototypes were found to differ across regions. The differences in prototypes between countries were substantially in agreement with a clustering reported by Ronen and Shenkar (1985; Ronen, 1986) on the basis of earlier studies on attitudinal, managerial, and organizational variables (see next section). As usual, there were similarities and differences. Vision and inspiration were rated highly everywhere, but participation was higher in north-west Europe than in south-east Europe, and administrative skills were more highly placed in the German-speaking countries than in Great Britain and Ireland. Three dimensions of country differences were found, called: (1) interpersonal directness and proximity, (2) modesty, and (3) autonomy. Further analyses per region within Europe showed within region dimensions that differed somewhat from the overall dimensions. For example, humane orientation was a more important determinant of differences on the first dimension in north-west Europe, while face saving and autonomy better differentiated countries in south-east Europe on this dimension. Brodbeck and his colleagues conclude that the findings validate a set of dimensions that represent core differences in leadership prototypes across Europe, and that this is relevant information for expatriate managers and consultants.

Many researchers, as well as managers (cf. Adler, 1986; Brodbeck et al., 2000), are convinced that cultural factors play an important role in managerial practices. Triandis (1994b) mentions several examples. Doktor (1983) found that Japanese managers spend a much longer time period on a single task than Americans; for tasks that occupy more than an hour the percentages are 41 and 10 respectively. Similarly, 18 percent of the Japanese and 49 percent of the American managers are busy with tasks that take less than nine minutes to complete. In Triandis's opinion this reflects the tendency of the Japanese to engage in long-term planning. Sinha (1984a) observed that in India more emphasis is placed on job satisfaction than on productivity, a finding that fits with the collectivistic tendencies of Indian societies. A third example by Triandis is the role of "face" in the sense of "losing face" or "gaining face" among the Chinese. This is considered an important value in business interactions (Redding & Ng, 1982).

This last example can serve to illustrate that the pattern of relationships between day-to-day practices and underlying cultural variables is almost never straightforward. Chinese business organizations, particularly in Hong Kong, have been described as resembling families with autocratic leadership. A condescending attitude toward subordinates and even scolding in public is not uncommon. Apparently the principle of "face" is less important in the personnel area than in other interpersonal dealings (cf., Redding & Wong, 1986). The cultural insider knows when issues of face apply and when not, but to the outsider with only partial knowledge, professed values and actual practices may seem quite contradictory.

A theoretical approach that seeks to take account of the obvious complexities and variations in leadership behavior is based on connectionism (Hanges, Lord, & Dickson, 2000). Connectionism or parallel distributed processing asserts that information processing often does not take place as a serial process; rather cognitive processes in neural networks occur simultaneously and in parallel (Rumelhart et al., 1986). Hanges and colleagues argue that a cognitive network consists of building blocks between which stable interconnections can develop through experience and learning, ultimately leading to schemas that are readily available, if they are required in a situation. In their connectionist frameworks they include elements like self, affect, beliefs, scripts, and values. One should realize that, unlike in the theorizing by Rumelhart and colleagues, the notions of connections and schemas are mainly metaphorical. They cannot be linked in an unambiguous way to neural processes. For the time being international questionnaire studies appear to be the main source of information on how leadership styles and practices are similar and different across cultures (cf. House et al., 1999).

## Decision making

Research on **decision making** varies from descriptive accounts to models in which probabilities of outcomes of imaginary bets are manipulated. An example of a rich descriptive analysis with low emphasis on theoretical formalization can be found in Janis and Mann (1977). Their work includes analyses of the decision-making process in single, but historically important, events. The use of biographical information next to knowledge derived from field studies and experiments allows for consideration of emotional and personal factors. There can be no doubt that incidental and personal factors influence decision outcomes. At the same time, it is evident that there are regularities in decision-making processes. The question is whether systematic cross-cultural variation can be discovered in these regularities.

Mann et al. (1998) administered a decision-making questionnaire, with subscales for various coping styles, to undergraduate students in Australia, New Zealand, and USA, and in Hong Kong, Japan, and Taiwan. The first three countries were qualified as more individualist, and the latter three as more collectivist, a distinction that we discussed in ch. 3 and to which we return in the next section. In the individualist countries students expressed more confidence in their decisions, while those in the collectivist countries scored higher on some styles like "buck-passing" (e.g., leaving decisions to others) and "avoidance." The authors report levels of statistical significance rather than the size of cross-cultural differences. Nevertheless, they could conclude that despite the differences these Western and East Asian student samples were more alike than different in self-reported decision styles.

Heller and Wilpert (1981) analyzed managerial decision making at the top levels of 129 organizations in the USA, five west European countries, and Israel. They postulated a continuum of power sharing that reaches from unshared unilateral decision making by the superior via shared (participatory) decision making, to the delegation of all power for certain decisions to the subordinate. Most managers greatly vary their behavior on the continuum, depending on the situation they are facing. Differences between countries were far less important than between situations. The extent of power sharing was found to be relatively high in France and Sweden and low in Israel and Spain. The overall trend in the results was that certain conditions foster participative decision making and that these conditions were quite similar across the range of countries studied. The balance between situational contingencies which lead to cultural convergence on the one hand, and on the other hand values and practices which lead to cultural divergence, clearly leaned to the former side in this study.

Much of the earlier cross-cultural research on decision making has been summarized by Wright (1985). He discussed research within organizational settings as well as experimental research. In organizations the most extensively studied topic was the supposed superiority of Japanese over American organizational efficiency. This has been attributed to a more consultative style of decision making that finds its expression in the *ringi* process, described in box 14.2. In descriptive studies based on impressions and clinical-style interviews (e.g., Abegglen, 1958) differences emerged that could be explained in terms of cultural factors. In studies with more systematic data collection (e.g., Pascale, 1978) there was a tendency toward striking similarities. Wright concluded that the picture was still unclear.

## Box 14.2 Decision-making by consensus

Martyn-Johns (1977) describes how a Javanese manager's decision style in the Indonesian subsidiary of an organization was seen by his international superiors as extremely authoritarian. Decisions were promulgated in instructions that were not to be questioned by anyone. A manager from Europe with a democratic style took over at a certain moment. He discussed issues at meetings and decisions were often taken by majority vote. However, his subordinates found this new manager more coercive and authoritarian. They objected that certain relevant matters could not be mentioned in an open discussion and that there was coercion of the minority by the majority, because even those who had expressed disagreement were held responsible for a decision once it had been taken.

According to Martyn-Johns there is extensive deliberation (*musjawarah*) in Java until everybody agrees what the best decision is under given circumstances and in the light of the various prevailing opinions. The ideal is to reach consensus, rather than to take a decision against the explicit opinion of a minority. Once consensus has been reached a decision made by the manager is supported by everyone and its implementation is not considered authoritarian.

Typical of decision making in Japanese organizations is the *ringi* procedure, whereby plans are drafted at the lower levels of an organization and employees are encouraged to develop their own ideas into a plan. Occasionally the initiative comes from a higher ranking person, but this is by no means the rule. A draft plan is circulated among the departments involved and can be changed repeatedly in the process. It gradually moves up the chain of command for approval. In this way the knowledge and experience of many employees is used and consensus is promoted. The *ringi* system fits in with the practice of broad consultation (*nemawashi*) in Japan. It is a bottom-up procedure of decision making that is supposed to lead to more involvement of employees with the organization and to a sense of commitment to the success of plans because everyone shares the responsibility. Also, the implementation of decisions tends to take little time. In the management literature the *ringi* procedure has been hailed occasionally as the key to the economic success of Japan. However, it also has weaknesses, such as the long time it can take for a plan to get through a bureaucracy and the large amount of paper work which results from it (e.g., Misumi, 1984).

One of the issues studied is the so-called "risky-shift" phenomenon. This refers to the tendency that in group discussions more hazardous decisions are reached than when individuals make decisions on their own. Brown (1965) has suggested that riskiness is valued in Western societies. Individuals want to take at least as much risk as their peers and in the course of a discussion they move to a more extreme position not to lag behind the others. If this is correct a "cautious shift" could be anticipated in cultures where caution is valued. Initially support was found for this idea by Carlson and Davis (1971), who studied the effect of group discussions on decisions in the USA and Uganda, the latter presumably a country where caution is seen as positive. Their results were criticized because of the possible culture inappropriateness of the American-designed stimuli (e.g., Mann, 1980). With more suitable methods Gologor (1977) found no tendencies toward risky shift in Liberia. Group decisions tended to be more extreme than individual decisions, but there was about as much polarization towards more cautious as toward more risky decisions. An interesting finding by Harrison (1975) is that in Zimbabwe group members of European descent shifted to more caution and those of African descent to more risk when race track bets had to be agreed upon in a small-group discussion.

The confidence that respondents have in their decisions was emphasized in a study by Poortinga and Spies (1972) with samples of white and black South African truck drivers. To reduce possible effects of prior educational experience, tasks of perception and motor skills were used in which the level of difficulty (and thus the expected outcome) could be adapted to the level of performance of a respondent. In this way the probability of success was set at an equal level for each respondent. The results of both samples fell well short of the maximum earnings because of overconfidence. But no significant intergroup difference was found with any of three different methods.

A quite consistent difference in probabilistic thinking was reported between Western (mainly British) and south-east Asian samples, including Malaysians, Indonesians, and Chinese (Wright, Phillips, & Wisudha, 1983). In their studies Wright and colleagues asked subjects to answer a question and then to indicate how confident they were about the correctness of their opinion. Respondents were usually overconfident, but Asians more so. They more often used absolute (yes/no) and less often intermediate judgments than Western respondents. Wright and Phillips (1980) ascribed this to a cultural difference in the tendency to use non-probabilistic as opposed to probabilistic thinking. To support this claim a variety of (mainly impressionistic) cultural antecedents were mentioned (Wright, 1985). Wright et al. (1983) found that the extent of cross-cultural differences varied between tasks and that the correlations between tasks were low. This points to situational specificity in dealing with uncertainty. Therefore, differences in scores might well be limited to a narrow range of situations. Also, a speculation by Wright that the Japanese would be non-probabilistic thinkers was not confirmed by Yates et al. (1989).

More recent research was reviewed by Weber and Hsee (2000). They described research based on decision-making models where a negative outcome may be weighed differently from a positive outcome (e.g., the risk of losing a sum of money outweighs a potential gain of the same value). Bontempo, Bottom, and Weber (1997) studied judgments of risk in lotteries. They found that the *size* of a potential loss had more impact on perceived risk among Chinese (Hong Kong, Taiwan) than among Western (Dutch and US American) students. However, the *probability* of a loss had relatively more effect on the perceived risk in the Chinese samples. Several factor-analytic studies of judgments of real-life risks (like hazardous technologies) have shown the same two factors, namely dread (catastrophic potential and lack of control) and risk of the unknown (unobservable and possible long-term harm) (Weber & Hsee, 2000). In studies in which Chinese respondents were compared with Westerners (mainly Americans) Chinese showed a higher preparedness to make risky investment choices, which were ascribed to the cushioning effects of Chinese social networks in the case of catastrophic outcomes. This interpretation was supported by results in an academic and a medical sphere, where such differences were not observed.

Weber and Hsee (2000) plead in their review for theory-based research with multiple methods and differentiation according to domain. Their recommendations appear to be quite similar to the notion of limited generalizability of cross-cultural differences discussed in chs. 11 and 12. This notion also fits with findings in studies on organizational decision making, mentioned above, in which situational contingencies were found to be quite prevalent.

## Work values and motives

The landmark study on **work-related values** was carried out by Hofstede (1980, 1983a) in the national subsidiaries of IBM. Through the 1990s this work was the most frequently cited source from the cross-cultural literature, with references not only in psychology and cultural anthropology, but also in the literature on management and on communication. The major report on results from forty countries was published in 1980. Later, Hofstede (1983a) included the results of another ten countries and three regions from which small or uneven samples had been tested. Data were collected in two rounds, around 1968 and around 1972. Seven different levels of occupation were distinguished ranging from managers to administrative personnel. Altogether there were more than 116,000 questionnaires in twenty languages. The survey instrument included some 160 questions of which 63, mainly pertaining to values, were used in the cross-cultural analysis (Hofstede, 1980, p. 66).

In ch. 3 Hofstede's work was discussed because of its relevance for social psychology. There we saw that Hofstede identified four dimensions, namely power distance, uncertainty avoidance, individualism–collectivism and masculinity–femininity. It is important to consider how these were derived. At the stage of pilot studies it had already become clear that items dealing with hierarchical relationships showed differences between countries. "How frequently are employees afraid to disagree with their managers?" became a core question to assess power distance. The index of uncertainty avoidance was developed along similar lines, following theoretical distinctions in the literature. The indices for individualism and masculinity resulted from a factor analysis of twenty-two (later fourteen) items inquiring about the importance of various work goals. These items more or less fitted Maslow's need hierarchy to distinguish between individuals (cf. below). A meaningful distinction between countries could only be obtained with factor analysis on a data matrix of work goals by countries. This country-level factor analysis yielded the two factors of individualism and masculinity.

To confirm the picture that had emerged factor analyses were carried out on the items relevant to all four factors. After some readjustments thirty-two items provided a three-factor solution explaining 49 percent of the variance at country level. The first factor was a combination of individualism and power distance (with reversed sign), the second factor represented masculinity, and the third factor corresponded to uncertainty avoidance. For conceptual reasons Hofstede maintained a distinction between the two dimensions of individualism and power distance that together constituted the first factor. He justified this with the argument that the correlations between the two dimensions $(r = -.67)$ virtually disappeared if variance due to national wealth was controlled for. It has often been suggested that Hofstede's dimensions were derived empirically (e.g. Ronen, 1986), but this is only partially true.

For each of the four dimensions country indices were computed. Hofstede saw these indices as reflecting broad underlying dimensions of culture. The interpretations were strengthened by extensive references to the literature about cross-cultural differences and by the use of data from other studies. In addition, data were collected with other value questionnaires on *ad hoc* samples of managers from various countries. The four dimensions were also correlated with seven economic, geographic, and demographic indicators. For example, the power distance dimension showed a correspondence with conformity versus independence, and with higher versus lower authoritarianism. Subordinates in low power distance countries negatively evaluated close supervision and preferred consultative decision making. The strongest predictor of the power distance indices across forty countries was geographical latitude. Hofstede explained this relationship as arising from the higher need for technology in enhancing human survival in colder countries. He did not postulate a direct causal relationship between environmental temperature and the power distance index, but saw the climatic factors at the beginning of a causal chain that through a long process of adaptation leads to cross-cultural differences in social structure (see also Van de Vliert, Kluwer, & Lynn 2000). Another example is the high correlation $(r = .82)$ between individualism and economic wealth (per capita GNP). In countries low on individualism conformity is liked, and autonomy is rated as less important, while in countries with high individualism, variety is sought and security is seen as less important.

Apart from the small numbers of items on which two of the factors were based, Hofstede's study has given rise to some other questions. Samples were drawn from a single company and although Hofstede rightly pointed to the advantage that samples were matched on a number of variables (Hofstede, 1979, p. 392), there was the disadvantage that they were not representative of the national populations to which the results were generalized (cf. ch. 11). There is another methodological problem. Hofstede's dimensions were identified at the group level and not at the individual level. Nevertheless, he saw a value as "a broad tendency to prefer certain states of affairs over others" (1980, p. 19). This is an individual-level rather than a country-level conceptualization (see ch. 11). Since individual-level data were collected it is surprising that dimensions could not be identified at this level.

The most serious difficulty is that in other studies, patterns and correlations expected on the basis of Hofstede's analysis often are not found. This was the case with the IDE (1981) study, mentioned in box 14.1. Ellis (1988) failed to find patterns of differences on value ratings between American and German subjects, that were predicted on the basis of their country indices. In the study of sex stereotypes by Williams and Best (1990a; see ch. 3) correlations between Hofstede's masculinity index and sex differences on three components of affective meaning failed to reach significance. A replication by Fernandez, Carlson, Stepina, and Nicholson (1997) showed substantial shifts in value classifications. Partial support was found by Van Oudenhoven (2001) in a study with business students from ten Western countries who rated companies on statements reflecting the four value dimensions. Another study by Hoppe (1990, reported in Smith and Schwartz, 1997), using ad hoc samples of managers from seventeen countries, found correlations of around $r = .60$ between average country indices on the four Hofstede scales and the original indices reported by Hofstede. However, Hoppe's attempt to replicate Hofstede's four factors was not successful.

An extensive replication study of Hofstede has been reported by Merritt (2000). An eighty-two-item questionnaire, including most of the items from Hofstede's original work value survey, was administered to more than 9,000 airline pilots in nineteen countries. The correlations between the four indices reported by Hofstede (1980) and the country scores of the pilots were $r = .74$ (power distance), $r = .16$ (masculinity), $r = .48$ (individualism) and $r = .25$ (uncertainty avoidance). Thus power distance and individualism were substantially replicated, but the replication failed for the other two dimensions.[3] It may be noted in passing that the two more consistent dimensions together formed one factor in Hofstede's original analysis, which was closely correlated with GNP.

Dimensions like those of Hofstede are attractive. They allow both managers and researchers to transcend "culture" as a fuzzy notion; they provide a "mapping of the nations of the world" (Smith & Schwartz, 1997). Especially the dimension of

---

[3] It may be noted that Merritt continued with a "conceptual replication" in which for forty-eight items the maximum correlations with Hofstede's indices were sought. Not surprisingly, in this matrix of forty-eight items by (only) nineteen countries some high correlations were also found for the other two dimensions. However, these correlations amount to overestimates, since there was no cross-validation, or correction for shrinkage (Wiggins, 1973). Such controls are needed to avoid capitalization on chance events. The questionable validity of the "conceptual replication" appears to be substantiated by its outcome: six of the twelve original Hofstede items were not part of the new set of item composites; and of the six items that were retained four ended up in a different dimension.

individualism–collectivism has been further developed. A major handbook of organizational psychology (Triandis, Dunnette, & Hough, 1994) has been organized in two parts, one part dealing with individualist and the other with collectivist countries. Many studies in the organizational literature take the distinction for granted in the explanation of virtually any cross-cultural difference between Eastern and Western countries (see, for example, reviews by Hui & Luk, 1997, and Aycan, 2000).

Another set of value dimensions was reported by Smith et al. (1996). As we have seen in ch. 3, the first two of these were labeled conservatism versus egalitarian commitment (combining values of ascription and particularism versus achievement and universalism), and utilitarian involvement versus loyal involvement (mainly represented by values of individualism versus collectivism).

In ch. 3 we also discussed relationships between various sets of dimensions. Another way to use these "maps of the world" is to see which nations are found in the same regions. This can be done with cluster analysis. Hofstede (1980) has reported the results of a cluster analysis. After some modifications of the outcome (on the basis of historical arguments), eight clusters remained: more developed Latin, less developed Latin, more developed Asian, less developed Asian, Near Eastern, Germanic, Anglo, and Nordic, while Japan formed a cultural area on its own. These clusters as well as those found in some studies of motivational and attitudinal variables, tend to group countries by geographical proximity (cf. Ronen, 1986; Griffith & Hom, 1987). The fact that the clusters by and large coincide with regions gives face validity to the instruments on which they are based. Hofstede (1983b) has drawn implications for managerial behavior from his findings. For example, harmony is important in countries with low individualism, and paternalistic management should be more acceptable in countries high on power distance. Such statements are open to empirical testing and can lead to gradual refinement of our understanding of cultural influences.

## Motives

Among the **motivation** (or need) theories that have inspired cross-cultural researchers the most prominent are those of McClelland (1961) and Maslow (1954). The basic argument in McClelland's work is that economic development cannot be explained without reference to social and psychological variables. He was struck by the apparent role which a motivation to get ahead plays in the process of national development; and he proposed the idea that achievement motivation is in part responsible for this. McClelland was able to demonstrate that correlations existed between economic development and the frequency of themes of achievement in a culture's literary products, usually with some temporal lag. An example is a significant correlation between country-level achievement scores derived from an analysis of the stories in children's books and estimates of economic growth (in per capita income and electricity production). More information on cross-cultural studies of achievement motivation can be found in Segall et al. (1999).

Maslow's need hierarchy has served as the theoretical basis for the first major international survey of motivation conducted by Haire et al. (1966). They slightly modified Maslow's scheme and investigated the following needs: security, social, esteem, autonomy, and self-actualization. The questionnaire on motivation was one of three scales; the other two were on leadership styles and managerial roles. Haire and colleagues obtained data from samples of at least some 200 managers in fourteen countries, nine from Europe, the USA, Argentina, Chile, India, and Japan. Subjects were recruited through employers' associations, universities, training centers, and individual companies. By comparing between-group and within-group variation the authors estimated that for most variables national differences comprised approximately one-quarter of the total variation in the data pool.

Of the various needs, self-actualization (i.e., realizing one's capacities) was rated as the most important in all countries, followed in most countries by the need for autonomy (i.e., the opportunity to think and act independently). Between-country differences in the importance of needs were relatively small; apparently managers are quite alike in what motivates them in their work situation. Relatively large differences were found in the satisfaction of needs. In all countries, the two most important needs were the least satisfied. The most satisfied managers (on all needs combined) came from Japan and the cluster of Nordic European countries. Managers from developing countries (which formed a separate cluster in this study) and from Latin European countries were the most dissatisfied.

Apart from the clusters already mentioned, there was an Anglo-American cluster, while Japan stood alone. Haire and colleagues interpreted the similarity of response patterns as a reflection of a uniform industrial culture. They attributed the differences between clusters to (unspecified) factors of national culture. At the same time they acknowledged another important factor, namely the level of industrialization which in their view led to a single cluster for three culturally diverse developing countries (Argentina, Chile, and India).

Later there was a shift away from research on the general needs and motives that are satisfied by work to the activity of working and the outcomes of work. The analysis of the meaning of working has a long history in social philosophy and more recently in the social sciences. Most famous is Weber's (1905/1976) treatise on the rise of capitalism as a result of Protestant religious dogma and work ethic. The most significant recent study (which did not support Weber's theory) has been reported by the Meaning of Working International Research team (MOW, 1987). The leading concept in this project was work centrality. This was defined as "a general belief about the value of working in one's life" (MOW, 1987, p. 17). To assess this concept respondents were asked directly how important working was for them, and also how important it was in relation to other life roles (leisure, community life, religion, and family). The importance of working was best illustrated by two findings. Eighty-six percent of all subjects indicated that they would continue to work even if they had sufficient money to live in comfort for the rest of their lives. The second finding was that working was second in importance among the five life roles; only family was rated higher.

The MOW study was based on a complex model with work centrality as the core. Societal norms are intermediate, and valued working outcomes and preferred working goals form a peripheral layer. To the model were further added antecedents and consequents of work centrality. Social norms (which can show cross-cultural differences) were seen as the basis for normative evaluations about work. A distinction was made between entitlements (the right to meaningful and interesting work) and obligations (the duty to contribute to society by working).

The study involved subjects from eight countries listed here in the order in which working was considered important (from high to low): Japan, (now former) Yugoslavia, Israel, USA, Belgium, Netherlands, (West) Germany, and Britain. Two kinds of samples were drawn in each country, a national sample ($n = 450$ or more) that was taken as representative for the country and various target groups ($n = 90$ approximately). These target groups were homogeneous with respect to demographic or work-related characteristics, such as age or occupation. In Yugoslavia there was no national sample; for this country estimates were derived from the results of the target groups.

The importance of working varied between occupations with the highest scores for professionals and the lowest for temporary workers. Skilled workers and the unemployed had medium scores on centrality of working. Except in Belgium and the USA women scored significantly lower than men, with the most noticeable gender difference in Japan. Differences between countries were about 1.5 times larger than between occupational groups. The Japanese had by far the highest score, a finding expected by the MOW team; the score was lowest in Britain. The second lowest position of Germany and the second highest position of the Yugoslavs were considered surprising. A tentative explanation for this pattern suggested by the MOW team was that the centrality of working is a non-linear function of the length of time since industrialization. The West European countries, with Britain in the lead, have the oldest history in this respect; Japan and Yugoslavia have only more recently become industrialized.

Meaningful differences were found for both the entitlements and the obligations aspect of societal norms. On the entitlements side the USA scored low and the Netherlands, Belgium, and Germany high. The Netherlands were low on obligations, Yugoslavia and Israel scored high. Of particular interest is the balance between these two variables, i.e. between the right to work and one's duty to do so. In Japan, Britain, Yugoslavia, and Israel these two variables were approximately balanced. In the USA there was more endorsement of duties than of rights. In the remaining three countries, Netherlands, Germany, and Belgium, entitlements were more emphasized than obligations. The MOW team believed (on intuitive grounds) that a balance between rights and duties would seem the most preferable state of affairs. Going a step further, one could speculate that an overemphasis on rights when it was coupled with a low work centrality (as in the Netherlands) might adversely affect the level of economic activity of a nation in the long run.

## Conclusions

In today's changing world cross-cultural research on work and organizations is a dynamic area. The radical changes in eastern Europe have had many implications, also for organizational psychology (Roe, 1995). Majority world psychologists try to define topics and engage in research that directly addresses the needs of their organizations and work force. Aycan (2000) argued that recruitment and selection, performance management, and employee health and well-being, are topics more related to human development than traditional issues like leadership, values, and so on. Moreover, the continuous struggle to come to grips with inherently complex and highly dynamic processes has led to a diversity of perspectives on behavior–culture relationships, some of which were mentioned in this chapter.

When detecting some cross-cultural difference in organizational data one may be wise to heed an advice by Drenth (1983, p. 570): "The researcher is still faced with ruling out other explanatory factors within the national context, such as economic conditions, level of national development, level of employment, type of product, etc. Clearly, not all national differences are caused by cultural factors ..." A summary presenting this difficulty more systematically, while at the same time making suggestions for its resolution has been given by Bhagat and McQuaid (1982, pp. 697–80). They made the following recommendations:

1 Researchers should examine in sufficient detail the rationale for doing their research cross-culturally.
2 Researchers should commit themselves to some theory in order to solve the methodological problems.
3 Researchers should be seriously concerned about suitable methodological strategies.
4 There is an obvious need for pooling of resources into multicultural research teams.

In this chapter we first discussed the role of culture in shaping organizational structure, and how cultural variables may play a lesser role in how organizations are structured, and perhaps a stronger role in how they are made to function by employees.

We then turned to managerial behavior mentioning research on leadership styles, and theories from Japan and India that also seem applicable outside these countries. A short overview of decision making in organizations expanded into a broader overview of decision making and risk taking, with more recent research showing limited and domain specific cross-cultural differences.

In the final section we addressed cross-cultural research on work values and motives, mentioning contemporary, frequently used dimensions of culture that have emerged largely from organization research.

## Key terms

contingency theory

decision making (by managers)

leadership styles

motivation (work-related)

organizational culture

organizational structure

work-related values

## Further reading

Aycan, Z. (2000). Cross-cultural industrial and organizational psychology: Contributions, past developments, and future directions. *Journal of Cross-Cultural Psychology, 31*, 110–28. In addition to providing a brief overview this article suggests ways for developing the field in directions more directly pertinent to health and well-being.

Hofstede, G. (1980). *Culture's consequences: International differences in work related values.* Beverly Hills, CA: Sage. The "classic" in which the origin of Hofstede's four value dimensions is described. (A new edition was published in 2001.)

Gelfand, M. J. (Ed.) (2000). Special issue on cross-cultural industrial and organizational psychology. *Applied Psychology: An International Review, 49*, 29–226. A collection of articles reviewing various aspects of cross-cultural research in the field of organization psychology.

Triandis, H. C., Dunnette, M. D., & Hough, L. M. (Eds.) (1994). *Handbook of industrial and organizational psychology.* Vol. 4 (2nd ed.). Palo Alto, CA: Consulting Psychologists Press. An extensive handbook on work and organizational psychology, with chapters on individualist and chapters on collectivist countries.

# 15  Communication and training

The intercultural communication literature has roots in linguistics (especially sociolinguistics), sociology, cultural anthropology, and psychology. Of these, psychology is probably the most obvious parent discipline, and particularly cross-cultural psychology. The first section of this chapter is on intercultural communication. There are three subsections of which the first looks at sojourners or expatriates and the difficulties they experience in adjusting to the new cultural environment. The second subsection draws attention to errors in communication between members of various cultural groups, and the third subsection asks what characteristics make a person competent in intercultural interactions. The second section is concerned with communication training, the preparation of sojourners to deal with people from a different cultural background. The last section is on international negotiations; in this section we also address some theoretical issues relevant to the topics discussed in this chapter.

## Intercultural communication

Concern for cultural factors in interpersonal communication has been increasing rapidly in recent decades. The expansion in international business and trade, exchange of students, technical assistance programs, and tourism, has brought about a corresponding increase in relatively short-term intercultural contacts. A growing number of people spend a limited period of time abroad, from a number of months to a number of years, for purposes of study or work or, occasionally, leisure. In addition, those who stay at home increasingly interact with foreign visitors and migrants who temporarily or permanently have taken up residence in a country.

## Sojourners

As we have seen in ch. 13, temporary migrants are collectively referred to as **sojourners,** or as expatriates. Relevant literature has been reviewed by Furnham and Bochner (1986; see also Ward, Bochner, & Furnham, 2001) in a book called "culture shock." This term has a meaning similar to what was called acculturative stress in ch. 13. Its origin is credited to the anthropologist Oberg (1960), who used it to indicate the difficulties that arise from exposure to an unfamiliar environment. Among other things Oberg referred to the strain of making new adaptations, a sense of loss, confusion about one's role, and feelings of anxiety. Other authors have described the experience of going to another culture in similar terms. Guthrie (1966) mentioned the frustration of subtle cultural differences that impede social interactions. In an extensive project with foreign students from 139 nations studying in eleven countries (Klineberg & Hull, 1979) a quarter reported feelings of depression. The difficulties experienced are not the same for all sojourners. Major variables include the distance between home culture and host culture, the type of involvement, the duration of contact, and the status of the visitor in the host country (cf. Bochner, 1982).

Torbiörn (1982) carried out a study with 800 Swedish expatriates stationed abroad. He obtained data from approximately thirty persons, businessmen and their wives, in each of twenty-six countries by means of a postal survey. Among the more important findings were that only 8 percent of the respondents reported being unhappy. This is a surprising result in view of the allegedly large proportion of overseas assignments that turn out unsuccessfully (up to 30 percent in the USA, according to Tung, 1981). It should be realized that Torbiörn had a biased sample, because business people are repatriated when they fail in their assignments. Torbiörn found no evidence that accompanying spouses were more frequently unhappy than the workers. However, it was confirmed that one cannot have a successful sojourn when one's family is unhappy.

Perhaps the most salient result of Torbiörn's study was that having friends among the nationals of the host country, rather than having contacts only with fellow expatriates, is an important determinant of satisfaction. Initially those who only mix with expatriates may have more positive experiences, but in the long run personal friendships with members of the host society are very important for the sojourner. This is a consistent finding also with other groups of expatriates, including students (Klineberg & Hull, 1979) and technical advisors (Kealey, 1989).

Sinangil and Ones (1997) did an investigation not unlike that of Torbiörn, but in a host country. They collected data from 220 expatriates working in Turkey as well as from a national co-worker of each expatriate. A factor analysis showed five factors, of which job knowledge and motivation were the most important for a successful assignment in the eyes of host nationals, while relational skills came second. The family situation emerged only as the fifth factor; in the light of Torbiörn's findings its effects are likely to be underestimated by host country nationals. However, the ratings did correlate with expatriates' adjustment and intentions to stay, pointing to factors of skills and motivation that are important for job performance, independent of culture.

It may be noted that a stay in a foreign country does not automatically lead to more positive attitudes towards the host country people. Available evidence suggests that there is more often a negative than a positive change during a sojourn, at least among university students (Stroebe, Lenkert, & Jonas, 1988).

The adjustment of sojourners to the new culture over the course of time has been found to follow a U-shaped curve, though not in all studies (Church, 1982). This could mean that sojourners initially have few problems; they are enthusiastic and fascinated by new experiences. After some time, feelings of frustration, loneliness, and anxiety take over. Still later, as the sojourner learns to cope, well-being increases again. The U-curve has been extended to a double U, or W, curve to include a period of adjustment after the return of sojourners to their homeland (cf. Brein & David, 1971). Initially there is the thrill of being back in the known environment and of meeting family and friends. Then disappointments occur because some of the more positive aspects of the life abroad are lost. Finally, after some time, readjustment follows.

Furnham and Bochner (1986) questioned the empirical validity of the U- or W-curves, because these were derived from cross-sectional rather than longitudinal studies, and because of the many uncertainties concerning the precise form and the time period of the curves. More generally, they objected to the clinical overtones of the culture shock notion in many writings. They also criticized theoretical approaches that presume negative or even pathological effects. Instead Furnham and Bochner advocated a social skills approach. Newcomers to a culture have problems because they are unfamiliar or not at ease with the social norms and conventions. Gradually sojourners will learn what they need to know in order to handle social encounters competently. Ward, Okura, Kennedy, and Kojima (1999) conducted a longitudinal study with Japanese students in New Zealand, who completed questionnaires assessing psychological and sociocultural adaptation at various times in the course of a year. They found that adjustment problems were greatest at the beginning and decreased over time.

## Communication difficulties

In earlier chapters we have indicated that modes of communication and the underlying processes are essentially universal. However, this does not preclude a variety of differences in actual communication patterns. In this context it is important to distinguish failures of communication that are obvious to the interacting persons, from subtle errors that easily escape one's notice.

Most important for human communication is language. It is also a very culture-specific medium. If two people do not share a common language their interactions are much restricted and they realize this. Less obvious are communication difficulties when command of a common language is less than perfect. Variations in pronunciation and usage of English have long been a point of concern in air traffic control (Ruffell Smith, 1975). Prosodic aspects of language, including stress and intonation contours, can also occasionally lead to misunderstandings. An example from the work of Gumperz (1982) may illustrate this. Indian and Pakistani women working in a staff cafeteria in Britain were seen as surly and uncooperative. Gumperz observed that the few words they said could be interpreted negatively. When serving out food a British assistant would say "gravy?" with a rising intonation. The Indian women would use the same word, but pronounce it with a falling intonation. To the people they served this sounded like a statement of fact that under the circumstances was redundant and sometimes rude. Listening to taped sequences of this type the migrant women at first could not hear any differences. After some training they began to recognize the point. Gumperz claims quite far-reaching effects; during the training it also became clear to the women why attitudes towards them had often been negative and they regained confidence in their ability to learn.

Although there are arguments for universality in politeness expressed in language (Brown & Levinson, 1987), there is evidence also that complications can occur in pragmatic aspects of language, including the taking of turns in conversations, exchange of compliments, politeness, and an indirect versus a direct style of communication (cf. Blum-Kulka, House, & Kasper, 1988, for a summary). Barnlund and Araki (1985) found Japanese to be less direct in paying compliments and more modest in expressing them verbally than Americans. More general differences of this kind lie perhaps at the basis of communication styles, like a direct versus an indirect style, or a personal versus a contextual style (Gudykunst, Ting-Toomey, & Chua, 1988).

Much the same can be said about non-verbal communication that was mentioned in ch. 7. We have seen that the expression of emotions may vary across cultures (display rules), and there are cross-cultural differences in the meaning of specific gestures. Also within our own culture we may misinterpret the intended meaning of an emblem (i.e., a gesture that can replace a verbal expression and is supposed to have a fairly clearly described meaning). Morris, Collett, Mansh, & O'shaughnessy (1979) found differences between respondents in the meaning attributed to specific emblems, even within the same regions of various European countries.

A quasi-experimental study by Li (1999) has provided evidence that in an intercultural situation the amount of information exchanged between two interaction partners can be less than in an intracultural situation. Chinese and Canadian university students in Canada were placed in a simulated physician–patient interaction, either in same-culture pairs or in different-culture pairs. The former pairs (Chinese as well as Canadian) communicated substantially more information. This study appears to support the generally held, but rarely substantiated, belief that intercultural communication difficulties reach further than incidental misunderstandings.

It is not yet very clear how often and how seriously intercultural encounters are disrupted by an insufficient "feeling" for prosodic and pragmatic aspects of language, or by errors of non-verbal communication. Unfamiliarity with social rules and customs adds to the ignorance and consequent ineptness of a stranger. The range of relevant variables can be extended to include stereotypes and prejudices, which also affect interpersonal interactions between sojourners and members of a host culture.

However, the most evident misunderstandings tend to arise out of specific conventions in everyday social situations. Triandis (1975) reports the example of the Greek villager inviting someone to dinner and mentioning that he is welcome "any time." For an American this amounts to a non-invitation; the vagueness of the time makes it non-committal. The Greek means to convey that his guest will be welcome at any time. More generally, Triandis states that effective intercultural communication requires "isomorphic attributions," i.e., participants in an interaction have to give the same interpretation to behavior.

## Intercultural competence

Which characteristics of the individual are correlates of effective communication? In the literature on **intercultural competence,** or communication competence, most answers to this question lean towards broad concepts, such as the adjustment and personal growth of the sojourner. There are also behavior-oriented answers in which more narrowly described domains such as attitudes, knowledge about other cultures, and directly observable behavior find favor. A further issue is whether competence is a quality of the communicator, of the perceiver, or of the dyadic system that they form together. This is related to the question of whether an individual who is competent in one culture is also competent in another culture, or in other words, whether the correlates of competence are the same everywhere (cf. Hammer, 1989; Ruben, 1989).

Empirical research on intercultural competence, or communication competence, mainly started in the 1960s among Peace Corps volunteers from the USA. At the time, a trait orientation in personality assessment was fashionable and several attempts were made to find the traits relevant for the prediction of successful volunteer candidates by means of self-report personality inventories. Kealey and Ruben (1983) have listed the traits claimed in a number of studies. Most of them, including honesty, empathy, display of respect, and flexibility, are rather vague and reflect general socially desirable interpersonal characteristics. The predictive success of these traits turned out to be disappointing. It was realized that part of the problem was the absence of well-defined criteria. The potential range of situations that sojourners are confronted with is very large, and the question can be asked whether intercultural competence over the whole range can be adequately predicted from personality variables.

Kealey and Ruben also found situational variables mentioned in the literature; these included job conditions, living conditions, health problems, realistic project objectives, political interference, and language difficulties. In addition, they listed criterion variables used to assess effectiveness. Apart from personality concepts such as strength of personality, one finds variables like social participation, local language ability, and appreciation of customs.

Kealey and Ruben distinguished three main components: (1) personal and family adjustment and satisfaction; (2) professional competence; and (3) cordial relations with members of the host country. Despite the poor predictive value found for personality trait measures, Kealey and Ruben maintained that the evidence presented supported the existence of what they call an "overseas type." They based this assertion on the similarity in personality traits that were thought relevant by various authors. The resulting profile was of a person who, among other things, was open and interested in others, with positive regard, self-confident, flexible, and professionally competent.

In one study (Kealey, 1989) the effectiveness of 277 Canadian technical advisors working in twenty different majority world countries was investigated. Some of these sojourners were tested prior to departure so that the predictive validity of personality variables could be investigated better than in most earlier studies. Another feature of this project was that interviewers went into the field and that data were obtained from peers of the advisors and of their host country counterparts in the various countries. Kealey's design included fourteen outcome variables, including difficulties in adjustment and stress, contacts with hosts, understanding, and effectiveness in transferring knowledge and skills. There were three situational variables; living conditions, job constraints, and hardship level. As predictors Kealey had twenty-one variables that included ratings by self on personality dimensions and interpersonal skills, ratings by peers on interpersonal skills, motives and attitudes, and work values.

The traditional personality variables assessed by self-reports and work values did not prove to be good predictors; motives and attitudes, and interpersonal skills rated by others, did clearly better. In a discriminant analysis 85 percent of the expatriates could be correctly classified as successful or unsuccessful on the basis of the predictor scores. The situational variables correlated with both predictor and outcome scores. Kealey interpreted this evidence as fitting a person by situation interactional model. However, the person variables explained more of the variance than the situation variables. Kealey argued that his results should serve to re-establish the value of personality traits for the prediction of success as an expatriate, since motives and attitudes and ratings by others (rather than by self), were the appropriate predictor variables.

A somewhat different interpretation can also do justice to the findings. Kealey included ratings by others, motives, and attitudes as indices of personality traits. Such variables would seem quite compatible with the social skills approach outlined by Furnham and Bochner (1986), if it is understood that not everybody is equally good at learning these skills. In a more recent review Kealey (1996) maintained his earlier position. However, the requirements that he has listed for a model cross-cultural collaborator consist of three categories of skills: (1) adaptation skills, including flexibility and stress tolerance, but also marital stability; (2) cross-cultural skills, including realism and involvement in culture; and (3) partnership skills, including openness to others and initiative. Thus, there appears to be some convergence between researchers on skills, rather than classical personality traits, as the type of qualities that define the "overseas type." At the same time, it should be noted that not all authors are as positive as Kealey about the advances that have been made in assessing intercultural competence (cf. Dinges & Baldwin, 1996).

Ogay (2000) critically reviewed the history of the field of intercultural communication, as developed mainly in the USA, from a more qualitative perspective. In particular, she argued that theories of intercultural competence, which produce lists of personal qualities like the capacity for decentration and empathy, actually fail to grasp the complexity of intercultural communication. She has a more positive opinion about models like that of Gudykunst (1995, see below) and the communication accommodation theory of Gallois, Giles, Jones, Cargile, and Ota (1995). The latter, in particular, has the advantage of treating macro-level dimensions, such as sociohistorical backgrounds, as an integral part of the communication between interacting groups. In the same light, she discusses the contribution of a model of "intercultural sensitivity" proposed by Bennett (1994). Ogay links these theories to current thinking on intercultural communication in the francophone countries (Abdallah-Pretceille & Camilleri, 1994; Mauviel, 1989; Porcher, 1994).

In her own empirical work, Ogay (2000) used youth exchange programs between the French- and German-speaking areas of Switzerland in order to assess traits before departure, processes during the exchange experience, and competencies developed from it. She concluded that existing competence models tend to be too static, and developed a framework of dynamic relationships between situational affordances and constraints, and the evolving representations of cultural differences.

## Communication training

For a long time the term **intercultural communication training** mainly referred to programs for special target groups, preparing for assignments outside the trainees' home country. As we shall see below, this is still an active area. However, there is a growing awareness that in a world that is becoming a global village and in multicultural societies, education on cultural matters should be part of the school curriculum. Brislin and Horvath (1997, p. 345) write: "Many of the goals of training and education are the same: increased awareness of cultural differences, increased knowledge, movement beyond stereotypes, introduction to emotional confrontations, coverage of different behaviors that meet similar everyday goals, and so forth." It can be argued that much of this education should be part of learning foreign languages (Krumm, 1997). According to Bennett, Bennett, and Allen (1999) language learning and intercultural learning can be combined so that linguistic competence and intercultural competence develop in parallel.

Most of the programs that exist in North America and western Europe are meant to prepare prospective expatriates for living and working in another culture. Some last for weeks or even months, others are a matter of a few hours. The longer programs usually include an intensive course in the language of the host country. Beyond language, much of the content of these programs is inspired by ideas and knowledge from intercultural communication studies. Descriptions of various techniques can be found in Weeks, Pedersen, and Brislin (1982), or in Brislin and Yoshida (1994).

Various attempts have been made to create some order in the diversity of available techniques. A convenient and simple scheme has been presented by Gudykunst and Hammer (1983; Gudykunst, Guzley, & Hammer, 1996). They propose a classification with two major distinctions, namely didactic versus experiential and culture general versus culture specific. The scheme can be presented as a figure with four quadrants (cf. fig. 15.1).

In the first quadrant are placed training methods, in which personal experiences of the trainees are considered important to help them recognize how their stereotypes and attitudes affect their behavior. These methods presumably improve communication competence in any culture. To this quadrant belong techniques that

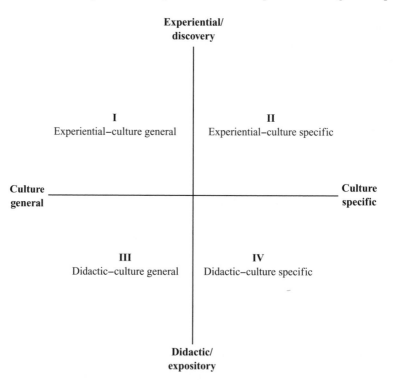

**15.1** A classification scheme for training techniques
From Gudykunst & Hammer, 1983

emphasize direct experience with people from various other cultures. This is re-alized in intercultural workshops with participants of various cultural origins, where those taking part learn to become more aware of the ways in which their own cultural backgrounds and values influence perceptions and interactions with others. A second kind of program entails sensitivity training (also called T-group training). The objectives of this kind of training, widely practiced in the 1960s and 1970s, are an increase in self-awareness and personal growth; those with self-knowledge presumably can also understand others, independent of their culture.

A third kind of technique is the culture-general simulation game. There exist a large number of these games, mostly based on similar principles. Imaginary "cultures" with contrasting values are specified in brief descriptions. The group of trainees is divided over the cultures; the subgroups receive one of the de-scriptions and have to familiarize themselves with their roles. Then follows some kind of interaction (e.g., bargaining for trade or a treaty). The games are designed so that the interactions are problematic and are likely to fail. At the end of the simulation there is a debriefing during which the reasons for the difficulties are discussed. Many of the games have been developed by training institutes for their own use and have not been published.

There are two important training techniques that belong to the second quad-rant. First, there are techniques that involve real bicultural contacts. They can take the form of a sensitivity training on an existing international conflict with members of the nations concerned in attendance. The limited evidence that is available shows that such programs are problematic, because of the strong iden-tification of participants with the views of their own group. The second group of methods is that of international workshops in which participants from two coun-tries together discuss critical incidents in interactions between people from their respective cultures.

The bottom half of fig. 15.1 refers to didactic programs, where trainees are taught by instruction. To the left quadrant (on culture-general didactic methods) belong traditional academic courses in cross-cultural psychology or intercultural communication. Gudykunst and colleagues (1996) mention here also videotapes, and "culture-general assimilators," a technique described below.

The most important form of didactic culture-specific training (the lower right quadrant of fig. 15.1) is language courses. In addition, there is a variety of brief-ings (area orientations) about the country trainees are going to visit, including information concerning its economic and political situation, problems that an ex-patriate is likely to face, and major customs and attitudes.

The technique that has been developed most systematically for intercultural training is the **culture assimilator**, also called the intercultural sensitizer. It was first developed by Fiedler, Mitchell, and Triandis (1971). It consists of a large number of short episodes describing interactions between people belonging to two different cultures, the target culture and the trainee's culture. Usually some criti-cal incident is described, such as an interaction in which something goes wrong. Each episode is followed by four or five possible reasons for the communication failure. The trainee has to choose the correct answer. In the ideal case there is one interpretation that is typically selected by members of the target culture. The other three or four are based on attributions likely to be made by members of the trainee's culture. After their choice the trainees are given feedback why their answer was correct or incorrect. In a good assimilator this feedback contains much cultural relevant information.

Most culture assimilators have been constructed for Americans who are trained for an assignment abroad (Albert, 1983), but the technique has been recommended elsewhere (e.g., Thomas & Wagner, 1999). Initially all culture assimilators were culture specific, but Brislin, Cushner, Cherrie, & Yong (1986) have constructed a culture-general assimilator that should increase the effectiveness of trainees independent of their cultural background and the culture they intend to visit. In box 15.1 one of the 100 items of this instrument is presented. Although we have no systematic evidence on this point, non-Westerners may find the topics and the concerns of the items rather "American." Nevertheless, this is a first step toward multicultural assimilators.

## Box 15.1  A culture assimilator item

Reprinted from Brislin, Cushner, Cherrie, and Yong (1986, pp. 212–13, 223)

**The eager teacher**

Upon graduating from college with a degree in English education with a Spanish minor, Rick Meyers accepted a position teaching English in a fairly large and progressive coeducational school in Merida, Mexico, capital city of the state of Yucatan. He had met the language director earlier that year while on a spring recess tour of Mexico and felt quite comfortable with him.

Eager to start the new school year off right, Rick spent a considerable amount of time in preparation of lessons and materials and in extra-help sessions with students. It seemed as if he was always doing something school related, often spending his lunch, free periods, and after-school hours with small groups of students.

Although his relationships with the students were growing, after the first few weeks, Rick noticed that his fellow teachers seemed cold and removed. He was seldom invited to after-school and weekend get-togethers or sought out during free times at school. Not sure what to make of this, Rick kept more and more to himself, feeling increasingly lonely and rejected.

What is the major issue of concern for Rick?

1  It is not common or acceptable for teachers in Mexico to show so much personal attention to students.
2  Rick has not spent the requisite amount of social time with his fellow workers.

## Box 15.1 (continued)

3 The other teachers were resentful as Rick was seen as someone special and was given attention by most of the students.
4 Rick expected to be perceived as an expert. When this was not the case, he was disappointed that his talents were not utilized by all.

### Rationales for the alternative explanations

After respondents have thought about the answers and made a choice, they are referred to another page of the book where a rationale is given for each of the five alternatives. (It has been found that subjects usually not only read the text with their own answer, but go over all the alternatives.) The following explanations are given by Brislin et al. for the item you just read:

1 While our validation sample suggested this as a possibility, one of the writer's first-hand experiences demonstrates otherwise. Especially in the larger and more progressive schools, contact between teachers and students is quite frequent and in many ways expected. Please choose again.
2 This is the best answer. Although skillful in his teaching and quite successful on the job, Rick's participation with other staff has been minimal. In many places, the degree of one's socializing with others is of critical importance. Although contrary to most Americans' desire to perform the task efficiently and well, attention must also be paid to social norms and expectations with colleagues to ensure success in the workplace.
3 There is no indication in the story that the students were responding to anything more than Rick's genuine offer of time and assistance. There is a better response. Please try again.
4 Although this may result in problems for some people in some situations, there is no indication that this is an issue for Rick. There is a better answer. Please choose again.

The construction of an assimilator is a tedious effort. It requires the collection of several hundred incidents. For each of these, likely attributions about the causes of miscommunication have to be found. The correct answer has to be identified. The items have to be validated by checking whether the distributions of answers by individuals from various cultures indeed are different (i.e., whether the attributions are indeed non-isomorphic). Finally, feedback information has to be written for each answer explaining why it is correct or incorrect.

Intercultural communication training programs tend to focus on internal psychological characteristics (whether in the form of traits or meanings) and how these are different cross-culturally. These programs help the appreciation that people in other groups may look at things in a way that differs from what we find in our own cultural environment. In a number of programs there is a related aspect, namely the role of stereotypes (mentioned in chs. 2 and 4). An additional emphasis in training follows from a diversified view on behavior–culture relationships as has been advocated in this book. In an ecocultural perspective the most important dimensions of cross-cultural differences include the actual economic conditions in which different people in the world live. Moreover, there is a variety of sociohistorically developed conditions. Among others this is elucidated by Ogay (2000). Similarly, Poortinga (1998b) referred to a training program for army officers preparing for UN peacekeeping missions, in which the importance of economic factors and associated conditions, like education and access to medical care, is emphasized.

Finally, a weak point of intercultural training programs is the lack of evaluation of their effects. Often a brief questionnaire is administered at the end of a training, but this indicates whether the trainees liked the program, rather than whether it was effective. Blake, Heslin, and Curtis (1996) have described how a proper evaluation study should be conducted, but they hardly refer to evaluation studies that meet these standards. However, some (positive) evidence is available for the culture assimilator technique (e.g., Albert, 1983; Cushner, 1989).

## Negotiation

The field of international negotiations provides an inexhaustible source of anecdotal evidence; sojourners who have been involved in international negotiations, especially of a commercial nature, can relate incidents which in their opinion illustrate in dramatic fashion the crucial importance of "culture." A telling example is the west European businessman who allegedly lost an important transaction in an Arab country, even after the papers had been signed, because he handed the contract over with his left hand.

An outside observer is inclined to see somewhat "odd" practices as a reflection of broader and more systematic differences. Observations tend to generalize to a more general trait, in earlier times indicated with the term "national character" (cf. ch. 4). Statements to the effect that one has to be careful with the X-people because of their formality, or that one has be patient in negotiations with the Y-people because they take a long time in reaching a decision, form an important part of the literature on negotiations that pays attention to cultural factors.

Negotiators are virtually unanimous in considering the substantive issues which are on the table as the most important determinants of the outcome of a negotiation process. On the relevance of cultural factors opinions differ, but many negotiators, from business as well as international diplomacy (e.g., Kaufmann, 1996), believe that an understanding of these factors is essential.

Information on how to best negotiate in a given culture can be obtained from different types of sources. However, it is important to realize that underlying principles apply everywhere (cf. Raiffa, 1982). Only specific strategies may differ, but the extent to which this actually happens is not very clear. Leung and Wu (1990) have listed variables reported in the literature. One difference they mentioned concerns persuasion styles, with negotiators from some countries more rational, others more emotional, and still others more ideological in their argumentation. Another dimension of differences is the degree of confrontation. Some cultures seek argumentation and competition, other are more restrained in their interactions. As far as initial offers in bargaining are concerned, in some cultures one finds more extreme initial bids than in others. Americans have been found to be generally moderate, they are also more inclined to make concessions and reciprocate concessions from others. Surveying the chapter by Leung and Wu, and the sources they refer to, one gains the impression that negotiators from the USA are less frequently attributed undesirable social traits. Since most studies originate from this country one may wonder how far the results are influenced by social stereotypes.

Books on business negotiations contain numerous prescriptions either for a specific country or for regions. Recommendations tend to be quite specific on what to do and what not, and what to watch out for (e.g., Harris & Moran, 1991; Kublin, 1995). Regions smaller than countries are rarely addressed.

Posses (1978), in a chapter called "Foreigners and foreign cultures," gives a host of general statements about culture as an influence on behavior. For example: "Across the foreign border, the negotiator must observe and note the alien movements carefully and distinguish them from his own in order to evaluate their positive or negative relation to the actions and responses of his foreign adversary" (p. 25). A little later (p. 29) we learn:

> Sometimes we may be thrust back by an apparent indifference. It may be a cultural convention, as it is in certain Oriental countries, for the Japanese or Chinese representative to appear impassive. Whereas in the Latin countries, the Spanish, the Portuguese or South American negotiators may be volatile about apparently irrelevant matters.

These quotes contain both tips and general descriptions, as well as stereotypical descriptions of national characteristics of people in specific countries or regions of the world.

In some instances anthropological theory provides the background for culture-general recommendations. The anthropologist Hall (1960) relates an imaginary story of an American negotiating an industrial contract with a state minister in a Central American country. Hall mentions time (speed of action, coming to the point), interpersonal space, orientation toward material wealth, interpersonal relations (friendship), and the status and meaning of agreements (including contracts) as important points to keep in mind. The article was largely based on an earlier book by Hall (1959). His recommendations go beyond the theory and no systematic empirical validation data are mentioned.

Many recommendations are written from the perspective of the businessman or diplomat from the USA (or to a lesser extent from Europe) who has dealings with some other country. Examples can be found in a reader edited by Binnendijk (1987). It contains chapters on six countries, mainly written by political scientists

and diplomats. In addition to existing literature their personal experiences as negotiators with the culture they describe, appear to be a main source of information.
Numerous statements are made about the "national character" of the countries
described. This serves as a background to explain national negotiation styles. About
the Chinese one learns, among other things, that:

> The most fundamental characteristic of dealings with the Chinese is their attempt
> to identify foreign officials who are sympathetic to their cause, to cultivate a
> sense of friendship and obligation in their official counterparts, and then to pur-
> sue their objectives through a variety of stratagems designed to manipulate feel-
> ings of friendship, obligation, guilt, or dependence. (Solomon, 1987, p. 3)

In the case of Japan it is important to recognize that negotiation implies social conflict and that the Japanese have been socialized to avoid conflict. The development of personal relationships is critical as they form the basis for future,
often long-lasting contacts (Thayer & Weiss, 1987). With the Egyptians "three
elements–a sense of national pride and historical continuity, acceptance of the
need for a strong ruler, and a highly developed bureaucratic tradition–are essential" for the understanding of their politics, nationally as well as internationally
(Quandt, 1987).

These few examples should give the general flavor of this literature that appears
to be mainly based on ad hoc observations of what has struck the author(s) as
odd, or as different from what one finds at home. Again, a problem hardly touched
upon is the validity of these descriptions.

Because of the confidential character of most international negotiations it is
difficult to carry out systematic studies in real-life settings. Publicly available
research is mainly based on archival data, self-reports of negotiators, and simulation studies. Personal accounts of diplomats were used by Cohen (1987) in a
study of intercultural communication in Egyptian–American diplomatic relations.
He obtained his materials largely from autobiographies of diplomats and interviews. Cohen uses a theoretical framework to describe his results, namely a theory
of conflict and culture by Ting-Toomey (1985). He is quite explicit that one can
never know to what extent intangible cultural factors have harmed relationships.
Still, he points to a series of disruptive events in Egypt–USA relationships (e.g.,
the Arab–Israeli wars of 1967 and 1973) where the recollections of some of the
diplomats involved make it plausible that cultural incompatibilities and misap-
prehensions played a contributory, if not a decisive, role. Cohen's main problem
is that each event in real life is embedded in a complex context from which it is
difficult to extract a decisive factor retrospectively.

There are also some major international negotiations in which social scientists
were involved, or which could be described quite accurately on the basis of available information (e.g., Faure & Rubin, 1993). The level of detail of the argument
makes the description of the actual process plausible, but any inference about underlying psychocultural factors remains post hoc.

Current cross-cultural theories are largely based on major dimensional distinctions, which we discussed in chs. 3 and 14. Hofstede (1989) has proposed a

set of hypotheses on the basis of the dimensions which have emerged from his earlier research (Hofstede, 1980) and that of Bond and colleagues (Chinese Culture Connection, 1987). Testable predictions include, for example, that large power distance will correlate with more centralized control and decision making, and that negotiators from countries high on uncertainty avoidance will prefer structured and ritualistic procedures. A theory by Ting-Toomey (1985) elaborates on Hall's (1976) distinction between low context and high context cultures. Within high context cultures much of the information in communication processes is shared by the sender and receiver of a message or is present in the context. Within low context cultures, much of the information is in the transmitted message. Most Western countries can be qualified as low context cultures, while Japan, Korea, and Vietnam are high context cultures.

A theoretical distinction for the entire area of intercultural communication is the anxiety/uncertainty theory formulated by Gudykunst (1995). The theory assumes that managing uncertainty and anxiety are central processes that influence the effectiveness of communication. Cross-cultural variations are related to conceptual dimensions as formulated by Hofstede, although Gudykunst sees his dimensions as individual-level variables. Most theorizing is centered around the dimension of individualism–collectivism (e.g., Gudykunst, 1999; Triandis, 2000a).

A richer theoretical frame has been suggested by Gelfand and Dyer (2000), who include, apart from major cultural dimensions, proximal social conditions (roles, deadlines, etc.), and psychological states of negotiators (judgment biases, motives, etc.) among the relevant parameters. However there is no empirical evidence on these modes.

Most research is on differences in negotiation, or more generally in communication, as found in one culture and compared to another. There are few studies on actual interactions between members of various cultures. Graham and colleagues (1992, 1994) have conducted some simulation studies in which members from different cultures interact. However, as a rule, research has not been intercultural, but rather cross-cultural. The same limitation applies to simulation studies where subjects in different cultures were brought into laboratory situations to negotiate as buyers or sellers of certain commodities (Graham, 1983; Graham, Mintu, & Rogers, 1988; Campbell, Graham, Jolibert, & Meissner, 1988). The contributions of cross-cultural psychology to the understanding of international negotiation and communication processes can only be limited, inasmuch as sound applicable knowledge is rather lacking. However, there can be no doubt that this is an area where there is a need for cross-cultural knowledge (Gärling, Kristensen, Backenroth-Ohsaka, Ekehammer, & Wessels, 2000).

## Conclusions

Intercultural communication and training is an area of increasing concern as people from different cultures and societies increasingly meet and interact. In this chapter we first discussed intercultural communication. We started from the situation of sojourners who are living in a new society. We then turned to errors in communication and the reasons that they are made. Intercultural communication training refers to programs designed to prepare sojourners for their assignment, but it should be broadened to include cultural knowledge and awareness in school curricula. The final section was on negotiations in an intercultural context. In this section we also briefly referred to theories on culture and communication.

Like in other applied areas there is an enormous array of theories and findings, but few of these have been endorsed by unambiguous evidence.

## Key terms

culture assimilator
intercultural competence
intercultural communication training
sojourners

## Further reading

Brislin, R., & Horvath, A.-M. (1997). Cross-cultural training and multicultural education. In J. W. Berry, M. H. Segall, & C. Kagitcibasi (Eds.), *Social and behavioral applications* (pp. 327–69). Vol. III of *Handbook of cross-cultural psychology* (2nd ed.). Boston, MA: Allyn and Bacon. A review chapter that addresses not only the more traditional field of training for sojourners, but also student education.

Gärling, T., Kristensen, H., Backenroth-Ohsaka, G., Ekehammer, B., & Wessels, M. G. (Eds.) (2000). Diplomacy and psychology. *International Journal of Psychology*, *35*, 81–176 (special issue). A series of articles on psychological dimensions of international conflict, justice, and negotiation.

Ghauri, P., & Usunier, J.-C. (Eds.) (1996). *International business negotiations*. Oxford: Pergamon. A set of chapters in which psychological and cultural factors are dealt with, mainly written from organizational sciences perspectives.

Landis, D., & Bhagat, R. S. (Eds.) (1996). *Handbook of intercultural training* (2nd ed.). Thousand Oaks, CA: Sage. An extensive collection of chapters addressing a range of issues in intercultural training.

Ward, C., Bochner, S., & Furnham, A. (2001). *The psychology of culture shock* (2nd ed.). Hove, UK: Routleclge. A thorough and integrative overview of research on the way sojourners adapt to living in other cultures.

# 16   Health behavior

This chapter considers the topic of health (both physical and mental) in relation to cultural context. It begins with a discussion of how culture and health may be related, taking a wide range of views into account. It then examines two core areas in this field, including the questions of how culture and mental illness might be linked in psychopathologies, and how positive mental health might be understood across cultures. When there are mental problems, the role of psychotherapy comes to the fore; attempts to relieve mental suffering can also be seen to be rooted in culture. Then we turn to the alternative of dealing with health problems before they arise. This involves increasing attempts to prevent health problems through health promotion; many of these attempts take cultural and psychological factors into account. A final section considers the large and complex question of the role of ecological and demographic factors in health promotion and health problems.

## Culture and health

In the past thirty years there has been a revolution in the way many people think about health: **promotion** and **prevention**, instead of only curing, are now the internationally sought goals, as indicated in the unanimous acceptance of the Alma Ata Declaration of Health for All by the Year 2000 (World Health Organization, 1978) and in the Ottawa Charter (World Health Organization, 1998) on health promotion. In these declarations there has been a shift away from "curing disease" once it has occurred, to the "prevention of disease" (through public health measures such as primary health care), and even more fundamentally to the "promotion of health" (through such factors as appropriate diet and exercise, and the avoidance of unhealthy substances).

With this shift in goals, there came as well a shift in approach, away from an exclusively high-technology biologically oriented strategy, to one that recognizes the potential role of the social and behavioral sciences in the health area (Aboud, 1998; Basic Behavioral Science Task Force, 1996; MacLachlan, 1997). In public education, mass communication, and behavior modification were seen a possibility of guiding the development of healthy behaviors or changing unhealthy ones. In this approach, improvement and control of social and environmental conditions (particularly poverty, but also crowding, technological change, and forced migration) were seen as ways to prevent some major health problems. Of course, medical technology has remained an important element in health, both in prevention and cure, but it is now more a matter of "appropriate technology" where the local population can understand, use, and sustain the technology provided to them. For example, sanitation and safe water can prevent, and oral rehydration can reduce, the effects of diarrheal disease; and the control of parasites and infections are often within reach for most populations, when behavioral and technical approaches are combined. These changes have brought about an increased emphasis on "community-based" programs, usually supplementing, rather than replacing, institution-based ones (e.g., Peat, 1997).

During the last three decades, not only was the approach to attaining and promoting health redefined, the actual definition of **health** was extended. In the Alma Ata Declaration (World Health Organization, 1978), health was defined as a "state of complete physical, mental and social well being, and not merely the absence of disease or infirmity." As a result, these positive aspects of health have become major topics of research and application, including such aspects as quality of life (Fernandez-Ballesteros, 1998; Orley & Kuyken, 1994), subjective well-being (Diener, 1996), and positive mental health (Minsel, Becker, & Korchin, 1991). Moreover, these positive qualities to health go beyond the physical, into the realms of psychological and social life. At the same time, health was viewed as a prerequisite for human development, both individual and national (see ch. 17), and was construed as the responsibility of everyone, not just as a professional responsibility of health specialists.

In the light of this movement and the development of medical anthropology (e.g., Frankenberg, 1988), cross-cultural psychology, attuned as it is to variations in both culture and individual behavior, is well placed to play an important and useful role in this newly redefined field. Psychology has already developed a number of new subfields ("behavioral medicine," "health psychology"), and a definable set of contributions can be made to health by these fields (Holtzman, Evans, Kennedy, & Iscoe, 1987). Cross-cultural psychology has begun to take a similar step (Aboud, 1998); while major strides have not yet been accomplished, it has been argued that the potential contribution is rather substantial (Dasen, Berry, & Sartorius, 1988). In some cases, for example in the culturally sensitive delivery of mental health services, the process of application has already yielded some benefits (Beardsley & Pedersen, 1997; Kazarian & Evans, 1998). We will be examining the evidence for these statements in this chapter.

It should be made clear at the outset that the role of social and behavioral science is not limited solely to mental health; the approach taken here is that psychology and cross-cultural psychology are just as relevant for physical and social health issues. This position is one that is shared with the World Health Organization (WHO) (1982, p. 4), which makes it quite explicit that:

> **psychosocial factors** have been increasingly recognized as key factors in the success of health and social actions. If actions are to be effective in the prevention of diseases and in the promotion of health and well being, they must be based on an understanding of culture, tradition, beliefs and patterns of family interaction.

Some specific ways in which cross-cultural psychology can contribute to such understanding are through the study of the shared and customary health activities of a cultural *group*, and then examining the health beliefs (what health is), attitudes, and values (the importance attached to health), and the actual health-related behaviors, of *individuals*.

This dual-level approach to health considers both the cultural and the individual levels to be worthy of study, using anthropological and psychological techniques. One framework for linking health behaviors to cultural contexts is shown in fig. 16.1 (Berry, 1998a). In keeping with the culture–individual distinction used in this text, ethnographic methods are employed to investigate and interpret

| Levels of Analysis | Categories of Health Phenomena | | | |
|---|---|---|---|---|
| | **Cognitive** | **Affective** | **Behavioural** | **Social** |
| **Community (Cultural)** | Health Conceptions and Definitions | Health Norms and Values | Health Practices | Health Roles & Institutions |
| **Individual (Psychological** | Health Knowledge and Beliefs | Health Attitudes | Health Behaviours | Interpersonal Relationships |

**16.1** Framework for examining relationships between cultural and individual levels of health phenomena
From Berry 1998a

collective health phenomena, following approaches used in medical anthropology and community-based studies. In parallel, individuals are studied with psychological methods, such as sampling, interviews, and observations.

The framework also divides health phenomena into four conventional categories in behavior science research. First, cognitive phenomena are the conceptions and definitions widely used in a cultural group, and the corresponding knowledge and beliefs held by individual members. As we noted earlier, the very definition of health has changed in the past few decades, from the absence of disease, to a more positive one, with health promotion and disease prevention being emphasized. While this is a historical example of differing definitions, there is substantial evidence of cultural variations as well.

These beliefs are known to carry on after culture contact. For example, Cook (1994) found differences across three ethnocultural groups (Chinese, Asian Indian, and AngloCeltic) in Canada in their health beliefs, using distinctions proposed earlier by Kleinman (1991): biomedical, psychosocial, and phenomenological. These were predicted on the basis of previous research on health in their cultures of origin. Chinese and Indian participants had stronger psychosocial beliefs about illness causation, and also preferred psychosocial treatment; and, of particular interest, those who had received more of their education in China or India revealed lower biomedical beliefs and intentions to use biomedical treatment. Thus, differing health beliefs (and behavior intentions) that are known to be present in home cultures continue to characterize ethnocultural groups after migration.

In studies of indigenous health beliefs (e.g., Dalal, 2000; Mulatu, 2000) there is strong support for such variations. For example in the work of Berry, Dalal and Pande (1994), beliefs about the origin (causes), control (what can be done), and outcome (possibility of cure or recovery) of physical disability varied substantially. In Bangladesh and parts of India, there was a strong belief in fate or cosmic influences, while in Canada and (Christian parts of) Indonesia, there was greater belief in personal actions causing, and being able to control, the problem. In the study by Mulatu, causes of mental illness in Ethiopia were thought to be mainly cosmic or supernatural (such as curses, spirit possession), with psychological, biological, and socio-environmental stressors also implicated. In both studies, there appears to be a stronger emphasis on health and illness being due to spiritual focus beyond one's control or responsibility. However, such beliefs may well be a significant factor in recovery from illness (Thoresen, 1999), and cannot be downplayed.

Beyond these cognitive aspects, people have differing evaluations of health. For some societies, health is a priority, with a large portion of national budgets spent on health care; in such societies, the value placed on health is high relative to other values, such as hedonistic or material aspects of life (see ch. 3). Similarly, individuals vary in their valuation of their own health, with some considering it to be paramount, and others regarding it as less important. For example, Dayan (1993) studied the value placed on health by three group of

Jews in Montreal (Orthodox, conservative, secular). Judaic law prescribes that health is given by God, and makes it the responsibility of individuals to sustain it; the value placed on health is thus a shared belief among practicing Jews. However, there is significant variation in the acceptance of this value across the three Jewish groups: Orthodox have the highest value, secular have the lowest, with conservatives in between. Moreover, these variations in health values were found to have a significant relationship with some health practices (such as substance abuse), and health status (such as better physical, but not mental, health).

Societal health practices and individual behaviors have also been studied cross-culturally. In some societies, practices are exclusively biomedical and technical, while in others they are rooted in folk and traditional conceptions and norms. Considerable study has been devoted to Indian (Ayurvedic) and Chinese health practices, and to the health behaviors of individuals. Beyond these well-known systems (with their own university training faculties), there are less comprehensive systems that nevertheless involve elaborate sets of practices. One such traditional medical system has been examined by Joshi (2000), in a Himalyan society (Jaunsari). Practitioners attempt to alleviate illness and suffering by bringing patients into greater harmony with natural and supernatural forces. Over 90 percent of Jaunsari make use of such practitioners (for problems ranging from fever and headache to having bad dreams and experiencing excessive crying), and the vast majority believe that their suffering is relieved by them.

Individual health behaviors can be illustrated by research on disability in India (Berry, Dalal, & Pande, 1994), which focussed on the relationship between causal beliefs and behaviors. Villagers commonly reported that during pregnancy mothers should eat little, so that there would be sufficient room in the abdomen for the fetus to grow. This resulted in fetal malnutrition, which in turn resulted in higher incidence of physical and communicative disabilities. Although the value the villagers placed on health was high, this belief and its associated behavior undermined their preferences.

Finally, social aspects of health include the ways in which a society organizes its health system (e.g., public, private), differential access due to socioeconomic status (Lynch & Kaplan, 1997; Wilkinson, 1996) and its component institutions (e.g., doctors, nurses, pharmacists). Some systems are hierarchical, some collegial; some are exclusive, others are widely accessible. All these factors vary cross-culturally, and have clear impact on the health status of individuals. At the interpersonal level, issues of sharing knowledge ("telling the patient"), empathy between healer and patient, even the use of touch for comforting, vary across cultures.

We now turn to an examination of the two central mental health issues confronting cross-cultural health psychologists (psychopathology and psychotherapy), and then consider other health domains, including cultural aspects of physical health.

## Psychopathologies across cultures

Reference was made in ch. 9 to the history of concern in psychological anthropology for abnormal psychological phenomena. At the same time, psychiatrists and clinical psychologists who were not associated with the school of psychological anthropology were developing an interest in similar phenomena; this area of activity has come to be known variously as the field of "cultural psychiatry," "transcultural psychiatry," "culture and psychopathology" (Good, 1992; Tanaka-Matsumi & Draguns, 1997), and "cultural clinical psychology" (Kazarian & Evans, 1998). It is a difficult area to comprehend, partly because of the specialist nature of the topic. There are a few integrated treatments of the field (see Yap, 1974; Murphy, 1981; Kleinman, 1991), and numerous edited volumes illustrate the range and depth of the material (e.g., Al-Issa, 1995; Desjarlais, Eisenberg, Good, & Kleinman, 1995).

### Box 16.1  A classification of mental disorders

To facilitate the international reporting of psychiatric illness, the World Health Organization (1992; see also Sartorius, 1991) has developed an International Classification of Mental and Behavioral Disorders (ICD 10). These are placed in the following categories:

1  organic mental disorders such as Alzheimer's disease, and dementia (due to such organic factors as Huntington and Parkinson disease);
2  mental disorders due to psychoactive substance use such as alcohol, tobacco, cannabis, sedatives, cocaine, and hallucinogens;
3  schizophrenia and delusional disorders such as paranoia, catatonic schizophrenia, and delusions;
4  affective disorders such as manic and depressive mood disorders;
5  neurotic disorders such as phobia, anxiety, obsession, amnesia, multiple personality, hypochondriasis and neurasthenia (fatigue syndrome);
6  physiological dysfunction such as anorexia, obesity, insomnia, sleep walking, and sexual dysfunctions (lack of desire, enjoyment, or response);
7  personality disorders such as impulsive, dependent personality, problems of gender identity, pathological gambling, fire-setting and stealing; also included are abnormalities of sexual preference (fetishism, exhibitionism, voyeurism, paedophilia (but *not* homosexuality);
8  mental retardation such as arrested mental development (low IQ);
9  developmental disorders such as language, aphasia, and reading problems; autism, and hyperkinesis.
10  childhood disorders such as sibling rivalry, tics, bedwetting, and stuttering.

Another widely used classification of these disorders has been developed: the DSM IV (American Psychiatric Association, 1994).

By "abnormal behaviors and states" psychologists and psychiatrists usually mean those features of an individual's behavior or experience that have been classified as an "illness" or a "disorder" (not just "eccentricities"), and are judged as strange or bizarre by others who interact with the individual in his or her daily life. They also go well beyond the more usual difficulties that are caused by stressful situations, which vary across cultures (Berry & Ataca, 2000). While more formal definitions are provided in the psychiatric literature, this everyday definition will allow us to designate the domain with which we are concerned. A listing of such mental disorders is provided in box 16.1; a more complete description of each category is available in textbooks of abnormal psychology (e.g., Sarason & Sarason, 1999). These disorders are of fundamental importance worldwide, since they account for substantial personal, social, and economic loss (World Bank, 1993).

The main theoretical issue (as outlined in ch. 12) regarding psychopathology cross-culturally is whether its phenomena are absolute (invariant across cultures in their origin, expression, etc.), universal (present in some form in all cultures, but subject to cultural influence on the factors that bring them on, expression, etc.), or culturally relative (unique to some cultures, and understandable only in terms of that culture). The relativist view gave rise to ethnopsychiatry (Devereux, 1980; Tseng, 2001) and is part of the move to understand "indigenous psychologies" of abnormal behavior. In reviewing the evidence we will focus on some selected areas of research that cover the range of disorders identified in box 16.1, beginning with the major organic and substance disorders, and ending with some of the "culture-bound syndromes."

## Organic and substance disorders

The most likely candidates for supporting the absolutist position are those disorders that are clearly rooted in some basic biological functions: these are the organic disorders, substance disorders, and serious forms of mental retardation (categories 1, 2, and 8 in box 16.1). While this position remains a logical possibility, there is little research actually available that would substantiate it, and those studies that are available suggest that cultural factors may affect rates and forms of expression. The physiological response to alcohol appears to vary across groups (Wolff, 1972), presumably for genetic reasons, but cultural norms about what, where, and how much alcohol to drink also vary, leading to quite different expressions of alcohol use across groups (e.g., Baxter et al., 1998; Korolenko, 1988). Thus, it makes little sense to even consider a culture-free abnormal behavior, since cultural factors appear to affect at least some aspects of mental disorders, even those that are so closely linked to human biology. The universalist (rather than the absolutist) position, seems to be the more tenable one at this point, and such a conclusion is clearly indicated by studies of the two major psychoses: schizophrenia and depression (categories 3 and 4 in box 16.1).

## Schizophrenia

This disorder has been identified in cross-cultural studies since the beginning of the twentieth century, using a variety of standard indicators (Murphy, 1982; Tanaka-Matsumi & Draguns, 1997). It is the most frequent mental disorder in the world, with incidence rates of new cases per year ranging from 1.5 to 4.2 per 100,000 (Jablensky et al., 1992). Commonly, the signs of the disorder are a lack of insight, auditory hallucinations, delusions of reference, and flatness of affect. There is evidence that to some degree it is inherited (cf. ch. 10), but also that certain cultural experiences may precipitate its onset. For example, Murphy (1982) proposed that culture can affect the risk of developing **schizophrenia** in four ways: through mistraining regarding the processing of information; through the complexity of information given to people; through expectations about having to make decisions when information is unclear; and through the degree to which schizophrenia-bearing families are discouraged or encouraged to have children. In addition to these possible cultural factors affecting the prevalence of the disorder, Murphy (1982) proposed that culture can also affect the definition, recognition, acceptance, and symptomatology of the disorder (the signs or behaviors through which the disorder is expressed); moreover it can also affect the course of the disorder (changes over time) and the response of the disorder to treatment.

There is evidence that cultural practices (in definitions and diagnostic preferences) may affect the apparent prevalence, and this may at least partially account for reported differences in rates across cultures. This subtle interaction between "true" rates in schizophrenia in different cultures and variations in diagnostic procedures has been highlighted in the work of Cooper et al. (1972) and in a major study by WHO (1973, 1979). In a detailed analysis of the Cooper et al. study, Leff (1977) has shown that there are differences in diagnoses of schizophrenia by hospital psychiatrists in New York and London (61.5 percent versus 33.9 percent of psychiatric patients respectively), but that this difference disappears when diagnoses are made by trained members of a research project using the same standard of diagnosis (29.2 percent versus 35.1 percent respectively).

The WHO studies went further afield, and included psychiatrists in nine centres (Colombia, Czechoslovakia, Denmark, India, Nigeria, Taiwan, UK, USA, and USSR) who were trained to use a standard diagnostic instrument (the Present State Examination), which has over 500 questions dealing with 107 symptoms. Over a hundred psychiatric patients were examined in each centre, and of the 1,202 patients, 77.5 percent were diagnosed as schizophrenic. A "core of common symptoms" appeared in all sites, including social and emotional withdrawal, delusions, and flat affect. However, profiles of symptoms did differ substantially from centre to centre. For example, the US schizophrenics differed from the Danish and Nigerian on symptoms of lack of insight and auditory hallucinations (fewer of both), while Nigerians had more frequent "other hallucinations" than the other two groups. Given this "common core" (and the reduction of variation in diagnosis when common instruments are employed) it has been concluded by the authors of the original studies, and by reviewers alike, that schizophrenia is best understood as a universal disorder, one that is recognizably present in all cultures, but that appears to respond to different cultural experiences in modes of expression.

This conclusion has been supported by two of the main cross-cultural researchers on schizophrenia: "the position of cultural relativism vis-à-vis the identification of schizophrenia in different populations finds little support" (Jablensky & Sartorius, 1988, p. 68). However, two cautions are necessary: first, the studies involved instruments, concepts, and researchers that were all Western oriented; and second, the patient populations were not a representative sample of world cultural variation (and were to some extent themselves acculturated to Western life). Hence, we cannot exclude entirely the possibility that the definition of schizophrenia will have to be further informed by cultural variations that have been insufficiently studied so far.

## Depression

The other major disorder that has been studied cross-culturally is that of depression (category 4 in box 16.1). While its symptoms are often less dramatic than those of schizophrenia, it has nevertheless received considerable empirical and theoretical attention (see Kaiser, Katz, & Shaw, 1998; Marsella, 1980). "Depression," in the non-psychotic sense, occurs often and for almost everyone; however, as a **psychopathology** it is characterized by a large set of problems and symptoms, including a sad mood, and a lack of energy, interest, and enjoyment. It is often accompanied by emotional changes (such as feelings of guilt, anger, and anxiety), physical changes (such as sleep disturbance, tiredness, and loss of appetite, weight, and strength), behavioral changes (such as crying, withdrawal, and agitation), and changes in self-evaluation (low self-esteem, pessimism, and feelings of hopelessness and worthlessness); severe depression may be accompanied by suicidal tendencies.

**Depression** was included, along with schizophrenia, in the Cooper et al. (1972) US–UK study, and in the further analysis by Leff (1977). Once again, there was a significant difference in hospital diagnosis (4.7 percent versus 24.1 percent in the USA and UK respectively), but this difference again largely disappeared when the research project psychiatrists carried out the diagnosis (19.8 percent versus 22.3 percent). Does this mean that apparent differences in rates and display of depression across cultures generally are due solely to the differential use of the depression diagnosis by psychiatrists? According to the comprehensive analysis of Marsella (1980), the answer is probably "no." The local cultural meaning of "being depressed" varies widely both with the patient's language family, and differentiation of emotional terminology (Leff, 1977); experience of acculturation to Western life style also tends to increase the prevalence of depression according to Prince (1968).

Going beyond these observed cultural correlates of depression, there are a number of elaborated theories that are proposed to account for both the origin of and variation in depression. These refer to aspects of family structure (extended families providing more elaborated social support, close mother–child relationships, and reduced risk of loss of loved ones); and mourning rituals (low depression may result from ritualized and overt expressions of grief). Marsella's (1980) own theory involves a cultural dimension of "epistemic orientations" (i.e., objective versus subjective orientation). In the relatively "objective" type of cultures there is an abstract language, and individuated self-structure; in contrast, a metaphorical language and more communal structure are found in "subjective" types of culture. According to Marsella, depression takes a primarily affective and cognitive form in cultures with objective orientations (and is experienced as a sense of isolation), while it takes a primarily somatic form in cultures with subjective orientations.

Despite these variations, most observers (e.g., Tanaka-Matsumi & Draguns, 1997, p. 455) believe that, as in the case of schizophrenia, a "common core" of symptoms of depression allow the disorder to be recognized in all cultures. These include anxiety, tension, lack of energy, and ideas of insufficiency. However, the expression of depression may differ across cultures (e.g., more frequent somatic symptoms in some cultures: Tung, 1994; Ulusahin, Basoglu, & Paykel, 1994). Depression thus qualifies as a universal, but like all other universals at the present time, the Western bias in research approach and in the populations studied may well have affected the conceptualization and descriptions, and hence this conclusion.

## Culture-bound syndromes

Culture-relative studies of psychopathology abound in the literature; there is apparently nothing more intriguing in this field than discovering another apparently unique way of "being mad!" The rich reports of **culture-bound syndromes** have fueled the relativist position and have led to the claim that there are unique, local forms of psychosis, not known outside of a particular culture.[1] A sample of these conditions is provided in box 16.2 in order to obtain a sense of their special and interesting qualities.

While many of these phenomena are limited to particular cultures, and while there are rich local interpretations and meanings for each condition, efforts in transcultural psychiatry have been made to discover some underlying similarities between them and the major disorders recognized by psychiatry generally (Simons & Hughes, 1985; Prince & Tcheng-Laroche, 1987), i.e., the question is raised whether these exotic, and apparently culturally determined syndromes, may be

---

[1] Not all such syndromes are locally recognized. In Japan, "salarymen" often spend time after work with their fellow employees, rather than going directly home. This has been called "The fear of going home syndrome"; however, when inquiries were made, a common response was "This is not a syndrome, it is normal!"

## Box 16.2 Culture-bound syndromes

In the literature of cultural psychiatry numerous "exotic" mental disorders have been described, and interpretations given in local terms, often with the indigenous name for the disorder entering into the medical literature. A sampling of some of the better-known syndromes follows.

*Amok* involves wild, aggressive behavior of limited duration (usually among males) in which there are attempts to kill or injure a person. It has been identified in south-east Asia (Malaysia, Indonesia, Thailand). *Amok* is a Bahasa Malay term meaning "to engage furiously in battle" (Westermeyer, 1973). It has obvious relations to the Viking behavior *berserker* practised just prior to entering battle (Leff, 1981). The terms "running amok" and "going berserk" are now in common usage, perhaps because the associated behaviors also occur in other societies.

*Brain fag* involves problems of academic learning, headache, and eye fatigue, and an inability to concentrate. It appears widely in West African students often just prior to school and university examinations (Prince, 1960), and is virtually unknown outside that culture area.

*Koro* involves the sensation that one's penis is retracting into the abdomen and the belief that when it is fully retracted death will result. Panic attempts to keep the penis from retracting can lead to severe physical damage.

*Latah* involves imitative behavior (usually among women) that seems beyond control; movements and speech are copied, and individuals in this state are compliant to commands to do things outside their usual range of behavior (e.g., to utter obscenities). Its onset is often the result of a sudden or startling stimulus. The term *latah* means "ticklish" in the Bahasa Malay language.

*Pibloqtoq* involves an uncontrollable urge to leave one's shelter, tear off one's clothes, and expose oneself to the Arctic winter weather. It has been identified in Greenland, Alaska, and the Canadian Arctic, and linked both to isolated environmental conditions, and to limited calcium uptake during long sunless winters.

*Susto* involves insomnia, apathy, depression, and anxiety, often among children, usually brought on by fright. Among the people of the Andean highlands, it is believed to result from contact with supernatural forces (witches, the evil eye, etc.), and to result in soul loss.

*Witiko* involves a distaste for ordinary food and feelings of depression and anxiety, leading to possession by the *witiko* spirit (a giant man-eating monster), and often resulting in homicide and cannibalism. It occurs among Canadian Indians and has been interpreted as an extreme form of starvation anxiety. If a cure is not attained, the *witiko* sufferer often pleads for death to avoid his cannibalistic desires.

*Anorexia nervosa* is a form of self-starvation, in the search for extreme thinness. It has been identified in Western industrial societies, with suggestions

that it is a culture-bound syndrome for affluent societies, and developing elite
sectors of other societies (Swartz, 1985; Di Nicola, 1990). However, in most
societies there is a positive correlation between social status and body weight
(Fedoroff & McFarlane, 1998).

The hallmark of all these syndromes is their apparently culturally unique
qualities; each is usually given an interpretation within the terms of its own
culture. The issue for transcultural psychiatry is whether they are also com-
prehensible within a universal framework of psychopathology (cf. Simons
& Hughes, 1985).

local expressions of some universal disorders already known and classified. An
early proposal at such a "classification" was made by Yap (1969), who later elaborated on it (1974). However, there are claims that these phenomena are
"unclassifiable," so that any such attempt would yield categories that are
"qualitatively of so diverse a nature that they cannot be systematically integrated
but by distortion" (Pfeiffer, 1982, p. 202).

Yap begins by distinguishing between unusual behaviors and those that may
signal an underlying disorder; this is similar to Honigmann's (1967) distinction between the socially abnormal and the psychiatrically abnormal: one is merely
eccentric, while the other is dysfunctional for society and the individual. By
concentrating on those exotic behaviors that are in the dysfunctional category we
can recognize that much of the unusual behavior reported in various parts of the
world is culturally patterned, even culture bound. Yap's distinction provides a basis
for his search for similarities in the various reports. He is able to subsume, using
his clinical judgment, many of the apparently culture-bound syndromes within
established diagnoses. For example, *latah* and *susto* are judged to be local cultural
expressions of a "primary fear reaction," while *amok* is a "rage reaction," and *witiko*
is a "possession state," all conditions recognized and described by general psychiatry. Yap recognized that his classification might be premature and even wrong in
some respects. However, he argued that the goal of organizing the mass of reports
of exotic syndromes was a scientifically valid one, and should be pursued.

What can be said about the universality of psychopathology? Aboud (1998,
pp. 251–6) has divided the answer to this general question into various components (see also Patel, 1995). First, all cultures appear to distinguish body from
mind, and to have separate categories for normal and abnormal behavior. Second, common symptoms are widespread across cultures, but there can be differences in expression, sometimes in the form of "culture-bound syndromes." Third,
how these symptoms are classified also appears to vary, even though there is
widespread use of ICD 10 and DSM IV. And finally, the course and outcome of
mental disorders are often culturally variable, but with only occasional culturally

unique features. It should be clear that most of this evidence points in the direction of a universalist position. On the one hand there appears to be important cultural patterning of those disorders that are most evidently biologically rooted (making the absolutist position untenable). On the other hand, initial attempts to discover some "common core" of symptoms of the major psychoses across cultures, and to identify underlying categorizing principles for the apparently "culture-bound" syndromes, have both yielded some success. Of course, such a conclusion must be a tentative one, awaiting further research from points of view, and samples, that are less clearly rooted in a single (Western) cultural tradition.

## Positive mental health

As noted earlier, the concept of health has changed to include not just the absence of problems, but is now construed in a more positive way. In keeping with its role as a promoter of health worldwide, the WHO has been sponsoring a long-term project on **quality of life** (QOL), (WHOQOL group, 1995; Orley & Kuyken, 1994). This project is rooted in the question: "What makes for a good or satisfying life?" As noted by Fernandez-Ballesteros (1998), the concept of QOL has wide use across disciplines such as economics, ecology, law, political science, and social welfare, in addition to health psychology. While the concept is shared, the findings do not always correlate; for example, it is often noted (e.g., Wilkinson, 1996) that increases in economic well-being are not necessarily related to subjective (psychological) well-being, or to health outcomes more generally.

The concept is also complex, a fact that stems from its multidisciplinary use. However, two basic dimensions have emerged, one representing objective factors in the cultural environment, and the other representing subjective appraisals and reactions to them. These two sets of factors have been termed "socio-environmental" and "personal" by Fernandez-Ballesteros (1998). Included in the first set are environmental quality, financial conditions, social support (etc.), and in the second set are life satisfaction, health, functional abilities, and leisure activities (etc.). In this distinction we see similarity to the field of cross-cultural psychology, where we attempt to link contextual to psychological variables. Overall, QOL has been defined as the product "of the dynamic interaction between external conditions of an individual's life and the internal perceptions of those conditions" (Browne et al., 1994, p. 235). However, in psychology the measurement of QOL has usually focussed on the subjective aspects, while estimates of the more objective conditions have been drawn from accounts given by the other disciplines.

Numerous scales have been developed to assess these subjective aspects, some of them intended for international comparative use. One such scale (Szabo, Orley, & Saxena, 1997), developed by the WHOQOL group, incorporated 100 items in six domains: physical, psychological, independence, social relationships, environment, and spiritual. Each domain included items representing various subfacets, and were responded to on five-point scales by participants in twelve countries. A major finding was that responses varied across cultures, possibly due to methodological problems, such as translation of items, and meanings assigned to descriptors on response scales (e.g., "very satisfied," "very dissatisfied").

At the core of the more personal facets of QOL is the notion of **subjective well-being** (SWB), defined as a person's cognitive and affective appraisal of his or her life. More specifically, it refers to life satisfaction and the balance between positive and negative affect in a person's life. Cross-cultural studies of SWB have been carried out for over fifty years. Generally, this research shows that for most people around the world positive affect predominates over negative affect (Veenhoven, 1994). However, there are rather large variations across countries. Using nationally representative samples, means on a ten-point scale range from highs (over 8.0) in Denmark, Australia, Iceland, and Switzerland, to lows (less than 5.0) in Yugoslavia, Nigeria, Panama, and Mexico. In another international survey (World Values Survey; De Moor, 1995), also using a ten-point scale, the same countries again scored high (plus Canada, Ireland, and Netherlands), but Russia, Bulgaria, and Latvia now scored in the lowest group.

How can these differences be accounted for? The first, and most important factors, are economic. Diener (1996) proposes that while SWB correlates positively with wealth (purchasing power) across nations (+.62), it is not the level of income, but recent increases in income that may predict SWB better within nations. This suggests that individuals may adapt to their economic circumstances, and respond more to changes in them than to their long-term financial situation. However, cultural factors other than economic ones may also play a role. Diener noted that SWB scores of some countries were higher than expected (on the basis of their economic situation), while others were lower: in the higher group were Argentina, Brazil, and Chile, while Russia and other East European countries were in the lower group; in contrast, Japan was an outlier, with high income, but low SWB. What these other cultural factors may be has not been determined. One possibility is religion (a factor that has often been suggested to increase happiness). However, Georgas et al. (2000) have shown that while an economic variable (affluence) correlates strongly with SWB, religion has virtually no relationship. Moreover, other variables, such as population size and density (indicative of crowding) also appear to have no impact. It is likely that there may be no single relationship that holds up across cultures: different factors may account for SWB in different cultures. For example, Veenhoven (1991) found that within poor countries, income correlated with SWB more strongly than it did in wealthy countries. Such variable relationships may well exist for other possible correlates of SWB.

Positive aspects of mental health (as distinct from pathologies) have also been studied (e.g., Minsel, Becker, & Korchin, 1991). Based on research on dimensions of personality, they investigated whether two main dimensions found previously (mental health, and behavior control) would also serve to characterize people's views about positive mental health. Samples of teachers in France, Germany, Greece, and the USA were asked to rate "how mentally healthy people behave and feel," using 186 person descriptions (such as attitudes to life, partner, and friends, abilities, temperament, and traits). Factor analyses (of all four samples combined, and separately) revealed that two orthogonal factors could explain the variance. The first factor (mental health) was defined as positive social attitudes, such as fairness, tolerance, warmth, helpfulness, and honesty, with its negative pole including emotional lability, anxiety, hostility, and unpredictability. The second factor (behavior control) was characterized at one pole by commitment to laws, rules, and moral principles, and devotion (to religion); at the other pole were traits such as atheism, sexuality, curiosity, and risk taking. While these two dimensions were found as well in each of the four samples, their generalizability so far is limited to Western industrial societies. Research in a wider range of cultural groups is required in order to determine whether such dimensions can characterize views about positive mental health more widely.

## Cultural factors in psychotherapy

Just as there are cultural factors involved in the development and display of psychopathology, so, too, are there cultural factors involved in the process of attempting to alleviate these problems (Beardsley & Pedersen, 1997; Pedersen, Draguns, Lonner, & Trimble, 1996). In every culture, there is a triangular relationship between the client, the therapist, and society. Usually, cultural beliefs and practices prevalent in a society enter into the psychotherapeutic process, because they form part of both the therapist's and patient's definitions and understandings of the problem. In the case of indigenous psychotherapy, and other health interventions, all three elements share a common culture, since no intercultural situation is involved. However, in the case of cross-cultural psychotherapy (across international borders; e.g., Sheikh & Sheikh, 1989), and for intercultural counselling (across groups within a country; e.g., Marin, 1999; Paniagua, 1994), since Western-based theory and method are frequently used to assist persons of other cultures, serious misunderstandings may result.

**Psychotherapy** is a general term that is employed to refer to any practice that involves a patient and a healer in a personal relationship, with the goal of alleviating the patient's suffering which is due to a psychological problem or disorder. According to Doi (1984), this interpersonal relationship is usually based upon a dependency need, although Prince (1980) questions whether this is an essential element in all forms of psychotherapy found across cultures. Note that the form of the therapy is usually psychological, rather than physical, although this distinction is not always easy to maintain in practice (Prince, 1980, pp. 292–3). What is common to all psychotherapeutic practices, in Prince's view (1980, p. 297) is that they serve to "mobilize the healing forces within the patient"; that is, coping mechanisms, and other psychological resources (such as resting, withdrawing, expectation, and hope) of the individual are drawn out: "most of the treatments that the healers offer are simply an exaggeration or extra development of . . . endogenous mechanisms" (p. 297). Prince (1984) has proposed that there may be a biological endogenous mechanism as well, noting that "there is now considerable experimental and circumstantial evidence that endogenously generated neurohormones produce analgesia, euphoria, amnesia, and altered states of consciousness." These neurohormones "are also generated by religious and other rituals that constitute an important element in many indigenous psychotherapeutic systems" (Prince, 1984, p. 62).

Indigenous psychotherapies can be found in virtually any society. Sometimes they are used in conjunction with Western psychiatry, sometimes alone. They correspond to what Kleinman (1991) has referred to as the traditional or popular sections of health practice. Because they are an inherent part of the triangle of cultural relationships discussed above, they are often effective. However, they may work for reasons other than this match or fit with the patients' beliefs. Jilek (1993) has noted that such healers are also more accessible to those needing help, that they tend to accept patients' descriptions of their problems, and that they are often empathetic and charismatic, leading to the establishment of a trusting and potentially more effective healing relationship. In Western industrialized societies psychotherapy tends to take the form of psychoanalytic therapy (deriving from the ideas of Sigmund Freud and his followers), or a number of other forms based on various theoretical positions in psychology (learning theory, gestalt theory, humanist theory, etc.). In this chapter we accept these as indigenous therapies of the West, but do not dwell on them, even though they are the most frequent basis for cross-cultural psychotherapy. Instead, we will focus on a few indigenous therapies that have been developed in non-Western cultures.

## Indigenous psychotherapy

Among the range of these indigenous psychotherapies are those rooted in Japanese culture and thought: *morita* therapy (Miura & Usa, 1970) and *naikan* therapy (Tanaka-Matsumi, 1979). According to Murase (1982, p. 317), both of these therapies are "revivalistic, and oriented towards a rediscovery of the core values of Japanese society." These core values are *amae* and *sunao*, and are related to *morita* and *naikan* respectively, although both values are thought to enter, to some extent, into both therapies.

Morita therapy was developed in Japan by the psychiatrist Morita (1874–1938) during the 1920s to treat psychoneurotic problems, and is based upon isolation and rest, rather than verbal interactions. According to Prince (1980, p. 299), Morita therapy lasts between four and eight weeks, and is divided into four stages:

1 Total bed rest and isolation for four to ten days; the patient is totally inactive and not permitted to converse, read, write, or listen to the radio.
2 For the next seven to fourteen days he is out of bed and allowed in the garden where he does light work; the patient begins to write a diary for the doctor but other human contact is forbidden.

3  For a further week or two he is instructed to do heavier work, continue the diary and attend lectures from the doctor on self-control, the evils of egocentricity, and so forth.

4  Finally, the patient gradually returns to full social life and his former occupation; the patient continues contact with the doctor and attends group sessions with other patients on an out-patient basis.

As we have seen in ch. 4, *amae* is a dependency need that is thought to be highly valued in Japanese life, and is opposite to the independence and control over one's own fate that is promoted during Western psychotherapy (Doi, 1984). Its relationship to Morita therapy is that one goal of Morita is to have patients accept the realities of life, rather than attempting to bring reality into line with their own needs and desires (Pedersen, 1981). This is similar to the distinction between primary and secondary control (Weisz et al., 1984) noted in ch. 1.

*Naikan* therapy is a kind of introspection, and comes from the Japanese terms *nai* ("inside") and *kan* ("looking"). Its goals are:

> (1) the discovery of personal, authentic guilt for having been ungrateful and troublesome to others in the past, and (2) the discovery of a positive gratitude towards individuals who have extended themselves on behalf of the client at some time in the past. In short, guilt and gratitude. When these goals are attained, a profound change in self-image and interpersonal attitude occurs. (Murase, 1982, p. 317)

The procedure involves the patient sitting quietly from 5.30 a.m. to 9 p.m. for seven days, introspecting the whole time, except for brief visits from an "interviewer" every ninety minutes. The patient is instructed to look at himself and his relationships with others from three perspectives:

> (1) Care received. The first instruction is to "recollect and examine your memories of the care and kindness that you received from a particular person during a particular time in your life". The client usually begins with an examination of his relationship to his mother, proceeds to talk about relationships with other family members, and then moves on to close persons, always following a progression from childhood to the present. For example, in the first day he may remember how his mother cared for him when he was sick in grammar school.
>
> (2) Repayment. During that particular period "recollect what you have done for that person in return".
>
> (3) Troubles caused. "Recollect what troubles and worries you have caused that person in that same period." (Murase, 1982, p. 317)

This examination is conducted in

> a boldly moralistic manner, placing the burden of blame on the client rather than "on others". Only in the earlier meetings when the interviewer is more lenient and tends to listen to what the client describes to him, are excuses, rationalizations or aggressions toward others permitted. (Murase, 1982, p. 318)

The interviewer's role is not like that of a therapist, but serves merely to supervise the patient's introspection and self-examination.

The value of *sunao* is widespread in Japan and has a variety of meanings, but at its core (in the interpersonal realm) it refers to being obedient or docile, accepting (rather than being assertive), in harmony with one's social environment (rather than egocentric), open minded, honest, and free from antagonism and rivalry. In the intrapersonal realm it refers to being relaxed, flexible, gentle, free from conflicts and frustrations, without bias and in tune with joy and gratitude (Murase, 1982, p. 321). While this is a rather broad "core," it does form a set of values that include being at peace with oneself and one's surroundings (again, similar to secondary control).

A case has been made (Murase, 1982, p. 322) that *sunao* is also relevant to Morita therapy. In Morita's view, non-acceptance of their own reality by patients is a main source of their psychological problems, and becoming more *sunao* is one way to re-establish harmony or peace:

> if they had a *sunao* mind it would be obvious to them that they have been trying to achieve the impossible. With a *sunao* mind they would be able to endure their anxiety and dissatisfaction. Accepting oneself means admitting one's weaknesses, demerits, discomforts, and undesirable feelings as they are. (Murase, 1982, p. 323)

While considerable attention has been devoted to these two Japanese forms of indigenous psychotherapy in the recent literature, most societies have examples of their own. In the survey by Prince (1980), there is a paradoxical redefinition of phenomena that in the West are often considered to be psychopathological to be psychotherapeutic in many other cultures. These include altered states of consciousness (see ch. 4), dream experience, trance (dissociation states), and various mystical states, including ecstasy. Since space does not permit a full review, we focus our attention on a single example, that of voodoo as practiced in Haiti (Bourguignon, 1984).

Voodoo is a synthesis of African, Roman Catholic, and local beliefs and practices into a folk religion that has served to give the people of Haiti a sense of unique identity. It has also served the purpose of healing (among other purposes), thus exhibiting the not uncommon link between religion and medicine found in many parts of the world. One of the most spectacular features of voodoo is ritual possession trance, in which saints (*loa*) enter into and "possess" the practitioner, who can either be a believer (with no special psychological problem), a patient, or a priest/doctor who seeks to heal.

Many varieties of possession have been identified by Bourguignon (1984), including the patient being possessed by harmful spirits of a dead person, the patient being possessed by protecting spirits, and the voodoo priest being possessed by spirits that assist in the diagnosis and cure of the patient. Thus, in voodoo healing there is an intimate matrix of relationships involving not just a patient and a therapist, but a patient-believer, a therapist-priest, and a variety of good and evil spirits, all set in a complex medico-religious belief system; this system in turn is rooted in a culture contact (acculturation) situation that led to its development, and set the stage for its widespread acceptance in the population.

What are we to make of these indigenous psychotherapies? Are they merely local superstitions that have no value, or perhaps only work to the extent that the superstitious believe in them? Or do they each have a status with respect to their sociocultural systems that parallels, for example, that of Freudian psychoanalysis in some Western societies? For some critics, both sets of practices may be dismissed as mere superstitions that work to some extent because, and only because, people believe they will work. Without "scientific foundations" or "proof" they could be dismissed easily by sceptics. However, Jilek (1993) has concluded that most indigenous psychotherapies do work at least as well as those employed in Western psychotherapy. Hence they cannot be dismissed as lacking in effectiveness. Moreover, a wide range of such (non-Western) indigenous psychotherapies (or their derivatives) are now being accepted into Western medical thought, as supplementary to other psychotherapeutic practices (Jilek, 1988). This more open-minded approach to psychotherapy parallels the acceptance of such practices as acupuncture (from Chinese medicine) and holistic theories (from *ayurvedic* medicine of India, and from elsewhere) by Western medicine. Perhaps, as Prince (1980) suggests, *all* of these practices are effective to some extent precisely because they are believed in, are accepted as part of the patient's all-encompassing cultural belief system. This belief permits the "mobilization of endogenous resources" noted earlier, as well as involving the family and the community, leading to relief for the sufferer. It may matter little what these beliefs and resources are, as long as they are accepted by the patient.

## Cross-cultural psychotherapy

This conclusion draws our attention to the second main question posed in this section: to what extent can cross-cultural psychotherapy work? That is, can medical beliefs and practices from one culture be effective in the healing process in another culture? Once again, it is useful to consider the absolute, universal, and relativist positions as points of view from which to approach the question. In the discussion of indigenous psychotherapies, we noted the existence of culturally unique ideas and practices that were part of a larger complex of cultural beliefs and values; and the claim in the literature is that they may have a positive effect in their local settings. We also noted some common dimensions to all of these approaches; the mobilization of one's own resources through medico-religious practices one believes in seems to be a central thread. Thus, it would be a reasonable, but tentative, conclusion that there might be some underlying universal basis for the healing process. A common core to psychotherapeutic practices may exist, but with different historical and cultural roots, and with highly varied cultural expressions.

Approaching the issue from the absolutist position, we may consider the attempts to employ Freudian psychoanalytic theory and practice in non-Western cultures, "as is," unmodified from its middle European Victorian era roots. Prince has asked the question:

> Are psychoanalytic formulations etic principles of human development and psychopathology? Psychoanalysts certainly believe this to be the case (Fenichel, 1955), but one crucial problem obstructs its verification. To validate psychoanalytic theory, it is necessary to apply the psychoanalytic technique cross-culturally, but this technique is impossible to employ beyond a very limited Western-educated elite. Prince (1980, p. 335)

If Prince's judgment is correct,[2] then we can dismiss psychoanalytic theory as a candidate for an absolute approach to psychotherapy (cf. Kakar, 1985). One may attempt cultural adaptations of various psychotherapies (see Draguns, 1981 for a discussion of these attempts), but in so doing one shifts from an absolutist position to at least a universalist one, as new cultural phenomena are taken into account.

## Cultural factors in health behavior

At the beginning of this chapter we noted that psychosocial and cultural factors (including many behavioral, social, and environmental factors) play an important role in health generally, not just in mental health. At this point we turn more explicitly to these relationships, focussing as much on the promotion of health and the prevention of illness, as on the curative aspects. In an overview by Dasen et al. (1988), a number of specific topics were addressed, including the way in which socialization practices, education, nutrition, acculturation, public health programs and the organization of health services can all help to promote health and prevent health problems. Many of these factors are given specific coverage in this text (e.g., socialization in ch. 2 and acculturation in ch. 13) and so do not need full attention here.

The new focus on health promotion and disease prevention has created a role for social and behavioral scientists in the development and implementation of public health programmes. For example, campaigns for the reduction of substance abuse, and of drinking and driving, and the advocacy of low-fat diets and exercise, are clearly activities in which social psychologists' expertise in attitude change, and clinical psychologists' expertise in behavior modification, could have a major part. In developing countries, similar roles have also been identified in such problem areas as parasite and other disease transmission (Aboud, 1998), and in increasing child survival (Harkness, Wyon, & Super, 1988). While these potential roles are self-evident for cross-cultural psychologists, Harkness et al. (1988, p. 240) note that there have been "only a handful of reports incorporating psychological, cultural, or social considerations into the design of research or intervention projects on disease prevention and control in developing

---

[2] Evidence that psychoanalysis can be used successfully in Africa has been presented by Parin, Morgenthaler, & Parin-Matthey (1966), and Ortigues & Ortigues (1966).

countries." Following are some examples, which may help to establish the legitimacy and usefulness of this involvement.

## Malaria

This is a major health problem in many tropical areas of the world, and has been increasing in recent years; in tropical counties, malaria represents a high proportion of reported medical cases, but due to under- or non-reporting, this is thought to represent only a fraction of actual incidence (World Health Organization, 2000). Malaria is transmitted by a parasite that requires mosquitoes as a host, and mosquitoes require stagnant water as a breeding environment.

Treatment of individuals with quinine or other drugs such as chloroquine (the "cure" orientation) has been the most common attack on the disease, although some individual "prevention" measures were widely used as well (e.g., the use of mosquito nets). New, more effective drugs for individual treatment, and the development of insecticides (notably, DDT) for mosquito control made it possible since the 1950s to mount a worldwide campaign to eradicate the disease.

While some regions became virtually malaria free, there has been a recent large-scale resurgence of the disease due to a growing resistance of mosquitoes and parasites to chemical treatment (both insecticides and drugs). Alternative approaches to controlling the disease, employing social and behavioral techniques have been advocated (Miller, 1984). For example, the Sarvodaya project in Sri Lanka has promoted public participation in the attempt to control mosquito populations, and in self-monitoring of people's own health. Local volunteers are trained to be on the lookout for stagnant water, to be vigilant about mosquito–human contacts, and to identify and report actual cases of malaria. This approach is in sharp contrast to the "vertical" approach which involves large-scale control spraying by "outsiders," and drug administration by professionals; the local population is encouraged to be responsible for its own health, rather than leaving it to others. Of course, "experts" are involved in teaching and training volunteers to use some basic technology (e.g., parasite and human surveys, draining of ponds), and in bringing about changes in attitudes towards health through public education, but it is clearly a program "belonging to" the local population. The project:

> has been organized as an alternative route to malaria control as part of a broad approach to community development through self-help. In contrast to the centrally organized, high-technology national malaria control program, the project was designed to put responsibility for malaria control with the villagers themselves. In contrast to the large regional groupings which are the administrative units of the national program, the project works through individual, culturally homogeneous villages. In this approach, the role of the behavioral sciences was conceived as important for understanding human behavior in relation to the transmission of malaria and in the organization of malaria control programs. (Harkness et al., 1988, p. 244)

Three behavioral factors were identified as important by the project researchers. First, initially villagers did not see malaria as a major or even as a solvable problem; the perception of malaria as a "disease" (rather than just one of life's ordinary problems), and the recognition that something could be done about it (rather than accepting it as part of one's "bad luck" or "fate") are specific areas of change that could be attempted using psychological techniques. Second, the perception of the earlier "vertical" control program (spraying and drug administration by outsiders) was examined; research showed that it was seen as heavy handed and noxious, requiring costly counter-measures based on traditional *ayurvedic* medicine. Third, the symbiotic relationship between human behavior and mosquito behavior can be clarified by behavioral science research; initial findings revealed patterns of mosquito habitat preference and territory, and of blood preference (animal blood is in fact preferred to human blood), but for a fuller understanding research is required to establish the behaviors on which to base effective control programs.

## Child survival

As a second example, Harkness et al. (1988) examined "child survival" (a more positive orientation than "child mortality"). The GOBI strategy (an acronym for the four points listed below) of UNICEF is aimed at improving child survival rates throughout the world, and concentrates on four techniques (Harkness et al., 1988, pp. 245–6):

1 Growth monitoring to identify early cases of growth failure and malnutrition.
2 Oral rehydration therapy for infants and children with severe diarrhea in order to reduce the high rate of mortality from fluid loss.
3 Breastfeeding promotion, for the direct nutritional and immunologic benefits as well as the indirect reduction of contamination from unsanitary bottle feeding.
4 Immunization against major infectious diseases of childhood.

While initial results have been impressive, there have also been some evident failures, and social-behavioral analysis of these problems has been instructive. For example, merely knowing about the nature and causes of a child health problem (such as neonatal tetanus caused by unsterile umbilical cord cutting) is apparently not sufficient to correct the problem. In addition, as research in Bangladesh by Chen, Rahman, and Sardar (1980) has shown, motivation to accept the anti-tetanus injections by the mothers proved to be critical. After a major effort, only 22 percent of mothers actually agreed to the inoculation, probably because:

> some mothers may have mistakenly associated the vaccinations with more familiar contraceptive injections; others feared harm to the fetus; and this biologically flawless procedure was perceived locally to be ineffective because the Bangla disease terms that cover tetanus also include other, unaffected, neonatal syndromes. (Harkness et al., 1988, p. 247)

## Malnutrition and psychological development

**Malnutrition** usually occurs in economically disadvantaged subgroups, whether in Western industrialized societies or in developing countries (Pinstrup-Anderson, Pelletier, & Alderman, 1995); hence, when assessing its relationships to psychological development, cultural issues are always at stake, and this area of research should benefit from taking the methodological knowledge of cross-cultural psychology into account. There are both theoretical and applied interests in this topic.

On the theoretical side, the purpose of research on malnutrition and psychological development is to seek a better understanding of the links between biological and psychological aspects of human development (Aboud, 1998). The theories in this respect have changed drastically over a very short time: in the early 1970s, the predominant hypothesis was a simple effect of reduced food intake on the number of brain cells, while now it is recognized that we are dealing with a very complex model of multiple interactions. The ultimate and applied purpose of such research is to better understand the causes of malnutrition (that go well beyond lack of food), and the mechanisms of its effects on psychological development, in order to be able to prevent malnutrition altogether, or at least minimize its ill effects. This is of crucial importance in developing countries, since 46 percent of children there experience stunting (chronic, long-term malnutrition), with severe impact on physical and psychological growth (UNICEF, 1996). Since malnutrition occurs in a complex ecological, economic, social, and cultural system, the solution is rarely as simple as providing more food, even though that may well have to be the first and most urgent measure (Barba, Guthrie, & Guthrie, 1982).

Before research on malnutrition and psychological functioning can even begin, a great deal of effort has to be devoted to the difficult question of the definition and measurement of nutritional status and protein–energy malnutrition (PEM). The assessment of clinical signs is notoriously unreliable and is applicable only to severe malnutrition. More indirect but practical are anthropometric growth measures. To simplify to the extreme, weight (in relation to age or height) indicates wasting, or current malnutrition, and height (for age) indicates stunting, or the effects of long-term (chronic) malnutrition (World Health Organization, 1995).

A large number of studies have attempted to assess the impact of malnutrition on intellectual development (for reviews, see Gorman, 1995; Grantham-McGregor, 1995; Martorell, 1997; Pollitt et al., 1996; Wachs, 1995). While results vary a great deal from study to study, it may be said that children recovering from severe clinical PEM (i.e., malnutrition needing hospitalization to avoid death), especially if it has occurred in the first two years of life and has lasted for several months, show a marked retardation in their intellectual development (in psychometric terms, of the order of ten IQ points). The effect may be long lasting if the child returns from the hospital to the same unfavorable environmental circumstances, while there would be complete resilience if the milieu were favorable to intellectual growth. The delays in motor and cognitive development negatively affect school performance, the ability to maximize educational opportunities, and social functioning later in life.

Chronic, moderate or mild malnutrition also has a measurable effect on cognitive development; in one West African study (Dasen et al., 1978), for example, the development of sensorimotor intelligence was delayed by about two months in moderately malnourished children aged nine to thirty months, when compared to a group of children (matched on sex and age) with normal nutritional status. All children eventually reached the last substage of sensorimotor intelligence, and no structural differences in cognitive processes were found; it is therefore doubtful whether such minor lags in development have any functional importance.

One review (Pelto, Dickin, & Engle, 1999) summarized the present state of findings in the following terms. Malnutrition causes both poor physical growth and developmental delays; it is causally related to mortality in infancy and early childhood, and interventions that reduce the incidence of malnutrition can be expected to reduce mortality dramatically. In many communities with endemic malnutrition, neither feeding practices nor the selection of foods for infants and young children from the locally available food sources are optimal. While many households in conditions of poverty potentially have the resources to provide adequate diets and use good feeding practices that support normal growth, there is a lack of knowledge and skills about how to do this. Feeding is a central aspect of caregiving in infancy and early childhood, and it is important to know about parental ethnotheories in this respect (Engle, Zeitlin, Medrano, & Garcia, 1996).

In considering the impact of malnutrition on development and later behavior, three possible routes have been proposed. The first or biological route is a direct influence of undernutrition on the development of the central nervous system (CNS) and on its functioning (Bedi, 1987). Until the early 1970s, this mechanism was thought to be the sole or major one, in both animal and man; the implications for the intervention were that food supplementation, during pregnancy and the early periods of life, would be sufficient to ensure optimal development. This proved to be a simplistic or at least insufficient model. A second route proposes that malnourished children are relatively passive, and engage in less exploration of their environment. They thus experience lower levels of stimulation than those required for normal development. Such passive behavior may become established and habitual, even after proper nutrition becomes available (Meeks-Gardner, Grantham-McGregor, Chang, Himes, & Powell, 1995). A third route of influence of malnutrition on behavior is the functional isolation (Levitsky & Strupp, 1984) that occurs when malnourished children become irritable and less engaging. This leads to less attention and to fewer social interactions. This functional isolation reduces learning opportunities and thus hinders psychological development (Aboud & Alemu, 1995).

These three mechanisms are not mutually exclusive, and they may interact, but it is currently thought that the second route is the most important one. For intervention programs, it implies that greater attention be paid to social and behavioral aspects in addition to food supplementation. Empirical data in favor of the second and third routes come from studies of the impact of malnutrition in the emotional and motivational spheres. Barrett (1984), for example, reviewed eight studies showing that malnutrition produced attentional impairments, reduced social responsiveness, and led to poor state control, difficulties in tolerating frustration, low activity levels, and lack of initiative and independence. This happened even in the absence of measurable cognitive impairment.

The findings of an impairment in social responsiveness, activity level, affect, attention, and interest in the environment are extremely important because, in addition to suffering the direct consequences of reduced psychological activity and learning, the malnourished child becomes a different type of stimulus both to peers and to caregivers. The latter tend to respond to the malnourished child less often and with less enthusiasm; the child in turn withdraws further from social interaction, and a sort of vicious circle is generated (Galler, Ricciuti, Crawford, & Kucharski, 1984.)

It is widely recognized that malnutrition is usually part of an ecologico-economico-sociocultural system that includes, in addition to the biological factor of suboptimal nutrition, other adverse environmental conditions. Examples of such conditions are poor housing, and sanitation, repeated exposure to infectious and parasitic diseases, inadequate health care, and poor feeding and child care practices. Research mainly based on anthropological, sociological, and epidemiological methods designates these characteristics as risk factors, a combination of which is likely to cause malnutrition, or to increase its ill effects (Ricciuti & Dorman, 1983; Grantham-McGregor, 1984).

The syndrome of malnutrition and poverty therefore occurs amid macro-environmental factors linked to the social and political systems (unequal distribution of wealth, lack of land ownership, agricultural policies favouring cash crops, etc.), and more generally speaking, to the world's unbalanced economy. A combination of unfavorable macro-environmental factors is usually found to indicate high risk of malnutrition, but even in the same unfavorable conditions, malnutrition does not occur in all families or all individuals. This indicates that other risk factors are linked to the family and home environment (e.g., large number of children in the family, absence or lack of involvement of father, stress in marital relationships, alcoholism), as well as to mother or caretaker characteristics (e.g., mother's age below nineteen or above thirty-five, unwanted pregnancy, birth spacing below two years, early weaning and bottle feeding in unfavorable circumstances, anxiety, stress, depression, and apathy). Some children are also more prone to suffer from malnutrition than others because of constitutional factors or their own medical history (premature birth, low birth weight, peri-natal medical complications, infectious and parasitic disease, etc.). It is important to consider the interaction among these risk factors, which can be additive or even multiplicative. The risk factors can also be compensated for by positive ones, interacting to prevent the occurrence of malnutrition or to alleviate its ill effects.

Dasen and Super (1988) have argued that, because malnutrition is not distributed uniformly among families living in the same high-risk conditions, it may be a wise strategy to concentrate future research on those who somehow manage to cope, instead of (or in addition to) those who do not. In terms of applications to prevention and intervention programs, it could be argued that a scheme based on the transfer of culturally familiar and acceptable coping mechanisms (Marsella & Dash-Scheuer, 1988) from one sector of a population to another within the same cultural group should be more efficient and more cost-effective than programs based on foreign models. Any intervention program should take into account the population's own strengths. Research is giving more attention to the factors that may foster positive deviance or resilience (Rutter, 1985; Tizard & Varma, 1992).

The evidence on long-term effects of intervention programs (e.g. Grantham-McGregor, Powell, Walker, Chang, & Fletcher, 1994; Ramey & Ramey, 1998) is now quite conclusive. The earlier the intervention, the better, but even programs addressed at pre-school children have a positive effect. The most effective programs combine nutritional supplementation with the teaching of feeding skills, which in turn provides an opportunity to teach other caregiving skills, such as responsive parenting to stimulate motor and cognitive development (Pelto et al., 1999). According to these authors, interventions to address nutrition (improving food and feeding practices) and to promote child development (responsive parenting) are both important, and there may be additional benefits in combining activities and integrating these interventions.

## Sexually transmitted diseases

The worldwide concern with the HIV/AIDS epidemic has stimulated much research by cross-cultural psychologists on sexual and reproductive health (Hynie, 1998) and health education (Pick, 1998). By 1996, around 30 million children and adults had contracted the HIV virus; nine million of these had developed AIDS, with over six million deaths. Infection rates are highest in sub-Saharan Africa (5.6 percent), followed by the Caribbean (1.7 percent) (UNAIDS, 1996).

The virus is transmitted in three ways: by unprotected heterosexual intercourse (accounting for around 70 percent of infections), and male (but not female) homosexual relations (around 10 percent); by blood (infected needles, and transfusions, accounting for 5 percent to 10 percent); and from mother to child during pregnancy, delivery or breastfeeding (around 10 percent of all cases, but these constitute 90 percent of all child cases). Other **sexually transmitted diseases** (STDs), such as syphillis, gonorrhea and herpes continue to infect thousands of people, but these diseases have been overshadowed by the rapid rise, and extraordinary fear, of HIV/AIDS. Since there are currently no known medicines that can cure or prevent HIV infections, considerable attention has been devoted to prevention; this is why behavioral and social sciences have been so prominent in this field (Mann, 1991). One approach has been to emphasize the ABCs of prevention: abstinence; be true to your lover; condom use. However, there are both psychological and cultural issues in such a prevention program, including the roles of men and women, norms regarding sexual behavior, attitudes towards condom use, communication media, and norms about open discussion of sexual relations.

For a long time, most prevention programs have employed an approach known as KAP (knowledge, attitudes, practices) to understand how a population is oriented to health problems (Aboud, 1998). For example: (K) "Have you ever heard of AIDS?" and "How does one get AIDS?" (A) "Do you feel at risk of AIDS?" (P) "Have you ever used a condom?" This initial stocktaking is used to provide information on which to base a prevention program, emphasizing K, A, or P, depending on the analysis. For example, if knowledge were widely present, and attitudes were appropriate (i.e., to reduce risk), then a program could deal directly with changing behavior. However, if neither the necessary knowledge nor attitudes were in place, then the program would need to start earlier in the KAP sequence. Such programs can also target specific populations, such as adolescents, engaged or married couples, or sex-workers and their clients, depending on survey results.

One comprehensive program with adolescents in Mexico (Pick, 1998) has included parts from design to implementation to evaluation. Called *Planeando tu Vida* (Planning your life), the program began with two diagnostic studies. The first survey was with various samples of female adolescents in Mexico City: those not yet sexually active; those active but not yet pregnant; and those in the last trimester of an unwanted pregnancy. Many factors were found to be associated with not being sexually active, including submission to family and sociocultural norms, high scholastic aspirations, and having communication about sex with one's mother. The second survey was with male adolescents, including those who had, and those who had not, impregnated an adolescent female. Among factors associated with not being sexually active were having high scholastic aspirations, high future orientation, and low risk taking.

These findings suggested that prevention might be enhanced by developing programs that emphasized biological, personal, family, and social factors in a person's sexuality. A pilot program included components that addressed communication, assertiveness, self-esteem, self-control, future planning, the anatomy and physiology of the reproductive system, and information about contraception and STDs. Evaluation of the pilot program used a pre-test–post-test design (with control group), and assessed KAP at the beginning, and four to eight months later.

Following some modification, a second program was delivered and evaluated using three randomly assigned groups: a *Planeando tu Vida* program group; a control group receiving a conventional sexuality education course; and a control group receiving no course at all. The post-test was administered eight months after the course delivery. Results showed that

> Sexually active adolescents who received *Planeando tu Vida* increased use of contraceptives, had fewer erroneous beliefs about sex than the control groups, and had increased knowledge regarding the correct use of birth control pills . . . and increased communication with partners about contraception, and with their mothers about sexuality. (Pick, 1998, p. 462)

With this evidence of success, the program has been implemented and evaluated in secondary schools both in Mexico City and throughout the country. Generally, the intended changes were observed in knowledge, attitudes, and practices of the adolescents. But of particular importance was the finding that if the program were taken prior to a person becoming sexually active, contraceptive use was more likely when that person became sexually active later; a case of true primary prevention. While such programs show immense possibility of success in the field of AIDS prevention, work in other countries (e.g., in Malawi by McAuliffe, 1998) suggest equally immense barriers. In one study (Lie, personal communication), the attitudinal barrier to condom use was very high: "You don't eat candy with the wrapper on!" Beliefs and attitudes are so strongly entrenched in some cultural and social systems (e.g., family; and male–female relations) that considerable effort will be required to achieve success worldwide.

## Ecology, population, and health

A persistent theme in this book is that ecology, culture, and behavior are continuously connected. In chs. 1 and 9, culture was defined both as adaptive to, and as changing, the ecosystem; behavior was portrayed as both being influenced by, and influencing, culture; and the ecosystem was seen as both affecting, and being affected by, individual behavior (see fig. 1.1). In the past two decades, there has been a growing awareness of these relationships as they impact on health, both societal and individual (McMichael, 1993; Rockett, 1999). The key links in these relationships have been identified as population increase (Erhlich & Erhlich, 1990; Livernash & Rodenburg, 1998), and social inequality (e.g., Wilkinson, 1996), both affecting the level and distribution of health resources and the potential for development (Clarke & Tabah, 1995; Lutz, 1994). Other ecological frameworks predicting health outcomes have also been proposed, for example, in the areas of physical disability (e.g., Cook, 1996) and psychological difficulties (Van Haaften & Van de Vijver, 1996).

### Fertility behavior

The growth of the world's population has been identified both by international groups, (e.g., UNEP, 1997), and by many countries, as a major problem. Depending on assumptions made, the world's population will grow to between 10.8 and 27.0 billion by the year 2150, with most of this increase taking place in the developing world. For example, in China (Ching, 1984; Jing & Zhang, 1998), concern about their rate of population increase led initially to a national policy of limiting families to one child, (now somewhat relaxed), in order to achieve "the four modernizations" (in industry, agriculture, science and technology, and defense). Generally, while the population in most economically developed countries is increasing only minimally, there is a rapid increase in developing countries (Livernash & Rodenburg, 1998). Are there social and behavioral factors that might help to explain these dramatic trends, and if so, can these same factors be employed to help control the increase?

At the outset, of course, the role of a number of other factors needs to be acknowledged: improved health care, including curative and preventative measures and improved nutrition, have both changed the pattern of infant survival and longevity. This change has been termed the "demographic-epidemiologic transition" (see Rockett, 1999), which is the period between the time when epidemics were brought under control (no longer causing relatively early deaths) and the time when fertility rates were reduced. During this period, massive growth in population has taken place; it is largely finished in the developed countries, but it is widely present in developing countries. As we have seen, the decline in disease has come about through combined biomedical and behavioral science interventions. The decline in fertility is also a product of both these sciences, with the medical sciences providing fertility control technology, and the behavioral sciences playing a major role in research and promotion of their use (e.g., the use of KAP programs, outlined in the previous section). In this section we examine some other social and psychological factors.

Early research by Fawcett (1973) highlighted a wide variety of factors, including the value of children to parents, family structure (including forms of marriage), knowledge and use of birth control technology, values and beliefs regarding abortion, and ability to plan for one's future. These factors (and other, non-psychological social variables) have begun to be considered as part of large systems, in which demographic, political, social, cultural, and psychological variables interact to affect population growth.

One psychological variable is the fundamental reasons adults give for having children. The question of why people have children has been the focus of a major international collaborative study called the Value of Children Study. It involved nine countries (Germany, Indonesia, Korea, the Philippines, Singapore, Taiwan, Thailand, Turkey, and the USA), with a total of over 20,000 adult respondents. While these societies are not representative of world cultural variation, they do include a range, of countries, and in most of these (all except Indonesia and Germany) nationally representative samples were drawn.

A basic approach taken in the study was that the "values attributed to children are conceptualized as intervening between antecedent background and social psychological variables, and consequent fertility-related outcome" (Kagitcibasi, 1984; see also Kagitcibasi, 1996). Two issues are of interest here: one is the reasons given for wanting children, and the other is the qualities one would like to see in one's children.

With respect to the first question, the "old age security value" of children is dominant for many societies; that is, children will provide for parents in their old age, not only materially, but socially and psychologically as well. In the survey, two relevant reasons were posed: "To have someone to depend on when you are old" (as a reason for having a child); and "To be sure that in your old age you will have someone to help you" (as a reason for wanting another child). Clear differences appeared across samples in response to both items. In Germany and the USA these reasons are generally judged to be "unimportant" (about 75 percent responded thus) but in Indonesia, the Philippines, Taiwan, Thailand, and Turkey, the responses ranged between about 70 percent and 98 percent judging them to be "very important"; Korea and Singapore were in between these two extremes.

With respect to the question about characteristics that are valued in children, there was again wide cultural variation. For example "obedience" is valued highly in Indonesia, the Philippines, Turkey, and Thailand, while "independence and self-reliance" are valued least in those countries. In contrast, "independence" is valued more in Korea, Singapore, and the USA, and "obedience" less in those countries. These values (and their distribution) correspond to some extent with the "compliance–assertion" dimension presented in ch. 2 on socialization practices. Analyses of such reasons for having children, when taken into account along with economic, political, and nutritional factors, provide a better basis for national and international programs in population planning.

More recent studies have been concerned with variations in fertility behavior within (rather than) across cultures. For example, in Turkey (Ataca, Sunar, & Kagitcibasi, 1998) a model was developed to predict fertility using background socialization and psychological factors. A sample of middle class mothers in Istanbul was divided into two groups. Low fertility ($n = 38$, with one or two children) and high fertility ($n = 37$, with three, four, or five children). The groups did not differ, in mean age or education. An interview focussed on sex differentiation in the mothers' early socialization (comparing their experiences with those of their brothers), including their education, dependence/obedience, independence/autonomy, performance of chores, and chastity. Responses were classified into a three-way distinction: traditional (socialization in favor of brother); non-traditional (in favor of the respondent); and egalitarian (no differentiation). The model also included the variables of gender role ideology, and self-esteem.

Results indicated that women who had been socialized in the traditional way had more children than those raised in an egalitarian way, had lower self-esteem, and shared decision making less with their husbands. Moreover, those who now had a more traditional gender role ideology had higher fertility. Overall, in a regression analysis, fertility was predicted by a younger age at marriage, a more traditional socialization, and lesser power in relationships with husbands.

To some extent these factors operating on fertility within Turkish society correspond to those found in other cross-cultural studies: essentially, the more "compliance" is emphasized in socialization (see ch. 2), and the more "traditional" is the role of women (see ch. 3), the larger the number of children.

## Health consequences

Increasing populations challenge resources and resource distribution in a society. The recognition of this fact is the main reason for national policy reforms that attempt to shorten the period between the time when increased lifespan arrives, and the time when reduced fertility is achieved (the "demographic transition"). For example, the "one child family" initiative in China (Jing & Zhang, 1998) has recognized that, as in all ecological thinking, one change is intimately linked with many other changes: economic growth requires a young and active population, but too many children undermine per capita wealth; one child per family (especially when she is a girl) interferes with traditional Chinese family and social values, but enhances per capita wealth, and so on.

Health outcomes are also part of this ecological system, as demonstrated by the discipline of epidemiology for more than a century. Population increases are usually accompanied by industrialization, which in turn creates pollutants, stress, hypertension, and a variety of diseases (of the lung, of the heart, cancer). These "webs of causation" are now well documented for many diseases (Rockett, 1999). At the same time, population increases and industrialization increase per capita wealth, which in turn allows for advances in medical research and health care. However, one of the most startling aspects of this relationship is that it is not the average (per capita) wealth, but the equitable distribution of that wealth (and of associated health services) that predict general health status and longevity (Wilkinson, 1996). This finding is one of the reasons that it is not the wealthiest nations that top the United Nations Human Development Index, but those that are moderately wealthy and have more egalitarian systems of distributing that wealth. It is not only countries that show this variation: death rates in the sinking of the *Titanic* were 2.8 percent for first class, 16.1 percent for second class and 45.3 percent for third class (Carroll & Smith, 1997); and mortality rates vary across states in the USA in relation to an index of inequality of income distribution (Kaplan, Pamuk, Lynch, Cohen, & Balfour, 1996). These inequalities in the distribution of health resources exist not only across social classes, and across regions within countries, but even more so across countries. International variation in the support for health is vast, with the least support going to those peoples who need it the most (Aboud, 1998; MacLachlan, 1997).

These relationships, between broad sets of variables, however, tell us little about what underlies the link between socioeconomic status and health. Chamberlain (1997) argues that studies of the experiences of individuals and families are essential if we are to discover why poverty and health are linked. His research shows how a number of factors intermix in this relationship, including contact with health providers, the meaning and value of health, and various health practices (diet, exercise, substance use).

## Conclusions

Applications of cross-cultural psychological perspectives and findings to issues of health can be seen as an extension of the movement to bring social and behavioral science to bear on health promotion and prevention strategies now underway nationally and internationally.

While the volume edited by Dasen et al. (1988) argued that there was much valuable knowledge now available, it concluded that little of it was ready for immediate use and application. There were two reasons advanced for this conclusion. One was that much cross-cultural psychological research has been conducted with a view to scientific discovery rather than to application; hence, a process of bridging or translating is necessary in order to move from one activity to the other. The second reason is rooted in a perspective espoused in the present book, namely that most human behaviors are intimately connected to the cultural context in which they develop:

> a "fact" that has been found to be successfully applicable in one particular context may well be quite irrelevant in another; any list of applications would look rather suspect to a cross-cultural social scientist. Is it not against too easy generalizations that the cross-cultural approach is raising a word of caution? While this point of view might be seen as a negative one, it can also be seen as an important advance: Cross-cultural psychology informs us that there are definite limits to the transcultural portability of knowledge (thereby reducing our potential for making mistakes), and it provides us with a set of perspectives, procedures, and methods that are helpful in carrying out work in other cultures. (Dasen et al., 1988, p. 299)

We therefore conclude that applications of cross-cultural psychology to health must proceed cautiously, and with a concern for validation in each cultural setting. Some important successes have been achieved (Harkness & Keefer, 2000). However, the health beliefs, attitudes, and behaviors in many societies are deeply rooted in their cultures, making them more difficult to understand, and less susceptible to cross-cultural change programs.

## Key terms

culture-bound syndromes
depression
health (definition)
malnutrition
prevention
promotion
psychopathology

psychosocial factors
psychotherapy
quality of life
schizophrenia
subjective well-being
sexually transmitted disease

## Further reading

Aboud, F. (1998). *Health psychology in global perspective.* Thousand Oaks, CA: Sage. A comprehensive textbook of concepts and findings in cross-cultural and international health research and programs.

Al-Issa, I. (Ed.) (1995). *Handbook of culture and mental illness.* Madison, WI: International University Press. A wide-ranging overview of how culture influences mental illness in many societies.

Beardsley, L., & Pedersen, P. (1997). Health and culture-centred interventions. In J. W. Berry, M. H. Segall, & C. Kagitcibasi (Eds.), *Social behavior and applications* (pp. 413–48). Vol. III of *Handbook of cross-cultural psychology* (2nd ed.). Boston, MA: Allyn & Bacon. A review chapter covering studies of how cultural factors contribute to health, and of applications of these findings in various cultures.

Kazarian, S., & Evans, D. (Eds.) (1998). *Cultural clinical psychology: Theory, research and practice.* New York: Oxford University Press. A collection of original articles examining the relationship between culture and a variety of health issues, with an emphasis on clinical practice.

MacLachlan, M. (1997). *Culture and health.* Chichester: Wiley. An informative and integrative discussion of how culture interacts with most major illnesses, and how this knowledge can be used for health promotion.

Tanaka-Matsumi, J., & Draguns, J. (1997). Culture and psychopathology. In J. W. Berry, M. H. Segall, & C. Kagitcibasi (Eds.), *Social behavior and applications* (pp. 449–91). Vol. III of *Handbook of cross-cultural psychology* (2nd ed.). Boston, MA: Allyn & Bacon. A very informative and integrative treatment of how culture interacts with most major illnesses, and how this knowledge can be used for health promotion.

# 17 Psychology and the majority world

In this chapter we examine critically the relationship between the science and practice of psychology as it has developed in the Western world, and the need for and use of psychology in the rest of the world. Psychological knowledge in the West (sometimes called WASP, for Western academic scientific psychology) is often of little relevance to the **majority world** (a term used, for example, by Kagitcibasi, 1996, for obvious reasons, and in preference to "developing" or "Third" World).

We begin with an examination of the impact of Western psychology on the rest of the world, taking into account the availability of, and the demand for, the flow of this knowledge and profession. Then we turn our attention to the concept and development of indigenous psychologies in many parts of the world. Finally, we consider the meaning of development as it applies to societies and countries, using psychological concepts and methods.

## Impact of Western psychology

As is clear to everyone involved in psychology internationally, the discipline and the profession are overwhelmingly rooted in, and practiced in, Western industrialized societies (Pawlik & Rosenzweig, 2000). The rest of the world has often assumed the roles of "consumers" or "subjects"; psychology is "sold to" or "tried out on" other peoples. The evidence for this state of affairs has been clearly presented by Sinha and Holtzman (1984), Sloan and Montero (1990), and Adair and Kagitcibasi (1995).

These roles, of course, are unlikely to be very useful for developing countries, since there may be a serious mismatch between what is available in Western psychology and what is needed by the majority world (Jahoda, 1973). Part of the answer to the problem is the development of a psychology that is sensitive to cultural variation; and so one might take the emergence of cross-cultural psychology as an important move in the right direction. While this is partly true, it is also the case that cross-cultural psychology has been guilty of using the majority world as a kind of "natural laboratory" and has been known to exploit its human resources in various other ways (Warwick, 1980). Indeed, for Warwick, "From the choice of topic to the publication and dissemination of the findings, cross-cultural research is inescapably bound up with politics" (p. 323); the cross-cultural work may involve differences in goals, differences in power, and differences in intended use (even to the extent of misuse) of the results. For others, the comparative method is inherently ethnocentric (Nisbet, 1971), and is rooted in the tradition of "social Darwinism," complete with its overtones of "racism and ethnocentrism" (Mazrui, 1968, pp. 69–70). These critical comments, and some more positive alternatives, have been well summarized by Schwendler (1984, p. 4), who considered how psychology, and knowledge more generally, can be made relevant to the needs of individuals and nations in the majority world.

It is possible to attempt to address these problems by employing some distinctions that have been made in cross-cultural psychology. We start with the observation that psychology can be exported and imported "as is" (from Western cultures to other countries). This represents a kind of "scientific assimilation," and has been referred to as psychology being done *in* a particular culture (Berry, 1978); it clearly resembles the imposed etic strategy (see ch. 12). Second, there are the parallel processes of developing **indigenous psychologies** locally, or adapting imported ones by indigenizing imported ones; this we refer to as a psychology *of* a particular culture, and resembles the emic strategy. Third, there are attempts to integrate all available psychologies into a universal psychology; this resembles the derived etic strategy.

Psychology is clearly a science rooted in Western culture, and like much of Western science and technology, psychology has been spread widely over the globe during the course of the twentieth century. While we argue in the next section that psychology need not be Western in character, that all societies can (and probably to some extent should) develop their own psychologies, the present state of affairs is one in which there is widespread scientific assimilation; others, both psychologists and general populations, have come to understand themselves in terms derived from Western psychological science. This export and import of psychology has led to psychology being done in other countries, without much regard for local cultural circumstances or needs.

For example, Lagmay (1984) for the Philippines, Melikan (1984) for the Gulf states, Salazar (1984) for Venezuela, Diaz-Guererro (1984) for Mexico and Durojaiye (1984) for Nigeria, have all analyzed how Western psychology has, in various ways, changed aspects of their respective societies. Lagmay (1984, p. 31) argued that the entry of Western (mainly American) psychology was a case of "cultural diffusion," and was part of a more general flow of cultural elements that included language, educational and legal systems, and the media. The overall impact of this fifty-year period of American colonization was that "Western Science and cultural concepts became part of the educated speech and thinking of all who went through the schools ... the language of research, interpretation and construction in the social sciences in the Philippines ... has been definitely American and Western" (p. 32). Such export and import of Western psychology is not likely to constitute an "appropriate psychology" for developing countries (Moghaddam & Taylor, 1986). Indeed, confusion can result when

> the techniques and ideology of modern psychology are ... overlaid, in some cases in considerable haste, upon an ideological background composed variously of Hinduism, Islam, Buddhism, Taoism, Confucianism, Shintoism and Marxism and Leninism, themselves occurring in a range of combinations. (Blowers & Turtle, 1987, p. 2)

In Venezuela, Salazar (1984, p. 114) has argued that "psychological technology is an imported commodity, like automobiles, computers and airplanes" and is part of the overall problem of developing world socioeconomic dependence (see also Montero & Sloan, 1988). However, unlike in the Philippines, Salazar (1984, p. 113) is skeptical that there has been any substantial value change in the culture as a whole, and wonders "whether psychological knowledge can affect value systems at all."

Between these two contrasting views probably lies the experience of most developing countries. On the one hand, psychology is only a small part of Western thought, and may not have direct and widespread impact on a functioning culture. On the other, psychology may be part of a broader package of acculturative influences that affect many of the core institutions (educational, work, religious) through which all or most people pass in the course of their development. While substantial acculturation may indeed take place (as outlined in ch. 13), it may be very difficult to specify the particular contribution of psychology to this process.

For sub-Saharan Africa (Nsamenang, 1995, 2001) has identified the problem succinctly: "Psychology is an ethnocentric science, cultivated mainly in the developed world and then exported to sub-Saharan Africa" (1995, p. 729). While considerable evidence points to this conclusion (e.g., Carr & MacLachlan, 1998) the question arises of how can there be export without there be a willingness to import. That is, there must be a "demand side" that corresponds to the "supply side" of this flow. While in principle it is possible for the majority world to turn its back on Western psychology (as many now advocate for a whole range of products and services that are available through globalization), there is an obvious imbalance in the relative power (political, economic) of the two sides (Berry, 2001b).

In this situation, psychologists in the majority world face a dilemma when they are called upon to explain or interpret the behavior of people to themselves. In opinion surveys, assessment for educational and work selection, and in clinical practice, psychologists are often in a position to be influential, both with the public at large and with key decision makers in government and other institutions. If their training, values, and technology are rooted in Western psychological science, and are minimally informed by local cultural and psychological knowledge, what likelihood is there that this influence will be culturally appropriate? Unless this likelihood is substantial, psychologists in developing countries may end up playing the role of inadvertent acculturators. Such training may be all the more unsuitable when it is so specialized (focussed on local Western topics) that the psychologist is ill equipped to deal with broader issues, set in complex local cultural settings (Moghaddam, 1989). The alternative to working with an imported psychology is to attempt to develop one locally.

Such alternatives have indeed been described. According to Carr and MacLachlan (1998), when faced with the dominant psychology, one can first try "to assimilate into the mainstream … by replicating Western studies in developing countries." However, second, when faced with the irrelevance of such work, some psychologists moved to a search for "positive aspects of cultural attributes." And third, that is replaced by an approach that "involves transcending both the conformity of stage 1 and the anti-conformity of stage 2, and assessing social reality independently of the 'need' for comparison with other cultures" (Carr & Maclachlan, 1998, p. 13). This last way of dealing with the problem has generated the burgeoning field of **indigenous psychologies** (Adair & Diaz-Loving, 1999; Kim & Berry, 1993; Sinha, 1997).

## Indigenous psychologies

By indigenous psychology we mean a system of psychological thought and practice that is rooted in a particular cultural tradition (see Enriquez, 1990; Kim, 1990). This notion can be linked to a number of other ones, including **ethnopsychology** (cf. the discussion of ethnoscience in ch. 9; see also Lillard, 1998), common sense or naive psychology (as proposed by Heider, 1958). The roots of ethnopsychology lie in the intellectual tradition of *Geisteswissenschaften* (cultural sciences) rather than the *Naturwissenschaften* (natural sciences; Kim & Berry, 1993). For Heelas and Lock (1981) indigenous psychology is to be understood in contrast to specialist psychology "those developed by academic psychologists who favor scientific experiments" (Heelas, 1981, p. 3), and is rooted in "the cultural views, theories, conjectures, classifications, assumptions and metaphors – together with notions embedded in social institutions – which bear on psychological topics" (Heelas, 1981, p. 3).

It is possible to discern some common threads among these various conceptions. First is the idea that cultural traditions give rise to psychological knowledge (including theories, methods, and data); second is the belief that the real stuff of psychology lies in the daily, mundane activity of people, rather than in contrived experimentally induced behavior; third is the implied emic orientation, requiring indigenous psychological knowledge to be achieved and interpreted in terms of local frames of reference. Taking these three themes together, we consider indigenous psychology to be a psychology of a cultural group based on the day-to-day behavior of its members, for which local points of view provide the paradigms that guide the collection and interpretation of psychological information.

Of course, Western psychology is one such indigenous psychology (Allwood, 1998), but because it has taken on the role and status of *the* psychology, the term is usually reserved for those psychologies that reflect the traditions, beliefs, and ideologies of non-Western societies. This has come about because to a certain extent indigenous psychologies have developed as a reaction to, or rejection of, the dominance of Western psychology in a culture (Sinha, 1997).

Indigenous psychologies attempt to develop a behavioral science that matches the sociocultural realities of people's own society. Indian scholars (Sinha, 1986, 1997; Sahoo, 1988) have sought the development of a psychology that reflects their historical and cultural traditions. In a comprehensive treatment, Sinha (1986) has identified the transfer of Western psychology to India "as part of the general process of Modernization" (p. 10) characterizing it as "completely isolated from the Indian tradition, and alien to the local intellectual soil" (p. 11), leading to endless "repetitions of foreign studies" (p. 33). Historically, Sinha notes four phases, beginning with a pre-independence period during which Indian psychology "remained tied to the apron strings of the West, and did not display any sign of maturing" (p. 36). Then came a period of post-independence expansion in which there was a burgeoning of research, but not so much for policy and action as for academic prestige.

The third period was one of problem-oriented research during which concerns for breaking the dependency were joined with those for more applied research. Finally came the period of **indigenization**, in which the imported Western psychology underwent a process of cultural transformation to become more informed by Indian social and cultural traditions, and relevant to Indian economic and political needs.

Sinha (1997) has presented a systematic account of this process in many parts of the majority world. His main position is composed of two complementary assertions. First is the need to embed every psychology in a specific cultural context. Second is the need to establish the universality of the empirical basis and principles of psychology. In his view, "indigenization is considered to be a vital step towards a universal psychology" (Sinha, 1997, p. 131; cf. Berry & Kim, 1993; Yang, 2000), and corresponds to the universalist approach taken in this book. His second position is to insist on the distinction between the product (indigenous psychology), and the process of indigenization. The first refers to a psychology with four attributes: it is psychological knowledge that is not external or imported; it is evidenced by the daily activities of people (rather than in experiments or tests); it is behavior that is understood in terms of local frames of reference; and it is composed of knowledge that is relevant to the life of a cultural population. In contrast, indigenization is a process of transforming the borrowed, transplanted, or imposed psychology in order to better suit the needs of a cultural population. To illustrate the substantial work being undertaken in one country (India), box 17.1 provides an overview of local research on indigenous and indigenization activity.

## Box 17.1 The surveys of psychological research in India

Of all developing countries India has by far the largest number of psychologists, the most universities and colleges with curricula in psychology, and the largest volume of research. A convenient overview can be found in four surveys of research on Indian psychology. The overall structure of scientific psychology is the same as in Euroamerican countries; the topics for the chapters in the first survey even followed the categorization of the Psychological Abstracts, and authors leave no doubt that Indian psychology finds its roots in the West. With respect to terminology, methods, and theories, the contents of the surveys are easily recognizable to the Euroamerican reader.

The editors of the surveys have each addressed the issue of the relevance of Indian psychology to the Indian context and social reality. The first editor (Mitra, 1972) noted that after the initial development of the discipline a stage of consolidation had been reached at the end of the 1960s. Two directions for further research were indicated: social and applied issues, and the development of a "hard-headed" science in the traditions of experimental psychology. It is perhaps significant that Mitra only elaborates on the first direction for research, noting several social problems that demand attention, preferably in an interdisciplinary context. The editor of the second survey (Pareek, 1981) noted a shift towards applied issues during the 1970s and he emphasized the potential of psychology to contribute to the solution of social problems. The summary chapter in the third survey on emerging trends in the 1980s by Pandey (1988) is largely devoted to the question of how the sociocultural context is being taken into account by Indian researchers. The various chapters still cover the whole area of psychology, but the table of contents of the Psychological Abstracts is no longer followed. The emphasis on applied issues is not only evident from the distribution of chapters, but also from the attention given to social relevance by various chapter authors. The fourth survey (Pandey, 2000/2001), in three volumes, continues this transition toward a psychology that is more concerned with Indian issues (both basic and applied). Chapter authors were encouraged by the editor to "to cover the development of indigenous concepts, methods, theories and cross-cultural research" and to "relate the psychological findings to the Indian sociocultural context" (Pandey, 2000, p. 9).

However, this concern with specifically Indian aspects has not yielded a psychology that is isolated from international psychology.

The trends that Pandey describes in his summary chapter are very much compatible with the notion of a universal psychology, as it has been developed in this book. He mentions the need for "outgrowing the alien framework" (p. 341), but argues that the emphasis on sociocultural context does not amount to a secessionist movement; the aim is rather to integrate the emerging Indian psychology into a more universal psychology. One area

**Box 17.1 (continued)**

where this orientation is becoming visible is that of psychological assessment, where translated tests from the West, instead of restandardized or locally constructed instruments, have long been dominant (cf. Kulkarni & Puhan, 1988). Another area is socio-economic change as it relates to national development (cf. Tripathi, 1988; Muthayya, 1988).

In the personality and clinical psychology area there have been attempts to construct theories and approaches to treatment that find their roots in the religious and philosophical traditions of Hinduism as laid down in the ancient scriptures. In some accounts (e.g., Kakar, 1982) the folkloristic and mythical aspects are hard to separate from scientific exploration; in other work, like that of Paranjpe (1984), an analytic and scientific orientation is followed and relationships and differences with Western conceptions are outlined. We have touched on Indian conceptions of personality in ch. 4, where it was noted that so far there are only few indigenous theories that lend themselves to a critical analysis of their validity. Still, it is particularly in this area that we expect a significant and lasting impact of Indian psychologists on the discipline.

Further work has been carried out by Paranjpe (1996) in concepts rooted in Indian culture. He notes that "psychological concepts, theories and techniques have been an integral part of the long and rich intellectual and cultural traditions of India" (p. 7). Some of these concepts have been described in ch. 4, together with some concepts of personality rooted in African and Japanese traditions. Another example of the development of an indigenous psychology from cultural foundations is the work of Diaz-Guerrero (1975, 1982, 1990), who has developed a Mexican psychology rooted in "historico-sociocultural premises," which he defined as a set of culturally significant statements that are held by a majority of persons in a culture. In Mexico these themes include affiliative obedience, machismo, respect, protection of women, and virginity.

Perhaps the most substantial set of writings on indigenous psychology has been produced by Enriquez (1981, 1993), who has consistently criticized Western influences on Filipino intellectual life. His alternative was to develop a *Sikolohiyang Pilipino* that is rooted in local culture and history. It emphasizes four areas of concern:

> 1) identity and national consciousness, specifically looking at the social sciences as the study of man and *diwa* [consciousness and meaning], or the indigenous conception and definition of the psyche, as a focus of social psychological research; 2) social awareness and involvement as dictated by an objective analysis of social issues and problems; 3) national and ethnic cultures and languages including the study of early or traditional psychology, called *kinagisnang sikolohiya* by Salazar (1983); and 4) bases and application of indigenous psychology

in health practices, agriculture, art, mass media, religion, etc. but also including the psychology of behavior and human abilities as demonstrated in Western psychology and found applicable to the Philippine setting. (Enriquez, 1989, p. 21)

The indigenous psychology movement has three primary areas of protest: it is against a psychology that perpetuates the colonial status of the Filipino mind; it is against the imposition on a majority world country of psychologies developed in and appropriate to industrialized countries; and it is against a psychology used for the exploitation of the masses. For Enriquez,

> The new consciousness, labeled *Sikolohiyang Pilipino* reflecting Filipino psychological knowledge, has emerged through the use of the local language as a tool for the identification and rediscovery of indigenous concepts and as an appropriate medium for the delineation and articulation of Philippine realities together with the development of a scientific literature which embodies the psychology of the Filipino people. (Enriquez, 1989, p. 21)

In his most comprehensive exposition, Enriquez (1993) portrayed *Sikolohyang Philipino* as the outcome of a long history of discrimination and resistance. He proposed two counteracting processes (indigenizing from without, and from within), the first being stimulated by (reaction to) the Western world (cf. "export"), and the second being stimulated by a fundamental interest in Filipino culture (cf. refusal to "import"). Enriquez went beyond explicating indigenous concepts, to indigenous methods (see also Sahoo, 1993), proposing that "asking around," interacting with people in their "natural habitat," and establishing and maintaining empathy are three ways of doing research on Filipino psychology that are culturally appropriate.

While it is difficult for a non-Filipino to comprehend some of the cultural meanings, it is relatively easy to understand both the underlying sentiments and the long-term implications of these views for a psychology of the Philippines.

In addition to these integrative approaches, a number of volumes have appeared that draw together a variety of research findings that are relevant to particular culture areas (e.g., Diaz-Guerrero & Pacheco, 1994, for Latin America; Nsamenang 1995 for Africa; Sinha, 1996, for Asia) or to specific countries (e.g., Bond, 1996 for China). These clearly represent an important and growing trend to achieve a psychology that is relevant to local cultural and regional phenomena.

An obvious advantage of an indigenous psychology is that there is likely to be a reasonable match between the psychological phenomena to be understood, and the description and interpretation of the phenomena. Numerous mismatches can be found in the literature, such as the attempt to understand Japanese or Indian achievement on the bases of American achievement motivation theory (e.g., de Vos, 1968). Historically, such mismatches have been the use of Freudian theory to comprehend father–son conflicts in Melanesia, and the use of Western intelligence tests to assess the cognitive competence of individuals in other cultures (see ch. 5).

A common criticism of indigenization is that there will be a proliferation of psychologies; if every population had its own psychology, an infinite regress to an individual psychology (for a population of one) is possible; or if not so minute, then regress to provincial, city, or village psychologies is envisaged. In addition to the problem of proliferation, Poortinga (1999) has argued that the indigenization of psychology places too much emphasis on differences in behavior found across cultures. Much of the field has paid insufficient attention to the discovery of psychological similarities, particularly the common processes and functions that underlie surface behavioral variation. In his view "those who argue for a culturalist interpretation of behavior have the obligation not only to show how (much) behavior differs per cultural population, but also how (much) it is the same" (Poortinga, 1999, p. 430).

Our view is that a balance has to be found (Berry, 2000a; Poortinga, 1997; Dasen & Mishra, 2000). On the one hand, it does not make sense to ignore the achievements of (a mainly) Western psychology, and to reinvent the wheel in each culture. On the other hand, the ethnocentrism of Western psychology makes it necessary to take other viewpoints on human behavior into account. One of the goals of cross-cultural psychology is the eventual development of a universal psychology that incorporates all indigenous (including Western) psychologies. We will never know whether all diverse data and cultural points of view have been incorporated into the eventual universal psychology, but we should cast our net as widely as possible in order to gather all the relevant information that is available.

## Psychology and national development

In ch. 13 we addressed the issue of change at both the population and individual levels; we distinguished between features of the two cultures in contact, and how they contributed to both cultural and psychological change. Within this framework, we can locate **national development** as change at the population-level (in economic, political, and social indicators) and at the individual-level (in attitudes, values, motives, etc.). For these changes, to constitute development, they need to be in the direction of some more valued end state than was present at the beginning of the process (see box 17.2). This definition of development

## Box 17.2 Psychology and development

The potential contribution of psychology to research and application in the area of national development is rather large. If we define development as the process of individuals and groups moving from some present state to some more valued end state, then psychology can contribute in the following ways:

## Box 17.2 (continued)

1 Understanding the present state: this is the obvious starting point for development, and many psychological constructs are relevant to its description: skills (cognitive, technical, social, etc.); attitudes to change; personality characteristics that may assist or prevent change; values concerning maintaining the past (or present) state of affairs; and interests in various change alternatives. That is, constructing a "psychological profile," or a study of the distribution of psychological characteristics in a population, should provide an understanding of the human resources upon which development may take place. Of course, there are political factors (such as the social organization and distribution of these resources), and economic factors (such as natural resources) that must enter into this present state description, but psychology does have something to contribute to the overall understanding of the current situation.

2 Understanding the valued end state: in the discussion of the local cultural meaning of "development" we saw that psychological research can draw out the local or indigenous meanings of a concept; this approach is one possible contribution of psychology to the study of national development. What, in fact, are the meanings assigned to "development" in various societies? Is it always associated with increased urbanization, industrialization, and organization (as the Western notion of "development" implies), or are there important cultural variations? The valued end state can also be studied by psychologists employing the conventional notions of aspirations, needs, values, and preferences. In short, "what do people want (if anything) out of life?" is a question that psychology can help to answer.

3 Understanding the process of change: how do people get from the present state to the future valued end state? In addition to the human and material resources mentioned earlier, people have motives, drives, coping mechanisms etc., all of which have an established place in psychology. Examining these dynamic factors, including the possibility of increasing their level and effectiveness of their organization in a population is an important potential contribution of psychology to national development.

4 Design, implementation, and evaluation of development programs: psychologists have usually enjoyed a solid training in research methods on human behavior. Cultural variations in behavior have usually been ignored, which is why many development programs have ended in failure. A psychology background can also be of immense help in a development team that is attempting to understand whether a particular development program is having its intended effects. In such areas as sampling, interviewing, the use of control groups, the statistical evaluation of change over time (including an informed choice between longitudinal and cross-sectional designs), psychology has a significant contribution to make.

fits generally into those views that have been expressed in the psychological literature over the past three decades (see Sinha, 1997, for a review).

However, criticism of such a definition also abounds in the literature. For example, Rist (1997; Rist & Sabelli, 1986) has questioned the very notion of national development, particularly its universality. Referring to development as one of the Western world's favorite myths, they systematically attack most of the accepted truths about development held by Western "developers." They assert that not every culture has a concept for "development," and that if there is, it may not be at all like the one in the "developer's" program. However, if the procedures outlined in box 17.2 are followed, misunderstandings about development should be discovered prior to the commencement of development programs. The very existence (or non-existence), and important variations in the meaning of development, should be revealed early in psychologically oriented research, and appropriate decisions can be made on these bases.

Others (e.g., Jahoda, 1974; Zaidi, 1979; Boesch, 1986) have seriously questioned the role that psychologists can play in majority world development. In particular, Mehryar (1984), has argued that psychology may not be capable of making a contribution to national development for a number of reasons. First is the very limited role that psychology has played so far in the development process in industrialized countries; how can it then presume to make a contribution to the process in the developing world? Second, the problems of development are

> by their very nature and etiology, unlikely to be solved by psychology, or other scientific disciplines ... any effort to "psychologise" these problems will not only be unproductive in terms of relieving the misery and backwardness of the people concerned, but it may in fact be misused by certain interest groups to obscure the real obstacles to development. (Mehryar, 1984, p. 161)

According to Mehryar (quoting Ardila, 1982) the problems to be solved are not psychological, but are basically political and economic. However, as we argued earlier, the role of psychology can be best viewed as being a partner with, or supplement to, political and economic sciences, not as the only or best orientation to the promotion of national development.

This complementary approach has been elaborated by Zaman and Zaman (1994). They argue that psychology has a role to play (along with other disciplines), but that the psychology that is employed has to be culturally appropriate. They propose three concepts that would be of use in Pakistan for development purposes. All three involve a joint focus on the individual and on the sociocultural context. For them, obviously relevant constructs are first, individual and affective feelings for efficacy; second, to attend more to feelings of helplessness; and third to consider human agency as a basic factor in development programs.

A role for psychology has also been claimed and articulated by Moghaddam, Branchi, Daniels, Apter, and Harré (1999). They call for an "appropriate psychology," one that recognizes cultural differences, but also power differences between the West and the majority world. When the psychology is inappropriate and the power differentials great, then there would be either or both "resistance" to, or failure of, the development program.

A major contribution to this debate has been made by Kagitcibasi. In her view, human development requires theoretical and empirical work at both the individual and cultural levels (Kagitcibasi, 1994, 1996; Kagitcibasi & Poortinga, 2000). This requires collaboration in research and application between psychologists and others in the field. In particular, she links the two meanings of development (ontogenetic and societal), arguing that without programs for optimal human (ontogenetic) development, there can be little hope of human (societal) development. This view is now becoming widely shared by those in other disciplines (e.g., Jayasuriya & Lee, 1994). While critical of some earlier forays by psychologists into the field (especially those who used the concept of "modernization," Kagitcibasi, 1998), she nevertheless advocates the relevance of psychology to a whole range of development issues (Kagitcibasi, 1996), including early childhood education, health, the role of family (especially the empowerment and training of mothers), and more generally the quality of social, cultural, and economic life (Kagitcibasi, 1996). A consideration of a range of possible ways to apply psychology is presented in box 17.3.

## Box 17.3 The utilization of psychology

There is a wide range of approaches to application in psychology, from the purely scientific to the client dominated. Heller (1986) has provided an overview. He distinguishes the following categories:

1 The traditional approach: science only: this includes experimental research, theory and model building. Application is not a necessary outcome and diffusion of knowledge is mainly through academic books and journals.

2 Building bridges between researcher and user: projects are developed by researchers, but are meant to have practical applications. Sometimes the researchers will be involved in the implementation of findings. Apart from diffusion through academic channels, there is also more popular dissemination.

3 Researcher–client equality: researcher and client discuss a problem area and formulate a research project. Initiative and active collaboration by the client is presumed. When the emphasis is on implementation rather than fact finding the method of "action research" is employed. Academic publications (usually requiring permission from the client) take second place to diffusion of knowledge via the client.

4 Client–professional exploration: advice or assistance is given to the client on the basis of knowledge and expertise available to the scientific adviser. Diffusion through publications is limited; the recommendations should lead to training or the implementation of changes in policy.

**Box 17.3  (continued)**

5 Client-dominated quest: the client calls on a specialist (e.g., counselor or personnel manager) or even someone untrained in the behavioral or social sciences. The best current knowledge as seen by this person is the basis for action. This kind of knowledge tends to be heavily influenced by personal experience and popular notions, called "common sense." Diffusion outside the client system is minimal.

The five categories differ along a number of dimensions. Basic research is usually paid for by universities or research foundations, while more applied research and client-dominated requests for help tend to be paid by the client. Basic research takes a long time to complete and the outcome is uncertain, while advice and interventions based on current insights are available immediately. As funds are more limited and the immediate needs more urgent, the scope for basic research become more restricted.

There is a persistent inequality between richer and poorer nations in the resources available for research as well as the number of professionals who possess scientific expertise. Since basic research is formulated primarily by scientists, it is the responsibility of the global scientific community to take other than local or national needs into account.

The application of knowledge based on research is primarily the concern of local experts. In the social and behavioral sciences where intimate knowledge of local circumstances is an essential requirement, the international community (which for any given developing society largely consists of outsiders) has a limited role to play. In the economically poorer countries the small numbers of local experts, the lack of facilities such as a good library, and the often overburdening workload impose serious limitations on the diffusion of scientific information and its use (Perez & Dasen, 1999).

In our view Heller's scheme leaves room for the incorporation of concerns such as those expressed by Mehryar and other majority world authors. In some of Heller's categories, the client and the researcher cooperate, or the client has the initiative. Appropriate discourse between the client (which may well be a society represented by local psychologists, who can express their society's concerns and check suggested solutions for their suitability) is an essential step on the road to useful research outcomes. This does little to alleviate the problems of unequal power in a political sense between societies, but it should help to create at least a mutual dependency between the psychologists involved in this process.

A collaborative interdisciplinary effort proved already fruitful for Ugorji and Berman (1974, psychologist and political scientist) who assessed the orientations of Igbo Nigerian villagers toward development (*oganihu*), and structural aspects of socioeconomic and political processes. At the psychological level, interviews focussed on beliefs about what makes for the "good life," understanding of notions such as "development" and "progress," attitudes toward change, knowledge of national development policy, and attitudes toward government officials and institutions. *Oganihu* was judged to have both positive and negative aspects. On the positive side were better housing, modern consumer goods, piped water, electricity, and improved roads, and hospitals. On the negative side were feelings of ambivalence, alienation, powerlessness, dependency, and dissatisfaction with government. It was believed that the most effective route to *oganihu* was by obtaining a formal education, leading in turn to a well-paid job. While life now was judged to be better than previously (in material terms), there was also a sense that moral decay had set in. This elaborate view of development in a Nigerian village is both a challenge to critics of the concept (who claim it to be only a Western notion), and an easily recognizable and probably widely shared orientation to life in many parts of the world.

The role of psychology in studying and promoting national development has been advocated particularly in India. For example, a journal entitled *Psychology and Developing Societies* was begun in 1989 at the initiative of D. Sinha. His interests have been directed as well toward the issue of poverty and its relationship to national development. Another Indian psychologist who has made a particularly important contribution to the study of national development is J. B. P. Sinha (1970, 1980, 1984b, 1990). His approach is an integrative one, in which psychology is seen as a "partner in development," both with other disciplines, and as practiced between psychologists from industrialized and developing countries. He has traced the evolving meaning of "development," and along with this change, the evolution of the roles played by psychologists. In the 1950s national development was generally

> taken as being synonymous to economic development, which was naturally the domain of economists ... however ... economic development of the newly independent nations did not obey the rational formula of saving, investment, and growth, because of the interfering effects of the socio-cultural features of the traditional societies. (J. B. P. Sinha, 1984b, p. 169)

Western views of "development" continued to hold sway, because Western psychologists and other social scientists tended to dominate any collaborative relationships that were forged (see Blackler, 1983, for substantial evidence of this point of view). It was only with the realization in the 1960s by some developing world psychologists that local or indigenous perspectives were necessary in order to study local problems that some progress began to be made. For example, Singh (1967) was able to show that Weber's theory linking the Protestant (Christian) ethic to economic growth (and its converse, that Hinduism restricted economic growth) was inappropriate if one looked at the relationship between religious ideology and economics from a Hindu perspective. For Indian scholars, "the Western models of development were embedded in Western values ... where the individual was and still is the agent as well as the recipient of social change" (J. B. P. Sinha, 1984b, p. 171). From a Western perspective this individual is open to new experience, relatively independent of parental authority, concerned with time and planning, willing to defer gratification, assumes mastery over nature, believes in determinism and science, has a wide cosmopolitan perspective, uses broad in-groups, and competes with standards of excellence (Triandis, 1984). Such individuals are not common in many developing countries, and so the question arises whether they are necessary for national development. Sinha does not think so. There are alternative psychological profiles that can serve as a basis for development. For example, cooperative behavior (rather than competition), carried out within a "nurturant" dependency relationship with the leader (Sinha, 1980, 1995; cf. ch. 14) can be a productive and satisfying form of economic activity. For J. B. P. Sinha (1984b, p. 173) human resource mobilization in India should focus on key individuals who are embedded in social groups and collectives that can be instruments of change.

With this proposal, we can observe one of the important contributions of cross-cultural psychology: knowledge and points of view gained from working in other cultures can give a much needed perspective, and provide alternative modes of action, for Western psychological research and application. To be of most value, cross-cultural psychology should be the two-way-street exemplified in this discussion of national development.

## Conclusions

The application of cross-cultural psychology to problem solving in diverse cultures has been the central theme of part III of this book. In principle, the discipline is poised to be of use in a number of domains (acculturation, intergroup relations, education, work, communication, and health). However, in this chapter we have attempted to establish some conceptual and practical limits to this enterprise. In particular, the need to make sure that the science and the problem are matched is paramount. Armed with basic knowledge from part I and with methodological and theoretical tools from part II, we believe that matching *is* possible. To accomplish this, however, working partnerships and two-way exchanges of psychological knowledge are required.

### Key terms

ethnopsychology
indigenization
indigenous psychologies
majority world
national development

## Further reading

Adair, J., & Kagitcibasi, C. (Eds.) (1995). National development of psychology: Factors facilitating and impeding progress in developing countries. *International Journal of Psychology, 30(6)* (special issue). A set of original articles that review and critically examine the development of psychology in various societies.

Bond, M. H. (Ed.) (1996). *The handbook of Chinese psychology.* Hong Kong: Oxford University Press. A volume with chapters on a variety of aspects of psychological functioning in a non-Western culture.

Kagitcibasi, C. (1996). *Family and human development across cultures: A view from the other side.* Hillsdale, NJ: Erlbaum. This book was mentioned with the further readings of ch. 2, but is also relevant for the perspective given on the role of psychology in the majority world.

Kim, U., & Berry, J. W. (Eds.) (1993). *Indigenous psychologies: Research and experience in cultural context.* Newbury Park, CA: Sage. A collection of original chapters by authors from various countries portraying their ideas and findings about psychologies that are indigenous to their cultures.

Sinha, D. (1997). Indigenizing psychology. In J. W. Berry, Y. H. Poortinga, & J. Pandey (Eds.), *Theory and Method* (pp. 129–69). Vol. I of *Handbook of cross-cultural psychology* (2nd ed.). Boston, MA: Allyn & Bacon. A review chapter that presents, organizes, and criticizes recent work on indigenous psychologies.

# Epilogue

&bull;

The reader will have realized that this book offers a selective presentation of a diverse field. Necessarily many important points of view, empirical research studies, and programs of application have not been mentioned, never mind
given substantive treatment. Our attention, however, has not been random, but
guided by an ecocultural framework that was made explicit at the outset. Central to this framework has been the view that individual human beings develop
and exhibit behaviors that are adaptive to the ecological and sociopolitical contexts in which they and their group find themselves.

We have also taken the position that psychological processes are shared,
species-wide characteristics. These common psychological qualities are nurtured,
and shaped by enculturation and socialization, sometimes further affected by
acculturation, and ultimately expressed as overt human behaviors. While set on
course by these transmission processes relatively early in life, behaviors continue
to be guided in later life by direct influence from ecological, cultural, and
sociopolitical factors. In short, we have considered culture, in its broadest sense,
to be a major source of human behavioral diversity producing variations on underlying themes. It is the common qualities that make comparisons possible, and
the variations that make comparisons interesting.

Our enterprise has some clearly articulated goals, and it is reasonable to ask
whether the field of cross-cultural psychology generally, and this book in particular, has met them. In our view, the third goal, as expressed in ch. 1 has *not*
been achieved: we are nowhere close to producing a universal psychology through
the comprehensive integration of results of comparative psychological studies.
However, we have taken some important steps toward this goal, both in terms of
demonstrating how human psychological functioning is similar across cultures
and how important differences in behavior repertoire emerge. Chapters 2 to 8
review empirical studies in various fields of cross-cultural psychology, showing
ample evidence of both pan-human psychological qualities, and variation in the
development and overt display of these qualities across cultures.

In part II of the book, we considered four areas of thinking and research that
define the four corners of the terrain within which cross-cultural psychology has
largely operated: culture, biology, method, and theory. This section essentially
provides an interpretive frame for the materials reviewed earlier, by linking them
to cognate disciplines and to fundamental issues of comparative science. By so
doing, we have intended to lift the whole of the first section above the level of

description to the level of possible (and alternative) interpretations. Central to this was the distinction between absolutism, relativism, and universalism as ways of thinking about the often subtle and complex interplay between psychological similarities and differences across cultures. While we have opted for a universalist stance, it is possible that future advances in the biological and cultural sciences will reinforce allegiance to absolutism or to relativism, at least for some parts of the total range of behaviors.

Cross-cultural psychological findings can be assessed not only against disciplinary, methodological, and theoretical criteria, but also against practical criteria in the world of day-to-day problems. In part III, again selectively, we considered areas of real concern to many people in many parts of the world. Using the findings, tools, and ideas drawn from basic research in cross-cultural psychology, we explored how a cross-cultural approach can begin to make a difference. In a rapidly changing, and increasingly interconnected world, concerns about acculturation and intercultural relations, about education, work, communication, health, and national development, have all come into the foreground and have stimulated many to direct their research toward these issues. Answers are partial, and much remains to be done, but the evidence we have marshaled points, we believe, to a central and important role for cross-cultural psychology in helping to deal with some of the major problems facing the world.

Scientific analysis does not exist in a vacuum; it ultimately has to be justified in terms of its demonstrated contribution, or prospect for future contribution, to human well-being. We realize that this is a steep order, and that the very definition of "human well-being" can be the topic of elaborate discussion. However, cross-cultural psychology has the pretension to look across the boundaries of one's own culture and from a global perspective the differences in well-being between societies are so striking that a debate on finer points soon becomes hypocritical. Despite globalization (which has been mainly profitable to those that control the means of production and distribution), the major divide between rich and poor societies in the world continues to exist, and cannot be ignored. This raises the question of what the specific expertise is of cross-cultural psychologists to ameliorate the situation. Looking at the history of psychology it is evident that its theoretical foundations are not very strong. Even the success of theories by giants like Freud, Piaget, and Vygotsky has been short lived, and many of their ideas have not stood up to later critical analysis.

Can we then pretend that in cross-cultural psychology there is a fund of knowledge that is ready for use to improve the situation, particularly of the poor in this world? We think that this is the case, if one is prepared to look for a balance between scientific restraint (using only well-tested knowledge) and the acceptance of risks because existing needs have to be addressed here and now. Such a balance was proposed explicitly at the end of ch. 16 in relation to health. However, for other areas of application as well, there will always be a question about how to achieve the optimal balance between using only well-established knowledge, and the need to act decisively to address important needs.

Of course, cross-cultural researchers are not just seekers of knowledge; they are inevitably part of an intercultural process, in which many factors other than obtaining information play a role. In some of the chapters we have touched upon political and ethical issues that are usually present: why is the research being done, whose interests will it serve, and with whom will the information be shared? While formerly *extractive* (see ch. 9), cross-cultural researchers now begin to recognize that the interests of the population investigated are part of their responsibility. Instead of merely studying a group, one should join them in analyzing matters that they consider of importance. This definitely holds as far as interventions are concerned. In fact, intervention programs should be constructed to meet the needs of a target population and with the explicit input of that population in the definition of needs to be addressed by a program and in the program objectives.

We also have shown (chs. 1, 9 and 10) that collaboration should not only include "cultural partners" but should extend to "disciplinary partners." Cross-cultural psychology is essentially an "interdiscipline," drawing not only on psychology, but also on other social, biological, and ecological sciences. This is an important scientific niche to occupy, since human problems (and hence the possibility of achieving human well-being) are obviously not uniquely psychological. Many contemporary issues have arisen because of social and political changes such as (de)colonization and globalization (sometimes verging on neocolonization). These contribute to migrant and refugee movements, economic and political inequalities, and to epidemics of psychological, social and physical problems (including racism, ethnic conflict and war, and the spread of HIV/AIDS). All of these problems have evident psychological and cultural dimensions. However, we need to take care that our central concern with cultural influences on behavior does not lead us to an exclusive focus on cultural differences in behavior. Such an emphasis was present earlier in our discipline, and may have sometimes fed into prejudice and intercultural hostility. Hence in this book, we have also emphasized the existence of both cultural similarities and of ongoing cultural change.

To live up to its promise the field of cross-cultural psychology will require three major changes: the development of persistent and collaborative work on particular topics; the incorporation of psychologists from *all* societies into this enterprise; and the convincing of our students and colleagues to accept the view that culture is indeed one of the most important contributors to human behavior. If this book stimulates any of these changes, then we will consider ourselves to be rewarded.

# Key terms

**Absolutism**: a theoretical orientation that considers human behavior as not essentially influenced by culture, and that studies behavior without taking a person's culture into account.

**Acculturation**: changes in a cultural group or individual as a result of contact with another cultural group (see also **psychological acculturation**).

**Acculturation strategies**: the way that individuals and **ethnocultural groups** orient themselves to the process of **acculturation**. Four strategies are: **assimilation, integration, separation**, and **marginalization**.

**Acculturative stress**: a negative psychological reaction to the experiences of **acculturation**, often characterised by anxiety, depression, and a variety of psychosomatic problems.

**Adaptation** (to acculturation): the process of dealing with the experiences of **acculturation**; a distinction is often made between psychological adaptation (feelings of personal well-being and self-esteem) and sociocultural adaptation (competence in dealing with life in the larger society).

**Adaptation** (biological): changes in the genetic make-up of a population through **natural selection** in reaction to demands of the environment.

**Adaptation** (social): changes in the behavior repertoire of a person or group in reaction to demands of the ecological or social environment.

**Affective meaning**: the connotative or emotional meaning which a word has in addition to its denotative or referential meaning.

**Aggression**: any act, usually intentional, that inflicts harm on one of more persons. Aggressive behaviors are often attempts to exercise social control via coercion, and may sometimes be perceived as justified, sometimes not.

**Allele**: variation of a single gene; alleles form the most important basis for individual differences within a species.

**Altered states of consciousness** (ASC): the name for a range of states of awareness including mystic experiences, meditation, hypnosis, trance, and possession.

**Antecedents of emotions**: situations that tend to lead to the emergence of certain emotions.

**Anthropology**: a scientific discipline that seeks to understand human societies in all their variety, and in various domains (cultural, social, biological, and psychological).

**Appraisal** (of emotions): the rapid and automatic evaluation of a situation in terms of its emotional significance.

**Assimilation**: the **acculturation strategy** in which people do not wish to maintain their own culture, and seek to participate in the larger society.

**Attachment**: the bonding between a mother and her young child during the first year of life, by many developmental psychologists throught to be of consequence through the entire lifespan.

**Attribution**: the explanations that individuals use for the causes of their own or other people's behavior, usually distinguishing between internal (psychological) and external (situational) causes.

**Basic color terms**: a set of words for major colors to which, according to some authors, all languages evolve.

**Basic emotions**: emotional states that presumably can be identified universally, often with reference to characteristic patterns of facial musculature.

**Behavior genetics**: the search for relationships between behavioral traits as they appear and underlying genetic determinants.

**"Big five" dimensions** (also the five-factor model, or FFM): five dimensions that tend to be seen as enduring dispositions, likely to be biologically anchored, and that together cover the main ways in which individual persons differ from each other in personality.

**Bilingualism**: the ability of persons to communicate with others in at least one other language beyond their mother tongue.

**Biological transmission,** see **Genetic transmission**

**Child training**: practices that are used by parents, and others, to ensure that **cultural transmission** takes place.

**Cognitive abilities**: various aspects of **general intelligence**, often assessed with different subtests in an intelligence battery.

**Cognitive anthropology**: a subdiscipline of anthropology that seeks to understand the relationship between culture and the cognitive life of the group.

**Cognitive styles**: a conception of cognitive activity that emphasizes the way in which cognitive processes are organized and used, rather than the level of development of cognitive abilities.

**Collative variables**: stimulus properties (such as novelty, complexity, and incongruity) that are thought to affect esthetic appreciation of art objects.

**Color categorization**: the way in which the colors of the visible spectrum are categorized by means of color names.

**Conformity**: the tendency of individuals to accept the majority or prevailing view about an issue, and to go along with the group norm.

**Contact hypothesis**: the proposition that contact between cultural and **ethnocultural groups,** and their members, will lead to more positive intercultural attitudes.

**Contextualized cognition**: a conception of cognitive activity that emphasizes the development and use of cognitive processes in relation to specific cultural contexts and practices.

**Contingency theory** (with respect to organizations): a group of theories addressing the question how, and how much, organizational structure is contingent upon (i.e., the consequence of) various kinds of contextual variables (cultural, political, technological, etc.).

**Convention** (also: cultural practice, cultural rule): explicitly or implicitly accepted agreement among the members of a group as to what is appropriate in some social interaction or in some field of activity.

**Cross-cultural psychology**: cross-cultural psychology is the study: of similarities and differences in individual psychological functioning in various cultural and ethnocultural groups; of the relationships between psychological variables and sociocultural, ecological, and biological variables; and of ongoing changes in these variables.

**Cross-ethnicity effect** (in face recognition): the tendency that individuals from groups with different facial features from our own group tend to look more alike to us.

**Cultural bias**: cross-cultural differences that are not related to the trait or concept presumably measured by an instrument (or by some other method), and that tend to distort the interpretation of these differences.

**Cultural distance**: the degree to which groups differ culturally, measured by ethnographic indicators, or by individuals' perception of such difference.

**Cultural evolution**: a view that cultures have changed over time in adaptation to their ecosystem and other influences.

**Cultural identity**: how individuals think and feel about themselves in to the cultural or **ethnocultural groups** with which they are associated.

**Cultural psychology**: a theoretical approach that sees culture and behavior as essentially inseparable; and that is closely linked to **cultural relativism** and **psychological anthropology**.

**Cultural relativism**: a view that cultures should be understood in their own terms, rather than being judged by the standards of other groups (see also **ethnocentrism**).

**Cultural transmission**: processes by which cultural features of a population are transferred to its individual members (see also **enculturation** and **socialization**).

**Cultural universals**: those cultural features that are present in all societies in some form, such as language, family, and technology.

**Culture**: the shared way of life of a group of people, including their artifacts (such as social institutions, and technology), and their symbols (such as communications and myths).

**Culture assimilator**: a series of short episodes describing incidents in the interaction between persons belonging to different cultures; intended for teaching intercultural communication.

**Culture-bound syndromes**: patterns of behavior that are said to occur only in a particular cultural group and that are considered to be abnormal or psychopathological.

**Culture-comparative research**: a research tradition in which similarities and differences in behavior are studied across cultures.

**Decision making** (by managers): decisions and processes of decision making, influenced by cultural variables related to styles of leadership and risk assessment.

**Depression**: a psychological illness characterized by sadness, a lack of energy, and of interest and enjoyment of life.

**Depth cues in pictures**: aspects of pictures that lead to a sensation of depth in observers (including, overlap of depicted objects, size at which various objects are represented, position of objects, etc.).

**Developmental niche**: a system in which the physical environment, sociocultural customs of child rearing, and psychological conceptions (beliefs, etc.) of parents, interact with the developing child.

**Discrimination**: the act of treating persons differently because of their membership in a cultural or **ethnocultural group**.

**Display rules**: cultural norms regarding the control and expression of emotions in various situations.

**Dual inheritance model** (Boyd & Richerson, 1985): a model postulating a cultural inheritance system that is based on social learning and that cannot be reduced to the genetic inheritance system.

**Ecocultural framework**: a conceptual approach to understanding similarities and differences in human behavior across cultures in terms of individual and group adapation to context.

**Emic approach**: the study of behavior in one culture, often emphasizing culture-specific aspects.

**Emotion components**: various aspects by which one emotional state can be distinguished from another, including facial expression, **appraisal, antecedents of emotions**, etc.

**Enculturation**: a form of **cultural transmission** by which a society transmits its culture and behavior to its members by surrounding developing members with appropriate models.

**Equivalence**: a condition for interpreting psychological data obtained from different cultures in the same way (also referred to as comparability of data); data can have structural equivalence (measuring cross-culturally the same trait), metric equivalence (measuring the same trait on scales with the same metric) and full score equivalence (measuring the same trait on the same scale).

**Ethnic attitudes**: positive or negative evaluations of individuals (or groups) because of their membership in a cultural or **ethnocultural group.**

**Ethnic stereotypes**: shared beliefs about the characteristics thought to be typical of members of a cultural or **ethnocultural group.**

**Ethnocentrism**: a point of view that accepts one's own group's standards as the best, and judges all other groups in relation to them.

**Ethnocultural group**: a group living in a **plural society** that is derived from a heritage cultural group, but which has changed as a result of **acculturation** in the larger society.

**Ethnographic archives**: a collection of ethnographic reports about various cultures, brought together into a form that can be used for comparative research (see also **Human Relations Area Files**).

**Ethnopsychology**: a perspective on human behavior that is rooted in a particular cultural worldview (see also **Indigenous psychologies**).

**Ethology**: the study by biologists of animal behavior in natural environments.

**Etic approach**: the comparative study of behavior across cultures, often assuming some form of universality of the psychological underpinnings of behavior.

**Evolutionary psychology**: a school of psychology based on the evolutionary thinking of **ethology** and **sociobiology.**

**Extraversion**: a personality dimension ranging from sociable and outgoing (extraverted) to quiet and passive (introverted).

**Fitness** (biological): the probability of survival and reproduction of an organism.

*g*: a view of **general intelligence** as an individual characteristic and, often, as an inborn capacity.

**Gender**: the socially ascribed roles (including behaviors and identities) that accompany the male and female sexes. While a person's sex is a biological given, gender is socially constructed.

**Gender role ideology**: normative beliefs about the behaviors thought to be appropriate for males and females.

**Gender stereotypes**: shared beliefs about the characteristics thought to be typical of males and females.

**Gene**: a segment of DNA that can be recognized by its specific locus and function; the gene is the functional unit of genetic material.

**General intelligence**: a unified view of the level of cognitive functioning of an individual person, derived from the positive correlations found between scores on a wide range of cognitive tests (especially intelligence batteries) (see also **g**).

**Genetic epistemology**: a theoretical approach that proposes a sequence of stages in the development of cognitive operations from birth to maturity.

**Genetic transmission** (also **biological transmission**): the transfer of genetic information from parents to their children. Each individual can be seen as representing a specific selection of genetic properties from the pool of genetic information present in the population.

**Health**: a state of complete physical, mental and social well-being, and not merely the absence of disease or infirmity.

**Holocultural approach**: a research method based on **ethnographic archives** that includes many societies in a single comparative study.

**Human ethology**: the use of methods and theories from **ethology** to study behavior in the human species.

**Human Relations Area Files (HRAF)**: an ethnographic archive of information about many of the world's societies organized by cultural topic.

**Independent self** and **interdependent self**: two ways of viewing oneself; namely as a separate, autonomous individual seeking independence from others, or as an individual inherently linked to others. (A similar distinction is between relational self and separated self.)

**Indigenization**: the transformation through which an imported psychology becomes a more culturally appropriate psychology.

**Indigenous personality concepts**: concepts that originated in non-Western cultures and are rooted in local views of human functioning (note that most concepts originate from Western indigenous views).

**Indigenous psychologies**: differing perspectives on human behavior that are rooted in particular cultural worldviews.

**Individualism and collectivism**: a distinction between the tendencies to be primarily concerned with oneself, or with one's group.

**Inference**: the interpretation of data in terms of some domain of behavior or trait to which the data are thought to pertain (see also **levels of inference**).

**Information processing**: the cognitive processes in the person during transformation from stimuli to responses; usually components of information processing are distinguished, such as an encoding, an inference, a mapping, and a response phase.

**Integration**: the **acculturation strategy** in which people wish to maintain their cultural heritage, and seek to participate in the larger society.

**Intercultural communication training**: preparation of prospective sojourners for assignments outside their home country by means of various kinds of training programs.

**Intercultural competence**: the competence of a person to interact adequately with others from a different cultural background; often considered as not only consisting of certain skills and knowledge, but also of more general personality traits.

**Larger society** (in acculturation): a term used to refer to the overall social composition and arrangements in a culturally diverse society, including its government, and its economic, educational, and legal institutions. It differs from another term (mainstream) which refers mainly to the dominant society.

**Leadership styles**: different ways in which leaders (notably managers in industrial organizations) influence the preformance of subordinates. Often a dimension is distinguished with concern for employees and concern for productivity as endpoints.

**Levels of analysis**: a concept that allows human phenomena to be studied and interpreted by various disciplines at various levels (such as individual, cultural, or ecological) without having to be reduced to explanations at a more basic level.

**Levels of inference** (or generalization): levels pertaining to the width or inclusiveness of behavioral domains and psychological traits in terms of which data are interpreted.

**Linguistic relativity** (also Whorfian hypothesis): the idea that there are important relationships between characteristics of a language and the ways of thinking found in speakers of that language.

**Locus of control**: a tendency to consider what happens to oneself either as a consequence of one's own actions (internal control) or as contingent upon forces beyond one's control, like other persons (external control).

**Majority world**: the countries in which the majority of the world population is living. The term is strongly associated with economic poverty and low educational opportunities.

**Malnutrition**: a state resulting from insufficient food intake, and indicated by low weight and height in relation to age.

**Marginalization**: the **acculturation strategy** in which people do not maintain their cultural heritage, and also do not participate in the **larger society**.

**Metacognition**: knowledge about one's own cognition, including capabilities and plans on how to carry out a task.

**Migration motivation**: the reasons that prompt individual to migrate from one society to another. "Push" motives are negative, inducing departure; "pull" motives are positive, attracting individuals to the new society.

**Moral development**: the development in individuals of principles about what is right and wrong behavior, and the reasons given for these principles.

**Motivation** (work-related): the complex of motives (or drives) and needs that presumably make people perform at work.

**Multicultural ideology**: a positive orientation of individuals to cultural diversity in **plural societies**, involving the acceptance of **ethnocultural groups** and their participation in the larger society.

**Multiculturalism**: a term used to refer to both the existence of, and a policy supporting the many **ethnocultural groups** living together in the **larger society**. It involves both the maintenance of diverse ethnocultural groups, and the participation of these groups in the larger society.

**National development**: a process of change in psychological, social, economic, and political features that leads a society toward achieving its own goals.

**Natural selection**: differential rates of reproduction for individual organisms in a given environment due to certain genetic features.

**Neuroticism** (or emotionality): a personality dimension ranging from instability (e.g., "moody," "touchy") to stability (even tempered).

**Ontogenetic development**: the systematic changes in the behavior of an individual person across the lifespan.

**Organizational culture**: deep-rooted beliefs, meanings, and values that are shared by the members of an organization, in distinction from other organizations. Sometimes the emphasis is more on practices prevalent in an organization, or on variables such as production techniques and attitudes of employees (the term organizational climate is also used, especially in the latter sense).

**Organizational structure**: the distribution of tasks in an organization. The total body of work that has to be performed is assigned to different divisions and subdivisions and ultimately to work groups and individuals with different tasks.

**Paradigm**: a metatheoretical, often philosophical, position on the nature of the phenomena studied in a science and the ways they can be studied.

**Parental ethnotheories** (also called parental beliefs, implicit developmental theories): a set of cultural beliefs and practices held by parents regarding the proper way to raise a child (see also **child training**).

**Personality traits**: characteristics of individual persons that are consistent over time and across situations, and through which they distinguish themselves from others.

**Phoneme category**: the speech sounds that are heard as the same phoneme by speakers of a language.

**Pleiotropy**: the variety of effects that one gene can have on the development of an organism.

**Plural society**: a society in which a number of **ethnocultural groups** live together within a shared political and economic framework.

**Prejudice**: a general negative orientation toward a cultural or **ethnocultural group** other than one's own (see also **ethnocentrism**).

**Prevention** (health): taking steps to avoid **health** problems before they appear, often through public education and public health programs.

**Promotion** (health): advocating and supporting the achievement of **health** through public education and public health programs.

**Psychological acculturation**: changes in the psychological features of persons as a result of their contact with another cultural group (see also **acculturation**).

**Psychological anthropology** (formerly known as culture and personality): a subdiscipline of **anthropology** that seeks to use and apply psychological concepts and methods to the understanding of cultural groups.

**Psychopathology**: a psychological illness that is considered by the community or experts to be reflected in strange or bizarre behavior.

**Psychosocial factors** (health): features (other than biophysical) of the ecological and sociopolitical environments that contribute to the attainment (or loss) of **health**.

**Psychotherapy**: practices that involve a patient and a healer in a personal relationship whose goal is to relieve the patient's suffering.

**Qualitative methodology**: approaches to research with an emphasis on the understanding of processes and meanings; often these cannot be experimentally or psychometrically examined or measured in terms of quantity, amount, etc.

**Quality of life** (QOL): a concept that emphasizes positive aspects of a person's life, in particular those that contribute to life satisfaction.

**Quantitative methodology**: approaches to research in which the measurement (in terms of quantity, amount, or frequency) is emphasized of the phenomena that are being examined.

**Relativism**: a theoretical orientation that assumes human behavior is strongly influenced by culture, and that it can only be studied by taking a person's culture into account.

**Schizophrenia**: a psychological illness characterized by lack of insight, hallucinations, and reduced affect.

**Sensory stimuli**: stimuli that solicit processes in the sensory organs (eye, ear, etc.), but are presumed to involve few other psychological functions, such as perception and cognition.

**Separation**: the **acculturation strategy** in which people wish to maintain their cultural heritage, and seek to avoid participation in the larger society.

**Sexually transmitted disease**: any disease that is contracted by sexual relations.

**Social construction of emotions**: the viewpoint that emotions are social constructions rather than biological givens and thus will differ essentially across cultures.

**Socialization**: a form of **cultural transmission** by which a society deliberately shapes the behavior of its developing members through instruction.

**Sociobiology**: the explanation of social behavior, including that of the human species, in terms of principles of evolutionary biology (cf. also **human ethology**).

**Sojourners** (also called expatriates): persons who live in another country for a certain period, varying from a number of weeks to a few years, and who have frequent interactions with local inhabitants for purposes of work or study.

**Spatial orientation**: the way persons locate objects and themselves in space; especially with respect to the question whether they use their own position for indications of direction (ego-referenced orientation) or have a preference for absolute or geocentric spatial coordinates.

**Subjective culture**: how members of a culture view themselves and how they evaluate their way of life.

**Subjective well-being**: a person's cognitive and affective appraisal of his or her life.

**Temperament**: characteristics of an individual's personality that are presumed to have a biological basis.

**Theories of mind**: the tendency to ascribe mental states to oneself and to others; theories of mind are used to understand other peoples' behaviors and psychological states and those of oneself.

**Tight–loose**: a dimension contrasting societies that are tightly structured and expect **conformity** from their members, with those that are more loosely knit and allow greater individual variability.

**Transfer of tests**: the use of tests with members of other cultural populations than the one for which they were originally designed.

**Universalism**: a theoretical orientation that considers basic psychological procsses as shared characteristics of all people, and culture as influencing their development and display.

**Universality**: psychological concepts, or relationships between concepts, are universal if they appear suitable for the description of the behavior of people in any culture.

**Universals in language**: characteristics thought to be found in all human languages.

**Validity**: the degree to which findings and interpretations have been shown to approximate a presumed state of affairs in reality, independent of the prior beliefs of scientists.

**Values**: conceptions of what is desirable, that influence the selection of means and ends of actions.

**Visual illusions**: systematic distortions in the visual perception of the objective reality as it presents itself to the perceiver (usually studied with simple figures, such as the Müller–Lyer, known to lead to such distortions).

**Work-related values**: desired states and outcomes (see **values**) derived from cross-cultural studies in organizations, ususally presented as value dimensions (e.g., individualism–collectivism, power distance).

# References

Abdallah-Pretceille, M., & Camilleri, C. (1994). La communication interculturelle. In C. Labat & G. Vermès (Eds.), *Cultures ouvertes, sociétés interculturelles: Du contact à l'interaction* (pp. 47–51). Paris: L'Harmattan.

Abegglen, J. C. (1958). *The Japanese factory*. Glencoe, IL: Free Press.

Aberle, D. F., Cohen, A. K., Davis, A., Levy, M., & Sutton, F. X. (1950). Functional prerequisites of society. *Ethics, 60*, 100–11.

Aboud, F. (1981). Ethnic self-identity. In R. C. Gardner & R. Kalin (Eds.), *A Canadian social psychology of ethnic relations* (pp. 37–56). Toronto: Methuen.

  (1988). *Children and prejudice*. Oxford: Basil Blackwell.

  (1998). *Health psychology in global perspective*. Thousand Oaks, CA: Sage.

Aboud, F., & Alemu, T. (1995). Nutritional status, maternal responsiveness and mental development of Ethiopian children. *Social Science and Medicine, 41*, 725–32.

Aboud, F., & Levy, S. (Eds.) (1999). Reducing racial prejudice, discrimination and stereotyping: Translating research into programmes. *Journal of Social Issues, 55*, 621–803.

Abrahamson, A. S., & Lisker, L. (1970). Discriminability along the voicing continuum: Cross-language tests. In *Proceedings of the Sixth International Congress of Phonetic Science* (pp. 569–73). Prague: Academia.

Abu-Lughod, L. (1986). *Veiled sentiments: Honor and poetry in a Bedouin society*. Berkeley, CA: University of California Press.

  (1991). Writing against culture. In R. Fox (Ed.), *Recapturing anthropology* (pp. 137–62). Santa Fe, NM: School of American Research.

Adair, J., & Diaz-Loving, R. (1999). Indigenous psychologies: The meaning of the concept and its assessment. *Applied Psychology, 48*, 397–402.

Adair, J., & Kagitcibasi, C. (Eds.) (1995). National development of psychology: Factors facilitating and impeding progress in developing countries. *International Journal of Psychology, 30*, 6 (special issue).

Aditya, R. N., House, R. J., & Kerr, S. (2000). Theory and practice of leadership: Into the new millennium. In C. L. Cooper & E. A. Locke (Eds.), *Industrial and organizational psychology: Linking theory with practice* (pp. 130–67). Oxford: Blackwell.

Adler, L. L. (Ed.) (1993). *International handbook of gender roles*. Westport, CT: Greenwood.

Adler, N. J. (1986). *International dimensions of organizational behavior*. Boston, MA: Kent.

Adorno, T., Frenkel-Brunswik, E., Levinson, D. J., & Sanford, R. N. (1950). *The authoritarian personality*. New York: Harper and Row.

Ager, A. (Ed.) (1999). *Refugees: Perspectives on the experience of forced migration*. London: Cassell.

Ainsworth, M. D. S. (1967). *Infancy in Uganda: Infant care and the growth of love.* Baltimore, MD: Johns Hopkins University Press.

Ainsworth, M. D. S., Blehar, M. C., Waters, E., & Wall, S. (1978). *Patterns of attachment: A psychological study of the strange situation.* Hillsdale, NJ: Erlbaum.

Alasuutari, P. (1995). *Researching culture: Qualitative method and cultural studies.* London: Sage.

Albas, D. C., McCluskey, K. W., & Albas, C. A. (1976). Perception of the emotional content of speech. *Journal of Cross-Cultural Psychology, 7,* 481–90.

Albert, R. D. (1983). The intercultural sensitizer or cultural assimilator: A cognitive approach. In D. Landis & R. W. Brislin (Eds.), *Handbook of intercultural training* (vol. II, pp. 186–217). New York: Pergamon.

Alcock, J. (1984). *Animal behavior: An evolutionary approach* (3rd ed.). Sunderland, MA: Sinauer Associates.

Aldwin, C. (1994). *Stress, coping and development.* New York: Guilford Press.

Al-Issa, I. (Ed.) (1995). *Handbook of culture and mental illness.* Madison, WI: International University Press.

Al-Issa, I., & Ondji, S. (1998). Culture and anxiety disorders. In S. Kazarian & D. Evans (Eds.), *Cultural clinical psychology: Theory, research and practice* (pp. 127–51). New York: Oxford University Press.

Al-Issa, I., & Tousignant, M. (Eds.) (1997). *Ethnicity, immigration and psychopathology.* New York: Plenum.

Allaire, Y., & Firsirotu, M. E. (1984). Theories of organizational culture. *Organization Studies, 5,* 193–226.

Allik, J., & Realo, A. (1996). The hierarchical nature of individualism and collectivism. *Culture and Psychology, 2,* 109–17.

Allison, A. C. (1964). Polymorphism and natural selection in human populations. *Cold Spring Harbor Symposium in Quantitative Biology, 24,* 137–49.

Allport, G. W. (1954). *The nature of prejudice.* Reading, MA: Addison-Wesley.

Allport, G. W., Vernon, P. E., & Lindzey, G. (1960). *A study of values.* Boston, MA: Houghton Mifflin.

Allwood, C. (1998). The creation and nature of indigenized psychologies from the perspective of the anthropology of knowledge. *Knowledge and Society, 11,* 153–72.

Altarriba, J. (Ed.) (1993). *Cognition and culture: A cross-cultural approach to cognitive psychology.* Amsterdam: North-Holland.

Altman, I., & Chemers, M. M. (1980). Cultural aspects of environment–behavior relationships. In H. C. Triandis & R. W. Brislin (Eds.), *Handbook of cross-cultural psychology* (vol. V, pp. 335–94). Boston, MA: Allyn and Bacon.

Altrocchi, J., & Altrocchi, L. (1995). Polyfaceted psychological acculturation in Cook Islanders. *Journal of Cross-Cultural Psychology, 26,* 426–40.

American Psychiatric Association (1994). *Diagnostic and statistical manual of mental disorders* (4th ed.). Washington, DC: American Psychiatric Association.

Amir, Y. (1969). Contact hypothesis in ethnic relations. *Psychological Bulletin, 71,* 319–41.
  (1986). *Intergroup cleavage in Israel.* Paper presented to International Congress of Applied Psychology, Jerusalem.

Amir, Y., & Ben-Ari, R. (1988). A contingency approach for promoting intergroup relations. In J. W. Berry & R. Annis (Eds.), *Ethnic psychology* (pp. 287–96). Lisse, Netherlands: Swets & Zeitlinger.

Amir, Y., & Sharon, I. (1987). Are social psychological laws cross-culturally valid? *Journal of Cross-Cultural Psychology*, *18*, 383–470.

Anand, B. K., Chhina, G. S., & Singh, B. (1961). Some aspects of electroencephalographic studies in yogis. *Electroencephalography and Clinical Neurophysiology*, *13*, 452–6.

Anastasi, A. (1982). *Psychological testing* (6th ed.). New York: Macmillan.

Andor, L. E. (1983). *Psychological and sociological studies of the black people of Africa, south of the Sahara: An annotated select bibliography*. Johannesburg: National Institute for Personnel Research.

APA (American Psychological Association) (1992). Ethical principles of psychologists and code of conduct. *American Psychologist*, *47*, 1597–611.

Aptekar, L., & Stöcklin, D. (1997). Children in particularly difficult circumstances. In J. W. Berry, P. R. Dasen, & T. S. Saraswathi (Eds.), *Basic processes and human development* (pp. 377–412). Vol. II of *Handbook of cross-cultural psychology* (2nd ed.). Boston, MA: Allyn and Bacon.

Archer, J. (1992). *Ethology and human development*. New York: Harvester Wheatsheaf.
  (1996). Sex differences in social behavior: Are the social role and evolutionary explanations compatible? *American Psychologist*, *51*, 909–17.

Ardila, R. (1982). Psychology in Latin America. *Annual Review of Psychology*, *33*, 103–22.

Argyle, M. (1988). *Bodily communication* (2nd ed.). London: Methuen.

Ariès, P. (1960). *L'enfant et la vie familiale sous l'Ancien Régime* [Child and family life in the Old Order]. Paris: Editions du Seuil.

Armstrong, R. E., Rubin, E. V., Stewart, M., & Kuntner, L. (1970). *Susceptibility to the Müller–Lyer, Sander parallelogram, and Ames Distorted Room illusions as a function of age, sex and retinal pigmentation among urban Midwestern groups*. Research report. Northwestern University, Department of Psychology.

Arnett, J. (1995). Broad and narrow socialization: The family in the context of cultural theory. *Journal of Marriage and the Family*, *57*, 617–28.

Aronowitz, M. (1992). Adjustment of immigrant children as a function of parental attitudes to change. *International Migration Review*, *26*, 86–110.

Asch, S. E. (1956). Studies in independence and conformity. *Psychological Monographs*, *70*, 1–70.

Ataca, B., Sunar, D., & Kagitcibasi, C. (1998). Variance in fertility due to sex-related differentiation in child-rearing practices. In H. Grad, A. Blanco, & J. Georgas (Eds.), *Key issues in cross-cultural psychology* (pp. 331–43). Lisse, Netherlands: Swets and Zeitlinger.

Au, T. K. (1983). Chinese and English counterfactuals: The Sapir–Whorf hypothesis revisited. *Cognition*, *15*, 155–87.
  (1984). Counterfactuals: In reply to Alfred Bloom. *Cognition*, *17*, 289–302.

Averill, J. R. (1980). A constructivist view of emotion. In R. Plutchik & H. Kellerman (Eds.), *Emotion: Theory, research, and experience*. Vol. I: *Theories of emotion* (pp. 305–39). New York: Academic Press.

Avis, J., & Harris, P. L. (1991). Belief-desire reasoning among Baka children: Evidence for a universal conception of mind. *Child Development*, *62*, 460–7.

Aycan, Z. (2000). Cross-cultural industrial and organizational psychology: Contributions, past developments, and future directions. *Journal of Cross-Cultural Psychology*, *31*, 110–28.

Aycan, Z., & Berry, J. W. (1996). Impact of employment-related experiences on immigrants' psychological well-being and adaptation to Canada. *Canadian Journal of Behavioural Science, 28,* 240–51.

Bacon, M., Child, I., & Barry, H. (1963). A cross-cultural study of correlates of crime. *Journal of Abnormal and Social Psychology, 66,* 291–300.

Baddeley, A. D. (1986). *Working memory.* Oxford: Oxford University Press.

Baillargeon, R. (1995). Physical reasoning in infancy. In M. S. Gazzaniga (Ed.), *The cognitive neurosciences* (pp. 181–204). Cambridge, MA: MIT Press.

(1998). Infants' understanding of the physical world. In M. Sabourin & F. Craik (Eds.), *Advances in psychological science* (vol. II, pp. 503–29). Hove, UK: Psychology Press.

Baker, C. (2000). *Foundations of bilingual education and bilingualism* (3rd ed.). Clevedon: Multilingual Matters.

Baker, C., & Prys Jones, S. (1998). *Encyclopedia of bilingualism and bilingual education.* Clevedon: Multilingual Matters.

Bali, S. K., Drenth, P. J. D., Van der Flier, H., & Young, W. C. E. (1984). *Contribution of aptitude tests to the prediction of school performance in Kenya: A longitudinal study.* Lisse, Netherlands: Swets & Zeitlinger.

Baltes, P. (1997). On the incomplete architecture of human ontogeny. *American Psychologist, 52,* 366–80.

Baltes, P., Lindenberger, U., & Staudinger, U. M. (1998). Life span theory in developmental psychology. In W. Damon (Chief Ed.) & R. M. Lerner (Ed.), *Handbook of child psychology.* Vol. I: *Theoretical models of human development* (5th ed., pp. 1029–143). New York: Wiley.

Bandura, A. (1977). *Social learning theory.* Englewood Cliffs, NJ: Prentice-Hall.

(1998). Personal and collective efficacy in human adaptation and change. In J. Adair, D. Belanger, & K. Dion (Eds.), *Advances in psychological science* (vol. I, pp. 51–71). Hove, UK: Psychology Press.

Banks, J., & Lynch, J. (Eds.) (1985). *Multicultural education in Western societies.* London: Holt, Rinehart and Winston.

Barba, C. V. C., Guthrie, H. A., & Guthrie, G. M. (1982). Dietary intervention and growth of infants and toddlers in a Philippine rural community. *Ecology & Nutrition, 11,* 235–44.

Barker, R. (1969). *Ecological psychology.* Stanford: Stanford University Press.

(1978). *Habitats, environments and human behavior.* San Francisco, CA: Jossey-Bass.

Barnlund, D. C., & Araki, S. (1985). Intercultural encounters: The management of compliments. *Journal of Cross-Cultural Psychology, 16,* 9–26.

Barrett, D. E. (1984). Malnutrition and child behavior: Conceptualization, assessment and an empirical study of social-emotional functioning. In J. Brozek & B. Schurch (Eds.), *Malnutrition and behavior* (pp. 280–306). Lausanne: Nestlé Foundation.

Barrett, P. T., Petrides, K. V., Eysenck, S. B. G., & Eysenck, H. J. (1998). The Eysenck Personality Questionnaire: An examination of the factorial similarity of P, E, N, and L across 34 countries. *Personality and Individual Differences, 25,* 805–19.

Barry, H. (1980). Description and uses of the Human Relations Area Files. In H. C. Triandis & J. W. Berry (Eds.), *Handbook of cross-cultural psychology.* Vol. II: *Methodology* (pp. 445–78). Boston, MA: Allyn and Bacon.

Barry, H., & Paxson, L. (1971). Infancy and early childhood: Cross-cultural codes. *Ethnology, 10,* 466–508.

Barry, H., & Schlegel, A. (Eds.) (1980). *Cross-cultural samples and codes*. Pittsburgh, PA: University of Pittsburgh Press.

Barry, H., Bacon, M., & Child, I. (1957). A cross-cultural survey of some sex differences in socialization. *Journal of Abnormal and Social Psychology, 55*, 327–32.

Barry, H., Child, I., & Bacon, M. (1959). Relation of child training to subsistence economy. *American Anthropologist, 61*, 51–63.

Barry, H., Josephson, L., Lauer, E., & Marshall, C. (1976). Agents and techniques for child training: Cross-cultural codes 6. *Ethnology, 16*, 191–230.

Bartlett, F. (1937). Psychological methods and anthropological problems. *Africa, 10*, 410–19.

Basic Behavioral Science Task Force (1996). Basic behavioral science research for mental health: Sociocultural and environmental processes. *American Psychologist, 51*, 723–31.

Baxter, B., et al. (1998). Incorporating culture into the treatment of alcohol abuse and dependence. In S. Kazarian & D. Evans (Eds.), *Cultural clinical psychology: Theory, research and practice* (pp. 215–45). New York: Oxford University Press.

Bayley, N. (1969). *Bayley scales of infant development*. New York: Psychological Corporation.

Beardsley, L., & Pedersen, P. (1997). Health and culture-centred interventions. In J. W. Berry, M. H. Segall, & C. Kagitcibasi (Eds.), *Social behavior and applications* (pp. 413–48). Vol. III of *Handbook of cross-cultural psychology* (2nd ed.). Boston, MA: Allyn and Bacon.

Becht, M. C., Poortinga, Y. H., & Vingerhoets, A. J. J. M. (2001). Crying across countries. In A. J. J. M. Vingerhoets & R. R. Cornelius (Eds.), *Adult crying: A biopsychosocial approach* (pp. 135–58). Hove, UK: Brunner-Routledge.

Bedford, O. (1994). *Guilt and shame in American and Chinese culture*. Unpublished Ph.D. dissertation, University of Colorado.

Bedi, K. (1987). Lasting neuroanatomical changes following undernutrition during early life. In J. Dobbing (Ed.), *Early nutrition and later achievement* (pp. 1–36). New York: Academic Press.

Beiser, M. (1999). *Strangers at the gate*. Toronto: University of Toronto Press.

Beiser, M., Barwick, C., Berry, J. W., daCosta, G., Fantino, A. M., Ganesan, S., Lee, C., Milne, W., Naidoo, J., Prince, R., Tousignant, M., & Vela, E. (1988). *After the door has been opened: Mental health issues affecting immigrants and refugees in Canada*. Ottawa: Ministry of Multiculturalism and Citizenship and Health and Welfare Canada.

Beiser, M., Johnson, P., & Turner, J. (1993). Unemployment, underemployment and depressive affect among Southeast Asian refugees. *Psychological Medicine, 23*, 731–43.

Belsky, J., Steinberg, L., & Draper, P. (1991). Childhood experience, interpersonal development, and reproductive strategy: An evolutionary theory of socialization. *Child Development, 62*, 647–70.

Ben-Ari, R., & Rich, Y. (1997). *Understanding and enhancing education for diverse students*. Ramat Gan: Bar Ilan University Press.

Benedict, R. (1932). Configurations of culture in North America. *American Anthropologist, 34*, 1–27.

(1934). *Patterns of culture*. New York: Mentor.

(1946). *The chrysanthemum and the sword*. Boston, MA: Houghton Mifflin.

Bennett, J. M., Bennett, M. J., & Allen, W. (1999). Developing intercultural competence in the language classroom. In R. M. Paige, D. M. Lange, & Y. A. Yershova (Eds.),

*Culture as the core: Integrating culture into the language curriculum.* CARLA Working Paper 15, 13–45. Minnesota: University of Minnesota.

Bennett, J. W. (1999). Classical anthropology. *American Anthropologist, 100,* 951–6.

Bennett, M. J. (1994). Towards ethnorelativism: A developmental model of intercultural sensitivity. In R. M. Paige (Ed.), *Education for the intercultural experience* (pp. 21–71). Yarmouth, ME: Intercultural Press.

Berk, R. A. (Ed.) (1982). *Handbook of methods for detecting item bias.* Baltimore, MD: Johns Hopkins University Press.

Berlin, B., & Berlin, E. A. (1975). Agueruna color categories. *American Ethnologist, 2,* 61–87.

Berlin, B., & Kay, P. (1969). *Basic color terms: Their universality and evolution.* Berkeley, CA: University of California Press.

Berlyne, D. E. (1960). *Conflict, arousal and curiosity.* New York: McGraw-Hill.

(1971). *Aesthetics and psychobiology.* New York: Appleton-Century-Crofts.

(1975). Extension to Indian subjects of a study of exploratory and verbal responses to visual patterns. *Journal of Cross-Cultural Psychology, 6,* 316–30.

(1980). Psychological aesthetics. In H. C. Triandis & W. J. Lonner (Eds.), *Handbook of cross-cultural psychology* (vol. III, pp. 323–61). Boston, MA: Allyn and Bacon.

Berlyne, D. E., Robbins, M. C., & Thompson, R. (1974). A cross-cultural study of exploratory and verbal responses to visual patterns varying in complexity. In D. E. Berlyne (Ed.), *Studies in the new experimental aesthetics* (pp. 259–78). New York: Wiley.

Bernard, H. (Ed.) (1998). *Handbook of methods in cultural anthropology.* Walnut Creek, CA: Altamira Press.

Berry, J. W. (1966). Temne and Eskimo perceptual skills. *International Journal of Psychology, 1,* 207–29.

(1967). Independence and conformity in subsistence-level societies. *Journal of Personality and Social Psychology, 7,* 415–18.

(1969). On cross-cultural comparability. *International Journal of Psychology, 4,* 119–28.

(1970a). Marginality, stress and identification in an acculturating Aboriginal community. *Journal of Cross-Cultural Psychology, 1,* 239–52.

(1970b). A functional approach to the relationship between stereotypes and familiarity. *Australian Journal of Psychology, 22,* 29–33.

(1971). Müller–Lyer susceptibility: Culture, ecology or race? *International Journal of Psychology, 6,* 193–97.

(1972). Radical cultural relativism and the concept of intelligence. In L. J. Cronbach & P. J. D. Drenth (Eds.), *Mental tests and cultural adaptation* (pp. 77–88). The Hague: Mouton.

(1974a). Canadian psychology: Some social and applied emphases. *Canadian Psychologist, 15,* 132–9.

(1974b). Psychological aspects of cultural pluralism. *Topics in Culture Learning, 2,* 17–22.

(1976a). *Human ecology and cognitive style: Comparative studies in cultural and psychological adaptation.* New York: Sage/Halsted.

(1976b). Sex differences in behaviour and cultural complexity. *Indian Journal of Psychology, 51,* 89–97.

(1978). Social psychology: Comparative, societal and universal. *Canadian Psychological Review, 19,* 93–104.

(1979). A cultural ecology of social behaviour. In L. Berkowitz (Ed.), *Advances in experimental social psychology* (vol. XII, pp. 177–206). New York: Academic Press.

(1980a). Acculturation as varieties of adaptation. In A. Padilla (Ed.), *Acculturation: Theory, models and some new findings* (pp. 9–25). Boulder, CO: Westview.

(1980b). Ecological analyses for cross-cultural psychology. In N. Warren (Ed.), *Studies in cross-cultural psychology* (vol. II, pp. 157–89). London: Academic Press.

(1980c). Social and cultural change. In H. C. Triandis & R. Brislin (Eds.), *Handbook of cross-cultural psychology* (vol. V, pp. 211–79). Boston, MA: Allyn and Bacon.

(1984a). Multicultural policy in Canada: A social psychological analysis. *Canadian Journal of Behavioural Sciences*, *16*, 353–70.

(1984b). Toward a universal psychology of cognitive competence. *International Journal of Psychology*, *19*, 335–61.

(1985). Cultural psychology and ethnic psychology: A comparative analysis. In I. Reyes-Lagunes & Y. H. Poortinga (Eds.), *From a different perspective* (pp. 3–15). Lisse: Swets & Zeitlinger.

(1989). Imposed etics-emics-derived etics: The operationalization of a compelling idea. *International Journal of Psychology*, *24*, 721–35.

(1990a). Psychology of acculturation. In J. Berman (Ed.), *Cross-cultural perspectives: Nebraska Symposium on motivation* (vol. 37, pp. 201–34). Lincoln, NE: University of Nebraska Press.

(1990b). The role of psychology in ethnic studies. *Canadian Ethnic Studies*, *22*, 8–21.

(1991). Cultural variations in field-dependence-independence. In S. Wapner & J. Demick (Eds.), *Field dependence-independence: Cognitive styles across the life span* (pp. 289–308). Hillsdale, NJ: Erlbaum.

(1992). Acculturation and adaptation in a new society. *International Migration*, *30*, 69–85.

(1994). Ecology of individualism–collectivism. In U. Kim et al. (Eds.), *Individualism and collectivism: Theory, method and applications* (pp. 77–84). Thousand Oaks, CA: Sage.

(1997a). Immigration, acculturation and adaptation. *Applied Psychology: An International Review*, *46*, 5–68.

(1997b). Preface. In J. W. Berry, Y. H. Poortinga, & J. Pandey (Eds.), *Theory and method* (pp. x–xv). Vol. I of *Handbook of cross-cultural psychology* (2nd ed.). Bostan, MA: Allyn and Bacon.

(1998a). Cultural and ethnic factors in health. In R. West et al. (Eds.), *Cambridge handbook of psychology, health and medicine* (pp. 84–96). New York: Cambridge University Press.

(1998b). Social psychological costs and benefits of multiculturalism: A view from Canada. *Trames*, *2*, 209–33.

(1999a). Aboriginal cultural identity. *Canadian Journal of Native Studies*, *19*, 1–36.

(1999b). Emics and etics: A symbiotic relationship. *Culture and Psychology*, *5*, 165–71.

(1999c). Intercultural relations in plural societies. *Canadian Psychology*, *40*, 12–21.

(2000a). Cross-cultural psychology: A symbiosis of cultural and comparative approaches. *Asian Journal of Social Psychology*, *3*, 197–205.

(2000b). Whatever happened to cognitive style? *Cross-Cultural Psychology Bulletin*, *33*, 19–23.

(2001a). A psychology of immigration. *Journal of Social Issues*, *57*, 615–31.

(2001b). Interamerican or Unter-American? Invited address. Interamerican Society of Psychology. Santiago, July *Trafficking in intemational psychology*.

Berry, J. W., & Ataca, B. (2000). Cultural factors in stress. In G. Fink (Ed.), *Encyclopedia of stress* (vol. I, pp. 604–11). San Diego: Academic Press.

Berry, J. W., & Bennett, J. A. (1989). Syllabic literacy and cognitive performance among the Cree. *International Journal of Psychology, 24*, 429–50.

(1992). Cree conceptions of cognitive competence. *International Journal of Psychology, 27*, 1–16.

Berry, J. W., & Cavalli-Sforza, L. L. (1986). *Cultural and genetic influences on Inuit art.* Unpublished report.

Berry, J. W., & Dasen, P. (Eds.) (1974). *Culture and cognition.* London: Methuen.

Berry, J. W., & Irvine, S. H. (1986). Bricolage: Savages do it daily. In R. Sternberg & R. Wagner (Eds.), *Practical intelligence: Nature and origins of competence in the everyday world* (pp. 271–306). New York: Cambridge University Press.

Berry, J. W., & Kalin, R. (1979). Reciprocity of inter-ethnic attitudes in a multicultural society. *International Journal of Intercultural Relations, 3*, 99–112.

(1995). Multicultural and ethnic attitudes in Canada: Overview of the 1991 survey. *Canadian Journal of Behavioural Science, 27*, 301–20.

Berry, J. W., & Kim, U. (1988). Acculturation and mental health. In P. Dasen, J. W. Berry, & N. Sartorius (Eds.), *Cross-cultural psychology and health: Towards applications* (pp. 207–36). London: Sage.

(1993). The way ahead: From indigenous psychologies to a universal psychology. In U. Kim & J. W. Berry (Eds.), *Indigenous psychologies* (pp. 277–80). Newbury Park, CA: Sage.

Berry, J. W., & Kostovcik, N. (1990). Psychological adaptation of Malaysian students in Canada. In A. H. Othman & W. R. A. Rahman (Eds.), *Psychology and socio-economic development* (pp. 155–62). Bangi: Penerbit Universiti Kebangsaan Malaysia.

Berry, J. W., & Sam, D. (1997). Acculturation and adaptation. In J. W. Berry, M. H. Segall, & C. Kagitcibasi (Eds.), *Social behavior and applications* (pp. 291–326). Vol. III of *Handbook of cross-cultural psychology.* (2nd ed.). Boston, MA: Allyn and Bacon.

Berry, J. W., & Wilde, G. J. S. (Eds.) (1972). *Social psychology: The Canadian context.* Toronto: McLelland & Stewart.

Berry, J. W., Dalal, A., & Pande, N. (1994). *Disability attitudes, beliefs and behaviors: A cross-cultural study.* Kingston: International Centre for Community-Based Rehabilitation.

Berry, J. W., Dasen, P. R., & Saraswathi, T. S. (Eds.) (1997). *Basic processes and human development.* Vol. II of *Handbook of cross-cultural psychology* (2nd ed.). Boston, MA: Allyn and Bacon.

Berry, J. W., Irvine, S. H., & Hunt, E. B. (Eds.) (1988). *Indigenous cognition: Functioning in cultural context.* Dordrecht: Nijhoff.

Berry, J. W., Kalin, R., & Taylor, D. (1977). *Multiculturalism and ethnic attitudes in Canada.* Ottawa: Supply and Services.

Berry, J. W., Kim, U., Minde, T., & Mok, D. (1987). Comparative studies of acculturative stress. *International Migration Review, 21*, 491–511.

Berry, J. W., Kim, U., Power, S., Young, M., & Bujaki, M. (1989). Acculturation attitudes in plural societies. *Applied Psychology, 38*, 185–206.

Berry, J. W., Lonner, W. J., & Leroux, J. (Eds.) (1973). *Directory of cross-cultural research and researchers.* Bellingham, WA: Center for Cross-Cultural Research.

Berry, J. W., Poortinga, Y. H., & Pandey, J. (Eds.). (1997). *Theory and method*. Vol. I of *Handbook of cross-cultural psychology* (2nd ed.). Boston, MA: Allyn and Bacon.

Berry, J. W., Segall, M. H., & Kagitcibasi, C. (Eds.) (1997). *Social behavior and applications*. Vol. III of *Handbook of cross-cultural psychology* (2nd ed.). Boston, MA: Allyn and Bacon.

Berry, J. W., van de Koppel, J. M. H., Sénéchal, C., Annis, R. C., Bahuchet, S., Cavalli-Sforza, L. L., & Witkin, H. A. (1986). *On the edge of the forest: Cultural adaptation and cognitive development in Central Africa*. Lisse, Netherlands: Swets & Zeitlinger.

Bertino, M., Beauchamp, G. K., & Jen, K. C. (1983). Rated taste perception in two cultural groups. *Chemical Senses*, *8*, 3–15.

Best, D. L., & Ruther, N. M. (1994). Cross-cultural themes in developmental psychology: An examination of texts, handbooks, and reviews. *Journal of Cross-Cultural Psychology*, *25*, 54–77.

Beveridge, W. M. (1935). Racial differences in phenomenal regression. *British Journal of Psychology*, *26*, 59–62.

(1940). Some differences in racial perception. *British Journal of Psychology*, *30*, 57–64.

Bhagat, R. S., & McQuaid, S. J. (1982). Role of subjective culture in organizations: A review and directions for future research. *Journal of Applied Psychology*, *67*, 653–85.

Biesheuvel, S. (1943). *African Intelligence*. Johannesburg: South African Institute of Race Relations.

(1954). The measurement of occupational aptitudes in a multi-racial society. *Occupational Psychology*, *18*, 189–96.

(1972). Adaptability: its measurement and determinants. In L. J. Cronbach & P. J. D. Drenth (Eds.), *Mental tests and cultural adaption* (pp. 47–62). The Hague: Mouton.

Billiez, J. (Ed). (1998). *De la didactique des langues à la didactique du plurilinguisme*. Grenoble: Université Stendhal, CDL-LIDILEM.

Billig, M. (1987). *Arguing and thinking: A rhetorical approach to social psychology*. Cambridge: Cambridge University Press/Paris: Editions de la Maison des Sciences de l'Homme.

Binnendijk, H. (Ed.) (1987). *National negotiating styles*. Washington, DC: Foreign Service Institute.

Birdwhistell, R. L. (1970). *Kinesics and context*. Philadelphia, PA: University of Philadelphia Press.

Birman, D. (1994). Acculturation and human diversity in a multicultural society. In E. Trickett, R. Watts, & D. Birman (Eds.), *Human diversity* (pp. 261–84). San Francisco, CA: Jossey-Bass.

Blackler, F. (Ed.) (1983). *Social psychology and developing countries*. Chichester: Wiley.

Blake, B. F., Heslin, R., & Curtis, S. C. (1996). Measuring impacts of cross-cultural training. In D. Landis & R. S. Bhagat (Eds.), *Handbook of intercultural training* (2nd ed., pp. 61–80). Thousand Oaks, CA: Sage.

Blake, R. R., & Mouton, J. S. (1964). *The managerial grid*. Houston, TX: Gulf Publishing.

Bleichrodt, N., & Van de Vijver, F. J. R. (Eds.) (2001). *Diagnostiek bij allochtonen* [Diagnostics with allochthonous peoples]. Lisse, Netherlands: Swets & Zeitlinger.

Bleichrodt, N., Drenth, P. J. D., & Querido, A. (1980). Effects of iodine deficiency on mental and psychomotor abilities. *American Journal of Physical Anthropology*, *53*, 55–67.

Bloom, A. (1981). *The linguistic shaping of thought: A study in the impact of language on thinking in China and the West.* Hillsdale, NJ: Erlbaum.

Blowers, G., & Turtle, A. (1987). *Psychology moving East.* Sydney: Sydney University Press.

Blum-Kulka, S., House, J., & Kasper, G. (1988). Investigating cross-cultural pragmatics: An introductory overview. In S. Blum-Kulka, J. House, & G. Kasper (Eds.), *Cross-cultural pragmatics: Requests and apologies* (pp. 1–34). Norwood, NJ: Ablex.

Boas, F. (1911). *The mind of primitive man.* New York: Macmillan.

Bochner, S. (1986). Observational methods. In W. J. Lonner & J. W. Berry (Eds.), *Field methods in cross-cultural research* (pp. 165–201). London: Sage.

Bochner, S. (Ed.) (1982). *Cultures in contact: Studies in cross-cultural interaction.* Oxford: Pergamon.

Bock, P. K. (1980). *Continuities in psychological anthropology: An historical introduction.* San Francisco, CA: Freeman.

(1988). *Rethinking psychological anthropology: Continuity and change in the study of human action.* New York: Freeman.

Bock, P. K. (Ed.) (1994). *Handbook of psychological anthropology.* Westport, CT: Greenwood.

Boesch, C. (1991). Teaching among wild chimpanzees. *Animal Behavior, 41,* 530–2.

(1993). Aspects of transmission in wild chimpanzees. In K. Gibson & T. Ingold (Eds.), *Tools, language and cognition in human evolution* (pp. 171–83). Cambridge: Cambridge University Press.

(1995). Innovation in wild chimpanzees (*Pan troglodytes*). *International Journal of Primatology, 16,* 1–16.

Boesch, E. E. (1976). *Psychopathologie des Alltags* [Psychopathology of everyday]. Berne: Huber.

(1980). *Kultur und Handlung* [Culture and action]. Berne: Huber Verlag.

(1986). Science, culture and development. In M. Gottstein & G. Link (Eds.), *Cultural development, science and technology in Sub-Saharan Africa* (pp. 19–29). Berlin: German Foundation for International Development.

(1991). *Symbolic action theory and cultural psychology.* Berlin: Springer-Verlag.

(1996). The seven flaws of cross-cultural psychology: The story of a conversion. *Mind, Culture and Activity, 3,* 2–10.

Bohnemeyer, J. (1998). *Time relations in discourse: Evidence from a comparative approach to Yukatek Maya.* Wageningen, Netherlands: Ponsen and Looijen.

Boldt, E. D. (1978). Structural tightness and cross-cultural research. *Journal of Cross-Cultural Psychology, 9,* 151–65.

Bolinger, D. (1978). Intonation across languages. In J. H. Greenberg (Ed.), *Universals of human language* (vol. II, pp. 471–524). Stanford, CA: Stanford University Press.

Bond, M. H. (1983). How language variation affects inter-cultural differentiation of values by Hong Kong bilinguals. *Journal of Language and Social Psychology, 2,* 57–76.

(1999). Unity in diversity: Orientations and strategies for building a harmonious multicultural society. In J. Adamopoulus & Y. Kashima (Eds.), *Social psychology and cultural context* (pp. 17–39). Thousand Oaks, CA: Sage.

Bond, M. H. (Ed.) (1986). *The psychology of the Chinese people.* Hong Kong: Oxford University Press.

(1988). *The cross-cultural challenge to social psychology.* Newbury Park, CA: Sage.

(1996). *The handbook of Chinese psychology.* Hong Kong: Oxford University Press.

Bond, R., & Smith, P. B. (1996). Culture and conformity: A meta-analysis of studies using Asch's line judgement task. *Psychological Bulletin*, *119*, 111–37.

Bontempo, R. N., Bottom, W. P., & Weber, E. U. (1997). Cross-cultural differences in risk perception: A model-based approach. *Risk Analysis*, *17*, 479–88.

Boorstin, D. J. (1985). *The discoverers*. New York: Vintage Books.

Born, M., Bleichrodt, N., & Van der Flier, H. (1987). Cross-cultural comparison of sex-related differences on intelligence tests: A meta-analysis. *Journal of Cross-Cultural Psychology*, *18*, 283–314.

Bornstein, M. H. (1973). Colour vision and colour naming: A psychophysiological hypothesis of cultural differences. *Psychological Bulletin*, *80*, 257–85.

(1991). *Cultural approaches to parenting*. Hillsdale, NJ: Erlbaum.

(1994). Cross-cultural perspectives on parenting. In G. d'Ydewalle, P. Eelen, & P. Bertelson (Eds.), *International perspectives on psychological science* (vol. II, pp. 359–69). Hove, UK: Erlbaum.

(1997). Selective vision. *Behavioral and Brain Sciences*, *20*, 180–1.

Bornstein, M. H., Kessen, W. H., & Weiskopf, S. (1976). The categories of hue in infancy. *Science*, *191*, 201–2.

Bornstein, M. H., Tal, J., Rahn, C., Galperín, C. Z., Pêcheux, M.-G., Lamour, M., Toda, S., Azuma, H., Ogino, M., & Tamis-LeMonda, C. S. (1992). Functional analysis of the contents of maternal speech to infants of 5 and 13 months in four cultures: Argentina, France, Japan and the United States. *Developmental Psychology*, *28*, 593–603.

Bouchard, T. J., McGue, M., Hur, Y.-M., & Horn, J. M. (1998). A genetic analysis of the California Psychological Inventory using adult twins reared apart and together. *European Journal of Personality*, *12*, 307–320.

Boucher, J. D., & Carlson, G. E. (1980). Recognition of facial expression in three cultures. *Journal of Cross-Cultural Psychology*, *11*, 263–80.

Bourguignon, E. (1976). *Possession*. Corte Madera, CA: Chandler and Sharp.

(1979). *Psychological anthropology: An introduction to human nature and cultural differences*. New York: Holt, Rinehart and Winston.

(1984). Belief and behaviour in Haitian folk healing. In P. Pedersen, N. Sartorius, & A. Marsella (Eds.), *Mental health services: The cross-cultural context* (pp. 243–66). London: Sage.

Bourguignon, E., & Evascu, T. (1977). Altered states of consciousness within a general evolutionary perspective: A holocultural analysis. *Behavior Science Research*, *12*, 197–216.

Bourhis, R., Moise, C., Perreault, S., & Senecal, S. (1997). Towards an interactive acculturation model: A social psychological approach. *International Journal of Psychology*, *32*, 369–386.

Bowerman, M. (1996). The origins of children's spatial semantic categories: Cognitive versus linguistic determinants. In J. J. Gumperz & S. C. Levinson (Eds.), *Rethinking linguistic relativity* (pp. 145–202). Cambridge: Cambridge University Press.

Bowlby, J. (1969). *Attachment and loss*. Vol. I: *Attachment*. New York: Basic Books.

Boyd, R., & Richerson, P. J. (1985). *Culture and the evolutionary process*. Chicago: the University of Chicago Press.

Bradshaw, J. L., & Nettleton, N. C. (1981). The nature of hemispheric specialization in man. *Behavioral and Brain Sciences*, *4*, 51–91.

Bragg, B. W. E., & Crozier, J. B. (1974). The development with age of verbal exploratory responses to sound sequences varying in uncertainty level. In D. E. Berlyne (Ed.), *Studies in the new experimental aesthetics* (pp. 91–108). Washington, DC: Hemisphere Publishing Corporation.

Brandt, M. E., & Boucher, J. D. (1985). Judgements of emotions from antecedent situations in three cultures. In I. Reyes Lagunes & Y H. Poortinga (Eds.), *From a different perspective: Studies of behaviour across cultures* (pp. 348–62). Lisse, Netherlands: Swets & Zeitlinger.

Brazelton, T. B. (1973). *Neonatal behavioural assessment scale*. London: National Spastics Society.

Breakwell, G., & Lyons, E. (Eds.) (1996). *Changing European identities*. Oxford: Butterworth-Heinemann.

Brein, M., & David, K. H. (1971). Intercultural communication and the adjustment of the sojourner. *Psychological Bulletin, 76*, 215–30.

Brettell, C., & Sargent, C. (Eds.) (1993). *Gender in cross-cultural perspective*. Englewood Cliffs, NJ: Prentice-Hall.

Brewer, M. (1991). The social self: On being the same and different at the same time. *Personality and Social Psychology Bulletin, 17*, 475–82.

Brewer, M., & Campbell, D. T. (1976). *Ethnocentrism and intergroup attitudes: East African evidence*. London: Sage.

Bril, B., & Lehalle, H. (1988). *Le développement psychologique: Est-il universel? Approches interculturelles*. Paris: Presses Universitaires de France.

Bril, B., & Sabatier, C. (1986). The cultural context of motor development: Postural manipulations in the daily life of Bambara babies (Mali). *International Journal of Behavioural Development, 9*, 439–43.

Bril, B., & Zack, M. (1989). Analyse comparative de l''emploi du temps postural' de la naissance à la marche. In J. Retschitzki, M. Bossel-Lagos, & P. R. Dasen (Eds.), *La recherche interculturelle*. Paris: L'Harmattan.

Brislin, R. W. (1974). The Ponzo illusion: Additional cues, age, orientation and culture. *Journal of Cross-Cultural Psychology, 5*, 139–61.

   (1980). Translation and content analysis of oral and written material. In H. C. Triandis & J. W. Berry (Eds.), *Handbook of cross-cultural psychology* (vol. II, pp. 389–444). Boston, MA: Allyn and Bacon.

   (1986). The wording and translation of research instruments. In W. J. Lonner & J. W. Berry (Eds.), *Field methods in cross-cultural research* (pp. 137–64). Beverly Hills, CA: Sage.

   (1997). *Understanding culture's influence on behavior* (2nd ed.). Fort Worth, TX: Harcourt.

Brislin, R. W. (Ed.) (1976). *Translation: Applications and research*. New York: John Wiley/Halsted.

Brislin, R. W., & Horvath, A.-M. (1997). Cross-cultural training and multicultural education. In J. W. Berry, M. H. Segall, & C. Kagikibasi (eds.), *Social behavior and applications* (pp. 327–69). Vol. III of *Handbook of cross-cultural psychology* (2nd ed.). Boston, MA: Allyn and Bacon.

Brislin, R. W., & Keating, C. (1976). Cross-cultural differences in the perception of a three-dimensional Ponzo illusion. *Journal of Cross-Cultural Psychology, 7*, 397–411.

Brislin, R. W., Cushner, K., Cherrie, C., & Yong, M. (1986). *Intercultural interactions: A practical guide*. Beverly Hills, CA: Sage.

Brislin, R. W., Lonner, W. J., & Thorndike, R. M. (1973). *Cross-cultural research methods*. New York: Wiley.

Brislin, R. W., & Yoshida, T. (Eds.) (1994). *Improving intercultural interactions: Modules for cross-cultural training programs*. Thousand Oaks, CA: Sage.

Brodbeck, F. C. et al. (2000). Cultural variation of leadership protoypes across 22 European countries. *Journal of Occupational and Organizational Psychology, 73*, 1–29.

Bronfenbrenner, U. (1979). *The ecology of human development*. Cambridge, MA: Harvard University Press.

Bronfenbrenner, U., & Ceci, S. J. (1994). Nature–nurture reconceptualized in developmental perspective: A bioecological model. *Psychological Review, 101*, 568–86.

Browne, J. P., O'Boyle, C. A., McGhee, H. M., Joyce, C. R. B., et al. (1994). Individual quality of life in the healthy elderly. *Quality of Life Research, 3*, 235–44.

Brown, P., & Levinson, S. C. (1987). *Politeness: Some universals in language use*. Cambridge: Cambridge University Press.

Brown, R. (1965). *Social psychology*. New York: Free Press.

Brown, R., & Gaertner, S. (Eds.) (2000). *Blackwell handbook of social psychology*. Vol. IV: *Intergroup processes*. Oxford: Blackwell.

Brown, R. W., & Lenneberg, E. H. (1954). A study of language and cognition. *Journal of Abnormal and Social Psychology, 49*, 454–62.

Brumann, C. (1999). Writing for culture: Why a successful concept should not be discarded. *Current Anthropology, 40*, 1–13.

Brunet, O., & Lézine, I. (1951; 3rd ed., 1971). *Le développement psychologique de la première enfance* [Psychological development in earliest infancy]. Paris: Presses Universitaires de France.

Brunswik, E. (1956). *Perception and the representative design of psychological experiments*. Berkeley, CA: University of California Press.

(1957). Scope and aspects of the cognition problem. In A. Gruber (Ed.), *Cognition: The Colorado Symposium*. Cambridge, MA: Harvard University Press.

Bullivant, B. (1985). Educating the pluralist person: Images of society and educational responses in Australia. In M. Poole, P. deLacey, & B. Randhawa (Eds.), *Australia in transition: Culture and life possibilities*. Sydney: Harcourt, Brace, Jovanovich.

Burridge, K. (1979). *Someone, no one: An essay on individuality*. Princeton, NJ: Princeton University Press.

Buss, D. M. (1989). Sex differences in human mate preferences: Evolutionary hypotheses tested in 37 cultures. *Behavioral and Brain Sciences, 12*, 1–49.

(1995). Evolutionary psychology: A new paradigm for psychological science. *Psychological Inquiry, 6*, 1–30.

Buss, D. M. et al. (1990). International preference in selecting mates. *Journal of Cross-Cultural Psychology, 21*, 5–47.

Buss, D. M., Haselton, M. G., Shackelford, T. K., Bleske, A. L., & Wakefield, J. C. (1998). Adaptations, exaptations and spandrels. *American Psychologist, 53*, 533–48.

Butcher, J. N. (Ed.) (1996). *International adaptations of the MMPI-2: Research and clinical applications*. Minneapolis, MN: University of Minnesota Press.

Butcher, J. N., & Pancheri, P. (1976). *A handbook of cross-national MMPI research*. Minneapolis, MN: University of Minneapolis Press.

Butcher, J. N. Lim, J., & Nezami, E. (1998). Objective study of abnormal personality in cross-cultural settings: The Minnesota Multiphasic Personality Inventory (MMPI-2). *Journal of Cross-Cultural Psychology, 29*, 189–211.

Byrne, B. M., & Campbell, T. L. (1999). Cross-cultural comparisons and the presumption of equivalent measurement and theoretical structure: A look beneath the surface. *Journal of Cross-Cultural Psychology*, *30*, 555–74.

Cacioppo, J. T., & Tassinary, L. G. (1990). Inferring psychological significance from physiological signals. *American Psychologist*, *45*, 16–28.

Calori, R., & Sarnin, P. (1991). Corporate culture and economic performance: A French study. *Organization Studies*, *12*, 49–74.

Camilleri, C. (1986). *Anthropologie culturelle et éducation* [Cultural anthropology and education]. Lausanne: Dalachaux and Nestlé.

(1991). La construction identitaire. *Les Cahiers Internationaux de Psychologie Sociale*, *9–10*, 91–104.

Camilleri, C., & Malewska-Peyre, H. (1997). Socialization and identity strategies. In J. W. Berry, P. R. Dasen, & T. S. Saraswathi (Eds.), *Basic processes and human development* (pp. 41–68). Vol. III of *Handbook of cross-cultural psychology* (2nd ed.). Boston, MA: Allyn and Bacon.

Camilleri, C., & Vinsonneau, G. (1996). *Psychologie et culture: Concepts et methodes* [Psychology and culture: Concepts and methods]. Paris: Armand Colin/Masson.

Campbell, D. T. (1957). Factors relevant to the validity of experiments in social settings. *Psychological Bulletin*, *54*, 297–312.

(1969). Reforms as experiments. *American Psychologist*, *24*, 409–29.

(1970). Natural selection as an epistemological model. In R. Naroll & R. Cohen (Eds.), *A handbook of method in cultural anthropology* (pp. 51–85). New York: Natural History Press.

(1974). Evolutionary epistemology. In P. A. Schilpp (Ed.), *The philosophy of Karl Popper* (pp. 413–63). La Salle, IL: Open Court Publishers.

(1975). On the conflicts between biological and social evolution and between psychology and moral tradition. *American Psychologist*, *30*, 1103–26.

(1988). Evolutionary epistemology. In E. S. Overman (Ed.), *Methodology and epistomology for social science: Selected papers of Donald T. Campbell* (pp. 393–434). Chicago, IL: University of Chicago Press.

Campbell, D. T., & Fiske, D. W. (1959). Convergent and discriminant validation by the multitrait-multimethod matrix. *Psychological Bulletin*, *56*, 81–105.

Campbell, N. C. G., Graham, J. L., Jolibert, A., & Meissner, H. G. (1988). Marketing negotiations in France, Germany, the United Kingdom and the United States. *Journal of Marketing*, *52*, 49–62.

Cann, R. L., Stoneking, M., & Wilson, A. C. (1987). Mitochondrial DNA and human evolution. *Nature*, *325*, 31–36.

Cantor, D. (Ed.) (1985). *Facet theory: Approaches to social research*. New York: Springer.

Cantor, N. & Mischel. W. (1977). Traits as prototypes: Effects on recognition memory. *Journal of Personality and Social Psychology*, *35*, 38–48.

(1979). Prototypes in person perception. In L. Berkowitz (Ed.), *Advances in Experimental Social Psychology* (vol. XII, pp. 3–52). New York: Academic Press.

Carballo, M. (1994). *Scientific consultation on the social and health impact of migration: Priorities for research*. Geneva: International Organization for Migration.

Carlson, J. A., & Davis, C. M. (1971). Cultural values and the risky-shift: A cross-cultural test in Uganda and the United States. *Journal of Personality and Social Psychology*, *20*, 392–9.

Carr, M., Kurtz, B. E., Schneider, W., Turner, L., & Borkowski, J. G. (1989). Strategy acquisition and transfer among American and German children: Environmental influences on metacognitive development. *Developmental Psychology, 25,* 765–71.

Carr, S., & MacLachlan, M. (1998). Psychology in developing countries: Reassessing its impact. *Psychology and Developing Societies, 10,* 1–20.

Carrithers, M., Collins, S., & Lukes, S. (Eds.) (1985). *The category of the person: Anthropology, philosophy, and history.* Cambridge: Cambridge University Press.

Carroll, D., & Smith, G. (1997). Health and socio-economic position. *Journal of Health Psychology, 2,* 275–82.

Carroll, J. B. (1993). *Human cognitive abilities: A survey of factor-analytic studies.* Cambridge: Cambridge University Press.

Carroll, J. B., & Casagrande, J. B. (1958). The function of language classifications in behavior. In E. Maccoby, T. Newcomb, & E. L. Hartley (Eds.), *Readings in social psychology* (3rd ed, pp. 18–31). New York: Holt, Rinehart & Winston.

Case, R. (1985). *Intellectual development: Birth to adulthood.* New York: Academic Press.

Case, R. (Ed.) (1992). *The mind's staircase: Exploring the conceptual underpinnings of children's thought and knowledge.* Hillsdale, NJ: Lawrence Erlbaum.

Case, R., & Griffin, S. (1990). Child cognitive development: The role of central conceptual structure in the development of scientific and social thought. In C. A. Hauert (Ed.), *Developmental psychology* (pp. 193–230). Amsterdam: North-Holland/Elsevier.

Cattell, R. B. (1965). *Scientific analysis of personality.* Harmondsworth: Penguin Books.

Cattell, R. B., Eber, H. W., & Tatsuoka, M. (1970). *The handbook for the Sixteen Personality factors questionnaire.* Champaign, IL: Institute for Personality and Ability Testing.

Cavalli-Sforza, L. L., & Bodmer, W. (1971). *The genetics of human populations.* New York: Freeman.

Cavalli-Sforza, L. L., & Feldman, M. (1981). *Cultural transmission and evolution: A quantitative approach.* Princeton, NJ: Princeton University Press.

Cavalli-Sforza, L. L., Menozzi, P., & Piazza, A. (1994). *The history and geography of human genes.* Princeton, NJ: Princeton University Press.

Ceci, S. J., Rosenblum, T., De Bruyn, E., & Lee, D. Y. (1997). A bio-ecological model of intellectual development: Moving beyond $h^2$. In R. J. Sternberg & E. Grigorenko (Eds.), *Intelligence, heredity, and environment* (pp. 303–22). Cambridge: Cambridge University Press.

Ceci, S. J., & Williams, W. (Eds.) (1999). *The nature–nurture debate.* Oxford: Blackwell.

Cervone, D., & Shoda, Y. (Eds.) (1999). *The coherence of personality: Social-cognitive bases of consistency, variability, and organization.* New York: Guilford Press.

Chamberlain, K. (1997). Socioeconomic health differentials: From structure to experience. *Journal of Health Psychology, 2,* 399–412.

Chan, S. fF. (2000). Formal logic and dialectical thinking are not incongruent. *American Psychologist, 55,* 1063–64.

Charmaz, K. (1995). Grounded theory. In J. A. Smith, R. Harré, & L. Van Langenhove (Eds.), *Rethinking methods in psychology* (pp. 27–49). London: Sage.

Chasiotis, A. (1999). *Kindheit und Lebenslauf: Untersuchungen zur evolutionären Psychologie der Lebensspanne* [Childhood and life course: Investigations into the evolutionary psychology of the lifespan]. Berne: Huber.

Chen, L., Rahman, M., & Sardar, A. (1980). Epidemiology and causes of death among children in a rural area of Bangladesh. *International Journal of Epidemiology, 9,* 25–33.

Chen, M. J., & Lin, Z. X. (1994). Chinese preschoolers' difficulty with theory-of-mind tests. *Bulletin of the Hong Kong Psychological Society*, *32/33*, 34–46.

Cheung, F. M., & Leung, K. (1998). Indigenous personality measures: Chinese examples. *Journal of Cross-Cultural Psychology*, *29*, 233–48.

Child, I. L. (1954). Socialization. In G. Lindzey (Ed.), *Handbook of social psychology* (vol. II, pp. 655–92). Cambridge, MA: Addison-Wesley.

  (1969). Esthetics. In G. Lindzey & E. Aronson (Eds.), *The handbook of social psychology* (vol. III, pp. 853–916). Reading, MA: Addison Wesley.

Child, J. (1981). Culture, contingency and capitalism in the cross-national study of organizations. In L. L. Cummings & B. M. Staw (Eds.), *Research in organizational behavior* (vol. III, pp. 303–56). Greenwich, CT: JAI Press.

Chinese Culture Connection (1987). Chinese values and the search for culture-free dimensions of culture. *Journal of Cross-Cultural Psychology*, *18*, 143–64.

Ching, C. C. (1984). Psychology and the four modernizations in China. *International Journal of Psychology*, *19*, 57–63.

Chodzinski, R. T. (1984). Counselling ethnic minorities. In R. Samuda, J. W. Berry, & M. Laferrière (Eds.), *Multiculturalism in Canada: Social and educational perspectives*. Toronto: Allyn and Bacon.

Choi, I., Nisbett, R., & Norenzayan, A. (1999). Causal attribution across cultures: Variation and universality. *Psychological Bulletin*, *125*, 47–63.

Chomsky, N. (1965). *Aspects of a theory of syntax*. Cambridge, MA: MIT Press.

  (1980). *Rules and representations*. Oxford: Blackwell.

  (2000). *New horizons in the study of language*. Cambridge: Cambridge University Press.

Church, A. T. (1982). Sojourner adjustment. *Psychological Bulletin*, *91*, 540–72.

  (2000). Culture and personality: Towards an integrated cultural trait psychology. *Journal of Personality*, *68*, 651–703.

Cissé, Y. (1973). Signes graphiques, représentations, concepts et tests relatifs à la personne chez les Malinka et les Bambasa du Mali [Graphic signs, representations, concepts and tests relative to personality among the Malinka and the Bambasa of Mali]. In Colloques Internationaux, *La notion de Personne en Afrique Noire* [The idea of the person in black Africa]. Paris: Editions du CNRS.

Clark, R., Anderson, N., Clark, V. R., & Williams, D. R. (1999). Racism as a stressor for African Americans: A biopsychosocial model. *American Psychologist*, *54*, 805–16.

Clarke, J., & Tabah, L. (Eds.) (1995). *Population–environment–development interactions*. Paris: CICRED.

Cohen, J. (1988). *Statistical power analysis for the behavioural sciences* (2nd ed.). Hillsdale, NJ: Erlbaum.

  (1994). "The earth is round (p< .05)". *American Psychologist*, *49*, 997–1003.

Cohen, R. (1970). Entry into the field. In R. Naroll & R. Cohen (Eds.), *Handbook of method in cultural anthropology* (pp. 220–45). New York: Natural History Press.

  (1987). Problems of intercultural communication in Egyptian-American diplomatic relations. *International Journal of Intercultural Relations*, *11*, 29–47.

Cole, M. (1975). An ethnographic psychology of cognition. In R. Brislin, S. Bochner, & W. Lonner (Eds.), *Cross-cultural perspectives on learning* (pp. 157–75). Beverly Hills, CA: Sage.

  (1988). Cross-cultural research in the sociohistorical tradition. *Human Development*, *31*, 137–57.

(1992a). Culture in development. In M. H. Bornstein & M. Lamb (Eds.), *Developmental psychology: An advanced textbook* (3rd ed., pp. 731–89). Hillsdale, NJ: Erlbaum.

(1992b). Context, modularity and the cultural constitution of development. In L. Winegar & J. Valsiner (Eds.), *Childrens' development within social contexts* (vol. II, pp. 5–31). Hillsdale, NJ: Erlbaum.

(1996). *Cultural psychology: A once and future discipline*. Cambridge, MA: Belknap.

Cole, M., & Scribner, S. (1974). *Culture and thought*. New York: Wiley.

(1977). Developmental theories applied to cross-cultural cognitive research. *Annals of the New York Academy of Sciences*, *285*, 366–73.

Cole, M., Gay, G., & Glick, J. (1968). A cross-cultural study of information processing. *International Journal of Psychology*, *3*, 93–102.

Cole, M., Gay, J., Glick, J., & Sharp, D. (1971). *The cultural context of learning and thinking*. New York: Basic Books.

Cook, P. (1994). Chronic illness beliefs and the role of social networks among Chinese, Indian and Angloceltic Canadians. *Journal of Cross-Cultural Psychology*, *25*, 452–65.

(1996). The application of an ecocultural framework to the study of disability programs in a rural and urban Indian community. In H. Grad, A. Blanco, & J. Georgas (Eds.), *Key issues in cross-cultural psychology* (pp. 355–70). Lisse, Netherlands: Swets & Zeitlinger.

Cook, T. D., & Campbell, D. T. (1979). *Quasi-experimentation: Design and analysis issues for field settings*. Chicago: Rand McNally.

Cooper, J. E., Kendell, R. E., Gurland, B. J., Sharpe, L., Copeland, J. R. M., & Simon, R. (1972). *Psychiatric diagnosis in New York and London*. London: Oxford University Press.

Costa, P. T., Jr, & McCrae, R. R. (1992). *Revised NEO Personality Inventory (NEO-PI-R) and NEO Five Factor Inventory (NEO-FFM) professional manual*. Odessa, FL: Psychological Assessment Resources.

(1994). "Set like plaster": Evidence for the stability of adult personality. In T. Heatherington & J. Weinberger (Eds.), *Can personality change?* (pp. 21–140). Washington, DC: American Psychological Association.

Cote, J. (1994). *Adolescent storm and stress: An examination of the Mead/Freeman controversy*. Hillsdale, NJ: Lawrence Erlbaum.

Cousins, S. (1989). Culture and selfhood in Japan and the US. *Journal of Personality and Social Psychology*, *56*, 124–31.

Creswell, J. W. (1998). *Qualitative inquiry and research design: Choosing among five traditions*. Thousand Oaks, CA: Sage.

Cronbach, L. J., Gleser, G. C., Nanda, H., & Rajaratnam, N. (1972). *The dependability of behavioral measurements*. New York: Wiley.

Cumming, P., Lee, E., & Oreopoulos, D. (1989). *Access to trades and professions*. Toronto: Ontario Ministry of Citizenship.

Cushner, K. (1989). Assessing the impact of a culture-general assimilator. *International Journal of Intercultural Relations*, *13*, 125–46.

Dabbs, J. M., & Morris, R. (1990). Testosterone, social class and antisocial behavior in a sample of 4,462 men. *Psychological Science*, *1*, 209–11.

Dacyl, J., & Westin, C. (Eds.) (2000). *Governance of cultural diversity*. Stockholm: CEIFO.

Dalal, A. (Ed.) (2000). Indigenous health beliefs and practices. *Psychology and Developing Societies*, *12(1)*, 1–103.

Daly, M., & Wilson, M. (1983). *Evolution and behavior* (2nd ed.). Boston, MA: Willard Grant Press.

D'Andrade, R. (1994). Introduction: John Whiting and anthropology. In E. Chasdi (Ed.), *Culture and human development: The selected papers of John Whiting* (pp. 1–13). New York: Cambridge University Press.

(1995). *The development of cognitive anthropology.* Cambridge: Cambridge University Press.

Darwin, C. (1998). *The expression of the emotions in man and animal* (3rd ed.). London Harper & Collins (1st ed., 1872).

Dasen, P. R. (1972). Cross-cultural Piagetian research: A summary. *Journal of Cross-Cultural Psychology, 7,* 75–85.

(1984). The cross-cultural study of intelligence: Piaget and the Baoulé. *International Journal of Psychology, 19,* 407–34.

(1988). Les activités quotidiennes d'enfants africains dans leur contexte naturel: La méthode des observations ponctuelles [The daily activities of African children in their natural setting: The method for precise observation]. *Enfance, 41,* 3–24.

(1998). Cadres théoriques en psychologie interculturelle [Theoretical frameworks in intercultural psychology]. In J. G. Adair, D. Bélanger, & K. L. Dion (Eds.), *Advances in psychological science. Vol. I : Social, personal, and cultural aspects* (pp. 205–27). Hove, UK: Psychology Press.

(1999). Représentations sociales de l'adolescence: Une perspective interculturelle. In B. Bril, P. R. Dasen, C. Sabatier, & B. Krewer (Eds.), *Propos sur l'enfant et l'adolescent: Quels enfants pour quelles cultures?* [Remarks on children and adolescents: Which children for which cultures?] (pp. 319–38). Paris: L'Harmattan.

(2000). Rapid social change and the turmoil of adolescence: A cross-cultural perspective. *International Journal of Group Tensions, 29,* 17–50.

Dasen, P. R., & de Ribaupierre, A. (1987). Neo-Piagetian theories: Cross-cultural and differential perspectives. *International Journal of Psychology, 22,* 793–832.

Dasen, P. R., & Heron, A. (1981). Cross-cultural tests of Piaget's theory. In H. C. Triandis & A. Heron (Eds.), *Handbook of cross-cultural psychology. Vol. IV: Developmental psychology* (pp. 295–342). Boston, MA: Allyn and Bacon.

Dasen, P. R., & Mishra, R. C. (2000). Cross-cultural views on human development in the third millennium. *International Journal of Behavioral Development, 24,* 428–34.

Dasen, P. R., & Super, C. M. (1988). The usefulness of a cross-cultural approach in studies of malnutrition and psychological development. In P. R. Dasen, J. W. Berry, & N. Sartorius (Eds.), *Health and cross-cultural psychology: Towards applications* (pp. 112–38). Newbury Park, CA: Sage.

Dasen, P. R., Berry, J. W., & Sartorius, N. (Eds.) (1988). *Cross-Cultural psychology and health: Towards applications.* Newbury Park, CA: Sage.

Dasen, P. R., Berry, J. W., & Witkin, H. A. (1979). The use of developmental theories cross-culturally, In L. H. Eckensberger, W. J. Lonner, & Y. H. Poortinga (Eds.), *Cross-cultural contributions to psychology* (pp. 69–82). Lisse, Netherlands: Swets and Zeitlinger.

Dasen, P. R., Dembele, B., Ettien, K., Kabran, K., Kamagaté, D., Koffi, D. A., & N'Guessan, A. (1985). N'glouló, l'intelligence chez les Baoulé. *Archives de Psychologie, 53,* 293–324.

Dasen, P. R., Inhelder, B., Lavallée, M., & Retschitzki, J. (1978). *Naissance de l'intelligence chez l'enfant Baoulé de Côte d'Ivoire* [The birth of intelligence among Baoulé children in the Ivory Coast]. Berne: Hans Huber.

Dasen, P. R., Mishra, R. C., & Niraula, S. (2000). *Ecology, language, and performance on spatial cognitive tasks*. Paper presented at the XVth congress of the IACCP, Pultusk, Poland, July 16–21.

Dasen, P. R., Ngini, L., & Lavallée, M. (1979). Cross-cultural training studies of concrete operations. In L. H. Eckensberger, W. J. Lonner, & Y. H. Poortinga (Eds.), *Cross-cultural contributions to psychology* (pp. 94–104). Amsterdam: Swets & Zeitlinger.

Davidson, G. R. (1994). Metacognition, cognition and learning: Old dubitations and new directions. *South Pacific Journal of Psychology*, 7, 18–31.

Davidson, G. R, & Freebody, P. (1988). Cross-cultural perspectives on the development of metacognitive thinking. *Hiroshima Forum for Psychology*, *13*, 21–31.

Davis, C. M., & Carlson, J. A. (1970). A cross-cultural study of the strength of the Müller–Lyer illusion as a function of attentional factors. *Journal of Personality and Social Psychology*, *16*, 403–10.

Dawson, J. L. M. (1967). Cultural and physiological influences upon spatial perceptual processes in West Africa (Parts 1 and 2). *International Journal of Psychology*, 2, 115–28, 171–85.

(1971). Theory and research in cross-cultural psychology. *Bulletin of the British Psychological Society*, *24*, 291–306.

Dayan, J. (1993). Health values, beliefs and behaviors of Orthodox, Reformed and Secular Jews. Unpublished MA Thesis, Queen's University.

De Moor, R. (1995). *Values in Western societies*. Tilburg: Tilburg University Press.

De Raad, B., Perugini, M., Hrebíčková, M., & Szarota, P. (1998). Lingua franca of personality: Taxonomies and structures based on the psycholexical approach. *Journal of Cross-Cultural Psychology*, *29*, 212–31.

de Vos, G. (1968). Achievement and innovation in culture and personality. In E. Norbeck, D. Price-Williams, & E. W. McCord (Eds.), *The study of personality* (pp. 348–70). New York: Holt, Rinehart & Winston.

De Waal, F. B. M. (1988). The communicative repertoire of captive bonobos (*pan paniscus*) compared to that of chimpanzees. *Behaviour*, *106*, 183–251.

(1995). Bonobo sex and society. *Scientific American*, *272(3)*, 58–64.

Deal, T. E., & Kennedy, A. A. (1982). *Corporate cultures: The rites and rituals of corporate life*. Reading, MA: Addison-Wesley.

Demetriou, A., & Efklides, A. (Eds.) (1994). *Intelligence, mind, and reasoning*. Amsterdam: Elsevier.

Demetriou, A., & Kazi, S. (2001). *Unity and modularity in the mind and the self: Studies on the relationships between self-awareness, personality, and intellectual development from childhood to adolescence*. London: Routledge.

Demetriou, A., Shayer, M., & Efklides, A. (Eds.) (1992). *Neo-Piagetian theories of cognitive development*. London: Routledge.

Denoux, P. (1993). Recherche interculturelle et psychologie de la différence. In F. Tanon & G. Vermes (Eds.), *L'individu et ses cultures* [Individuals and their cultures]. Paris: L'Harmattan.

Denzin, N. K., & Lincoln, Y. S. (Eds.) (2000a). *Handbook of qualitative research* (2nd ed.). Thousand Oaks, CA: Sage.

Denzin, N. K., & Lincoln, Y. S. (2000b). Introduction: The discipline and practice of qualitative research. In N. K. Denzin & Y. Lincoln (Eds.), *Handbook of qualitative research* (2nd ed., pp. 1–28). Thousand Oaks, CA: Sage.

Deprez, C. (1994). *Les enfants bilingues: Langues et familles* [Bilingual children: Languages and families]. Paris: Didier CREDIF.

Deregowski, J. B. (1968). Difficulties in pictorial depth perception in Africa. *British Journal of Psychology, 59*, 195–204.

(1972). Reproduction of orientation of Kohs-type figures: A cross-cultural study. *British Journal of Psychology, 63*, 283–96.

(1977). A study of orientation errors in response to Kohs-type figures. *International Journal of Psychology, 12*, 183–91.

(1980a). *Illusions, patterns and pictures: A cross-cultural perspective.* London: Academic Press.

(1980b). Perception. In H. C. Triandis & W. Lonner (Eds.), *Handbook of cross-cultural psychology* (vol. III, pp. 21–115). Boston, MA: Allyn and Bacon.

(1989). Real space and represented space: Cross-cultural perspectives. *Behavioral and Brain Sciences, 12*, 51–119.

Deregowski, J. B., & Bentley, A. M. (1986). Perception of pictorial space by Bushmen. *International Journal of Psychology, 21*, 743–52.

(1987). Seeing the impossible and building the likely. *British Journal of Psychology, 78*, 91–7.

Deregowski, J. B., & Byth, W. (1970). Hudson's pictures in Pandora's box. *Journal of Cross-Cultural Psychology, 1*, 315–23.

Deregowski, J. B., & Parker, D. M. (1994). The perception of spatial structure with oblique viewing, an explanation for Byzantine perspective? *Perception, 23*, 5–13.

Deregowski, J. B., & Serpell, R. (1971). Performance on a sorting task: A cross-cultural experiment. *International Journal of Psychology, 6*, 273–81.

Deregowski, J. B., Muldrow, E. S., & Muldrow, W. F. (1972). Pictorial recognition in a remote Ethiopian population. *Perception, 1*, 417–25.

DeRidder, R., & Tripathi, R. C. (Eds.) (1992). *Norm violation and intergroup relations.* New York: Oxford University Press.

Desjarlais, R., Eisenberg, L., Good, B., & Kleinman, A. (1995). *World mental health.* New York: Oxford University Press.

Devereux, G. (1980). *Basic problems of ethnopsychiatry.* Chicago, IL: University of Chicago Press.

Diaz-Guerrero, R. (1975). *Psychology of the Mexican: Culture and personality.* Austin, TX: University of Texas Press.

(1979). The development of coping style. *Human Development, 22*, 320–31.

(1982). The psychology of the historic-sociocultural premise. *Spanish Language Psychology, 2*, 382–410.

(1984). Transference of psychological knowledge and its impact on Mexico. *International Journal of Psychology, 19*, 123–34.

(1990). A Mexican ethnopsychology. In U. Kim & J. W. Berry (Eds.), *Indigenous psychologies: Experience and research in cultural context.* Newbury Park, CA: Sage.

Diaz-Guerrero, R., & Pacheco, A. (Eds.) (1994). *Ethnopsicologia: Scientica Nova.* San Juan: Corripio.

Diener, E. (1996). Subjective well-being in cross-cultural perspective. In H. Grad, A. Blanco, & J. Georgas (Eds.), *Key issues in cross-cultural psychology* (pp. 319–30). Lisse, Netherlands: Swets & Zeitlinger.

Diener, E., Diener, M., & Diener, C. (1995). Factors predicting subjective well-being of nations. *Journal of Personality and Social Psychology, 69*, 851–64.

Diener, E., Suh, E. M., Lucas, R. E., & Smith, H. L. (1995). Subjective well-being: Three decades of progress. *Psychological Bulletin, 125*, 276–302.

Dinges, N. G., & Baldwin, K. D. (1996). Intercultural competence: A research perspective. In D. Landis & R. S. Bhagat (Eds.), *Handbook of intercultural training* (2nd ed., pp. 105–23). Thousand Oaks, CA: Sage.

DiNicola, V. (1990). Anorexia multiform: Self starvation in historical and cultural context. *Transcultural Psychiatric Research Review, 27*, 245–86.

Dissanayake, E. (1992). *Homo aestheticus: Where art comes from and why*. New York: Free Press.

Dittrich, A., Von Arx, S., & Staub, S. (1985). International study on altered states of consciousness (ISASC): Summary of results. *German Journal of Psychology, 9*, 319–39.

Dobkin de Rios, M. (1989). Power and hallucinogenic states of consciousness among the Moche. In C. Ward (Ed.), *Altered states of consciousness and mental health: A cross-cultural perspective* (pp. 285–99). Newbury Park, CA: Sage.

Dobzhansky, T., Ayala, F. J., Stebbins, G. L., & Valentine, J. W. (1977). *Evolution*. San Francisco: Freeman.

Doi, T. (1973). *The anatomy of dependence*. Tokyo: Kodanska International.

  (1984). Psychotherapy: A cross-cultural perspective from Japan. In P. Pedersen, N. Sartorius, & A. Marsella (Eds.), *Mental health services: The cross-cultural context* (pp. 267–79). London: Sage.

Doise, W. (1982). *L'Explication en psychologie sociale*. Paris: Presses Universitaires de France.

Doktor, R. (1983). Culture and management of time: A comparison of Japanese and American top management top practice. *Asia Pacific Journal of Management, 1*, 65–70.

Dona, G., & Berry, J.W. (1994). Acculturation attitudes and acculturative stress of Central American refugees in Canada. *International Journal of Psychology, 29*, 57–70.

Doty, R. L. (1986). Cross-cultural studies of taste and smell perception. In D. Duvall, D. Muller-Schwarze, & R. Silverstein (Eds.), *Clinical signals in vertebrates* (vol. IV). New York: Plenum.

Dougherty, J. W., & Keller, C. (1982). Task autonomy: A practical approach to knowledge structure. *American Ethnologist, 9*, 763–74.

Draguns, J. (1981). Cross-cultural counselling and psychotherapy: History, issues, current status. In A. Marsella & P. Pedersen (Eds.), *Cross-cultural counselling and psychotherapy* (pp. 3–27). New York: Pergamon.

Drenth, P. J. D. (1983). Cross-cultural organizational psychology: Challenges and limitations. In S. H. Irvine & J. W. Berry (Eds.), *Human assessment and cultural factors* (pp. 563–80). New York: Plenum.

Drenth, P. J. D., & den Hartog, D. H. (1999). Culture and organizational differences. In W. J. Lonner, D. L. Dinnel, D. K. Forgays, & S. A. Hayes (Eds.), *Merging past, present, and future in cross-cultural psychology* (pp. 489–502). Lisse, Netherlands: Swets & Zeitlinger.

Drenth, P. J. D., & Groenendijk, B. (1984). Work and organizational psychology in cross-cultural perspective. In P. J. D. Drenth, H. Thierry, P. J. Willems, & C. J. De Wolff (Eds.), *Handbook of work and organizational psychology* (vol. II, pp. 1197–230). New York: Wiley.

  (1997). Organisatiepsychologie in cross-cultureel perspectief. [Organizational psychology in cross-cultural perspective]. In P. J. D. Drenth, Hk. Thierry, & Ch. J. de Wolff (Eds.),

*Nieuw handboek arbeids- en organisatiepsychologie* [New handbook of work and organizational psychology] (vol. II, pp. 1407–51). Houten: Bohn.

Drenth, P. J. D., Van der Flier, H., & Omari, I. M. (1983). Educational selection in Tanzania. *Evaluation in Education*, *7*, 93–217.

Du Toit, B. M. (1968). Pictorial depth perception and linguistic relativity. *Psychologia Africana*, *11*, 51–63.

DuBois, C. (1944). *The people of Alor*. New York: Harper and Row.

Ducci, L, Arcuri, L.W., Georgis, T., & Sinseshaw, T. (1982). Emotion recognition in Ethiopia. *Journal of Cross-Cultural Psychology*, *13*, 340–51.

Duckitt, J. (1994). *The social psychology of prejudice*. New York: Praeger.

Duncan, H. F., Gourlay, N., & Hudson, W. (1973). *A study of pictorial perception among Bantu and White primary school children in South Africa*. Johannesburg: Witwatersrand University Press.

Durham, W. H. (1982). Interactions of genetic and cultural evolution: Models and examples. *Human Ecology*, *10*, 289–323.

Durojaiye, M. (1984). The impact of psychological testing on educational and personnel selection in Africa. *International Journal of Psychology*, *19*, 135–44.

Dyal, J .A. (1984). Cross-cultural research with the locus of control construct. In H. M. Lefcourt (Ed.), *Research with the locus of control construct* (vol. III, pp. 209–306). New York: Academic Press.

Dziurawiec, S., & Deregowski, J. B. (1986). Construction errors as a key to perceptual difficulties encountered in reading technical drawings. *Ergonomics*, *29*, 1203–12.

Eagly, A. (1978). Sex differences in influenceability. *Psychological Bulletin*, *85*, 85–116.

Eagly, A. H., & Wood, W. (1999). The origins of sex differences in human behavior: Evolved dispositions versus social roles. *American Psychologist*, *54*, 408–23.

Eckensberger, L. H. (1972). The necessity of a theory for applied cross-cultural research. In L. J. Cronbach & P. J. D. Drenth (Eds.), *Mental tests and cultural adaptation* (pp. 99–107). The Hague: Mouton.

(1979). A metamethodological evaluation of psychological theories from a cross-cultural perspective. In L. H. Eckensberger, W. J. Lonner, & Y. H. Poortinga (Eds.), *Cross-cultural contributions to psychology* (pp. 255–75). Lisse, Netherlands: Swets & Zeitlinger.

(1987). *Boesch dynamic action theory: A bridge between theory and practice, between general laws and context*. Arbeiten der Fachrichtung Psychologie. Universität des Saarlandes, 113.

(1996). Agency, action, and culture: Three basic concepts for cross-cultural psychology. In J. Pandey, D. Sinha, & D. P. S. Bhawuk (Eds.), *Asian contributions to cross-cultural psychology* (pp. 72–102). New Delhi: Sage.

Eckensberger, L. H., & Meacham, J. A. (1984). Essentials of action theory: A framework for discussion. *Human Development*, *27*, 166–72.

Eckensberger, L. H., & Reinshagen, H. (1980). Kohlbergs Stufentheorie der Entwicklung des moralischen Urteils: Ein Versuch ihrer Reinterpretation im Bezugsrahmen handlungstheoretischer Konzepte [Kohlberg'stage theory of the development of moral judgement: An attempt at reinterpretation in the context of action theoretical concepts]. In L. H. Eckensberger & R. K. Silbereisen (Eds.), *Entwicklung sozialer Kognitionen: Modelle, Theorien, Anwendung* [The development of social cognition: Models, theories, applications] (pp. 65–131). Stuttgart, Germany: Klett-Cotta.

Eckensberger, L. H., & Zimba, R. (1997). The development of moral judgement. In J. W. Berry, P. R. Dasen, & T. S. Saraswathi (Eds.), *Basic processes and human development* (pp. 299–338). Vol. II of *Handbook of cross-cultural psychology* (2nd ed.). Boston, MA: Allyn and Bacon.

Edgerton, R. (1974). Cross-cultural psychology and psychological anthropology: One paradigm or two? *Reviews in Anthropology, 1,* 52–65.

Edwards, A. L. (1970). *The measurement of personality traits by scales and inventories.* New York: Holt, Rinehart and Winston.

Edwards, C. P. (1986). Cross-cultural research on Kohlberg's stages: The basis for consensus. In S. Modgil & C. Modgil (Eds.), Lawrence Kohlberg: Consensus and controversy (pp. 419–30). London: Falmer Press.

Edwards, J. (1984). The social and political context of bilingual education. In R. Samuda, J. W. Berry, & M. Laferrière (Eds.), *Multiculturalism in Canada: Social and educational perspectives* (pp. 184–200). Toronto: Allyn and Bacon.

Efron, D. (1972). *Gesture, race and culture.* The Hague: Mouton. [Originally published 1941].

Eibl-Eibesfeldt, I. (1975). *Ethology: The biology of behavior* (2nd ed.). New York: Holt, Rinehart and Winston.

(1979). Human ethology: Concepts and implications for the sciences of man. *The Behavioral and Brain Sciences, 2,* 1–57.

(1989). *Human ethology.* New York: Aldine de Gruyter.

Eimas, P. D. (1975). Auditory and phonetic coding of the cues for speech: Discrimination of the [r-l] distinctions by young infants. *Perception and Psychophysics, 18,* 341–7.

Ekman, P. (1973). Cross-cultural studies of facial expression. In P. Ekman (Ed.), *Darwin and facial expression* (pp. 169–222). New York: Academic Press.

(1980). *The face of man.* New York: Garland Press.

(1993). Facial expression and emotion. *American Psychologist, 48,* 384–92.

(1994). Strong evidence for universals in facial expression: A reply to Russell's mistaken critique. *Psychological Bulletin, 115,* 268–87.

Ekman, P. (Ed.) (1982). *Emotion in the human face* (2nd ed.). Cambridge, UK: Cambridge University Press.

Ekman, P., & Davidson, R. J. (Eds.) (1994). *The nature of emotions: Fundamental questions.* New York: Oxford University Press.

Ekman, P., & Friesen, W. V. (1969). The repertoire of nonverbal behavior: Categories, origins, usage and coding. *Semiotica, 1,* 49–98.

(1971). Constants across cultures in the face and emotion. *Journal of Personality and Social Psychology, 17,* 124–9.

(1986). A new pancultural expression of emotion. *Motivation and emotion, 10,* 159–68.

Ekman, P., Friesen, W. V., O'Sullivan, M., Diacoyanni-Tarlatris, I., Krause, R., Pitcairn, T., Scherer, K., Chan, A., Heider, K., LeCompte, W. A., Ricci-Bitti, P. E., & Tomita, M. (1987). Universals and cultural differences in the judgements of facial expressions of emotion. *Journal of Personality and Social Psychology, 53,* 712–17.

Ekstrand, L. H., & Ekstrand, G. (1986). Developing the emic/etic concepts for cross-cultural research. In L. H. Ekstrand (Ed.), *Ethnic minorities and immigrants in a cross-cultural perspective* (pp. 52–66). Lisse, Netherlands: Swets & Zeitlinger.

Eldering, L., & Kloprogge, J. (Eds.) (1989). *Different cultures, same school: Ethnic minority children in Europe.* Amsterdam: Swets & Zeitlinger.

Eldering, L., & Leseman, P. P. M. (Eds.) (1999). *Effective early education.* New York: Falmer Press.

Ellis, B. B. (1988). Hofstede's culture dimensions and Rokeach's values: How reliable is the relationship? In J. W. Berry & R. C. Annis (Eds.), *Ethnic psychology: Research and practice with immigrants, refugees, native peoples, ethnic groups and sojourners.* (pp. 266–74). Lisse, Netherlands: Swets & Zeitlinger.

(1989). Differential item functioning: Implications for test translations. *Journal of Applied Psychology, 74,* 912–21.

Ellis, B. B., Becker, P., & Kimmel, H. D. (1993). An item reponse theory evaluation of an English verion of the Trier Personality Inventory (TPI). *Journal of Cross-Cultural Psychology, 24,* 133–48.

Ellis, H. D., Deregowski, J. B., & Shephard, J. W. (1975). Description of white and black faces by white and black subjects. *International Journal of Psychology, 10,* 119–23.

Ember, C., & Ember, M. (1988). *Guide to cross-cultural research using the HRAF archive.* New Haven: HRAF Press.

Ember, M., & Ember, C. (1998). *Cultural anthropology* (9th ed.). New York: Prentice-Hall.

Endler, N., & Parker, J. (1990). Multidimensional assessment of coping. *Journal of Personality and Social Psychology, 58,* 844–54.

Engeström, Y. (1993). Developmental studies of work as a testbench of acitivity theory: The case of primary care medical practice. In S. Chaitklin & J. Lave (Eds.), *Understanding practice: Perspectives on activity and context* (pp. 64–103). Cambridge: Cambridge University Press.

Engle, P. L., Zeitlin, M., Medrano, Y., & Garcia, L. H. (1996). Growth consequences of low income Nicaraguan mothers' theories about feeding one year olds. In C. Super & S. Harkness (Eds.), *Parental cultural belief systems* (pp. 428–46). New York: Guilford Press.

Enriquez, V. G. (1981). *Decolonizing the Filipino psyche.* Quezon City: Psychology Research and Training House.

(1989). *Indigenous psychology and national consciousness.* Tokyo: Institute for the Study of Languages and Cultures of Asia and Africa.

(1993). Developing a Filipino psychology. In U. Kim & J. W. Berry (Eds.), *Indigenous psychologies: Research and experience in cultural context* (pp. 152–69). Newbury Park, CA: Sage.

Enriquez, V. G. (Ed.). (1990). *Indigenous psychologies.* Quezon City: Psychology Research and Training House.

Erhlich, P., & Erhlich, A. (1990). *The population explosion.* New York: Simon and Schuster.

Erlandson, D. A., Harris, E. L., Skipper, B. L., & Allen, S. D. (1993). *Doing naturalistic inquiry: A guide to methods.* Newbury Park, CA: Sage.

Eysenck, H. J. (1967). *The biological basis of personality.* Springfield, IL: Charles Thomas.

(1988). The biological basis of intelligence. In S. H. Irvine & J. W. Berry (Eds.), *Human abilities in cultural context* (pp. 70–104). New York: Cambridge University Press.

Eysenck, H. J., & Eysenck, S. B. G. (1975). *Manual of the Eysenck Personality Questionnaire.* San Diego, CA: Hodder and Stoughton.

Faucheux, C. (1976). Cross-cultural research in social psychology. *European Journal of Social Psychology, 6,* 269–322.

Faure, G. O., & Rubin, J. Z. (Eds.) (1993). *Culture and negotiation: The resolution of water disputes.* Newbury Park, CA: Sage.

Fawcett, J. T. (1973). *Psychological perspectives on population.* New York: Basic Books.

Feather, N. (1975). *Values in education and society.* New York: Free Press.

Fedoroff, I., & McFarlane, T. (1998). Cultural aspects of eating disorders. In S. Kazarian & D. Evans (Eds.), *Cultural clinical psychology: Theory, research and practice* (pp. 152–76). New York: Oxford University Press.

Fehr, B., & Russell, J. A. (1984). Concept of emotion viewed from a prototype perspective. *Journal of Experimental Psychology: General, 113*, 464–86.

Feldman, D. (1975). The history of the relationship between environment and culture in ethnological thought: an overview. *Journal of the History of the Behavioural Sciences, 110*, 67–81.

Ferguson, G. (1956). On transfer and the abilities of man. *Canadian Journal of Psychology, 10*, 121–31.

Fernald, A. (1992). Meaningful melodies in mothers' speech to infants. In H. Papoušek, U. Jurgens, & M. Papoušek (Eds.), *Nonverbal vocal communication: Comparative and developmental approaches* (pp. 263–81). Cambridge: Cambridge University Press.

Fernald, A., Taeschner, T., Dunn, J., Papoušek, M., Boysson-Bardies, B., & Fukui, A. (1989). A cross-language study of prosodic modifications in mothers' and fathers' speech to preverbal infants. *Journal of Child Language, 16*, 477–501.

Fernandez, D. R., Carlson, D. S., Stepina, L. P., & Nicholson, J. D. (1997). Hofstede's country classification 25 years later. *Journal of Social Psychology, 137*, 43–54.

Fernandez-Ballesteros, R. (1998). Quality of life: Concept and assessment. In J. Adair, D. Belanger, & K. Dion (Eds.), *Advances in psychological science: Social, personal and cultural aspects* (pp. 387–406). Hove, UK: Psychology Press.

Fernando, S. (1993). Racism and xenophobia. *Innovation in Social Sciences Research* (Special Issue on Migration and Health), *6*, 9–19.

Feuerstein, R. (1979). *The dynamic assessment of retarded performers.* Baltimore, MD: University Park Press.

Fiati, T. A. (1992). Cross-cultural variation in the structure of children's thought. In R. Case (Ed.), *The mind's staircase: Exploring the conceptual underpinnings of children's thought and knowledge* (pp. 319–42). Hillsdale, NJ: Lawrence Erlbaum.

Fiedler, F. E., Mitchell, T., & Triandis, H. C. (1971). The culture assimilator: An approach to cross-cultural training. *Journal of Applied Psychology, 55*, 95–102.

Figge, H. H. (1973). Zur Entwicklung und Stabilisierung von Sekundärpersönlichkeiten im Rahmen von Besessenheitskulten [About the development and stabilisation of secondary personalities in the context of possession cults]. *Confinia Psychiatrica, 16*, 28–37.

Fijneman, Y., Willemsen, M., & Poortinga, Y. H. in cooperation with Erelcin, F. G., Georgas, J., Hui, H. C., Leung, K., & Malpass, R. S. (1996). Individualism–collectivism: An empirical study of a conceptual issue. *Journal of Cross-Cultural Psychology, 27*, 381–402.

Fischer, A. H. (1991). *Emotion scripts: A study of social and cognitive factors in emotions.* Leiden: DSWO Press.

Fischer, K. W., Knight, C. C., & Van Parys, M. (1993). Analyzing diversity in developmental pathways: Methods and concepts. In R. Case & W. Edelstein (Eds.), *The new structuralism in cognitive development. Theory and research on individual pathways. Contributions to Human Development* (vol. XXIII, pp. 33–56). Basel: Karger.

Fish, J. M. (1997). How psychologists think about race. *General Anthropology, 4(1)*, 1–4.

(2000). What anthropology can do for psychology: Facing physics envy, ethnocentrism, and a belief in race. *American Anthropologist, 102*, 552–63.

Fishman, J. (1960). A systematization of the Whorfian hypothesis. *Behavioral Science*, *5*, 323–38.

Fiske, A. P. (1991). *Structures of social life: The four elementary forms of human relations*. New York: Free Press.

  (1993). Social errors in four cultures: Evidence about universal forms of social relations. *Journal of Cross-Cultural Psychology*, *24*, 463–94.

Fiske, A., P. Kitayama, S., Markus, H., & Nisbett, R. (1998). The cultural matrix of social psychology. In D. Gilbert, S. Fiske, & G. Lindzey (Eds.), *Handbook of social psychology* (pp. 915–81). New York: McGraw-Hill.

Fiske, D. W. (1971). *Measuring the concepts of personality*. Chicago, IL: Aldine.

Flatz, G., & Rotthauwe, H. W. (1977). The human lactase polymorphism: Physiology and genetics of lactose absorption and malabsorption. *Progress in Medical Genetics*, *2*, 205–49.

Flavell, J. H. (1963). *The developmental psychology of Jean Piaget*. New York: Van Nostrand.

  (1974). The development of inferences about others. In T. Mischel (Ed.), *Understanding other persons* (pp. 66–116). Oxford: Basil Blackwell & Mott.

  (1976). Metacognitive aspects of problem-solving. In L. B. Resnick (Ed.), *The nature of intelligence* (pp. 231–5). Hillsdale, NJ: Lawrence Erlbaum.

Flavell, J. H., Zhang, X. D., Zou, H., Dong, Q., & Qi, S. (1983). A comparison between the development of the appearance–reality distinction in the People's Republic of China and the United States. *Cognitive Psychology*, *15*, 459–66.

Flynn, J. R. (1987). Massive IQ gains in 14 nations: What IQ tests really measure. *Psychological Bulletin*, *101*, 171–91.

  (1999). Searching for justice: The discovery of IQ gains over time. *American Psychologist*, *54*, 5–20.

Fodor, J. (1983). *Modularity of mind*. Cambridge, MA: MIT Press.

Fontaine, J. (1999). *Culturele vertekening in Schwartz' waardeninstrument* [Cultural bias is Schwartz's value instrument]. Ph.D Thesis. Leuven: University of Leuven.

Fontaine, J. R. J., Poortinga, Y. H., Setiadi, B., & Markam, S. S. (in press). "Shame" and "guilt" in Indonesian and Dutch cognitive emotion structure. *Cognition and Emotion*.

Fox, N. A. (1995). Of the way we were: Adult memories about attachment experiences and their role in determining infant–parent relationships: A commentary on Van Ijzendoorn (1995). *Psychological Bulletin*, *117*, 404–10.

Frank, H., Harvey, O. J., & Verdun, K. (2000). American responses to five categories of shame in Chinese culture: A preliminary cross-cultural construct validation. *Personality and Individual Differences*, *28*, 887–96.

Frankenberg, R. (1988). Culture and medical anthropology. *Medical Anthropology Quarterly*, *2*, 324–37.

Fraser, S. (Ed.) (1995). *The bell curve wars: Race, intelligence, and the future of America*. New York: Basic Books.

Freeman, D. (1983). *Margaret Mead and Samoa: The making and unmaking of an anthropological myth*. Cambridge, MA: Harvard University Press.

Freud, S. (1938). *An outline of psychoanalysis*. London: Hogarth.

Fridlund, A. J. (1997). The new ethology of human facial expression. In J. A. Russell & J. N. Fernández-Dols (Eds.), *The psychology of facial expression* (pp. 103–29). Cambridge: Cambridge University Press.

Frijda, N. H. (1986). *The emotions*. Cambridge: Cambridge University Press.

  (1993). Appraisal and beyond. *Cognition and emotion*, *7*, 225–31.

Frijda, N. H., & Jahoda, G. (1966). On the scope and methods of cross-cultural research. *International Journal of Psychology*, *1*, 109–27.

Frijda, N. H., Kuipers, P., & Ter Schure, E. (1986). Relations among emotion, appraisal, and emotional action readiness. *Journal of Personality and Social Psychology*, *57*, 212–28.

Frijda, N. H., Markam, S., Sato, K., & Wiers, R. (1995). Emotions and emotion words. In J. A. Russell, J-M. Fernández-Dols, A. S. Manstead, & J. C. Wellenkamp (Eds.), *Everyday conceptions of emotion* (pp. 121–44). Dordrecht, Netherlands: Kluwer.

Fromkin, V. A. (1978). *Tone: A linguistic survey*. New York: Academic Press.

Fromm, E. (1941). *Escape from freedom*. New York: Farrar and Rinehart.

Frost, P. J., Moore, L. F., Louis, M. R., Lundberg, C. C., & Martin, J. (Eds.) (1985). *Organizational culture*. Beverly Hills, CA: Sage.

Fuller, J. L., & Thompson, W. R. (1978). *Foundations of behavior genetics*. St. Louis: The Mosby Company.

Furby, L. (1973). Implications of within-group heritabilities for sources of between-group differences: IQ and racial differences. *Developmental Psychology*, *9*, 28–37.

Furnham, A., & Alibhai, N. (1985). The friendship networks of foreign students: A replication and extension of the functional model. *International Journal of Psychology*, *20*, 709–22.

Furnham, A., & Bochner, S. (1986). *Culture shock: Psychological reactions to unfamiliar environments*. London: Methuen.

Furnham, A. & Shiekh, S. (1993). Gender, generational and social support correlates of mental health in Asian immigrants. *International Journal of Social Psychiatry*, *39*, 22–33.

Galler, J. R., Ricciuti, H. N., Crawford, M.A., & Kucharski, L. T. (1984). The role of mother–infant interactions in nutritional disorders. In J. Galler (Ed.), *Nutrition and behavior* (pp. 269–304). New York: Plenum.

Gallois, C., Giles, H., Jones, E., Cargile, A. C., & Ota, H. (1995). Accommodating to intercultural encounters. Elaborations and extensions. In R. L. Wiseman (Ed.), *Intercultural communication theory* (vol. XXIX, pp. 115–47). Thousand Oaks, CA: Sage.

Garcia, J., & Koelling, R. A. (1966). Relation of cue to consequence in avoidance learning. *Psychonomic Science*, *4*, 123–4.

Gardner, R. C., & Lambert, W. E. (1972). *Attitudes and motivation in second language learning*. Rowley, MA: Newbury House.

Gardner, R. C., Wonnacott, E., & Taylor, D. (1968). Ethnic stereotypes: A factor analytic investigation. *Canadian Journal of Psychology*, *22*, 35–44.

Gärling, T., Kristensen, H., Backenroth-Ohsaka, G., Ekehammer, B., & Wessels, M. G. (Eds.) (2000). Diplomacy and psychology. *International Journal of Psychology*, *35*, 81–176 (special issue).

Gasché, J. (1992). A propos d'une expérience d'éducation bilingue au Perou.: L'indigénisation d'un programme; sa critique de l'anthropologie [On an experience of bilingual education in Peru: The indigenisation of a programme; its critique of anthropology]. *Journal de la Société Suisse de Américanistes*, *53–4*, 131–42.

Gatewood, J. B. (1985). Actions speak louder than words. In J. W. D. Dougherty (Ed.), *Directions in cognitive anthroplogy*. Chicago, IL: University of Illinois Press.

Gauvain, M. (1993). Sociocultural processes in the development of thinking. In J. Altarriba (Ed.), *Cognition and culture* (pp. 299–316). Amsterdam: North-Holland.

(1995). Thinking in niches: Sociocultural influences on cognitive development. *Human Development, 38,* 25–45.

(2001). *The social context of cognitive development.* New York: Guilford Press.

Gazzaniga, M. S. (Ed.) (1996). *The cognitive neurosciences.* Cambridge, MA: MIT Press.

Geber, M. (1958). The psycho-motor development of African children in the first year and the influence of maternal behaviour. *Journal of Social Psychology, 47,* 185–95.

Geber, M., & Dean, M. F. (1957). The state of development of newborn African children. *Lancet, 272,* 1216–19.

Geertz, C. (1965). The impact of the concept of culture on the concept of man. In J. Platt (Ed.), *New views on the nature of man.* Chicago, IL: University of Chicago Press.

(1973). *The interpretation of cultures.* New York: Basic Books.

(1984). From the native's point of view: On the nature of anthropological understanding. In R. A. Shweder & R. A. LeVine (Eds.), *Culture theory: Essays on mind, self, and emotion* (pp. 123–36). New York: Cambridge University Press.

Geertz, H. (1961). *The Javanese family.* New York: Free Press.

Geiger, L. (1880). *Contributions to the history of the development of the human race.* London: Trübner & Co.

Gelfand, M. J. (Ed.) (2000). Special issue on cross-cultural industrial and organizational psychology. *Applied Psychology: An International Review, 49,* 29–226.

Gelfand, M. J., & Dyer, N. (2000). A cultural perspective on negotiation: Progress, pitfalls and prospects. *Applied Psychology: An International Review, 49,* 62–99.

Georgas, J. (1993). Ecological-social model of Greek psychology. In U. Kim & J. W. Berry (Eds.), *Indigenous psychologies* (pp. 56–78). Newbury Park, CA: Sage.

Georgas, J., & Papastylianou, D. (1998). Acculturation and ethnic identity: The remigration of ethnic Greeks to Greece. In H. Grad, A. Blanco, & J. Georgas (Eds.), *Key issues in cross-cultural psychology* (pp. 114–27). Lisse, Netherlands: Swets & Zeitlinger.

Georgas, J., Van de Vijver, A. J. R., & Berry, J. W. (2000). *The ecocultural framework, ecosocial indices and psychological variables in cross-cultural research.* Paper presented at the IACCP congress, Pultusk, Poland, July.

Gergen, K. J. (1994). Exploring the postmodern: Perils or potentials? *American Psychologist, 49,* 412–16.

Gergen, M. M., & Gergen, K. J. (2000). Qualitative inquiry: Tensions and transformations. In N. K. Denzin & Y. Lincoln (Eds.), *Handbook of qualitative research* (2nd ed., pp. 1025–46). Thousand Oaks, CA: Sage.

Gesell, A. (1940). *The first five years of life: A guide to the study of the preschool child (Part I).* New York: Harper.

Gesell, A., & Amatruda, C. (1947). *Developmental diagnosis.* New York: Harper Bros.

Ghauri, P., & Usunier, J.-C. (Eds.) (1996). *International business negotiations.* Oxford: Pergamon.

Gibbons, J. L. (2000). Adolescence in international and cross-cultural perspective: An introduction. *International Journal of Group Tensions, 29,* 3–16.

Gibson, J. J. (1966). *The senses considered as perceptual systems.* Boston, MA: Houghton Mifflin.

Gilligan, C. (1992). *In a different voice: Psychological theory and women's development.* Cambridge, MA: Harvard University Press.

Ginges, J., & Cairns, D. (2000). Social representations of multiculturalism: A facet analysis. *Journal of Applied Social Psychology, 30,* 1345–70.

Girndt, T. (2000). *Cultural diversity and work-group performance: Detecting the rules.* Ph.D. thesis. Tilburg: Tilburg University.

Girndt, T., & Poortinga, Y. H. (1997). Interculturele communicatie: Conventies en mis-verstanden [Intercultural communication: Conventions and misunderstandings]. *De Psycholoog*, *32*, 299–304.

Glacken, C. J. (1967). *Traces of the Rhodesian shore*. Berkeley, CA: University of California Press.

Glazer, N. (1997). *We are all multiculturalists now*. Cambridge, MA: Harvard University Press.

Goldin-Meadow, S., & Mylander, C. (1998). Spontaneous sign systems created by deaf children in two cultures. *Nature*, *391*, 279–81.

Goldstein, A. P. (1983). Causes, controls and alternatives to aggression. In A. P. Goldstein & M. H. Segall (Eds.), *Aggression in global perspective*. Elmsford: Pergamon.

Gologor, E. (1977). Group polarization in a non-risk-taking culture. *Journal of Cross-Cultural Psychology*, *8*, 331–46.

Gombrich, E. H. (1977). *Art and illusion: A study in the psychology of pictorial representation* (5th ed.). Oxford: Phaidon Press.

Good, B. (1992). Culture and psychopathology: Directions for psychiatric anthropology. In T. Schwartz, G. White, & C. Luts (Eds.), *New directions in psychological anthropology* (pp. 181–205). New York: Cambridge University Press.

Goodall, J. (1986). *The chimpanzees of Gombe*. Cambridge, MA: Harvard University Press.

Goodenough, W. (1956). Componential analysis and the study of meaning. *Language*, *32*, 195–216.

(1980). Ethnographic field techniques. In H. C. Triandis & J. W. Berry (Eds.), *Methodology*. Vol. II of *Handbook of cross-cultural psychology* (2nd ed.). Boston, MA: Allyn and Bacon.

Goody, J., & Watt, I. (1968). The consequences of literacy. In J. Goody (Ed.), *Literacy in traditional societies* (pp. 27–68). New York: Cambridge University Press.

Gorman, K. (1995). Malnutrition and cognitive development. *Journal of Nutrition, Supplement*, *125*, 2239–445.

Goto, H. (1971). Auditory perception by normal Japanese adults of sounds of "l" or "r." *Neuropsychologia*, *9*, 317–23.

Gottlieb, G. (1998). Normally occurring environmental and behavioral influences on gene activity: From central dogma to probabilistic epigenesis. *Psychological Review*, *105*, 792–802.

Gottlieb, G., Wahlsten, D., & Lickliter, R. (1998). The significance of biology for human development: A developmental psychobiological system view. In W. Damon (Chief Ed.) & R. M. Lerner (Vol. Ed.), *Handbook of child psychology*. Vol. I: *Theoretical models of human development* (5th ed., pp. 233–73). New York: Wiley.

Gough, H., & Heilbrun, A. B. (1965). *Adjective check list manual*. Palo Alto, CA: Consulting Psychologists Press.

(1983). *The Adjective Check List manual – 1983 edition*. Palo Alto, CA: Consulting Psychologists Press.

Gould, J. L., & Marler, P. (1987). Learning by instinct. *Scientific American*, *256(1)*, 62–73.

Gould, S. J. (1991). Exaptation: A crucial tool for evolutionary psychology. *Journal of Social Issues*, *47*, 43–65.

Gould, S. J., & Lewontin, R. C. (1979). The spandrels of San Marco and the Panglossian paradigm: A critique of the adaptationist programme. *Proceedings of the Royal Society of London (Series B)*, *205*, 581–98.

Government of Canada (1971). *Policy statement to House of Commons on multiculturalism*. Ottawa: Government of Canada.

Graham, J. A., & Argyle, M. (1975). A cross-cultural study of the communication of ex-traverbal meaning of gestures. *International Journal of Psychology*, *10*, 57–67.

Graham, J. L. (1983). Brazilian, Japanese, and American business negotiations. *Journal of International Business Studies*, *14*, 47–61.

Graham, J. L., Evenko, L. I., & Rajan, M. N. (1992). An empirical comparison of Soviet and American business negotiations. *Journal of International Business Studies*, *16*, 387–418.

Graham, J. L., Kim, D. K., Lin, C., & Robinson, M. (1988). Buyer–seller negotiations around the Pacific rim: Differences in fundamental exchange processes. *Journal of Consumer Research*, *15*, 48–54.

Graham, J. L., Mintu, A. T., & Rodgers, W. (1994). Exploration of negotiation behaviors in ten foreign cultures using a model developed in the US. *Management Science*, *40*, 70–95.

Grant, G. V. (1970). *The development and validation of a classification battery constructed to replace the General Adaptability Battery*. Report C/Pers 181. Johannesburg: National Institute for Personnel Research.

Grantham-McGregor, S. (1984). Social background of childhood malnutrition. In J. Brozek & B. Schürch (Eds.), *Malnutrition and behavior: Critical assessment of key issues* (pp. 358–74). Lausanne: Nestlé Foundation.

   S. M. (1995). A review of the effect of severe malnutrition on mental development. *Journal of Nutrition, Supplement*, *125*, 2233–8.

Grantham-McGregor, S. M., Powell, C., Walker, S., Chang, S., & Fletcher, P. (1994). The long-term follow-up of severely malnourished children who participated in an intervention program. *Child Development*, *65*, 428–39.

Graves, T. D. (1967). Psychological acculturation in a tri-ethnic community. *South-western Journal of Anthropology*, *23*, 337–50.

Grey, J. A. (1981). A critique of Eysenck's personality theory. In H. J. Eysenck (Ed.), *A model of personality* (pp. 246–76). Berlin, Germany: Springer-Verlag.

Green, J. (1987). Le langage et son double–The language and its shadow. Texte bilingue. Paris: Seuil.

Greenberg, J. H. (1957). The nature and uses of linguistic typologies. *International Journal of American Linguistics*, *23*, 68–77.

Greenberg, J. H. (Ed.) (1963). *Universals of language*. Cambridge, MA: MIT Press.

   (1978). *Universals of human language* (vols. I–IV). Stanford, CA: Stanford University Press.

Greenfield, P. M. (1976). Cross-cultural research and Piagetian theory: Paradox and progress. In K. F. Riegel & J. A. Meacham (Eds.), *The developing individual in a changing world* (vol. I, pp. 322–33). The Hague: Mouton.

   (1994). Independence and interdependence as developmental scripts: Implications for theory, research, and practice. In P. M. Greenfield & R. C. Cocking (Eds.), *Cross-cultural roots of minority child development* (pp. 1–37). Hillsdale, NJ: Erlbaum.

   (1997a). You can't take it with you: Why ability assessments don't cross cultures. *American Psychologist*, *52*, 1115–24.

   (1997b). Culture as process: Empirical methods for cultural psychology. In J. W. Berry, Y. H. Poortinga, & J. Pandey (Eds.), *Theory and method* (pp. 301–46). Vol. I of *Handbook of cross-cultural psychology* (2nd ed.). Boston, MA: Allyn and Bacon.

   (2000). What psychology can do for anthropology, or why anthropology took postmodernism on the chin. *American Anthropologist*, *102*, 564–76.

Gregory, R. L. (1966). *Eye and brain*. London: World University Library.

Griesel, R. D., Richter, L. M., & Belciug, M. (1990). Electro-encephalography and performance in a poorly nourished South African population. *South African Medical Journal*, *78*, 539–43.

Griffith, R. W., & Hom, P. W. (1987). Some multivariate comparisons of multinational managers. *Multivariate Behavioral Research*, *22*, 173–91.

Griffiths, R. (1970). *The abilities of young children. A comprehensive system of mental measurement for the first 8 years of life*. London: Young & Son.

Grosjean, F. (1982). *Life with two languages: An introduction to bilingualism*. Cambridge, MA: Harvard University Press.

Gross, P. R., Levitt, N., & Lewis, M. W. (Eds.) (1996). *The flight from science and reason*. Annals of the New York Academy of Sciences. Vol. 775.

Grossarth-Maticek, R., & Eysenck, H. J. (1990). Personality, stress and disease: Description and validity of a new inventory. *Psychological Reports*, *66*, 355–73.

Guanzon-Lapeña, Ma. M., Church, A. T., Carlota, A. J., & Katigbak, M. S. (1998). Indigenous personality measures: Philippine examples. *Journal of Cross-Cultural Psychology*, *29*, 249–70.

Guba, E. G., & Lincoln, Y. S. (1994). Competing paradigms in qualitative research. In N. K. Denzin & Y. S. Lincoln (Eds.), *Handbook of qualitative research* (pp. 105–17). Thousand Oaks, CA: Sage.

Gudykunst, W. B. (1995). Anxiety/Uncertainty Management (AUM) theory: Current status. In R. L. Wiseman (Ed.), *Intercultural communication theory* (pp. 8–58). Thousand Oaks, CA: Sage.

  (1999). Individualistic and collectivistic perspectives on communication: An introduction. *International Journal of Intercultural Relations*, *22*, 107–34.

Gudykunst, W. B., & Bond, M. (1997). Intergroup relations across cultures. In J. W. Berry, M. H. Segall, & C. Kagitcibasi (Eds.), *Social behavior and applications* (pp. 119–61). Vol. III of *Handbook of cross-cultural psychology* (2nd ed.). Boston, MA: Allyn and Bacon.

Gudykunst, W. B., & Hammer, M. R. (1983). Basic training design: Approaches to intercultural training. In D. Landis & R. W. Brislin (Eds.), *Handbook of intercultural training* (vol. I, pp. 118–54). New York: Pergamon.

Gudykunst, W. B., Guzley, R. M., & Hammer, M. R. (1996). Designing intercultural training. In D. Landis & R. S. Bhagat (Eds.), *Handbook of intercultural training* (2nd ed., pp. 61–80). Thousand Oaks, CA: Sage.

Gudykunst, W. B., Ting-Toomey, S, & Chua, E. (1988). *Culture and interpersonal communication*. Newbury Park, CA: Sage.

Guerraoui, Z., & Troadec, B. (2000). *Psychologie interculturelle* [Intercultural psychology]. Paris: Armand Colin.

Gumperz, J. J. (1982). *Discourse strategies*. Cambridge: Cambridge University Press.

Gumperz, J. J., & Levinson, S. C. (1996). Introduction: Linguistic relativity re-examined. In J. J. Gumperz & S. C. Levinson (Eds.), *Rethinking linguistic relativity* (pp. 1–18). Cambridge: Cambridge University Press.

Gustafsson, J.-E. (1984). A unifying model for the structure of intellectual abilities. *Intelligence*, *8*, 179–203.

Guthrie, G. M. (1966). Cultural preparation for the Philippines. In R. B. Textor (Ed.), *Cultural frontiers of the Peace Corps*. Cambridge, MA: MIT Press.

Guthrie, G. M., & Lonner, W. J. (1986). Assessment of personality and psychopathology. In W. J. Lonner & J. W. Berry (Eds.), *Field methods in cross-cultural research* (pp. 231–64). Beverly Hills, CA: Sage.

Hagen, M. A., & Jones, R. K. (1978). Cultural effects on pictorial perception: How many words is one picture really worth? In R. D. Walk & H. L. Pick (Eds.), *Perception and experience* (pp. 171–209). New York: Plenum.

Hagendoorn, L. (1993). Ethnic categorization and outgroup exclusion: The role of cultural values and social stereotypes in the construction of ethnic hierarchies. *Ethnic and Racial Studies, 16*, 26–51.

Haidt, J., & Keltner, D. (1999). Culture and facial expression: Open-ended methods find more expressions and a gradient of recognition. *Cognition and Emotion, 13*, 225–66.

Haire, M., Ghiselli, E. E., & Porter, L. W. (1966). *Managerial thinking: An international study*. New York: Wiley.

Hall, E. T. (1959). *The silent language*. New York: Doubleday.
  (1960). The silent language in overseas business. *Harvard Business Review, 38*, 87–96.
  (1966). *The hidden dimension*. New York: Doubleday.

Hallowell, A. I. (1945). Sociopsychological aspects of acculturation. In R. Linton (Ed.), *The science of man in the world crisis* (pp. 310–32). New York: Columbia University Press.

Hallpike, C. P. (1986). *The principles of social evolution*. Oxford: Clarendon Press.

Halpern, D. (1993). Minorities and mental health. *Social Science and Medicine, 36*, 597–607.

Hambleton, R. K. (1994). Guidelines for adapting educational and psychological tests: A progress report. *European Journal of Psychological Assessment, 10*, 229–44.

Hambleton, R. K., Swaminathan, H., & Rogers, H. J. (1991). *Fundamentals of item response theory*. Newbury Park, CA: Sage.

Hamilton, D. L. (Ed.) (1981). *Cognitive processes in stereotyping and intergroup behavior*. Hillsdale, NJ: Erlbaum.

Hamilton, W. D. (1964). The genetical evolution of social behavior, I, II. *Journal of Theoretical Biology, 7*, 1–52.

Hammer, M. R. (1989). Intercultural communication competence. In M. K. Asante & W. B. Gudykunst (Eds.), *Handbook of international and intercultural communication* (pp. 247–60). Newsbury Park, CA: Sage.

Hammersley, M. (1992). *What's wrong with ethnography: Methodological explorations*. London: Routledge.

Hanges, P. J., Lord, R. G., & Dickson, M. W. (2000). An information-processing perspective on leadership and culture: A case of connectionist architecture. *Applied Psychology: An International Review, 49*, 133–61.

Hardin, C. L., & Maffi, L. (Eds.) (1997). *Colour categories in thought and language*. Cambridge: Cambridge University Press.

Hardonk, M. M. (1999). *Cross-cultural universals of aesthetic appreciation in decorative band patterns*. Nijmegen, Netherlands: NICI.

Harkness, S., & Keefer, C. H. (2000). Contributions of cross-cultural psychology to research and interventions in education and health. *Journal of Cross-Cultural Psychology, 31*, 92–109.

Harkness, S., & Super, C. H. (Eds.) (1995). *Parents' cultural belief systems: Their origins, expressions, and consequences*. New York: Guilford Press.

Harkness, S., Wyon, J., & Super, C. (1988). The relevance of behavioural sciences to disease prevention and control in developing countries. In P. Dasen, J. W. Berry, & N. Sartorius (Eds.), *Cross-cultural psychology and health: Towards applications* (pp. 239–55). London: Sage.

Harley, T. R. (1995). *The psychology of language: From data to theory*. Hove, UK: Psychology Press.

Harlow, H. F., & Harlow, M. K. (1962). Social deprivation in monkeys. *Scientific American*, *207*, 136–46.

Harris, P., & Heelas, P. (1979). Cognitive processes and collective representations. *Archives Européennes de Sociologie*, *20*, 211–41.

Harris, P. R., & Moran, R. T. (1991). *Managing cultural differences*. Houston, TX: Golf.

Harrison, D. E. (1975). Race track shift: A cross-cultural study. *South African Journal of Psychology*, *5*, 10–15.

Haviland, J. B. (1998). Guugu Yimithirr cardinal directions. *Ethos*, *26*, 25–47.

Hays, W. L. (1988). *Statistics* (4th ed.). New York: Holt, Rhinehart & Winston.

Hebb, D. O. (1949). *The organization of behavior*. New York: Wiley.

Hector, H. (1958). A new pattern completion test. *Journal of the National Institute for Personnel Research*, *7*, 132–4.

Heelas, P. (1981). Introduction. In P. Heelas & A. Lock (Eds.), *Indigenous psychologies: The anthropology of the self*. London: Academic Press.

  (1986). Emotion talk across cultures. In R. Harré (Ed.), *The social construction of emotions* (pp. 234–66). Oxford: Blackwell.

Heelas, P., & Lock, A. (Eds.) (1981). *Indigenous psychologies: The anthropology of the self*. London: Academic Press.

Heider, F. (1958). *The psychology of interpersonal relations*. New York: Wiley.

Heider, K. G. (1991). *Landscapes of emotion: Mapping three cultures of emotion in Indonesia*. New York: Cambridge University Press.

Heller, F. A. (1985). Some theoretical and practical problems in multinational and cross-cultural research on organizations. In P. Joynt & M. Wasner (Eds.), *Managing in different countries* (pp. 11–22). Oslo: Universitetsforlaget.

  (1986). Introduction and overview. In F. Heller (Ed.), *The use and abuse of social science* (pp. 1–18). London: Sage.

Heller, F. A., & Wilpert, B. (1981). *Competence and power in managerial decision-making*. Chichester: Wiley.

Hendrix, L. (1985). Economy and child training reexamined. *Ethos*, *13*, 246–61.

Hermans, H., & Kempen, H. (1998). Moving cultures: The perilous problems of cultural dichotomies in a globalizing society. *American Psychologist*, *53*, 1111–20.

Herrnstein, R. J., & Murray, C. (1994). *The bell curve: Intelligence and class structure in American life*. New York: Free Press.

Herskovits, M. J. (1938). *Aculturation: The study of culture contact*. New York: Augustin.

  (1948). *Man and his works: The science of cultural anthropology*. New York: Knopf.

Hewlett, B. S. (1992). Husband–wife reciprocity and the father–infant relationship among Aka Pygmies. In B. S. Hewlett (Ed.), *Father–child relations: Cultural and biosocial contexts* (pp. 153–76). New York: Aldine De Gruyter.

Hewstone, M., Stroebe, W., & Stephenson, G. (Eds.) (1996). *Introduction to social psychology: A European perspective*. Oxford: Blackwell.

Heymans, G. (1932). *Inleiding tot de special psychologie* [Introduction to special psychology] (vols. I & II, 2nd printing). Haarlem: De Erven Bohn.

Hick, W. E. (1952). On the rate of gain of information. *Quarterly Journal of Experimental Psychology*, *34*, 11–26.

Hinde, R. A. (1982). *Ethology: Its nature and relations with other sciences*. Oxford: Oxford University Press.

(1987). *Individuals, relationships and culture*. Cambridge: Cambridge University Press.

(1992). Developmental psychology in the context of other behavioral sciences. *Developmental Psychology*, *28*, 1018–29.

Ho, D. Y. F. (1996). Filial piety and its psychological consequences. In M. H. Bond (Ed.), *Handbook of Chinese psychology* (pp. 155–65). Hong Kong: Oxford University Press.

(2000). Dialectical thinking: Neither Eastern nor Western. *American Psychologist*, *55*, 1064–65.

Ho, E. (1995). Chinese or New Zealander? Differential paths of adaptation of Hong Kong Chinese adolescent immigrants in New Zealand. *New Zealand Population Review*, *21*, 27–49.

Hocoy, D. (1998). Empirical distinctiveness between cognitive and affective elements of ethnic identity, and scales for their measurement. In H. Grad, A. Blanco, & J. Georgas (Eds.), *Key issues in cross-cultural psychology* (pp. 128–37). Lisse, Netherlands: Swets & Zeitlinger.

Hofstede, G. (1979). Value systems in forty countries: Interpretation, validation and consequences for theory. In L. Eckensberger, W. Lonner & Y. H. Poortinga (Eds.), *Cross-cultural contributions to psychology* (pp. 389–407). Lisse, Netherlands: Swets & Zeitlinger.

(1980). *Culture's consequences: International differences in work related values*. Beverly Hills, CA: Sage.

(1983a). The cultural relativity of organizational practices and theories. *Journal of International Business Studies*, 14, 75–89.

(1983b). Dimensions of national cultures in fifty countries and three regions. In J. B. Deregowski, S. Dziurawiec, & R. C. Annis (Eds.), *Expectations in cross-cultural psychology* (pp. 335–55). Lisse, Netherlands: Swets & Zeitlinger.

(1989). Cultural predictors of national negotiation styles. In F. Mauter-Markhof (Ed.), *Processes of international negotiations* (pp. 193–202). Boulder, CO: Westview Press.

(1991). *Cultures and organizations: Software of the mind*. London: McGraw-Hill.

(2001). *Culture's consequences* (2nd ed.). Thousand Oaks, CA: Sage.

Hofstede, G., & Bond, M. H. (1984). Hofstede's culture dimensions: An independent validation using Rokeach's value survey. *Journal of Cross-Cultural Psychology*, 15, 417–33.

Hofstede, G., & Spangenberg, J. (1987). Measuring individualism and collectivism at occupational and organizational levels. In C. Kagitcibasi (Ed.), *Growth and progress in cross-cultural psychology*. Lisse, Netherlands: Swets and Zeitlinger.

Hofstede, G., Neuijen, B., Ohayv, D. D., & Sanders, G. (1990). Measuring organizational cultures: A qualitative/quantitative study across twenty cases. *Academy of Management Journal: Administrative Science Quarterly*, *35*, 286–316.

Holland P. W., & Wainer, H. (Eds.) (1993). *Differential item functioning*. Hillsdale, NJ: Erlbaum.

Holm, A., & Dodd, B. (1996). The effect of first written language on the acquisition of English literacy. *Cognition*, *59*, 119–47.

Holtzman, W., Evans, R., Kennedy, S., & Iscoe, I. (1987). Psychology and health: Contributions of psychology to the improvement of health and health care. *International Journal of Psychology*, *22*, 221–67.

Honigmann, J. J. (1967). *Personality in culture*. New York: Harper and Row.

Hoorens, V., & Poortinga, Y. (2000). Behavior in social context. In K. Pawlik & M. Rosenzweig (Eds.), *International handbook of psychology* (pp. 40–63). London: Sage.

Hoosain, R., & Salili, F. (1987). Language differences in pronunciation speed for numbers, digit span, and mathematical ability. *Psychologia: An International Journal of Psychology*, *30*, 34–38.

Hopkins, B. (1977). Considerations of comparability of measures in cross-cultural studies of early infancy from a study on the development of black and white infants in Britain. In Y. H. Poortinga (Ed.), *Basic problems in cross-cultural psychology* (pp. 36–46). Lisse, Netherlands: Swets and Zeitlinger.

Hopkins, B., & Westra, T. (1990). Motor development, maternal expectations, and the role of handling. *Infant Behavior and Development*, *13*, 117–22.

Hoppe, M. H. (1990). *A comparative study of country elites: International differnces in work-related values and learning and their implications for management training development.* Unpublished Ph.D. thesis. Chapel Hill, NC: University of North Carolina.

Hopper, P. J., & Thompson, S. A. (1984). The discourse basis for lexical categories in universal grammar. *Language*, *60*, 703–52.

Horenczyk, G. (1996). Migrant identities in conflict: Acculturation attitudes and perceived acculturation ideologies. In G. Breakwell & E. Lyons (Eds.), *Changing European identities* (pp. 241–50). Oxford: Butterworth-Heinemann.

House, R. J. et al. (1999). Cultural influences on leadership and organizations: Project GLOBE. In W. F. Mobley, M. J. Gessner, & V. Arnold (Eds.), *Advances in global leadership* (vol. I, pp. 171–233). Stamford, CT: JAI Press.

Hsu, F. L. K. (Ed.) (1961). *Psychological anthropology* (1st ed.). Homewood, IL: Dorsey/ (1972) (2nd ed.). Cambridge, MA: Schenkman.

Huang, H. S., & Hanley, J. R. (1994). Phonological awareness and visual skills in learning to read Chinese and English. *Cognition*, *54*, 73–98.

Hudson, W. (1960). Pictorial depth perception in sub-cultural groups in Africa. *Journal of Social Psychology*, *52*, 183–208.

(1967). The study of the problem of pictorial perception among unacculturated groups. *International Journal of Psychology*, *2*, 89–107.

Hui, C. H. (1982). Locus of control: A review of cross-cultural research. *International Journal of Intercultural Relations*, *6*, 301–23.

Hui, C. H., & Luk, C. L. (1997). Industrial/organizational psychology. In J. W. Berry, M. H. Segall, & C. Kagitcibasi (Eds.), *Social behavior and applications* (pp. 371–411). Vol. III of *Handbook of cross-cultural psychology* (2nd ed.). Boston, MA: Allyn and Bacon.

Hui, C. H., & Yee, C. (1994). The shortened individualism–collectivism scale: Its relationship to demographic and work related variables. *Journal of Research in Personality*, *28*, 409–24.

Humphreys, L. G. (1985). Race differences and the Spearman hypothesis. *Intelligence*, *9*, 275–83.

Hunt, E. B. (1997). Nature vs. nurture: The feeling of vujà dé. In R. J. Sternberg & E. Grigorenko (Eds.), *Intelligence, heredity, and environment* (pp. 531–51). Cambridge: Cambridge University Press.

Hunt, E. B., & Agnoli, F. (1991). The Whorfian hypothesis: A cognitive psychology perspective. *Psychological Review*, *98*, 377–89.

Hurh, W. M., & Kim, K. C. (1990). Adaptation stages and mental health of Korean male immigrants in the United States. *International Migration Review*, *24*, 456–79.

Hwang, K.-K., & Yang, C.-F. (Eds.) (2000). Indigenous, cultural and cross-cultural psychologies. *Asian Journal of Social Psychology*, *3*, 183–293 (special issue).

Hynie, M. (1998). The AIDS/HIV pandemic. In F. Aboud (Ed.), *Health psychology in global perspective* (pp. 94–122). Newbury Park, CA: Sage.

IDE (Industrial Democracy in Europe International Research Group) (1981). *Industrial democracy in Europe*. Oxford: Clarendon Press.

Ikebe, O. (1999). *The concept of Amae: A new interpretation and examination in cross-cultural validity*. Unpublished paper, University of Leuven.

Inglehart, R. (1997). *Modernization and postmodernization: Cultural, economic and political change in 43 societies*. Princeton, NJ: Princeton University Press.

Inglehart, R., & Baker, W. (2000). Modernization, culture change and the persistance of traditional values. *American Sociological Review, 65,* 19–51.

Ingman, M., Kaessmann, H., Pääbo, S., & Gullensten, U. (2000). Mitrochondrial genome variation and the origins of modern humans. *Nature, 408,* 708–12.

Inkeles, A. (1997). *National character: A psycho-social perspective*. New Brunswick: Transaction Books.

Irvine, S. H. (1979). The place of factor analysis in cross-cultural methodology, and its contribution to cognitive theory. In L. Eckensberger, W. Lonner, & Y. H. Poortinga (Eds.), *Cross-cultural contributions to psychology* (pp. 300–41). Lisse, Netherlands: Swets & Zeitlinger.

Irvine, S. H., & Berry, J. W. (1988). The abilities of mankind: A reevaluation. In S. Irvine & J. W. Berry (Eds.), *Human abilities in cultural context* (pp. 3–59). New York: Cambridge University Press.

Irvine, S. H., & Berry, J. W. (Eds.) (1988). *Human abilities in cultural context*. New York: Cambridge University Press.

Izard, C. E. (1971). *The face of emotion*. New York: Appleton-Century-Crofts.

(1977). *Human emotions*. London: Plenum Press.

(1994). Innate and universal facial expressions: Evidence from developmental and cross-cultural research. *Psychological Bulletin, 115,* 188–299.

Jablensky, A., & Sartorius, N. (1988). Is schizophrenia universal? *Acta Psychiatrica Scandinavica, 78,* 65–70.

Jablensky, A., Sartorius, N., Ernberg, G., Anker, M., et al. (1992). Schizophrenia: Manifestations, incidence and course in different cultures. *Psychological Medicine, Monograph. Supplement, 20,* 1–97.

Jahoda, G. (1954). A note on Ashanti names and their relationship to personality. *British Journal of Psychology, 45,* 192–5.

(1971). Retinal pigmentation, illusion susceptibility and space perception. *International Journal of Psychology, 6,* 199–208.

(1973). Psychology and the developing countries: Do they need each other? *International Social Science Journal, 25,* 461–74.

(1974). Applying cross-cultural psychology to the Third World. In J. W. Berry & W. Lonner (Eds.), *Applied cross-cultural psychology* (pp. 3–7). Lisse, Netherlands: Swets & Zeitlinger.

(1975). Retinal pigmentation and space perception: A failure to replicate. *International Journal of Psychology, 97,* 133–4.

(1977). In pursuit of the emic–etic distinction: Can we ever capture it? In Y. H. Poortinga (Ed.), *Basic problems in cross-cultural pychology* (pp. 55–63). Lisse, Netherlands: Swets & Zeitlinger.

(1978). Cross-cultural study of factors influencing orientation errors in the reproduction of Kohs-type figures. *British Journal of Psychology, 69,* 45–57.

(1979). A cross-cultural perspective on experimental social psychology. *Personality and Social Psychology Bulletin*, 5, 142–8.

(1980). Theoretical and systematic approaches in cross-cultural psychology. In H. C. Triandis & W. W. Lambert (Eds.), *Handbook of cross-cultural psychology*. Vol. I: *Perspectives* (pp. 69–141). Boston, MA: Allyn and Bacon.

(1981). The influence of schooling on adult recall of familiar stimuli: A study in Ghana. *International Journal of Psychology*, 16, 59–71.

(1982). *Psychology and anthropology: A psychological perspective*. London: Academic.

(1983). The cross-cultural emperor's conceptual clothes: The emic–etic issue revisited. In J. B. Deregowski, S. Dziurawiec, & R. C. Annis (Eds.), *Expectations in cross-cultural psychology* (pp. 19–38). Lisse, Netherlands: Swets & Zeitlinger.

(1984). Do we need a concept of culture? *Journal of Cross-Cultural Psychology*, 15, 139–52.

(1986). Nature, culture and social psychology. *European Journal of Social Psychology*, 16, 17–30.

(1990a). Our forgotten ancestors. In J. J. Berman (Ed.), *Cross-cultural perspectives: Nebraska symposium on motivation*, 37 (pp. 1–40). Lincoln, NE: University of Nebraska Press.

(1990b). Variables, systems, and the problem of explanation. In F. J. R. Van de Vijver & G. J. M. Hutschemaekers (Eds.), *The investigation of culture* (pp. 115–30). Tilburg: Tilburg University Press.

(1999). *Images of savages: Ancient roots of modern prejudice in western culture*. London: Routledge.

Jahoda, G., & Krewer, B. (1997). History of cross-cultural and cultural psychology. In J. W. Berry, Y. H. Poortinga, & J. Pandey (Eds.), *Theory and method* (pp. 1–42). Vol. I of *Handbook of cross-cultural psychology* (2nd ed.). Boston, MA: Allyn and Bacon.

Jahoda, G., & McGurk, H. (1974a). Development of pictorial depth perception: Cross-cultural replication. *Child Development*, 45, 1042–7.

(1974b). Pictorial depth perception in Scottish and Ghanaian children: A critique of some findings with Hudson's test. *International Journal of Psychology*, 9, 255–67.

Jahoda, G., & Stacey, B. (1970). Susceptibility of geometrical illusions according to culture and professional training. *Perception and Psychophysics*, 7, 179–84.

Jahoda, G., Cheyne, W. M., Deregowski, J. B., Sinha, D., & Collingbourne, R. (1976). Utilization of pictorial information in classroom learning: A cross-cultural study. *AV Communication Review*, 24, 295–315.

Janis, I. L., & Mann, L. (1977). *Decision making: A psychological analysis of conflict, choice and commitment*. London: Free Press.

Jasinskaja-Lahti, I., & Liebkind, K. (1999). Exploration of the ethnic identity among Russian-speaking immigrant adolescents in Finland. *Journal of Cross-Cultural Psychology*, 30, 527–39.

Jayasuriya, L., & Lee, N. (Eds.) (1994). *Social dimensions of development*. Perth: Academic Books.

Jayasuriya, L., Sang, D., & Fielding, A. (1992). *Ethnicity, immigration and mental illness: A critical review of Australian research*. Canberra: Bureau of Immigration Research.

Jensen, A. R. (1980). *Bias in mental testing*. New York: Free Press.

(1982). Reaction time and psychometric g. In H. J. Eysenck (Ed.), *A model for intelligence* (pp. 93–132). Berlin, Springer-Verlag.

(1985). The nature of Black–White difference on various psychometric tests: Spearman's hypothesis. *Behavioral and Brain Sciences*, 8, 193–263.

(1998). *The g factor. The science of mental ability.* Westport, CT: Praeger.

Ji, L.-J., Peng, K., & Nisbett, R. (2000). Culture, control and perception of relationships in the environment. *Journal of Personality and Social Psychology, 78*, 943–55.

Jilek, N. G. (1988). *Indian healing: Shamanic ceremonialism in the Pacific Northwest.* Vancouver, BC: Hancock House.

Jilek, W. (1993). Traditional medicine relevant to psychiatry. In N. Sartorius et al. (Eds.), *Treatment of mental disorders: A review of effectiveness* (pp. 341–90). Washington, DC: American Psychiatric Press.

Jing, Q., & Zhang, H. (1998). China's reform and challenges for psychology. In J. Adair, D. Belanger, & K. Dion (Eds.), *Advances in psychological science.* Vol. I: *Social, personal and cultural aspects* (pp. 271–91). Hove, UK: Psychology Press.

Joe, R. C. (1991). *Effecten van taaltonaliteit op het cognitief functioneren: Een cross-cultureel onderzoek.* [Effects of tonality in language on cognitive functioning]. Tilburg, Netherlands: Tilburg University Press.

Jones, E. E., & Nisbett, R. (1972). The actor and the observer: Divergent perceptions of the causes of behavior. In E. E. Jones (et al.) (Eds.), *Attribution: Perceiving the causes of behavior* (pp. 79–94). Morristown, NJ: General Learning Press.

Jöreskog, K., & Sörbom, D. (1999). *LISREL 8.30.* Chicago, IL: Scientific Software International.

Joshi, P. C. (2000). Relevance and utility of traditional medical system in a Himalayan tribe. *Psychology and Developing Societies, 12*, 5–29.

Kagitcibasi, C. (1984). Socialization in a traditional society: A challenge to psychology. *International Journal of Psychology, 19*, 145–57.

(1987). Individual and group loyalties: Are they compatible? In C. Kagitcibasi (Ed.), *Growth and progress in cross-cultural psychology.* Lisse, Netherlands: Swets & Zeitlinger.

(1990). Family and socialization in cross-cultural perspective: A model of change. In J. Berman (Ed.), *Cross-cultural perspectives: Nebraska Symposium on Motivation, 1989* (pp. 135–200). Lincoln, NE: University of Nebraska Press.

(1993). Is psychology relevant to global human development issues? *American Psychologist, 50*, 293–300.

(1994a). A critical appraisal of individualism and collectivism: Toward a new formulation. In U. Kim, H. C. Triandis, C. Kagitcibasi, S.-C. Choi, & G. Yoon (Eds.), *Individualism and collectivism* (pp. 52–65). Thousand Oaks, CA: Sage.

(1994b). Human development and societal development. In A.-M. Bouvy, F. J. R. van de Vijver, & P. Boski (Eds.), *Journeys in cross-cultural psychology* (pp. 3–24). Lisse, Netherlands: Swets & Zeitlinger.

(1996). *Family and human development across cultures: A view from the other side.* Hillsdale, NJ: Erlbaum.

(1997a). Individualism and collectivism. In J. W. Berry, M. H. Segall, & C. Kagitcibasi (Eds.), *Social behavior and applications* (pp. 1–49). Vol. III of *Handbook of cross-cultural psychology*, 2nd ed. Boston, MA: Allyn and Bacon.

(1997b). Whither multiculturalism? *Applied Psychology: An International Review, 46*, 44–9.

(1998). Whatever happened to modernization? *Cross-Cultural Psychology Bulletin, 32*, 8–11.

Kagitcibasi, C., & Poortinga, Y. H. (2000). Cross-cultural psychology: Issues and overarching themes. *Journal of Cross-Cultural Psychology, 31*, 129–47.

Kaiser, A., Katz, R., & Shaw, B. (1998). Cultural issues in the management of depression. In S. Kazarian & D. Evans (Eds.), *Cultural clinical psychology: Theory, research and practice* (pp. 177–214). New York: Oxford University Press.

Kakar, S. (1982). *Shamans, mystics and doctors*. Delhi: Oxford University Press.

(1985). Psychoanalysis and non-Western cultures. *International Review of Psychoanalysis, 12*, 441–8.

Kalin, R., & Berry, J. W. (1995). Ethnic and civic self-identity in Canada: Analyses of the 1974 and 1991 national surveys. *Canadian Ethnic Studies, 27*, 1–15.

(1996). Interethnic attitudes in Canada: Ethnocentrism, consensual hierarchy and reciprocity. *Canadian Journal of Behavioural Science, 28*, 253–61.

Kalin, R., & Tilby, P. (1978). Development and validation of a sex-role ideology scale. *Psychological Reports, 42*, 731–8.

Kalmus, H. (1969). Ethnic differences in sensory perception. *Journal of Biosocial Science, Supplement 1*, 81–90.

Kaplan, G., Pamuk, E., Lynch, J., Cohen, R., & Balfour, J. (1996). Inequality in income and mortality in the United States. *British Medical Journal, 312*, 999–1003.

Kardiner, A., & Linton, R. (1945). *The individual and his society*. New York: Columbia University Press.

Kasamatsu, A., & Hirai, T. (1966). An electroencephalographic study of the Zen meditation. *Folia Psychiatrica et Neurologica Japonica, 20*, 315–36.

Kashima, Y. (2000). Conceptions of culture and person for psychology. *Journal of Cross-Cultural Psychology, 31*, 14–32.

Kashima, Y., Yamaguchi, S., Kim, U., Choi, S.-C., Gelfand, M., & Yuki, M. (1995). Culture, gender and self: A perspective from individualism–collectivism research. *Journal of Personality and Social Psychology, 69*, 925–37.

Kaufmann, J. (1996). *Conference diplomacy* (3rd ed.). London: Macmillan.

Kay, P., & McDaniel, C. K. (1978). The linguistic significance of the meanings of basic color terms. *Language, 54*, 610–46.

Kay, P., Berlin, B., Maffi, L., & Merrifield, W. (1997). Color naming across languages. In C. L. Hardin, & L. Maffi (Eds.), *Colour categories in thought and language* (pp. 21–58). Cambridge: Cambridge University Press.

Kazarian, S., & Evans, D. (Eds.) (1998). *Cultural clinical psychology: Theory, research and practice*. New York: Oxford University Press.

Kealey, D. J. (1989). A study of cross-cultural effectiveness: Theoretical issues, practical applications. *International Journal of Intercultural Relations, 13*, 387–428.

(1996). The challenge of international personnel selection. In D. Landis & R. S. Bhagat (Eds.), *Handbook of intercultural training* (2nd ed., pp. 81–105). Thousand Oaks, CA: Sage.

Kealey, D. J., & Ruben, B. D. (1983). Cross-cultural personnel selection criteria, issues and methods. In D. Landis & R. W. Brislin (Eds.), *Handbook of intercultural training* (vol. I, pp. 155–75). New York: Pergamon.

Keefer, C. H., Dixon, S., Tronik, E., & Brazelton, T. B. (1978). Gusii infants' neuromotor behavior. Paper presented at the International Conference on Infant Studies, Providence, RI.

Keller, H. (1997). Evolutionary approaches. In J. W. Berry, Y. H. Poortinga, & J. Pandey (Eds.), *Theory and method* (pp. 215–55). Vol. I of *Handbook of cross-cultural psychology* (2nd ed.). Boston, MA: Allyn and Bacon.

Keller, H., & Eckensberger, L. (1998). Kultur und Entwicklung. In H. Keller (Ed.), *Lehrbuch Entwicklungpsychologie* (pp. 57–96). Berne: Hans Huber.

Keller, H., & Greenfield, P. M. (2000). History and future of development in cross-cultural psychology. *Journal of Cross-Cultural Psychology, 31*, 52–62.

Keller, H., Schölmerich, A., & Eibl-Eibesfeldt, I. (1988). Communication patterns in adult–infant interactions in western and non-western cultures. *Journal of Cross-Cultural Psychology, 19*, 427–45.

Kendon, A. (1984). Did gestures escape the curse at the confusion of Babel? In A. Wolfgang (Ed.), *Nonverbal behavior: Perspectives, applications, intercultural insights* (pp. 75–114). Lewiston, NY: Hogrefe.

Kenrick, D. T., & Keefe, R. C. (1992). Age preferences reflect sex differences in human reproductive strategies. *Behavioral and Brain Sciences, 15*, 75–133.

Kermoian, R., & Leiderman, P. H. (1986). Infant attachment to mother and child caretaker in an East African community. *International Journal of Behavioural Development, 9*, 455–70.

Kessen, W. (1979). The American child and other cultural inventions. *American Psychologist, 34*, 815–20.

Kessler, R. C., Mickelson, K., & Williams, D. (1999). The prevalence, distribution and mental health correlates of perceived discrimination in the United States. *Journal of Health and Social Behavior, 40*, 208–30.

Kettlewell, H. B. D. (1959). Darwin's missing evidence. *Scientific American, 200 (3)*, 48–53.

Khandwalla, P. N. (1988). Organizational effectiveness. In J. Pandey (Ed.), *Pychology in India: The state of the art* (vol. III, pp. 97–215). New Delhi: Sage.

Kilbride, P. L. (1980). Sensorimotor behavior of Baganda and Samia infants: A controlled comparison. *Journal of Cross-Cultural Psychology, 11*, 131–52.

Kim, U. (1990). Indigenous psychology: Science and applications. In R. Brislin (Ed.), *Applied cross-cultural psychology* (pp. 142–60). Newbury Park, CA: Sage.

Kim, U., & Berry, J. W. (Eds.) (1993). *Indigenous psychologies: Research and experience in cultural context.* Newbury Park, CA: Sage.

Kim, U., Triandis, H. C., Kagitcibasi, C., Choi, S.-C., & Yoon, G. (Eds.) (1994). *Individualism and collectivism: Theory, method and application.* Thousand Oaks, CA: Sage.

Kim, Y. Y. (1988). *Communication and cross-cultural adaptation: An integrative theory.* Clevedon: Multilingual Matters.

Kimmel, H. D., Van Olst, E. H., & Orlebeke, J. F. (Eds.) (1979). *The orienting reflex in humans.* New York: Wiley.

Kimura, D. (1999). *Sex and cognition.* Cambridge, MA: MIT Press.

Kish, L. (1965). *Survey sampling.* New York: Wiley.

Kitayama, S., & Markus, H. R. (1994). Introduction to cultural psychology and emotion research. In S. Kitayama & H. R. Markus (Eds.), *Emotion and culture: Empirical studies of mutual influence* (pp. 1–22). Washington, DC: American Psychological Association.

Kitayama, S., Markus, H. R., Matsumoto, H., & Norasakkunit, V. (1997). Individual and collective processes in the construction of the self: Self-enhancement in the United States and self-criticism in Japan. *Journal of Personality and Social Psychology, 72*, 1245–67.

Kleinman, A. (1991). *Rethinking psychiatry: From cultural category to personal experience.* New York: Free Press.

Klineberg, O. (1940). *Social psychology.* New York: Henry Holt.

(1980). Historical perspectives: Cross-cultural psychology before 1960. In H. C. Triandis & W. W. Lambert (Eds.), *Handbook of cross-cultural psychology.* Vol. I: *Perspectives* (pp. 31–68). Boston, MA: Allyn and Bacon.

Klineberg, O., & Hull, W. F. (1979). *At a foreign university: An international study of adaptation and coping.* New York: Praeger.

Kloos, P. (1988). *Door het oog van de anthropoloog* [Through the eye of the anthropologist]. Muiderberg: Coutinho.

Kluckhohn, C. (1951). Values and value orientations in the theory of action. In T. Parsons & E. Shils (Eds.), *Toward a general theory of action.* Cambridge, MA: Harvard University Press.

(1957). *Mirror for man.* New York: Premier Books.

Kluckhohn, F., & Strodtbeck, F. (1961). *Variations in value orientations.* Evanston, IL: Row, Peterson.

Knapen, M. T. (1962). *L'enfant Mukongo: Orientation de base du système éducatif et développement de la personnalité* [The Mukongo child: Basic orientation of the education system and the development of the personality]. Louvain: Ed. Nauwelaerts.

Kohlberg, L. (1981). From *is* to *ought*: How to commit the naturalistic fallacy and get away with it in the study of moral development. In L. Kohlberg (Ed.), *Essays on moral development: The philosophy of moral development* (vol. I, pp. 101–89). San Francisco: Harper & Row.

(1984). *Essays on moral development: The psychology of moral development* (Vol. II). San Francisco: Harper & Row.

Kohlberg, L., Levine, C., & Hewer, A. (1983). Moral stages: A current formulation, and a response to critics. In J. A. Meacham (Ed.), *Contributions to human development* (vol. X). New York: Karger.

Kojima, H. (1999). Ethnothéorie des soins et de l'éducation des enfants au Japon. Une perspective historique. In B. Bril, P. R. Dasen, C. Sabatier, & B. Krewer (Eds.), *Propos sur l'enfant et l'adolescent: Quels enfants pour quelles cultures?* [Remarks on children and adolescents: Which children for which cultures?] (pp. 185–206). Paris: L'Harmattan.

Konner, M. (1981). Evolution of human behavior development. In R. H. Munroe, R. L. Munroe, & B. B. Whiting (Eds.), *Handbook of cross-cultural human development* (pp. 3–51). New York: Garland.

(1988). The aggressors. *New York Times Magazine,* 14 August, 33–4.

Kornadt, H.-J., & Tachibana, Y. (1999). Early child-rearing and social motives after nine years: A cross-cultural longitudinal study. In W. J. Lonner, D. L. Dinnel, D. K. Forgays, & S. A. Hayes (Eds.), *Merging past, present and future in cross-cultural psychology* (pp. 429–41). Lisse, Netherlands: Swets & Zeitlinger.

Korolenko, C.P. (1988). The peculiarities of alcoholism in the North. In H. Linderholm (Ed.), *Circumpolar Health 87* (pp. 36–7). Oulu: Nordic Council for Arctic Medical Research.

Kottak, C. (1999). The new ecological anthropology. *American Anthropologist, 101,* 23–35.

Krech, D., Crutchfield, R., & Ballachey, E. (1962). *Individual in society.* New York: McGraw-Hill.

Krishnan, A., & Berry, J. W. (1992). Acculturative stress and acculturation attitudes among Indian immigrants to the United States. *Psychology and Developing Societies, 4,* 187–212.

Kroeber, A. L. (1917). The superorganic. *American Anthropologist, 19,* 163–213.

(1939). *Cultural and natural areas of North America*. Berkeley, CA: University of California Press.

(1949). The concept of culture in science. In A. L. Kroeber (Ed.), *The nature of culture* (pp. 118–35). Chicago, IL: Chicago University Press.

Kroeber, A. L., & Kluckhohn, C. (1952). *Culture: A critical review of concepts and definitions*. Cambridge, MA: Peabody Museum, Vol. 47, no. 1.

Krumm, H. J., (1997). Der Erwerb und die Vermittlung von Fremdsprachen. [Acquiring and transmitting foreign languages]. In F. E. Weinert (Ed.), *Psychologie des Unterrichts und der Schule* (pp. 503–34). Göttingen: Hogrefe.

Kublin, M. (1995). *International negotiating: A primer for American business professionals*. New York: International Business Press.

Kuhn, T. S. (1962). *The structure of scientific revolutions*. Chicago, IL: Chicago University Press.

Kulkarni, S. G., & Puhan, B. N. (1988). Psychological assessment: Its present and future trends. In J. Pandey (Ed.), *Psychology in India: The state of the art* (vol. I, pp. 19–91). New Delhi: Sage.

Kumagai, H. A., and Kumagai, A. K. (1986). The hidden "I" in Amae: "Passive love" and Japanese social construction. *Ethos*, *14*, 305–319.

Kuwano, S., Namba, S., & Schick, A. (1986). A cross-cultural study on noise problems. In A. Schick, H. Höge & G. Lazarus-Mainka (Eds.), *Contributions to psychological acoustics* (pp. 370–95). Oldenburg: Universität Oldenburg.

Laaksonen, O. (1988). *Management in China during and after Mao in enterprise, government, and party*. Berlin: Walter de Gruyter.

Laferrière, M. (1984). Languages, ideologies and multicultural education. In R. Samuda, J. W. Berry, & M. Laferrière (Eds.), *Multiculturalism in Canada: Social and educational perspectives* (pp. 171–83). Toronto: Allyn and Bacon.

Lagmay, A. (1984). Western psychology in the Philippines: Impact and response. *International Journal of Psychology*, *19*, 31–44.

Lakatos, I. (1974). Falsification and the methodology of scientific research programmes. In I. Lakatos & A. Musgrave (Eds.), *Criticism and the growth of knowledge* (pp. 91–196). Cambridge: Cambridge University Press.

Laland, K. N., Odling-Smee, J., & Feldman, M. W. (2000). Niche construction, biological evolution, and cultural change. *Behavioral and Brain Sciences*, *23*, 131–75.

Lamb, M. (Ed.) (1986). *The father's role: Applied perspectives*. New York: Wiley.

Lambert, W. E. (1967). A social psychology of bilingualism. *Journal of Social Issues*, *23*, 91–109.

(1977). The effects of bilingualism on the individual: Cognitive and sociocultural consequences. In P. A. Hornby (Ed.), *Bilingualism: Psychological, social and educational implications*. New York: Academic Press.

(1980). The social psychology of language: A perspective for the 1980's. In H. Giles, W. Robinson, & P. Smith (Eds.), *Language: Social psychological perspectives* (pp. 415–24). Oxford: Pergamon.

Lambert, W. E., & Anisfeld, E. (1969). A note on the relationship of bilingualism and intelligence. *Canadian Journal of Behavioural Science*, *1*, 123–8.

Lambert, W. E., & Tucker, R. (1972). *Bilingual education of children: The St. Lambert study*. Rowley, MA: Newbury House.

Lammers, C. J., & Hickson, D. J. (Eds.) (1979). *Organizations alike and unlike: International and interinstitutional studies in the sociology of organizations*. London: Routledge and Kegan Paul.

Landis, D., & Bhagat, R. S. (Eds.) (1996). *Handbook of intercultural training* (2nd ed.). Thousand Oaks, CA: Sage.

Langaney, A., Hubert van Blyenburgh, N. H., & Sanchez-Mazas, X. (1992). *Tous parents, tous différents.* Paris: Chabaud.

Lantz, D., & Stefflre, V. (1964). Language and cognition revisited. *Journal of Abnormal and Social Psychology, 69,* 472–81.

Laroche, M., Kim, C., Hui, M., & Joy, A. (1996). An empirical study of multidimensional ethnic change. *Journal of Cross-Cultural Psychology, 27,* 114–31.

Laroche, M., Kim, C., Hui, M., & Tomiuk, M. (1998). Test of a nonlinear relationship between linguistic acculturation and ethnic identification. *Journal of Cross-Cultural Psychology, 29,* 418–33.

Lave, J., & Wenger, E. (1991). *Situated learning: Legitimate peripheral participation.* Cambridge: Cambridge University Press.

Lawlor, M. (1955). Cultural influences on preference for designs. *Journal of Abnormal and Social Psychology, 51,* 690–2.

Lazarus, R. S. (1990). Theory-based stress measurement. *Psychological Inquiry, 1,* 3–13.

  (1991). Psychological stress in the workplace. *Journal of Social Behavior and Personality, 6,* 1–13.

Lazarus, R. S., & Folkman, S. (1984). *Stress, appraisal and coping.* New York: Springer.

LCHC (Laboratory of Comparative Human Cognition) (1982). Culture and intelligence. In R. Sternberg (Ed.), *Handbook of human intelligence* (pp. 642–719). New York: Cambridge University Press.

  (1983). Culture and cognitive development. In P. H. Mussen & W. Kessen (Eds.), *Handbook of child psychology* (vol. I, pp. 295–356). New York: Wiley.

Leconte, F. (1997). *La famille et les langues* [Family and languages]. Paris: L'Harmattan.

Lee, R. B., & DeVore, I. (Eds.) (1976). *Kalahari hunter-gatherers.* Cambridge, MA: Harvard University Press.

Leff, J. (1977). International variations in the diagnosis of psychiatric illness. *British Journal of Psychiatry, 131,* 329–38.

  (1981). *Psychiatry around the globe: A transcultural view.* New York: Dekker.

Leibowitz, H. W., Brislin, R., Perlmutter, L., & Hennessey, R. (1969). Ponzo perspective illusion as a manifestation of space perception. *Science, 166,* 1174–6.

Lenneberg, E. H. (1953). Cognition in linguistics. *Language, 29,* 463–71.

  (1967). *Biological foundations of language.* New York: Wiley.

Lens, W., & Hermans, I. (1988). *Organizational climate and the individual motivational orientations of managers: A correlational study.* Louvain: University of Louvain.

Leung, K., & Bond, M. H. (1989). On the empirical identification of dimensions for cross-cultural comparison. *Journal of Cross-Cultural Psychology, 20,* 133–51.

Leung, K., & Wu, P. G. (1990). Dispute processing. In R. G. Brislin (Ed.), *Applied cross-cultural psychology* (pp. 209–31). Thousand Oaks, CA: Sage.

Levelt, W. J. M. (2000). Psychology of language. In K. Pawlik & M. R. Rosenzweig (Eds.), *The international handbook of psychology* (pp. 151–66). London: Sage.

Levenson, R. W., Ekman, P., Heider, K., & Friesen, W. V. (1992). Emotion and autonomic nervous system activity in the Minangkabau of West-Sumatra. *Journal of Personality and Social Psychology, 62,* 972–88.

LeVine, R. A. (1977). Child rearing as cultural adaptation. In H. Leiderman, S. Tulkin, & A. Rosenfeld (Eds.), *Culture and infancy.* New York: Academic Press.

(1982). *Culture, behaviour and personality* (2nd ed.). Chicago, IL: Aldine.

(1999). An agenda for psychological anthropology. *Ethos, 27,* 15–24.

LeVine, R. A., & Campbell, D. T. (1972). *Ethnocentrism.* New York: Wiley.

Levinson, S. C. (1998). Studying spatial conceptualization across cultures: Anthropology and cognitive science. *Ethos, 26,* 7–24.

Levi-Strauss, C. (1962). *La pensée sauvage.* Paris: Plon (trans. 1966, *The savage mind.* London: Weidenfeld & Nicolson).

Levistsky, D. A., & Strupp, N. J. (1984). Functional isolation in rats. In J. Brozek & B. Schürch (Eds.), *Malnutrition and behavior: Critical assessment of key issues* (pp. 411–20). Lausanne: Nestlé Foundation.

Levy, R. I. (1984). The emotions in comparative perspective. In K. R. Scherer & P. Ekman (Eds.), *Approaches to emotion* (pp. 397–412). Hillsdale, NJ: Erlbaum.

Lewin, K. (1936). *Principles of topological psychology.* New York: McGraw-Hill.

Lewis, J., & Mercer, J. (1978). The system of multicultural pluralistic assessment: SOMPA. In W. Coulter & H. Morrow (Eds.), *Adaptive behaviour: Concepts and measurement.* New York: Grune and Stratton.

Lewis, M., Ramsay, D. S., & Kawakami, K. (1993). Differences between Japanese infants and Caucasian American infants in behavioral and cortisol responses to inoculation. *Child Development, 64,* 1722–31.

Lewis, O. (1966). *La vida.* New York: Random House.

Lewontin, R. C. (1972). The apportionment of human diversity. *Evolutionary Biology, 6,* 381–98.

(1978). Adaptation. *Scientific American, 239(3),* 156–69.

Li, H. Z. (1999). Communicating information in conversations: A cross-cultural comparison. *International Journal of Intercultural Communication, 23,* 387–409.

Li, J. C., Dunning, D., & Malpass, R. S. (1998). Cross-racial identification among European-Americans: Basketball fandom and the contact hypothesis. Paper presented at the biennial meeting of the American Psychology-Law Society, Redondo Beach, CA, March 1998.

Liebkind, K. (1996). Vietnamese refugees in Finland: Changing cultural identity. In G. Breakwell & E. Lyons (Eds.), *Changing European identities* (pp. 227–40). London: Butterworth-Heinemann.

(2000). Acculturation. In R. Brown & S. Gaertner (Eds.), *Blackwell Handbook of Social Psychology.* Vol. IV: *Intergroup processes* (pp. 386–404). Oxford: Blackwell.

Liebkind, K., & Jasinskaja-Lahti, I. (2000). The influence of experiences of discrimination on psychological stress: A comparison of seven immigrant groups. *Journal of Community* and *Applied Social Psychology, 10,* 1–16.

Liebkind, K., & McAlister, A. (1999). Extended contact through peer modeling to promote tolerance in Finland. *European Journal of Social Psychology, 29,* 765–80.

Likert, R. (1967). *The human organization: Its management and values.* New York: McGraw-Hill.

Lillard, A. (1998). Ethnopsychologies: Cultural variations in theories of mind. *Psychological Bulletin, 123,* 3–32.

Lin, N., Dean, A., & Ensel, N. (Eds.) (1986). *Social support, life events and depression.* New York: Academic Press.

Lincoln, Y., & Guba, E. G. (2000). Paradigmatic controversies, contradictions, and emerging conflicts. In N. K. Denzin & Y. Lincoln (Eds.), *Handbook of qualitative research* (2nd ed., pp. 163–88). Thousand Oaks, CA: Sage.

Linton, R. (1936). *The study of man*. New York: Appleton-Century-Crofts.

(1940). *Acculturation in seven American Indian tribes*. New York: Appleton-Century.

Lipiansky, E. M. (1992). *Identité, communication* [Identity, communication]. Paris: Presses Universitaires de France.

Little, T. D. (1997). Mean and covariance structures (MACS) analyses of cross-cultural data: Practical and theoretical issues. *Multivariate Behavioral Research, 32*, 53–76.

Liu, L. A. (1985). Reasoning counterfactually in Chinese: Are there any obstacles? *Cognition, 21*, 239–70.

Livernash, R., & Rodenburg, E. (1998). Population change, resources and the environment. *Population Bulletin, 53*, 2–40.

Lloyd, B. (1977). Culture and colour coding. In G. Vessey (Ed.), *Communication and understanding* (pp. 140–60). Brighton: Harvester Press.

Lockett, M. (1983). Organizational democracy and politics in China. In C. Crunch & F. Heller (Eds.), *Organizational democracy and political processes* (pp. 591–635). Chichester: Wiley.

Loehlin, J. C. (1992). Genes and environment in personality development. Newbury Park, CA: Sage.

Loehlin, J. C., Horn, J. M., & Willerman, L. (1989). Modeling IQ change: Evidence from the Texas Adoption Project. *Child Development, 60*, 993–1004.

Lomax, A., & Berkowitz, N. (1972). The evolutionary taxonomy of culture. *Science, 177*, 228–39.

Longabaugh, R. (1980). The systematic observation of behavior in naturalistic settings. In H. C. Triandis & J. W. Berry (Eds.), *Handbook of cross-cultural psychology*. Vol. I: *Perspectives* (pp. 57–126). Boston, MA: Allyn and Bacon.

Lonner, W. J. (1980). The search for psychological universals. In H. C. Triandis & W. W. Lambert (Eds.), *Handbook of cross-cultural psychology*. Vol. I: *Perspectives* (pp. 143–204). Boston, MA: Allyn and Bacon.

Lonner, W. J., & Adamopoulos, J. (1997). Culture as antecedent to behavior. In J. W. Berry, Y. H. Poortinga, & J. Pandey (Eds.), *Theory and method* (pp. 43–83). Vol. I of *Handbook of cross-cultural psychology* (2nd ed). Boston, MA: Allyn and Bacon.

Lonner, W. J., & Berry, J. W. (1986). Sampling and surveying. In W. J. Lonner & J. W. Berry (Eds.), *Field methods in cross-cultural research* (pp. 85–110). London: Sage.

Lonner, W. J., & Berry, J. W. (Eds.) (1986). *Field methods in cross-cultural research*. London: Sage.

Lonner, W. J., & Sharp, D. (1983). Psychological differentiation in a rural Yucatec Mayan village. In S. H. Irvine & J. W. Berry (Eds.), *Human assessment and cultural factors* (pp. 191–209). New York: Plenum.

Lucy, J. A. (1997). Linguistic relativity. *Annual Review of Anthropology, 26*, 291–312.

Lucy, J. A., & Schweder, R. A. (1979). Whorf and his critics: Linguistic and nonlinguistic influences on color memory. *American Anthropologist, 81*, 581–615.

Ludwig, A. M. (1969). Altered states of consciousness. In C. C. Tart (Ed.), *Altered states of consciousness* (pp. 9–22). New York: Wiley.

Lumsden, C. J., & Wilson, E. O. (1981). *Genes, mind and culture: The coevolutionary process*. Cambridge, MA: Harvard University Press.

Lundström, S. (1986). Opening address to IACCP Conference. In L. Ekstrand (Ed.), *Ethnic minorities and immigrants in a cross-cultural perspective* (pp. 9–13). Amsterdam: Swets and Zeitlinger.

Luria, A. R. (1971). Towards the problem of the historical nature of psychological processes. *International Journal of Psychology, 6,* 259–72.

(1976). *Cognitive development: Its cultural and social foundations.* Cambridge, MA: Harvard University Press.

Lutz, C. (1988). *Unnatural emotions: Everyday sentiments on a Micronesian atoll and their challenge to western theory.* Chicago, IL: University of Chicago Press.

Lutz, W. (Ed.) (1994). *Population–development–environment.* Berlin: Springer-Verlag.

Lynch, J., & Kaplan, G. (1997). Understanding how inequality in the distribution of income affects health. *Journal of Health Psychology, 2,* 297–314.

Ma, H. K. (1988). The Chinese perspective on moral judgement development. *International Journal of Psychology, 23,* 201–27.

(1989). Moral orientation and moral judgement in adolescents in Hong Kong, mainland China, and England. *Journal of Cross-Cultural Psychology, 20,* 152–77.

MacArthur, R. S. (1967). Sex differences in field dependence for the Eskimo: Replication of Berry's findings. *International Journal of Psychology, 2,* 139–40.

Maccoby, E., & Jacklin, C. (1974). *The psychology of sex differences.* Stanford, CA: Stanford University Press.

MacDonald, K. (1998). Evolution, culture and the five-factor model. *Journal of Cross-Cultural Psychology, 29,* 119–49.

MacLachlan, M. (1997). *Culture and health.* Chichester: Wiley.

MacLin, O. H., Malpass, R. S., & Honaker, S. (2001). Racial categorization of faces: The ambiguous race face effect. *Psychology, Public Policy and Law, 7,* 134–52.

Maddieson, I. (1978). Universals of tone. In J. H. Greenberg (Ed.), *Universals of human language* (vol. II, pp. 335–65). Stanford, CA: Stanford University Press.

Magnus, H. (1880). Untersuchungen über den Farbensinn der Naturvölker. *Physiologische Abhandlungen,* ser. 2, no. 7. Jena: Fraher.

Magnusson, D., & Endler, N. S. (Eds.) (1977). *Personality at the crossroads: Current issues in interactional psychology.* Hillsdale, NJ: Erlbaum.

Main, J., & Solomon, J. (1990). Procedures for identifying infants as disorganized/disoriented during the Ainsworth strange situation. In T. M. Greenberg, D. Cicchetti, & E. M. Cummings (Eds.), *Attachment in the preschool years: Theory, research and intervention* (pp. 121–60). Chicago, IL: University of Chicago Press.

Main, M., Kaplan, N., & Cassidy, J. (1985). Security in infancy, childhood and adulthood: A move to the level of representation. In I. Bretherton & E. Waters (Eds.), *Monographs of the Society for Research in Child Development, 50,* nos. 1–2.

Malinowski, B. (1924). Special Foreword. In W. H. R. Rivers, *Social Organization.* London: Kegan Paul, Trench, Trubner.

(1931). Introduction to C. R. Aldrich, *The primitive mind and modern civilization.* New York: AMS Press.

(1944). *A scientific theory of culture.* Chapel Hill, NC: University of North Carolina Press.

Malpass, R. S. (1977). Theory and method in cross-cultural psychology. *American Psychologist, 32,* 1069–79.

(1996). Face recognition at the interface of psychology, law and culture. In H. Grad, A. Blanco, & J. Georgas (Eds.), *Key issues in cross-cultural psychology* (pp. 7–21). Lisse, Netherlands: Swets & Zeitlinger.

Malpass, R. S., & Kravitz, J. (1969). Recognition for faces of own and other races. *Journal of Personality and Social Psychology, 13,* 333–4.

Malpass, R. S., & Poortinga, Y. H. (1986). Strategies for design and analysis. In W. J. Lonner & J. W. Berry (Eds.), *Field methods in cross-cultural research* (pp. 47–84). Beverly Hills, CA: Sage.

Mandell, A. J. (1980). Toward a psychobiology of transcendence: God in the brain. In T. Davidson & R. Davidson (Eds.), *The psychobiology of consciousness* (pp. 379–464). New York: Plenum.

Mange, E. J., & Mange, A. P. (1999). *Basic human genetics* (2nd ed.). Sunderland, MA: Sinauer.

Mann, C. W. (1940). Mental measurements in primitive communities. *Psychological Bulletin, 37*, 366–95.

Mann, J. (1991). Global AIDS: Critical issues for prevention in the 1990s. *International Journal of Health Sciences, 21*, 553–9.

Mann, L. (1980). Cross-cultural studies of small groups. In H. C. Triandis & R. W. Brislin (Eds.), *Handbook of cross-cultural psychology* (vol. V, pp. 155–209). Boston, MA: Allyn and Bacon.

Mann, L., Radford, M., Burnett, P., Ford, S., Bond, M., Leung, K., Nakamura, H., Vaughan, G., & Yang, K.-S. (1998). Cross-cultural differences in self-reported decision-making style and confidence. *International Journal of Psychology, 33*, 325–35.

Marcoen, A. (1995). Filial maturity of middle-aged adults in the context of parent care: Model and measures. *Journal of Adult Development, 2*, 125–36.

Marin, G. (1999). Subjective culture in health interventions. In J. Adamopoulos & Y. Kashima (Eds.), *Social psychology and cultural context* (pp. 139–50). Thousand Oaks, CA: Sage.

Marin, G., Balls-Organista, P., & Chung, K. (Eds.) (2001). *Acculturation*. Washington, DC: American Psychological Association.

Markus, H. R., & Kitayama, S. (1991). Culture and the self: Implications for cognition, emotion and motivation. *Psychological Review, 98*, 244–53.

  (1994). The cultural shaping of emotion: A conceptual framework. In S. Kitayama & H. R. Markus (Eds.), *Emotion and culture: Empirical studies of mutual influence* (pp. 339–51). Washington, DC: American Psychological Association.

Marsella, A. J. (1980). Depressive experience and disorder across cultures. In H. C. Triandis & J. Draguns (Eds.), *Handbook of cross-cultural psychology*. Vol. VI: *Psychopathology* (pp. 237–89). Boston, MA: Allyn and Bacon.

Marsella, A. J., & Dash-Scheuer, A. (1988). Coping, culture, and healthy human development: A research and conceptual overview. In P. R. Dasen, J. W. Berry, & N. Sartorius (Eds.), *Health and cross-cultural psychology: Towards applications* (pp. 162–78). Newbury Park, CA: Sage.

Marsella, A. J., De Vos, G., & Hsu, F. L. K. (Eds.) (1985). *Culture and the self: Asian and western perspectives*. London: Tavistock.

Marsh, H. W., & Byrne, B. M. (1993). Confirmatory factor analysis of multigroup–multimethod self-concept data: Between-group and within-group invariance constraints. *Multivariate Behavioral Research, 28*, 313–49.

Martorell, R. (1997). Undernutrition during pregnancy and early childhood: consequences for cognitive and behavioral development. In M. E. Young (Ed.), *Early child development: Investing in our children's future* (pp. 39–83). Amsterdam: Elsevier.

Martyn-Johns, T. A. (1977). Cultural conditioning of views of authority and its effect on the business decision-making process with special reference to Java. In Y. H. Poortinga

(Ed.), *Basic problems in cross-cultural psychology* (pp. 344–52). Lisse, Netherlands: Swets & Zeitlinger.

Maslow, A. H. (1954). *Motivation and personality*. New York: Harper.

Massimini, F., & Delle Fave, A. (2000). Individual development in a bio-cultural perspective. *American Psychologist, 55,* 24–33.

Matsumoto, D. (1992). American–Japanese cultural differences in the recognition of universal facial expressions. *Journal of Cross-Cultural Psychology, 23,* 72–84.

(1996). *Culture and psychology.* Pacific Grove, CA: Brooks/Cole.

(1999). Culture and self: An empirical assessment of Markus and Kitayama's theory of independent and interdependent self-construals. *Asian Journal of Social Psychology, 2,* 289–310.

Matsumoto, D., & Hearn, V. (1991). Culture and emotion: Display rule differences between the United States, Poland, and Hungary. Unpublished manuscript.

Maurice, M. (1979). For a study of the "societal effect": Universality and specificity in organization research. In C. J. Lammers & D. J. Hickson (Eds.), *Organizations alike and unlike* (pp. 42–60). London: Routledge and Kegan Paul.

Maurice, M., Sorge, A., & Warner, M. (1980). Societal differences in organizing manufacturing units: A comparison of France, West Germany and Great Britain. *Organization Studies, 1,* 59–86.

Mauviel, M. (1989). La communication interculturelle: Approche conceptuelle [Intercultural communication: Conceptual approach]. *Intercultures, 7,* 39–57.

Maxwell, J. (1992). Understanding and validity in qualitative research. *Harvard Educational Review, 62,* 279–300.

Mazrui, A. (1968). From social Darwinism to current theories of modernization. *World Politics, 21,* 69–83.

Mazur, A. (1985). A biosocial model of status in face-to-face primate groups. *Social Forces, 64,* 377–402.

McAuliffe, E. (1998). AIDS: Barriers to behavior change in Malawi. In H. Grad, A. Blanco, & J. Georgas (Eds.), *Key issues in cross-cultural psychology* (pp. 371–86). Lisse, Netherlands: Swets & Zeitlinger.

McCarthy, J. J., & Prince, A. (1990). Foot and word in prosodic morphology: The Arabic broken plural. *Natural Language and Linguistic Theory, 8,* 209–83.

McClelland, D. C. (1961). *The achieving society.* Princeton, NJ: Van Nostrand.

McCluskey, K., Albas, D., Niemi, R., Cuevas, C., & Ferrer, C. (1975). Cross-cultural differences in the perception of the emotional content of speech. *Developmental Psychology, 11,* 551–5.

McCrae, R. R. (2000). Trait psychology and the revival of personality and culture studies. *American Behavioral Scientist, 44,* 10–31.

McCrae, R. R., & Costa, P. T., Jr. (1996). Toward a new generation of personality theories: Theoretical contexts for the Five-Factor Model. In J. S. Wiggins (Ed.), *The five-factor model of personality: Theoretical perspectives* (pp. 51–87). New York: Guilford Press.

McCrae, R. R., Costa, P. T., Jr., Del Pilar, G. H., Rolland, J.-P., & Parker, W. D. (1998). Cross-cultural assessment of the five-factor model: The revised NEO personality inventory. *Journal of Cross-Cultural Psychology, 29,* 171–88.

McCrae, R. R., Yik, M. S. M., Trapnell, P. D., Bond, M. H., & Paulhus, D. L. (1998). Interpreting personality profiles across cultures: Bilingual acculturation and peer rating studies of Chinese undergraduates. *Journal of Personality and Social Psychology, 74,* 1041–55.

McGrew, W. C. (1992). *Chimpanzee material culture*. Cambridge: Cambridge University Press.

McGurk, H., & Jahoda, G. (1975). Pictorial depth perception by children in Scotland and Ghana. *Journal of Cross-Cultural Psychology*, *6*, 279–96.

McLeod, K. A. (1984). Multiculturalism and multicultural education: Policy and practice. In R. Samuda, J. W. Berry, & M. Laferrière (Eds.), *Multiculturalism in Canada: Social and educational perspectives* (pp. 30–49). Toronto: Allyn and Bacon.

McLuhan, M. (1971). *The Gutenberg galaxy: The making of typographic man*. London: Routledge and Kegan Paul.

McMichael, A. (1993). *Planetary overload: Global environmental change and the health of the human species*. Cambridge: Cambridge University Press.

McNaughton, N. (1989). *Biology and emotion*. Cambridge: Cambridge University Press.

McNett, C. (1970). A settlement pattern scale of cultural complexity. In R. Naroll & R. Cohen (Eds.), *A handbook of method in cultural anthropology* (pp. 872–86). New York: Natural History Press.

McShane, D., & Berry, J. W. (1988). Native North Americans: Indian and Inuit abilities. In S. H. Irvine & J. W. Berry (Eds.), *Human abilities in cultural context* (pp. 385–426). New York: Cambridge University Press.

Mead, M. (1928). *Coming of age in Samoa: A psychological study of primitive youth for Western civilization*. New York: Morrow Quill Paperbacks.

Meeks-Gardner, J. M., Grantham-McGregor, S. M., Chang, S. M., Himes, J. H., & Powell, C. A. (1995). Activity and behavioral development in stunted and non-stunted children and response to nutritional supplementation. *Child Development*, *66*, 1785–97.

Mehyrar, A. (1984). The role of psychology in national development: Wishful thinking and reality. *International Journal of Psychology*, *19*, 159–67.

Meissner, C. A., & Brigham, J. C. (2001). Thirty years of investigating the own-race bias in memory for faces: A meta-analytic review. *Psychology, Public Policy and Law*, *7*, 3–35.

Melikan, L. (1984). The transfer of psychological knowledge to the Third World countries and its impact on development: The case of five Arab Gulf oil producing states. *International Journal of Psychology*, *19*, 65–78.

Merritt, A. (2000). Culture in the cockpit: Do Hofstede's dimensions replicate? *Journal of Cross-Cultural Psychology*, *31*, 283–301.

Mesquita, B., & Frijda, N. H. (1992). Cultural variations in emotions: A review. *Psychological Bulletin*, *112*, 179–204.

Mesquita, B., Frijda, N. H., & Scherer, K. R. (1997). Culture and emotion. In J. W. Berry, P. R. Dasen, & T. S. Saraswathi (Eds.), *Basic processes and human development* (pp. 255–97). Vol. II of *Handbook of cross-cultural psychology* (2nd ed.). Boston, MA: Allyn and Bacon.

Messick, S. (1995). Validity of psychological assessment. *American Psychologist*, *50*, 741–9.

Miller, G. A. (1987). Meta-analysis and the culture-free hypothesis. *Organization Studies*, *8*, 309–25.

Miller, J. G. (1984). Culture and the development of everyday social explanation. *Journal of Personality and Social Psychology*, *46*, 961–78.

(1988). Bridging the content–structure dichotomy: Culture and the self. In M. H. Bond (Ed.), *The cross-cultural challenge to social psychology* (pp. 266–81). Newbury Park, CA: Sage.

(1997a). A cultural psychology perspective on intelligence. In R. Sternberg & E. Grigorenko (Eds.), *Intelligence, heredity and environment* (pp. 269–302). Cambridge: Cambridge University Press.

(1997b). Theoretical issues in cultural psychology. In J. W. Berry, Y. H. Poortinga, & J. Pandey (Eds.), *Theory and method* (pp. 85–128). Vol. I of *Handbook of cross-cultural psychology* (2nd ed.). Boston, MA: Allyn and Bacon.

Miller, J. G., Bersoff, D. M., & Harwood, R. L. (1990). Perceptions of social responsibilities in India and the United States: Moral imperatives or personal decisions. *Journal of Personality and Social Psychology, 58*, 33–47.

Miller, K. F., & Stigler, J. W. (1987). Counting in Chinese: Cultural variation in a basic cognitive skill. *Cognitive Development, 2*, 279–305.

Minsel, B., Becker, P., & Korchin, S. (1991). A cross-cultural view of positive mental health. *Journal of Cross-Cultural Psychology, 22*, 157–81.

Mischel, W. (1968). *Personality and assessment.* New York: Wiley.

(1973). Toward a cognitive social learning reconceptualization of personality. *Psychological Review, 80*, 252–83.

Mishra, R. C. (1997). Cognition and cognitive development. In J. W. Berry, P. R. Dasen, & T. S. Saraswathi (Eds.), *Basic processes and human development* (pp. 143–76). Vol. II of *Handbook of cross-cultural psychology* (2nd ed.). Boston, MA: Allyn and Bacon.

Mishra, R. C., Sinha, D., & Berry, J. W. (1996). *Ecology, acculturation and adaptation: A study of Adivasi in Bihar.* New Delhi: Sage.

Misumi, J. (1984). Decision-making in Japanese groups and organizations. In B. Wilpert & A. Sorge (Eds.), *International perspectives on organizational democracy* (vol. II, pp. 525–39). Chichester: Wiley.

(1985). *The behavioral science of leadership.* Ann Arbor, MI: University of Michigan Press.

Mitra, S. K. (Ed.) (1972). *A survey of research in psychology.* Bombay: Popular Prakashan.

Miura, M., & Usa, S. (1970). A psychotherapy of neuroses: Morita therapy. *Psychologia, 13*, 18–34.

Miyawaki, K., Strange, W., Verbrugge, R., Liberman, A. M., Jenkins, J. J., & Fujimura, O. (1975). An effect of linguistic experience: The discrimination of [r] and [l] by native speakers of Japanese and English. *Perception and Psychophysics, 18*, 331–40.

Modgil, S., Verma, G. K., Mallick, K., & Modgil, C. (Eds.) (1986). *Multicultural education: The interminable debate.* London: Falmer Press.

Moghaddam, F. (1989). Specialization and despecialization in psychology: Divergent processes in the three worlds. *International Journal of Psychology, 24*, 103–16.

Moghaddam, F., & Taylor, D. M. (1986). What constitutes an "appropriate psychology" for the developing world? *International Journal of Psychology, 21*, 253–67.

Moghaddam, F., Branchi, C., Daniels, K., Apter, M., & Harré, R. (1999). Psychology and national development. *Psychology and Developing Societies, 11*, 119–42.

Moghaddam, F. M., Ditto, B., & Taylor, D. (1990). Attitudes and attributions related to symptomatology in Indian immigrant women. *Journal of Cross-Cultural Psychology, 21*, 335–50.

Mohanty, A. (1994). *Bilingualism in a multilingual society: Implications for cultural integration and education.* Keynote address, International Congress of Applied Psychology, Madrid, July 1994.

Mohanty, A., & Perregaux, C. (1997). Language acquisition and bilingualism. In J. W. Berry, P. R. Dasen, & T. S. Saraswathi (Eds.), *Basic processes and human develop-*

*ment* (pp. 217–53). Vol. II of *Handbook of cross-cultural psychology* (2nd ed.). Boston, MA: Allyn and Bacon.

Montagu, A. (1997). *Man's most dangerous myth: The fallacy of race* (6th ed.). Thousand Oaks, CA: Altamira Press.

Montero, M., & Sloan, T. (1988). Understanding behavior in conditions of economic and cultural dependency. *International Journal of Psychology*, *23*, 597–617.

Moore, F. W. (1971). The outline of cultural materials: contemporary problems. *Behaviour Science Notes*, *6*, 197–89.

Moran, E. (1990). *The ecosystem approach in anthropology*. Ann Arbor, MI: University of Michigan Press.

Morris, C. R. (1956). *Varieties of human values*. Chicago, IL: Chicago University Press.

Morris, D., Collett, P., Marsh, P., & O'Shaughnessy, M. (1979). *Gestures: Their origin and distribution*. London: Johnathan Cape.

Morris, M., & Peng, K. (1994). Culture and cause: American and Chinese attributions for social and physical events. *Journal of Personality and Social Psychology*, *67*, 949–71.

Moscovici, S. (1972). Society and theory in social psychology. In J. Israel & H. Tajfel (Eds.), *The Context of Social Psychology* (pp. 17–68). London: Academic Press.

(1982). The phenomenon of social representations. In R. M. Farr & S. Mocovici (Eds.), *Social representations* (pp. 3–70). Cambridge: Cambridge University Press.

MOST (Management of Social Transformations Programme) (1995). *Multiculturalism: A policy response to diversity*. Paris: UNESCO.

MOW (Meaning of Working International Research Team) (1987). *The meaning of working*. London: Academic Press.

Mulatu, M. S. (2000). Perceptions of mental and physical illness in Northwestern Ethiopia: Causes, treatments and attitudes *Journal of Health Psychology*, *4*, 531–49.

Mulatu, M. S., & Berry, J. W. (2001). Cultivating health through multiculturalism. In M. MacLachlan (Ed.), *Promoting health across cultures* (pp. 15–35). Chichester: Wiley.

Munroe, R. H., & Munroe, R. L. (1994a). Field observations of behavior as a cross-cultural method. In P. K. Bock (Ed.), *Handbook of psychological anthropology* (pp. 255–77). Westport, CT: Greenwood.

(1994b). *Cross-cultural human development* (2nd ed.). Prospect Heights, IL: Waveland Press.

Munroe, R. H., Munroe, R. L., Westling, E., & Rosenberg, J. (1997). Infant experience and late-childhood dispositions: An eleven-year follow-up among the Logoli of Kenya. *Ethos*, *25*, 359–72.

Munroe, R. L., & Munroe, R. H. (1975). *Cross-cultural human development*. Monterey, CA: Brooks/Cole.

(1986). Field work in cross-cultural psychology. In W. J. Lonner & J. W. Berry (Eds.), *Field methods in cross-cultural research* (pp. 111–36). London: Sage.

(1997). A comparative anthropological perspective. In J. W. Berry, Y. H. Poortinga, & J. Pandey (Eds.), *Theory and method* (pp. 171–213). Vol. I of *Handbook of cross-cultural psychology* (2nd ed.). Boston, MA: Allyn and Bacon.

Murase, T. (1982). Sunao: A central value in Japanese psychotherapy. In A. Marsella & G. White (Eds.), *Cultural conceptions of mental health and therapy* (pp. 317–29). Dordrecht: Reidel.

Murdock, G. P. (1937). Comparative data on the division of labor by sex. *Social Forces*, *15*, 551–3.

(1949). *Social structure*. New York: Macmillan.

(1967). *Ethnographic atlas*. Pittsburgh, PA: University of Pittsburgh Press.

(1975). *Outline of world cultures* (5th ed.). New Haven, CT: Human Relations Area Files.

Murdock, G. P., & White, D. (1969). Standard cross-cultural sample. *Ethnology, 8,* 329–69.

Murdock, G. P., Ford, C. S., & Hudson, A. E. (1971). *Outline of cultural materials* (4th ed.). New Haven, CT: Human Relations Area Files.

Murphy, H. B. M. (1965). Migration and the major mental disorders. In M. B. Kantor (Ed.), *Mobility and mental health* (pp. 221–49). Springfield, IL: Thomas.

(1981). *Comparative psychiatry*. Berlin: Springer-Verlag.

(1982). Culture and schizophrenia. In I. Al-Issa (Ed.), *Culture and psychopathology* (pp. 221–49). Baltimore, MD: University Park Press.

Muthayya, B. C. (1988). Dynamics of rural development. In J. Pandey (Ed.), *Psychology in India: The state of the art* (vol. II, pp. 225–78). New Delhi: Sage.

Muthén, B. O. (1991). Multilevel factor analysis of class and student achievement components. *Journal of Educational Measurement, 28,* 338–54.

Naidoo, J. C. (1992). The mental health of visible ethnic minorities in Canada. *Psychology and Developing Societies, 4,* 165–86.

Naidu, R. K. (1983). A developing program of stress research. Paper presented at the seminar on Stress, Anxiety and Mental Health. Allahabad, December.

Naroll, R. (1962). *Data quality control*. New York: Free Press.

(1970a). What have we learned from cross-cultural surveys? *American Anthropologist, 72,* 1227–88.

(1970b). The culture bearing unit in cross-cultural surveys. In R. Naroll & R. Cohen (Eds.), *Handbook of method in cultural anthropology* (pp. 721–65). New York: Natural History Press.

(1970c). Galton's problem. In R. Naroll & R. Cohen (Eds.), *Handbook of method in cultural anthropology* (pp. 974–89). New York: Natural History Press.

(1983). *The moral order: An introduction to the human situation*. Newbury Park, CA: Sage.

Naroll, R., & Cohen, R. (Eds.) (1970). *Handbook of method in cultural anthropology*. New York: Natural History Press.

Naroll, R., Michik, G., & Naroll, F. (1980). Holocultural Research Methods. In H. C. Triandis & J. W. Berry (Eds.), *Handbook of cross-cultural psychology*. Vol. II: *Methodology* (pp. 479–521). Boston, MA: Allyn and Bacon.

Naveh-Benjamin, M., & Ayres, T. J. (1986). Digit span, reading rate, and linguistic relativity. *Quarterly Journal of Experimental Psychology, 38 A,* 739–51.

Neisser, U., Boodoo, G., Bouchard, T. J., Boykin, W. A., Brody, N., Ceci, C. J., Halpern, D. F., Loehlin, J. C., Perloff, R., Sternberg, R. J., & Urbina, S. (1996). Intelligence: Knowns and unknowns. *American Psychologist, 51,* 77–101.

Nguyen, H., Messe, L., & Stollak, G. (1999). Toward a more complex understanding of acculturation and adjustment. *Journal of Cross-Cultural Psychology, 30,* 5–31.

Nisbet, R. (1971). Ethnocentrism and the comparative method. In A. Desai (Ed.), *Essays on modernization of underdeveloped societies* (vol. I, pp. 95–114). Bombay: Thacker.

Nkounkou-Hombessa, E. (1988). *Le développement psycho-moteur du bébé Kongo-Lari. Environnement culturel et aspects cognitifs* [The psychomotor development of the Congo-Lari baby: Cultural enviornment and cognitive aspects]. Thesis, Université René Descartes, Paris V.

Noh, S., Beiser, M., Kaspar, V., Hou, F., & Rummens, J. (1999). Perceived racial discrimination, depression and coping. *Journal of Health and Social Behavior, 40,* 193–207.

Norman, W. T. (1963). Toward an adequate taxonomy of personality: Replicated factor structure in peer nomination personality ratings. *Journal of Abnormal and Social Psychology, 66,* 574–83.

Nsamenang, A. B. (1992). *Human development in cultural context: A third world perspective.* Newbury Park, CA: Sage.

(1995). Factors influencing the development of psychology in Sub-Saharan Africa. *International Journal of Psychology, 30,* 729–38.

(2001). Perspective africaine sur le développement social: Implications pour la recherche développementale interculturelle [The African perspective on social development: Implications for intercultural developmental research]. In C. Sabatier & P. R. Dasen (Eds.), *Contextes, cultures, développement et éducation. Autres enfants, autres écoles* (pp. 39–52). Paris: L'Harmattan.

Oberg, K. (1960). Cultural shock: Adjustment to new cultural environments. *Practical Anthropology, 7,* 177–82.

Ogay, T. (2000). *De la compétence à la dynamique interculturelle: Théories de la communication interculturelle et échanges de jeunes entre Suisse romande et alémanique* [Competence in intercultural dynamics: Theories of intercultural communication and exchange of youngsters between French and German Switzerland]. Berne: Peter Lang.

Ogbu, J. U. (1978). *Minority education and caste: The American system in cross-cultural perspective.* New York: Academic Press.

Oliver, R. A. C. (1932). The musical talents of natives in East Africa. *British Journal of Psychology, 22,* 333–43.

(1933). The adaptation of intelligence tests to tropical Africa, I, II. *Overseas Education, 4,* 186–91; *5,* 8–13.

Ombrédane, A. (1954). *L'exploration de la mentalité des noirs au moyen d'une épreuve projective: Le Congo TAT* [Exploration of the mentality of blacks by means of a projective test: The Congo TAT]. Brussels: Institut Royal Colonial Belge.

Ongel, U., & Smith, P. B. (1994). Who are we and where are we going? JCCP approaches its 100th issue. *Journal of Cross-Cultural Psychology, 25,* 25–53.

Orlansky, H. (1949). Infant care and personality. *Psychological Bulletin, 46,* 1–48.

Orley, J., & Kuyken, W. (Eds.) (1994). *Quality of life assessment: International Perspectives.* Berlin: Springer-Verlag.

Ortigues, M. E., & Ortigues, E. (1966). *Oedipe africain* [African Oedipus]. Paris: Plon.

Osgood, C. E. (1977). Objective cross-national indicators of subjective culture. In Y. H. Poortinga (Ed.), *Basic problems of cross-cultural psychology* (pp. 200–35). Lisse, Netherlands: Swets & Zeitlinger.

(1979). From yang and yin to *and* or *but* in cross-cultural perspective. *International Journal of Psychology, 14,* 1–35.

(1980). *Lectures on language performance.* New York: Springer-Verlag.

Osgood, C. E., May, W. H., & Miron, M. S. (1975). *Cross-cultural universals of affective meaning.* Urbana, IL: University of Illinois Press.

Osgood, C. E., Suci, G. J., & Tannenbaum, P. H. (1957). *The measurement of meaning.* Urbana, IL: University of Illinois Press.

Otake, T., Hatano, G., Cutler, A., & Mehler, J. (1993). Mora or syllable? Speech segmentation in Japanese. *Journal of Memory and Language, 32,* 258–78.

Ouchi, W. G. (1981). *Theory Z: How American business can meet the Japanese challenge.* Reading, MA: Addison-Wesley.

Ouellet, F. (Ed) (1988). *Pluralisme et école* [Pluralism and school]. Montreal: Institut Québécois de Recherche sur la Culture.

Overman, E. S. (Ed.) (1988). *Methodology and epistemology for social science: Selected papers of Donald T. Campbell*. Chicago: University of Chicago Press.

Pääbo, S. (2001). The human genome and our view of ourselves. *Science, 291*, (Number 5507), 1219–20.

Pande, N., & Naidu, R. K. (1992). Anasakti and health: A study of non-attachment. *Psychology and Developing Societies, 4*, 91–104.

Pandey, J. (Ed.) (1988). *Psychology in India: The state of the art* (vols. I–III). New Delhi: Sage.

  (2000). *Psychology in India Revisited: Developments in the discipline*. Vol. I: *Psychological foundations and human cognition*. New Delhi: Sage.

  (2001a). *Psychology in India Revisited: Developments in the discipline*. Vol. II: *Personality and health psychology*. New Delhi: Sage.

  (2001b). *Psychology in India Revisited: Developments in the discipline*. Vol. III: *Applied social and organizational psychology*. New Delhi: Sage.

Paniagua, F. (1994). *Assessing and treating culturally diverse clients*. Thousand Oaks, CA: Sage.

Papoušek, H., & Papoušek, M. (1992). Innnate and cultural guidance of infants' integrative competencies: China, the United States and Germany. In M. H. Bornstein (Ed.), *Cultural approaches to parenting*. Hillsdale, NJ: Erlbaum.

  (1995). Intuitive parenting. In M. H. Bornstein (Ed.), *Handbook of parenting* (vol. II, pp. 117–36). Mahwah, NJ: Erlbaum.

Paranjpe, A. C. (1984). *Theoretical psychology: The meeting of East and West*. New York: Plenum.

  (1996). Some basic psychological concepts from the intellectual tradition of India. *Psychology and Developing Societies, 8*, 7–28.

Paranjpe, A. C. (1998). *Self and identity in modern psychology and Indian thought*. New York: Plenum.

Pareek, U. (Ed.) (1981). *A survey of research in psychology, 1971–76*. Bombay: Popular Prakashan.

Parin, P., Morgenthaler, G., & Parin-Matthey, G. (1966). *Les blancs pensent trop: 13 entretiens psychoanalytiques avec les Dogons* [The whites think too much: 13 psychoanalytic interviews with the Dogons]. Paris: Payot.

Parker, I., & Shotter, J. (Eds.) (1990). *Deconstructing social psychology*. London: Routledge.

Pascale, R. T. (1978). Communication and decision making across cultures: Japanese and American comparisons. *Administrative Science Quarterly, 23*, 91–110.

Pascual-Leone, J. (1980). Constructive problems for constructive theories: The current relevance of Piaget's work and a critique of information-processing simulation psychology. In R. Kluwe & H. Spada (Eds.), *Developmental models of thinking* (pp. 263–96). New York: Academic Press.

  (1984). Attention, dialectic and mental effort: Toward an organismic theory of life stages. In M. L. Richards, F. A. Commons, & C. Armon (Eds.), *Beyond formal operations* (pp. 182–215). New York: Praeger.

Patel, V. (1995). Explanatory models of mental illness. *Social Science and Medicine, 40*, 1291–8.

Paunonen, S. V., & Ashton, M. C. (1998). The structured assessment of personality across cultures. *Journal of Cross-Cultural Psychology, 29*, 150–70.

Pawlik, K., & Rosenzweig, M. (Eds.) (2000). *International handbook of psychology*. London: Sage.

Peabody, D. (1967). *Trait inferences: Evaluative and descriptive aspects.* Journal of Personality and Social Psychology Monographs, 7.

(1985). *National characteristics.* Cambridge: Cambridge University Press.

Peal, E., & Lambert, W. E. (1962). The relation of bilingualism to intelligence. *Psychological Monographs, 76,* 1–23.

Peat, M. (1997). *Community-based rehabilitation.* London: Saunders.

Pedersen, P. (1981). Alternative futures for cross-cultural counselling and psychotherapy. In A. Marsella & P. Pederson (Eds.), *Cross-cultural counselling and psychotherapy* (pp. 22–58). New York: Pergamon.

Pedersen, P., Draguns, J., Lonner, W., & Trimble, J. (Eds.) (1996). *Counselling across cultures* (4th ed.). Thousand Oaks, CA: Sage.

Peeters, H. (1988). Vijf eeuwen gezin in Nederland [Five centuries of nuclear family in the Netherlands]. In H. Peeters, L. Dresen-Coenders, & T. Brandenberg (Eds.), *Vijf eeuwen gezinsleven* (pp. 11–30). Nijmegen, Netherlands: SUN.

(1996). *Psychology: The historical dimension.* Tilburg: Syntax Publishers.

Pelto, P. J. (1968). The difference between "tight" and "loose" societies. *Transaction,* April, 37–40.

Pelto, P. J., & Pelto, G. H. (1981). *Anthropological research.* Cambridge: Cambridge University Press.

Pelto, G., Dickin, K., & Engle, P. (1999). *A critical link: Interventions for physical growth and psychological development: A review.* Geneva: World Health Organization.

Peng, K., & Nisbett, R. (1999). Culture, dialectics and reasoning about contradiction. *American Psychologist, 54,* 741–54.

Peng, K., Nisbett, R., & Wong, N. (1997). Validity problems comparing values across cultures, and possible solutions. *Psychological Methods, 2,* 329–44.

Pepitone, A. (1976). Toward a normative and comparative biocultural social psychology. *Journal of Personality and Social Psychology, 34,* 641–53.

Pepitone, A., & Triandis, H. C. (1987). On the universality of social psychological theories. *Journal of Cross-Cultural Psychology, 18,* 471–98.

Perez, S., & Dasen, P. R. (1999). Educational research. *Prospects* (Special Issue), *29,* 327–34.

Perregaux, C. (1994). *Les enfants à deux voix: Des effets du bilinguisme sur l'apprentissage de la lecture* [Children with two voices: Effects of bilingualism on learning to read]. Berne: Lang.

(2000). Approches interculturelles et didactiques des langues: Vers des intérêts partagés en sciences de l'éducation? [Intercultural and teaching approaches to languages: Towards shared interests in the science of education?] In P. R. Dasen & C. Perregaux (Eds.), *Pourquoi des approches interculturelles en sciences de l'éducation?* [Why intercultural approaches in the science of education?] (pp. 181–201). Brussels: DeBoeck Université (Collection "Raisons éducatives" vol. 3).

Peters, I. J., & Waterman, R. H. (1982). *In search of excellence: Lessons from America's best run companies.* New York: Harper and Row.

Peters, L. G., & Price-Williams, D. (1983). A phenomenological overview of trance. *Transcultural Psychiatric Review, 20,* 5–39.

Petersen, A. C. (1988). Adolescent development. *Annual Review of Psychology, 39,* 583–607.

Pettigrew, T., & Tropp, L. (2000). Does intergroup contact reduce prejudice? Recent meta-analytic findings. In S. Oskamp (Ed.), *Reducing prejudice and discrimination* (pp. 93–114). Mahwah, NJ: Lawrence Erlbaum.

Pettigrew, T. F. (1979). The ultimate attribution error: Extending Allport's cognitive analysis of prejudice. *Personality and Social Psychology Bulletin*, *5*, 461–576.

Pfeiffer, W. (1982). Culture-bound syndromes In I. Al-Issa (Ed.), *Culture and psychopathology*. Baltimore, MD: University Park Press.

Pheysey, D. C. (1993). *Organizational cultures: Types and transformations*. London: Routledge.

Phinney, J. (1990). Ethnic identity in adolescents and adults: A review of research. *Psychological Bulletin*, *108*, 499–514.

  (1999). An intercultural approach in psychology: Cultural contact and identity. *Cross-Cultural Psychology Bulletin*, *33*, 24–31.

  (2000). Identity formation across cultures: The interaction of personal, societal and historical change. *Human Development*, *43*, 27–31.

Piaget, J. (1966). Nécessité et signification des recherches comparatives en psychologie génétique. [Need and significance of cross-cultural studies in genetic psychology]. *Journal International de Psychologie*, *1*, 3–13. Reprinted in J. W. Berry & P. R. Dasen (Eds.), *Culture and Cognition* (pp. 299–309). London: Methuen, 1974]

  (1970). Piaget's Theory. In P. H. Mussen (Ed.), *Carmichael's manual of child psychology* (3rd ed., pp. 703–32). New York: Wiley.

  (1972). *The principles of genetic epistemology*. London: Routledge & Kegan Paul.

  (1975). La psychogenèse des connaissances et sa signification epistémologique. In M. Piatelli-Palmarini (Ed.), *Théories du langage, théories de l'apprentissage:* Paris: Editions du Seuil.

Pick, S. (1998). Sexual and reproductive health education in Latin America. In J. Adair, D. Belanger, & K. Dion (Eds.), *Advances in psychological science: Social, personal and cultural aspects* (Vol. I, pp. 455–511). Hove, UK: Psychology Press.

Pike, K. L. (1967). *Language in relation to a unified theory of the structure of human behavior*. The Hague: Mouton.

Pinstrup-Anderson, P., Pelletier, D., & Alderman, H. (Eds.) (1995). *Child growth and nutrition in developing countries*. Ithaca, NY: Cornell University Press.

Piontkowski, U., Florack, A., Hoelker, P., & Obdrzalek, P. (2000). Predicting acculturation attitudes of dominant and non-dominant groups. *International Journal of Intercultural Relations*, *24*, 1–26.

Plomin, R., & Caspi, A. (1998). DNA and personality. *European Journal of Personality*, *12*, 387–407.

Plomin, R., & Daniels, D. (1987). Why are children of the same family so different from one another? *Behavioral and Brain Sciences*, *10*, 1–16.

Plomin, R., & De Fries, J. (1998). The genetics of cognitive abilities and disabilities. *Scientific American*, May, 62–9.

Plomin, R., DeFries, J. C., McClearn, G. E., & Rutter, M. (1997). *Behavioral genetics* (3rd ed.). New York: Freeman.

Plotkin, H. C., & Odling-Smee, F. J. (1981). A multiple-level model of evolution and its implications for sociobiology. *The Behavioral and Brain Sciences*, *4*, 225–68.

Poggie, J., & Lynch, R. (Eds.) (1974). *Rethinking modernization*. New York: Greenwood.

Pollack, R. H. (1963). Contour detectability thresholds as a function of chronological age. *Perceptual and Motor Skills*, *17*, 411–17.

Pollack, R. H., & Silvar, S. D. (1967). Magnitude of the Müller–Lyer illusion in children as a function of pigmentation of the fundus oculi. *Psychonomic Science*, *8*, 83–4.

Pollitt, E., Golub, M., Gorman, K., Grantham-McGregor, S., Levitsky, D., Schurch, B., Strupp, B., & Wachs, T. (1996). A reconceptualization of the effects of undernutrition on children's biological, psychosocial, and behavioral development. *Social Policy Report, Society for Research in Child Development, 10,* 1–21.

Poortinga, Y. H. (1971). Cross-cultural comparison of maximum performance tests: Some methodological aspects and some experiments. *Psychologia Africana,* Monograph Supplement, No. 6.

(1972). A comparison of African and European students in simple auditory and visual tasks. In L. J. Cronbach & P. J. D. Drenth (Eds.), *Mental tests and cultural adaptation* (pp. 349–54). The Hague: Mouton.

(1985a). Empirical evidence of bias in choice reaction time experiments. *The Behavioral and Brain Sciences, 8,* 236–7.

(1985b). How and why cultural or ethnic groups are suposed to be different: A classification of inferences. Paper presented at IACCP Conference, Malmö, June 1985.

(1989). Equivalence of cross-cultural data: An overview of basic issues. *International Journal of Psychology, 24,* 737–56.

(1992a). Is there no child in the experimental bathwater? A comment on Misra and Gergen. *International Journal of Psychology, 28,* 245–8.

(1992b). Towards a conceptualization of culture for psychology. In S. Iwawaki, Y. Kashima, & K. Leung (Eds.), *Innovations in cross-cultural psychology* (pp. 3–17). Lisse, Netherlands: Swets & Zeitlinger.

(1993). Cross-culturally invariant personality variables: A study in India and The Netherlands. In G. L. Van Heck, P. Bonaiuto, I. J. Deary, & W. Novack (Eds.), *Personality psychology in Europe* (vol. IV, pp. 105–53). Tilburg: Tilburg University Press.

(1995). The use of tests across cultures. In T. Oakland & R. K. Hambleton (Eds.), *International perspectives on academic assessment* (pp. 187–206). Boston, MA: Kluwer.

(1997). Towards convergence? In J. W. Berry, Y. H. Poortinga, & J. Pandey (Eds.), *Theory and method* (pp. 347–87). Vol. I of *Handbook of cross-cultural psychology* (2nd ed.). Boston, MA: Allyn and Bacon.

(1998a). Cultural diversity and psychological invariance: Methodological and theoretical dilemmas of (cross-)cultural psychology. In J. G. Adair, D. Bélanger, & K. L. Dion (Eds.), *Advances in psychological science: Social, personal and cultural aspects* (vol. I, pp. 229–46). Hove, UK: Psychology Press.

(1998b). Economic factors: A comment. *Cross-Cultural Psychology Bulletin, 32,* (*3*), 9.

(1999). Do differences in behaviour imply a need for different psychologies? *Applied Psychology, 48,* 419–32.

Poortinga, Y. H., & Foden, B. I. M. (1975). A comparative study of curiosity in black and white South African students. *Psychologia Africana,* Monograph, Supplement 8.

Poortinga, Y. H., & Malpass, R. S. (1986). Making inferences from cross-cultural data. In W. J. Lonner & J. W. Berry (Eds.), *Field methods in cross-cultural research* (pp. 17–46). Beverly Hills, CA: Sage.

Poortinga, Y. H., & Soudijn, K. (in press). Behavior–culture relationships and ontogenetic development. In H. Keller, Y. H. Poortinga, & A. Schölmerich (Eds.), *Biology, culture and development: Integrating diverse perspectives.* Cambridge: Cambridge University Press.

Poortinga, Y. H., & Spies, E. (1972). An attempt to compare risk taking in two culturally different groups. *Psychologia Africana, 14,* 186–99.

Poortinga, Y. H., & Van de Vijver, F. J. R. (1987). Explaining cross-cultural differences: Bias analysis and beyond. *Journal of Cross-Cultural Psychology, 18,* 259–82.

(1997). Is there no cross-cultural evidence in colour categories of psychological laws, only of cultural rules? *Behavioral and Brain Sciences, 20,* 205–6.

(2000). How different are personality traits cross-culturally, and how are they different? Review of *The importance of psychological traits: A cross-cultural study* by John E. Williams, Robert C. Satterwhite, and José L. Saiz. *Contemporary Psychology, 45,* 89–91.

Poortinga, Y. H., & Van der Flier, H. (1988). The meaning of item bias in ability tests. In S.H. Irvine & J. W. Berry (Eds.), *Human abilities in cultural context* (pp. 166–83). New York: Cambridge University Press.

Poortinga, Y. H., & Van Hemert, D. A. (2001). Personality and culture: Demarcating between the common and the unique. *Journal of Personality, 69,* 1033–1060.

Poortinga, Y. H., Schoots, N. H., & Van de Koppel, J. M. H. (1993). The understanding of Chinese and Kurdish emblematic gestures by Dutch subjects. *International Journal of Psychology, 28,* 31–44.

Poortinga, Y. H., Van de Vijver, F. J. R., Joe, R. C., & Van de Koppel, J. M. H. (1987). Peeling the onion called culture. In C. Kagitcibasi (Ed.), *Growth and progress in cros-cultural psychology* (pp. 22–34). Lisse, Netherlands: Swets & Zeitlinger.

Popper, K. R. (1959). *The logic of scientific discovery.* New York: Basic Books.

Porcher, L. (1994). La communication interculturelle au carrefour des générations [Intercultural communication between generations]. In C. Labat & G. Vermes (Ed.), *Cultures ouvertes, sociétés interculturelles. Du contact à l'interaction* [Open cultures, intercultural societies: From contact to interaction] (pp. 52–61). Paris: L'Harmattan.

Posner, M. I. (1978). *Chronometric explorations of mind.* Hillsdale, NJ: Lawrence Erlbaum.

Posses, F. (1978). *The art of international negotiations.* London: Business Books.

Post, R. H. (1962). Population differences in red and green color vision deficiency: A review, and a query on selection relaxation. *Eugenics Quarterly, 9,* 131–46.

(1971). Possible cases of relaxed selection in civilized populations. *Human Genetics, 13,* 253–84.

Preiswerk, R., & Perrot, D. (1978). *Ethnocentrism and history.* New York: NOK (originally French [1975]. *Ethnocentrisme et histoire.* Paris: Anthropos).

Premack, D., & Woodruff, G. (1978). Does the chimpanzee have a theory of mind? *Behavioral and Brain Sciences, 1,* 515–26.

Prince, R. (1960). The "brain fag" syndrome in Nigerian students. *Journal of Mental Science, 106,* 550–70.

(1968). The changing picture of depressive symptoms in Africa. *Canadian Journal of African Studies, 1,* 177–92.

(1980). Variations in psychotherapeutic procedures. In H. C. Triandis & J. Draguns (Eds.), *Handbook of cross-cultural psychology.* Vol. VI: *Psychopathology* (pp. 291–349). Boston, MA: Allyn and Bacon.

(1984). Shamans and endorphins: Exogenous and endogenous factors in psychotherapy. In P. Pedersen, N. Sartorius, & A. Marsella (Eds.), *Mental health services: The cross-cultural context* (pp. 59–77). London: Sage.

Prince, R., & Tcheng-Laroche, F. (1987). Culture-bound syndromes and international disease classifications. *Culture, Medicine and Psychiatry, 11,* 18–23.

Przeworski, A., & Teune, H. (1970). *The logic of comparative social inquiry.* New York: John Wiley.

Pugh, D. S., & Hinings, C. R. (Eds.) (1976). *Organizational structure: Extensions and replications.* London: Saxon House.

Puhan, B. N. (1982). *Issues in psychological measurement.* Agra: National Psychological Corporation.

Quandt, W. B. (1987). Egypt: A strong sense of national identity. In H. Binnendijk (Ed.), *National negotiating styles* (pp. 105–24). Washington, DC: Foreign Service Institute.

Rabain, J. (1979). *L'enfant du lignage.* Paris: Payot.

(1989). Pratiques de soin et interaction meìe–enfant dans un contexte d'émigration [Love and interaction practices between mother and child in the context of emigration]. In J. Retschitzki, M. Bossel-Lagos, & P. R. Dasen (Eds.), *La recherche interculturelle* [Intercultural research] (pp. 31–44). Paris: L'Harmattan.

Raiffa, H. (1982). *The art and science of negotiation.* Cambridge, MA: Harvard University Press.

Ramey, C. T., & Ramey, S. L. (1998). Early intervention and early experience. *American Psychologist, 53,* 109–20.

Ratner, C. (1997). *Cultural psychology and qualitative methodology: Theoretical and empirical considerations.* New York: Plenum.

Ray, V. F. (1952). Techniques and problems in the study of human color perception. *South Western Journal of Anthropology, 8,* 251–59.

Realo, A., Allik, J., & Vadi, M. (1997). The hierarchical structure of collectivism. *Journal of Research in Personality, 31,* 93–116.

Rebelsky, F. (1967). Infancy in two cultures. *Nederlands Tijdschrift voor de Psychologie, 22,* 379–87.

Redding, S. G., & Ng, M. (1982). The role of "face" in the organizational perception of Chinese managers. *Organization Studies, 3,* 201–19.

Redding, S. G., & Wong, G. Y. Y. (1986). The psychology of Chinese organizational behaviour. In M. H. Bond (Ed.), *The psychology of Chinese people* (pp. 267–95). Oxford: Oxford University Press.

Redfield, R., Linton, R., & Herskovits, M. J. (1936). Memorandum on the study of acculturation. *American Anthropologist, 38,* 149–52.

Relethford, J. H. (1997). *The human species: An introduction to biological anthropology* (3rd ed.). Mountain View, CA: Mayfield.

Reuning, H., & Wortley, W. (1973). Psychological studies of the Bushmen. *Psychologia Africana,* Monograph, Supplement No. 7.

Reynolds, P. D. (1986). Organizational culture as related to industry, position and performance: A preliminary report. *Journal of Management Studies, 23,* 333–45.

Reynolds, V., Falger, V., & Vine, I. (Eds.) (1987). *The sociobiology of ethnocentrism.* London: Croom Helm.

Rhee, E., Uleman, J., & Lee, H. (1996). Variations in collectivism and individualism by ingroup and culture: Confirmatory factor analyses. *Journal of Personality and Social Psychology, 71,* 1037–54.

Rhee, E., Uleman, J., Hoon, L., & Roman, R. (1995). Spontaneous self-descriptions and ethnic identities in individualistic and collectivistic cultures. *Journal of Personality and Social Psychology, 69,* 142–52.

Ricciuti, H. N., & Dorman, R. (1983). Interaction of multiple factors contributing to high-risk parenting. In R. A. Hoekelman (Ed.), *Minimizing high-risk parenting.* Media, PA: Harwal.

Richmond, A. (1993). Reactive migration: Sociological perspectives on refugee movements. *Journal of Refugee Studies*, *6*, 7–24.

Riemann, R., & De Raad, B. (Eds.) (1998). Behavior genetics and personality. *European Journal of Personality*, *12*, 303–410.

Rimé, B., Mesquita, B., Philippot, P., & Boca, S. (1991). Beyond the emotional event: Six studies on the social sharing of emotion. *Cognition and Emotion*, 5, 435–65.

Rimé, B., Philippot, P., Boca, S., & Mesquita, B. (1992). Long lasting cognitive and social consequences of emotion: social sharing and rumination. In W. Stroebe & M. Hewstone (Eds.), *European Review of Social Psychology* (vol. III, pp. 225–58). New York: Wiley.

Rist, G. (1997). *Development: From western origin to global faith*. London: Zed Books.

Rist, G., & Sabelli, F. (Eds.) (1986). *Il était une fois le développement* [Once upon a time there was development]. Lausanne: Editions d'en Bas.

Rivers, W. H. R. (1901). Vision. In *Physiology and psychology*, Part I: *Reports of the Cambridge Anthropological Expedition to Torres Straits* (vol. II). Cambridge: Cambridge University Press.

(1924). *Social organization*. London: Kegan Paul, Trench, Trubner & Co.

Robbins, S. R. (1987). *Organization theory: Structure, design and applications*. Englewood Cliffs, NJ: Prentice-Hall.

Roberson, D., Davies, I., & Davidoff, J. (2000). Color categories are not universal: Replications and new evidence from a stone-age culture. *Journal of Experimental Psychology: General*, *129*, 369–89.

Rockett, I. (1999). Population and health: An introduction to epidemiology. *Population Bulletin*, *54*, 1–43.

Roe, R. (1995). Developments in Eastern Europe in work and organizational psychology. In C. L. Cooper & I. T. Robertson (Eds.), *International Review of Industrial and Organizational Psychology* (vol. X, pp. 275–349). Chichester, UK: Wiley.

Rogoff, B. (1990). *Apprenticeship in thinking: Cognitive development in social context*. New York: Oxford University Press.

Rogoff, B., & Waddell, K. J. (1982). Memory for information organized in a scene by children from two cultures. *Child Development*, *53*, 173–81.

Rogoff, B., Mistry, J., Göncü, A., & Mosier, C. (1993). *Guided participation in cultural activity by toddlers and caregivers*. Monographs of the Society for Research in Child Development, 58 (8) (no. 236).

Rohner, R. (1984). Toward a conception of culture for cross-cultural psychology. *Journal of Cross-Cultural Psychology*, *15*, 111–38.

Rokeach, M. (1973). *The nature of human values*. New York: Free Press.

Romaine, S. (1989). *Bilingualism*. Oxford: Blackwell.

Romney, A., & D'Andrade, R. (1964). Cognitive aspects of English kin terms. *American Anthropologist*, *66*, 146–70.

Romney, A. K., & Moore, C. (1998). Toward a theory of culture as shared cognitive structures. *Ethos*, 26, 314–37.

Ronen, S. (1986). *Comparative and multinational management*. New York: Wiley.

Ronen, S., & Shenkar, O. (1985). Clustering countries on attitudinal dimensions: A review and synthesis. *Academy of Management Review*, *10*, 435–54.

Rosaldo, M. (1980). *Knowledge and passion: Ilongot notions of self and social life*. Cambridge: Cambridge University Press.

Rosch (Heider), E. (1972). Universals in color naming and memory. *Journal of Experimental Psychology*, *93*, 10–20.

(1977). Human categorization. In N. Warren (Ed.), *Studies in cross-cultural psychology* (vol. I, pp. 1–49). London: Academic Press.

Rosch, E. (1978). Principles of categorization. In E. Rosch & B. B. Lloyd (Eds.), *Cognition and categorization* (pp. 27–48). Hillsdale, NJ: Erlbaum.

Rosenzweig, M. (1999). Continuity and change in the development of psychology around the world. *American Psychologist, 54*, 252–9.

Ross, L. (1977). The intuitive scientist and his shortcomings. In L. Berkowitz (Ed.), *Advances in experimental social psychology* (vol. X, pp. 174–220). New York: Academic Press.

Rotter, J. B. (1954). *Social learning and clinical psychology*. Englewood Cliffs, NJ: Prentice-Hall.

(1966). Generalized expectancies for internal versus external control of reinforcement. *Psychological Monographs, 80* (Whole no. 609).

Royal Anthropological Institute (1951). *Notes and queries on anthropology* (6th ed.). London: Routledge.

Ruben, B. D. (1989). The study of cross-cultural competence: Traditions and contemporary issues. *International Journal of Intercultural Relations, 13*, 229–40.

Ruffell Smith, H. (1975). Some problems of voice communication for international aviation. In A. Chapanis (Ed.), *Ethnic variables in human factors engineering* (pp. 225–30). Baltimore, MD: Johns Hopkins University Press.

Rumelhart, D. E., McClelland, J. L., & the PDP Research Group (1986). *Parallel distributed processing: Explorations in the microstructure of cognition*. Cambridge, MA: MIT Press.

Rushton, J. P. (1988). Race differences in behaviour: A review and evolutionary analysis. *Journal of Personality and Individual Differences, 9*, 1009–24.

(1995). *Race, evolution and behavior*. New Brunswick: Transaction.

Russell, J. A. (1983). Pancultural aspects of the human conceptual organization of emotions. *Journal of Personality and Social Psychology, 45*, 1281–8.

(1991). Culture and the categorisation of emotions. *Psychological Bulletin, 110*, 426–50.

(1994). Is there universal recognition of emotion from facial expression? A review of cross-cultural studies. *Psychological Bulletin, 115*, 102–41.

(1995). Facial expressions of emotion: What lies beyond minimal universality? *Psychological Bulletin, 118*, 379–91.

Russell, P. A, Deregowski, J. B., & Kinnear, P. R. (1997). Perception and aesthetics. In J. W. Berry, P. R. Dasen, & T. S. Saraswathi (Eds.), *Basic processes and human development* (pp. 107–42). Vol. II of *Handbook of cross-cultural psychology* (2nd ed.). Boston, MA: Allyn and Bacon.

Russon, A. E. (1999). Naturalistic approaches to orangutan intelligence and the question of enculturation. *International Journal of Comparative Psychology, 12*, 181–202.

(in press). Compartive developmental perspectives on culture: The great apes. In H. Keller, Y. H. Poortinga, & A. Schölmerich (Eds.), *Biology, culture and development: Integrating diverse perspectives*. Cambridge: Cambridge University Press.

Rutter, M. (1985). Resilience in the face of adversity: Protective factors and resistance to psychiatric disorder. *British Journal of Psychiatry, 147*, 598–611.

Ruzgis, P. (1994). Culture and intelligence: Cross-cultural investigation of implicit theories of intelligence. *Voprosy-Psikhologii, 1*, 142–6.

Ryder, A., Alden, L., & Paulhus, D. (2000). Is acculturation undimensional or bidimensional? A head-to-head comparison in the prediction of personality, self-identity and adjustment. *Journal of Personality and Social Psychology, 79*, 49–65.

Sabatier, C. (1999). Adolescents issus de l'immigration: Les clichés à l'épreuve des faits [Adolescents formed by immigration: Testing clichés against facts]. In B. Bril, P. R. Dasen, C. Sabatier, & B. Krewer (Eds.), *Propos sur l'enfant et l'adolescent: Quels enfants pour quelles cultures?* [Remarks on children and adolescence: Which children for which cultures?] (pp. 357–82). Paris: L'Harmattan.

Sahlins, M. (1976). Colors and cultures. *Semiotica*, *16*, 1–22.

   (1977). *The use and abuse of biology*. London: Tavistock Publications.

Sahlins, M., & Service, E. (Eds.) (1960). *Evolution and culture*. Ann Arbor, MI: University of Michigan Press.

Sahoo, F. (1993). Indigenization of psychological measurement: Parameters and operationalization. *Psychology and Developing Societies*, *5*, 1–14.

Sahoo, F. (Ed.) (1988). *Psychology in Indian context*. Agra: National Psychological Corporation.

Saito, A. (Ed.) (2000). *Bartlett, culture and cognition*. London: Psychology Press.

Salazar, J. (1984). The use and impact of psychology in Venezuela. *International Journal of Psychology*, *19*, 113–22.

Salazar, J. M., & Salazar, M. A. (1998). Permanence and modification in national identities. In J. Adair, D. Bélanger, & K. Dion (Eds.), *Advances in psychological science*. Vol. I: *Social, personal and cultural aspects* (pp. 247–70). Hove, UK: Psychology Press.

Sam, D. L., & Berry, J. W. (1995). Acculturative stress among young immigrants in Norway. *Scandinavian Journal of Psychology*, *36*, 10–24.

Samuda, R., Berry, J. W., & Laferrière, M. (Eds.) (1984). *Multiculturalism in Canada: Social and educational perspectives*. Toronto: Allyn and Bacon.

Santa, I. L., & Baker, L. (1975). Linguistic influences on visual learning. *Memory and Cognition*, 3, 445–50.

Sapir, E. (1949). *Culture, language and personality*. Berkeley, CA: University of California Press.

Sarason, I., & Sarason, B. (1999). *Abnormal psychology*. Toronto: Prentice-Hall.

Saraswathi, T. S. (1999). Adult–child continuity in India: Is adolescence a myth or an emerging reality? In T. S. Saraswathi (Ed.), *Culture, socialization and human development: Theory, research and applications in India* (pp. 213–32). New Delhi: Sage.

Sartorius, N. (1991). The classification of mental disorders in the 10th ICD. *European Psychiatry*, *6*, 315–22.

Saucier, G., & Goldberg, L. R. (2001). Lexical studies of indigenous personality factors: Premises, products and prospects. *Journal of Personality*, *69*, 847–79.

Saunders, B. A. C. (1992). *The invention of colour terms*. Utrecht, Netherlands: ISOR.

Saunders, B. A. C., & Van Brakel, J. (1997). Are there non-trivial constraints on colour categorizations? *Behavioral and Brain Sciences*, *20*, 167–228.

Saxe, G. B. (1981). Body parts as numerals: A developmental analysis of numeration among remote Oksapmin village populations in Papua New Guinea. *Child Development*, *52*, 302–16.

Saxe, G. B., & Moylan, T. (1982). The development of measurement operations among the Oksapmin of Papua New Guinea. *Child Development*, *53*, 1242–8.

Schein, E. H. (1985). *Organizational culture and leadership*. San Francisco: Jossey-Bass.

Scherer, K. R. (1981). Speech and emotional states. In J. Darby (Ed.), *Speech evaluation in psychiatry* (pp. 189–220). New York: Grune and Stratton.

   (1986). Vocal affect expression: A review and a model for further research. *Psychological Bulletin*, *99*, 143–65.

(1997a). The role of culture in emotion-antecedent appraisal. *Journal of Personality and Social Psychology*, *73*, 902–22.

(1997b). Profiles of emotion-antecedent appraisal: Testing theoretical predictions across cultures. *Cognition and Emotion*, *11*, 113–50.

Scherer, K. R., & Walbott, H. G. (1994). Evidence of universality and cultural variation of differential emotion response patterning. *Journal of Personality and Social Psychology*, *66*, 310–28.

Scherer, K. R., Wallbott, H. G., & Summerfield, A. B. (Eds.) (1986). *Experiencing emotion: A cross-cultural study*. Cambridge: Cambridge University Press.

Scherer, K. R., Wallbott, H., Matsumoto, D., & Kudoh, T. (1988). Emotional experience in cultural context: A comparison between Europe, Japan and the United States. In K. R. Scherer (Ed.), *Faces of emotion* (pp. 5–30). Hillsdale, NJ: Erlbaum.

Schlegel, A., & Barry III, H. (1986). The cultural consequences of female contribution to subsistence. *American Anthropologist*, *88*, 142–50.

(1991). *Adolescence: An anthropological enquiry*. New York: Free Press (Macmillan).

Schliemann, A., Carraher, D., & Ceci, S. (1997). Everyday cognition. In J. W. Berry, P. R. Dasen, & T. S. Saraswathi (Eds.), Basic processes and human development (pp. 177–216). Vol. II of *Handbook of cross-cultural psychology* (2nd ed.). Boston, MA: Allyn and Bacon.

Schmitz, P. (1992a). Immigrant mental and physical health. *Psychology and Developing Societies*, *4*, 117–31.

(1992b). Acculturation styles and health. In S. Iwawaki, Y. Kashima, & K. Leung (Eds.), *Innovations in cross-cultural psychology* (pp. 360–70). Amsterdam: Swets & Zeitlinger.

(1994). Acculturation and adaptation process among immigrants in Germany. In A. M. Bouvy, F. J. R. van de Vijver, & P. Schmitz (Eds.), *Journeys into cross-cultural psychology* (pp. 142–57). Amsterdam: Swets & Zeitlinger.

Schraw, G. (1998). On the development of adult metacognition. In C. Smith & T. Pourchot (Eds.), *Adult learning and development: Perspectives from educational psychology* (pp. 89–106). Mahwah, NJ: Lawrence Erlbaum.

Schraw, G., & Moshmann, D. (1995). Metacognitive theories. *Educational Psychology Review*, *7*, 351–71.

Schwartz, S. H. (1994). Are there universal aspects in the structure and contents of human values? *Journal of Social Issues*, *50*, 19–45.

Schwartz, S. H., & Bilsky, W. (1990). Toward a theory of the universal content and structure of values: Extensions and cross-cultural replications. *Journal of Personality and Social Psychology*, *58*, 878–91.

Schwartz, S. H., & Sagiv, L. (1995). Identifying culture specifics in the content and structure of values. *Journal of Cross-Cultural Psychology*, *26*, 92–116.

Schwartz, T., White, G., & Lutz, C. (Eds.) (1992). *New directions in psychological anthropology*. New York: Cambridge University Press.

Schwarzer, R., Hahn, A., & Schröder, H. (1994). Social integration and social support in a life crisis: Effects of macrosocial change in East Germany. *American Journal of Community Psychology*, *22*, 685–706.

Schwendler, W. (1984). UNESCO's project on the exchange of knowledge for endogenous development. *International Journal of Psychology*, *19*, 3–15.

Scribner, S. (1979). Modes of thinking and ways of speaking: Culture and logic reconsidered. In R. O. Freedle (Ed.), *New directions in discourse processing* (pp. 223–43). Norwood, NJ: Ablex.

Scribner, S., & Cole, M. (1981). *The psychology of literacy.* Cambridge, MA: Harvard University Press.

Searle, W., & Ward, C. (1990). The prediction of psychological and sociocultural adjustment during cross-cultural transitions. *International Journal of Intercultural Relations, 14,* 449–64.

Segall, M. H. (1979). *Cross-cultural psychology: Human behavior in global perspective.* Monterey, CA: Brooks/Cole.

(1983). On the search for the independent variable in cross-cultural psychology. In S. H. Irvine & J. W. Berry (Eds.), *Human assessment and cultural factors* (pp. 127–38). New York: Plenum.

(1984). More than we need to know about culture, but are afraid not to ask. *Journal of Cross-Cultural Psychology, 15,* 153–62.

(1999). Why is there still racism if there is no such thing as "race"? In W. J. Lonner, D. L. Dinnel, D. K. Forgays, & S. H. Hayes (Eds.), *Merging past, present, and future in cross-cultural psychology* (pp. 14–26). Amsterdam: Swets & Zeitlinger.

Segall, M. H., Campbell, D. T., & Herskovits, K. J. (1966). *The influence of culture on visual perception.* Indianapolis, IN: Bobbs-Merrill.

Segall, M. H., Dasen, P. R., Berry, J. W., & Poortinga, Y. H. (1990). *Human behavior in global perspective: An introduction to cross-cultural psychology.* New York: Pergamon.

(1999). *Human behavior in global perspective: An introduction to cross-cultural psychology* (rev. 2nd ed.). Boston, MA: Allyn and Bacon.

Segall, M. H., Ember, C., & Ember, M. (1997). Aggression, crime and warfare. In J. W. Berry, M. H. Segall, & C. Kagitcibasi (Eds.), *Social behavior and applications* (pp. 213–54). Vol. III of *Handbook of cross-cultural psychology.* (2nd ed.). Boston, MA: Allyn and Bacon.

Segalowitz, N. S. (1980). Issues in the cross-cultural study of bilingual development. In H. C. Triandis & A. Heron (Eds.), *Handbook of cross-cultural psychology.* Vol. IV: *Developmental* (pp. 55–92). Boston, MA: Allyn and Bacon.

Semin, G., & Zwier, S. (1997). Social cognition. In J. W. Berry, M. H. Segall, & C. Kagitcibasi (Eds.), *Handbook of cross-cultural psychology.* Vol. III: *Social behavior and applications* (pp. 51–75). Boston, MA: Allyn and Bacon.

Serpell, R. (1976). *Culture's influence on behavior.* London: Methuen.

(1993). *The significance of schooling: Life journeys in an African society.* Cambridge: Cambridge University Press.

Serpell, R., & Deregowski, J. B. (1980). The skill of pictorial perception: An interpretation of cross-cultural evidence. *International Journal of Psychology, 15,* 145–80.

Shaver, P., Schwartz, J., Kirson, D., & O'Connor, C. (1987). Emotion knowledge: Further exploration of a prototype approach. *Journal of Personality and Social Psychology, 52,* 1061–86.

Shaver, P., Wu, S., & Schwartz, J. C. (1992). Cross-cultural similarities and differences in emotion and its representation: A prototype approach. In M. S. Clark (Ed.), *Review of Personality and Social Psychology.* Vol. XIII: *Emotion* (pp. 175–212). Newbury Park, CA: Sage.

Shaw, J. B. (1990). A cognitive categorization model for the study of intercultural management. *Academy of Management Review, 15,* 626–45.

Sheikh, A., & Sheikh, K. (Eds.) (1989). *Eastern and Western approaches to healing.* New York: Wiley.

Shepard, L. A., Camilli, G., & Averill, M. (1981). Comparisons of procedures for detecting test-item bias with both internal and external ability criteria. *Journal of Educational Statistics, 6*, 317–75.

Shweder, R. A. (1979a). Rethinking culture and personality theory. Part I: A critical examination of two classical postulates. *Ethos, 7*, 255–78.

(1979b). Rethinking culture and personality theory. Part II: A critical examination of two more classical postulates. *Ethos, 7*, 279–311.

(1980). Rethinking culture and personality theory. Part III: From genesis and typology to hermeneutics and dynamics. *Ethos, 8*, 60–94.

(1984a). Anthropology's romantic rebellion against the enlightment, or there's more to think than reason and evidence. In R. A. Shweder & R. A. LeVine (Eds.), *Culture theory: Essays on mind, self and emotion* (pp. 27–66). Cambridge: Cambridge University Press.

(1984b). Preview. In R. A. Shweder & R. A. LeVine (Eds.), *Culture theory: Essays on mind, self, and emotion* (pp. 1–24). Cambridge: Cambridge University Press.

(1990). Cultural psychology–what is it? In J. W. Stigler, R. A. Shweder, & G. Herdt (Eds.), *Cultural psychology: Essays on comparative human development* (pp. 1–43). Cambridge: Cambridge University Press.

(1991). *Thinking through cultures: Expeditions in cultural psychology*. Cambridge, MA: Harvard University Press.

Shweder, R. A., & Bourne, E. J. (1984). Does the concept of the person vary cross-culturally? In R. A. Shweder & R. LeVine (Eds.) *Culture theory* (pp. 158–99). New York: Cambridge University Press.

Shweder, R. A., & Sullivan, M. A. (1993). Cultural psychology: Who needs it? *Annual Review of Psychology, 44*, 497–527.

Shweder, R. A., Goodnow, J., Hatano, G., LeVine, R. A., Markus, H., & Miller, P. (1998). The cultural psychology of development: One mind, many mentalities. In W. Damon (Chief Ed.) & R. M. Lerner (vol. Ed.), *Handbook of child psychology*. Vol. I: *Theoretical models of human development* (5th ed., pp. 865–923). New York: Wiley.

Shweder, R. A., Mahapatra, M., & Miller, J. G. (1990). Culture and moral development. In J. W. Stigler, R. A. Shweder, & G. Herdt (Eds.), *Cultural psychology: Essays on comparative human development* (pp. 130–204). Cambridge: Cambridge University Press.

Sigel, I. E., McGillicuddy-De Lisi, A., & Goodnow, J. J. (Eds.) (1992). *Parental belief systems: The psychological consequences for children* (2nd ed.). Hillsdale, NJ: Erlbaum.

Silvar, S. D., & Pollack, R. H. (1967). Racial differences in pigmentation of the fundus oculi. *Psychonomic Science, 7*, 159–60.

Silverman, D. (1993). *Interpreting qualitative data: Methods for analyzing talk, text, and interaction*. London: Sage.

Simons, R., & Hughes, C. C. (Eds.) (1985). *The culture-bound syndromes*. Dordrecht: Reidel.

Sinaiko, H. W. (1975). Verbal factors in human engineering: Some cultural and psychological data. In A. Chapanis (Ed.), *Ethnic variables in human engineering* (pp. 159–77). Baltimore, MD: Johns Hopkins University Press.

Sinangil, H. K., & Ones, D. S. (1997). Empirical investigations of the host country perspective in expatriate management. *New Approaches to Employee Managment, 4*, 173–205.

Singh, A. K. (1967). Hindu culture and economic development in India. *Conspectus, 1*, 9–32.

Singh, N. K., & Paul, O. (1985). *Corporate soul: Dynamics of effective management.* New Delhi: Vikas.

Sinha, D. (1979). Perceptual style among nomads and transitional agriculturalist Birhors. In L. Eckensberger, W. Lonner, & Y. H. Poortinga (Eds.) *Cross-cultural contributions to psychology* (pp. 83–93). Lisse, Netherlands: Swets and Zeitlinger.

——— (1984). Psychology in the context of Third World development. *International Journal of Psychology, 19,* 17–29.

——— (1986). *Psychology in a Third World country: The Indian experience.* New Delhi: Sage.

——— (1989). Research in psychology in the developing world. *Psychology and Developing Societies, 1,* 105–26.

——— (1990). Interventions for development out of poverty. In R. W. Brislin (Ed.), *Applied cross-cultural psychology* (pp. 77–97). Newbury Park, CA: Sage.

——— (1996). Culture as the target and culture as the source: A review of cross-cultural psychology in Asia. *Psychology and Developing Societies, 8,* 83–106.

——— (1997). Indigenizing psychology. In J. W. Berry, Y. H. Poortinga, & J. Pandey (Eds.), *Theory and method* (pp. 129–69). Vol. I of *Handbook of cross-cultural psychology* (2nd ed.). Boston, MA: Allyn and Bacon.

Sinha, D., & Holtzman, W. (Eds.) (1984). The impact of psychology on Third World development. *International Journal of Psychology,* 1984, *19* (Special Issue, Nos. 1 & 2).

Sinha, J. B. P. (1970). *Development through behaviour modification.* Bombay: Allied Publishers.

——— (1980). *The nurturant task leader.* New Delhi: Concept Publishing House.

——— (1984a). A model of effective leadership styles in India. *International Studies of Management and Organization, 14,* 86–98.

——— (1984b). Towards partnership for relevant research in the Third World. *International Journal of Psychology, 19,* 169–77.

Skelton, T., & Allen, T. (Eds.) (1999). *Culture and global change.* London: Routledge.

Skinner, B. F. (1957). *Verbal behavior.* New York: Appleton-Century-Crofts.

Sloan, T., & Montero, M. (Eds.) (1990). Psychology for the Third World. *Journal of Social Issues, 46* (3) (special issue).

Slobin, D. I. (1996). From "thought and language" to "thinking for speaking." In J. J. Gumperz & S. C. Levinson (Eds.), *Rethinking linguistic relativity* (pp. 70–96). Cambridge: Cambridge University Press.

Slobin, D. I. (Ed.) (1985–97). *The cross-linguistic study of language acquisition* (vols. I–V). Mahwah, NJ: Erlbaum.

Smith, J. A., Harré, R., & Van Langenhove, L. (Eds.) (1995). *Rethinking methods in psychology.* London: Sage.

Smith, P. B., & Bond, M. H. (1998). *Social psychology across cultures* (2nd ed.). Hemel Hempstead: Harvester/Wheatsheaf.

Smith, P. B., & Peterson, M. F. (1988). *Leadership, organizations and culture: An event management model.* London: Sage.

Smith, P. B., & Schwartz, S. H. (1997). Values. In J. W. Berry, M. H. Segall, & C. Kagitcibasi (Eds.), *Social behavior and applications* (pp. 77–118). Vol. III of *Handbook of cross-cultural psychology* (2nd ed.). Boston, MA: Allyn and Bacon.

Smith, P. B., Dugan, S., & Trompenaars, F. (1996). National culture and the values of organizational employees. *Journal of Cross-Cultural Psychology, 27,* 231–64.

Smith, P. B., Trompenaars, F., & Dugan, S. (1995). The Rotter locus of control scale in 43 countries: A test of cultural relativity. *International Journal of Psychology, 30,* 377–400.

Snarey, J. R. (1985). Cross-cultural universality of social-moral development: A critical review of Kohlbergian research. *Psychological Bulletin*, 87, 202–32.

Snustad, D. P., & Simmons. M. J. (1997). *Principles of genetics* (2nd ed.). New York: Wiley.

Social Science Research Council (1954). Acculturation: An exploratory formulation. *American Anthropologist*, 56, 973–1002.

Sokal, A. D. (1996a). Transgressing the boundaries. *Social Text*, 46–7, 217–52.

(1996b). Transgressing the boundaries: An afterword. *Philosophy and Literature*, 20, 338–46.

Solomon, R. H. (1987). China: Friendship and obligation in Chinese negotiation style. In H. Binnendijk (Ed.), *National negotiating styles* (pp. 1–16). Washington, DC: Foreign Service Institute.

Sommerlad, E., & Berry, J. W. (1970). The role of ethnic identification in distinguishing between attitudes towards assimilation and integration of a minority racial group. *Human Relations*, 23, 23–9.

Sonke, C. J., Poortinga, Y. H., & De Kuijer, J. H. J. (1999). Cross-cultural differences in cognitive task performance: The influence of stimulus familiarity. In W. J. Lonner, D. L. Dinnel, D. K. Forgays, & S. A. Hayes (Eds.), *Merging past, present, and future in cross-cultural psychology* (pp. 146–58). Lisse, Netherlands: Swets & Zeitlinger.

Sow, I. (1977). *Psychiatrie dynamique africaine* [Dynamic African psychiatry]. Paris: Payot.

(1978). *Les structures anthropologiques de la folie en Afrique noire* [The anthropological structures of madness in black Africa]. Paris: Payot.

Spearman, C. (1927). *The abilities of man*. London: Macmillan.

Spielberger, C. D., Gorsuch, R., & Lushene, R. (1970). *Manual for the State-Trait Anxiety Questionnaire*. Palo Alto, CA: Consulting Psychologists Press.

Sporer, S. L. (2001). Recognizing faces of other ethnic groups: Data in search of theory. *Psychology, Public Policy and Law*, 7, 170–200.

Stephan, W. G., & Stephan, C. W. (1996). *Intergroup relations*. Boulder, CO: Westview Press.

Stern, P. (1999). Learning to be smart: An exploration of the culture of intelligence in a Canadian Inuit community. *American Anthropologist*, 101, 502–14.

Sternberg, R. J. (1977). *Intelligence, information processing, and analogical reasoning: The componential analysis of human abilities*. New York: Wiley.

Sternberg, R. J., & Grigorenko, E. (Eds.) (1997a). *Intelligence, heredity and environment*. New York: Cambridge University Press.

(1997b). Are cognitive styles still in style? *American Psychologist*, 52, 700–12.

Sternberg, S. (1969). The discovery of processing stages: Extension of Donders' method. *Acta Psychologica*, 30, 276–315.

Stevenson, H. W., & Stigler, J. W. (1992). *The learning gap: Why our schools are failing and what we can learn from Japanese and Chinese education*. New York: Summit Books.

Stewart, V. M. (1973). Tests of the "carpentered world" hypothesis by race and environment in America and Zambia. *International Journal of Psychology*, 8, 83–94.

Stigler, J. W., & Perry, M. (1990). Mathematics learning in Japanese, Chinese and Amerian classrooms. In J. W. Stigler, R. A. Shweder, & G. Herdt (Eds.), *Cultural psychology: Essays on comparative human development* (pp. 328–53). New York: Cambridge University Press.

Stigler, J. W., Lee, S. W., & Stevenson, H. W. (1986). Digit memory span in Chinese and English: Evidence for a temporary limited store. *Cognition*, 23, 1–20.

Strange, W., & Jenkins, J. J. (1978). Role of linguistic experience in the perception of speech. In R. D. Walk & H. L. Pick (Eds.), *Perception and experience* (pp. 125–69). New York: Plenum.

Strelau, J. (1998). *Temperament: A psychological perspective*. New York: Plenum.

Strelau, J., Angleitner, A., Newberry, B. H. (1999). *Pavlovian Temperament Survey (PTS): An international handbook*. Berne: Hogrefe.

Strodtbeck, F. (1964). Considerations of meta-method in cross-cultural research. In A. K. Romney & R. D'Andrade (Eds.), Transcultural studies of cognition. *American Anthropologist, 66*, 223–29.

Stroebe, W., Lenkert, A., & Jonas, K. (1988). Familiarity may breed contempt: The impact of student exchange on national stereotypes and attitudes. In W. Stroebe, A. W. Kruglanski, D. Bar-Tal, & M. Hewstone (Eds.), *The social psychology of intergroup conflict* (pp. 167–87). Berlin: Springer Verlag.

Strohschneider, S., & Güss, D. (1998). Planning and problem solving: Differences between Brazilian and German students. *Journal of Cross-Cultural Psychology, 29*, 695–716.

Sturtevant, W. (1964). Studies in ethnoscience. *American Anthropologist, 66*, 99–124.

Suarez-Orozco, M. M., Spindler, G., & Spindler, L. (Eds.) (1994). *The making of psychological anthropology*. Fort Worth, TX: Harcourt Brace.

Sumner, W. G. (1906). *Folkways*. New York: Ginn & Co.

Super, C. M. (1976). Environmental effects on motor development: The case of "African infant precocity". *Developmental Medicine and Child Neurology, 18*, 561–7.

Super, C. M., & Harkness, S. (1986). The developmental niche: A conceptualization at the interface of child and culture. *International Journal of Behavioral Development, 9*, 545–69.

Super, C., M. & Harkness, S. (1997). The cultural structuring of child development. In J. W. Berry, P. R. Dasen, & T. S. Saraswathi (Eds.), *Basic processes and human development* (pp. 1–39). Vol. II of *Handbook of cross-cultural psychology* (2nd ed.). Boston, MA: Allyn and Bacon.

Super, C. M., Harkness, S., Van Tijen, N., Van der Vlugt, E., Fintelman, M., & Dijkstra, J. (1996). The three R's of Dutch childrearing and the socialization of infant arousal. In S. Harkness & C. M. Super (Eds.), *Parents' cultural belief systems: Their origins, expressions, and consequences* (pp. 447–65). New York: Guilford.

Sussman, N. M., & Rosenfeld, H. M. (1982). Influence of culture, language and sex on conversational distance. *Journal of Personality and Social Psychology, 42*, 66–74.

Swartz, L. (1985). Anorexia nervosa as a culture-bound syndrome. *Social Science and Medicine, 20*, 725–30.

Swets, J. A. (Ed.) (1964). *Signal detection and recognition by human observers*. New York: Wiley.

Symons, D. (1979). *The evolution of human sexuality*. Oxford: Oxford University Press.

Szabo, S., Orley, J., & Saxena, S. (1997). An approach to response scale development for cross-cultural questionnaires. *European Psychologist, 2*, 270–6.

Taft, R. (1977). Coping with unfamiliar culture. In N. Warren (Ed.), *Studies in cross-cultural psychology* (pp. 121–51). London: Academic Press.

Tajfel, H. (Ed.) (1978). *Differentiation between social groups*. London: Academic Press.

Takano, Y., & Osaka, E. (1999). An unsupported common view: Comparing Japan and the US on individualism/collectivism. *Asian Journal of Social Psychology, 2*, 311–41.

Tanaka-Matsumi, J. (1979). Cultural factors and social influence techniques in Naikan therapy: A Japanese self-observation method. *Psychotherapy: Theory, Research and Practice*, *16*, 385–90.

Tanaka-Matsumi, J., & Draguns, J. (1997). Culture and psychopathology. In J. W. Berry, M. H. Segall, & C. Kagitcibasi (Eds.), *Social behavior and applications* (pp. 449–91). Vol. III of *Handbook of cross-cultural psychology* (2nd ed.). Boston, MA: Allyn and Bacon.

Tangney, J. P. (1990). Assessing individual differences in proneness to shame and guilt: Development of the Self-Conscious Affect and Attribution Inventory. *Journal of Personality and Social Psychology*, *59*, 102–11.

    (1992). Situational determinants of shame and guilt in young adulthood. *Personality and Social Psychology Bulletin*, *18*, 199–206.

Tanon, F. (1994). *A cultural view on planning: The case of weaving in Ivory Coast*. Tilburg: Tilburg University Press.

Tayeb, M. H. (1988). *Organizations and national culture: A comparative analysis*. London: Sage.

Taylor, D. M. (1981). Stereotypes and intergroup relations. In R. C. Gardner & R. Kalin (Eds.), *A Canadian social psychology of ethnic relations* (pp. 151–71). Toronto: Methuen.

Taylor, D. M., & Moghaddam, F. M. (1994). *Theories of intergroup relations: International social psychological perspectives*. Westport, CT: Praeger.

Textor, R. (1967). *A cross-cultural summary*. New Haven, CT: Human Relations Area Files.

Thayer, N. B., & Weiss, S. E. (1987). Japan: The changing logic of a former minor power. In H. Binnendijk (Ed.), *National negotiating styles* (pp. 45–74). Washington, DC: Foreign Service Institute.

Thelen, E. (1995). Motor development: A new synthesis. *American Psychologist*, *50*, 79–95

Thomas, A. (Ed.) (1993). *Kulturvergleichende Psychologie: Eine Einführung* [Culture-comparative psychology: An introduction]. Berne: Hogrefe.

Thomas, A., & Wagner K. H. (1999). Von der Fremdheitserfahrung zum interkulturellen Verstehen [From experiencing strangeness to intercultural understanding]. *Praxis*, *46*, 227–36.

Thomas, J. (1988). The role played by metalinguistic awareness in second and third language learning. *Journal of Multilingual and Multicultural Development*, *9*, 235–47.

Thompson, W. R. (1980). Cross-cultural uses of biological data and perspectives. In H. C. Triandis & W. W. Lambert (Eds.), *Handbook of cross-cultural psychology* (vol. I, pp. 205–52). Boston, MA: Allyn and Bacon.

Thoresen, C. (1999). Spirituality and health. *Journal of Health Psychology*, *4*, 291–434 (Special Issue).

Thouless, R. H. (1933). A racial difference in perception. *Journal of Social Psychology*, *4*, 330–9.

Thurstone, L. L. (1938). *Primary mental abilities*. Psychometric Monographs, No. 1.

Tinbergen, N. (1963). On aims and methods of ethology. *Zeitschrift für Tierpsychologie*, *20*, 410–33.

    (1969). Ethology. In R. Harré (Ed.), *Scientific thought 1900–1960* (pp. 238–68). Oxford: Clarendon Press (reprinted in Tinbergen, N. [1973]. *The animal and its world* [vol. II, pp. 130–60]. London: Allen and Unwin).

Ting-Toomey, S. (1985). Toward a theory of conflict and culture. *International and Intercultural Communication Annual*, *9*, 71–86.

Titchener, E. B. (1916). On ethnological tests of sensation and perception. *Proceedings of the American Philisophical Society, 55*, 204–36.

Tittle, C. K. (1982). Use of judgemental methods in item bias studies. In R. A. Berk (Ed.), *Handbook of methods for detecting test bias* (pp. 31–63). Baltimore, MD: Johns Hopkins University Press.

Tizard, B., & Varma, V. (Eds.). (1992). *Vulnerability and resilience in human development: A Festschrift for Ann and Alan Clarke.* London: Kingsley.

Tobin, J. J., Wu, D. Y. H., & Davidson, D. H. (1989). *Preschool in three cultures: Japan, China and the United States.* New Haven, CT: Yale University Press.

Tomasello, M. (1999). *The cultural origins of human cognition.* Cambridge, MA: Harvard University Press.

Tomasello, M., Kruger, A. C., & Ratner, H. H. (1993). Cultural learning. *Behavioral and Brain Sciences, 16*, 495–552.

Tomkins, S. S. (1962). *Affect, imaginary and consciousness.* Vol. I: *The positive emotions.* New York: Springer.

(1963). *Affect, imaginary and consciousness.* Vol. II: *The negative emotions.* New York: Springer.

Tooby, J., & Cosmides, L. (1992). The psychological foundations of culture. In J. Barkow, L. Cosmides, & J. Tooby (Eds.), *The adapted mind: Evolutionary psychology and the generation of culture* (pp. 19–136). New York: Oxford University Press.

Torbiörn, I. (1982). *Living abroad.* New York: Wiley.

Triandis, H. C. (1972). *The analysis of subjective culture.* New York: Wiley.

(1975). Culture training, cognitive complexity and interpersonal attitudes. In R. Brislin, S. Bochner, & W. Lonner (Eds.), *Cross-cultural perspectives on learning* (pp. 39–77). Beverly Hills, CA: Sage.

(1978). Some universals of social behavior. *Personality and Social Psychology Bulletin, 4*, 1–16.

(1980). Introduction. In H. C. Triandis & W. W. Lambert (Eds.), *Handbook of cross-cultural psychology.* Vol. I: *Perspectives* (pp. 1–14). Boston, MA: Allyn and Bacon.

(1984). Toward a psychological theory of economic growth. *International Journal of Psychology, 19*, 79–95.

(1988). Collectivism *vs* individualism: A reconceptualization of a basic concept in cross-cultural social psychology. In C. Bagley & G. K. Verma (Eds.), *Personality, cognition and values* (pp. 60–95). London: Macmillan.

(1989). The self and social behavior in differing cultural contexts. *Psychological Review, 96*, 506–20.

(1990). Theoretical concepts of use to practitioners. In R. Brislin (Ed.), *Applied cross-cultural psychology.* Newbury Park, CA: Sage.

(1993). Collectivism and individualism as cultural syndromes. *Cross-Cultural Research, 27*, 155–80.

(1994a). *Culture and social behavior.* New York: McGraw-Hill.

(1994b). Cross-cultural industrial and organizational psychology. In H. C. Triandis, M. D. Dunnette, & L. M. Hough (Eds.) (1994), *Handbook of industrial and organizational psychology* (vol. IV, 2nd ed.). Palo Alto, CA: Consulting Psychologists Press.

(1995). *Individualism and collectivism.* Boulder, CO: Westview.

(1996). The psychological measurement of cultural syndromes. *American Psychologist, 51*, 407–15.

(2000a). Culture and conflict. *International Journal of Psychology*, *35*, 145–52.

(2000b). Dialectics between cultural and cross-cultural psychology. *Asian Journal of Social Psychology*, *3*, 185–96.

Triandis, H. C. (Ed.) (1980). *Handbook of cross-cultural psychology*. Boston, MA: Allyn and Bacon.

Triandis, H. C., & Gelfand, M. (1998). Converging measurement of horizontal and vertical individualism and collectivism. *Journal of Personality and Social Psychology*, *74*, 118–28.

Triandis, H. C., & Vassiliou, V. (1972). A comparative analysis of subjective culture. In H. C. Triandis, *The analysis of subjective culture* (pp. 299–335). New York: Wiley.

Triandis, H. C., Dunnette, M. D., & Hough, L. M. (Eds.) (1994). *Handbook of industrial and organizational psychology* (vol. IV, 2nd ed.). Palo Alto, CA: Consulting Psychologists Press.

Triandis, H. C., Malpass, R., & Davidson, A. R. (1971). Cross-cultural psychology. *Biennial Review of Anthropology*, *1*, 1–84.

Triandis, H. C., McCusker, C., & Hui, C. H. (1990). Multimethod probes of individualism and collectivism. *Journal of Personality and Social Psychology*, *59*, 1006–20.

Tripathi, R. C. (1988). Applied social psychology. In J. Pandey (Ed.), *Psychology in India: The state of the art* (vol. II, pp. 225–78). New Delhi: Sage.

Troadec, B. (2001). Le modèle écoculturel: Un cadre pour la psychologie comparative [The ecocultural model: A framework for comparative psychology]. *International Journal of Psychology*, *36*, 53–64.

Tseng, W.-S. (Ed.) (2001). *Handbook of cultural psychiatry*. San Diego CA: Academic Press.

Tulviste, P. (1991). *The cultural-historical development of verbal thinking*. New York: Nova Science Publishers.

Tung, M. (1994). Symbolic meanings of the body in Chinese culture and "somatization". *Culture, Medicine and Psychiatry*, *18*, 483–92.

Tung, R. L. (1981). Selection and training of personnel for overseas assignments. *Columbia Journal of World Business*, Spring 69–78.

Turiel, E. (1983). *The development of social knowledge: Morality and convention*. Cambridge: Cambridge University Press.

(1998). The development of morality. In W. Damon & N. Eisenberg (Eds.), *Handbook of developmental psychology*. Vol. III: *Social, emotional and personality development* (pp. 863–932). New York: Wiley.

Tweed, R., Conway, L., & Ryder, A. (1999). The target is straw or the arrow is crooked. *American Psychologist*, *54*, 837–8.

Tylor, E. B. (1871). *Primitive culture* (2 vols.). London: Murray.

Udy, S. H. (1970). *Work in traditional and modern society*. Englewood Cliffs, NJ: Prentice-Hall.

Ugorji, R., & Berman, B. (1974). Orientations of Umuaro Igbo villagers to development. In J. W. Berry & W. J. Lonner (Eds.), *Applied cross-cultural psychology* (pp. 52–7). Amsterdam: Swets & Zeitlinger.

Ulusahin, A., Basoglu, M., & Paykel, E. (1994). A cross-cultural comparative study of depression symptoms in British and Turkish clinical samples. *Social Psychiatry and Psychiatric Epidemiology*, *29*, 31–9.

UNAIDS (1996). *HIV/AIDS: The global epidemic*. Geneva: UNAIDS and WHO.

UNEP (1997). *Global environment outlook*. New York: Oxford University Press.

UNICEF (1996). *The state of the world's children*. Oxford: Oxford University Press.

Valentine, T. (1991). A unified account of effects of distinctiveness, inversion and race on face recognition. *Quarterly Journal of Experimental Psychology*, *43A*, 161–204.

Valentine, T., & Endo, M. (1992). Towards an exemplar model of face processing: The effects of race and distinctiveness. *Quarterly Journal of Experimental Psychology*, *44A*, 671–703.

Valsiner, J. (1987). *Culture and the development of children's action*. New York: Wiley.

Valsiner, J., & Lawrence, J. (1997). Human development in culture across the life span. In J. W. Berry, P. R. Dasen, & T. S. Saraswathi (Eds.), *Basic processes and human development* (pp. 69–106). Vol. II of *Handbook of cross-cultural psychology* (2nd ed.). Boston, MA: Allyn and Bacon.

Van Bezooijen, R., Otto, S. A., Heenan, T. A. (1983). Recognition of vocal expressions of emotion: A three-nation study to identify universal characteristics. *Journal of Cross-Cultural Psychology*, *14*, 387–406.

Van de Koppel, J. M. H., & Schoots, N. H. (1986). Why are all trains painted yellow? Conventies in het acculturatieproces. *Nederlands Tijdschrift voor de Psychologie*, 41, 189–96.

Van de Vijver, F. J. R. (1997). Meta-analysis of cross-cultural comparisons of cognitive test performance. *Journal of Cross-Cultural Psychology*, *28*, 678–709.

(in press). Inductive reasoning in Zambia, Turkey and The Netherlands: Establishing cross-cultural equivalence. *Intelligence*.

Van de Vijver, F. J. R., & Hambleton, R. K. (1996). Translating tests: Some practial guidelines. *European Psychologist*, *1*, 89–99.

Van de Vijver, F. J. R., & Leung, K. (1997a). Methods and data analysis of comparative research. In J. W. Berry, Y. H. Poortinga, & J. Pandey (Eds.), *Theory and method* (pp. 257–300). Vol. I of *Handbook of cross-cultural psychology* (2nd ed.). Boston, MA: Allyn and Bacon.

(1997b). *Methods and data analysis for cross-cultural research*. Newbury Park, CA: Sage.

Van de Vijver, F. J. R., & Poortinga, Y. H. (1982). Cross-cultural generalization and universality. *Journal of Cross-Cultural psychology*, *13*, 387–408.

(1991). Testing across cultures. In R. K. Hambleton & J. Zaal (Eds.), *Advances in educational and psychological testing* (pp. 277–308). Boston: Kluwer.

(1994). Methodological issues in cross-cultural studies on parental rearing behavior and psychopathology. In C. Perris, W. A. Arrindell, & M. Eisemann (Eds.), *Parenting and psychopathology* (pp. 173–97). New York: Wiley.

(1997). Towards an integrated analysis of bias in cross-cultural assessment. *European Journal of Psychological Assessment*, *13*, 21–9.

(in press). Structural equivalence in multicultural research. *Journal of Cross-Cultural Psychology*.

Van de Vijver, F. J. R., & Tanzer, N. K. (1997). Bias and equivalence in cross-cultural assessment: An overview. *European Review of Applied Psychology*, *47*, 263–79.

Van de Vijver, F. J. R., Helms-Lorenz, M., & Feltzer, M. (1999). Acculturation and cognitive performance of migrant children in The Netherlands. *International Journal of Psychology*, *34*, 149–62.

Van de Vliert, E., Kluwer, E. S., & Lynn, R. (2000). Citizens of warmer countries are more competitive and poorer: Culture or chance? *Journal of Economic Psychology*, *21*, 143–65.

Van den Heuvel, K., & Poortinga, Y. H. (1999). Resource allocation by Greek and Dutch students: A test of three models. *International Journal of Psychology*, *34*, 1–13.

Van der Flier, H., Mellenbergh, G. J., Adèr, H. J., & Wyn, M. (1984). An iterative item bias detection method. *Journal of Educational Measurement*, *21*, 131–45.

Van der Werff, J. J. (1985). Heymans' temperament dimensions in personality research. *Journal of Research in Personality, 19*, 279–87.

Van Haaften, E. H., & Van de Vijver, F. J. R. (1996). Psychological consequences of environmental degradation. *Journal of Health Psychology, 1*, 411–29.

(1999). Dealing with extreme environmental degradation: Stress and marginalization of Sahel dwellers. *Social Psychiatry and Psychiatric Epidemiology, 34*, 376–82.

Van Hemert, D. A., Van de Vijver, F. J. R., Poortinga, Y. H., & Georgas, J. (in press). *Structure and score levels of the Eysenck Personality Questionnaire across individuals and countries. Personality and Individual Differences.*

Van Herk, H. (2000). *Equivalence in cross-national context: Methodological and empirical issues in marketing research.* Ph. D. thesis. Tilburg: Tilburg University.

Van Ijzendoorn, M. H. (1995). Adult attachment representations, parental responsiveness, and infant attachment: A meta-analysis on the predictive validity of the adult attachment interview. *Psychological Bulletin, 117*, 387–403.

Van Lancker, D., & Fromkin, V. A. (1973). Hemispheric specialization for pitch perception: Evidence from Thai. *Journal of Phonetics, 1*, 101–9.

(1978). Cerebral dominance for pitch contrasts in tone language speakers and in musically untrained and trained English speakers. *Journal of Phonetics, 6*, 1–23.

Van Leest, P. F. (1997). *Persoonlijkheidsmeting by allochtonen* [Personality measurement with migrants]. Lisse, Netherlands: Swets & Zeitlinger.

Van Leeuwen, M. S. (1978). A cross-cultural examination of psychological differentiation in males and females. *International Journal of Psychology, 13*, 87–122.

Van Muijen, J. J., Koopman, P. L., & De Witte, K. (1996). *Focus op organisatiecultuur* [Focus on organizational culture]. Schoonhoven: Academic Service.

Van Oudenhoven, J. P. (2001). Do organizations reflect national cultures? A 10-nation study. *International Journal of Intercultural Relations, 25*, 89–107.

Van Oudenhoven, J. P., & Willemsen, T. M. (Eds.) (1989). *Ethnic minorities: Social psychological perspectives.* Amsterdam: Swets & Zeitlinger.

Van Zon, M. (1997). *Speech processing in Dutch: A cross-linguistic approach.* Ph. D. thesis. Tilburg: Tilburg University.

VanderSteene, G., Van Haassen, P. P., De Bruyn, E. E. J., Coetsier, P. Pijl, Y. J., Poortinga, Y. H., Spelberg, H. C., & Stinissen, J. (1986). *WISC-R: Wechsler Intelligence Scale for Children-Revised. Nederlandstalige Uitgave.* Lisse, Netherlands: Swets & Zeitlinger.

Veenhoven, R. (1991). Is happiness relative? *Social Indicators Research, 20*, 333–54.

(1993). *Happiness in nations: Subjective appreciation of life in 56 nations, 1945–1992.* Rotterdam: RISBO.

Vega, W., & Rumbaut, R. (1991). Ethnic minorities and mental health. *Annual Review of Sociology, 17*, 56–89.

Vega, W., Kolody, B., Valle, R., & Weir, J. (1991). Social networks, social support, and their relationship to depression among immigrant Mexican women. *Human Organization, 50*, 154–62.

Vernon, P. A. (Ed.). (1987). *Speed of information-processing and intelligence.* Norwood, NJ: Ablex.

Vernon, P. E. (1969). *Intelligence and cultural environment.* London: Methuen.

(1979). *Intelligence, heredity and environment.* San Francisco, CA: Freeman.

Verster, J. M. (1991). Speed of cognitive processing: Cross-cultural findings on structure and relation to intelligence, tempo, temperament, and brain function. In P. L. Dann,

S. H. Irvine, & J. M. Collis (Eds.), *Advances in computer-based human assessment* (pp. 103–47). Dordrecht: Kluwer.

Vinden, P. G. (1996). Junín Quechua children's understanding of mind. *Child Development, 67,* 1707–16.

(1999). Children's understanding of mind and emotion: A multiculture study. *Cognition and Emotion, 13,* 19–48.

Vinsonneau, G. (1997). *Culture et comportement.* Paris: Armand Colin.

Vogel, F., & Motulsky, A. G. (1979). *Human genetics: Problems and approaches.* Berlin: Springer-Verlag.

Vorster, J., & Schuring, G. (1989). Language and thought: Developmental perspectives on counterfactual conditionals. *South African Journal of Psychology, 19,* 34–8.

Vouilloux, D. (1959). Etude de la psychomotricité d'enfants africains au Cameroun: Test de Gesell et réflexes archaïques [Study of psychomotor ability in African children in Cameroon: Gesell test and archaic reflexes]. *Journal de la Société des Africanistes, 29,* 11–18.

Vroomen, J., Van Zon, M., & De Gelder, M. (1996). Cues to speech segmentation: Evidence from juncture misperceptions and word spotting. *Memory and Cognition, 24,* 744–55.

Vygotsky, L. S. (1978). *Mind in society: The development of higher psychological processes.* Cambridge, MA: Harvard University Press.

Wachs, T. (1995). Relation of mild-to-moderate malnutrition to human development: Correlation studies. *Journal of Nutrition, Supplement, 125,* 22455–545.

Wagner, D. A. (1977). Ontogeny of the Ponzo illusion: Effects of age, schooling and environment. *International Journal of Psychology, 12,* 161–76.

(1978). Memories of Morocco: The influence of age, schooling and environment on memory. *Cognitive Psychology, 10,* 1–28.

(1981). Culture and memory development. In H. C. Triandis & A. Heron (Eds.), *Handbook of cross-cultural psychology: Developmental psychology* (vol. IV, pp. 178–232). Boston, MA: Allyn and Bacon.

(1993). *Literacy, culture and development: Becoming literate in Morocco.* New York: Cambridge University Press.

Wahi, S., & Johri, R. (1994). Questioning a universal theory of mind: mental–real distinctions made by Indian children. *Journal of Genetic Psychology, 155,* 503–8.

Wallace, A. C. (1959). Cultural determinants of response to hallucinatory experiences. *AMA Archives of General Psychiatry, 1,* 58–69.

Ward, C. (1996). Acculturation. In D. Landis & R. Bhagat (Eds.), *Handbook of intercultural training* (2nd ed., pp. 124–47). Thousand Oaks, CA: Sage.

Ward, C. (Ed.) (1989). *Altered states of consciousness and mental health.* Newbury Park, CA: Sage.

Ward, C., & Kennedy, A. (1992). Locus of control, mood disturbance and social difficulty during cross-cultural transitions. *International Journal of Intercultural Relations, 16,* 175–94.

(1993). Where is the "culture" in cross-cultural transition? Comparative studies of sojourner adjustment. *Journal of Cross-Cultural Psychology, 24,* 221–49.

(1995). Crossing cultures: The relationship between psychological and sociological dimensions of cross-cultural adjustment. In J. Pandey, D. Sinha, & P. Bhawuk (Eds.), *Asian contributions to cross-cultural psychology* (pp. 289–306). New Delhi: Sage.

Ward, C., & Rana-Deuba, A. (1999). Acculturation and adaptation revisited. *Journal of Cross-Cultural Psychology*, *30*, 422–42.

Ward, C., & Searle, W. (1991). The impact of value discrepancies and cultural identity on psychological and socio-cultural adjustment of sojourners. *International Journal of Intercultural Relations*, *15*, 209–25.

Ward, C., Bochner, S., & Furnham, A. (2001). *The psychology of culture shock*. Hove, UK: Routledge.

Ward, C., Okura, Y., Kennedy, A., & Kojima, T. (1999). The U-curve on trial: A longitudinal study of psychological and sociocultural adjustment during cross-cultural transition. *International Journal of Intercultural Relations*, *22*, 277–91.

Warren, N., & Parkin, J. M. (1974). A neurological and behavioral comparison of African and European newborns in Uganda. *Child Development*, *45*, 966–71.

Warwick, D. (1980). The politics and ethics of cross-cultural research. In H. C. Triandis & W. W. Lambert (Eds.), *Handbook of cross-cultural psychology*. Vol. I: *Perspectives* (pp. 310–71). Boston, MA: Allyn and Bacon.

Wassmann, J., & Dasen, P. R. (1994a). Yupno number system and counting. *Journal of Cross-Cultural Psychology*, *25*, 78–94.

(1994b). "Hot" and "cold": Classification and sorting among the Yupno of Papua New Guinea. *International Journal of Psychology*, *29*, 19–38.

(1998). Balinese spatial orientation: Some empirical evidence for moderate linguistic relativity. *The Journal of the Royal Anthropological Institute, incorporating Man (N.S.)*, *4*, 689–711.

Weber, E. U., & Hsee, C. K. (2000). Culture and individual decision making. *Applied Psychology: An International Review*, *49*, 32–61.

Weber, M. (1976). *The Protestant Ethic and the spirit of capitalism*. New York: Charles Scribner's Sons.

Weeks, W. H., Pedersen, P. B., & Brislin, R. W. (1982). *A manual of structured experiences for cross-cultural learning*. Chicago, IL: Intercultural Press.

Weisz, J., Rothbaum, F., & Blackburn, T. (1984). Standing out and standing in: The psychology of control in America and Japan. *American Psychologist*, *39*, 955–68.

Wellman, H. M. (1990). *The child's theory of mind*. Cambridge, MA: MIT Press.

Werner, C., Brown, B., & Altman, I. (1997). Environmental psychology. In J. W. Berry, M. H. Segall, & C. Kagitcibasi (Eds.), *Social behavior and applications* (pp. 255–90). Vol. III of *Handbook of cross-cultural psychology* (2nd ed.). Boston, MA: Allyn and Bacon.

Werner, E. E. (1972). Infants around the world: cross-cultural studies of psycho-motor development from birth to two years. *Journal of Cross-Cultural Psychology*, *3*, 111–34.

Werner, H. (1957). The concept of development from a comparative and organismic point of view. In D. B. Harris (Ed.), *The concept of development* (pp. 125–48). Minneapolis, MN: University of Minnesota Press.

Werner, O., & Campbell, D. T. (1970). Translating, working through interpreters and the problem of decentering. In R. Naroll & R. Cohen (Eds.), *A handbook of method in cultural anthropology* (pp. 398–419). New York: Natural History Press.

Wertsch, J. V., & Tulviste, P. (1992). L. S. Vygotsky and contemporary developmental psychology. *Developmental Psychology*, *28*, 548–57.

Westermeyer, J. (1973). On the epidemicity of Amok violence. *Archives of General Psychiatry*, *28*, 873–6.

Wexley, K. N., & Yukl, G. A. (1984). *Organizational behavior and personnel psychology* (rev. ed.). Homewood, IL: Irwin.

Whiten, A., Goodall, J., McGrew, W. C., Nishida, T., Reynolds, V., Sugiyama, Y., Tutin, C. E. G., Wrangham, R. W., & Boesch, C. (1999). Cultures in chimpanzees. *Nature*, *399*, 682–5.

Whiting, B. B. (1976). The problem of the packaged variable. In K. Reigel & J. Meacham (Eds.), *The developing individual in a changing world* (vol. I, pp. 303–9). Mouton: The Hague.

Whiting, B. B., & Whiting, J. W. M. (1988). Foreword to Adolescents in a Changing World series. In V. C. Burbank (Ed.), *Aboriginal adolescence: Maidenhood in an Australian community* (pp. vii–xiv). New Brunswick, NJ: Rutgers University Press.

Whiting, J. W. M. (1968). Methods and problems in cross-cultural research. In G. Lindzey & E. Aronson (Eds.), *Handbook of social psychology* (vol. II, pp. 693–728). Reading, MA: Addison-Wesley.

 (1974). A model for psychocultural research. *Annual Report*. Washington, DC: American Anthropological Association.

 (1981). Environmental constraints on infant care practices. In R. L. Munroe, R. M. Munroe, & B. B. Whiting (Eds.), *Handbook of cross-cultural human development* (pp. 151–81). New York: Garland Press.

 (1994). Fifty years as a behavioral scientist: Autobiographical notes. In E. Chasdi (Ed.), *Culture and human development: The selected papers of John Whiting* (pp. 14–41). New York: Cambridge University Press.

Whiting, J. W. M., & Child, I. (1953). *Child training and personality*. New Haven, CT: Yale University Press.

Whiting, J. W. M., Kluckhohn, R., & Anthony (1958). The function of male initiation ceremonies at puberty. In E. Maccoby, T. Newcomb, & E. Hartley (Eds.), *Readings in social psychology* (3rd ed., pp. 359–70). New York: Holt.

WHOQOL Group (1995). The World Health Organization Quality of Life Assessment: Position paper from the World Health Organization. *Social Science and Medicine*, *42*, 1403–9.

Whorf, B. L. (1956). *Language, thought and reality*. J. Carroll (Ed.). Cambridge, MA: MIT Press.

Wierzbicka, A. (1994). Emotion, language, and cultural scripts. In S. Kitayama & H. R. Markus (Ed.), *Emotion and culture: Empirical studies of mutual influence* (pp. 133–96). Washington, DC: American Psychological Association.

 (1996). *Semantics: Primes and universals*. Oxford: Oxford University Press.

 (1998). Angst. *Culture & Psychology*, *4*, 161–88.

 (1999). *Emotions across languages and cultures: Diversity and universals*. Cambridge: Cambridge University Press.

Wiggins, J. S. (1973). *Personality and prediction: Principles of personality assessment*. Menlo Park, CA: Addison-Wesley.

Wilkinson, R. (1996). *Unhealthy societies: The affliction of inequality*. London: Routledge.

Willemsen, M. E., & Van de Vijver, F. J. R. (1997). Developmental expectations of Dutch, Turkish-Dutch, and Zambian mothers: Towards an explanation of cross-cultural differences. *International Journal of Behavioral Development*, *21*, 837–54.

Williams, J. E., & Best, D. L. (1990a). *Measuring sex stereotypes: A thirty nation study*. (2nd ed.). London: Sage.

 (1990b). *Sex and psyche: Gender and self viewed cross-culturally*. Newbury Park, CA: Sage.

Williams, J. E., Satterwhite, R. C., & Saiz, J. L. (1998). *The importance of psychological traits: A cross-cultural study*. New York: Plenum.

Williams, T. R. (1967). *Field methods in the study of culture*. New York: Holt, Rinehart and Winston.

Wilson, E. O. (1975). *Sociobiology: The new synthesis*. Cambridge, MA: Belknap Press-Harvard University Press.

Wimmers, R. H., Savelsbergh, G. J. P., Van der Kamp, J., & Hartelman, P. (1998). A developmental transition modeled as a cusp catastrophe. *Developmental Psychobiology*, *32*, 23–35.

Wimmers, R. H., Savelsbergh, G. J. P., Beek, P. J., & Hopkins B. (1998). Evidence for a phase transition in the early development of prehension. *Developmental Psychobiology*, *32*, 235–48.

Winkelman, M. (1986). Trance states: A theoretical model and cross-cultural analysis. *Ethos*, *14*, 174–203.

Winter, W. (1963). The perception of safety posters by Bantu industrial workers. *Psychologia Africana*, *10*, 127–35.

Wissler, C. (1923). *Man and culture*. New York: Thomas Y. Crowell.

Witkin, H., & Berry, J. W. (1975). Psychological differentiation in cross-cultural perspective. *Journal of Cross-Cultural Psychology*, *6*, 4–87.

Witkin, H. A., Dyk, R. B., Paterson, H. F., Goodenough, D. R., & Karp, S. (1962). *Psychological differentiation*. New York: Wiley.

Witkin, H. A., Goodenough, D. R., & Oltman, P. (1979). Psychological differentiation: Current status. *Journal of Personality and Social Psychology*, *37*, 1127–45.

Wober, M. (1966). Sensotypes. *Journal of Social Psychology*, *70*, 181–9.

(1975). *Psychology in Africa*. London: International African Institute.

Wolff, P. H. (1972a). Ethnic differences in alcohol sensitivity. *Science*, *175*, 449–50.

(1972b). Vasomotor sensitivity to alcohol in diverse Mongoloid populations. *American Journal of Human Genetics*, *25*, 193–9.

World Bank (1993). *World development report: Investing in health*. Oxford: Oxford University Press.

World Health Organization (1973). *Report of the International Pilot Study of Schizophrenia*, Vol. I. Geneva: WHO.

(1978). *Primary Health Care: Report of the International Conference at Alma Ata*. Geneva: WHO.

(1979). *Schizophrenia: An international follow-up study*. New York: Wiley.

(1982). *Medium term programme*. Geneva: WHO.

(1988). *Charter for action to achieve health for all by the year 2000 and beyond*. Geneva: WHO.

(1990). *International classification of diseases*. Geneva: WHO.

(1992). *The ICD–10 classification of mental and behavioral disorders*. Geneva: WHO.

(1995). *World Health Organization Expert Committee on physical status: The use and interpretation of anthropometry*. Geneva: WHO.

(2000). *World health statistics annual, 1999*. Geneva: WHO.

Wortley, W. W., & Humphriss, D. (1971). Study of acuity of vision of South African Whites, Bantu and Bushmen. *Psychologia Africana*, *14*, 11–19.

Wright, G. N. (1985). Organizational, group and individual decision making in cross-cultural perspective. In G. N. Wright (Ed.), *Behavioral decision making* (pp. 149–65). New York: Plenum.

Wright, G. N., & Phillips, L. D. (1980). Cultural variation in probabilistic thinking: Alternative ways of dealing with uncertainty. *International Journal of Psychology*, *15*, 239–57.

Wright, G. N., Phillips, L. D., & Wisudha, A. (1983). Cultural comparison on decision making under uncertainty. In J. B. Deregowski, S. Dziurawiec, & R. C. Annis (Eds.), *Expositions in cross-cultural psychology* (pp. 387–402). Lisse, Netherlands: Swets & Zeitlinger.

Wundt, W. (1913). *Elemente der Völkerpsychologie* (2nd ed.). Leipzig: Alfred Kroner Verlag.

Wyndham, C. H. (1975). Ergonomic problems in the transition from peasant to industrial life in South Africa. In A. Chapanis (Ed.), *Ethnic variables in human factors engineering* (pp. 115–34). Baltimore, MD: Johns Hopkins University Press.

Yang, K.-S. (2000). Monocultural and cross-cultural indigenous approaches. *Asian Journal of Social Psychology*, *3*, 241–63.

Yang, K. S., & Bond, M. H. (1990). Exploring implicit personality theories with indigenous or imported constructs: The Chinese case. *Journal of Personality and Social Psychology*, *58*, 1087–95.

Yap, P. M. (1969). The culture-bound reactive syndromes. In W. Caudill & T.-Y. Lin (Eds.), *Mental health research in Asia and the Pacific*. Honolulu: East West Centre Press.

(1974). *Comparative psychiatry*. Toronto: University of Toronto Press.

Yates, J. F., Ying, Zhu, Ronis, D. L., Deng-Feng, Wang, Shinotsuka, H., & Toda, M. (1989). Probability judgment accuracy: China, Japan, and the United States. *Organizational Behavior and Human Decision Processes*, *43*, 145–71.

Young, M., & Evans, D. (1997). The well being of Salvador refugees. *International Journal of Psychology*, *32*, 289–300.

Zaidi, H. (1979). Applied cross-cultural psychology: Submissions of a cross-cultural psychologist from the Third World. In L. Eckensberger, W. Lonner, & Y. H. Poortinga (Eds.), *Cross-cultural contributions to psychology* (pp. 236–43). Lisse, Netherlands: Swets & Zeitlinger.

Zaman, A., & Zaman, R. (1994). Psychology and development: A conceptual itinerary. *Psychology and Developing Societies*, *6*, 1–20.

Zempléni-Rabain, J. (1970). L'enfant Wolof de 2 à 5 ans (Sénégal): Echanges corporels et échanges médiatisés par les objets. *Revue de Neuropsychiatrie Infantile*, *18*, 785–98.

Zhang, J. X., & Bond, M. H. (1997). Personality and filial piety among college students in two Chinese societies. *Journal of Cross-Cultural Psychology*, *29*, 402–17.

Zheng, X., & Berry, J. W. (1991). Psychological adaptation of Chinese sojourners in Canada. *International Journal of Psychology*, *26*, 451–70.

Zimba, R. F. (in press). Indigenous conceptions of childhood and social realities: Development in Southern Africa. In H. Keller, Y. H. Poortinga, & A. Schoelmerich (Eds.), *Between biology and culture: Perspectives on ontogenetic development*. Cambridge: Cambridge University Press.

# Author index

Abdallah-Pretceile, M., 413
Abegglen, J. C. 396
Aberle, D. F., 55, 84, 232
Aboud, F., 357, 424, 425, 434, 442, 445–6, 449, 453–4
Abramson, A. S., 148
Abu-Loghud, L., 190, 228
Adair, J. A., 459
Adèr, H. J., 310
Aditya, R. N., 391
Adler, L. L., 79
Adler, N. J., 395
Adorno, T., 245
Ager, A., 349
Agnoli, F., 149, 163, 164
Ainsworth, M. D. S., 27, 28
Alasuutari, P., 234
Albas, C. A., 182
Albas, D. C., 182
Albert, R. D., 416, 418
Alcock, J., 276
Alden, L., 356
Alderman, 445
Aldwin, C., 364, 365
Alemu, T., 446
Alibhai, N., 369
Al-Issa, I., 352, 428, 454, 454
Allaire, Y., 390
Allen, S. D., 291
Allen, T., 346
Allen, W., 413
Allik, J., 68, 71
Allison, A. C., 261
Allport, G. W., 59, 374, 375
Allwood, C., 460
Altarriba, J., 149, 171
Altman, I., 185
Altrocchi, J., 370
Altrocchi, L., 370
Amatruda, C., 24
American Psychiatric Association, 428
Amir, Y., 53, 373–4, 376
Anand, B. K., 110
Anastasi, A., 47
Andor, L. E., 201

Angleitner, A., 91
Anisfeld, E., 169
Anker, M., 430
Annis, R. C., 138, 141
Aptekar, L., 44
Apter, M., 466
Araki, S., 410
Archer, J., 74, 272
Arcuri, L. W., 178
Ardila, R., 466
Argyle, M., 183–5
Ariès, P., 43
Armstrong, R. E., 206
Arnett, J., 32
Aronowitz, M., 366
Asch, S. E., 58
Ashton, M. C., 95
Ataca, B., 356, 362, 429, 452
Au, T. K., 152
Averill, J. R., 186
Averill, M., 310
Avis, J., 134
Ayala, F. J., 269
Aycan, Z., 366, 377, 402, 405, 406
Ayres, T. J., 130
Azuma, H., 27

Backenroth-Ohsaka, G., 421, 422
Bacon, M., 31, 32, 33, 34, 35, 58, 82, 139
Baddeley, A. D., 130
Bahuchet, S., 138, 141
Baillargeon, R., 48
Baker, C., 168, 380
Baker, L., 152
Baker, W., 63
Baldwin, K. D., 413
Balfour, J., 453
Bali, S. K., 122
Ballachey, E., 229
Balls-Organista, P., 383
Baltes, P., 45
Bandura, A., 13, 49, 281
Banks, J., 379
Barba, C. V. C., 445
Barker, R., 301, 302

# Subject index

abilities, 115, 121–5
abnormal behavior *see* psychopathology
absolutism, 4, 132, 180, 324–6, 387, 429
accommodation, 131
acculturation, 11, 14, 21, 77, 119, 345–70,
 472
 attitudes, 353–7
 behavioral changes, 360–1
 contact, 144, 349, 351–2
 cultural level, 349–50, 352
 definition, 349–50
 framework, 351
 ideology, 357
 individual characteristics, 366
 influences, 458
 moderating variables, 364–6
 psychological level, 350–1
 scientific, 457–8
 social support, 369
 strategies, 353–7, 378
 transmission, 20
 U-curve, 368
acculturative stress, 352, 361, 364–5
achievement motivation, 402
achievement training, 32–5
action theory, 329–31
activity (dimension), 77, 174
activity settings, 331, 352, 365, 368, 369–70
adaptation, 2, 12, 13
 acculturation, 352, 369–71
 biological, 11–3, 259, 261–3, 274–6
 cultural, 11–13
 economic, 370
 psychological, 370
 social, 231–2
 sociocultural, 370
adjective check list, 75, 79, 95
adjustment, 409
adolescence, 39
adult attachment, 29
affective meaning, 174–6
 activity, 174–5
 evaluation, 174–5
 potency, 174–5
 sub-universals, 175

uniquenesses, 175
universals, 175
affluence, 69, 119, 436
 *see also* GNP
affordances, 15, 338–40
African infant precocity, 23
African personality, 104–7
 psychosis, 106
 neurosis, 106
aggregation error, 303
aggression, 82–3
 inculcation, 82
agreeableness, 93
agriculture, 34–6, 58, 138–41, 270,
 385
alcoholic flush, 200
allele, 256–8, 260
 dominant, 258
 recessive, 258
 homozygotic, 257, 260
 heterozygotic, 257–60
allocation of subjects, 296–7
Alma Ata Declaration, 423
altered states of consciousness, 109–13
 criteria for, 109–10
alternative explanations, 197, 286–7
alternative moralities, 41
altruism, 276, 282
*amae*, 107–8, 438–9
amok, 433–4
analogies, 274
analysis of equivalence, 304–10
 stimulus content, 304–6
 judgmental methods, 304–6
 translation, 306
*anasakti*, 109
*anorexia nervosa*, 433
antecedents, 2, 320–3, 334, 340
 *see also* components (emotions)
anthropology, 7–9, 225–53
 cognitive, 249–53
 psychological, 241–9
 relationship with psychology, 7–8, 227
anxiety/uncertainty theory, 421
appearance–reality distinction, 135